BROOKS/COLE PUBLISHING COMPANY
PACIFIC GROVE, CALIFORNIA

Death and Dying
Life and Living

Charles A. Corr
Southern Illinois University
at Edwardsville

Clyde M. Nabe
Southern Illinois University
at Edwardsville

Donna M. Corr
St. Louis Community College
at Forest Park

ITP™ The trademark ITP is used under license.

Brooks/Cole Publishing Company
A Division of Wadsworth, Inc.

Printed in the United States of America

10   9   8   7   6   5   4   3   2   1

Library of Congress Cataloging-in-Publication Data
Corr, Charles A.
    Death and dying, life and living / Charles A. Corr, Clyde M. Nabe,
Donna M. Corr.
        p.   cm.
    Includes bibliographical references and index.
    ISBN 0-534-21138-0
    1. Death—Psychological aspects.   2. Bereavement—Psychological
aspects.   3. Death.   I. Nabe, Clyde   II. Corr, Donna M.
III.   Title.
BF789.D4C67   1993
155.9'37—dc20   93-3208
                                                            CIP

Sponsoring Editor: *Vicki Knight*
Marketing Representative: *Susan Hays*
Editorial Assistant: *Lauri Banks-Wothe*
Production Editor: *Penelope Sky*
Manuscript Editor: *Lorraine Anderson*
Permissions Editor: *Roxane Buck*
Interior and Cover Design: *Sharon L. Kinghan*
Cover Photo: *© Joseph Kayne*
Art Coordinator: *Susan Haberkorn*
Interior Illustration: *Laurie Albrecht*
Photo Editor: *Larry Molmud*
Photo Researcher: *Sue C. Howard*
Typesetting: *Weimer Graphics*
Cover Printing: *Phoenix Color Corporation*
Printing and Binding: *Arcata Graphics/Fairfield*

Credits continue after indexes.

To Herman Feifel
and to the memory of Richard A. Kalish

both of whom, in person and through their own publications, encouraged us and so many others who have worked in the field of death, dying, and bereavement.

Life glitters between two darknesses; or mysteries.

C. Leach, *Letter to a Younger Son* (1981, p. 47)

Death is no enemy of life; it restores our sense of the value of living. Illness restores the sense of proportion that is lost when we take life for granted. To learn about value and proportion we need to honor illness, and ultimately to honor death.

A. W. Frank, *At the Will of the Body* (1991, p. 120)

Brief Contents

Contents

PART II   DYING   101

Chapter 5   Coping with Dying   103

Preface

This is a book about *death,* about *dying,* and about *bereavement.* We use the phrase "death and dying" in the title because it has become a familiar shorthand designation for understanding and appreciating all death-related events. This book is also about *life* and *living.* In fact, our real concern is to examine life and living from the special perspective of death and dying. Thus, nearly all of the individuals we discuss are alive: the people who are facing death, those who are coping with dying or bereavement, those who are contemplating suicide or struggling with decisions about euthanasia, the children whom we wish to teach about the place of death in life, and our readers.

This book is a resource that can stand on its own as a primary text for undergraduate and graduate courses in death, dying, and bereavement, and can be used to good effect as a supplementary text in related courses. The volume can also be consulted as a helpful reference in the field.

We want to introduce readers to the interesting and challenging issues in this subject area. In particular, we have provided a solid pedagogic foundation upon which readers can rely as they pursue their own insights, emphases, and special interests in this challenging field of study.

Our overall orientation is drawn from Richard Kalish's allegory, "The Horse on the Dining-Room Table," which appears as the prologue to this book. The main point is that we human beings cannot magically make death disappear from our lives, nor can we erase completely the sadness and other forms of distress associated with many death-related experiences. But we are not completely impotent. We can talk about death together, share insights and attitudes, learn from each other, and strive to cope more effectively. All of this will enable us to lead more productive lives in the face of death.

Our field has grown rapidly since the publication of Herman Feifel's *The Meaning of Death* (1959) and Elisabeth Kübler-Ross's *On Death and Dying* (1969). This book reflects that fact—that is, we do not merely repeat what has been said in the past. Instead, we provide new explanations of old ideas and emphasize fresh new insights, whether they are our own or others'.

Features

The book is arranged in topical groupings whose contents, balance, and sequence have been tested in our own classroom teaching. But individuals can easily adapt the material to their own needs and preferences. Chapters that we have grouped together can be studied in any order.

Each chapter opens with a brief vignette or case study, and closes with both questions for review and discussion and a list of suggested readings. We have paid careful attention to chapter length and readibility, and we have made judicious use of tables, figures, boxes, and artwork to highlight the text.

Two special features of this book are our consistent use of task-based approaches and our attention to developmental perspectives in interactions with death and dying. For example, we examine tasks involved in coping with dying, coping with bereavement, funeral and memorial rituals, and grieving youngsters. The developmental perspective enables us to study death-related issues in ways that emphasize the experiences of individuals at different points in the life cycle. The task-based approach and the developmental perspective also help empower those who are involved with death and dying by showing them how to cope with these challenges in order to live as well as they can. Finally, in describing those who are coping with death-related issues, providing care, or otherwise involved with illness, dying, and bereavement, we highlight all four of the dimensions that are involved: the physical, the psychological, the social, and the spiritual.

Organization

Death-related encounters and death-related attitudes are central elements in everyone's experiences of life and living. In Part 1, we establish this fact as a historical and cultural context that is influential throughout the book. We explore death-related encounters and attitudes in depth in Chapters 1 and 2. In Chapter 3, we describe our basic conceptual framework, which is taken from Robert Kastenbaum's notion of the many elements of the "death system" in every society. In Chapter 4, we consider the ways in which cultural differences within the United States affect death-related encounters, attitudes, and practices. The literature in this area is neither well nor uniformly developed. Because a responsible appreciation of diversity within this country requires sensitivity to cultural differences, we encourage readers to supplement this book with culturally specific reports about death, dying, and bereavement, drawn both from their own experiences and from extracurricular research.

In Parts 2 and 3, we examine coping and helping: coping with dying and helping those who are coping with dying; coping with bereavement and helping those who are coping with bereavement. These parts also include separate chapters on hospice principles and caring for the dying, and on funeral practices and other memorial rituals.

In Part 4, we adopt a developmental perspective, which we value for its sensitivity to differences across the human life cycle. Accordingly, in four separate chapters we give individual attention to the death-related experiences of children, adolescents, adults, and the elderly.

In Part 5, four chapters address the legal, conceptual, and moral issues that so frequently test our societal relations to death, dying, and bereavement.

In Part 6, separate chapters are devoted to HIV infection and AIDS and to education about death, dying, and bereavement. Each of these subjects is significant in its own right; together they illustrate the interplay of the many themes explored in the book as a whole.

Our epilogue is an excerpt from the poignant poem, "How Could I Not Be Among You?", written by Ted Rosenthal after the diagnosis of his acute leukemia at age 31 and not long before his death three years later. A classic piece of literature in our field, the poem vividly expresses Rosenthal's deeply felt concern that we live as fully as we can and not waste the limited time that is given to us.

Acknowledgments

We have learned a great deal from our students and our professional colleagues, and above all from the many unselfish individuals who shared the insights they derived from their personal experiences of death, dying, and bereavement. We have striven to learn our lessons well and to convey them effectively and helpfully. We also wish to thank the following people who read the manuscript and suggested improvements: David Balk, Kansas State University; Kenneth Doka, College of New Rochelle; Nancy Falvo, Clarion University of Pennsylvania; Mal Goldsmith, Southern Illinois University at Edwardsville; Joseph Heller, California State University, Sacramento; Martha Loustaunau, New Mexico State University; Sarah O'Dowd, Community College of Rhode Island; Thomas Paxson, Southern Illinois University at Edwardsville; Constance Pratt, Rhode Island College; and Rita S. Santanello, Belleville Area College. We appreciate the assistance of Dr. Sandra Bertman, of the School of Medicine at the University of Massachusetts at Worcester. Finally, we are grateful for the support we have received in our professional work during many years at Southern Illinois University at Edwardsville and Saint Louis Community College at Forest Park.

We have worked diligently to say what we want to say, to be responsible to our subjects, to reflect the strengths and limitations of the available literature, to acknowledge current issues and concerns, to achieve broad topical coverage, and to shape the whole to our readers' advantage. But we make no false claims of covering every aspect of all the uncountable areas affected by death, dying, and bereavement. There are many opportunities to supplement this book with study, research, and teaching.

We would be happy to receive comments about this book or suggestions for improving it, outlines or syllabi of courses in which it has been used, and references, handouts, or other supplementary materials. Communications on these and related matters may be sent to us directly in care of Box 1433, Southern Illinois University, Edwardsville, IL 62026.

Charles A. Corr
Clyde M. Nabe
Donna M. Corr

The Horse on the Dining-Room Table
by Richard A. Kalish

I struggled up the slope of Mount Evmandu to meet the famous guru of Nepsim, an ancient sage whose name I was forbidden to place in print. I was much younger then, but the long and arduous hike exhausted me, and, despite the cold, I was perspiring heavily when I reached the plateau where he made his home. He viewed me with a patient, almost amused, look, and I smiled wanly at him between attempts to gulp the thin air into my lungs. I made my way across the remaining hundred meters and slowly sat down on the ground—propping myself up against a large rock just outside his abode.

We were both silent for several minutes, and I felt the tension in me rise, then subside until I was calm. Perspiration prickled my skin, but the slight breeze was pleasantly cool, and soon I was relaxed. Finally I turned my head to look directly into the clear brown eyes, which were bright within his lined face. I realized that I would need to speak.

"Father," I said, "I need to understand something about what it means to die, before I can continue my studies." He continued to gaze at me with his open, bemused expression. "Father," I went on, "I want to know what a dying person feels when no one will speak with him, nor be open enough to permit him to speak, about his dying."

He was silent for three, perhaps four, minutes. I felt at peace because I knew he would answer. Finally, as though in the middle of a sentence, he said, "It is the horse on the dining-room table." We continued to gaze at each other for several minutes. I began to feel sleepy after my long journey, and I must have dozed off. When I woke up, he was gone, and the only activity was my own breathing.

I retraced my steps down the mountain—still feeling calm, knowing that his answer made me feel good, but not knowing why. I returned to my studies and gave no further thought to the event, not wishing to dwell upon it, yet secure that someday I should understand.

Many years later I was invited to the home of a casual friend for dinner. It was a modest house in a typical California development. The eight or ten other guests, people I did not know well, and I sat in the living room—drinking Safeway Scotch and bourbon and dipping celery sticks and raw cauliflower into a watery cheese dip. The conversation, initially halting, became more animated as we got to know each other and developed points of contact. The drinks undoubtedly also affected us.

Eventually the hostess appeared and invited us into the dining room for a buffet dinner. As I entered the room, I noticed with astonishment that a brown horse was sitting quietly on the dining-room table. Although it was small for a horse, it filled much of the large table. I caught my breath, but didn't say anything. I was the first one to enter, so I was able to turn to watch the other guests. They responded much as I did—they entered, saw the horse, gasped or stared, but said nothing.

The host was the last to enter. He let out a silent shriek—looking rapidly from the horse to each of his guests with a wild stare. His mouth formed soundless words. Then in a voice choked with confusion he invited us to fill our plates from the buffet. His wife, equally disconcerted by what was clearly an unexpected horse, pointed to the name cards, which indicated where each of us was to sit.

The hostess led me to the buffet and handed me a plate. Others lined up behind me—each of us quiet. I filled my plate with rice and chicken and sat in my place. The others followed suit.

It was cramped, sitting there, trying to avoid getting too close to the horse, while pretending that no horse was there. My dish overlapped the edge of the table. Others found other ways to avoid physical contact with the horse. The host and hostess seemed as ill-at-ease as the rest of us. The conversation lagged. Every once in a while, someone would say something in an attempt to revive the earlier pleasant and innocuous discussion, but the overwhelming presence of the horse so filled our thoughts that talk of taxes or politics or the lack of rain seemed inconsequential.

Dinner ended, and the hostess brought coffee. I can recall everything on my plate and yet have no memory of having eaten. We drank in silence—all of us trying not to look at the horse, yet unable to keep our eyes or thoughts anywhere else.

I thought several times of saying, "Hey, there's a horse on the dining-room table." But I hardly knew the host, and I didn't wish to embarrass him by mentioning something that obviously discomforted him at least as much as it discomforted me. After all, it was his house. And what do you say to a man with a horse on his dining-room table? I could have said that I did not mind, but that was not true—its presence upset me so much that I enjoyed neither the dinner nor the company. I could have said that I knew how difficult it was to have a horse on one's dining-room table, but that wasn't true either; I had no idea. I could have said something like, "How do you feel about having a horse on your dining-room table?", but I didn't want to sound like a psychologist. Perhaps, I thought, if I ignore it, it will go away. Of course I knew that it wouldn't. It didn't.

I later learned that the host and hostess were hoping the dinner would be a success in spite of the horse. They felt that to mention it would make us so uncomfortable that we wouldn't enjoy our visit—of course we didn't enjoy the evening anyway. They were fearful that we would try to offer them sympathy, which they didn't want, or understanding, which they needed but could not accept. They wanted the party to be a success, so they decided to try to make the evening as enjoyable as possible. But it was apparent that they—like their guests—could think of little else than the horse.

I excused myself shortly after dinner and went home. The evening had been terrible. I never wanted to see the host and hostess again, although I was eager to seek out the other guests and learn what they felt about the occasion. I felt confused about what had happened and extremely tense. The evening had been grotesque. I was careful to avoid the host and hostess after that, and I did my best to stay away altogether from the neighborhood.

Recently I visited Nepsim again. I decided to seek out the guru once more. He was still alive, although nearing death, and he would speak only to a few. I repeated my journey and eventually found myself sitting across from him.

Once again I asked, "Father, I want to know what a dying person feels when no one will speak with him, nor be open enough to permit him to speak, about his dying."

The old man was quiet, and we sat without speaking for nearly an hour. Since he did not bid me leave, I remained. Although I was content, I feared he would not share his wisdom, but he finally spoke. The words came slowly.

"My son, it is the horse on the dining-room table. It is a horse that visits every house and sits on every dining-room table—the tables of the rich and of the poor, of the simple and of the wise. This horse just sits there, but its presence makes you wish to leave without speaking of it. If you leave, you will always fear the presence of the horse. When it sits on your table, you will wish to speak of it, but you may not be able to.

"However, if you speak about the horse, then you will find that others can also speak about the horse—most others, at least, if you are gentle and kind as you speak. The horse will remain on the dining-room table, but you will not be so distraught. You will enjoy your repast, and you will enjoy the company of the host and hostess. Or, if it is your table, you will enjoy the presence of your guests. You cannot make magic to have the horse disappear, but you can speak of the horse and thereby render it less powerful."

The old man then rose and, motioning me to follow, walked slowly to his hut. "Now we shall eat," he said quietly. I entered the hut and had difficulty adjusting to the dark. The guru walked to a cupboard in the corner and took out some bread and some cheese, which he placed on a mat. He motioned to me to sit and share his food. I saw a small horse sitting quietly in the center of the mat. He noticed this and said, "That horse need not disturb us." I thoroughly enjoyed the meal. Our discussion lasted far into the night, while the horse sat there quietly throughout our time together.

PART I

DEATH

With respect to death, there are some aspects in which each of us is like *every* other human being who has ever lived or who is now alive, other aspects in which each of us is only like *some* other human beings who have ever lived or who are now alive, and still other aspects in which each of us is like *no* other human being who has ever lived or who is now alive. One important part of the study of death, dying, and bereavement is to sort out these various aspects: the universal, the particular, and the uniquely individual. We begin here with the particular: with contemporary American society, its evolving historical character, and some of the many cultural differences within that society.

Every human being lives within a particular historical and cultural framework. Individuals are born within such frameworks or migrate from one framework to another, as, for example, when they emigrate from one part of the world to another. This does not mean that every individual and/or minority group within a particular society must share every aspect of the social and death-related experiences that characterize that society as a whole. In fact, specific individuals and members of distinct groups within the society can be expected to have their own unique experiences with life and death. The four chapters that follow attempt to describe both the broad context of the larger American society and representative examples of the many cultural differences that are alive and well within that general framework.

An old joke claims that the only two unchanging things in life are death and taxes. Actually, tax structures are frequently altered and patterns of experience with death are also subject to change. What can be misleading is the intimate familiarity that people develop with their own particular way of living (including its unique tax structure) and their own characteristic pattern of death-related experiences. Often, these social structures and experiential patterns are taken for granted. Without giving the matter much thought, individuals may assume that everyone in a particular society shares these structures and patterns in the same way. One might even think that all other people who are now living throughout the world or who have been alive at different times in human history did or still do share similar social structures and experiential patterns.

In fact, social structures and patterns of experience with death that are typical for many within American society at present may be very different from those of specific cultural groups within the larger society or those found in the United States in an earlier period of history. In turn, each of these is likely to differ in many ways from the current structures and patterns in many other countries.

It is useful, therefore, to begin our study of death, dying, and bereavement by drawing attention to prominent features of patterns of death-related experiences and to take note of their relationships to significant social and cultural variables. This helps us to know ourselves more fully and to appreciate the settings within which we take up all of the other issues addressed in this book.

The four chapters in this part consider two fundamental features: the historical and cultural patterns typical of experiences with death in the United States, and the societal structures relevant to death-related experiences. Death-related experiences and mortality patterns influence society, just as society in its own ways helps to shape experiences with death. One might argue that general alterations in the society itself are the primary factors, with changes in death-related experiences and mortality patterns playing a later, narrower, and usually subordinate role.

In the chapters that follow, death-related experiences and social structures are examined first in terms of encounters with death and then in terms of attitudes toward death. Encounters and attitudes are distinguishable aspects of the totality of human experience that shape each other in a complex series of interactions. Certain kinds of encounters with death generate particular attitudes about death, just as particular attitudes encourage or discourage specific involvements or encounters with death. In the complex web of experience, encounters and attitudes are so closely intertwined as to be almost inextricable. In Chapters 1 and 2, they are separated somewhat artificially to facilitate individual analysis.

Following the broad historical and cross-cultural comparisons between death-related encounters and attitudes set forth in Chapters 1 and 2, Chapter 3 focuses more directly on a number of significant aspects of the contemporary scene in the United States, and Chapter 4 emphasizes cultural differences within that society. This illuminates several very special features of the ways in which individuals live with the changing face of death in our own society as we approach the end of the twentieth century. It also establishes and permits us to bring forward some of the central themes that will reappear from time to time throughout this book.

CHAPTER 1

Changing Encounters with Death

Death and life: Two dimensions of the same reality. To interpret this drawing rotate the image one quarter turn to the left and then one quarter turn to the right.

To approach death, dying, and bereavement as a topic of serious and sustained study, we begin by considering some typical ways in which 20th-century Americans meet up with death. Significant features of these encounters are not always obvious, nor are these the only possible ways in which humans have interacted or might interact with mortality. Earlier peoples did not, and many peoples in other parts of the world today do not, experience mortality as we do.

What this means is that encounters with death, dying, and bereavement are always, to some degree, the product of a historical process and a social or cultural context. Thus, it is useful to look at some of the historical, social, and cultural factors that are most influential in shaping death-related encounters. In this chapter, we consider the following principal factors: mortality rates; average life expectancy; changing causes of death; dying trajectories; and locations where death occurs. In addition, we consider some of the social changes that have altered encounters with death in our society.

Three Contemporary Encounters with Death

We stand beside the bed of a man who is apparently unconscious. He is thin, pale, and breathing shallowly. A plastic mask covers his nose and mouth. A tube runs from the mask to an outlet in the wall. In the arm closest to us, a needle is sticking into a vein. From that needle, another tube runs to a bag of fluid hanging from a metal pole near the head of the bed. Another person, a close family member, stands on the other side of the bed. There are no chairs nearby. Outside the small window in the room, one can see only a brick wall. The room is a hospital room; sterile, unfamiliar, uncomfortable. We wonder what to say, what to do.

We approach a large white brick house. Walking in the front door, we are greeted by an attendant and directed to a parlor on the right. Through a wide archway, we see a spacious room. Around the edges of the room are big chairs and occasionally a couch; at one end, a number of folding chairs have been set out in rows. As we enter the room, we see at one end a long rectangular box. Floral displays stand around and on top of the box. Half of the lid of the box stands open, revealing the silent, unmoving, recumbent figure of a woman. Many people are gathered in this room. They sit or stand in small groups, talking quietly. Some laugh; some weep; some appear to be dazed. We have come to the viewing of a body in a funeral home. For us, it is in many ways an alien physical environment and an unfamiliar personal and social context. We wonder what to say, what to do.

We sit in our own living room, next to a young child who is obviously upset. She weeps and seems now angry, now frightened. Her parents have brought her here so that we can sit with her while they attend the funeral of the child's brother. She asks us uncomfortable questions about where her

Sitting, waiting, and anticipating.

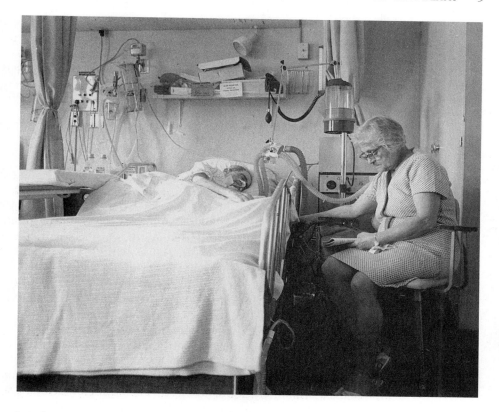

brother is and why her parents are so upset. Her parents have told us not to discuss the death of the boy with her. They don't want her to think about it because "she is too young and cannot understand death." We wonder what to say, what to do.

Encountering Death in America Today

Each of the preceding examples depicts experiences associated with the events of death, dying, and bereavement for many Americans living toward the end of the 20th century. Most adults—urban or rural; Caucasian American, African American, Asian American, Hispanic American, or Native American; Christian, Jewish, Muslim, or Buddhist—have lived through or can easily imagine such moments.

These examples illustrate three factors that are likely to complicate encounters with death in our society. First, individuals in our society who are involved in death-related situations may not have had much prior experience with death. Thus, their behavioral repertoire in the face of death is likely to be sorely limited. Second, because Americans live in a multicultural society, they may find themselves in unfamiliar social or cultural contexts when they are obliged to deal with death. This means that they may not be clear about what to say or do in such situations. Third, American adults often find themselves unsure of how to talk about death with children. These and other distinctive features of the ways in which death is encountered in our society are the focus of this chapter.

Mortality Rates

Much can be learned about experiences with death from a study of relevant statistics. For example, we can study *mortality rates*, for the population as a whole or for selected subgroups within our society (Kain, 1988). A mortality rate is determined by choosing some specific group of people and determining how many members of that group die during a particular time period. For instance, we might study white males living in the United States in the year 1992. Dividing the number of deaths among these males by the total number of such males in the overall population, we obtain a mortality rate for that year. For convenience, this number is usually expressed as some number of deaths per 1,000 persons (Shryock, Siegel, & Associates, 1980).

Note that the determination of any mortality rate depends upon the availability of a fund of demographic statistics. These statistics derive from birth, death, and census records, which are familiar features of modern society. Where those records are absent or have not been maintained carefully, as in the past or in many poor and impoverished societies today, statistical accuracy must give way to more or less imprecise estimates.

Changing Mortality Rates in the United States

When one studies the available data concerning mortality rates, it quickly becomes obvious that Americans—and, in general, those who reside in other modern or developed societies around the world today—live in a privileged time (Preston, 1976). Just 100 years ago, mortality rates were considerably higher than they are today—at least in the industrialized nations of the modern world. This is clear from the data in Table 1.1. In 1900, the mortality rate for the total American population of approximately 76 million people was 17.2 deaths per 1,000 in the population (Lerner, 1970; National Center for Health Statistics, 1991). By 1954 that rate had dropped to 9.2 per 1,000 (United States Bureau of the Census, 1975, 1991). This is a drop of nearly 47 percent in just 54 years—a stunning alteration unparalleled in any other period in human history. Nevertheless, as Table 1.1 and Figure 1.1 show, by 1990 the overall American mortality rate had dropped even lower to 8.6 per 1,000 in a much larger population, nearing 250 million people. It is increasingly difficult to reduce overall mortality rates as they get lower and lower (contrast a decline of nearly 47 percent from 1900–1954 with a decline of only 6.5 percent from 1954–1990). Thus,

TABLE 1.1   Death Rates by Gender and Age, All Races, United States, 1900 and 1990, per 1,000 Population

Age (In Years)	1900 Both Sexes	Males	Females	1990 Both Sexes	Males	Females
All ages	17.2	17.9	16.5	8.6	9.2	8.1
Under 1	162.4	179.1	145.4	9.7	10.8	8.6
1–4	19.8	20.5	19.1	0.5	0.5	0.4
5–14	3.9	3.8	3.9	0.2	0.3	0.2
15–24	5.9	5.9	5.8	1.0	1.5	0.5
25–34	8.2	8.2	8.2	1.4	2.0	0.7
35–44	10.2	10.7	9.8	2.2	3.1	1.4
45–54	15.0	15.7	14.2	4.7	6.1	3.4
55–64	27.2	28.7	25.8	12.0	15.5	8.8
65–74	56.4	59.3	53.6	26.5	34.9	19.9
75–84	123.3	128.3	118.8	60.1	78.9	48.8
85 and over	260.9	268.8	255.2	153.3	180.6	142.7

SOURCE: United States Bureau of the Census, 1975; National Center for Health Statistics, 1993.

in recent years overall mortality rates in the United States have tended to level out. Perhaps they are approaching a minimum level below which they are not likely to go.

Improvements in overall mortality rates have fundamental significance in terms of contemporary experiences with death. Above all, they mean that most living Americans are likely to have fewer direct encounters with natural death than did our great-grandparents. The typical American alive today will have lived through fewer deaths of family, friends, and neighbors than did his or her ancestors at the same time of life. This has led Fulton (1976, p. 85) to write with only some exaggeration of a "death-free generation"—one that enters adulthood, marries, and has children without having encountered the death of a close family relative. For such a generation, it is perhaps not surprising that when death actually does occur, it seems a stranger, an alien figure that has no natural or appropriate place in human life.

Differences in Changing Mortality Rates: Gender and Class

But this is not the whole story. It is true that substantial declines in mortality rates during the 20th century are found in nearly every segment of the population in the United States. There are, however, differences among these declines that can be examined in terms of a number of significant variables, the most prominent of which are gender, race, and social class (Antonovsky, 1967; Gove, 1973; Kitagawa & Hauser, 1973; Stillion, 1985). We will consider racial and cultural differences in Chapter 4. Here, we focus on gender and class differences.

If we look at gender differences, mortality rates for males in the United States declined from 17.9 per 1,000 population in 1900 to 9.2 per 1,000 in 1990, while similar rates for females declined from 16.5 to 8.1 (see Table 1.1). That is,

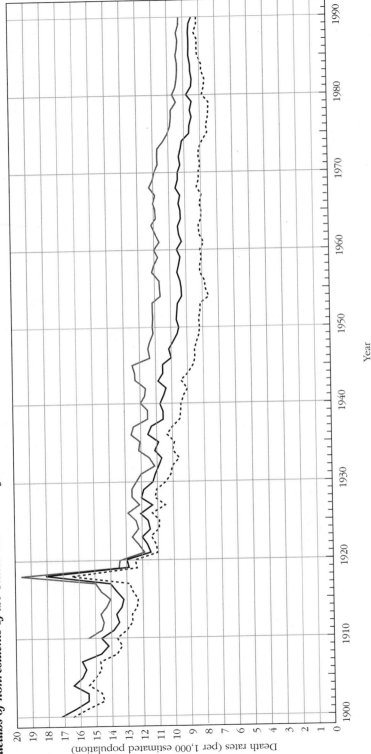

FIGURE 1.1 Death rates by gender, for all races, United States, 1900–1990, per 1,000 estimated population. Note: Prior to 1933, includes death-registration states only. Beginning 1959, includes Alaska. Beginning 1960, includes Hawaii. Beginning 1970, excludes deaths of nonresidents of the United States. Data from National Center for Health Statistics, 1991 and 1993.

*Consoling a
grieving child.*

females began with a lower rate at the beginning of the century and achieved an even lower mortality rate at the end of the period (Retherford, 1975).

Similarly, Goldscheider (1971) demonstrated the well-known point that members of lower socioeconomic classes tend on average to have higher mortality rates than members of middle and upper socioeconomic classes within the same society. The reason for this is that the latter are likely to have the advantages of better education, housing, nutrition, access to health care, and financial resources. This part of the story is perhaps obvious, although there are some subtler differences. For example, middle-class males and upper-class females may have lower mortality rates than upper-class males. At least this is true when the middle-class males have productive jobs, good health insurance, and low levels of stress; when the upper-class females do not work outside the home, have all the advantages of their husbands' socioeconomic position, and have ample opportunities for healthful exercise; and when the upper-class males are subject to high job-related stress and have few opportunities to address that stress in healthful ways.

Differences in Changing Mortality Rates: Infants and Children

Another important difference concerning those who die in the United States has to do with infants and children. At the beginning of this century death came much more frequently to the very young in the United States than it does today. Mortality rates for infants—newborns and children under 1 year of age—were more than 17 times higher in 1900 than in 1990: 162.4 infant deaths per 1,000 live births versus 9.2 per 1,000 (National Center for Health Statistics, 1991, 1993). This is a huge reduction in infant mortality rates in less than a century.

Nevertheless, infant mortality rates were not as low as they might have been in 1900 nor are they as low as they might be as we near the year 2000. The United States was the richest country in the world in 1900; it remains so today. But in 1900, the United States did not enjoy lower infant mortality rates than those found elsewhere around the globe. And as of 1988, at least 19 other countries had lower infant mortality rates than the United States (United Nations, 1992). It has been persuasively argued (Preston & Haines, 1991) that the relatively high infant mortality rates in 1900 in the United States resulted not from neglect or from a lack of resources but from inadequacies in our understanding of the range of factors that cause or contribute to death and of how to reduce their influence. However, the factors that contributed to relatively high infant mortality rates in 1900 are unlikely to be as influential today. (For additional information on infant mortality rates, see Figure 4.2 in Chapter 4.)

Great decreases in infant mortality rates are obviously most significant for those infants who do not die today in our society but who would have died if past conditions had continued to prevail. However, these statistics also have important implications for other members of society. For example, people who were parents in 1900 were far more likely to experience the death of at least one (and often more than one) of their children than those who are parents in the latter half of the century (Rosenblatt, 1983; Uhlenberg, 1980). Similarly, youngsters in 1900 were far more likely to experience the death(s) of one or more of their brothers or sisters than are children today.

There is another important fact about plunging infant mortality. Being born was not just life-threatening for babies: it was also life-threatening for their mothers. Mortality rates among pregnant women, women in the process of giving birth, and women immediately after the birth of a child were much higher in our own society in times gone by than they are today. Maternal mortality rates of 608 per 100,000 live births in 1915 had been supplanted by rates of 8.2 per 100,000 in 1990. (For additional information on maternal mortality rates, see Figure 4.3 in Chapter 4.)

Of course, death is always a greater threat to vulnerable populations than it is to those who are healthy and well off. Mortality rates at the turn of the century were high for the sick, the weak, and the aged, and they continue to be high for similar groups today. But nowadays mortality rates for nearly every vulnerable group are much lower than they were in times past. Those who are most vulnerable to death today are not as fortunate as their less-vulnerable contemporaries, but as a group they are far better off than their counterparts were in 1900. Many deaths are now avoided that would have taken place in the past or that might still take place in other societies today.

TABLE 1.2   Estimated Average Life Expectancy Across Human History

Period and Society	Average Life Expectancy
Prehistoric times	18
Ancient Greece	20
Ancient Rome	22
England during the Middle Ages	33
Massachusetts Bay Colony, North America, 17th century	35
Nineteenth-century England and Wales	41
Ten death-registration states in the United States, 1900	47

SOURCE: Lerner, 1970.

Average Life Expectancy

Average life expectancy is closely related to mortality rates and is another significant feature in the changing pattern of our encounters with death. Average life expectancy is determined by studying some particular population and marking not just how many people in that population die in a particular period of time, but how old the people are who die. In this way, one might find out how many of the people who died were between 0 and 10 years old, 10–20 years old, and so on. By carrying out the relevant computations, one can determine the average life expectancy for the population as a whole.

Drawing upon very fragmentary evidence, scholars have made estimates of average life expectancy in various societies across history (see Table 1.2). In our own society, it is common knowledge that average life expectancy has for many years exceeded, for the first time in human history, the biblical promise of "three score and ten" (that is, 70 years; see Figure 1.2). This has resulted from a steady increase during the first third of the century—with a few exceptions, most notably the influenza epidemic of 1918—associated with improved quality of life and environmental conditions, followed by a more rapid increase associated with the introduction of the sulfa drugs in the late 1930s and of penicillin during World War II. The rate of this increase has slowed since 1954, but average life expectancy continues to rise gradually even as we approach the end of the century.

Several comments might be made concerning alterations in average life expectancy during the twentieth century. First, such increases are immediately and inversely correlated with declining mortality rates. That is, when death rates go down, average life expectancy goes up, and vice versa. Second, it is not the case that no one in the periods and societies represented in Table 1.2 lived beyond the estimated averages. Many did. That is the whole point of averages: some individuals exceed and some fall below the average figure. Third, average life expectancy is originally and most rapidly increased by decreasing the number of deaths occurring in the early years of life. That is, if more people survive birth, infancy, and childhood, average life expectancy for the population as a whole will rise proportionately. This is precisely what has taken place in our society during the past century.

One implication of this last comment is that as time passes becomes more and more difficult to extend average life expectancy. That is, as it becomes

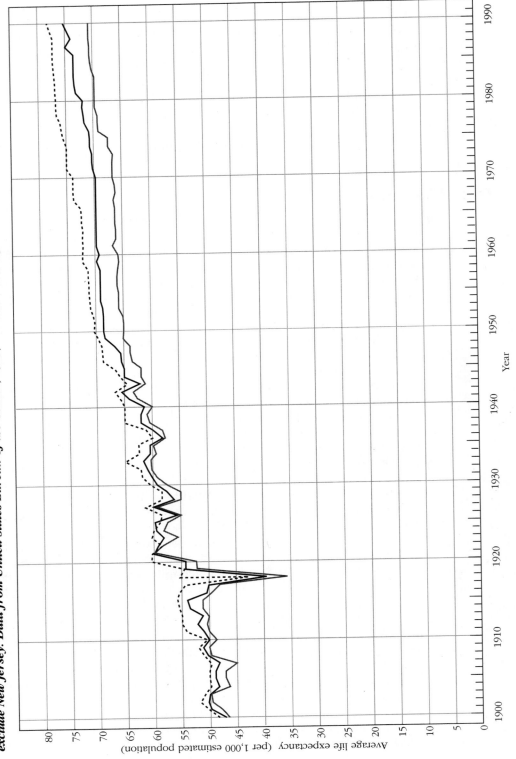

FIGURE 1.2 *Average life expectancy by gender, for all races, United States, 1900–1990 (per 1,000 estimated population). Note: Prior to 1933, includes death-registration states only. Beginning 1959, includes Alaska. Beginning 1960, includes Hawaii. 1962 and 1963 exclude New Jersey. Data from United States Bureau of the Census, 1975; National Center for Health Statistics, 1993.*

increasingly difficult to lower mortality rates among the young, improvements in mortality rates among mature adults and the elderly will have a less significant impact upon overall average life expectancy. Most of the early and relatively easy victories have already been won in the campaign to lower mortality rates and increase average life expectancy; the battles that lie ahead are much more difficult. This helps to explain why the rate of increase in average life expectancy in the United States has slowed almost to a standstill in recent years.

Like mortality rates, average life expectancy varies for different populations. For example, as a group women enjoy a significantly higher average life expectancy than do men in the United States (78.8 years versus 71.8 years, according to data for 1990), much as Caucasian Americans do over African Americans (76.1 years versus 69.1 years, according to 1990 data) and members of other minority groups (National Center for Health Statistics, 1993).

During the twentieth century, overall average life expectancy in the United States has increased from fewer than 50 years to around 75 years. This is a gain of approximately 50 percent in a period of less than 100 years! The significance of this alteration lies in its implications for our encounters with death. As average life expectancy increases, it is the elderly whom we experience more and more as the dying—so much so that in our society death is associated in many people's minds almost exclusively with the aged.

Causes of Death

Another way to describe differentiating factors in contemporary experiences with death is to look at *causes of death*. For instance, around the turn of the century in our society a large number of deaths were due to *communicable diseases* (see Table 1.3). These are acute diseases that can be transmitted or spread from person to person.

Earlier cultures experienced sporadic waves of these communicable diseases. From time to time, epidemics of such diseases as influenza, cholera, scarlet fever, measles, smallpox, and tuberculosis would run through human communities. Perhaps the most famous of these epidemics, at least for Europeans, was the black (bubonic) plague of the 14th century, which killed nearly 25 million people in a total European population much smaller than that of today (Gottfried, 1983).

Communicable diseases are often accompanied by sets of symptoms that include diarrhea, nausea, vomiting, headache, fever, and muscle ache. In cultures where antibiotics were or are not available—that is, anywhere in the world before 1930, and in many undeveloped or poverty-stricken portions of the world today—those providing physical care for people with communicable diseases mainly dealt or deal with these symptoms rather than with their underlying causes. That is, they offered or offer such things as shelter from the elements, a warm fire, a place to rest, hot food (chicken soup!), and a cool cloth to wipe a feverish brow. Pasteur's discovery in the late 19th century that communicable diseases are caused by microbial agents, the subsequent devel-

TABLE 1.3   The Ten Leading Causes of Death, in Rank Order, All Races, United States, 1900 and 1990

Rank	Cause of Death	Deaths per 100,000 Population	Percentage of All Deaths
	1900		
	All causes	1,719.1	100.0
1	Influenza and pneumonia	202.2	11.8
2	Tuberculosis (all forms)	194.4	11.3
3	Gastritis, duodenitis, enteritis, etc.	142.7	8.3
4	Diseases of the heart	137.4	8.0
5	Vascular lesions affecting the central nervous system	106.9	6.2
6	Chronic nephritis	81.0	4.7
7	All accidents	72.3	4.2
8	Malignant neoplasms (cancer)	64.0	3.7
9	Certain diseases of early infancy	62.6	3.6
10	Diphtheria	40.3	2.3
	1990		
	All causes	863.8	100.0
1	Diseases of the heart	289.5	35.5
2	Malignant neoplasms (cancer)	203.2	23.5
3	Cerebrovascular diseases	57.9	6.7
4	Accidents & adverse effects	37.0	4.3
5	Chronic obstructive pulmonary diseases & allied conditions	34.9	4.0
6	Pneumonia and influenza	32.0	3.7
7	Diabetes mellitus	19.2	2.2
8	Suicide	12.4	1.4
9	Chronic liver disease & cirrhosis	10.4	1.2
10	Human immunodeficiency virus infection	10.1	1.2

SOURCE: United States Bureau of the Census, 1975; National Center for Health Statistics, 1993.

opment of antimicrobial drugs (antibiotics), and general improvements in quality of life gradually brought these diseases under control in developed parts of the world.

Today, relatively few people in developed countries die of communicable diseases, with the exception of infection by the Human Immunodeficiency Virus (HIV) and Acquired Immunodeficiency Syndrome (AIDS). However, HIV/AIDS is an important exception here, having risen to become the 10th-ranking cause of death in the United States in 1990, crowding "homicide and legal intervention" into 11th place by a fraction of a percentage point (National Center for Health Statistics, 1993). Apart from this exception and mortality arising from accidents or suicide, in our society death is largely the result of the long-term wearing out of bodily organs, a deterioration associated with lifestyle, environment, and aging. That is, people in our society die mainly of a set of chronic conditions or causes called *degenerative diseases*. In fact, the three leading causes of death in our society as a whole—diseases of the heart, malignant neoplasms (cancer), and cerebrovascular diseases—all fall into the category of degenerative diseases.

Deaths produced by degenerative diseases have their own typical characteristics. For example, vascular diseases (coronary attacks, strokes, embolisms, aneurysms, and so on) sometimes cause quick, unanticipated deaths. However, although the outcome or exposure of the underlying condition may be sudden (as is suggested by the term *stroke*), these diseases themselves usually develop slowly over time and generally produce a gradual (but often unnoticed) debilitation. Of course, such debilitation may not occur; the first symptom may be a dramatic, unexpected, almost instantaneous death. The dying associated with such a death may be relatively painless—in one's sleep or after a rapid onset of unconsciousness. But deaths resulting from degenerative diseases may also be quite painful—even heart attacks do not necessarily lead to "easy" deaths.

Dying Trajectories

Different causes of death are typically associated with different patterns of dying. These patterns have been called *dying trajectories* (Glaser & Strauss, 1968). Their differences are marked primarily by duration and shape. *Duration* refers to the time involved between the onset of dying and the arrival of death, whereas *shape* designates the course of the dying process, whether one can predict how it will advance, and whether or not death is expected or unexpected. Some dying trajectories involve a swift or almost instantaneous onset of death, and others last a long time; some can be anticipated, others are ambiguous or unclear (perhaps involving a series of remissions and relapses), and still others give no advance warning at all (see Figure 1.3).

In general, communicable diseases lead to a relatively brief dying trajectory. That is, the period of time from the onset of the infection until its resolution, either in death or in recovery, is usually short. This period of time during which one may be seriously incapacitated by communicable diseases is usually measured in days or weeks.

In many contemporary societies, degenerative diseases can often be identified and treated. When such treatment is successful, it may restore quality and long life to persons with such diseases. In other circumstances, it may only have the effect of prolonging the dying of such people, at least insofar as that dying is related to the same condition rather than to some other intervening event. This prolongation of living or of the dying period is characteristically measured in terms of months and even years.

For example, the degenerative disease that is currently the second leading cause of death in our society and that is likely soon to become the leading cause of death is neoplastic disease or cancer in all of its various forms. Cancer is one of the most dreaded diseases in our culture. It remains a frightening diagnosis, even though it much less frequently carries with it a prognosis of imminent death than it did 25 years ago. Perhaps much of the fear of cancer has to do with the dying processes associated with it. Familiar images of cancer usually involve intense, chronic dying producing pain and discomfort for a long period of time. These images have been reinforced by the popular media and by the personal stories of a number of prominent individuals (for exam-

FIGURE 1.3   *Some contrasting dying trajectories.*

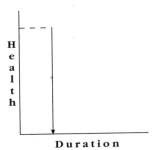

D u r a t i o n

Sudden death occurring at an
unpredictable point in life

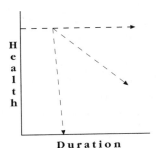

D u r a t i o n

A predictable point of resolution
for a life-threatening condition,
following which there may be
ongoing health, decline in health,
or death

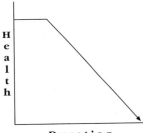

D u r a t i o n

Slow, steady decline in health
with a predictable time of
death (chronic illness)

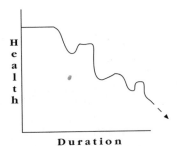

D u r a t i o n

Slow, ambiguous decline in
health with an unpredictable
time of death

ple, Lear, 1980; Rosenbaum, 1988; Ryan & Ryan, 1979; Wertenbaker, 1957).
Nevertheless, this may not be an entirely appropriate depiction of cancer. Not
all cancers are fatal, some do not involve much pain or discomfort, and much
depends upon family predisposition and individual circumstances. But
images associated with death persist long beyond their original justification
(Parsons, 1951; Sontag, 1978), and those that we have described are familiar to
most contemporary Americans.

Notice that the dying process associated with degenerative diseases is
considerably different from the one associated with communicable diseases.
In general, the former is lengthier, even much lengthier, it is often far less
predictable, and it may be linked with long-term pain and suffering, loss of
physical control over one's body, or loss of one's mental faculties. Diseases of
this sort include motor neuron disease (for example, amyotrophic lateral
sclerosis or "Lou Gehrig's disease"), Alzheimer's disease, Parkinson's disease, muscular dystrophy, and multiple sclerosis. As we have noted, HIV
infection is an exception to this classification, representing as it does a communicable disease that develops into the chronic complications of AIDS,

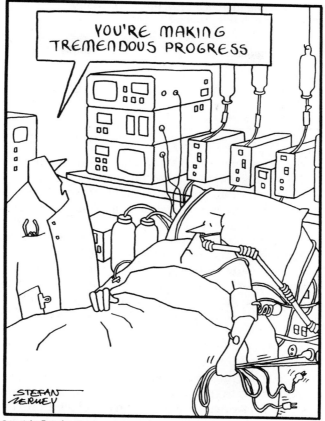

Copyright © Stefan Verwey.

which resemble degenerative diseases in their overall pattern (Fee & Fox, 1992).

The relative prominence of degenerative diseases changes our experiences with dying and death. Although death is less frequently encountered in our society, when it does occur it is often associated with a more protracted and more ambiguous dying trajectory. Death arising from degenerative diseases is more likely to become a drain on physical and emotional resources. Caregivers will be required to provide care for much longer periods of time. The physical care they are required to provide most frequently has to do with the management of increasing debilitation and often (but not always) chronic, high-intensity pain or other sources of distress.

*P*lace of Death

If one were present at the deathbed of a person 100 years ago, one would almost certainly have been in that person's home. That is where most peo-

TABLE 1.4   Deaths by Place of Death, United States, 1988 (Based on Reports from 44 States)

	Number	Percent
Total	2,171,196	100.0
In hospital or medical center	1,296,206	59.7
Not in hospital or medical center[a]	874,148	39.0
Place unknown	842	———

[a] Includes all other institutions and entries.
SOURCE: National Center for Health Statistics, 1991.

ple—perhaps as many as 80 percent—died: in their own beds (Lerner, 1970). This means that they were surrounded by sights, sounds, smells, and people that were quite familiar to them. Hospitals or other sorts of health care institutions were not typical of death-related experiences in our society in previous eras and may not now be characteristic of death-related experiences in many underdeveloped parts of the world. In the past, one certainly did not leave the comforts of home—one's own bed, one's own friends and family—to go somewhere else to die. By contrast, the majority of people in our society today die in a public institution of some sort (usually a hospital or long-term care facility)—in a strange place, in a strange bed, and surrounded mostly by strangers (National Center for Health Statistics, 1991; see Table 1.4).

When most people died at home, their primary health care providers usually were members of their extended family. The care provided was largely palliative—that is, care for symptoms. If there was fever, a cool cloth was offered along with frequent washings of the person. Food was familiar, prepared as usual; favorite food selections could be provided by people who knew one's preferences. When one grew frightened, people who knew one well were there to hold one's hand, sit with one, read or recite words of comfort, and share their love.

When death was near, the family also was near, in the same or next room. After death, the family would clean and clothe the body—the last act of love in a lifelong drama. The body might well be left in the bed while friends and neighbors "visited." Or perhaps the body was placed in a coffin (sometimes handmade by family members—another last action for the deceased) and laid out in the parlor for a wake or visitation. After the funeral, the body might have been lowered by the family into a grave that they might also have dug in a nearby family plot or churchyard. As a mark of special honor, it would have been the family that would have filled in the grave. The struggles of one family to do this are well depicted in Faulkner's novel *As I Lay Dying* (1930).

In this sort of situation, death is familiar. Most members of a family would have seen, heard, and touched death by way of the dead body of a family member. Children, too, were included here. If grandmother was dying in her bed in the same house, children participated by talking with her, sitting with her, or helping with small chores. Children obviously were present during the wake (since it was held in the home) and the funeral. Death would not have been a stranger in these children's lives.

All of this has changed for most (but not all) Americans. In 1949, 49.5 percent of all deaths in our society occurred in some sort of health care institution (mainly in a hospital). By 1958 and continuing through 1988, some 60 percent of all deaths in the United States took place in an institution; more than 53 percent in a hospital or medical center and slightly more than 6 percent in some sort of long-term care facility (Lerner, 1970; National Center for Health Statistics, 1991). What has happened in our society is that for many, death has gradually been moved out of the family home. In turn, families have more and more become spectators at a family member's death, rather than participants or primary caregivers. When many Americans die today, they are away from the people they know best and with whom they have shared personal, long-term histories. Personal interests, values, needs, preferences are largely unknown by the people providing care. This is not a criticism of professional caregivers; our point is only to note that they are different from those who would have provided care in the past.

Because dying persons are now often out of the home, death is unknown to many of us. In these circumstances, family members may not be present at the moment of death in our society. Except among certain groups (for example, some Mormons, Jews, and Amish), the last loving actions—cleaning and dressing the body—for most persons who die in our society are performed by strangers: nurses, nurse's aides, funeral directors. (A funeral director once told us that he sees it as his job to keep the family from having anything to do. Although that is surely well meaning, it simply forces them into the helpless, empty inertia of bystanders.) The body is most likely taken from the place where death occurred to a funeral home. There, after preparation, the family sees the body mysteriously appear, dressed, arranged, made up. In many ways, the actual event of death is hidden or removed from the lives of most people. At the cemetery, at least in many places today, the family may also be removed from the grave site before the casket is lowered into the grave, or the last separation may take place at a chapel near the cemetery entrance and at a distance from the grave site (Raether, 1989).

What all this means is that direct experience with all facets of natural human death has been diminished in our society. Care for the dying and care of the dead has been moved away from the family and out of the home for many in our society (although this is changing somewhat with the support of hospice and other home-care programs). Thus, many may have little experience with the moments immediately before, at the time of, or immediately after the death of someone they love. For these individuals, death is increasingly distanced—some would say estranged or made alien—from the mainstream of life's events.

How Did These Patterns Develop?

When we think about changing encounters with death, several factors rise to our attention. Studying mortality rates, we find that they already had begun to

A visitation at a contemporary American funeral home.

decrease in a noticeable way in the middle to latter half of the 19th century. What was happening that could account for this decrease?

The earliest and most important factor was *industrialization*. This historical and social phenomenon had several immediate consequences. Among them were increased production of food, better clothing, and better housing, all of which supported a healthier population. That is, improvements in the general standard of living meant that death became a less familiar visitor in human lives.

Another implication of industrialization was that methods of communication and transportation improved. This can easily be shown to be significant in affecting mortality rates. The development of more effective means of communication (for example, telegraph and telephone) and more effective means of transportation (for example, rail systems, better highways, more efficient trucking) changed the pattern of encounters with death. For instance, now when crops failed in one place, that fact could be made known to people in other areas, surpluses from elsewhere could be moved to that place, and malnutrition and starvation could be alleviated or eliminated. High death rates from hunger and malnutrition in some poor societies in recent years have exposed deficiencies in just these aspects of those societies. Food shipped from other parts of the world often goes to waste when bottled up by inadequate port and distribution facilities.

The second major factor in reducing mortality rates involved *public health measures*. That is, as disease came to be better understood, isolation of those with communicable diseases (quarantine), separation of drinking water sources from sewage, and other improvements in basic sanitation contributed to declining mortality rates.

During this early period of decline in overall mortality rates, average life expectancy improved only slowly. Fewer people died, but young people—infants in particular—continued to die at high rates. Nutrition and preventive health measures had to be understood better before overall death rates, and particularly deaths in infancy, could be reduced further. When such measures were pursued in increasingly effective ways, average life expectancy showed significant gains in the late 1930s and 1940s.

This brings us to the second quarter of the twentieth century and the third major factor in reducing mortality rates, *modern medicine*. By this time, the hospital had begun to be a major contributor to health care. The biomedical model of disease had become dominant with its tendencies to emphasize cure over prevention. Physicians were now important in providing health care, and that health care was no longer largely palliative but had become curative in many important ways. To provide this sort of health care, special technologies were developed, and many of these technologies were quite expensive. Thus, they were localized in particular places, mainly hospitals. Health care was usually not delivered to where the sick person was; rather, the person with disease was delivered to the place where health care was located.

Medicine had now become an important factor in reducing mortality rates and in accelerating changes that had begun much earlier. Especially since the introduction of successful antibiotics—largely a post–World War II phenomenon—modern medicine has become the source of many of the improvements in mortality rates and in the average life expectancy rates of contemporary peoples, at least in the industrialized nations. All of these factors affect both overall mortality rates and infant mortality rates, although the latter have tended to lag behind the former and only approached their current levels in the late 1950s and 1960s.

And so we arrive at our world: for many people today death is removed in numerous important ways from the home and from the mainstream of contemporary living. Of course, this does not mean that death no longer comes into our world in any form. And how it comes into our world differs depending on certain variables. How our family, our ethnic group, our local community encounters and deals with death and dying has a strong impact on our personal experiences. For example, some ethnic groups (see Chapter 4) resist the tendencies often found elsewhere in our society to institutionalize the dying.

We will all die, sooner or later. And we will all have encounters with death, dying, and bereavement throughout the course of our lives. What this chapter has shown is that those encounters will typically be different for us from those that we would have had in times past in our own country or that we would have at present in other parts of the world. Our encounters with death in the United States today are an important component in a very special set of experiences. In many ways, these experiences represent very desirable improvements over the lot of other human beings; in other ways, they have less favorable implications. Both aspects of those changing experiences with death will be explored further in subsequent chapters.

Summary

In this chapter, we have learned about contemporary encounters with death, especially those found in the developed societies of North America and western Europe. We have examined those encounters both in themselves and as they differ from mortality patterns in the same societies in the past or in developing societies in other parts of the world at present. In our society today, mortality rates are lower overall, average life expectancy is longer, people die mainly of degenerative rather than communicable diseases, and more people die in institutions than at home. In addition, we have examined some changes in society that are correlated with these changes in mortality patterns.

QUESTIONS FOR REVIEW AND DISCUSSION

1. Two types of statistical data can be used to illustrate changes in encounters with death in American society: mortality rates and average life expectancy. How have these changed over the last 100 years in the United States? How have these changes affected your encounters with death, dying, and bereavement?

2. People in American society 100 years ago often died of communicable diseases; today they often die of degenerative diseases. How do we distinguish these two sorts of causes of death, and what are the associated patterns of dying typically like? How might these different causes of death affect your encounters with death, dying, and bereavement?

3. This chapter has noted changes in the locations where people typically die in American society. Think about how encounters with death are likely to be different when a person dies at home and when a person dies away from home (for example, in an institution like a hospital or nursing home). How will these changes in location affect the encounters with death of the person who is dying and of those who are his or her survivors?

4. An important issue to think about is what might account for the changes noted in this chapter related to encounters with death. Think about how the following factors have affected these encounters: (a) improved general living conditions (better nutrition and shelter); (b) improved communication and transportation; (c) public health measures; and (d) modern medicine. Which of these first and most greatly affected encounters with death?

Account for each factor's effect on encounters with death, dying, and bereavement.

SUGGESTED READINGS

Note that this list and those that follow at the end of the other chapters in this book focus almost exclusively on book-length publications. Bibliographical data for these publications is given in the reference list at the end of this volume.

The basic materials and principles of demography are described in the following sources:

Centers for Disease Control. *Morbidity and Mortality Weekly Report.* Provides current information and statistics about disease.

National Center for Health Statistics. *Monthly Vital Statistics Report.* Provisional data for a particular month or year appear approximately three to four months later; final data appear approximately two to two-and-a-half years later.

National Center for Health Statistics. *Vital Statistics of the United States.* Published annually; annual data appear in print approximately three years later.

National Safety Council. *Accident Facts.* Published annually.

Shryock, H. S., Siegel, J. S., & Associates. (1980). *The Methods and Materials of Demography.*

United States Bureau of the Census. (1975). *Historical Statistics of the United States, Colonial Times to 1970, Bicentennial Edition.*

United States Bureau of the Census. *Statistical Abstract of the United States.* Published annually; reflects data from two to three years earlier.

Connections between mortality rates and socioeconomic factors are examined in the following:

Benjamin, B. (1965). *Social and Economic Factors Affecting Mortality.*

Cohen, M. N. (1989). *Health and the Rise of Civilization.*

Goldscheider, C. (1971). *Population, Modernization, and Social Structure.*

Kitagawa, E. M., & Hauser, P.M. (1973). *Differential Mortality in the United States: A Study in Socioeconomic Epidemiology.*

Preston, S. H. (1976). *Mortality Patterns in National Populations: With Special Reference to Recorded Causes of Death.*

Differences in mortality rates arising from age or gender are considered in the following:

Preston, S. H., & Haines, M. R. (1991). *Fatal Years: Child Mortality in Late Nineteenth-Century America.*

Retherford, R. D. (1975). *The Changing Sex Differential in Mortality.*

Stillion, J. M. (1985). *Death and the Sexes: An Examination of Differential Longevity, Attitudes, Behaviors, and Coping Skills.*

CHAPTER 2

Changing Attitudes Toward Death

This chapter examines societal attitudes associated with death. The term *attitude* arose in art; originally it meant the disposition or posture of a figure in statuary or painting. In turn, that idea led to the notion of a posture of the body that could be related to a particular mental state. From there, *attitude* came to be associated with some "settled behaviour or manner of acting, as representative of feeling or opinion" (Simpson & Weiner, 1989, I, p. 771).

These definitions contribute to a better understanding of what an attitude is. It is a way of presenting oneself to or being in the world. If one's bodily posture (one's attitude) includes an upraised fist, a general tenseness, and a facial grimace as one leans toward another person, the posture itself will affect how that particular encounter goes. Compare this first attitude with one that includes open arms, a smile, and a generally relaxed body. This is what needs to be emphasized: one's way of being in the world, or how one meets the world, influences which encounters one has and how those encounters go. Of course, it also works the other way around; one's encounters influence one's bodily postures and habits of mind.

In this chapter, the role that attitudes play in death-related experiences is illustrated through a brief example taken from Amish life in the United States (compare Bryer, 1979; Hostetler, 1980; Zielinski, 1975) and is explained through an analysis of the ways in which encounters and attitudes interact in death-related experiences. The main portion of the chapter consists of a description of Western attitudes toward death; a concluding case study involves the Puritans in 17th-century New England.

The Death of an Amish Man

John Stolzfus bore one of the most common names in the Old Order Amish community in eastern Pennsylvania where he had lived all of his life. The Stolzfus family traced its roots through 18th-century immigrants from Alsace to Swiss origins in the 16th-century Anabaptist movement. The Anabaptists were persecuted in Europe for their rejection of infant baptism (on the grounds that children come into the world without a knowledge of good and evil, and thus do not need to be baptized as infants in order to remove sin). The Amish (named after their founder, Jacob Ammann) are one of the few groups that survive today from the Anabaptist movement. No Amish remain in Europe, but some 90,000 can be found in the United States and Canada.

As a member of a close-knit Amish community, John Stolzfus centered his life on religious beliefs and practice, a large extended family, and work on a farm. The Old Order Amish are known for their distinctive dress (plain, dark clothes fastened with hooks and eyes, broad-brimmed hats, and full beards without mustaches for the men; bonnets and long, full dresses for the women), their use of horse-drawn buggies instead of automobiles, their pacifism, and their rejection of many modern devices (such as telephones, highline electricity, and tractors with pneumatic tires).

These are the outward expressions of a slow-changing culture that is determined to follow biblical injunctions: "Be not conformed to this world" (Rom. 12:2) and "Be ye not unequally yoked together with unbelievers" (2 Cor. 6:14). Amish society essentially turns inward to community (*Gemeinschaft*) in order to worship God, moderate the influences of humanity's evil circumstances, and preserve values in ethical relationships through obedience and conformity. The community emphasizes a blend of religion and culture: an emphasis on oral tradition (the *Ordnung*), shared practical knowledge, closeness to nature, respect for elders, striving for self-sufficiency, and smallness in social scale (usually, 30 to 40 households in geographical proximity take turns in hosting biweekly religious services in their homes).

The Stolzfus family rose with the sun and went to bed shortly after nightfall. As a child, John was assigned chores that contributed to meeting the needs of his family. This sort of work continued during his school years. John's schooling did not extend beyond the eighth grade, since members of the community judged that this was sufficient for the sort of lives that they had chosen to lead and they were wary that further formal education might only tend to subvert their traditional beliefs and values. Like most of his peers, John was baptized at the age of 18 into his local church district, and he soon married a young woman from the same community one November day.

At first, the young couple lived with John's family and he continued to work on their farm. Eventually, through a small inheritance and with some financial help from their families, John and his wife bought a small piece of their own land to farm. The birth of their first three children, building their own house, and the great communal activity of raising a large barn on their farm all marked a very productive period in John's life.

Shortly after the birth of their fifth child, John's first wife died of an infection. Relatives helped with the care of the children and with some of the work on the expanding farm until John found one of his wife's unmarried cousins who was willing to marry him and take on the role of mother for his existing children and for the additional children that they would have together. After that, life went on for many years in a quiet and steady way. Eventually, the offspring from both of John's marriages grew up and were themselves married. John and his second wife did not stand out in any special way, but they did become respected members of their community, he as a deacon or minister to the poor in the church, and she for her work in church groups and for her quiet presence at community gatherings.

Eventually, after what he thought of as a good life, John began to decline in vigor and in his ability to get around. In accordance with Amish custom, a small house (called a "grandfather house") was built next to the main farmhouse, and John retired there. After his retirement, John concentrated on reading his beloved Bible, whittling simple wooden toys, and spending time with his grandchildren. When he could no longer get out of bed, both John and other members of his community realized that his death was not far off. Gradually, Amish neighbors of all ages began to come by in order to pray together and say goodbye one last time. John spoke openly of his coming death and used these visits to encourage others to prepare for and calmly accept their own deaths. At the age of 82, John Stolzfus died peacefully one night in his own bed, as one of his daughters sat quietly in a nearby rocking chair and two of his grandchildren slept in their own beds in the same room.

The family cleaned and dressed John's body in the traditional white garments. Then the body was placed in a six-sided wooden coffin that had been made ready a few weeks before and the coffin was laid out in the central room of the house on top of several planks and two sawhorses covered by a plain sheet. Friends helped with many of these arrangements and made sure that those who had known John were notified of his death. That evening, the next day, and the following evening, other members of the community came to the house to bring gifts of food and to offer practical, emotional, and spiritual support to John's family. Several people took turns sitting with the body through the night until the grave could be dug and other preparations made for the funeral. In keeping with the whole of his life, John Stolzfus's funeral was a simple event, a familiar ritual that involved members of the community in the services, the burial, a communal meal afterward, and a recognized pattern of consolation activities during the following weeks and months. No one was shocked or surprised by this death or by its surrounding events. Experience, tradition, and shared attitudes had prepared individuals and the community as a whole to support each other and to contend with the cycles of life and death in their midst.

Death-Related Attitudes

Chapter 1 examined how death-related events thrust themselves into human life. These encounters constitute one important element of experiences with death. The present chapter explores a second important aspect of those experiences: our attitudes toward death. When events in the world come to our attention, we are already in a particular posture; that is, our beliefs, feelings, and habits of thought lead us to receive information and process encounters in selective ways. For instance, we pay attention to what one person is saying, even while we ignore other communications going on in the background—or vice versa. Death-related attitudes are both products and determinants of at least some of our encounters with the world. Thus, the central issue relating to attitudes concerns the ways in which patterns of belief and feeling enter into what we think and do, especially as our attitudes become dispositions or habitual ways of thinking about and acting in the world.

What this means is that we human beings *contribute to* our experiences of the world. We are not mere passive receivers of information. We shape and form our knowledge of what is happening, depending upon our prior beliefs and feelings. We meet the world from a particular stance, in specific ways. The Amish do this in their own special ways; everyone does it in some way or other.

This is not to deny that what is happening in the world helps to shape in its own ways our knowledge and understanding of the world. Death-related encounters certainly do play an important role in shaping death-related attitudes. But it works the other way around, too. Attitudes also help to shape encounters. For instance, unlike the example of John Stolzfus, most people in the United States today who are dying are doing so in a hospital or other institution. Consequently, their deaths may be physically removed from the presence of family members and friends. That makes such deaths remote from those individuals. Most people in these circumstances do not meet up with death very often. This contributes to and supports a belief that death is or should be invisible. In addition, if one's habitual way of behaving in the face of someone else's stress is to withdraw because it creates discomfort, then one is likely to stay away from the hospital where someone is dying. In these ways, *attitudes* toward death (for example, "death is stressful—stay away from stressful situations") influence encounters. In other words, the attitudes that one holds may tend to encourage one to withdraw or become remote from encounters with death.

So our encounters with and attitudes about death interact to shape our knowledge and understanding of it. People's experiences with death are complex and multidimensional. As has been seen, the structure of encounters with death in the United States has changed dramatically over time for most Americans. This may be less true for the Amish, whose roots and current practices are closely bound to a culture that reflects attitudes that are not typical of most contemporary Americans. Not surprisingly, the attitudes of most Americans today are different from those of the Amish and have changed from those of earlier eras. Now it will be useful to study more closely large-scale changes in Western attitudes toward death.

Western Attitudes Toward Death

To understand death-related attitudes across Western history, it is useful to pay attention to descriptions proposed by historians, sociologists, and anthropologists. In particular, our attention will focus most strongly on the work of a French cultural historian, Philippe Ariès (1974b, 1981). In his studies, Ariès examined how attitudes toward death have changed in Western society from the early Middle Ages to the present. Although the bulk of his evidence came from France, Ariès also looked at examples from other parts of Europe and from the United States.

Ariès found that he could differentiate distinct changes in attitudes toward death over roughly the last 1,500 years. He divided these attitudes into five basic patterns (see Table 2.1). Ariès further described each basic pattern by dividing it into two primary components: attitudes toward death itself and attitudes toward the dead. This basic two-part analysis will be employed throughout this chapter.

Each of the five basic patterns can be associated with a different period in Western history. But, as Ariès clearly indicated, these patterns and their accompanying attitudes do not simply come into being and then pass from view. It is probably more accurate to see specific patterns of attitudes as being *dominant* in a particular historical period, but also as continuing to exist in later periods. So today one may find examples of many, if not all, of these attitudes depending upon where one looks and whom one studies. More significantly, several of these attitudes can coexist in any society and in any individual. This is the main point: to recognize the different possibilities that may characterize society's attitudes toward death.

TABLE 2.1   Death-Related Attitudes in Western Thought: Five Patterns and Two Themes According to Philippe Ariès

Tame Death	Death of the Self	Remote and Imminent Death	Death of the Other	Death Denied; Forbidden Death
THEME 1: ATTITUDES TOWARD DEATH				
The moment of death is familiar, simple, and public	The moment of death is a final ordeal; it affects the Last Judgment by God of the person			The moment of death is banished from view
Focus is on the community	Focus is on the dying person		Focus is on survivors	Focus is on survivors (or bureaucrats?)
Death is a sleep, until the Second Coming of Christ	Death leads to heaven or hell	Death is a natural event but is also frightening; ambivalence is the main feature	Death is an intolerable separation from the beloved; it is a sleep awaiting a reunion. Death is also a release into nature; there is little mention of God or hell.	Death is dirty and indecent
Afterlife is nonthreatening	Afterlife may involve suffering			
THEME 2: ATTITUDES TOWARD THE DEAD				
Bodies are buried in common graves in cemeteries near churches; the powerful are buried in the churches themselves	For upper classes, coffins are used and the grave site is marked; others still buried in common graves	Cemeteries move away from churches; serve *only* as burial grounds	Private graves are common; cult of the dead (visiting graves, etc.)	Coffins are "caskets"
Cemeteries are public squares		Fascination with cadaver; dissection becomes a "fashionable art"	The dead are disembodied spirits that may continue to be in this world; rise of "spiritualism"	Emphasis is on visitation, attempt to make dead appear to be "alive" ("sleeping")
		Survivors keep some part of the dead loved one (heart or hair); the "eroticization" of death		

SOURCE: Ariès, (1981).

Human beings are complex creatures. Their attitudes are likely to be equally complex toward any subject that is as central to human life as is death. Recognizing this complexity, we undertake to disentangle different sorts of attitudes so that each can be studied more clearly. Holding each of these strands apart for investigation helps to clarify their individual roles within the overall fabric of human experience, although in everyday life they run together and intertwine.

Tame Death

Ariès (1981) used the phrase *tame death* to describe the first typical pattern of death-related attitudes. He explained that he chose this title to contrast with contemporary attitudes in which death seems to be regarded as a wild force, beyond our control and often not subject to human domination.

Ariès used this first pattern as a standard; he tested all the other patterns against it. Tame death is the most basic pattern in the sense that it is the most pervasive and the most persistent. Ariès believed that this pattern is present today. For instance, he argued that many working-class people in the West display some of these attitudes. Such attitudes are also found in many people in rural areas.

The attitude that sees death as tame emerged in antiquity. By the early Middle Ages (fifth to eighth centuries, perhaps), the dominant attitude toward death was one of familiarity. Ariès wrote that this attitude toward death has two essential characteristics: death has a familiar simplicity and it is a public event.

Death did not come as a surprise to people who had this attitude. The dying person knew that he or she was dying. No attempt was made to evade death; instead, an accepted and expected ritual was associated with death. Dying persons lay quietly on their backs, crossed their arms on their chests, and prayed. Ariès reported that dying persons who viewed death as tame may have felt some regret for the loss of their lives, but basically they calmly accepted the inevitable. They may also have reviewed things they had owned and friends they had loved. Such dying persons asked forgiveness of friends, and commended first the friends and then themselves to God. Then communication ceased and the person waited calmly for death. Routine, simple, easeful: this is the picture of death for these persons.

This calm simplicity was related to a belief about what death is. For most people in Christian Europe at that time, death was believed to be a sleep. Those who died were thought to sleep until the Second Coming of Christ. At that moment, the saints would enter a heavenly home; those who were not saints would remain forever asleep. In either case, death would be peaceful and nonthreatening.

The second characteristic of this pattern of attitudes associated with death is that death was always a public event. In fact, people who shared this attitude thought of a vile and ugly death as one that was sudden and solitary. Until the 18th century, the dying person was, and preferred to be, surrounded by friends, family, neighbors, and other members of the community who chose

A repository for bones, in France.

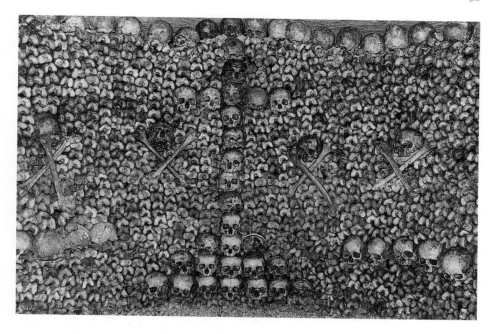

to be present. In part, this was because the individual was not believed to be preeminently important in this scene; the community mattered most. Death was a social event that affected the entire community, and the whole community, not just the individual who died, had to deal with it. Thus, death was not to be accomplished alone.

Tame death is also characterized by a particular attitude toward the dead. Ancient people had feared the proximity of the dead, who were thought of as impure. Thus, the dead were not allowed to remain inside towns; ancient cemeteries were outside of towns. This set of attitudes continued until the early Middle Ages, when the pattern that Ariès called tame death came into being. Then, as Christianity became the dominant mode of thought in the West, the earlier set of attitudes began to change. People wanted to be buried near the bodies of the martyrs, presumably because the martyrs' relics would protect them at the Second Coming, and basilicas began to be built in these places. So when death became a tame feature of human experience, the dead had ceased to inspire fear. Living people now moved around near the dead with no anxiety, and eventually all cemeteries were moved near churches. The poor were buried on top of each other in large, unmarked common graves in churchyards, while the powerful were buried individually within the grounds of the churches or inside the church buildings themselves, below the floor.

As bodies piled up in small churchyards, their bones were dug up periodically to make way for new bodies. The bones were placed in open attics around the cemeteries—the charnels. Seeing the bones provided lessons about the universality of death and decay. Meanwhile, cemeteries also became centers of social life; marketing, judicial proceedings, and social gatherings occurred in them. They were the public squares of their time.

Michelangelo's
The Last
Judgment *in the*
Sistine Chapel,
Rome.

   Two conclusions follow: death and the dead are familiar in these circumstances; present-day attitudes in society, generally, are quite different from those described as involving tame death.

Death of the Self

Slowly, another pattern evolved. By the 12th and 13th centuries, Western attitudes toward death had changed. Ariès (1985) dramatized one aspect of these changes by describing sculptures found in medieval cathedrals. Prior to the 11th century, when reference was made to the next world, an image of the Second Coming of Christ was dominant. In this image, Christ was portrayed in glory, surrounded by the saints (including the dead members of the church). But in the 12th century another image began to play a larger and larger role:

the image of the Last Judgment, where the just are separated from the damned. This change in the dominant imagery reveals that no longer could persons be assured of their own salvation. Hence, people began to feel anxiety about what would happen to them after death.

For anxiety to arise about personal salvation, individuals must have a strong sense of self. According to Ariès, this is an important factor in the changes that occurred. Recognition of the significance of the individual was beginning to increase. Biography—the history of a life, my life—now became important. This can be seen in the increasing prevalence of the notion that a book of life, a record or register of what the individual had done, was kept by God or in heaven. According to this notion, the deeds that made up a life were weighed after death. Eventually this idea was replaced with another: people began to see the moment of death as the final ordeal of the individual. At that moment—just preceding the actual event of death—the dying individual supposedly witnessed a struggle between a patron saint and the devil for his or her soul. The patron saint pointed to good deeds accomplished, the devil pointed to bad deeds, and a judgment was rendered. How one behaved at this moment was believed to be crucial because it could determine the outcome and decide the meaning of the person's whole life. Needless to say, the moment of death became laden with great anxiety. This was the origin of the notion of the *ars moriendi*, the art of dying well (Beaty, 1970; Kastenbaum, 1989a; O'Connor, 1942). Elements of an outlook involving a struggle between one's patron saint and the devil can be found in many people's attitudes today.

Several notions come together in this description. The afterlife was no longer seen as nonthreatening. The idea that suffering—everlasting suffering—is one possible outcome of death helped to make death a dreadful event. But there was also a new notion developing here—namely, that what happens after death no longer affects the whole human being, body and soul. By the 14th century, Western thought clearly distinguished the soul from the body, and death was understood to be the separation of the soul from the body.

The body was now seen by many as a "bag of excrement." It was itself corruption; illness was believed to come from the body. At death, the body simply proceeded on its essential, inevitable path toward total corruption. Thus, during the 14th to the 16th centuries an image frequently associated with death was the *transi*—a half-decomposed corpse. The *danse macabre* or "dance of death" also became a popular image (Kastenbaum, 1989c; Kurtz, 1934; Meyer-Baer, 1970). That dance was portrayed as occurring in a cemetery, with the dead (usually drawn as transi) leading the living—to death. So the body simply ended up decayed, as mere bones, to be stored in the charnels. That part of the person was gone. What was left to survive, either to experience heavenly ecstasy or infernal torment, was the soul.

The second central theme in Ariès's analysis involves attitudes toward the dead. It has already been shown that an emphasis upon death of the self included a fascination with the dead body: it was frequently portrayed in a half-decomposed state. This fascination showed up in other ways. Much of northern Europe at this time began to cover the face of the corpse. (People in Mediterranean countries resisted this and continued to insist that the face be uncovered.) Eventually, the prevailing custom became one of hiding the body from view. It was either sewn into a shroud or placed in a coffin. Still later, even this was not enough; the coffin itself had to be covered by a cloth (the pall).

The place of burial during this period was either in church or in the cemetery next to the church. A tendency to mark the grave with some sort of sign or structure developed throughout this period. In the ancient world, the burial site, at least for the powerful and wealthy, would have been marked by a tomb. But by the 5th century, graves had become anonymous; this persisted until the 11th century. After the 12th century, the poor (who were the vast majority)— and children—continued to be buried in anonymous, common graves. But the powerful and wealthy began to mark their graves again. Here too, one sees an indication of the rise of the significance of the individual. This second period indeed emphasized the death of the self.

Remote and Imminent Death

According to Ariès (1981), the 16th to the 18th centuries make up an important transition period in Western attitudes toward death. During this time, events worked to change dramatically how people felt and what they believed about death. Many of the changes occurred within a European community that was still dominated by religious modes of thinking. But with the Renaissance and the reformations in religious institutions, changes were set into motion that permanently altered how people thought about, felt about, and reacted to death.

Ariès reported that in the human community two invaders from nature have always been feared: sex and death. The ancient world and medieval Europe kept at bay these invaders of the *civitas* or social community by carefully controlling what people believed and how they behaved with regard to sex and death. But the ancient controls were changing. In the centuries now under consideration, the cultural reins on nature—especially on death—that kept death (at least apparently) tamed were loosening. From now on, death would seem to be untamed, wild, invasive. Ariès claimed that before this period, people generally did not fear death; now they would begin to fear it.

This involves a paradox. Death was proclaimed to be a natural event, not a supernatural one. For example, the notion from the previous period that a struggle goes on at the deathbed for the soul of the dying person was denied. Instead, calm acceptance of one's mortality was expected; this was a natural event. People sought a "beautiful" and "edifying" death. But at the same time, the whole scene had to be carefully controlled. Real effort was expended to keep death at a distance, because death was seen to be frightening. In other words, death was both nearby (natural, beautiful) and at a distance (untamed, dangerous, something to be feared)—both *remote and imminent*. In this single, oxymoronic phrase, Ariès captured the tone of this period: the attitude toward death was primarily one of ambivalence.

Attitudes toward the dead also changed. Fascination with the cadaver deepened. But the old fascination (with the decomposed body—the transi) was replaced by a fascination with the structure of the body itself. The body (like death) was seen as purely natural; at death, the soul left the body and the body decomposed back into the natural ingredients from which it had originated. This separation was nothing to be feared. (What people of this period did come to fear was the disembodied shadow, the "ghost.") At the same time, the belief also arose that we could learn something about life by studying the cadaver. Dissection became a fashionable art and a social event.

This period also saw the rise of a new concern about cemeteries. New cemeteries were situated at a distance from churches (eventually even outside of the towns). These are the ancestors of our modern cemeteries, for they served only one purpose: they were specialized places for burial, not places for social life. Note that this relocation made the dead more remote from the living. Few people were now being buried in churches or in churchyards; nearly everyone was buried in the cemetery.

The dread fascination of the period is seen in several other phenomena. Ariès claimed that with the breakdown of the old taming controls on sex and death, these two invaders penetrated the unconscious and became mixed. In these centuries, one finds for the first time an eroticizing of death. Death is often portrayed now as being inseparable from violence and pain (as in the case of the Marquis de Sade, whose name and deeds have given us the term *sadism*, who linked love and cruelty in the form of a sexual perversion involving the inflicting of pain upon another). Death could now even inspire love and desire. By the 18th century this would reach its climax in stories about the love of the dead. This aspect can also be seen in the practice of keeping some part of the body of the dead loved one. Early in the period this was often the heart; later, people would keep a lock of hair.

For Ariès, this period was one in which people struggled to keep death-related feelings and behavior under tight control, but that control was very fragile. Anxiety, fear, and fascination marked this period. Of course, many people today are also ambivalent about death, although perhaps not in identical ways.

Death of the Other

Many of the seeds planted in the uncertainty and ambiguity regarding death in the 17th and 18th centuries bloomed in the 19th century. The emphasis in this new pattern of feelings, beliefs, and behaviors was on the death of the other—that is, on relationships broken by death. Death was now seen as an intolerable separation. If death for the dying individual still was thought of as the separation of the soul from the body, it was also seen—and this somehow seemed at least as important, if not more important—as the separation of those bound together by human affections. Immortality was believed to begin in this world, in the hearts of those who remembered. Death and the dead body were said to be beautiful; those who died were believed to have been released from suffering.

Death was once again (at least usually) seen as a peaceful, waiting sleep. But whereas in earlier periods the sleeping dead were awaiting the end time, now they were waiting for the reunion with loved ones in the next life. (In Arthur Barron's documentary film *Death* [1969], the brother of a dying man claims that their dead mother is calling him—the notions of longing, yearning, and reunion are at least implicit.)

This notion of a reunion was new. In fact, Ariès found that in the first decades of this period dramatic changes in attitudes occurred very quickly, more quickly than ever before. Many people are still so influenced by these new attitudes, and they are so pervasive, that they are taken for granted. For instance, the notion of a reunion after death with those we love is frequently encountered today. A young girl once described to one of us how she and her mother had baptized their new dog. Their aim in doing this seems to have been to ensure that when they reached the next life, not only would they be reunited with loved persons, but even the household pet would be there, too!

Ariès identified two essential components of the romantic (19th-century) idea of death: first, as already noted, the notion of a reunion, and second, the notion of death as a release into the immensity of the beyond. The vision of God played at best a secondary role; immersion in nature—where nature was infinite—was a more widely accepted concept of what death involves.

Several aspects of this view should be noted. Death was not expected to involve suffering. Hell had virtually disappeared in 19th-century descriptions of the afterlife. American literature carefully described daily life in the afterlife (often called heaven) as remarkably like life in this world. Thus, one child observed in an interview that "when you die, God takes care of you like your mother did when you were alive—only God doesn't yell at you all the time" (Adler, 1979, p. 46).

Second, the notion that death involved the separation of the soul from the body was developed a bit further (19th-century writers liked to talk about the "spirit," rather than the soul). The dead were thought of as "pseudo-living" (Ariès's word), disembodied spirits. Sometimes the spirit of the dead person would continue to be present in this world—at first, near the site of the body. (Thus arose the notion that cemeteries are haunted, dangerous, fearful places.) Later, the spirit would haunt the place where it had lived and loved. (Thus arose the haunting of bedrooms, houses, and such.)

This notion of the dead as spirits gave rise to the new phenomenon of spiritualism. Ariès traces the rise of this movement to the United States. It was here that people first began (mainly in the 19th century) to try to communicate with the spirits of dead persons. This again reflects the intolerability of the separation brought about by death. That separation must be overcome, by communicating with the spirit, or by placing the graves of lovers next to each other under one memorial slab, or by the survivor going down into the grave of the deceased lover and touching or kissing the coffin.

These descriptions perhaps help to make plain why Ariès called the modern period "death untamed." One gets the impression that feelings, beliefs, and behaviors are now indeed nearly out of control. Part of this may be due to the fact that whereas in earlier historical periods human affections were distributed among a larger number of individuals, now human affection was limited to a smaller number of family members. So much feeling concentrated on so few persons helped to make the death of those persons intolerable.

Even though death was thought of as beautiful, not ugly, in this outlook, Ariès believed that this romantic view actually continued the process of hiding death. It was carefully concealed under the mask of beauty.

The romantic "death of the other" also generated wholly new ways to deal with the dead. For example, by the 18th century complaints were being made about the unsanitary character of cemeteries. Whereas earlier people did not seem to mind odors associated with cemeteries (remember how they once were public marketplaces?), now people did mind these odors. Similarly, burial in churches was now attacked on the grounds that it made the churches "unclean." Eventually, it was argued that all cemeteries should be relocated outside of the towns; in fact, many were dug up and physically transferred to such new sites.

In addition, as the cemeteries were moved and as burial became a function of the civil government (rather than of the church), private graves also came to be recommended. Bodies were no longer to be buried on top of each other; now they were only to be buried next to each other. This was a complete break with the past. When private graves became popular—as they did very quickly—the notions of granting the resting place in perpetuity and of the hereditary ownership of the cemetery plot arose. At this point, the cemetery became the focus of all piety for the dead. People wanted markers now; tombs became places to go to remember, to meditate, to pray, and to mourn. Perhaps not surprisingly, the experts announced that cemeteries were in fact not unclean or unhygienic. The visit to the cemetery had been born. Ariès called this pattern a new cult, the cult of the dead. It is well represented by Mount Auburn Cemetery outside Boston, which was dedicated in September 1831 and which is a model of the American "rural" or "garden" cemetery whose art and architecture were intended to instruct the living, inculcate morality, and cultivate the finer emotions (French, 1975; Zanger, 1980).

Most Americans today can recognize this romantic idea of death. Much of what the 19th century passed on has been accepted, while other aspects have been revised, and fresh contributions have been made to a new pattern of attitudes toward death and the dead.

Death Denied

The changes that produced the pattern of attitudes typical of the 20th century occurred rapidly. The pattern of death denied or forbidden death (Gorer, 1965a) has been adopted by so many people in Western society that it seems to many people to be inevitable and natural. That is, many people believe that the ways they currently think and feel about death are typical of all peoples everywhere and at all times. This is a large misperception, as this analysis so far should have demonstrated.

Ariès claimed that an absolutely new attitude toward dying appeared in the 20th century, virtually reversing the customs surrounding death. Much of contemporary American society now sees death as dirty and indecent. It is thought to be somehow offensive or unacceptable to die in public. Death has been made into a solitary, private action. Thus, in contemporary society many appear to believe that the dying person prefers to be left alone to die. Others have disagreed (for example, Hinton, 1967).

Ariès traced the development of this notion to a variety of sources. Whereas earlier peoples thought of death as a public drama in which the chief actor and director was the dying person, attention is now turned away from the dying person to others, a process that was already well under way in the 19th century. So, when one thinks about the death of the other today, the focus of attention is on *our* response to the other person's death. This perhaps reaches its logical climax in our century. The feelings and sensibilities of those around the dying person take precedence. If they are made uncomfortable by the death, then that must be dealt with most vigorously.

The simplest way to protect survivors from the odors, sights, sounds, and feelings associated with death is to remove death from their presence. So contemporary society often banishes death. According to Ariès, when a death occurs in much of today's society, one can hardly tell that anything has happened. Society no longer observes a pause in its ongoing rhythms of working and playing. Except for the brief funeral period—which involves only the closest associates of the dead person and only those who choose to participate—the surface of societal life is unmarked by the death of one of its members. The message seems to be that nothing—or at least nothing important—has happened.

To accomplish this, another sort of hiding must occur. One must hide not just the facts about the expected outcome, one must also hide the emotional response to those facts. Thus, many Americans avoid situations in which feelings might be shown. This is true both before and after a death. In other words, many in contemporary society have also adopted an attitude toward mourning that is historically quite unusual. According to this attitude, mourning is morbid, even pathological. A similar attitude can be found in responses to other losses today in which individuals attempt to avoid or hide from strong negative feelings. In medieval and early modern history, mourning was more a social than an individual activity. It was the community that was threatened by a death; hence, the community's needs had to be met by the mourning rituals. These rituals exposed the anguish of the community and provided ways of assuaging that anguish.

In the 19th century, mourning began to take on an added function. Increasingly, it was seen as a means for survivors to express the suffering associated with the intolerable loss of the loved one. Society shared this suffering with survivors and sought to help the bereaved overcome it. But in the 20th century, society often refuses to share in the suffering of the bereaved. The bereaved are more or less isolated, as the dying person is often isolated. Except in very controlled circumstances (for example, the funeral and the visitation) and ways of expression, grief is to be expressed in private.

Ariès (1981) also pointed to another way in which death has been banished in our society. He described the "medicalization" of Western society. Prior to the 1880s, physicians played little or no role in deathbed scenes. But late in the 19th century, visits to physicians became important, even necessary, steps when illness entered one's life. Death now seemed less and less a natural, necessary phenomenon. People began to believe that technology could achieve almost anything, including the prevention of death. When death occurred, it was an "accident." To prevent this accident from occurring, more and more people went to technological centers of treatment—hospitals and other similar institutions. By the 1930s and 1940s, death had become an event that occurred in hospitals. By 1950, this removal of death to the hospital was widespread. Death was now banished from the home. The result was that death could be kept hidden much more effectively. After all, neighbors and relatives might drop into the home. They were less likely to drop into the hospital, especially given that institution's rules about visiting hours. Thus, Gorer's (1965b) research in England revealed that in only one fourth of the deaths were survivors actually present at the time of death.

Perhaps the ultimate banishment of death occurs when no one is present at the moment of death: the dying person is alone in a room and is unconscious. Here the dying person has lost all control over and any say in his or her death. Death no longer belongs to the dying person, nor even to the family. As Ariès said, death belongs now to bureaucrats.

Attitudes toward the dead show a similar pattern of denial. By 1857, according to Ariès, children's coffins—and eventually all coffins—no longer looked like coffins. They had become caskets. The term *casket* originated as a diminutive form of *cask*, a small box or chest for jewels, letters, or other things of value; caskets themselves were works of art, as tombs used to be. But the 20th century rejected the 19th-century cult of the dead. All memorial activities were now focused on the visit to the deceased. And when people go to a visitation, what they experience is the illusion of life. Morticians carefully work to erase signs of death. Dead bodies are no longer frightening or beautiful, as they were in earlier centuries; now they are "not dead"! After the Civil War in the United States, embalming became an important part of the care of the dead. In American society today, the point of embalming appears to be not so much to preserve the dead body as to keep it from showing signs of death.

Ariès (1974a) concluded that these profound changes in attitudes toward death in Western societies constitute a "reversal of death," which has three central characteristics: (1) the dying person is deprived of his or her own death; (2) mourning is denied; and (3) new funerary rites are invented in the United States.

The Puritans of 17th-Century New England

The critical role of attitudes in shaping the character of experiences with death can be illustrated in one final example: that of the Puritans of 17th-century New England. This example has been chosen because it draws upon a historical group in the United States and because it differs in so many ways from contemporary death-related attitudes. It also reminds us once again that the patterns that Ariès has described are not strictly sequential; one pattern does not simply replace another, and different attitudinal patterns (or different aspects of a pattern) may be emphasized by different groups.

The Puritans originated as a reformist group within the Church of England. Their mission, as Thomas Cartwright (1574, p. 1) wrote, was not "innovation but a renovation, and the doctrine not new but renewed." In particular, the Puritans wished to do away with bishops and with the episcopal structure of the church, along with a number of other "popish" practices that they saw as undesirable remnants from the Roman Catholic church. For both religious and political reasons, the influence of this Puritan point of view rose and fell at different times during the 16th and 17th centuries.

Those Puritans who came to America found a new land in which they were free to uphold their beliefs and practice their religion as they wished. The New England Puritans established thriving settlements in various colonies, but their presence was particularly notable in Massachusetts during the middle and latter portions of the 17th century. Here, they emphasized the importance of preaching and conversion through an intense personal experience.

For the Puritans, everything that existed or happened was part of a divine purpose. At the same time, they viewed human history since the betrayal of Adam and Eve as one long descent into ever-deepening depravity. In this situation, no human being could be truly worthy of salvation, nor could any good works earn the favor of God's grace. Nevertheless, the Puritans believed that God, in His infinite mercy and love, had chosen a select and predetermined few for salvation.

The great question for each individual Puritan was whether or not he or she was a member of God's holy elect. No one could ever have confident knowledge concerning the answer to that question. To think that one did have such knowledge would be to think that one understood the all-knowing mind of God. More likely, to believe that one was assured of salvation was good evidence that one had actually succumbed to the seductive falsehoods of Satan. Confidence in the "sure and certain hope of resurrection to eternal life" was simply not open to the Puritans.

Nevertheless, the question of personal salvation preoccupied individual Puritans. Each Puritan struggled continuously with his or her conscience to discern, in the midst of innumerable signs of personal depravity, at least some indicators or "marks" that he or she might be among the chosen few. As Stannard (1977, pp. 75, 79) has written, Puritanism was "a faith marked by a never-ending, excruciating uncertainty . . . [in which] the Puritans were gripped individually and collectively by an intense and unremitting fear of death, while *simultaneously* clinging to the traditional Christian rhetoric of viewing death as a release and relief for the earthbound soul." For the Puritans, one must constantly recognize one's own utter and total depravity, while at the same time praying earnestly for a salvation that one is helpless to secure.

Puritan preachers dwelt vividly upon the contrast between the potential terrors and bliss of the afterlife. Those who were not among the elect were subject to the eternal torment of the damned. Those who actually were among the elect were themselves troubled by lack of certainty even up to the very moment of death. Thus, as Stannard (1977, p. 89) has argued, "the New England Puritans, despite their traditional optimistic rhetoric, were possessed of an intense, overt fear of death—the natural consequence of what to them were three patently true and quite rational beliefs: that of their own utter and unalterable depravity; that of the omnipotence, justness, and inscrutability of God; and that of the unspeakable terrors of Hell."

It is interesting to note how these attitudes toward death among the New England Puritans worked themselves out with regard not only to individual adults, but also to children and to society as a whole in the late 17th century. The Puritan world view combined a deep love of children with a strong sense of their depravity and sinful pollution (so different, in this latter regard, from the Amish). Also, the era of the Puritans in New England was a time when infants and children were actually at great risk of dying, and when parents gave birth to many children in the expectation that few would remain alive to care for them in the hour of their own deaths. Perhaps for both these reasons, in their personal relationships with their children Puritan parents were advised to maintain an attitude of "restraint and even aloofness, mixed with . . . an intense parental effort to impose discipline and encourage spiritual precocity" (Stannard, 1977, p. 57).

Puritan children were constantly reminded of the likelihood that they might die at any moment. They were threatened with the dangers of personal judgment and damnation in which even their own parents might testify against them. The expectation of reunion with parents after death was denied to them. And they were reminded of the guilt they would bear if through sinfulness they should bring harm to their parents. In this vein, books for children, including even the *New England Primer* (1727/1962) from which they learned the alphabet, were designed to remind young readers of the imminence and possible consequences of death. How different this is from attitudes of today, or even from 19th-century emphases, such as those in one of the famous McGuffey's *Readers* (1866), which stressed eternal reunion of children and parents after death for a new life in heaven (see "What Is Death? A Victorian Dialogue"; also Minnich, 1936a, 1936b; Westerhoff, 1978).

Burial practices are a particularly good indicator of death-related attitudes among the New England Puritans. At first, absence of ceremony and restraint of emotion reflected the Puritan reaction to the excesses of "papist" practices. That is, the corpse was regarded as a meaningless husk, burial was swift and simple, and excessive displays of sadness or grief were discouraged. Funeral sermons were not delivered at the time of burial and were not very different from other forms of preaching.

In the latter half of the 17th century, however, Puritan society in New England experienced many changes that threatened the prospects for its holy mission. Several important early leaders died (for example, John Winthrop,

What Is Death? A Victorian Dialogue

Child: 1. *Mother, how still the baby lies!*
            I can not hear his breath;
            I can not see his laughing eyes;
            They tell me this is death.

         2. *My little work I thought to bring,*
            And sit down by his bed,
            And pleasantly I tried to sing;
            They hushed me: he is dead!

         3. *They say that he again will rise,*
            More beautiful than now;
            That God will bless him in the skies;
            O mother, tell me how!

Mother: 4. *Daughter, do you remember, dear,*
            The cold, dark thing you brought,
            And laid upon the casement here?
            A withered worm, you thought.

         5. *I told you, that Almighty power*
            Could break that withered shell;
            And show you, in a future hour,
            Something would please you well.

         6. *Look at that chrysalis, my love;*
            An empty shell it lies;
            Now raise your wondering glance above,
            To where yon insect flies!

Child: 7. *O yes, mamma! how very gay*
            Its wings of starry gold!
            And see! it lightly flies away
            Beyond my gentle hold.

         8. *O mother! now I know full well,*
            If God that worm can change,
            And draw it from this broken cell,
            On golden wings to range;

         9. *How beautiful will brother be*
            When God shall give him wings,
            Above this dying world to flee,
            And live with heavenly things!

        10. *Our life is like a summer's day,*
            It seems so quickly past:
            Youth is the morning, bright and gay,
            And if 'tis spent in wisdom's way,
            We meet old age without dismay,
            And death is sweet at last.

SOURCE From McGuffey, *McGuffey's New Fourth Eclectic Reader* (1866); pp. 109–110.

An invitation to the funeral of Sir William Phips (1651–1695).

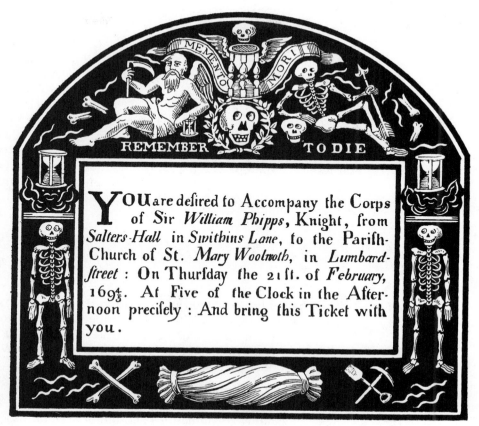

MEMENTO MORI

REMEMBER   TO DIE

YOU are desired to Accompany the Corps of Sir *William Phipps*, Knight, from *Salters-Hall* in *Swithins Lane*, to the Parish-Church of St. *Mary Woolnoth*, in *Lumbard-street*: On Thursday the 21st. of *February*, 169⁴⁄₅. At Five of the Clock in the After-noon precisely: And bring this Ticket with you.

Thomas Shepard, John Cotton, and Thomas Hooker), a civil war in England and an ensuing official doctrine of religious toleration isolated the New England Puritans in their stress on doctrinal righteousness, and growing immigration and mercantilism in America produced an increasingly complex society in which the Puritan community was waning in numbers and signifi-cance (Stannard, 1977).

In reaction, the embattled New England Puritans developed more and more elaborate funeral practices. For example, gloves were sent to friends and acquaintances as a form of invitation to the funeral, church bells were rung on the day of the funeral, a funeral procession conducted the coffin to the burial ground, and those who returned to the church or home of the deceased after the burial would be given food and distinctively designed, costly funeral rings as tokens of attendance. As the deaths of Puritan leaders and community pillars were experienced, prayer was conducted at the funeral and funeral sermons took on the form of eulogies. Gravestones carved with elaborate verses praising the moral and religious character of the deceased began to mark the sites of burial. Clearly, a special set of atti-tudes toward death existed in Puritan New England, shaped by deeply held beliefs and implemented in earnest practice.

Summary

This chapter has revealed that the beliefs, feelings, behaviors, and underlying values that constitute the dominant pattern of death-related attitudes in the United States today are just one pattern among many possible patterns. These distinctive attitudes are the outcome of a changing and developing path. They are not the eternal essence of how human beings everywhere and throughout all time think about, feel about, or behave in the face of death. This is evident from Ariès's survey of Western history and from the two specific examples considered in this chapter, the Amish in America today and the New England Puritans of the 17th century. Patterns of death-related attitudes have changed before; they can, and will, change again.

QUESTIONS FOR REVIEW AND DISCUSSION

1. This chapter has discussed attitudes toward death, dying, and bereavement. Think about how the chapter has described attitudes. How do these differ from encounters (as discussed in Chapter 1)? Why is it helpful to distinguish between these aspects of human experience? How might they influence each other as components in human experience?

2. This chapter described in some detail two particular sets or patterns of attitudes regarding death: those of the Amish and those of the Puritans in New England. Note similarities and differences in these sets of attitudes. How did or do the attitudes of these two groups affect their encounters with death, dying, and bereavement?

3. Much of this chapter focused on Philippe Ariès's description of five patterns of attitudes toward death found in the West. He related these patterns to historical periods, but they can be found throughout many epochs. Which of the five patterns seems most familiar to you? Which aspects of each of the five patterns can you find in your own experience?

4. In the discussion of the five patterns of Western attitudes toward death, Ariès distinguishes between attitudes toward death and attitudes toward the dead. Describe one significant feature of each of the patterns related to these two aspects.

SUGGESTED READINGS

Concerning death-related attitudes and their interpretation, see:

Becker, E. (1973). *The Denial of Death.*
Lonetto, R., & Templer, D. I. (1986). *Death Anxiety.*

The views of Philippe Ariès are set forth in three books:

Ariès, P. (1974). *Western Attitudes Toward Death: From the Middle Ages to the Present.*
Ariès, P. (1981). *The Hour of Our Death.*
Ariès, P. (1985). *Images of Man and Death.*

Along with these, one should read the following celebrated and oft-reprinted essay, which influenced Ariès's analysis of attitudes in today's society:

Gorer, G. (1965). "The Pornography of Death."

On the art of dying (*ars moriendi*) and the *danse macabre*, see:

Beaty, N. L. (1970). *The Craft of Dying.*
Boase, T.S.R. (1972). *Death in the Middle Ages: Mortality, Judgment and Remembrance.*
Kurtz, L. P. (1934). *The Dance of Death and the Macabre Spirit in European Literature.*
Meyer-Baer, K. (1970). *Music of the Spheres and the Dance of Death: Studies in Musical Iconology.*
O'Connor, M. C. (1942). *The Art of Dying Well: The Development of the Ars Moriendi.*

Depictions of various attitudes toward death in Western art, literature, and popular culture can be found in the following:

Bertman, S. L. (1991). *Facing Death: Images, Insights, and Interventions.*
Enright, D. J. (Ed.). (1983). *The Oxford Book of Death.*
Weir, R. F. (Ed.). (1980). *Death in Literature.*

Consult the following concerning death-related attitudes in America:

Dumont, R., & Foss, D. (1972). *The American View of Death: Acceptance or Denial?*
Farrell, J. J. (1980). *Inventing the American Way of Death: 1830–1920.*
Hostetler, J. A. (1980). *Amish Society.*
Mack, A. (Ed.). (1974). *Death in American Experience.*
Stannard, D. E. (1977). *The Puritan Way of Death: A Study in Religion, Culture, and Social Change.*

CHAPTER 3

The Contemporary American Death System

After studying contemporary death-related attitudes and practices in the United States, some writers (such as Gorer, 1965a; Kübler-Ross, 1969) have concluded that this is a death-denying society, one from which death has largely been exiled as a social or public presence. Others (such as Dumont & Foss, 1972; Weisman, 1972) have challenged this conclusion by considering the same issue from different points of view. For example, it has been asked whether the American view of death need be one of either acceptance or denial. Can it not include elements of both postures simultaneously?

This chapter highlights selected factors related to death, dying, and bereavement that either have worked to shape American society or reflect what it has become. The discussion begins with a description of the situation of one young person who is growing up in the United States during the last decade of the 20th century. Then two theoretical models—Goldscheider's contrast between ''uncontrolled'' and ''controlled'' death, and Kastenbaum's notion of a societal death system—are examined as a foundation for surveying some of the most prominent features of the contemporary American death system. That survey emphasizes language about death, media news reports and entertainment programs, and various forms of human-induced death. The chapter closes by identifying four enduring themes that emerge from this analysis and that will reappear throughout the book.

Growing Up with Death in the United States

Drew Weisman was a junior in high school when several events caused him to pay attention to issues associated with death, dying, and bereavement. First, his older sister, Rachel, enrolled in a death and dying course at her community college. Drew was aware that an elective course at his high school dealt with some of these topics, but he had not included that course in his plans for the rest of his high school career.

Almost every evening at supper Rachel would bring up some issue from her course. One night, it was the hospice movement; another night, it was World War II and the Holocaust. At least the latter was a topic in which Drew had some interest, since he had built and owned quite a collection of scale models of propeller-driven military aircraft. Also, everyone in Drew's family was familiar with the story of the brutal Nazis and their horrific attempt to eradicate the Jews. In fact, Drew's grandparents had been among the last to escape to America from Europe just before the Nazis closed the doors to further Jewish emigration.

Drew remembered long, lazy Sabbath afternoons when he was a young child and his grandparents would reminisce about prewar life in Europe and the terrible things that had happened to relatives who had stayed behind. Sometimes, Drew wondered what it might have been like if those relatives had also been able to come to America. He used to ask himself unanswerable questions: Would they have had their own children and grandchildren if they had lived? What would it have been like to grow up with those young people who had never been born?

One evening, Rachel was talking—as usual—about her course, when she happened to mention nuclear weapons. She had just said that since the Soviet Union had disintegrated and was no longer a superpower, there was now much less danger from nuclear weapons. But their younger sister, Sarah, immediately protested that with nuclear power plants all around the world, including a big one not too far away in their own state, one of those plants might somehow break down and spread radiation or other lethal contaminants all over the surrounding landscape. Sarah was very upset about this possibility. Drew was not as fearful as Sarah seemed to be about this subject, but it did make him think about the possibility of his own death.

Apart from his unknown European relatives, no one who was really important in Drew's life had ever died. From time to time, Drew did feel some concern about his elderly grandparents, especially his Grandpa Alvin, to whom he was quite close. But he always dismissed these troublesome thoughts quickly and went back to building his model planes or doing his homework.

When Drew was a boy, his pet dog, Butch, had been run over by a car. That was a terrible experience. Drew had felt awful for many weeks and had decided never to have another pet.

One cold, icy day last year, two boys from the high school had been killed in an automobile accident. There had been a memorial service that students were encouraged to attend, and counselors were around in the halls for several days afterward, but the boys who died had not really been part of Drew's group and he had felt no need to take part in the service.

Drew knew that people said that youngsters who grew up in the "television generation" would experience reports or depictions of nearly 20,000 deaths on the tube before they left high school. And he was aware of a number of popular rock and country songs whose lyrics were about various forms of death and loss. But Drew thought that no one really paid any attention to television (except for sports), and he said that he just listened to the music, not the lyrics, in those songs.

In the end, Drew told himself that he had plenty of time to learn about dying or death. And he did not see much point to all the weeping and wailing Rachel described as part of what she called "good grief." That was probably just another of those catchy phrases from her textbook.

"Uncontrolled" Versus "Controlled" Death

One way of interpreting the personal experiences of Drew Weisman and the death-related encounters and attitudes that we have analyzed on a much larger scale in Chapters 1 and 2, is to imagine a contrast between two broad models of social interaction with death (Goldscheider, 1971). One model is characterized by what appears to be a relative lack of control in dealings with death:

high overall mortality rates, high infant and maternal mortality rates, a significant degree of variation between places and fluctuation over time in death rates, low average life expectancy, strong influence of communicable diseases as leading causes of death, relatively swift and anticipated dying trajectories, and many deaths in the home, often accompanied by attitudes emphasizing familiarity with death. In other words, as Goldscheider has written, "life under extreme conditions of the noncontrol of mortality is precariously short, death is ever-present, shrouded in mystery and uncertainty, and is concentrated among the very young" (p. 126). This is a model of *uncontrolled death*, associated with death-related experiences in the preindustrial world of the past or in underdeveloped parts of the world today.

The other model is characterized by an apparently high degree of control in dealings with death: greatly reduced overall mortality rates along with significant reductions in infant and maternal mortality rates, little variation between places or fluctuation over time in death rates, high average life expectancy, an emphasis upon degenerative diseases as leading causes of death, relatively slow and ambiguous dying trajectories, and a high degree of institutionalization of death, often accompanied by attitudes emphasizing death of the other and seeking to distance society from death or to treat it as a forbidden, even pornographic or inherently offensive, topic. This is a model of *controlled death*, associated with death-related experiences in the United States and other developed areas of the world in the latter part of the 20th century. This model is close to the world of Drew Weisman and his contemporaries.

Of course, despite the fact that human beings have always tried to influence the nature of their experiences with death, those experiences never have been and never will be completely controlled. Death itself marks the ultimate limit of human control, as do many of the experiences associated with death. These two models, therefore, represent extreme examples of how things might be, rather than strict historical realities. But it is worth noting the degree and the ways in which many human beings in contemporary society struggle to influence what is permitted or acceptable both in encounters with and in attitudes toward death.

Death-related encounters can be altered either by changes in society or by interventions that bear directly on mortality patterns. On the one hand, improvements to food, clothing, and shelter make for a better society in which to live and also cause mortality rates to decline and the lethality of some causes of death to diminish. On the other hand, one can alter mortality patterns directly in some ways without otherwise doing much to change society. The most celebrated example of this occurred after World War II when DDT spraying virtually wiped out mosquito-breeding grounds on the island of Sri Lanka (then called Ceylon) (Goldscheider, 1971). Since mosquitoes were the primary carriers of malaria, which had been one of the leading causes of death in Sri Lanka, mortality patterns were directly and immediately affected. Not much else had been changed in Sri Lankan society, but this single change in mortality patterns subsequently led to many social changes, such as rapid population growth and problems with housing and food supplies.

A contemporary scene in an American hospital.

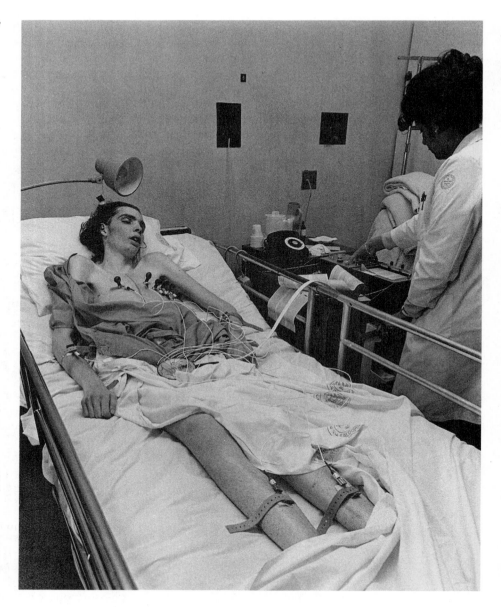

The Death System in Every Society

A more complex and helpful perspective for understanding the death-related experiences of individuals and societies is Kastenbaum's (1972) notion of the *death system*. Kastenbaum defined a death system as the "sociophysical network by which we mediate and express our relationship to mortality" (p. 310). By this, he meant that every society works out, more or less formally and explicitly, a system that it inserts between death and its citizens and that interprets the former to the latter. This is one way to acknowledge the importance of social systems, social realities, and processes of socialization in human interactions with death, dying, and bereavement (Charmaz, 1980; Parsons, 1951). According to Kastenbaum (1972), each societal death system has its own constitutive elements and characteristic functions.

Elements of a death system include the following:

- *People*—individuals defined by their more-or-less permanent or stable roles in the death system, such as funeral directors, lawyers, florists, and life insurance agents
- *Places*—specific locations that have assumed a death-related character, such as cemeteries, funeral homes, health care institutions, and the "hallowed ground" of a battlefield or disaster
- *Times*—occasions that are associated with death, such as Memorial Day, Good Friday, or the anniversary of a death
- *Objects*—things whose character is somehow linked to death, such as death certificates, hearses, obituaries and death notices in the newspaper, weapons, tombstones, gallows, or electric chairs
- *Symbols*—things that have come to signify death, such as a black arm band, a skull and crossbones, certain solemn organ music, and certain words or phrases

Functions of a death system are as follows:

- *To give warnings and predictions*, as in the case of civil defense sirens
- *To prevent death*, as in the case of emergency medical care
- *To care for the dying*, as in the case of modern hospice programs
- *To dispose of the dead*, as in the case of funeral directors, cemeteries, and crematories
- *To work toward social consolidation after death*, as in the case of funeral rituals or self-help groups for the bereaved
- *To help make sense of death*, as in the case of certain religious or philosophical systems
- *To bring about socially sanctioned killing* either of humans or of animals, as in the case of some aspects of police protection, training for war, and capital punishment

The significant claim in the idea of a death system is that such a system will be found in some form in every society. The death system may be formal, explicit, and widely acknowledged in some of its aspects; it may be largely hidden and often unspoken in other aspects. As Blauner (1966) has shown, many small, primitive, tribal societies must organize themselves in large measure around death's recurrent presence; in large, modern, impersonal societies the social implications of death are often less disruptive, less prominent, and more contained. Thus, the death system in contemporary American society appears to act in many important ways to keep death at a distance from the mainstream of life and to gloss over many of its harsh aspects. But no society is without some system for coping with the fundamental realities that death presents to human existence; and one issue to examine in every society is the

> ### What Sort of Death System Have We Created?
>
> We have created systems which protect us in the aggregate from facing up to the very things that as individuals we most need to know.
>
> SOURCE From Evans, *Living with a Man Who Is Dying* (1971), p. 83.

nature of its death system and the effectiveness with which it functions. The remainder of this chapter considers several prominent aspects of the contemporary American death system and four enduring themes that emerge from that system.

Death and Language

One obvious way in which the death system in the United States strives to control death and to influence how death is experienced is evident in language patterns—that is, in language about death and in death-related language. Linguistic usage reflects strong social messages concerning appropriate emotions and behaviors regarding death.

Language About Death

A familiar point made about discussions of death, dying, and bereavement in contemporary American society is that people often go to great lengths to avoid saying the words *dead* and *dying*. In place of this direct language, individuals commonly employ *euphemism*—that is, substitution of a word or expression of comparatively pleasant or inoffensive associations in place of a harsher or more offensive one that would more precisely designate what is intended. Thus, people don't die; they merely "pass away." In principle, euphemisms are pleasing ways of speaking; in practice, they usually involve "prettifying" language in order to seem more delicate, "nice," or socially acceptable and to avoid seeming disagreeable, impolite, or nasty. While use of euphemism is not necessarily undesirable in itself, it can become excessive and reflect an unwillingness to confront realities of life and death directly.

Euphemisms that relate to death are familiar to most users and students of language (Neaman & Silver, 1983; Rawson, 1981) and arise from many contexts. Long before recent interest in "thanatology" (itself a euphemism for death-related studies), these figures of speech were recognized by scholars (for example, Pound, 1936). Terms like "kicked the bucket" (originally, a graphic description of one way of committing suicide by hanging) or "bought the farm" are euphemistic descriptions of death. The "dearly departed" have been "called home," "laid to rest," or "gone to their reward." Much the same is true for those who "conk out," who are "cut down," or whose "number is up." Anyone who is "on his last legs" has "run the good race," "is down for the long count," and "it's curtains." The precise status of those who are "no longer with us" is not quite clear.

Professional caregivers sometimes say that they "lost" Mr. Smith last night or that he "expired." Such language always has some original foundation. One has lost the company of a spouse or friend who has died; the spirit or last breath has gone out of the person. But those who use such expressions today are usually not thinking of such linguistic justifications. This form of speech is most often the result of an unwillingness to speak directly. It resembles the bureaucratic hyperbole of health care, which twists death into the contortions of "negative patient care outcome," or the dissimulations of counterespionage, which disguises its activities in discussions of "terminating with extreme prejudice."

The change in labels from "undertaker" (a marvelously graphic old word) to "mortician" (with its roots in the Latin word *mors*, death) to "funeral director" or "funeral services practitioner" reflects both a euphemistic tendency and a broadened vocational scope.

Language is more effective as a vehicle for accurate communication when people speak directly in ways that are neither camouflaged nor brutal. Consider the state to which society has come in trying to express in ordinary language what veterinarians do to very sick, old, or infirm cats and dogs. They "put them to sleep." What meaning does that convey to young children who are then urged to take a nap? It can be quite a challenge to try to express the same point in some other way in colloquial but effective English. Thus, some say that animals are "put out of their misery" or "put down." Does that help to explain things? Are such animals simply "killed" or "euthanized"? Not among the people who speak to the authors of this book.

Euphemisms are not solely linked to death. On the contrary, they are ways to stand back from or cover over all sorts of taboo topics. Consider, for example, common expressions for genital organs or excretory functions. Both the New England Puritans of the 17th century and adherents to the romantic movement in the United States during the 19th century firmly suppressed talk about sexuality even as they readily spoke of death (usually for moral or religious purposes). Late in the 20th century, it often seems that people have simply inverted these attitudes and practices so as to be tongue-tied about death but all too verbose about sex.

Note that direct speech and candor are not always desirable. Frankness can be admirable or out of place. This is equally true for avoidance. Both overemphasis and underemphasis, whether on sexuality or on death, are equally unbalanced postures. Both distort and demean central realities of life.

Still, as Neaman and Silver (1983, pp. 144–145) have noted, contemporary American society is special:

At no other time in history has a culture created a more elaborate system of words and customs to disguise death so pleasantly that it seems a consummation devoutly to be wished. . . .

The motives for euphemizing death are in many ways similar to those for disguising our references to pregnancy and birth. Great superstition surrounded these events, as did great distaste and a sense of social impropriety. Propelled by these feelings, we have attempted to strip death of both its sting and its pride—in fact to kill death by robbing it of its direct and threatening name. The terms change and the euphemisms grow, but the evasion of the word "death" survives.

Linguistic and other contemporary modes of avoidance of death are more than detours around the unpleasant. Euphemisms become problematic whenever they are no longer held in check by personal experience. Most euphemisms originated in a rich soil of experiential contact with death. As death-related experiences have become increasingly attenuated and diminished in our society, these essential roots of language have dried up. The problem with an overabundance of euphemisms in recent American talk about death is the way in which they reveal and themselves contribute to a kind of distancing from important and fundamental events of life itself.

Death-Related Language

One might be tempted to conclude from the preceding that death-related language is simply absent from most ordinary speech. Such a conclusion would be "dead wrong." In talk about actual events pertaining to death and dying, it is quite common for language about death to be avoided. But in a curious reversal—some might call it a paradox—in talk about events that do not have to do with actual death and dying, death language is frequently employed (see, for example, Partridge, 1966; Wentworth & Flexner, 1967; Weseen, 1934).

Most people in contemporary American society speak quite openly about dead batteries, dead letters, a deadpan expression, a dead give-away, deadlines, and being dead drunk. Everyone knows people who are dead tired, dead on their feet, dead certain, dead beat or dead broke, deadly dull, deadlocked, dead to the world, scared to death. Marksmen who hit the target dead center have a dead eye or are dead shots. Gamblers recognize a "dead man's hand," while truckers "deadhead" back to home with an empty vehicle. Parents may be "worried to death" about children who "will be the death" of them. Those who are embarrassed may "wish they were dead" or that they "could just die." Orville Kelly (1977), a man with a life-threatening illness, reported an encounter with a friend who said, "I'm just dying to see you again" (p. 186).

Similarly, in today's society when one has nothing else to do one may be said to be "killing time." There is quite a difference between a ladykiller who is "fit to kill" and a killjoy. And everyone knows just what it means to "die on base," "flog a dead horse," or "kill the lights." To "kill a bottle of whiskey" leaves us with a "dead soldier." Good comedians "slay" their audiences, who "die of laughter"; poor comedians "die on their feet."

In these and many other similar linguistic phrases, death-related language emphasizes and exaggerates what is said. To be dead right is to be very right, completely right, absolutely right, the rightest one can be. Death-related language dramatizes or intensifies a word or phrase that might have seemed insufficiently forceful on its own or too weak to convey the intended meaning or depth of feeling. It trades on the ultimacy and finality of death to heighten in the manner of the superlative.

If we place this familiar use of death-related language alongside common euphemisms, what do we learn about society today? It appears that death language is avoided when we speak of death itself, but it is employed with enthusiasm when we are not speaking of death itself. There seems to be an inverse ratio here: when death is more real, people speak about it in less direct ways, and vice versa. Thus, some of the ways in which people talk about death have an odd topsy-turvy quality.

Language is powerful. Quite frequently, naming seems to both define and determine reality. Possibly that is why death-related language can be employed so easily in safe situations that have nothing to do with death itself. Surely, these same qualities are the motivations for euphemisms that seek to soften death or allude to it obliquely.

Death and the Media

The media play an important role in our contemporary American death system. News reports and entertainment programs are perhaps most representative of that role.

Vicarious Death Experiences: News Reports in the Media

Many Americans do not have much direct personal experience with natural human death, but most people in the United States have experienced in a vicarious or secondhand way hundreds, perhaps thousands, of violent or traumatic deaths. These vicarious experiences come to us through news reports in newspapers and magazines, on the radio, and—above all—on television. Almost any night one can learn about some form of human-induced death—all one has to do is to watch the evening news reports on television. Here, homicide, suicide, war, and other forms of traumatic death are the staple "newsworthy" events.

A phenomenon noticed during the Vietnam War, with its nightly reports of body counts and electronic scenes of bleeding, dying bodies, was a growing sense of psychological immunity to the impact of violent death among the general public. Experiencing violent death in a vicarious way does not seem to have the same impact as being there in person. Watching someone be shot to death on a smaller-than-life-size television screen or a larger-than-life-size movie screen is quite different from direct participation in the event. These media deaths are distant or remote for most people, and death itself may remain outside our actual experience despite frequent vicarious encounters with its surrogates.

The eternal flame at the grave of President John F. Kennedy (1917–1963).

One reason for the remote or distanced quality of these newsworthy events is that they are a highly selective portrait of death in today's society and around the world. That which is newsworthy is by definition out of the ordinary. The news media are preoccupied with the deaths of special persons or with special sorts of death. As a result, they depict death in a selective and distorted way to individuals in a society that has less and less contact with the realities of natural human death. Ordinary people who die in ordinary ways are not newsworthy; they are tucked away in death announcements on the back pages of a newspaper or silently omitted from the television news.

Death announcements are an exception to the rules of newsworthiness. They are the brief notices mentioning the fact of death, the names of survivors, and the plans (if any) for funeral or burial services. Typically, these death announcements appear in small type (a characteristic that has become a source of complaint among some elderly or visually impaired readers), in alphabetized columns, near the classified advertisement section of our newspapers. Such a location is not surprising, since death announcements are essentially public notices paid for by survivors. That is, death announcements are quite different from obituaries, which are the news stories that the media run to mark the deaths of prominent persons. By contrast, death announcements very much resemble paid advertisements, and like the classifieds they record quite ordinary events of everyday life.

The very selectivity of the criterion of newsworthiness carries along with it a certain reassurance. That is, it encourages people to comfort themselves with a little story of the following sort: Since I am not a very special person and since I do not expect to die in any very special way, I can distance myself from the staple fare of newspapers and television, and thus from unpleasant associations with death. In other words, the specialized and highly selective drama of death in media news reports is abstract and insubstantial; it lacks the definite shape, feelings, texture, and concreteness of one's own life. Having been shocked by so many out-of-the-ordinary, newsworthy events, people often become thick-skinned, passive spectators, hardened against the personal import of death. It is just one more among many distant and unusual phenomena paraded before us in a regular, unending, and not always very interesting series.

Moreover, the unusual modes of death reported so selectively in the media may come to be seen as themselves ordinary or typical. By contrast, one's own death—which is not perceived as anything like these secondhand experiences—appears less likely and less proximate. Selectivity in the external events dramatized by the news media may become the first step toward a topsy-turvy set of perceptions in the unspoken inner world of one's own psyche.

Fantasized Death: Entertainment

The distortion of death in news reports is compounded in many of the entertainment programs in the media. Death is hardly absent from the entertainment media; on the contrary, it is frequently present, but often in very unrealistic ways. Think of cowboy, war, or gangster movies, along with police or military shows and science fiction fantasies on television. What is remarkable about the typical portrayal of death in these media is that it is most often so very unrealistic or fantasized. Those who die are unimportant people or "bad guys," heroes and heroines repeatedly survive extreme peril, actors die one week and reappear unharmed the next, and grief following a death is mostly noticeable for its absence. Murders take place, but audiences are chiefly interested in whether or not the detective can identify their perpetrator. Killings do occur, but they usually satisfy a sense of poetic justice and their consequences are not of much interest. The realities of death and dying are rarely apparent.

Children's cartoons on television are sharp examples of this very special vision of death, because they simplify the complexities of other entertainment forms. Because attention spans in the audiences for these cartoons are short and distraction is always likely, the plot must be gripping and it must continually reassert its hold over viewers. Thus, these cartoon programs frequently emphasize action, as in cats chasing mice or dogs chasing cats. In the well-known "Roadrunner" cartoon series, Wile E. Coyote relentlessly pursues the flightless bird only to be caught over and over again in his own traps. He is apparently the repeated victim of horrible death experiences. But in fact he always survives and usually enjoys instant resurrection. In other words, he just keeps getting killed; he never dies. Delight, joy, and renewed activity follow so rapidly upon destruction that there is no time for grief. The cartoon is about the ongoing action of an endless chase. It is not really about death, although inevitably it communicates many messages about that subject.

Recently, death has become an even more vivid presence in adult entertainment. In the good old days, no one ever bled when shot or stabbed in a movie. Fistfights erupted in saloons, six-guns blazed away, actors staggered against walls and crumpled in death—but all the while their clothes were clean and their hats usually remained firmly on their heads. Now, blood, gore, and crashing automobiles have become standard fare. Today's movie and television viewers witness so much artificial blood and apparent mayhem that they have become jaded and are no longer easily surprised or impressed.

Again, death has been distorted through a process of selectivity and fantasization. Of course, selectivity is unavoidable in reporting the news or telling a story, and fantasy is neither unhealthy nor undesirable in itself. The games, songs, and fairy tales of childhood have long been full of fantasy and death, and children have coped with it without major difficulty, simply by holding on to the essential distinction between fantasy and reality. The problem in our society is a looser grip on the realities of life and death, coupled with a growing and evolving presence of fantasy. Selectivity and fantasy become dangerous in media communications about death when they substitute for or supplant a balanced appreciation of life.

Human-Induced Death

Human-induced death is familiar within the contemporary American death system. It is represented here by five types of this sort of death: accidents, homicide, war, the Holocaust, and the nuclear shadow. Suicide is explored in Chapter 17. These are examples of what some have called "horrendous death" (Leviton, 1991a, 1991b).

Accidents

Accidents are the fourth leading cause of death in the United States for the population as a whole, and the leading cause among all persons aged 1 to 36 (Dixon & Clearwater, 1991; National Safety Council, 1991). This statistic has resulted from the relative decline in importance of communicable diseases and the increasing prevalence of fast-paced, stress-filled lifestyles in a highly developed technological society. In 1990, 93,500 Americans died in accidents and 9 million suffered disabling injuries. Among the fatalities, the largest share (46,300) involved motor vehicles.

As Americans have become more safety conscious—driving more carefully, wearing seat belts, not driving after consuming alcoholic beverages—accident-related deaths have declined in number in the United States. Still, the total number of such deaths remains substantial. Also, if one assumes that each accidental death involves an average of ten survivors, nearly one million persons were affected by such deaths in the United States in 1990.

Members of almost every societal subgroup—males and females, young and old, Caucasians and African Americans—can be killed in automobile accidents, but some groups experience more deaths from this cause than do others. For example, more than twice as many males as females die in vehicular accidents. African-American females have the lowest mortality rates from vehicular accidents; 15–24-year-old males have the highest rates (56.6 per 100,000).

These deaths contrast with some basic assumptions about mortality patterns in contemporary society. For example, in automobile accidents it is the young who are most likely to die, not the elderly. Also, these deaths are sudden, unexpected, and violent. Often the person killed is badly disfigured in the accident, perhaps even burned. So the scenario may go like this: a knock on the door (or a telephone call) by a police officer leads to the announcement that someone is dead. Disbelief and denial may follow; he (or she) had just driven to a movie! How could *death* intervene? If the body is disfigured, the survivors may never see it again. If not and if the body is delivered to a hospital, requests to authorize organ donation may pose unexpected challenges to shocked family members. An air of unreality may pervade the experience; grief and mourning following such a death may be complicated.

Homicide

Human beings have always killed each other. One primordial myth of Western society involves the first pair of human siblings and shows this first case of sibling rivalry erupting into the murder of Abel by Cain. History is full of fascinating and horrifying tales of murder, often involving close relatives such as a father (Oedipus), mother (Orestes), or brother (Cain). And yet some societies frown so heavily on homicide that it is virtually unheard of in them. For instance, among Native Americans the Hopi are a culture in which murder is unknown throughout the recorded history of that society (that is, since the 17th century).

In contemporary American society, homicide is a well-recognized phenomenon. In 1990, it was the 11th leading cause of death in the society as a whole (National Center for Health Statistics, 1993), but it was even more significant among some subgroups. For example, among African Americans the rate of deaths from homicide is more than six times that of Caucasian Americans, while in the total population the homicide rate for males is more than three times that for females (United States Bureau of the Census, 1991). In terms of age, the highest rates of homicide are found in the 15- to 24-year-old group and (close behind) the 25- to 34-year-old group. Together, these two groups account for nearly 60 percent of all deaths due to homicide in the United States. Thus, the highest rate of all homicides is among African-American males and homicide is the leading cause of death for young African Americans (Ewing, 1990; Stark, 1991).

Death by homicide is usually sudden and unexpected. Typically, it involves a short transition from the act of violence to the death. Since it happens most frequently among younger members of society, it also runs against an expected picture of who dies. This sort of death presents special problems for survivors: they are faced with an unexpected death in circumstances that might be unclear and that carry some social stigma. If the agent is identified, this may further complicate the grief of survivors. Often, the agent is a family member; nearly 50 percent of those murdered are killed by family members, friends, or acquaintances. In addition, the outcome of his or her trial may be uncertain and the families of victims are often deliberately shut out of the proceedings. A sense of outrage, fed by impressions of injustice and lack of control, may complicate the mourning (Magee, 1983; Redmond, 1989).

One way in which death is experienced as a result of homicide is particularly vicious: random murders by "drive-by" shootings. Such shootings lead to violent, human-induced death that often results merely from being in the wrong place at the wrong time. Subsequently, life may seem very fragile and even cheap. Such attitudes are not likely to increase social stability.

War

Elliot (1972) documented 110 million human-induced deaths resulting from wars in this century alone. In so doing, he noted that such statistics are far from reliable. The number of actual combatants (soldiers) killed may be relatively reliable; those who keep such statistics are likely to be people who have some interest in getting an accurate count. But the number of noncombatants killed is likely to be considerably less reliable. It is often difficult to obtain an accurate count when one is dealing with large numbers of dead and when health concerns are of first priority. In addition, some may not wish to know how many civilians were killed. A prime example of this is the 1991 war in Iraq and Kuwait. Americans were given the impression that this war resulted in very few deaths; that is, few American soldiers were killed. It was suggested that more Iraqi soldiers were killed, even though accurate counts were not presented. But there was little mention of the numbers of civilians killed in the heavy bombing of Iraqi targets before the ground war got under way. So that figure of 110 million mentioned above is likely to be low, perhaps even very low.

Moreover, the overall number of combat-related deaths must surely have risen since Elliot's work in 1972. War or conflict in different forms has continued since that time in Vietnam, Cambodia, Afghanistan, Lebanon, Ethiopia, Yugoslavia, and elsewhere. In addition, many others have died because of political choices—for example, those who starved in Ethiopia and Somalia (because food had not been delivered to the hungry); those who were shot in Tienanmen square; victims of violence in Chile and Peru. Even before the century is over, Elliot's numbers must surely be raised considerably. It has been a bloody period for human-induced violent death.

Ours is the century of two (announced) world wars and many other regional and local conflicts. It is also the century of major (bloody) revolutions—for example, the Russian and the Chinese. It is a century in which (as Elliot reported) people have died in the following ways:

1. Privation technologies, accounting for 62 million deaths in
    a. camps, such as the enclosed ghettos of Poland, prisoner of war camps, the Nazi concentration camps, and Russian labor camps
    b. cities, as in the siege of Leningrad by German forces in World War II
    c. rural areas, such as people dying in transit, or from economic blockades and scorched earth tactics
2. Hardware technologies, accounting for 46 million deaths from big guns, aerial bombs, small arms fire, and mixed causes
3. Chemical and other technologies, such as gas chambers and germ warfare, accounting for the deaths of 1–2 million people

In the long run, the analysis provided by Elliot proves curiously ineffective. That is, the fact that 62 million people died of starvation or untreated disease or just physical depletion may be so incomprehensible that we may be unmoved by it. Thus, Elliot (1972) wrote the following about the "big guns": "As deaths from big guns increase, they also help to bring about an *increase* in deaths from small arms. . . . It is a question of the big guns *creating an environment* of death on the scale of macro-violence" (p. 132).

In fact, this sort of understanding can be broadened: the numbers of deaths from human-induced violence in the 20th century have created an environment of death, too. Violent death is curiously accepted in a way in which "natural" deaths (for example, dying from disease) are not. Watching "Dirty Harry" kill ("blow away") a dozen people in a Clint Eastwood movie barely moves audiences; watching one person die (in reality or in a film like *Terms of Endearment*) is often much more agonizing.

As the number of human-induced deaths has grown in recent years, a shift in their quality has also taken place. More and more, such deaths have taken on an *impersonal or distanced* character. For example, in times gone by wars were fought face to face. Often they were confined to professionals (for example, the Hessians who were hired to fight in the American Revolution) and to specified sets of conditions (for example, daytime). Now war is more often an impersonal experience, fought at a distance or under conditions when the "enemy" is rarely seen. Those involved include not just soldiers but entire populations. Few innocent persons are spared the threat of death as war has come to be waged.

It is no wonder, then, that when Americans today think of death, in addition to the long, protracted dying associated with degenerative disease, they most often think of death near their homes in an automobile accident or of bullets, bombs, or beatings associated with violent social conflict, ethnic strife, and international combat. By contrast, even today in other death systems around the world, large numbers of people die of malnutrition, contaminated water, communicable diseases, stresses involved in relocation, and other more prosaic (and often preventable) causes.

In addition to its direct role as a context of high numbers of human-induced deaths, World War II also introduced two new and distinct elements to the world's death systems: the Holocaust and the nuclear threat. These deserve special attention here, not only as part of recent history but also for their ongoing significance in the lives of contemporary human beings.

The Holocaust

One can find many examples in human history of terrible atrocities committed by one group of people against others that resulted in large numbers of deaths. From World War II, there are the relatively isolated examples of the saturation bombings that leveled Dresden and Coventry, or the fire bombings that destroyed large parts of Tokyo. But one could also cite numerous historical attempts at genocide or the destruction of entire population groups. Nevertheless, what became under the Nazis a systematic program to eliminate whole classes of people from the face of the earth can still be regarded as unique for its scope and political or ideological basis (Bauer, 1982; Dawidowicz, 1975; Pawelczynska, 1979; Reitlinger, 1968).

According to the Nazis' perverted philosophy, whole categories of people—the Jews, gypsies, Jehovah's Witnesses, homosexuals, and others—were classified as *Untermensch*, subhuman. In a manner roughly similar to that in which political prisoners, members of the resistance, criminals, or prisoners of war were treated, these proscribed groups were at first rounded up and shipped off to "concentration camps." One example of how this was expected to proceed was a plan to transport the entire Jewish population of Europe to the island of Madagascar off the East African coast (without, of course, requesting permission to do so from either the island's inhabitants or those to be relocated) where they would be left to make do as best they could.

In practical terms, however, the relocation camps soon became work camps as the Nazis sought to extract every bit of property, possessions, skill, and energy from what was now essentially a slave labor force working on behalf of the German war effort. Thus, gold and jewelry, shoes and clothing, eyeglasses and prostheses, hairbrushes and toothbrushes, and hanks of women's hair were all "harvested" from those transported to the camps. Harsh living and working conditions, meager rations, and brutal pressure of all sorts that has been amply detailed by firsthand witnesses (for example, Kulka, 1986;

Levi, 1986) weakened and killed many prisoners, who then had to be replaced with fresh transports.

Worse yet, at a point in 1941 a decision was made to go a step further: what had essentially been prison and work camps now often became "extermination camps" (*Vernichtungslager*). The term itself is significant: one kills a human being, but one exterminates a less-than-human pest. In search of efficiency, the first methods—bludgeoning, hanging, and shooting people to death, machine gunning and burying them in mass graves, and using engine exhaust gasses to suffocate those who were being transported in closed vans to locations where their bodies were burned or interred—were replaced by the infamous gas chambers and crematories of the *Vernichtungslager*.

This final stage of the Holocaust reached its peak of depravity in southwestern Poland at a former military barracks on the edge of the city of Auschwitz (Oswiecim)—whose gate still proclaims the infamous and cruelly ironic motto *"Arbeit macht frei"* ("Work makes us free")—and its newly constructed satellite about two miles away in the countryside at Birkenau (Brzezinka). Here, in the words of the camp commander (Hoess, 1959, p. 160), was developed "the greatest human extermination center of all time." And here (but elsewhere also), cruel and hideous experiments were undertaken under the guise of medical research (Lifton, 1986).

It is thought that in this place alone, at least two million people died from the time when the first prisoners arrived (June 14, 1940)—and especially after September of 1941, when the use of cyanide gas was first tested—until January 27, 1945, when the Soviet army liberated the camp and freed some 7,000 remaining prisoners (Bauer, 1982; Dawidowicz, 1975). It is reported that toward the end, some 80 percent of the people (mainly women, children, and the elderly) who arrived at Auschwitz-Birkenau in the daily transports (which tied up a large number of railroad cars that were desperately needed by the German military for the war effort) went directly to their deaths from the notorious "selections" held at railside as they arrived at the camp.

Nothing quite like this had been seen in the world prior to the 1940s. To visit Auschwitz many years after the Holocaust is to confront an enormous incongruity between what is in many ways an ordinary, even banal, setting, and innumerable images of horror that must endure as a reminder of the dark side of human capacity (Corr, 1993c; Czarnecki, 1989). Perhaps that is why some writers (such as MacMillan, 1991; Wiesel, 1960) have employed the devices of literature to convey in imaginative and evocative ways messages about the Holocaust that are not always effectively transmitted in other ways. In any event, Yehuda Bauer (1986, p. xvii) has articulated the basic lesson for all who lived through and after the events of the Holocaust: "We have the choice between the Holocaust as a warning and the Holocaust as a precedent." The ongoing impact of this lesson is evident in the United States Holocaust Memorial Museum in Washington, DC, which was dedicated in April, 1993, and in the many other U.S. and Canadian institutions in the United States that promote such reflections, such as those listed in the directory of the Association of Holocaust Organizations (Shulman, 1933).

The entrance gate to the Nazi death camp at Auschwitz ("Work makes us free.").

Nuclearism

As if the Holocaust were not sufficient, the advent of the nuclear era in August of 1945 introduced another sort of death-related experience for which there again is no adequate historical precedent. In Hiroshima and Nagasaki, mass death became an instantaneous reality at the hands of a far-distant enemy for the very first time. It is estimated that at least 100,000 persons died immediately at Hiroshima on August 6, 1945, 50,000 more died at Nagasaki three days later, and a like number were injured or harmed by radiation. Blast, fire, and the enduring effects of radiation killed people, destroyed property, and contaminated the land in ways that had never been possible before. Both the quantity and the quality of all subsequent death-related experiences were fundamentally altered in ways that reporters (such as Lustig, 1977), scholars (such as Lifton, 1964, 1967), and novelists (such as Hersey, 1948) have all sought to understand and interpret.

Elliot (1972) identified the cities bombed with nuclear weapons as examples of a "total death environment": "Imagine a plate half a mile in diameter placed over the centre of the city. Ninety per cent of the people under the plate were killed. Extend the plate to one mile: in the further area, sixty per cent of the people were killed . . . that's your total death environment" (pp. 92–93).

In a total death environment, death is the primary, if not the only, symbol. The nearest earlier centuries could come to this was perhaps an area decimated by a plague (but that was not human-induced death), or a battlefield such as those in the American Civil War where perhaps 50,000 soldiers were killed in one day's fighting (but those deaths were not spread over a whole population; they mainly involved only those engaged to fight). War in our century has changed dramatically.

In the years since 1945, much more powerful nuclear weapons have been developed. Such weapons can now be launched from the ground, from high in the air, and from deep under the seas. Delivery on target is supposedly much more accurate. Multiple warheads can attack many objectives simultaneously. Above all, the level of destruction that can be achieved has increased many times. For the first time in human history, nuclear weaponry has made it possible for opposing powers to destroy each other many times over (Arkin & Fieldhouse, 1985). It has not yet been determined whether human beings have the ability to destroy the full range of human and other forms of life on our planet. But clearly, death and destruction can now be brought down upon humankind in a degree and form that is far beyond the wildest dreams—or nightmares—of human beings over nearly the whole of recorded history.

In recent years, the nuclear era has also shown itself to have another face as nuclear power has become a source of much-needed energy supplies. Here, the initial appearance is benign and welcome; and in many ways it has remained so. But accidents in the nuclear reactors at Three Mile Island in Pennsylvania in 1979 and at Chernobyl in Ukraine in 1986 have shown that even a peaceful source of nuclear energy can pose a potential or an actual threat to large areas of the world. Explosion, fire, and local irradiation, however lethal they may be to the surrounding territory, are as nothing compared to the airborne radiation and long-term contamination of land, water, food supplies, and people such as followed the events at Chernobyl.

How are these dangers associated with nuclear weaponry and nuclear power to be kept in check? And how should they be balanced against needs for self-defense and for sources of energy to sustain quality in living? More broadly, what does it mean to live under the nuclear shadow? For some, apparently the subject does not bear thinking about; they simply put it out of their minds. For others, the power of the threat and the difficulty of doing anything about it diminish their joy in living and their sense of promise for the future. For all, it is a new and unprecedented dimension in death-related experiences in the late 20th century.

Four Enduring Themes

In reflecting upon the changing face of death in contemporary America, it is worthwhile to note four enduring themes that will reemerge from time to time throughout the remainder of this book.

The first of these themes is *limitation and control.* We humans would like to achieve complete control over the whole of our lives, but that is not possible. We are finite, limited beings. We strive to impose our wills upon ourselves, other people, things in the world, and the events of life, only to be reminded again and again that our influence has limits. That is not necessarily a bad thing, but it does mean that part of living has to do with coming to terms with what we can and cannot change. Death is real. Dying is inevitable— although it may occur at different times and in different ways. Losses of many sorts cannot be avoided. Grief is a consequence of loving. Life is transient, but it can be good.

A second theme has to do with *individuality and community.* American culture often stresses individual freedom, personal rights, autonomy, and independence. Each of these has value and should be valued. Death, dying, and bereavement are all ultimately lived out in individual ways. But death, dying, and bereavement also teach individuals about the human community and universal needs that apply to all. Death-related events are shared experiences in which both individuals and human communities participate. American society, in particular, is struggling against ways in which it has become alienated and estranged from death. It is a society in which individuals are seeking to reestablish interdependence and constructive modes of community within themselves, with others, and between themselves and their God or nature.

A third important theme in our story is *vulnerability and resilience.* The discussion thus far has mainly concerned human vulnerability to dying, death, grief, fantasized presentations of death, violence, and the nuclear shadow. That vulnerability is real. The pain that may be associated with it can be intense. Sometimes it is so overwhelming as to drain from life all of the energy, joy, and other positive qualities that had made it worth living, as when bereavement leads to clinical depression. But death also teaches about human resilience. Humans are capable of facing death and responding to its reality in ways that can be ennobling and awesome. So death can remind individuals about both the boundaries and the potential of the human spirit.

Finally, a fourth of many possible themes in this analysis of changing experiences with death is *quality in living and the search for meaning.* As Orville Kelly showed (1975), the prospect of one's own imminent death can encourage efforts to "make today count." The ways in which death puts the values of life at risk can lead humans to search for sources of inspiration and frameworks within which enduring meaning can be established. Some of this may involve a philosophical quest or a religious conviction and trust. At bottom, this search rests upon faith that life is ultimately good and confidence that it can also be meaningful. Even as humans are limited, alone, vulnerable, and hesitant in facing the challenges of dying, death, and bereavement, they can learn to influence the course of their own lives, share together, achieve resilience, and create meaning.

Quality in living and the search for meaning are subjects addressed by the psychologist and Holocaust survivor Viktor Frankl (1984, p. 86), who wrote that even in the greatest adversity, "everything can be taken from a man but one thing: the last of the human freedoms—to choose one's attitude in any given set of circumstances, to choose one's own way." Socrates put this another way when he said that "the really important thing is not to live, but to live well" (*Crito*, 48b).

Summary

This chapter has identified several of the most important features of the contemporary American death system, with an emphasis upon the distinctive aspects of its death-related encounters and attitudes toward death. The pattern is a mixed one. Relatively more control over death than was experienced in the past is combined with disturbing encounters with accidental death and homicide. Evident discomfort in talking about death, signaled by euphemistic language, stands alongside the popularity of death-related language in areas not related to death. Highly selective and fantasized portraits of death in the media coincide with the forbidding shadows of war, the Holocaust, and the nuclear threat. As a result of these and other factors, individuals in the United States today are left to resolve issues of limitation and control, individuality and community, vulnerability and resilience, and quality in living and the search for meaning.

QUESTIONS FOR REVIEW AND DISCUSSION

1. This chapter described Kastenbaum's notion of the "death system." There are five elements of a death system: people, places, times, objects, and symbols. Think about the death system within which you live. What elements (that is, what people, places, and so on) of this system have you encountered?

2. What role do the media play in the contemporary death system in the United States? How do they contribute—perhaps in some helpful ways; perhaps in some unhelpful ways—to your coping with death, dying, and bereavement?

3. In the 20th century, violence has become an even larger factor in encounters with death. What role (if any) have accidents, homicides, and war played in your encounters with death? Think about whether your encounters (direct or indirect) with death have included a component of violence. How might this have affected your attitudes toward death?

4. This chapter closed with a discussion of four enduring themes that run throughout all of the subsequent chapters: (a) limitation and control, (b) individuality and community, (c) vulnerability and resilience, and

(d) quality in living and the search for meaning. How do these four themes relate to what you have learned so far in the first three chapters?

SUGGESTED READINGS

On 20th-century experiences with death and some of the ways in which they have been influenced by societal institutions and practices, see:

Charmaz, K. (1980). *The Social Reality of Death: Death in Contemporary America.*
Elliot, G. (1972). *The Twentieth Century Book of the Dead.*
Sontag, S. (1978). *Illness as Metaphor.*
Sudnow, D. (1967). *Passing On: The Social Organization of Dying.*

For euphemisms and death-related language, consult:

Neaman, J. S., & Silver, C. G. (1983). *Kind Words: A Thesaurus of Euphemisms.*
Partridge, E. (1966). *A Dictionary of Slang and Unconventional English.*
Rawson, H. (1981). *A Dictionary of Euphemisms and Other Doubletalk.*
Wentworth, H., & Flexner, S. B. (Eds.). (1967). *Dictionary of American Slang (with Supplement).*
Weseen, M. H. (1934). *A Dictionary of American Slang.*

Among the many historical, biographical, and literary accounts arising from World War II and the Holocaust, see:

Bauer, Y. (1982). *A History of the Holocaust.*
Camus, A. (1947/1972). *The Plague.*
Czarnecki, J. P. (1989). *Last Traces: The Lost Art of Auschwitz.*
Dawidowicz, L. S. (1975). *The War Against the Jews 1933–1945.*
Hersey, J. (1948). *Hiroshima.*
Kulka, E. (1986). *Escape from Auschwitz.*
Levi, P. (1986). *Survival in Auschwitz; and, The Reawakening: Two Memoirs.*
Lifton, R. J. (1967). *Death in Life: Survivors of Hiroshima.*
MacMillan, I. (1991). *Orbit of Darkness.*
Pawelczynska, A. (1979). *Values and Violence in Auschwitz: A Sociological Analysis.*
Reitlinger, G. (1968). *The Final Solution: The Attempt to Exterminate the Jews of Europe 1939–1945.*
Wiesel, E. (1960) *Night.*

On nuclearism, see:

Arkin, W., & Fieldhouse, R. (1985). *Nuclear Battlefields.*
Gould, B. B., Moon, S., & Van Hoorn, J. (Eds.). (1986). *Growing Up Scared? The Psychological Effect of the Nuclear Threat on Children.*
Lifton, R. J. (1979). *The Broken Connection.*

For broader analyses of "horrendous death," see:

Leviton, D. (Ed.). (1991). *Horrendous Death, Health, and Well-Being* and *Horrendous Death and Health: Toward Action.*

CHAPTER 4

Cultural Differences and Death

The broad account of experiences with death, dying, and bereavement that has been set forth thus far in this part—describing death-related encounters and attitudes, along with prominent features of the contemporary death system in the United States—is not the whole story. The reason for this is that American society is not a single, homogeneous entity. On the contrary, our society embraces within its boundaries a kaleidoscope of cultural, social, racial, ethnic, and religious groupings.

Much of what has been discussed thus far is a background shared by all individuals in American society. That is, everyone living in the United States today (except perhaps a few social isolates) is compelled, to one extent or another, to interact with our society's death system. For example, some appropriately designated official must declare a person to be dead. However, members of different social groups interact with our society's death system in ways appropriate to their particular values.

For that reason, in this chapter—and elsewhere throughout this book—special attention is paid to some of the many ways in which cultural differences affect death-related experiences. Following a short vignette, this chapter will consider some of the constraints that limit what can be said about cultural differences in the field of death, dying, and bereavement; identify three principal areas around which to organize this description of cultural differences; and describe what is known about each of these areas in relationship to four selected cultural groups in America. Throughout, the analysis draws upon the general social and cultural background provided in Chapters 1–3 and points forward both to the issue-oriented chapters that follow and to broader studies of cultural differences outside the borders of the United States.

A Happy Funeral

A charming picture book for young readers entitled *The Happy Funeral* (Bunting, 1982) tells the story of two young Chinese-American sisters who are preparing to take part in their grandfather's funeral. When their mother first tells May-May and Laura of their grandfather's death, she says that he is going to have a happy funeral. The girls are puzzled about what that means. "It's like saying a sad party. Or hot snow. It doesn't make sense" (p. 1). Mom explains: "When someone is very old and has lived a good life, he is happy to go" (p. 1).

May-May and Laura are still puzzled and they are unclear about many of the events that subsequently take place. Although they loved their grandfather and are clearly expected to be participants in this community event, the girls have not had much experience with death and funerals. They are insiders to the community, but in many ways outsiders to what is about to happen. They do not expect to be happy at their grandfather's funeral.

At the funeral home, bunches of flowers are everywhere and incense sticks burn in front of Grandfather's casket. There are many gifts for Grandfather's "journey to the other side," such as a map of the spirit world, some food, and half a comb (Grandmother keeps the other half, to be rejoined when she is reunited with her husband after her own death). A cardboard house, paper play money, and pictures of various objects (for example, a drawing of Chang, the big black dog that Grandfather had when he was a boy, and a picture of a red car with a silver stripe of the kind that Grandfather never had in this life) are burned, with the idea that they will become real when they turn into smoke and rise to the spirit world.

At the funeral service in the Chinese Gospel Church, there are more flowers and a big photograph of Grandfather framed in roses. The adults talk about Grandfather's fine qualities and the many good things that he did. Some of the adults cry and Laura feels a big lump in her throat when she realizes how small Grandmother is and that she is even older than Grandfather. When the ceremony is over, a woman gives a small candy to each of the mourners "to sweeten your sorrow" (p. 22). Then Grandfather's casket is put in a glass-sided car and his photograph is propped on the roof of one of the two flower cars. With a marching band playing spirited music, the cars parade throughout the streets of Chinatown. That part is a happy funeral.

At the cemetery, Grandfather's casket is placed on a wooden table next to a big hole in the ground. The minister says that Grandfather is going to his spiritual reward, but Laura tries to think of him flying the wonderful kites that he used to make. Throughout all of these events, Laura has been alternating between warm memories and feelings of sadness, between smiles and tears. Finally, she realizes that although she and May-May were not happy to have their grandfather die, his funeral really was a happy one because he was ready for his death and he left a good legacy through his well-lived life and everyone's fond memories of him. Mom "never said it was happy for us to have him go" (p. 38).

Constraints on What Can Be Said About Cultural Differences

Whatever anyone might wish to say about cultural differences in relationship to death, dying, and bereavement is limited by three primary constraints that must be kept firmly in mind. First, to open a door to the many cultural groups within the broad panorama of American society is immediately to confront a dazzling plurality of population clusters. We have chosen in this chapter to study the special qualities of death-related experiences in four groups—African Americans, Hispanic Americans, Asian Americans, and Native Americans—but these are just four of many cultural groups that could be selected for study and none of these groups is a single, undifferentiated entity.

For example, Morris (1991) has offered an interesting description of attitudes and customs concerning the end of life in two groups of conservative Russian religious isolates who now reside in Oregon (Old Believers and Molokans). And Herz and Rosen (1982) have identified four primary patterns of belief and behavior in Jewish-American families that influence ways in which these families respond to sickness, death, and loss: (1) the family as the central source of support and emotional connectedness; (2) suffering as a shared family and community value; (3) the prominence of intellectual achievement and financial success; and (4) the premium placed on the verbal expression of feelings. Obviously, there are many more cultural groups than can be studied in a single chapter.

Furthermore, there are many interesting differences within the four groups that are to be considered here. Among African Americans, there are rural and urban, rich and poor, Christian and Muslim. Among Hispanic Americans, there are Puerto Ricans, Mexican Americans, Cuban Americans, and immigrants from Central or South America. Among Asian Americans, there are people who trace their ancestries to the very different societies of Cambodia, China, Japan, Korea, Vietnam, and other Pacific countries. And among Native Americans (or "First Nation Peoples" as they have recently begun to call themselves in Canada), there are literally hundreds of distinct groupings (for example, Navajo, Zuni, Dakota, Seminole) who can trace their ancestral homes to nearly every part of the North American continent.

The second constraint relevant here is the state of current knowledge about issues related to death, dying, and bereavement. This constraint refers both to knowledge of these subjects in general and especially to more particular questions involving cultural differences. Research, teaching, and publication in the field of death, dying, and bereavement is primarily a phenomenon of the second half of the 20th century. Prior to this time, there were scattered scholarly reports, especially in selected fields of study such as anthropology and history. But investigations from a wide range of perspectives really only began to appear more frequently during the 1950s and 1960s. Such investigations could not be said to have reached an acceptable degree of depth, breadth, and maturity until the 1970s and thereafter.

Even today, there are obvious gaps in the literature, not-well-studied topics, and opportunities for much additional research. For example, most of what is known about various cultural groups in the field of death, dying, and bereavement is based upon a few studies in various locales throughout the United States. Just a moment's reflection, however, suffices to show that what might be true of some African Americans in New York City might not be equally valid for African Americans living in rural Alabama. Among Hispanic Americans, Mexican Americans in Texas are a different community from Mexican Americans living in California, and of course Mexican Americans are a different cultural group from Puerto Ricans in New York City. Thus, when one explores the literature on cultural differences in death-related experiences, a repeated refrain is heard: there is a dearth of data and much less analysis about how ethnic minorities in America deal with these issues.

When combined, these first two constraints mean that in present circumstances much remains unknown about death, dying, and bereavement. These limitations are especially evident with regard to specialized cultural aspects of those topics. While some data and some analyses are available, they are limited in many respects and often require that conclusions be carefully qualified. That is why what follows are really sketches of cultural differences, the beginnings of the fuller portraits that will emerge when researchers seize the opportunities now available to set forth richer materials and more detailed analyses in these important subject areas.

A third constraint to bear in mind is the need to avoid the danger of stereotypes. Everyone who is discussed in this chapter is simultaneously an American, a member of some particular cultural group, and an individual person. No one of them in any aspect of his or her death-related experiences is simply identical with any other individual—even with other members of his or her own cultural group.

For example, Japanese Americans reflect this in the very precise distinctions they make among generations: "Issei" are members of the older, first generation who were born in Japan, came to live in the United States between 1890 and 1924, often spoke English only poorly if at all, lived much of their lives in Japanese enclaves, and usually had strong ties to the attitudes and practices of their ancestors; "Nisei" are members of the intermediate or second generation who were born in America between 1910 and 1940, attended American schools, and spoke English as their main language, but who wished to maintain some links to the attitudes and practices of their ancestors; "Sansei" are members of a third generation, born after World War II in America to American parents (of Japanese ancestry), who often are in many ways indistinguishable in their education, attitudes, and practices from American peers who have no cultural or ethnic links to Japan (Kitano, 1976). These distinctions illustrate the need to avoid lumping people (such as all Japanese Americans) together in stereotypical ways and the value of respect for individuality in any multicultural account of death, dying, and bereavement.

Three Areas of Investigation

For each of the cultural groups discussed in this chapter, three areas of investigation will be considered: encounters with death, attitudes toward death, and death-related practices.

Encounters with Death

Different cultural groups may experience different kinds of encounters with death, either in terms of the level of mortality within a particular group or in terms of its causes. For example, mortality rates are generally higher in poor, rural, and ghetto areas than in more affluent, urban, and middle-class regions. And infant mortality rates, a particularly sensitive social and economic barometer, may vary between subgroups in the broad American society. Also, average life expectancy varies for different populations, as in the case of women who, as a group, enjoy a significantly higher average life expectancy than do men in American society. This chapter will explore some of these differences in the demography of death.

TABLE 4.1   Resident Population of the United States, 1900 and 1989

	1900[a]		1989[b]	
	Number	Percent	Number	Percent
Total population	75,994,000	100.0	248,240,000	100.0
Male	38,816,000	51.1	120,982,000	48.7
Female	37,178,000	48.9	127,258,000	51.3
Caucasian Americans	66,809,000	87.9	208,961,000	84.0
African Americans	8,834,000	11.6	30,660,000	12.3
Hispanic origin[c]	(NA)		20,505,000	8.2
Asian Americans and Pacific Islanders	(NA)		6,881,000	2.8
Native Americans	(NA)		1,737,000	0.7

[a] June 1; excludes Alaska and Hawaii.
[b] July 1; except total population, which is the figure for April 1, 1990.
[c] Persons of Hispanic origin may be of any race.
Source: United States Bureau of the Census, 1991.

Attitudes Toward Death

Different cultural groups may share attitudes toward death or they may have quite distinct attitudes as part of their own unique death systems. That is, as members of the larger society, they are likely to share some of the elements and functions of the American death system (for example, ways of maintaining demographic records or of investigating homicides); as members of sub-groups within the society, they are likely to experience unique involvements with death that help to mark out their groups' distinctive aspects.

Death-Related Practices

Death-related encounters and attitudes are expressed differently in the practices of different cultural groups. These practices include attitudes toward health care, death-related communications, care of the dying, customs at the moment of death, and funeral and mourning rituals. Practices of this sort usually reflect the basic attitudes and values of the community. Thus, they often have much to teach about the particular cultural group and its unique ways of coping with death, dying, and bereavement.

African Americans

African Americans are the single largest minority group in American society (see Table 4.1), a group that accounted for more than 12 percent of all deaths in the United States in 1988 (see Table 4.2). African Americans are linked in many ways by origins on the African continent, the history of slavery and slave trading, and experiences of discrimination. Slavery itself was a practice with many death-related implications. These included the killings involved in taking individuals prisoner and removing them from their tribal homes, suffering and death during transport to the New World, harsh living and working condi-

TABLE 4.2 *Deaths in the United States by Race or National Origin and Gender, 1988*

	Both Sexes	Percent	Male	Percent	Female	Percent
All races	2,167,999	100.0	1,125,540	51.9	1,042,459	48.1
Caucasian Americans	1,876,906	86.5	965,419	51.4	911,487	48.6
African Americans	264,019	12.2	144,228	54.6	119,791	45.4
Hispanic origin[a]	54,713	0.3	33,124	60.5	21,589	39.5
Asian Americans and						
Pacific Islanders	18,963	0.09	11,155	58.8	7,808	41.2
Chinese Americans	4,958	0.02	2,968	59.9	1,990	40.1
Filipino Americans	3,667	0.02	2,481	67.7	1,186	32.3
Japanese Americans	3,655	0.02	1,942	53.1	1,713	46.9
Other Asian						
Americans						
or Pacific Islanders	6,683	0.03	3,764	56.3	2,919	43.7
Native Americans	7,917	0.04	4,617	58.3	3,300	41.7
Others	194	———	121	———	73	———

[a] Based upon 26 reporting states and the District of Columbia; not included in totals for all races.
Source: National Center for Health Statistics, 1991.

tions on this side of the Atlantic, and all that is entailed in being treated as objects who could become the property of others. That background influences many aspects of contemporary African-American experiences with death in America. As Kalish and Reynolds (1981) have written, "to be Black in America is to be part of a history told in terms of contact with death and coping with death" (p. 103).

Encounters with Death

As noted in Chapter 1, substantial declines in mortality rates during the 20th century are found in nearly every segment of the population in the United States. There are, however, differences among these declines. During the period from 1900 to 1974, mortality rates for African Americans consistently exceeded those for Caucasian Americans (see Figure 4.1; Kitagawa & Hauser, 1973). Nevertheless, in 1974 for the first time overall mortality rates for African Americans were lower than those for Caucasian Americans, and this new pattern of African-American statistical advantage continued through 1990. This does not mean that all groups of African Americans display lower mortality rates than their Caucasian-American counterparts. In fact, African-American males are generally less well off than their Caucasian-American counterparts in this regard. Nevertheless, African-American females have significantly lower mortality rates than do their Caucasian-American counterparts.

Historical disadvantages in mortality rates for African Americans during much of this century may not have resulted simply from ethnicity. Many minority groups in American society are disadvantaged in terms of socioeconomic standing, and disadvantages of that sort almost always reveal themselves in higher death rates (Benjamin, 1965). Poverty, inadequate access to health care, and higher incidences of life-threatening behavior have immediate and unhappy implications for death rates. Because cultural and socioeconomic factors of this sort are so complex and closely intertwined, it is

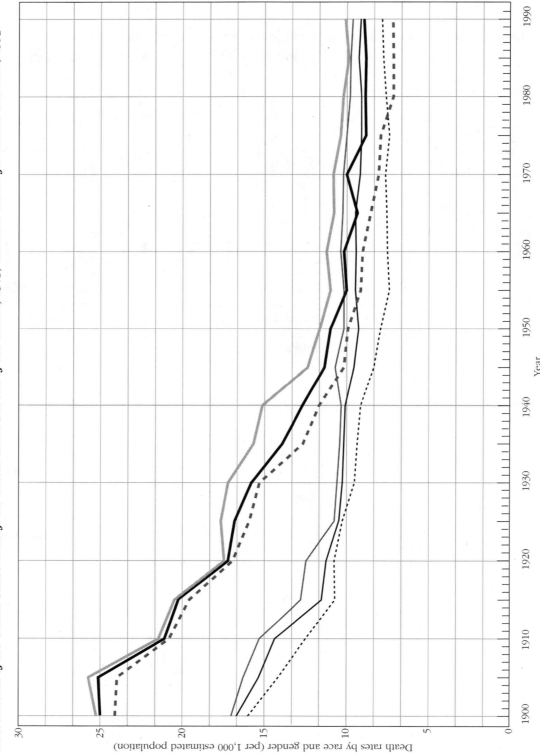

FIGURE 4.1 *Death rates by race and gender, United States, 1900–1990, per 1,000 estimated population. Note: Prior to 1933, includes death-registration states only. Beginning 1959, includes Alaska. Beginning 1960, includes Hawaii. Beginning 1970, excludes deaths of nonresidents of the United States. Data from United States Bureau of the Census, 1975; National Center for Health Statistics, 1993.*

Caucasian-American   African-American

difficult to identify or rank causal factors influencing mortality rates for the African-American population as a whole. However, correlations between membership in the group and the statistical likelihood of dying at an earlier age than a member of the Caucasian-American population are clearly evident.

There are various ways of describing the situation facing African Americans today. For example, for an African-American infant born in the late 20th century, average life expectancy is more than seven years lower than for a white infant (Gee & Veevers, 1985; National Center for Health Statistics, 1993). By middle age, African Americans are at greater risk than their Caucasian counterparts in the United States of dying from most causes. Although a "crossover" effect has frequently been reported when the later age groups are studied (that is, at that point mortality rates are higher among Caucasian Americans than among African Americans), at least one study (Berkman, Singer, & Manton, 1989) did not find this to be true.

McCord and Freeman (1990) dramatized the mortality situation encountered by African Americans by showing that African-American males living in Harlem are less likely to reach the age of 65 than men living in Bangladesh, one of the poorest countries in the world. According to these authors, the "situation in Harlem is extreme, but it is not an isolated phenomenon. . . . Similar pockets of high mortality have been described in other U.S. cities" (p. 176).

Death rates due to violence are higher among African Americans, so much so that the main cause of death among young African-American males is homicide, especially homicide involving firearms (Fingerhut, Ingram, & Feldman, 1992; Ropp, Visintainer, Uman, & Treloar, 1992; Wishner, Schwarz, Grisso, Holmes, & Sutton, 1991). Infant mortality rates were more than twice as high among African Americans in 1990 as among Caucasian Americans (see Figure 4.2; Powell-Griner, 1988). In addition, while maternal death rates at the time of childbirth have decreased dramatically for all Americans over the past 100 years, they remain more than four times higher among African Americans (see Figure 4.3; Lee, 1977). Finally, there is a higher incidence of and lower survival rates with cancer among African Americans (Polednak, 1990).

These differences do not themselves directly reveal the underlying factors from which they result. Nevertheless, in studies in which other factors were held constant, some aspects of these higher mortality rates and lowered life expectancies were found to be more directly related to socioeconomic status than to ethnicity (Polednak, 1990). This should not be surprising. For instance, Powell-Griner (1988) reported that higher risks of infant mortality are associated with illegitimacy, blue-collar families, inadequate prenatal care, and low birth weight. In many instances, these factors are not unrelated to each other; where they are added together they are likely to converge in a way that puts the infant at higher risk of premature death.

In terms of life-threatening behavior, the suicide rate among African Americans is lower than among Caucasian Americans, and it reaches a peak in the young adult (20–35) age group (Heacock, 1990). However, such rates are increasing among young African-American males, even more rapidly than among young white males (Heacock, 1990).

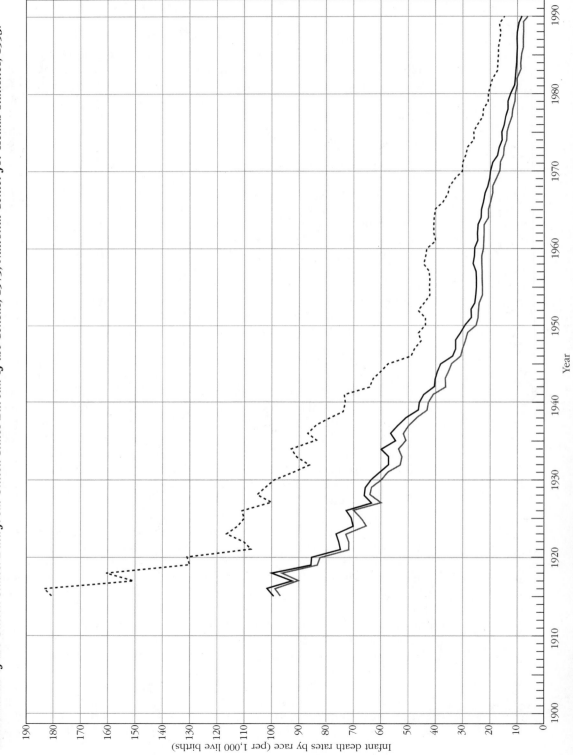

FIGURE 4.1 *Death rates by race and gender, United States, 1900–1990, per 1,000 estimated population. Note: Prior to 1933, includes death-registration states only. Beginning 1959, includes Alaska. Beginning 1960, includes Hawaii. Beginning 1970, excludes deaths of nonresidents of the United States. Data from United States Bureau of the Census, 1975; National Center for Health Statistics, 1993.*

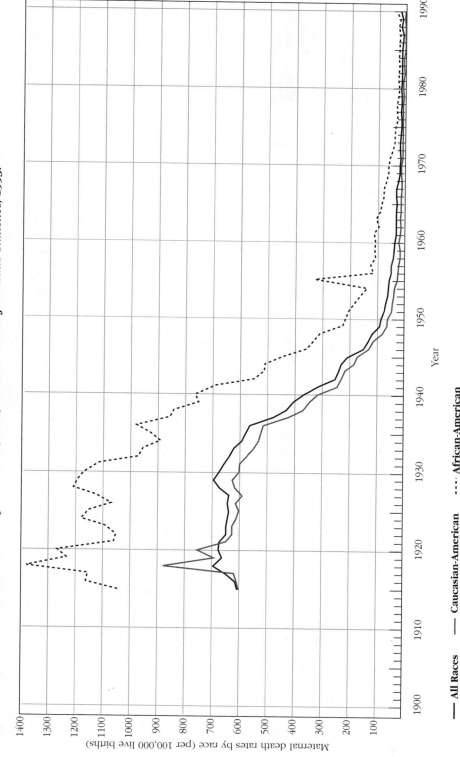

FIGURE 4.3 *Maternal death rates by race, United States, 1915–1990, per 100,000 live births. Note: Prior to 1933, includes birth-registration states only. Beginning 1959, includes Alaska. Beginning 1960, includes Hawaii. 1963 figures by race exclude data for residents of New Jersey. Beginning 1970, excludes deaths of nonresidents of the United States. 1972 deaths based on a 50-percent sample. Data from United States Bureau of the Census, 1975; National Center for Health Statistics, 1993.*

Maternal death rates by race (per 100,000 live births)

Year

—— All Races   —— Caucasian-American   ---- African-American

Last, as early as 1986 it was noted that "Blacks and Hispanics comprise a disproportionately high percentage of AIDS cases" (Institute of Medicine, 1986, p. 102). In addition, later data from 1990 revealed that deaths associated with HIV infection represent the tenth leading cause of death in the population as a whole; the seventh leading cause of death for African Americans, and the eighth leading cause of death for Hispanic Americans (National Center for Health Statistics, 1993). Thus, deaths associated with HIV infection signal an additional disequity related to cultural differences in American society.

Attitudes Toward Death

The systematic study of attitudes and behaviors associated with death, dying, and bereavement among African Americans has hardly begun. Kalish and Reynolds (1981) published one report about such attitudes and behaviors among African Americans in Los Angeles in 1976. They found that individuals in the study relied on friends, church associates, and neighbors for support when dealing with these issues. That is, Kalish and Reynolds found that family relationships were not as important among African Americans as they were among other groups in their study. But this may have been related to the population studied: this pool of African Americans reported the shortest average residence in California, so they may simply have had fewer family members around upon whom they could rely.

And the role of the family in African-American society is described somewhat differently by Brown (1990). He reported that the family is central to the care provided for the terminally ill among African Americans. This care was seen by the African Americans in Brown's study as a "public" rather than a "private" matter, meaning that the extended family, friends, and neighbors may all get involved. Brown suggested that African Americans are reluctant to place terminally ill persons in a hospital or nursing home, preferring instead to keep them at home. This seems to reinforce Brown's claim that for African Americans there is a "strong sense of family loyalty" (p. 76) and to signal the need for professional health care workers to be sensitive to cultural differences among those whom they serve (Leininger, 1988, 1991).

It is important to be wary of overgeneralizations and stereotypes here. As Brown (1990) reported, *middle-class* African Americans may have taken over attitudes and behaviors that are closer to those of the dominant society than are the attitudes and behaviors of other African Americans. In other words, African Americans are as influenced by socioeconomic class, geographical location, and historical heritage as are members of other groups, so their reactions are varied and personal.

Death-Related Practices

African Americans in the Kalish and Reynolds study (1981) saw themselves as freely expressive in times of grief and regarded funerals as important (see also

An African-American community grieving for someone who died violently.

Hines, 1986). Similarly, funeral directors were held in high regard by the study group. Another author (Jackson, 1980) has argued that African Americans view death as a moment in which recognition can be provided for the deceased person's ability to stand up to others and (in the case of males) for the individual's masculinity. Thus, what happens at the funeral (how many persons are present, the appearance of the casket, and so on) can be quite important. Kalish and Reynolds (1981) reported that their informants were likely at the funeral to touch but not kiss the body of the deceased. They were also unlikely to visit the grave.

This might be compared to what Devore (1990) wrote. She argued that African Americans "revert" to the ways of their African ancestors at the time of mourning. This means in part that anyone from the community closely associated with the family who wants to can come to the home of the survivors to offer condolences and any help that might be needed. Devore also described a typical African-American funeral as including "singing by choirs, soloists, and the congregation, testimony of friends, resolutions from church and community organizations, as well as acknowledgement of telegrams from those who could not attend, flowers and sympathy cards" (p. 57). The obituary (which tells the life story of the deceased) is read and a eulogy is presented by a minister. Devore also reported that African Americans exhibit their emotions openly in response to the eulogy; in fact, a funeral among African Americans "allows for unrestrained grief" (p. 60).

Finally, both Brown (1990) and Davidson and Devney (1991) identified a distrust of the medical community on the part of many African Americans. If this is accurate, this attitude might be responsible for other findings. For instance, Davidson and Devney (1991) linked such mistrust to the fact that African Americans also have relatively low organ donor rates, with only 8.8 percent of donated organs coming from the African-American community. Such distrust may also play a role in other situations. For example, it may help to account for poor prenatal care leading to higher infant mortality rates or for the fact that many African Americans prefer to care for dying persons at home.

Hispanic Americans

Hispanics are the second-largest minority group in the continental United States, representing a total population of more than 20 million persons (see Table 4.1). Within this group, some 63 percent are of Mexican origin, approximately 13 percent originated in Puerto Rico, 5 percent are Cuban Americans, and some 18 percent have other origins (mostly in Central and South America) (Soto & Villa, 1990). Some people of Hispanic origin are recent immigrants, others have lived in the continental United States for generations, and all Puerto Ricans have been U.S. citizens since 1917.

Encounters with Death

Efforts to study mortality rates among Hispanic Americans face particular difficulties (Rosenwaike & Bradshaw, 1988). Most of the data collected on mortality rates come from records in county offices. Such records usually record race, but few designate ethnicity. Official government documents (for example, United States Bureau of the Census, 1991) warn that persons of Hispanic origin may be of any race. More important, when Hispanic Americans are classified as Caucasians, few records separate out these persons from the broader group of "Anglo" whites.

In these circumstances, efforts to determine numbers of deaths (see Table 4.2) and death rates among Hispanic Americans often must be based on indirect evidence. The usual method is to look for a Spanish surname. Obviously, this can be misleading: other ethnic groups (such as Italians or Portuguese) may have similar surnames, and a woman who has married out of the original family and has adopted her spouse's surname is lost to the count (as are her children). This means that what is said here about Hispanic-American encounters with death is very tentative.

In general, when compared to other white males, Hispanic-American males have lower mortality rates from heart disease, cancer, and suicide, but higher death rates from infections, diabetes, pneumonia, influenza, accidents, and homicide. Death rates among females with Spanish surnames are similar to other white females' rates of death from heart disease and cancer; lower than other white females' rates of death from accidents and suicide; and higher than other white females' rates of death from infections, diabetes, and homicide.

However, mortality rates for Hispanic Americans born in the United States approach those of the rest of the white population (Rosenwaike & Bradshaw, 1989). Also, as Hispanic-American groups adjust to their surrounding culture, they often take on many of the characteristics of that culture, further confounding claims about that which is distinct to the Hispanic-American experience with death, dying, and bereavement (Salcido, 1990; Soto & Villa, 1990). Unfortunately, that is not true with regard to the HIV/AIDS epidemic, which, as noted earlier, is disproportionately prevalent among Hispanic Americans and African Americans.

Heacock (1990) studied suicide among Puerto Ricans in Manhattan. He found that Puerto Rican men had the highest rate of completed suicides among Hispanics in New York. Puerto Rican women also made more suicide attempts than members of other Hispanic subgroups in New York City. Heacock also reported that suicides in the Southwest occurred at younger ages among Mexican Americans, a point confirmed by other authors (for example, Markides, 1980). Kalish and Reynolds (1981) pointed out that the reported rate of suicide among Mexican Americans in Los Angeles was low. But all of these data are dependent upon what is reported, and several authors (such as Hoppe & Martin, 1986) have remarked that among Hispanics (and African Americans) many deaths that are suicides may not be reported as such (for example, they may be reported as accidents or homicides). Again, the lack of conclusive data makes all of this quite tentative.

Attitudes Toward Death

Among Hispanic Americans, family and religion appear to play influential roles in shaping attitudes and behaviors related to death, dying, and bereavement. For example, Kalish and Reynolds (1981) described the Mexican-American families in their study as tightly knit and as maintaining a strong locus of emotional support in the family unit. Accordingly, when a member is dying in a hospital, the family typically arranges shifts of visitors and may "camp in." Garcia-Preto (1986) reported this for Puerto Ricans in New York, too. In addition, she wrote that "Puerto Ricans place great value on seeing a dying relative, resolving whatever conflicts may exist, and saying a final good-bye. . . . Not being able to be present during the illness or time of death of someone close to them makes the loss more difficult to accept" (pp. 33–34).

However, the nature of the Mexican-American family may be changing in important ways. For example, Salcido (1990) reported a rise in the number of single-family households among Mexican Americans. These are families that may not behave exactly as did others studied previously.

Kalish and Reynolds (1981) also reported that 90 percent of the Mexican Americans whom they studied in Los Angeles were Roman Catholic. This may be one reason why Mexican Americans in this study were opposed to allowing someone to die even if that person wished to do so.

In regard to other attitudes and behaviors around the dying, additional generalizations have been made about Hispanic Americans. Eisenbruch (1984) reported on conflicts between the expectations of health care providers and the attitudes and behaviors of many Puerto Ricans living in New York City. For example, an accepted grief reaction in this population group (but one often not looked on favorably by health care providers) includes "el ataque," consisting of "seizurelike patterns, with a hyperkinetic episode, a display of histrionics or aggression, and sometimes the climax of stupor" (Eisenbruch, 1984, p. 335). This response is regarded in the Puerto Rican community as normal for women; following a code of "machismo," the men show no grief. Campos (1990) reported that Puerto Ricans regard death as an adversity that should be met with fatalism and pessimism, and seem to try to protect dying persons from knowing their prognoses. And Garcia-Preto (1986) suggested that Puerto Ricans typically care for the ill at home, choosing hospitalization only when there is no other alternative.

Kalish and Reynolds (1981) found Mexican Americans more likely than other groups to call for a priest when a person is dying; indeed, the "last rites" may be performed several times. They also found this group to express intense feelings of grief and to believe that it takes time to express such feelings properly. Mexican Americans hold part of the grieving process to involve the gathering together of a large support group, which includes people from the community, friends, and family members (Salcido, 1990).

Death-Related Practices

In terms of funeral practices, Moore (1980) reported that Mexican Americans originally had voluntary self-help associations. When a member of such an association died, other members would be assessed for the costs of the funeral. Moore concluded that the funeral is the single most important family ceremony for this population group; members come from remote points, as they are expected to do. To have a socially effective funeral in this group, a certain level of expense and a certain number of people must be present. In such funerals, children are present and "women rather than men are the focus of interest and emotion" (Moore, 1980, p. 85).

Eisenbruch (1984) noted that among Puerto Ricans in New York City the wake may continue for several days. This reinforces the finding noted earlier by Kalish and Reynolds (1981) that Hispanic Americans believe that it takes time properly to express one's feelings of grief. According to Campos (1990), during the wake and funeral Puerto Ricans strongly prohibit any speaking ill of the person who has died.

Kalish and Reynolds (1981) also reported that the Mexican Americans in their study wore black for the longest time by comparison with other groups whom they studied, visited graves more frequently, and wanted to spend more time during the burial at the grave site than some cemetery officials found

Grieving at the coffin.

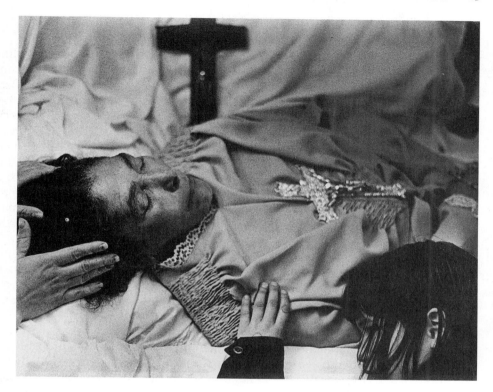

desirable. They found that behavior of this last sort sometimes led to conflict with professionals in the funeral and cemetery industries when they were unfamiliar with the practices of the group or uninformed about their rationale.

These descriptions of Hispanic-American mourning and funeral practices have been reinforced by Campos (1990), who found that Puerto Ricans prefer lengthy formal mourning periods. Another report described a family of Mexican Americans in which adults and children at the wake touched the body and made the sign of the cross on it (Soto & Villa, 1990). These individuals also stayed at the grave site until the body was lowered into the grave. Last, it has been noted that a typical expression of sympathy in Spanish is "Siento mucho su perdida" (Soto & Villa, 1990, p. 123), which they translate as "I feel your loss very much." This is different from merely expressing regrets to another over his or her pain as a bereaved person.

Asian Americans

As of 1988, there were an estimated 6.9 million residents of the United States whose origins trace back to Asia or the Pacific islands (see Table 4.1). The largest of these communities (each constituting some 20 to 23 percent of the total) are Chinese Americans, Filipino Americans, and Japanese Americans.

Encounters with Death

Asian-American deaths in the United States in 1988 are outlined in Table 4.2. When added together, the deaths in this group total just under 19,000 and represent fewer than 0.1 percent of all deaths for that year in a population that totals almost 3 percent of the U.S. resident population.

Mortality rates for specific Asian-American communities can be illustrated through Yu's (1986) report that mortality rates among Chinese Americans are lower than among Caucasian Americans and have been so since the middle 1960s. Causes of death among Chinese Americans show similarities to those among Caucasian Americans: the four leading causes in both groups are heart disease, cancer, cerebrovascular disease, and accidents. Moreover, for each of the six leading causes of death, mortality rates are higher among foreign-born Chinese than among Chinese Americans born in the United States. One curiosity is that cancer rates for the buccal (mouth) cavity and pharynx are higher for Chinese Americans than for Caucasian Americans; it is uncertain whether this is due to a genetic susceptibility to this form of cancer or some other (perhaps dietary) factor. Another point to note is that infant mortality rates for Chinese Americans appear to be significantly lower than for Caucasian Americans (Yu, 1982).

Available data on suicide for Asian Americans suggest that relatively high suicide rates in this population in the early 1950s (probably related to cultural isolation, stress, loneliness, and depression) had given way by the early 1980s to rates that are generally below those of the general population (McIntosh, 1989a). Among Chinese Americans, rates of suicide appear to be highest among elderly women (Yu, 1986). In general, suicide rates among Asian Americans are highest among the aged for Chinese, Japanese, and Filipino Americans (McIntosh & Santos, 1981a). Kalish and Reynolds (1981) reported that they found very low homicide rates for their Japanese-American sample and that suicides are often concealed among this group.

Attitudes Toward Death

Kalish and Reynolds (1981) found that communication is carefully controlled within the Japanese-American community in Los Angeles that they studied. This means that even when members of this community are dying and in distress, health care providers may have difficulty determining this, since such persons are often quite restrained in communicating what they are feeling. Similarly, Eisenbruch (1984) reported that Chinese Americans are "stoic" in the face of death. Furthermore, the strong tendency displayed by many Asian Americans not to question authority is an attitude that carries through to interactions with health care providers (Manio & Hall, 1987). But this can lead to miscommunication; for example, the health care provider may fail to perceive a patient's pain because that person chooses to "save face" in front of a stranger.

Another consequence of this attitude is found in the fact that both Japanese Americans (Hirayama, 1990) and Cambodian Americans (Lang, 1990) may be unlikely to tell seriously ill persons that they are dying. In general, Asian Americans prefer themselves to die at home (Kalish & Reynolds, 1981) and try to keep the elderly at home (Manio & Hall, 1987).

For many Asian Americans, death allows for a continued relationship between the deceased and the survivors (Eisenbruch, 1984; Kalish & Reynolds, 1981). Thus, Kalish and Reynolds (1981) reported that 100 percent of their Japanese-American respondents believed that those who had died watch over those who remain alive on earth. Accordingly, funerals and other memorialization activities are likely to be regarded as important social events because by taking care of the ancestors in this way, one insures that the ancestors will contribute to the well-being of surviving descendants.

Death-Related Practices

Funerals are very important to Japanese Americans (Hirayama, 1990; Kalish & Reynolds, 1981). What is appropriate at a funeral is determined by a (preferably Japanese-American) funeral director. Strict rituals are preferred, so that everyone knows his or her role. Many of the people who take part in Japanese-American funerals attend as representatives of the various groups to which the deceased was related, rather than in a private or individual capacity. Thus, Japanese Americans are likely to have large, well-attended funeral ceremonies because of the large numbers of persons who are expected to attend.

When people attend such funerals, they bring gifts (*koden*) that have the effect of serving as a sort of group insurance. Much of this is similar to the practices in Samoan-American funerals (which carefully blend Samoan tradition, elaborate Christian ceremony, and the realities of a new environment), including the practice of giving both money and fine mats (Ablon, 1970; King, 1990).

According to Kalish and Reynolds (1981), in Japanese-American society the wake and funeral are often held in the evening as a combined event; on the next day, a private service will likely be held at the grave site or crematorium. Japanese Americans are not likely to touch the body of the deceased person. They typically cremate the body of the deceased and may also send the remains (or part of the remains) back to Japan to be buried near ancestors (Kalish & Reynolds, 1981).

Concerning other Asian-American customs, Lee (1986) reported that people in large Chinatown communities tried to retain some traditional funeral practices, such as burning paper money, "funeral marches around the community, and a funeral dinner for relatives and friends" (p. 35). And Manio and Hall (1987) found that Asian Americans often make extensive photographic records of the funeral.

In light of beliefs in a continued interaction between the living and the deceased, within which the well-being of living descendants is at least partly related to the care taken by deceased ancestors, it is not surprising that Japa-

A Vietnamese memorial service in Boston.

nese Americans visit grave sites on a frequent basis to express their ongoing concern and care for their ancestors (Kalish & Reynolds, 1981).

Japanese Americans in the Kalish and Reynolds (1981) study were reported to have very conservative mourning traditions. Few members of these groups were reported to believe that remarriage, or even dating after the death of a spouse, was appropriate. Nevertheless, they also held that wearing black was not necessary.

Native Americans

Readily available information about Native Americans' death-related encounters, attitudes, and practices is limited, not always reliable, and not easily subject to generalization. There are hundreds of Native-American tribal groups in the United States and Canada, varying in size from fewer than 100 members (for example, Picuris Pueblo in New Mexico) to more than 100,000 members (for example, the Navajo) (Marquis, 1974). Each Native-American group has its own set of encounters, beliefs, patterns of behavior, and rituals.

One official estimate placed the total population of Native Americans in the United States as of July, 1989, at more than 1.7 million (see Table 4.1).

However, not all Native Americans live within a tribal group or on tribal lands, where data about their death-related experiences could conveniently be located and identified. In fact, it has been estimated that some 60 percent of Native Americans now live in urban areas in North America, where they may be invisible in many ways to an external observer (Thompson & Walker, 1990). Furthermore, it has been reported that there are some 6.7 million additional individuals who claim partial Native-American ancestry (United States Congress, 1986). For all of these reasons, generalizations about death, dying, and bereavement may be particularly inappropriate or hazardous for this relatively small but very heterogeneous portion of American society.

Encounters with Death

Official government documents (see Table 4.2) report 7,917 deaths of Native Americans in 1988, which suggests an overall mortality rate of 4.6 percent. However, these are aggregate figures, which are subject to all of the limitations just noted. Death is likely to be encountered in quite different ways among very different Native-American groups.

Typically, Native Americans have died most frequently from infectious diseases, tuberculosis, diabetes mellitus, cirrhosis, and accidents. However, as these causes are reduced in significance and the average life expectancy of Native Americans has increased, cancer has become more important as a cause of death in these groups (Michalek & Mahoney, 1990). However, few studies have been made of cancer incidence among Native Americans (Michalek & Mahoney, 1990). What is available indicates that both Native-American males and females have lower rates than other groups for all disease sites combined; however, females have increased rates of cervical cancer. Overall, Native Americans also have the least favorable survival rates from cancer.

With respect to infant mortality rates, Campbell (1989) stated that in 1982 these rates among Native Americans nationwide were below the national average for all races. He also found that the leading cause of infant death among Native Americans was Sudden Infant Death Syndrome—at twice the national average.

Mahoney (1991) found high mortality rates from automobile accidents among Native-American populations in New York State. In fact, these rates were nearly double the overall rate in the United States. The largest portion (73.7 percent) of these deaths occurred among males (Mahoney, 1991). Carr and Lee (1978) found motor vehicle accidents to be the leading cause of death among Navajo males and the second leading cause among females on the reservation. Campbell (1989) makes a similar report concerning Native Americans in Montana. In addition, Olson and her colleagues (Olson, Becker, Wiggins, Key, & Samet, 1990) reported that deaths due to motor vehicle crashes were exceptionally high among Native-American children in New Mexico.

High vehicular mortality rates among Native-American populations may in part be attributed to their living in areas where people live far apart from one another and where roads are often in poor condition. In these circumstances, increased motor vehicle use is necessary, but it is also more dangerous, given the condition of the roads. All this is compounded when alcoholism is another contributing factor.

Thompson and Walker (1990) discussed what they believe is a myth, that there are high suicide rates among Native Americans. One commonly hears this reported as fact. According to some authors (such as Van Winkle & May, 1986), however, this claim is based on small numbers of suicides over short time spans and among small population bases. In fact, Webb and Willard (1975) determined that there is no single, common Native-American pattern for suicides, and Thompson and Walker (1990) argued that suicide rates in the various tribes seem most closely related to suicide rates in their surrounding populations. If that is correct, then Native-American rates of suicide should be compared to rates among others in the areas in which the Native Americans live. In other words, no overall statistic for Native American suicide rates is really reliable, since such rates vary markedly from area to area and tribe to tribe (McIntosh, 1983).

Still, this myth persists and even influences beliefs among Native-Americans themselves. Thus, Levy and Kunitz (1987) reported that the Hopi have become concerned about suicide rates among themselves, even though "Hopi suicide rates are no higher than those of the neighboring counties" (p. 932). Furthermore, they found no evidence that Hopi suicide rates are increasing.

The only generalization that does appear to be valid is that suicide among Native Americans is largely a phenomenon of young males, since suicide rates among the elderly are low in this minority group (McIntosh & Santos, 1981b; Thompson & Walker, 1990).

Attitudes Toward Death

Commentators (such as Brown, 1987; Hultkrantz, 1979) have suggested that Native Americans tend to view life and death not in a linear but in a circular or interwoven fashion. Thus, death is regarded as a part of life. Within this general outlook, however, death-related attitudes of specific Native-American groups may range from acceptance without anxiety to a high level of fear. For example, Carr and Lee (1978) reported that among Navajos, death taboos "favor bringing the sick into the hospital to die rather than permitting them to die at home" (p. 280) so that the home will not be polluted by the experience of death. In the face of great heterogeneity, we can perhaps best illustrate distinctive qualities of Native-American attitudes toward death, dying, and bereavement by focusing on a single community—the Hopi—and its unique outlook.

For the Hopi all of life is interconnected, and since "death" merely involves moving from one form of life to another, the "dead" are involved in what happens in this life. There is constant interaction between the ancestors and those living today in the Hopi villages in Arizona.

Still, Kennard (1932) reported that the Hopi speak only reluctantly of the dead. Anyone who thinks too much about the dead or that "other life" may bring about his or her own death. In fact, in the Hopi view any death—even after an illness—"is attributed to the will or lack of strength of the individual" (p. 494).

However, each person also has his or her own "road"; old persons who die are seen as having reached the end of their personal roads, so the death of such a person is more or less accepted. But if someone young or middle-aged dies, there is a more complex response. Depending on the perceived cause of the death ("trouble," a conflict too strong for the person's will to overcome; or a deliberate willing of one's own death), responses will differ. There may be anxiety, fear, or anger. Kennard (1932) reported on a woman who slapped the face of a corpse, saying "You are mean to do this to me" (p. 495).

The Beagleholes (1935) studied Hopi living on the reservation in the first third of this century. At that time, they also reported that the Hopi were reluctant to discuss death. According to their informants, no special behavior occurred in the presence of someone who was dying, although they reported that people sometimes left to avoid becoming afraid so that they in turn would not become sick or even die. The adult left in the house took care of the corpse. The body was left in the clothes it was wearing at the time of its death; an adult male was wrapped in buckskin, an adult female in her wedding blanket. The hair was washed. The body was put into a sitting position and tied together in that position. A related male made prayer feathers (these are spiritual objects, helping to carry the spirit to the other world); one prayer feather was tied to the hair or under each foot, one was placed in each hand, and one was laid over the navel. The face was covered with raw cotton (perhaps symbolizing a cloud—a *kachina*—which the spirit would eventually become). Food was sometimes placed with the body. A male, accompanied by other males, then carried the body to the cemetery. A hole was dug; the body was placed in it facing west. The hole was filled in and a stick was placed in the grave to serve as a ladder for the spirit to climb to depart to the west (the home of the ancestors). The persons involved in dealing with the corpse then purified themselves, and the survivors thereafter tried to forget the deceased.

Death-Related Practices

In terms of practices associated with mourning, Hanson (1978) reported on a striking case of a Hopi man in San Francisco. A death of a family member was followed by his having auditory hallucinations. This was thought by officials at a local psychiatric authority to represent psychosis. But Hanson's agency returned the young man to his reservation where he could participate in tribal rituals related to the burial of the dead. His hallucinations stopped. As Hanson remarked, "practices that are difficult to understand are usually interpreted as indicators of psychopathology by the dominant society" (p. 20).

That Hopi man was not unique. Hopi women frequently report hallucinations as part of the mourning process (Matchett, 1972). In cases described by Matchett, the experiences were apparently neither like a seance nor like a dream, but allowed the beholder to converse with, describe in visual detail, and even struggle with the figure that appeared to them.

In Canada, people from remote areas who have acute life-threatening illnesses or long-term chronic illnesses are normally referred for treatment in

The grave of a Native American child.

urban tertiary-care hospitals. For First Nation peoples, one effect of this practice is to remove them from their home communities and to locate death in the alien cultural environment of an urban hospital. A report from Winnipeg described ways in which trained native interpreters acted as mediators for Cree, Ojibway, and Inuit patients who were terminally ill: as language translators; as cultural informants who could describe native health practices, community health issues, and cultural perspectives on terminal illness and postmortem rituals to clinical staff; as interpreters of biomedical concepts to native peoples; and as patient and community advocates—for instance, by enabling them to return to their communities to spend their final days with their families (Kaufert & O'Neil, 1991).

With respect to grief and its expression, two reports are helpful. The first concerns Cree people living east of James Bay in the Province of Quebec (Preston & Preston, 1991). For the Cree, death is regarded as "at once a commonplace event and one with much significance" (p. 137). Since they place great value on personal autonomy and competence, they strive not to interfere in the lives of others. "The ideal for Cree grieving is an immediate, shared, emotional release, with mutual support for those most at loss and perhaps at risk. But the release of crying and support is soon followed by a return to outward self-reliance and composure, though the inward, private feelings may still be strong" (Preston & Preston, 1991, p. 155).

A second report concerns the Tanacross Athabaskans of east central Alaska (Simeone, 1991). For these people, activities after death involve both a funeral and a memorial potlatch. The funeral has to do with preparing the corpse, building a coffin and grave fence, and conducting a Christian religious service. The work of preparing the body and building the funeral structures is assumed by nonrelatives, because the spirit of the dead person is thought to be danger-ous to relatives. However, it is relatives who prepare a three-day ceremony involving feasting, dancing, singing, oratory, and a distribution of gifts (such as guns, beads, and blankets) on the last night to those who have fulfilled their obligations. This ceremony is the memorial potlatch, which "marks the sepa-ration of the deceased from society and is the last public expression of grief" (Simeone, 1991, p. 159). The gifts that are distributed objectify and personal-ize the grief of the hosts. Through the whole ceremony of the potlatch, social support is provided and strong emotions of grief are given legitimate expres-sion in the Tanacross Athabaskan community, but the larger social context is one that contains grief in a culture that values emotional reserve.

Broader Studies of Cultural Differences

This chapter has focused on the experience of death in four different cultural groups within the United States. One might go further than this to enter into cross-cultural studies of death-related experiences outside the boundaries of the United States. Such studies could offer additional information from other parts of the world that is relevant to our field of study (Palgi & Abramovitch, 1984); important similarities and differences could be identified (see "And What Do You Die of in Africa?") That sort of information would add to the comparisons and contrasts set forth in this chapter. Some resources for such broader cross-cultural research in the field of death, dying, and bereavement are identified in the suggested readings at the end of this chapter and some exam-ples of the results of such work are occasionally cited throughout this book.

Summary

Without going beyond the four groups selected for analysis in this chapter, the first thing to be learned is that there is a rich diversity in the death-related experiences of the many different cultural groups in American society. Each of these groups is both a part of the larger society in which we all share and a distinct entity with its own unique death system. Normally, membership within such a cultural group is a matter of birth and socialization; we do not choose such membership. And it can be difficult to overcome long-standing

And What Do You Die of in Africa?

You die of the things you die of everywhere: you die of microscopic germs; of accident and murder; of politics and poverty; of rooms in hotels and hospitals; of love and lack of love; of madness and silly obsessions; of the spirit that leaves you; of bad habits and time; but most of all you die of yourself and the private poison of loneliness.

SOURCE From Harrison, *Three Hunters* (1989), p. 234.

experiences of our group as the norm, and other groups as outsiders who vary from the norm. But all of us can learn from the other cultural groups around us. Taking part in the death-related practices of such groups (when outsiders are permitted to do so), reading about their attitudes and rituals, and sharing personal experiences (for example, through discussions in a course on death, dying, and bereavement) can enrich us, both as individuals and as citizens in a multicultural society.

QUESTIONS FOR REVIEW AND DISCUSSION

1. This chapter focused attention on cultural differences in encounters with, attitudes toward, and practices in the face of death, dying, and bereavement. That is, we might say that this chapter showed us four different "death systems." What major factors do you note as being *unique* to each of the four groups described? What major factors do you note as being *similar* among each of the four groups described?

2. How would you describe the relationship between death-related encounters and attitudes, on the one hand, and death-related practices, on the other hand, in any one or more of the four population groups discussed in this chapter?

3. How would you describe the relationship between your own death-related encounters and attitudes, on the one hand, and your own death-related practices, on the other hand?

SUGGESTED READINGS

Book-length studies of cultural differences and of different cultural experiences with death within American society include the following:

Coffin, M. M. (1976). *Death in Early America: The History and Folklore of Customs and Superstitions of Early Medicine, Burial and Mourning.*

Irish, D. P., Lundquist, K. F., & Nelson, V. J. (Eds.). (1993). *Ethnic Variations in dying, death, and grief: Diversity In Universality.* Washington, DC: Taylor & Francis.

Kalish, R. A., & Reynolds, D. K. (1981). *Death and Ethnicity: A Psychocultural Study.*

Leininger, M. (1978). *Transcultural Nursing: Concepts, Theories, and Practices.*

McGoldrick, M., Pearce, J. K., & Giordano, J. (Eds.). (1982). *Ethnicity and Family Therapy.*

Mindel, C. H., Habenstein, R. W., & Wright, R. (1988). *Ethnic Families in America: Patterns and Variations* (3rd ed.).

Parry, J. K. (Ed.). (1990). *Social Work Practice with the Terminally Ill: A Transcultural Perspective.*

Radin, P. (1973). *The Road of Life and Death: A Ritual Drama of the American Indians.*

Stannard, D. E. (Ed.). (1975). *Death in America.*

For examples of reports on death-related experiences outside American society, see:

Abrahamson, H. (1977). *The Origin of Death: Studies in African Mythology.*

Brodman, B. (1976). *The Mexican Cult of Death in Myth and Literature.*

Counts, D. R., & Counts, D. A. (Eds.). (1991). *Coping with the Final Tragedy: Cultural Variation in Dying and Grieving.*

Craven, M. (1973). *I Heard the Owl Call My Name.*

Danforth, L. M. (1982). *The Death Rituals of Rural Greece.*

Goody, J. (1962). *Death, Property, and the Ancestors: A Study of the Mortuary Customs of the LoDagaa of West Africa.*

Kalish, R. A. (Ed.). (1980). *Death and Dying: Views from Many Cultures.* Includes some North American contributions.

Kurtz, D. C., & Boardman, J. (1971). *Greek Burial Customs.*

Lewis, O. (1970). *A Death in the Sanchez Family.*

Rosenblatt, P. C., Walsh, P. R., & Jackson, D. A. (1976). *Grief and Mourning in Cross-Cultural Perspectives.*

Scheper-Hughes, N. (1992). *Death Without Weeping: The Violence of Everyday Life in Brazil.*

PART II

DYING

There is a sense in which every living thing is dying or moving toward death from the moment of its birth. However, this stretches our normal, everyday usage of the word *dying* so far as to render it useless for most of its customary purposes. Clearly, a difference exists between the universal condition shared by all living things and the processes that are involved in the ending of a life. Even if all of us are dying in some generic sense, some of us are more actively dying than others.

In common practice, many people act as if those who are dying are already dead or as good as dead. This, too, is unhelpful; it is incorrect and hurtful. One major theme of the following three chapters is to draw attention to the many ways in which dying persons are (and continue to be, as long as they are dying) living human beings. Death is the outcome of dying, not its equivalent.

But still, when does dying begin? A number of answers have been suggested: when a fatal condition develops; when that condition is recognized by a physician; when knowledge of that condition is communicated to the person involved; when that person realizes and accepts the facts of his or her condition; when nothing more can be done to reverse the condition and to preserve life (Kastenbaum, 1989d). It is not clear whether any or all of these are sufficient to define the state of dying. The situation is reminiscent of a statement attributed to the English statesman Edmund Burke (1729–1797), that it is difficult to determine the precise point at which daytime becomes nighttime, even though everyone can easily distinguish between light and darkness.

This suggests that it might be more helpful to focus not on *when* dying begins, but on *what is involved in dying*. Pattison (1977) suggested that in many instances it might be useful to think of what he called a "living-dying interval" (see Figure II.1). By this, he meant a period of time between the normal processes of living in which all of us could become (but most of us actually are not yet) involved in dying and the point at which death occurs. Further, Pattison proposed that the living-dying interval be subdivided into three phases: (1) an acute crisis phase; (2) a chronic living-dying phase; and (3) a terminal phase culminating in death. In addition, Pattison advanced the idea that each of these subperiods might be focused on a different variable: rising anxiety generated by the critical awareness of impending death in the acute crisis phase; a variety of potential fears and challenges in the chronic living-dying phase; and issues concerning hope and different types of death in the terminal phase.

FIGURE II.1 *The living–dying interval. From E. M. Pattison, 1977 (p. 44).*

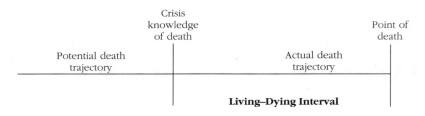

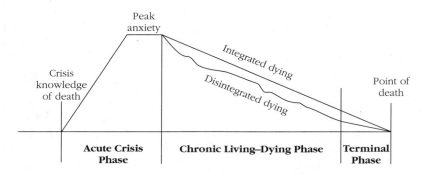

One need not accept this analysis of dying and its elements to realize that dying is not always simple or uncomplicated. That is, dying can hold the same complexity and richness as all other aspects of living. The aim of the three chapters that follow is to seek a better understanding of some of the dimensions of dying that are most significant for human beings. Chapter 5 explores what is involved in coping with dying, together with two major theoretical models designed to aid understanding of such coping. Chapter 6 investigates ways in which individuals can help those who are coping with dying. And Chapter 7 looks at hospice principles and the basic ways in which our society has organized itself to care for those who are coping with dying.

CHAPTER 5

Coping with Dying

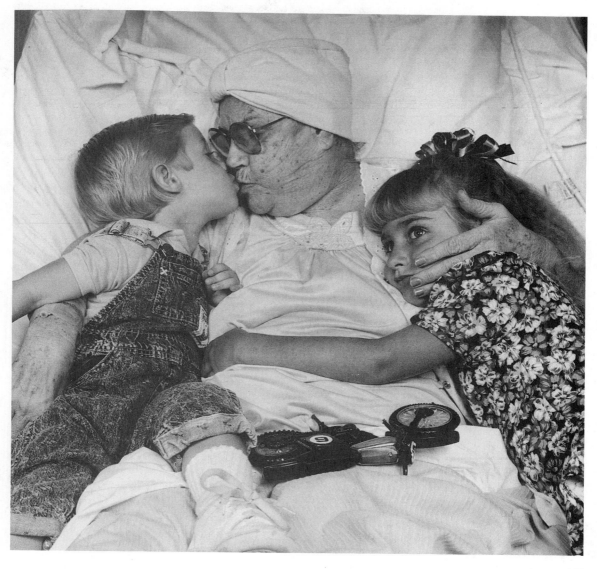

Dying at home among the living.

An individual with an illness that puts his or her life in jeopardy or who is in the process of ending that life is above all else a *person*, a living human being. There may be much that is distinctive or special about individuals with life-threatening or terminal illnesses, because the pressures of dying often underscore the preciousness of living. But like all other living persons, those who are dying have a broad range of needs and desires, hopes, fears and anxieties, joys and sufferings.

Dying is part of our experience of life and living; death does not take place until life, living, and dying have ended. One cannot already be dead and yet still be dying. To be dead is to be through with dying; to be dying is still to be alive. It is important to understand this correctly, for it is fundamental to much that follows.

Dying persons are not merely individuals within whom biochemical systems are malfunctioning. That may be important, but it is not the whole story. Dying is a human experience, not just a matter of anatomy and physiology. If the latter were true, we could safely ignore the other dimensions of dying persons and treat them merely as physical objects. However, we should not do that. *Dying persons are living human beings.*

In fact, each person who is dying is a complex and unique entity, inter-mixing physical, psychological, social, and spiritual dimensions (Saunders, 1967). Psychological difficulties, social discomfort, and spiritual suffering may be just as powerful, pressing, and significant for a dying person as physical distress. To focus on any one of these dimensions alone is to be in danger of ignoring the totality of the person and overlooking what matters most to him or her. Those who have kept company with and actively listened to persons who are dying will know this to be true.

This chapter investigates a series of issues that relate to dying persons and those who are involved with such persons. It begins with a short, concrete example of one such person and one of his visitors. After that is a discussion of some fears, anxieties, and concerns of those who are dying, some of the things that are involved in coping with living and dying, and two key variables in the form of dying trajectories and awareness contexts. The latter half of the chapter is devoted to an analysis of two models—one based on stages, the other on tasks—that have been proposed to explicate what is involved in coping with dying.

A Dying Person

He was in his middle 30s; tall, gaunt, nearly bald. He lay in the bed, looking tired and bored. We sat and talked for nearly an hour. He had had a bout of cancer many years earlier; chemotherapy had forced it into remission. Recently it had recurred, and now it was no longer responding to the drugs that had worked before, so an experimental drug was being used. This meant that each month he spent some time in the hospital receiving the new drug. That process and its attendant side effects left him tired. Each time he went back home, he slowly built up strength so that he could go back to work. Then it would be time for him to come back to the hospital for another treatment.

I listened and tried to allow him to take the conversation where he wanted it to go. He talked about his disappointments, his anxiety, his hope. Underneath the conversation was the theme of approaching death. While he seldom addressed it directly, the topic was frequently indicated in oblique ways. Uncertain of whether or not he had gained much from our conversation, I left his room. When I returned to that room later to talk to his roommate, he called me over and we continued our earlier conversation. My general impression was that he was glad to see me; perhaps he had discovered that he could discuss whatever he wanted with me, and I would listen.

Fears, Anxieties, and Concerns of Those Who Are Dying

Death has many meanings—for example, as organizer of time, as punishment, as transition, as loss (Kalish, 1985a). Because of this, fears and anxieties related to death take many forms. In general, *fear* has to do with apprehension or concern directed toward some specific focus, while *anxiety* means that we are worried or troubled in a broader or more diffuse way. With respect to death, there are four broad categories within which one might organize typical areas of concern: (1) fears related to dying and the dying process (for example, fear of pain or dependence, fear of various sorts of losses that may be experienced while one is dying; (2) fears related to death itself and its meaning (for example, fear of being dead, fear of nonexistence or nonbeing, fear of loss of self or loss of identity); (3) fears related to the consequences of death, whether for oneself or for those whom the individual loves (for example, fear of the unknown, fear of judgment and/or punishment, fear of what will happen to people, things, or plans that are left behind); and (4) fears related to the death or dying of others (for example, fear of separation from someone who is loved, fears associated with problems experienced during the dying of another) (Simpson, 1979).

The fact that death-related fears or anxieties can take many forms should not be surprising, since they arise from the very divergent attitudes that different societies and individuals have toward life and living. In recent years, such fears and anxieties have been the object of active study that has sought to employ different research approaches and to be sensitive to a wide variety of demographic, situational, and other variables (see, for example, Lonetto & Templer, 1986; Neimeyer, 1988).

This chapter concentrates on concerns about death among those who are coping with dying. On this topic, Davidson (1979, p. 169) offered the following report: "In 1969 I directed a study at the University of Chicago to see what a majority of terminally ill patients would rank as their major problem. The overwhelming majority ranked 'abandonment' as their major problem, with 'loss of self-management' and 'intractable pain' as their second and third greatest problems. 'Fear of death' ranked ninth." In other words, dying persons in this study indicated that they were most concerned about (1) being deserted or rejected by significant persons in their lives; (2) losing control or the ability to manage their own lives; and (3) being in overwhelming pain or distress. This reveals a mixture of physical, psychological, social, and spiritual concerns. Physical concerns are not necessarily foremost, nor are concerns that relate directly to death itself. This suggests that coping with dying may be more complex than it first appears and may be closely linked to what is involved in coping with living.

Coping with Living, Coping with Dying

Coping has been defined as "constantly changing cognitive and behavioral efforts to manage specific external and/or internal demands that are appraised as taxing or exceeding the resources of the person" (Lazarus & Folkman, 1984, 141; compare Monat & Lazarus, 1991). This is a useful definition in many ways. First, it focuses on *processes* of coping, with special reference to their changing character and the specific demands to which they respond. Second, it emphasizes *efforts to manage* those demands—that is, not just traits that characterize internal feeling states, but whatever one is thinking or doing in the endeavor to cope. Third, it identifies coping as those efforts that address demands that are appraised as *taxing or exceeding the resources* of the person, thus associating coping with situations involving psychological stress and distinguishing coping from routine, automatized, adaptive behaviors that do not require effort. Fourth, it *does not confuse coping with outcome*—that is, coping includes any efforts to manage stressful demands, however successful or unsuccessful such efforts might be. And fifth, it emphasizes efforts to *manage* demands, not necessarily to *master* them—that is, one may attempt to master the situation, but often one is content to accept, endure, minimize, or avoid stressful demands.

In trying to understand coping with living and coping with dying, it is important to know what individuals who are coping are actually thinking or doing in specific contexts of stressful demands (Hinton, 1984; Silver & Wortman, 1980). This requires that one adopt a dynamic outlook rather than a static point of view that emphasizes general attributes or personality dispositions (White, 1974). That is, one must ask what the person is actually thinking or doing as the stressful encounter unfolds, not just what he or she might do, should do, or usually does. Because coping involves shifting processes as the relationship between the person and his or her environment changes, it may involve different forms of coping at different times—for example, problem-solving strategies may supplant defensive responses. Thus the focus of the individual's coping is critical.

With respect to efforts involved in managing a life transition or crisis, Moos and Schaefer (1986) have described the following five major sets of adaptive coping tasks (p. 11):

1. Establish the meaning and understand the personal significance of the situation.
2. Confront reality and respond to the requirements of the external situation.
3. Sustain relationships with family members and friends as well as with other individuals who may be helpful in resolving the crisis and its aftermath.
4. Maintain a reasonable emotional balance by managing upsetting feelings aroused by the situation.
5. Preserve a satisfactory self-image and maintain a sense of competence and mastery.

Further, they have organized nine major types of coping skills into three broad focal domains, as follows (Moos & Schaefer, 1986, pp. 14–19):

Appraisal-focused coping

1. *Logical analysis and mental preparation*—Paying attention to one aspect of the crisis at a time, breaking a seemingly overwhelming problem into small, potentially manageable bits, drawing on past experiences, and mentally rehearsing alternative actions and their probable consequences.
2. *Cognitive redefinition*—Cognitive strategies by which an individual accepts the basic reality of a situation but restructures it to find something favorable.
3. *Cognitive avoidance or denial*—An array of skills aimed at denying or minimizing the seriousness of a crisis.

Problem-focused coping

4. *Seeking information and support*—Obtaining information about the crisis and alternate courses of action and their probable outcome.

5. *Taking problem-solving action*—Taking concrete action to deal directly with a crisis or its aftermath.
6. *Identifying alternative rewards*—Attempts to replace the losses involved in certain transitions and crises by changing one's activities and creating new sources of satisfaction.

Emotion-focused coping

7. *Affective regulation*—Efforts to maintain hope and control one's emotions when dealing with a distressing situation.
8. *Emotional discharge*—Openly venting one's feelings . . . and using jokes and gallows humor to help allay constant strain.
9. *Resigned acceptance*—Coming to terms with a situation and accepting it as it is, deciding that the basic circumstances cannot be altered, and submitting to "certain" fate.

What is especially valuable in this schematization is the breadth of the task work that it details and the diverse emphases that can be involved in any individual's coping. Moos and Schaefer (1986, p. 13) noted that "the word *skill* underscores the positive aspects of coping and depicts coping as an ability that can be taught and used flexibly as the situation requires." In short, these authors recognized that coping outcomes depend upon a background context (involving demographic and personal factors, event-related factors, and physical and social environmental factors), the way(s) in which an individual appraises cognitively the perceived meaning of the event or challenge, and how one applies coping skills to adaptive tasks.

Coping with Illness

This understanding of coping can be applied, in the first place, to those who are coping with illness. In today's society, the first signs of stress and demands for coping are likely to be associated with initial indicators of illness or disease (Doka, 1993). For example, I might notice a small growth, feel an unusual pain, or become aware of a decline in my functioning. At first, I may simply ignore the indicator. That is, I might appraise it as not being significant or I might direct attention to minimizing my feelings about its presence. Eventually, I may find myself compelled to decide whether to investigate its significance. Perhaps I will seek medical or other advice for investigation or diagnosis of the potential problem. Instead, I might put that off for many reasons—for example, lack of ready access to such advice, lack of medical insurance or personal funds to pay for such advice, or simply the hope that things will get better and "it" will go away on its own.

If a serious but treatable condition is diagnosed, I may have to cope with decisions about cure-oriented interventions of various sorts. For example, if my diagnosis involves some type of cancer, one or more of the following interventions may be proposed: (1) a surgical intervention in the form of efforts to remove a malignant growth; (2) a medical intervention in the form of chemotherapy (drugs designed to kill the cancerous cells or at least to retard their growth); or (3) a radiological intervention in the form of radiotherapy (also designed to destroy unwanted cells or halt their growth). In contemporary medical practice, it is not uncommon to recommend a multimodal therapeutic intervention in which surgery is preceded and/or followed by "adjuvant" therapies such as chemotherapy and radiotherapy.

At some point, however, cure-oriented interventions may no longer have much to offer when their potential benefits are balanced against their physical and psychosocial costs. Or no relevant cure-oriented intervention may be available, either for this disease as such or for the stage at which it has been discovered and diagnosed. In any of these circumstances, the individual may be faced with decisions to discontinue cure-oriented interventions and to turn, perhaps, to interventions that are designed to minimize discomforting symptoms.

Coping with Dying: Dying Persons

The needs of dying persons are both complex and highly personal. In part, they are shaped by social, cultural, and religious influences, as well as by family practices and personal experiences. As a result, each individual will cope with his or her own dying in his or her own way. Some may not have much time to understand or to cope with their own dying. Others may have time, but may be confused as to whether or not they really are seriously ill, facing a life-threatening situation, or dying. They might ask themselves questions such as the following: Is this really a dire illness? Am I already dying? Will I be dead soon?

Davidson's report (1979) suggests that most dying persons will be anxious about challenges they are currently facing. But the range of fears, anxieties, and concerns can be very broad, as we have already noted. What the proximity of death sets before each of us is a very individual matter, influenced by our current situation and our stage of development (discussed in Part 4).

How one copes with any challenge is also quite personal. For the most part, coping is learned behavior. Thus, Davidson (1975, p. 28) noted that "we are born with the *ability* to adapt to change, but we all must *learn* how to cope with loss." As individuals move through life, they observe how others around them cope with separation, loss, and endings—the "necessary losses" (Viorst, 1986) or "little deaths" (Purtillo, 1976) that none of us can completely avoid. Some will try out in their own lives strategies that they have watched others use in coping. Others will simply rely upon methods that have proved satisfactory to them in the past. When it comes to dealing with the issues that confront us in life, the aim for each individual is to acquire a repertoire of coping skills that responds to his or her needs and that enables that person to adapt in satisfactory ways.

All of the ways in which one learns to cope are not likely to be of equal value. Some ways of coping are useful in most situations. Some have value in certain situations but not in others. Some merely appear to be effective ways of coping, even while they are actually counterproductive. Some ways of coping may be satisfactory to one person but hurtful to others. But the better we learn to cope with past and present losses, the more likely we are to be able to cope successfully with losses in the future.

So in each particular situation, we can ask: How and to what extent is the individual coping? Why is he or she coping in this particular way? What does he or she perceive as that which needs to be coped with? These questions apply to coping with dying as well as to coping with all other challenges in living. For that reason, although there are significant differences between death and other sorts of losses, how one copes with the ''little deaths'' throughout life may be indicative of how one is likely to cope with the large crises involved in death itself.

Coping with Dying: Other Persons

Coping with dying is not solely confined to ill and dying persons. Coping with dying is also a challenge for others who are drawn into such situations. These include the family members and friends of the dying person as well as the volunteer and professional caregivers who attend to the dying person. The experience of dying resonates deeply within the personal sense of mortality and limitation of all who are drawn into its processes. A family member who says to a dying person, ''Don't die on me,'' may be conveying anguish at the pending loss of a loved one. A caregiver who says, ''We lost Mr. Smith last night,'' may be expressing awareness of his or her inability to prevent the coming of death. In the case of families, it is especially important to note that people who are coping with dying do so both as individuals and as members of a family system that influences their coping (Rosen, 1990).

Coping with dying is usually multifaceted. It involves more than one person, more than one perception of what is going on, more than one set of motivations, and more than one way of coping. Those who wish to understand coping with dying need to identify each person who is involved in that activity and listen carefully to what his or her coping reveals. Only by listening can we hope to understand what the coping means for each individual in each particular situation. Sensitivity to outward behaviors, to underlying feelings, and to key variables is essential in such listening.

Dying Trajectories and Awareness Contexts

Two key variables in coping with dying have been described by Glaser and Strauss (1965, 1968). These are the nature of the dying trajectory and the degree to which those who are involved are aware of and share information about dying. These variables describe both the individual situation and the social context within which coping with dying takes place.

All dying persons do not move toward death at the same rates of speed or in the same ways. The process of dying or coming-to-be-dead has its own distinctive characteristics in each individual case. As we have already noted in Chapter 1, Glaser and Strauss (1968) have suggested that we should understand *dying trajectories* in terms of two principal variables: duration and shape. Some trajectories involve an up-and-down history—remission, relapse, remission, and so on—often in a rather unpredictable way. Other dying trajectories make relatively steady progress toward death. In some cases, the dying trajectory may be completed in a very brief, almost instantaneous, span of time; in other cases, it may be slow, extending over a period of weeks, months, or even years.

Obviously, there are variations on these simple patterns. For example, the time when death will occur or the moment when the process will resolve itself so that its ultimate outcome is clear may or may not be predictable. We may know that the person will die, when the death will occur, and how it will take place, or we may be unclear about one or more of these points. These are the proximate patterns within which dying and coping with dying are lived out in our society.

Awareness contexts have to do with social interactions among those who are coping with dying. They were first studied by Glaser and Strauss (1965), who argued that once a person is discovered to be dying, the relationships between that person and his or her close associates and health care providers can take at least four basic forms.

1. *Closed awareness* is a context in which the person who is dying does not realize that fact. The staff, and perhaps the family, may know that the person is dying, but the information has not been conveyed to the dying person, nor does he or she even suspect it. Many have thought it desirable not to convey diagnostic and prognostic information to dying persons. As a matter of fact, however, this sort of knowledge usually cannot be hidden for long. Communication is achieved in complex, subtle, and sometimes unconscious ways, and awareness is likely to develop at several levels. For example, changes in one's own body associated with progression of the disease, along with alterations in the behaviors of others or changes in their physical appearances, often lead to some recognition that all is not well.

2. *Suspected awareness* identifies a context in which the ill person may begin to suspect that he or she has not been given all of the information that is relevant to his or her situation. For a variety of reasons—for example, tests, treatments, or other behaviors that do not seem to correspond with the supposed problem—the person who is ill may begin to suspect that more is going on than is being said. This may undermine trust and complicate future communications.

3. *Mutual pretense* describes a context that was once (and may still be) quite common, in which the relevant information is held by all the individual parties in the situation but is not shared between them. In other words, mutual pretense involves a kind of shared drama in which everyone involved acts out a role intended to say that things are not as they know them to be. "It is the horse on the dining-room table," as Kalish told us in the prologue to this book. As mutual pretense is lived out it may even be

conducted so as to cover over embarrassing moments when the strategy of dissembling fails temporarily. This is a fragile situation; one slip can cause the entire structure to collapse. Mutual pretense requires constant vigilance and a great deal of effort. Consequently, it is extremely demanding for everyone involved.

4. *Open awareness* describes a context in which the dying person and everyone else realize and are willing to discuss the fact that death is the prognosis. Those who share a context of open awareness may or may not actually spend much time discussing the fact that the person is dying. On some occasions, one or the other person may not want to talk about it right then. After all, as has aptly been said, "no one is dying 24 hours a day." But there is no pretense; when everyone is ready and able to discuss the realities of the situation, they are willing to do so.

These are four different sorts of awareness contexts, not necessarily stages in a linear progression from inhibitedness to openness. The important point is that social interactions are likely to be affected by the awareness context of coping with dying. All awareness contexts bring with them some potential costs and some potential benefits. At some moments, for example, the anxiety and grief of the family member (or staff person) raised by the oncoming death of a loved one may make discussion of that event too difficult. Avoidance of reality can get some people through a difficult moment and thus may, in certain circumstances, be a productive way of coping.

In general, however, open awareness allows for honest communication. It permits each involved person to participate in the shared grief of an approaching loss. Important words of concern and affection can be spoken. Ancient wounds can be healed. Unfinished business—between the dying person and his or her family members, friends, or God—can be addressed. These benefits come at the cost of having to admit and face powerful feelings (such as anger, sadness, perhaps guilt) and recognized facts (for instance, jobs uncompleted, choices unmade, paths not taken). This can be quite difficult and painful. Nevertheless, for many persons these costs are preferable to those associated with lack of openness. Always, one balances costs against benefits in both the short and the long run.

Coping with Dying: A Stage-Based Approach

For many, it has seemed important to carry the discussion of coping with dying forward into an identification of widespread patterns in such coping. The person who awakened the widest audience for discussion of this topic was a Swiss-American psychiatrist, Dr. Elisabeth Kübler-Ross (Gill, 1980). In her book *On Death and Dying* (1969), Kübler-Ross reported the results of a series of interviews that focused on psychosocial reactions in persons who were dying. In particular, she developed a theoretical model of five stages: (1) denial—"Not me"; (2) anger—"Why me?"; (3) bargaining—"Yes me, but . . . "; (4) depression, which can be of two sorts—a reactive depression responding to past and present losses, or a preparatory, often silent, depression that anticipates losses that are yet to come; and (5) acceptance, which is described as a stage "almost void of feelings." Kübler-Ross understood these stages as "defense mechanisms" that "will last for different periods of time and will replace each other or exist at times side by side" (p. 138). In addition, she maintained that "the one thing that usually persists through all these stages is *hope*" (p. 138).

In other words, Kübler-Ross argued convincingly that people who are dying are people who are in a stressful situation. Because they are living people, like people in other stressful situations, they employ or develop a number of different ways of coping. Some people when confronted with an object that blocks their forward journey in life speed up their personal engines and charge full speed ahead, crashing into and perhaps through the barrier. Other persons who encounter a roadblock back away and try to find some way around it. Others simply remain stationary, not moving forward, not seeking a way around. Still other people go off in some different direction, seeing the roadblock as something that cannot be overcome and that demands that some other road be taken. So dying persons may cope by withdrawing, or by becoming angry, or by finding what has occurred in their lives up to now that might make death acceptable. One major point to be underlined again is that *different people cope in different ways*.

Kübler-Ross's stages had an immediate attractiveness. They identified common psychosocial responses to difficult situations, responses with which we are all familiar. In addition, they drew attention to the human aspects of living with dying, to the strong feelings experienced by those who are coping with dying, and to what Kübler-Ross called the "unfinished business" that many want to address. Kübler-Ross said that her book is "simply an account of a new and challenging opportunity to refocus on the patient as a human being, to include him in dialogues, to learn from him the strengths and weaknesses of our hospital management of the patient. We have asked him to be our teacher so that we may learn more about the final stages of life with all its anxieties, fears, and hopes" (p. xi).

Three important lessons follow from this approach (Corr, 1993a):

1. Those who are coping with dying are still alive and often have unfinished needs that they want to address.
2. We cannot be or become effective providers of care unless we listen actively to those who are coping with dying and identify with them their own needs.
3. We need to learn from those who are dying and coping with dying in order to come to know ourselves better (as limited, vulnerable, finite, and mortal; but also as resilient, adaptable, interdependent, and lovable).

These are lessons about all who are dying and coping with dying; about becoming and being a provider of care; and about living our own lives.

But however much one may admire the underlying lessons from the work of Kübler-Ross and however fashionable her stage-based model may have become in the popular mind, the structure of this model has attracted a good deal of criticism. The early research literature (for example, Metzger, 1979; Schulz & Aderman, 1974) did not support this model. In fact, since the publication of Kübler-Ross's book in 1969, there has been no independent confirmation of the validity or reliability of her model, and Kübler-Ross has advanced no further evidence on its behalf. On the contrary, some of the most knowledgeable and sophisticated clinicians who work with the dying have made known their view that the model is inadequate, superficial, and misleading (for example, Feigenberg, 1980; Pattison, 1977; Shneidman, 1980; Weisman, 1977). Widespread acclaim in the popular arena contrasts with sharp criticism in the scholarly world and suggests that different factors may be at work in these competing assessments of Kübler-Ross's model (Klass, 1982; Klass & Hutch, 1985).

One serious and thorough evaluation of this stage-based model raised the following points: (1) the existence of these stages as such has not been demonstrated; (2) no evidence has been presented that people actually do move from Stage 1 through Stage 5; (3) the limitations of the method have not been acknowledged; (4) the line is blurred between description and prescription; (5) the totality of the person's life is neglected in favor of the supposed stages of dying; and (6) the resources, pressures, and characteristics of the immediate environment, which can make a tremendous difference, are not taken into account (Kastenbaum, 1991).

If one thinks for a moment about the traits that Kübler-Ross has described as stages, one can see that they are so broadly formulated that they can designate a variety of reactions. For example, "denial" can describe the following range of responses: (1) I am not ill; (2) I am ill, but it is not serious; (3) I am seriously ill, but not dying; (4) I am dying, but death will not come for a long time; or (5) I am dying and death will come shortly (Weisman, 1972). Similarly, "acceptance" may take the form of an enthusiastic welcoming, a surly resignation, or a variety of other responses. Also, the trait of "depression" must mean "sadness," not clinical depression, which is a psychiatric diagnosis or illness, not a normal coping process.

In fact, there are not just five ways in which to cope with dying. Also, there is no reason to think that the particular five ways identified by Kübler-Ross are interlinked as *stages* in a larger process. To some extent Kübler-Ross agreed with this latter point, insofar as she argued for fluidity, give and take, or an ability to jump around from one stage to another. That suggests that the language of stages, with its associated implications of linear progression and regression, is not really appropriate for a cluster of disconnected coping strategies.

Another problem with this model—for which its author is not wholly responsible—is that it has been misused by many people. There is some irony in this. After all, Kübler-Ross set out to argue that dying persons are mistreated when they are objectified—that is when they are treated as a "liver case" or as a "cardiac case." Unfortunately, since the publication of *On Death and Dying*, some people have come to treat dying persons as a "case of anger" or a "case of depression," others have told ill persons that they have already been angry and should now move on to bargaining or depression, and still others have become frustrated by those whom they view as "stuck" in the dying process. All of this simply forces those who are coping with dying into a preestablished

framework that reduces their individuality to little more than an instance of one of five categories (anger, or depression, or . . .) in a schematic process. That is why one person who was coping with dying said, "Being invisible I invite only generalizations" (Rosenthal, 1973, p. 39).

All of this suggests that the language of stages and the metaphor of a linear theory (*first* one denies, *then* one is angry, *then* one might retreat to renewed denial, and so on) are simply not adequate as a basis for understanding coping with dying. Furthermore, it is not sufficient to say that a person is "in denial" or has "reached acceptance" if one is to understand that individual in more than a superficial and potentially misleading way.

For these reasons, it has been suggested that it would be better to speak of a broad range of responses to the experience of dying. Essentially, this is the approach taken in the metaphor of a "hive of affect" for coping with dying (Shneidman, 1973, p. 7). In this metaphor, one thinks of a hive (or a busy, buzzing, active set) of feelings, attitudes, and such, to which a person returns from time to time, now journeying forth with this posture (for example, anger), now with that one (for example, denial). The person may return to the hive and experience the same feelings again and again, sometimes one day after another, sometimes with long intervals in between.

Nevertheless, a better model for coping with dying is still needed. An alternative model in this area has been suggested by Corr (1992a) and is described in the following section. It is intended to apply to dying persons and to all of the other individuals who are drawn into coping with dying. Like any account of coping with dying, such a model must help us to understand the efforts that all of these people are making to manage challenges that arise from that which has already happened in dying, that which is in the process of taking place, and that which is yet to come (Stedeford, 1984).

Coping with Dying: A Task-Based Approach

A task-based model for coping with dying avoids metaphors that emphasize a passive or reactive way of understanding such coping. As Weisman (1984) has noted, coping involves more than an automatic response or a defensive reaction. Coping is, or at least can be, a process with a *positive* orientation that seeks to resolve problems or adapt to challenges in living. Defenses merely seek to ward off problems. That may be useful initially (and sometimes on later occasions)—for example, as a way of obtaining time in which to mobilize resources. But a posture of defense is a *negative* one; it channels energy into avoiding problems, rather than coping with them or achieving some kind of adaptive accommodation.

Tasks represent work that can be undertaken in coping with dying. When one is coping with dying, like all other work, one can always choose not to take on a particular task. One can proceed with a task, leave it for another time, or work on it for a while and then set it aside. In the face of a series of tasks, one can choose to undertake all or none of them, to attempt this one or that one. The main point is that choice provides empowerment.

In every concrete situation, one must draw up an individual list of tasks that present themselves to each person who is coping with dying. But in principle, one can identify four primary areas of task work that relate to coping with dying. Clues to the identity of these areas come from the previous discussion of the four dimensions in the life of a human being: the physical, the psychological, the social, and the spiritual. The basic types of tasks for coping with dying suggested by these four dimensions are summarized in Table 5.1.

TABLE 5.1   Task Work in Coping with Dying

Area of Task Work	Basic Types of Tasks in Coping with Dying
Physical	To satisfy bodily needs and to minimize physical distress in ways that are consistent with other values.
Psychological	To maximize psychological security, autonomy, and richness.
Social	To sustain and enhance those interpersonal attachments that are significant to the person concerned and to address social implications of dying.
Spiritual	To identify, develop, or reaffirm sources of spiritual energy and in so doing to foster hope.

Source: Corr, 1992a.

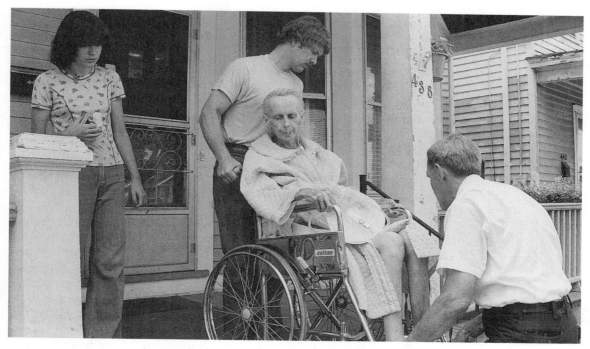

Daily activities can be enjoyed during the dying process.

Physical Tasks

Bodily needs are fundamental to maintaining biological life and functioning. As Maslow (1971) has shown, satisfaction of fundamental bodily needs is usually the indispensable foundation upon which the work of meeting higher needs can be built. In addition, *physical distress* cries out for relief both for its own sake and in order that the rest of life can be appreciated. For example, it is unlikely that individuals who are experiencing intense pain, severe nausea, or active vomiting will have rich psychosocial or spiritual interactions. This area identifies tasks in coping with such matters as pain, nausea, or constipation, and in satisfying such needs as hydration and nutrition.

A qualification is necessary, however, since humans can and sometimes do choose to subordinate bodily needs and physical distress to the service of other values. For example, martyrs endure torture for the sake of spiritual values and individuals have been known to sacrifice their own lives for the sake of protecting those whom they love. More simply, individuals who are dying may choose to accept a slightly higher degree of pain or discomfort in order to be able to stay at home, rather than enter an institution in which constant supervision by skilled professionals could achieve a higher standard in the management of distressing physical symptoms. Others who are offered the support of in-home services may prefer to be in an institution, where they have less fear of falling and lying unattended for hours.

Psychological Tasks

The second important area of tasks in coping with dying concerns psychological security, autonomy, and richness. Like the rest of us, individuals who are coping with dying seek a sense of *security* even in a situation that may in many ways not be safe. For example, suppose they are dependent on others to provide needed services. They need to be assured that those providers are reliable.

Also, most individuals who are coping with dying wish to retain their own *autonomy*, insofar as that is possible. Autonomy means the ability to govern or be in charge of one's own life (*auto* = self + *nomous* = regulating). In fact, no one has control over the whole of one's life; each person is limited and all are interdependent in a host of ways. Autonomy designates the shifting degrees and kinds of influence that individuals are able to exercise within everyday constraints. Nevertheless, for many persons, it is important to retain some degree of self-government. Some may wish to make the big decisions in their lives on their own; others may simply wish to designate who should make decisions on their behalf. Some may turn over much of the management of their own bodies to professionals, even while they retain authority over some symbolic decisions. An outsider cannot say in advance how autonomy will or should be exercised; that would undercut the very notion of *self*-regulation.

For many people, achieving a sense of security and autonomy contributes to a *psychological richness in living*. Many who are terminally ill appreciate a regular shave and haircut, or an opportunity to use a favorite bath powder and to dress in a comfortable and attractive way. Some dying persons may find it important to their psychological well-being to have a taste of a favorite food or to continue a lifelong habit of sipping a small glass of wine with meals.

Social Tasks

The third task area concerns two interrelated aspects of social living. Each of us is involved in attachments to other persons in our society, as well as in relationships to the society itself and to its subordinate groups. One set of tasks in this social area has to do with sustaining and enhancing the interpersonal attachments that we value. Note that it must be the individual who decides which of these attachments he or she values, and that these decisions may alter as one lives through the process of coping with dying. If the significance of each attachment is not subject to individual decision making, then autonomy is constrained in a fundamental way.

The second set of social tasks has to do with *societal implications* of dying. Society correctly wishes to protect its citizens from harm, to prohibit them from certain sorts of behavior, to ensure that their property is properly handed over to their heirs, to offer certain sorts of assistance and benefit. Social groups have their own religious and cultural rituals, expectations, and prohibitions. Like all other events in living, dying and death implicate people in social systems. These systems are constructed and implemented by individuals, but they represent the interests of the group. Social tasks in coping with dying include interacting with social systems, responding to demands that continue to be made upon us by society and its social organizations (for example, hospital bills and income taxes may still need to be paid), and drawing upon their resources as needed (for example, by obtaining hospital equipment, transportation assistance, or "Meals on Wheels" services from charitable organizations).

Spiritual Tasks

A fourth set of tasks in coping with dying concerns sources of spiritual energy and hope. One may find the source of one's *spiritual energy* in a personal god, an impersonal nature, or an individual value system. The focus of the energy source is not as important as its effectiveness in invigorating and enriching our lives. The task may be to find such a focus for the first time, to develop a neglected focus, or to reaffirm a highly valued focus. When time permits, coping with dying often throws individuals back on a process much like "life review," as it has been described in the elderly. This involves a recall and evaluation of what one has done and been during one's life, and an attempt to define the meaning of one's life.

Doka (1993) has identified three principal spiritual tasks for those who are dying: (1) to find meaning in life; (2) to die appropriately, consistent with one's self-identity (which includes being able to interpret and understand death); and (3) to find hope that extends beyond the grave. This last task recognizes that an important aspect of spirituality in human lives is identifying and sustaining *hope.*

Three points can be made about hope in relationship to coping with dying. First, this sort of hope can reflect many concerns. In fact, changes in the focus of hope are found in many individuals who are dying (Pattison, 1977). For example, an individual may now hope to live out his or her life without pain or discomfort, to live long enough to see his or her grandchild born, or to have time to say, "Thank you. I love you. Goodbye." What this means is that hope need not be seen only in terms of cure.

Second, how one acts on one's hopes depends very much on the individual and his or her culture, history, environment, and condition. Third, hope is grounded in reality and is really about one's faith or trust in the meaning and goodness of life. One aspect of facing dying is to determine, in the light of one's spiritual convictions (whether they be personal, religious, or philosophical in origin), whether life is still basically good.

Advantages of a Task-Based Approach

The value of a task-based approach is fourfold (Corr, 1992a). First, it offers opportunities for improved understanding of the full range of thoughts and behaviors that are involved in coping with dying. Second, it supports empowerment of those who are coping with dying by allowing them to choose which tasks to address and how. Third, it encourages participation in coping with dying because it recognizes that each person has at least two sets of tasks in coping with dying: one conducted on his or her own behalf and another conducted in relation to the needs of others who are involved. And fourth, it provides guidelines for helpers and caregivers that arise from respect for the tasks and coping efforts that have been selected by those who are being helped.

Even in times of great stress and difficulty, when options seem limited, individuals are compelled to cope with dying. Their freedom lies in choosing the ways in which they will cope. A task-based approach applies to all who are involved in coping with dying. The person who is dying, his or her family members and friends, and his or her volunteer or professional caregivers all face potential tasks that they might pursue and have individual decisions to make about working on coping tasks. Moreover, the set of tasks each person needs to work on is interrelated with the tasks that confront others.

For example, family members may have tasks related to their own needs, as well as tasks related to their responsibilities to assist the dying person. For themselves, they may need to rest or find some relief from the burdens of caregiving; for the ill person, they may need to be available to provide companionship and a sense of security. Similarly, the dying person faces some tasks related to his or her own needs and others related to the needs of family members or caregivers. He or she may need to decline further efforts at cure because they are too burdensome and offer too little promise of help; in so doing, that person may need to help family members or caregivers accept this decision and become reconciled to what it means for how soon death will arrive.

Often, as individuals are dying they narrow the scope of their world of interest. They may no longer care about international politics or their former duties at work or their large circle of friends. Instead, they may increasingly focus upon their own needs and their attachments to a progressively smaller number of individuals who are perceived as important in their lives. In this way, they may gain freedom from responsibilities that are now judged to be more burdensome or less compelling than before. The scope of their interests, hopes, and tasks has shifted. There is no obvious set of tasks on which each person *must* focus.

Those who surround the dying person may not experience a similar freeing from responsibilities. Their everyday lives and obligations may continue as before, although they may be adjusted temporarily to meet the current situation. At the same time, these individuals are forced to confront new tasks entailed in coping with the dying of a person whom they love. And they are often asked to help the dying person meet his or her own tasks. Life can become very much more complicated for these people who are not themselves dying but who are nevertheless coping with dying.

It may be useful to summarize once again the purpose of this outline of fundamental task areas in coping with dying. The task areas describe general categories of work for all who are coping with dying (not just the dying person). Tasks may or may not be undertaken; some may be more or less necessary or desirable. The main concern of this account of a task-based approach has only been to describe areas of potential task work in coping with dying. No burden is imposed merely by describing task areas. On the contrary, a task-based model is intended precisely to foster empowerment and participation in coping with dying.

Tasks of this sort are never completed. For the dying person, they end with death; for those who live on, similar tasks continue in coping with bereavement. These task areas may also serve as guidelines for helping those who are coping with dying, as will be seen in Chapter 6.

Summary

This chapter has explored coping with dying. In so doing, it has attempted to describe coping processes in ways that do justice to the many elements that enter into such coping and the many differences among individuals who are engaged in such coping. Coping with dying is clearly linked to coping with living, even though special issues are undoubtedly involved in dying. Thus, it is important that any account of coping with dying be holistic and individualized. Special attention has been paid to fears, anxieties, and concerns of those who are dying, to dying trajectories and awareness contexts, and to stage-based and task-based models for interpreting coping with dying.

QUESTIONS FOR REVIEW AND DISCUSSION

1. Think about some moment in your life when you were quite ill. What was most stressful for you at that time? If you felt fear, what were the sources of your greatest fears? What did you want other people to do for or with you at that time? Now try to imagine yourself in a similar situation, only adding that the illness is a life-threatening one. What would be similar about these two situations? How might your answers to the preceding questions be different?

2. This chapter focused on the notion of coping. In what ways in the past have you coped with stressful situations? Choose someone you know well and reflect on how she or he copes with stress. What strengths and limitations do you note in your own ways of coping and in this other person's methods of coping?

3. If you think about the coping of dying persons as involving tasks, how might this affect your understanding of a dying person's needs? That is, how might this model of coping affect your interactions with dying persons?

SUGGESTED READINGS

Some personal accounts of coping with life-threatening illness or dying (autobiographical, biographical, and fictional) are found in the following:

Alsop, S. (1973). *A Stay of Execution.*

Broyard, A. (1992). *Intoxicated by My Illness, and Other Writings on Life and Death.*

Cousins, N. (1979). *Anatomy of an Illness as Perceived by the Patient: Reflections on Healing and Regeneration.*

Craven, M. (1974). *I Heard the Owl Call My Name.*

De Beauvoir, S. (1964/1973). *A Very Easy Death.*

Evans, J. (1971). *Living with a Man Who Is Dying: A Personal Memoir.*

Faulkner, W. (1930). *As I Lay Dying.*

Frank, A. W. (1991). *At the Will of the Body: Reflections on Illness.*

Gunther, J. (1949). *Death Be Not Proud.*

Hanlan, A. (1979). *Autobiography of Dying.*

Jury, M., & Jury, D. (1978). *Gramps: A Man Ages and Dies.*

Kelly, O. (1975). *Make Today Count.*

Lerner, G. (1978). *A Death of One's Own.*

Lerner, M. (1990). *Wrestling with the Angel: A Memoir of My Triumph over Illness.*

Mandell, H., & Spiro, H. (Eds.) (1987). *When Doctors Get Sick.*

Rosenthal, T. (1973). *How Could I Not Be Among You?*

Ryan, C., & Ryan, K. M. (1979). *A Private Battle.*

Tolstoy, L. (1884/1960). *The Death of Ivan Ilych and Other Stories.*

Wertenbaker, L. T. (1957). *Death of a Man.*

Zorza, V., & Zorza, R. (1980). *A Way to Die.*

Researchers, scholars, and clinicians write about various aspects of coping with dying in the following:

Brim, O., Freeman, H., Levine, S., & Scotch, N. (Eds.). (1970). *The Dying Patient.*

Davidson, G. W. (1975). *Living with Dying.*

Doka, K. J. (1993). *Living with Life-Threatening Illness: A Guide for Patients, Families, and Caregivers.*

Glaser, B., & Strauss, A. (1965). *Awareness of Dying.*

Glaser, B., & Strauss, A. (1968). *Time for Dying.*

Hinton, J. (1967). *Dying.*

Kavanaugh, R. E. (1972). *Facing Death.*

Kübler-Ross, E. (1969). *On Death and Dying.*

Pattison, E. M. (1977). *The Experience of Dying.*

Rosen, E. J. (1990). *Families Facing Death: Family Dynamics of Terminal Illness.*

Weisman, A. D. (1972). *On Dying and Denying: A Psychiatric Study of Terminality.*

Analyses of stress and coping strategies appear in the following:

Lazarus, R. S., & Folkman, S. (1984). *Stress, Appraisal, and Coping.*

Monat, A., & Lazarus, R. S. (Eds.). (1991). *Stress and Coping: An Anthology* (3rd ed.).

Selye, H. (1978). *The Stress of Life* (rev. ed.).

Weisman, A.D. (1984). *The Coping Capacity: On the Nature of Being Mortal.*

Special problems associated with long-term, chronic diseases are examined in the following:

Greenblatt, M. H. (1972). *Multiple Sclerosis and Me.*

Mace, N. L., & Rabins, P. V. (1991). *The 36–Hour Day* (rev. ed.).

Webster, B. D. (1989). *All of a Piece: A Life with Multiple Sclerosis.*

Weisman, M-L. (1982). *Intensive Care: A Family Love Story.*

CHAPTER 6

Helping Those Who Are Coping with Dying

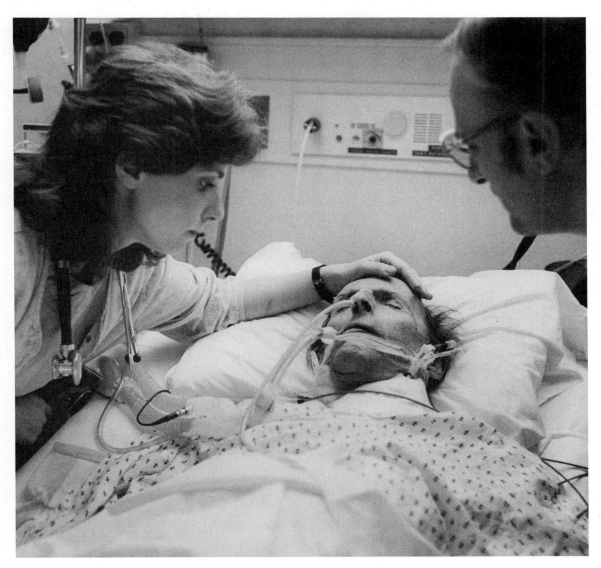

Chapter 5 examined the needs and concerns of dying persons and of everyone else who is drawn into the processes of coping with dying. This chapter turns attention to what can be done to care for or help all of these people. The chapter begins by illustrating the roles of helpers through the example of Carol and Bill Johnson, and by noting the complementary roles of the specialized professional tasks and the unspecialized human tasks in caring for those who are coping with dying. Next, it explores four primary dimensions of care and the role of tasks as guidelines for helpers. Finally, separate sections are devoted to the topics of palliative care, hope, and effective communication, because those topics underlie nearly all of this analysis.

Two Helpers: Carol and Bill Johnson

Carol Johnson is a nurse who had worked with dying persons in various settings before becoming involved in a hospice program. In all of these settings, Carol came to appreciate the role of basic professional care. Helping to wash and bathe people made them feel better and also prevented sores and other complications associated with confinement to a bed. Much the same could be said for moving people in bed, or transferring them to a wheelchair, or walking with them to exercise stiff muscles.

Carol recognized that especially when the ill person was at home, but sometimes also in the nursing home or hospital, family caregivers could often take part in this sort of care. Frequently, they wished to participate in the care of the person whom they loved, and that person usually appreciated their efforts on his or her behalf. As a result, Carol made a special effort to teach family members how to participate in care and to prepare them for the things that might happen to a loved one who was seriously ill or dying.

After Carol had worked in the hospice program for a while, her husband, Bill, asked her if there was some way in which he could contribute to the program. Bill had been impressed by the spirit of the hospice team and by what Carol had told him about its achievements in helping people even when they were very close to death. Bill knew that the hospice program made a special effort to include volunteers in its caregiving team. Nevertheless, he was still a bit hesitant at first, but after he attended the hospice's volunteer training program he felt more confident about his own role. After working with several dying persons and their families, Bill recognized that he had much to contribute by helping with practical chores, by taking an interest in people who often felt so isolated and overwhelmed by what was happening, by simply being present and listening to their concerns, and by making regular reports to the other members of the team about what was occurring.

Many people commented to Carol and Bill that their work with dying persons must be morbid and depressing. But Carol knew that it was far more depressing to work with people who did not want to be helped, who resisted help and refused to cooperate, or who took their feelings out on those who were caring for them. Carol and Bill found that most of those who were coping

Some Thoughts About Caring

The common diagnostic categories into which medicine places its patients are relevant to disease, not to illness. They are useful for treatment, but they only get in the way of care. . . . Caring has nothing to do with categories; it shows the person that her life is valued because it recognizes what makes her experience particular. One person has no right to categorize another, but we do have the privilege of coming to understand how each of us is unique. . . . Terms like pain or loss have no reality until they are filled in with an ill person's own experience. Witnessing the particulars of that experience, and recognizing all its differences, is care.

SOURCE From Frank, *At the Will of the Body* (1991), pp. 45–49.

with dying were grateful for any attempt to help them. Carol and Bill took great satisfaction in helping to improve quality of life and foster individual dignity during the time before death, even though it was sad when death came to someone for whom they had cared.

Carol and Bill were especially encouraged when the wife of a person who had died in their hospice program wrote to them several months later to express her gratitude. She was grateful that they had helped her to fulfill her own desire and her husband's last wish, that he could be at home with her as long as possible before his death. Her sadness at his loss was tempered by her knowledge that she had done everything that she could have done for her husband and for herself. She thanked Carol and Bill and their colleagues because she knew that this could not have been achieved without their help.

Caring for the Dying: Human and Professional Tasks

Caring for the dying is not an activity to be carried out only by people who are specially trained to do so. Certainly, dying persons and others who are coping with dying are people with special needs, some of which can best or perhaps only be met by individuals with special expertise. For example, a dying person may have a special need for a physician's prescription for narcotic analgesics or a sacramental act by a member of the ordained clergy. But much of the care required is not related to special needs; it involves fundamental concerns common to all living human beings, even though they are concerns that may take on a special intensity under the pressures of coping with dying.

For example, dying persons need to eat, they need to exercise their bodies, minds, and spirits, and they need above all to be cared *about*, not just cared *for*. For most of the 24 hours in each day, the care that dying persons need is not specialized care. This care can be provided by any of us. A hand held, a grief or joy shared, and a question listened to and responded to: these are human moments of caring, and they can be provided by any human being who is willing and able to care. In short, "the secret of the care of patients is still caring" (Ingles, 1974).

In Chapter 5, we noted that persons who are dying are most likely to be concerned about such matters as being abandoned, losing control over their own bodies and lives, and being in overwhelming pain or distress. Dame Cicely Saunders, founder of St. Christopher's Hospice in London and initiator of the modern hospice movement, has been reported (Shephard, 1977) to have phrased this in a slightly different way in language addressed primarily to helpers. She said that dying persons ask three things of their caregivers: (1) "Help me" (minimize my distress); (2) "Listen to me" (let me direct things or at least be heard); and (3) "Don't leave me" (stay with me; give me your presence).

It is important to recognize the many ways in which we can help those who are coping with dying. Even when we cannot do something specific to help, all of us—professionals and nonprofessionals alike—can listen to and stay with the dying persons and their significant others in our communities. This is the lesson that Carol and Bill Johnson learned in their work with those who are coping with dying.

To provide adequate care for the dying, we must address the many fears, anxieties, needs, and desires of dying persons. The same applies to family members and friends of the dying person—those significant others who are also coping with dying. We may be more or less successful in meeting these responsibilities because of lack of time, energy, information, or resources. But if we are serious about providing good care, we ought not to fail to address these needs because of lack of understanding or attention to what is needed by those who are coping with dying. This chapter seeks to provide information and draw attention to ways in which help can be provided to those who are coping with dying.

Dimensions of Care

There are four primary dimensions of care for those who are coping with dying: physical, psychological, social, and spiritual (Saunders, 1967; Woodson, 1976). Here, each of these will be considered in turn, with special attention to their application to dying persons. These dimensions are also relevant to others who are coping with dying: family members and friends of the dying person, as well as professional and volunteer helpers/caregivers.

Physical Aspects

For many dying persons, one of the most pressing needs is the control of *physical* pain or distress. When pain is present, it must be carefully understood. Only recently has pain begun to be studied in its own right (for example, Benoliel & Crowley, 1974; Melzack & Wall, 1989, 1991). One can distinguish between at least two sorts of pain: acute pain and chronic pain.

Acute pain is a form of pain that is essential to human life. Those who do not feel this sort of pain—for example, when they touch a hot stove—are in danger of serious harm. When individuals are ill, a physician often obtains the sort of information needed to make an accurate diagnosis by eliciting careful, specific descriptions of pain or distress. For instance, acute pain associated with kidney stones guides both diagnosis and treatment. Consequently, acute pain is not always or completely undesirable, given our present human condition; rather, it may make possible enhancement of both the quality and the quantity of our lives. Of course, dying persons may experience acute pain, too. They may develop symptoms—including physical pain—that may or may not be directly related to the illness that threatens their lives. In this regard, Saunders has reminded caregivers that toothache hurts just as much when you are dying (*Until We Say Goodbye*, 1980).

Chronic pain, however, does not serve the functions that acute pain does. For example, chronic pain does not serve to assist in diagnosis because that diagnosis has already been made. Nor does chronic pain protect the person from dangers in the environment. It is just there, always there. Dull or invasive, sharp or intermittent, chronic pain forms the backdrop of whatever the person is doing at the moment. When it is intense, it can become the whole focus of attention of those who are experiencing such pain (LeShan, 1964).

In terminal illness, chronic pain is associated with a disease that will lead to death. Proper care of the dying person must involve efforts to manage or at least to diminish distress arising from this sort of pain. It may not always be possible to eradicate chronic pain completely, but to reduce pain from agony to ache is an impressive achievement. Care of the dying has shown that chronic pain can be controlled or at least greatly diminished in nearly every case (Baines, 1981; Lipman, 1980; Twycross & Lack, 1983). Needless pain in terminal illness is a tragedy when good research has taught so much about the nature of pain and the role of analgesics in its management (Melzack, 1990). Appropriate medications and supportive therapy can see to it that chronic pain need not so fill the consciousness of dying persons that they can pay attention to nothing else but their pain.

The challenge for therapeutic interventions is to select just the right drug(s) to meet the need(s) of the individual, to achieve just the right balance of responses to requirements (without overmedication), and to employ an appropriate route of administration. The philosophy of pain management in terminal illness has often emphasized administration of medications via oral routes (in liquid or capsule form) to avoid the pain of injections. Nevertheless, both injections and suppositories have been recognized as appropriate in certain cases (for instance, when rapid results achievable by injections are required or when individuals are nauseated). More recently, these have been supplemented by slow-release analgesic tablets, long-term continuous infusion devices (similar to those used for insulin by some diabetics), and patient-controlled analgesia (whereby individuals have some measure of control and autonomy in administering their own medications, often resulting in less overall medication than might otherwise have been employed).

Drug therapy is not the *only* method of controlling chronic pain. As research achieves better a understanding of the nature of disease, it is evident that most pain has a psychological component. Thus, McCaffery and Beebe (1989, p. 7) have written, "Pain is whatever the experiencing person says it is, existing whenever the experiencing person says it does." That is, pain is distress as it is perceived by an individual. Pain management may seek to alter the threshold or the nature of that perception, just as it may block the pathways or the effects of a noxious stimulant. So biofeedback, guided imagery, meditation, and techniques of self-hypnosis may also assist persons to control their pain or to manage its effects. Also, good psychological care may encourage individuals to keep muscles and joints active, thereby helping to lessen the degree of physical pain that occurs when a person remains immobile. These therapies are not in opposition to, but can work alongside medications and other interventions.

When drug therapies are used, research has demonstrated that many dying persons, including long-term patients with far-advanced cancer, can tolerate large doses of strong narcotics without becoming "doped up" or "knocked out" (Twycross, 1979b, 1982). The goal is not total anesthesia (unconsciousness), but rather analgesia (an insensibility to pain). This can be achieved in most cases by choosing the correct medication(s) for the situation and by carefully titrating or balancing dosages against the nature and level of pain.

If the right drug is used and the dose is titrated to the precise level needed to control pain—and *no* further—then the pain is well managed. The right drug is crucial. Pain may arise from a variety of sources—for example, direct damage to tissue, pressure, or inflammation. Each source of pain and each route of transmission may require its own appropriate medication. Also, each drug must be selected in terms of the needs of an individual patient, its method of administration, the time intervals at which it will be given, and potential problems with side effects or interactions with other drugs that the patient may be taking. For example, some drugs like Demerol are quick-acting and potent. This makes them very useful for dealing with episodes of acute pain. But a drug like this may not retain its efficacy long enough to suit someone scheduled for doses every four hours. If so, a dying person for whom this sort of drug is prescribed may be back in pain every third hour after the drug is administered. This is *not* good care.

That *addiction* does not occur, even when strong narcotics are prescribed in high doses for dying persons, has been shown by research (for example, Twycross, 1976) and is now well known (Porter & Jick, 1980). The psychological "high" and subsequent craving for steadily escalating doses that characterize addiction are not found. This may have to do with ways in which medications are administered and absorbed in the body: usually they are given by mouth or intramuscular injections rather than as intravenous injections.

Dying persons may become *physically dependent* upon strong narcotics, but that occurs frequently in other situations—for example, in the use of insulin by some diabetics. Thus, it has been recognized for many years that physical dependence without underlying emotional disorder is easily terminated and does not constitute an additional problem ("Medical Ethics," 1963). Dependence only means that one cannot withdraw the drug abruptly or while it is still required without harmful side effects. Otherwise, it is as if the body uses the drug to deal with the pain it is experiencing, and it signals when the drug or dose are not correct. Too small or too weak a dose will allow pain to return; too large or too powerful a dose will induce drowsiness.

Once individuals learn that their pain really can and will be controlled, the dose provided can often be reduced (Twycross & Lack, 1983). Such persons no longer are fearful and tense in the face of *expected* pain. Hence, effective drug therapeutics provide a sense of security that relaxes anxiety. Addressing such psychosocial components of pain can lower the threshold of analgesia and may make it easier to manage discomfort. Thus, relaxation may actually allow individuals to tolerate more pain, so that a lower drug dose can be used.

Dying persons may also experience other physical symptoms that can be just as distressing as or even more distressing than physical pain (Saunders, 1984). These symptoms include constipation (a common side effect of narcotics), diarrhea, nausea, and vomiting. Sometimes there is weakness or reduction in available energy, loss of appetite, or shortness of breath. Similarly, loss of hair, dark circles around the eyes, and changes in skin color may also be matters of concern to individuals who place high value on self-image and how they present themselves to others. In addition, if someone lies in bed for long periods of time, skin ulcers or bedsores can become a potential source of added discomfort. Diminishing this sort of distress has always been a concern of effective care for the dying.

Dehydration illustrates an issue that is frequently encountered in dying persons (Zerwekh, 1983). An intravenous infusion might be used, but that method adds another source of pain to the burdens of terminally ill persons. In addition, it may overload with fluid a body that is weak and whose organ systems may no longer be functioning effectively. Often, small sips of juice or other fluid, ice chips, or flavored mouth swabs may be adequate to maintain quality of life. This teaches us that effective care for dying persons must address all of their distressing physical symptoms and must do so in ways that are suited to their current situation. Such care may require intervention on the part of physicians, nurses, and other professional caregivers, but it is clear that family caregivers and significant others also have important roles to play in these situations, especially when they are shown how to be most helpful to the ill person.

Psychological Aspects

Another set of concerns revolves around psychological needs. These issues are capable of making care providers even more uncomfortable than those having to do with a dying person's physical needs. It is difficult to be with someone in physical pain, but many would-be helpers are even more uncomfortable in the face of so-called negative feelings. Nevertheless, someone who

Meditation on the Patient's Fear

I observe the Phisician, with the same diligence, as hee the disease; I see hee feares, and I feare with him: I overtake him, I overrun him in his feare, and I go the faster, because he makes his pace slow; I feare the more, because hee disguises his feare, and see it with more sharpnesse, because hee would not have me see it.

SOURCE From Donne, *The complete poetry and selected prose of John Donne* (1624/1952), p. 1181.

is dying is likely to express these sorts of feelings at one time or another. Such a person may experience anger and sadness, anxiety and fear. It is in the face of these feelings in particular that people often wonder, "What is the right thing to say or to do?"

Often, there is no specific and universal right thing to say or to do, but that does not mean there is nothing to say or to do. In fact, one can say and do many things to be helpful. However, to hunt for some way to make all fear, anger, or sadness disappear is to begin a hopeless search. These feelings are real, and they must be lived through. A student once announced to us that she believed someone informed of a prognosis of impending death would become sad or "depressed," an emotion she thought of as undesirable; she said she would seek any means to prevent it from occurring, or if it did occur, to end it.

This is a stance that is unrealistic. If someone is given unhappy news—of any sort—sadness is a likely and *appropriate* response. Furthermore, some people—including many professional caregivers—too quickly identify sadness with depression. But to realize that one is going to die is to be faced with a loss—and in the face of loss, human beings grieve.

Anger is another of those feelings that may be particularly discomforting. People who are coping with dying often feel lots of anger. They are angry because of the losses they are experiencing, and they are angry because others—apparently for no justifiable reason—are enjoying happy, healthy, and satisfying lives. Further, because of physical or other restrictions, the dying person's anger may be limited in the ways in which it can be expressed. Not surprisingly, strong feelings may be projected onto others—that is, directed at whatever or whomever is most readily available, whether or not that is an appropriate target.

It may help to realize that this sort of anger needs to be identified, acknowledged, and expressed. Feelings like this cannot simply be made to go away. Feelings are real; one cannot just stop feeling what one is feeling. Nor is it reasonable to expect that strong feelings should always be suppressed. For example, anger and an outpouring of adrenalin go together; the emotional anger must be worked off, much like the physical rush of adrenalin. It may not be very consoling when one is the object of growls, complaints, or screaming to realize that there is usually nothing personal in such expressions of anger and other strong feelings. Nonetheless, this is often the case.

Two special gifts to a dying person: presence and active listening.

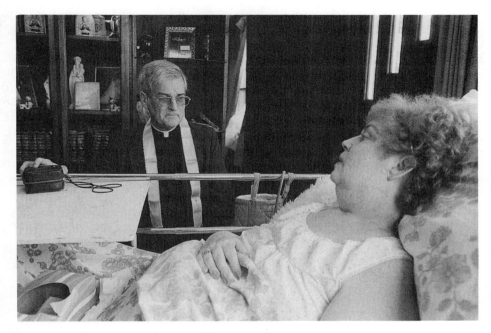

In such situations, it may be important to learn to be comfortable with one's discomfort. That is, our task as helpers is not to discover the magical "right" thing to say to make dying persons no longer have such feelings. Letting them talk about why they feel as they do and giving them "permission" to do so through bodily or verbal cues—*really* listening to them—may be the most helpful thing one can do.

In addition, many dying persons have reported that for someone to say to them "I know how you feel" is *not* helpful. For one thing, this is almost certainly not true. Most individuals have not really been in the situation of the other person to whom such a remark is made. And no one can really experience the feelings of another individual. Also, such a remark is often perceived as an attempt to minimize or trivialize the feelings of the person to whom it is addressed.

How can people who are experiencing "negative" feelings be helped? If this question means, How can someone make them stop having those feelings? the question may say more about *our* discomfort with their feelings and *our* need to end that discomfort than it does about the needs of those who are coping with dying. Two things should be noted here. First, outsiders cannot *make* anyone feel different or better. Second, that may often be an *inappropriate* goal. Dying people must live with and through their feelings, just as they must live with and through all of the rest of their life experiences. They can be helped to do that by assistance in identifying their feelings, by acknowledgment of their feelings as appropriate to their particular situations (if that is, in fact, the case), and by permission for them to vent or share their feelings.

There are no magic formulas here. There are no cookbooks for the right behaviors or statements. Nevertheless, what does seem to help people who

On Being a Good Listener

If I am a good listener, I don't interrupt the other nor plan my own next speech while pretending to be listening. I try to hear what is said, but I listen just as hard for what is not said and for what is said between the lines. I am not in a hurry, for there is no preappointed destination for the conversation. There is no need to get there, for we are already here; and in this present I am able to be fully present to the one who speaks. The speaker is not an object to be categorized or manipulated, but a subject whose life situation is enough like my own that I can understand it in spite of the differences between us. If I am a good listener, what we have in common will seem more important than what we have in conflict.

This does not mean that I never say anything, but I am more likely to ask questions than to issue manifestos or make accusations.

SOURCE From Westphal, *God, Guilt, and Death* (1984), p. 12.

are coping with dying is for someone to listen to them and to take seriously what they are feeling. This is one thing that can be done to help. Helpers can *be present* to such persons (physically, emotionally, existentially) and can listen *attentively* to what they say. If helpers turn off their own internal monologues, if they stop hunting around for the "right" response, and if they just *listen*, that can help. It helps because it says to the other person, loudly and clearly, "You matter; you and your feelings are real and important to me." It also helps because what they need can be heard, rather than what others think they need. This is compassion or empathy, which reaches out to understand and feel along with the other person. It is quite different from pity, which always commiserates with the other individual from a hierarchical and distant standpoint. As Garfield (1976, p. 181) insisted, "The largest single impediment to providing effective psychosocial support to the terminal patient is the powerful professional staff distinction between 'US' and 'THEM.'"

Something else that can be done to help, at least in most cases, is to *touch* the person. Some people are uncomfortable with physical touch. They keep a fairly large personal space around themselves, and they may resent and resist intrusion by others into that space. But sickness may break down some of these barriers. For example, a body massage may be *psychologically* helpful. Often, it is also helpful for a friend or concerned person to touch one's wrist or arm, hold one's hand, or give a hug. Not everyone responds favorably to this; each person is an individual with individual expectations and values. Those who seek to be helpful must respect the dying person's values on this point. But for many persons who are coping with dying, gentle touch is psychologically healing.

Many of the psychological needs of dying persons can be met by anybody, whether that person is a professional caregiver or not. If there are psychological needs that run deeper and that interfere with the individual's quality in living, a professional counselor or therapist may be helpful. After all, if the goal is to provide whatever care is needed in order to make this time in life as good as possible, the lesson must be that no particular expertise or mode of care should be looked upon as irrelevant just because the person might be dying.

For example, one hospice psychiatrist made an important contribution by painstakingly sorting out the origins and consequences of different confusional states, and the approaches in caring that are applicable to each (Stedeford, 1978). Similarly, the expertise of psychiatrists and psychotherapists might also be useful when terminal illness is associated with clinical depression or other forms of mental illness.

There is no evidence that terminal illness on its own is associated with suicidal tendencies or other psychiatric problems (Achté & Vauhkonen, 1971; Brown, Henteleff, Barakat, & Rowe, 1986). Thus, Stedeford (1979, pp. 13–14) has suggested that as a general rule in the care of those who are coping with dying, "sophisticated psychotherapy is not as necessary as are sensitivity, a willingness to follow the patient rather than lead him, some knowledge of the psychology of dying, and the ability to accept the inevitability of death."

In the end, one's ability to meet the needs of a dying person depends upon one's ability to begin to cope with the reality of one's own impending death. Failure to do so often complicates the ability to help in this area. Thus, the fundamental criterion for all aspects of caring for dying persons and their family members is that caring must be made relevant and must be seen to be relevant to the needs of the person whom one is trying to help. Caregivers must always ask, "What is the relative value of the various available methods of treatment *in this particular patient?*" (Cade, 1963, p. 3).

Social Aspects

The *social* needs of dying persons are often just as pressing as physical and psychological needs. These needs are expressed, first of all, in the special person-to-person relationships that most individuals form with one or more people who occupy cherished roles in their lives. It is to these special people that one brings one's intimate achievements and tribulations. Within these relationships individuals seek safety and security. In their shelter, one makes plans, works through problems, and defines that which is meaningful. Here love is expressed most basically in the sharing of two lives. Often, it is sufficient merely to be in the company of such a special person in order to feel a bit better and less beset by the problems of living.

Individuals who are coping with dying can be helped when the interpersonal attachments that they value are fostered and encouraged. When energy levels are low, they may not be able to sustain all of the relationships that once were important to them. Their circle of personal involvements may change its shape, size, or character. But those who are coping with dying may want to be shown how to uphold the most significant of these relationships. They will want to continue to give care to and to receive care from the special people in their lives. Sensitivity to the identities of these special people, to the nature of their attachments with the person who is coping with dying, and to ways in

Sharing life and loving while dying.

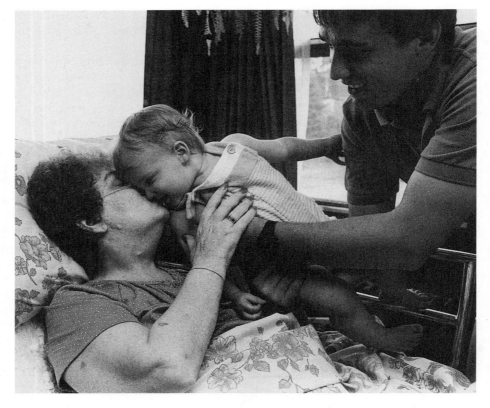

which such relationships can be maintained and nurtured is an important part of caring and helping.

Social needs also include concerns about one's role and place in the family, in the work force, and in the community at large. For example, economic concerns may be or seem to be very important. In our society, many people worry about how their families will survive economically, given the costs of health care and the disappearance of the income that the dying person had formerly provided. There are other concerns, too: Will that project I started at work be completed? What will happen to my business (students, parishioners, clients, customers, stockholders, employees)? How will my spouse be able to cope with being a single parent of young children? Who will take care of my aged parents or aging spouse?

These are the sorts of questions that arise for many people who are dying. One responds in helpful ways to these concerns first of all by allowing those who are coping with dying to talk about their concerns, and then by being an advocate for such persons. That is, one can listen and try to help these people to find resources that may be of assistance with their specific (or not so specific) problems. Sometimes advocacy involves acting on behalf of or in place of others in order to try to serve their needs. In many other situations, advocacy involves enabling or empowering individuals to act for themselves in seeking to satisfy their requirements. Note that it can be *dis*empowering to take over the work of coping from the other person; it may be sufficient to help that person recognize his or her options and think about ways to go about fulfilling his or her own needs. Playing social roles offers an excellent opportunity for people to assert and maintain autonomy. Social workers, family therapists, counselors, and lawyers are often able to be of help in areas of social need.

Spiritual Aspects

Dying persons often raise questions that are *spiritual* in nature. What is my relationship to God? Where is God in all of this? Why is there so much pain in human life? What does my life mean—to me, to the people closest to me, in the larger scheme of things? Have I achieved the goals I most wanted to achieve? Searching for meaning in this way within one's life may or may not involve a religious formulation or affiliation.

Once more, one cannot *provide* for any individual the answers to such questions. When asked, one may share with others one's convictions in this area. But when dying persons ask these questions out loud, they may not be very interested in *our* responses. When we first used to sit with people and hear such questions, we would guardedly begin to "answer" them. Sometimes these persons would just look at us and appear to listen to us; sometimes they just went on with *their* talking over our replies. Frequently, when we stopped talking, they would continue with *their* own thoughts on these matters. Eventually, we learned that individuals most often ask these questions as a way of articulating issues in their own minds. Talking is a way of developing their own thinking. Sometimes, they are attempting to determine whether we will allow them to "spin out" their own answers. Again, what is usually being asked for here is for someone to be *present* and to *listen*.

Dying persons need to work out their own answers to these questions (International Work Group on Death, Dying, and Bereavement, 1990; Ley & Corless, 1988; Wald & Bailey, 1990). It is their life, after all. They must find their own meaning(s) for it. In popular terms, they must be permitted to "sing their own songs" or "tell their own stories" (Brady, 1979). Sometimes dying persons ask for someone who can specifically provide them with information that they want. Often, they can be helped by those who can affirm that their lives continue to be, just as they have been, important and meaningful to others.

Enhancing opportunities for creativity near the end of life can be an important way of helping individuals with spiritual tasks. In practice, this illustrates how the spiritual dimensions of a person's life blend with psychological, social, and physical dimensions. For example, one hospice has developed a rich program that offers creative opportunities in music, literature, drama, visual arts, movement and dance, gardening and nature, needlework and fabric arts, and metalsmithing (Bailey et al., 1990). Artistic endeavors of this sort reflect specifically human qualities in coping with living and dying. They can be undertaken in diverse settings where helpers can join together in natural ways with those who are coping with dying.

One last word really has to do with all of the dimensions in which one might seek to help a person who is coping with dying. Because the person has dealt with an issue once does not mean that the issue is now settled. The feeling (anger or sadness, fear or joy) or issue may come around again. The question—Who is going to see to it that my child gets a good education? What does my dying at 26 mean?—is likely to be spoken again later. Caregivers need to be ready to listen to this person, wherever he or she is today, *at this moment*. There is no fixed goal at which the dying person—and those who are listening to that person—has to arrive. Although it may be unwise to put off a question or request—death is always an unexpected visitor—still, one can rest assured that there will always be more questions, needs, desires, and concerns. No one ever finishes *all* of the business of life, if for no other reason than that each moment lived brings *new* business.

Tasks as Guidelines for Helping

One important aim of a task-based approach to coping with dying is to identify guidelines for helping those who are coping with dying. This can be achieved in the following ways.

Helping Others with Their Tasks

If those who are dying or those who are coping with dying in some other way (as a family member, lover, friend, or caregiver for the dying person) face many tasks in their coping, then it may become the responsibility of a helper (whether a professional or layperson) to facilitate and assist that individual with his or her task work. Of course, the individual may not wish to have this sort of assistance. Or it may be that the individual is attempting to carry out his or her perceived tasks through some behavior (for example, suicide) that is morally or legally unacceptable to the one who is asked to help. The ways in which any one person chooses to live out his or her life do not necessarily impose obligations on others. But these ways often can become a reference point that can guide the work of helpers, and this is particularly true for areas of task work as they are perceived by individuals who are coping with dying.

Careful observation of the ways in which the individual who is coping with dying perceives and responds to potential tasks can shape specific approaches in helping. For example, a dying person may express a need to get in contact with an estranged relative. That might lead a helper to assist in making a telephone call or in writing a letter, or it might become appropriate (if the dying person so wishes) for the helper to make the first contact as an intermediary with the estranged relative.

In the case of a family member who is caring for a dying person at home, the helper might become aware that what is most needed is some temporary relief from the physical burdens of care or some time off for psychological or social rejuvenation. In these circumstances, the helper might offer to take over some of the physical care that is needed in order to permit the family caregiver to have time for uninterrupted sleep or rest. Similarly, the helper might just sit with the dying person so that the family caregiver can leave the confines of the house to shop, see a movie, or seek some other form of rejuvenation. In other circumstances, a perceptive helper might offer to take young children out for a day in the park so that a dying person and his or her spouse might have some time alone together.

Rosen (1990) has described a number of ways in which to assist families who are facing the death of one of their members. His recommendations are grounded in the use of a genogram or three-generation family tree that describes the family's structure, history, and relationships (see McGoldrick & Gerson, 1985, 1988). This provides a rich portrait of dynamics within the family and its own resources that might be mobilized by a helper. On this basis, Rosen has shown how one might use literary and cinematic materials to help families, as well as practices ("rituals") with which they are familiar and specific suggestions ("coaching") to direct their attention and energies to tasks that they need to address.

These are only a few examples. The principle that coping tasks can become guidelines for helpers must always be realized in *concrete*, *specific*, and *individual* circumstances. For example, as they talk together, a dying person and a helper might agree upon a number of coping tasks that could be undertaken. But an astute helper will then permit the dying person to determine which (if any) tasks should be undertaken first and when, and even to change those decisions as time passes. This enhances the autonomy of the dying person and acknowledges the measure of control that he or she still retains at a time when so many other things may be out of control. Here the helper fosters a sense of security even when there is much that is not safe in the dying person's life.

Individuals who are coping with dying may surprise us with their choices of tasks that are important to them at any given moment. They may be more concerned to have a beloved pet in their company than to permit visits from some human beings who are not very close friends. They may still be preoccupied with how they look or with a diet program. They may find more comfort in talking to a hospital janitor than to a psychiatrist. They may be more grateful to someone who cleans their eyeglasses, gives them a back rub, or trims their ingrowing toenails than to the chaplain who offers lofty spiritual advice. They may be more interested in one last taste of a fast food hamburger and French fried potatoes—what the British describe as "a little of what you fancy" (Willans, 1980)—than in the carefully planned offerings of the dietary department.

The reason for all of this is that dying persons are living human beings. They need to sing their own songs, to live out their own lives in ways that they find appropriate, and not to be "killed softly" by somebody else's song. This is not to imply that passivity is the central principle for helpers. One can suggest things to do, pose options, and make opportunities. Sometimes it is important to urge people rather strongly to do that which they do not want to do but which serves their own needs in ways they may not yet have realized or appreciated. Experienced caregivers learn when to be a bit insistent in matters like this and when to back off. But in the end, primacy of decision making must rest with the person being helped, not with the helper.

When one learns that someone is coping with dying, strong feelings well up and one's urge may be to try to make everything right again. Most often, that is not possible. But one should not conclude that nothing is possible. As long as an individual is alive, it is always possible to do something to improve or contribute to the quality of his or her life. For this, it is desirable to move toward (not away from) the person who is coping with dying. Helpers need to listen to and be guided by that person in their roles; otherwise, they are merely imposing their own agenda upon the other person.

What one does is not always or even mainly of primary importance. What counts is that one's actions show that one cares. Often, the action can be something simple and concrete. The gesture may not be accepted; it may not even be acknowledged. Dying persons (like everyone else) can be grumpy or exhausted. For those who care, that will not matter too much, because the gesture is made for the sake of the other person, not for one's own sake.

Helpers should begin where they are, with their own talents and limitations. Sharing honest emotions or feelings of uncertainty is not a bad way to start. Laughing, listening in an interested and nonjudgmental way, and just silently being present are often appreciated. Avoiding insensitive clichés is a good idea. Offering help in specific and practical ways is desirable. Conveying one's own sense of hope and sharing (often in nonverbal ways) one's conviction that the life of the other person is and has been meaningful in one's own life can be an eloquent form of caring. Holding a dying person's hand and crying with that person speaks volumes when words are not really possible.

Helping Helpers and Oneself

A task-based approach to coping with dying reminds helpers that they also have their own coping to consider (Corr, 1992c; Grollman, 1980). That is, helpers are also human beings with needs and limitations. One does not have to be dying to be important. Helpers must not overburden their own resources. Otherwise, they may become unable to be of any further assistance. The best helpers are those who operate from a foundation in a rich and satisfying life of their own, not from a sense that they are overwhelmed by stressors and problems of their own.

In the videotape *The Heart of the New Age Hospice* (1987), one woman described the foundation for helping others in the following way: "Duty without love is preposterous. Duty with love is acceptable. Love without duty is divine." Helpers cannot operate solely from their own need to be needed. They must care about those whom they are helping, but their love for others must also include themselves. The best helpers are those who can also take care of themselves and who take time to meet their own needs. This may require some self-awareness on the part of the helper in question.

In recent years, stress and what is called "burnout" on the part of care providers and other helpers have been the subject of much study (for example, Selye, 1978). One interesting result is that stress more often arises from the situation within which one is working and the colleagues with whom one works than from the fact that one is working with dying persons and others who are coping with dying (Vachon, 1979, 1987). In each case, then, one must carefully examine the particular factors from which stress arises and the mediators that may modify that stress in various ways (Friel & Tehan, 1980). In addition, thoughtful programs to address stress include such elements as careful staff selection, training, supervision, and support. When this is coupled with the development of an individual philosophy of care and attention to one's own needs for care (whether self-care or care from others), helping those who are coping with dying need not be more stressful than many other activities in our society (Harper, 1977; LaGrand, 1980; Lattanzi, 1983, 1985).

Good helpers may need to be open to suggestions and support from other persons—even from the dying person or the family unit whom they are helping. Indeed, when they are freed from the burden of distressing symptoms and made to feel secure, dying persons can often be very thoughtful and sensitive in caring for those around them. In short, none of us is without needs in coping with someone else's mortality or with our own mortality. We all can benefit from help as we look to our own tasks in coping.

Palliative Care

Most of the helping discussed thus far can be subsumed under the heading of *palliative care*. Palliative care means addressing *symptoms* rather than their underlying causes. In other words, palliative care is essentially an affirmation of life and a rejection of the statement that "there is nothing more that we can do." This rejection stands even when there is no reasonable expectation of benefit from cure-oriented interventions.

In fact, there may be many reasons why underlying causes cannot be addressed. For example, there may exist no available intervention that is capable of halting or reversing the development of a particular disease; all of the available interventions (surgery, radiation, chemotherapy, or other less conventional therapies) may already have been attempted without success; before it was identified, the disease may already have progressed beyond the point at which it was open to cure-oriented interventions; or the individual in question may have refused further interventions (for example, on religious or ethical grounds, or because they involve unwanted side effects).

When traditional or conventional therapies are unavailable or not appropriate for a life-threatening illness, attention often turns to new or unconventional forms of therapy. However, the realities usually confronted in such situations must be respected: (1) the sudden appearance of new cure-oriented interventions is often unlikely; (2) even if such interventions do abruptly appear, the condition of this particular person may already have deteriorated so far that he or she may derive little benefit from them; and (3) unconventional therapies are called "unconventional" precisely because research or clinical experience has not established their efficacy. Still, nothing in this book is meant to stand in opposition to cure-oriented interventions—old or new, conventional or unconventional—when they are feasible, relevant, and desirable. Our concern is to point out that for those who are dying, much can be done to ameliorate distressing symptoms, both in conjunction with or in the absence of cure-oriented interventions. That is the sphere of palliative care.

To be unable to provide a cure is not to be in the situation of no longer being needed or useful. It is also incorrect to think of palliative care as the opposite of active treatment (an inaccurate phrase used most often to mean cure-oriented treatment), for that portrays palliation as merely some passive mode of care. In fact, "the care of the dying patient is an active treatment peculiar to the dying patient" (Liegner, 1975, p. 1048). That is, palliative care is an active and aggressive mode of care, but one whose focus has shifted from a primary emphasis on cure to a primary emphasis on the mitigation of distressing symptoms. In this sense and as was evident in the example of Carol and Bill Johnson at the outset of this chapter, palliative care is very important both to dying persons who may no longer reasonably expect to obtain a cure and to their family members.

In fact, more often than not, health care providers mainly provide some form of palliative care, even in situations involving diseases that are not life-threatening. This can be illustrated in the familiar example of the common cold. There is no cure for the common cold (or for many other unexceptional maladies). But aspirin, decongestants, antiexpectorants, antihistamines, medications to dry up unwanted secretions, and other interventions are usually employed to improve the quality of life when individuals have a cold and cough. Remedies of this sort usually correct or compensate for deficiencies related to illness or disability. In the case of the common cold, symptoms are palliated until the body's own resources fight off the underlying virus. Thus, palliative care is an important aspect of our approach to many familiar health care situations.

The point for this book is that palliative care is especially significant for those who are dying. For them, it makes the difference between another good day of living and another terrible day of dying. Thus, Saunders (1976, p. 674) observed that palliative care represents "the unique period in the patient's illness when the long defeat of living can be gradually converted into a positive achievement in dying." An achievement of this sort is one to which we might all aspire or seek to assist. It is an achievement that Victor and Rosemary Zorza (1980) described after the death of their 25-year-old, fiercely independent daughter, when they were able to say that "her personality was intact, her identity hadn't been drowned in drugs or crushed by pain" (p. 226)—in short, she was able to die as she had lived.

Hope

This brings us back to the subject of *hope*. Sometimes it is said that there is no more hope for dying persons, that they are hopeless cases. Such assertions reveal a narrow understanding of the role that hope plays in human lives (Corr, 1981). We hope for all sorts of things. I hope that someone will (continue to) love me. He hopes that he can have his favorite food for dinner tonight. She hopes to be able to see her sister again. Many of us hope to live as long as we possibly can. Some dying persons hope to live until a special birthday or holiday, or until the birth of a new grandchild. Perhaps all of us hope that our own situation and the situations of those whom we love will be better after our deaths. In the meantime, most of us hope that whatever it is that is making us uncomfortable will be removed from our lives. This last hope—like many other hopes that we may entertain—cannot always be realized. Still, it is only *one* hope among many.

Few situations in life are ever completely *hopeless*. So when someone says, "This situation is hopeless," it may just signify a failure of imagination. Often, it represents the point of view of an outsider (for example, a care provider) and his or her judgment that there is no likelihood of cure for the person in the situation. Usually, a statement of this sort indicates that the speaker has focused exclusively on a single hope or a narrow range of hopes that cannot be realized in a specific set of circumstances.

However, "hope, which centers on fulfilling expectations, may focus on getting well, but more often focuses on what yet can be done" (Davidson, 1975, p. 49). Hope is a characteristically human phenomenon (Veninga, 1985). But it is fluid, often altering its focus to adapt to changes in the real circumstances within which we find ourselves. In other words, we must listen carefully to each individual in order to determine the object of his or her hope. And we must distinguish between hope, which is founded in reality, and unrealistic wishes, which merely express our fanciful desires.

Effective Communication

In the past, our death system often advised us not to speak candidly to dying persons about their diagnoses and prognoses (for example, Oken, 1961). It was thought that candor would undercut hope and the will to live or even encourage people to end their own lives. There is, in fact, no evidence that that did or does take place. Even so, the key issues in effective communication are whether or not specific acts of communication are responsive to the needs of dying persons and are carried out in a thoughtful and caring way (Zittoun, 1990). That is, the content of the communication may not be as important as the ways in which it is expressed and understood. One can brutalize a vulnerable person with the truth, just as one can harm with falsehood.

For the most part, our death system now encourages speaking with greater candor to dying persons about their diagnoses and prognoses (Novack et al., 1979). This is because nowadays much emphasis is placed upon informed consent and the rights of patients (President's Commission, 1982; Rozovsky, 1990). Consent to professional intervention or any sort of supportive treatment cannot be freely given unless it is based upon information needed to understand the current situation, the nature of the proposed interventions, and their likely outcomes. Even in the direst of situations, the necessary information can be provided in a caring manner and consent obtained in ways that foster the dignity of all who are involved.

So communication is an important part of fostering hope and quality in living when individuals are coping with dying. And the ways in which one communicates with those whom one is trying to help can become a model for all helping interactions (Buckman, 1988, 1992). The resulting challenge to helpers appears on two fundamental levels: (1) to keep company with the dying and with others who are coping with dying—even when that requires one to be comfortable with one's own discomfort and to do nothing more than to sit together quietly in silence; and (2) to learn how to identify and respond effectively to the particular physical, psychological, social, and spiritual tasks that are part of a specific individual's coping with dying.

Summary

This chapter has explored ways in which professional and laypersons can provide care to those who are coping with dying. It has considered four primary dimensions in such care and a task-based model as a source of guidelines for helping both others and oneself. All of this is a part of effective palliative care, with its emphases upon maximizing present quality in living, effective communication, and realistic hope.

QUESTIONS FOR REVIEW AND DISCUSSION

1. Think about some moment in your life when someone you loved was quite ill or dying. What was most stressful for you at that time? What did you do or what might you have done to help the person who was ill or dying? What did you do or what might you have done that you now think was unhelpful to the person who was ill or dying?

2. This chapter has described four dimensions or aspects of care for the dying: physical, psychological, social, and spiritual. Think about someone whom you know who was or is dying (or use the example of the Amish man described near the beginning of Chapter 3 or the dying person described

near the beginning of Chapter 5). In the case that you choose to reflect on, how did these four dimensions or aspects of care show up?

3. This chapter suggested that hope is or can be important both for dying persons and for those who are helping such persons. How can hope be important for those who know they will soon be dead or for those who know that the person for whom they are caring will soon be dead? What does hope mean to you?

4. This chapter suggested that effective communication is or can be important both for dying persons and for those who are helping such persons. Why is communication important for the dying and their helpers? What makes for effective communication among such people? What is an example from your own experience of poor communication? Of good communication?

SUGGESTED READINGS

The lives and motivations of two pioneering women who have done much to help the dying in recent years are described in the following:

DuBoulay, S. (1984). *Cicely Saunders: The Founder of the Modern Hospice Movement.*
Gill, D. L. (1980). *Quest: The Life of Elisabeth Kübler-Ross.*

Researchers, scholars, and clinicians write about various ways in which to help those who are coping with dying in the following books:

Bailey, S. S., Bridgman, M. M., Faulkner, D., Kitahata, C. M., Marks, E., Melendez, B. B., & Mitchell, H. (1990). *Creativity and the Close of Life.*
Buckman, R. (1988). *I Don't Know What to Say: How to Help and Support Someone Who Is Dying.*
Buckman, R. (1992). *How to Break Bad News: A Guide for Health Care Professionals.*
Callanan, M., & Kelley, P. (1992). *Final Gifts: Understanding the Special Awareness, Needs, and Communications of the Dying.*
Cantor, R. C. (1978). *And a Time to Live: Toward Emotional Well-Being During the Crisis of Cancer.*
Melzack, R., & Wall, P. D. (1989). *The Challenge of Pain* (rev. ed.).
Melzack, R., & Wall, P. D. (Eds.). (1991). *Textbook of Pain* (3rd ed.).
Rosen, E. J. (1990). *Families Facing Death: Family Dynamics of Terminal Illness.*
Stedeford, A. (1984). *Facing Death: Patients, Families and Professionals.*
Twycross, R. G., & Lack, S. A. (1983). *Symptom Control in Far Advanced Cancer: Pain Relief.*

Support for helpers is another important aspect of assisting those who are coping with dying:

Corr, C. A. (1992). *Someone You Love Is Dying: How Do You Cope?*
Grollman, E. A. (1980). *When Your Loved One Is Dying.*
Harper, B. C. (1977). *Death: The Coping Mechanism of the Health Professional.*
Vachon, M.L.S. (1987). *Occupational Stress in the Care of the Critically Ill, the Dying, and the Bereaved.*

CHAPTER 7

Hospice Principles and Caring for the Dying

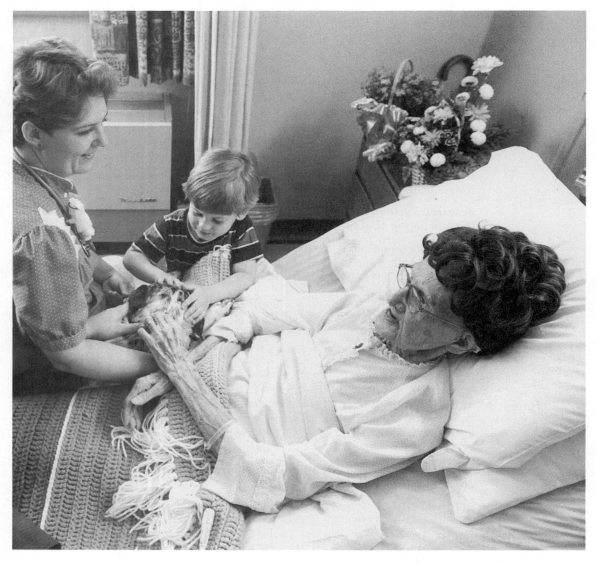

This chapter describes some of the ways in which helping principles have been embodied in formal programs of care for those who are coping with dying. A program of this sort may be associated with an institution, defined as "a complex interaction of professionals, para-professionals, and the public, on informational, economic, and occupational levels, in identifiable physical environments, whose coordinated decisions and actions have magnified public impact" (Jonsen & Helleghers, 1974, p. x). Two well-known institutions in our society that may have some role in caring for the dying are hospitals or medical centers and long-term care facilities (often called nursing homes). Dying persons have also been cared for in our society by home care programs and hospice programs. For all of these institutions or programs, this chapter asks two related questions: (1) What, in principle, are the desirable elements of a program concerned with care of those who are living while dying? and (2) How, in practice, do actual institutions or programs in our society undertake this work?

This chapter pays particular attention to hospice programs—the newest of the programs in our society that are involved in caring for the dying, the one that has been specifically designed for this purpose, and the one that may be least familiar to readers. The term *hospice* designates both a philosophy of care and an organized program that seeks to implement that philosophy.

As a philosophy or approach to care, hospice is a form of palliative care for those who are coping with dying. The hospice philosophy is described here in terms of ten principles of care. As an organization or practical program for delivering care to those who are coping with dying, hospice stands alongside hospitals, long-term care facilities, and other forms of home care that address (at least in part) similar needs. An outline of the historical development and contemporary role of these institutions and programs indicates how each responds to the needs of those who are coping with dying.

In short, this chapter moves forward from the guidelines for individual helpers discussed in Chapter 6 to present a model for formal programs of care and discuss the institutional realities of care in our societal death system. Those topics are introduced here through an example of a woman who received care from all of the programs that may play some role in caring for the dying in our society.

Glenda Williams: Illness, Dying, and Death in Institutions

Glenda Williams was 38 years old when she first felt a small lump in her left breast. Until that unforgettable moment alone in her shower, Glenda had thought that she had a charmed and very satisfying life. She had finished college, begun a promising career, married a bit later than most these days, and had two healthy children, Drew and Cindy, who were 12 and 10 years old at the time of her shattering discovery.

Glenda had had her regular medical checkup about nine months earlier. She had been given a clean bill of health, which was always a relief in view of her mother's mastectomy five years earlier. Thus, when she first felt that tiny lump in her breast, Glenda's initial thoughts were about her family. What would this all mean for Cindy's role in her school drama group's performance just six weeks off, or for the long-planned family trip to Europe with Drew's choral group in the summer? And what about Dave, who had had so many disappointments at work and with his own parents lately? Dave was a good provider who often told Glenda how much he loved her. But Glenda knew that she was the strong one in the family upon whom Dave and the children relied.

"It just can't be cancer! It must be a cyst! If I wait a few days, it probably will just shrivel up and go away." Glenda wanted so very much to believe all of these things that she told herself.

But it did not get better or go away. After some time, Glenda went to see her family physician. That led to a swift referral to a specialist, some tests, and the awful moment when Glenda had to tell Dave what she now knew to be the truth and they had to make a quick decision about treatment. One possibility was simply to do nothing; other possibilities involved various degrees of invasiveness and disfigurement. For Glenda, it was essential to involve her family in this decision, as they would be involved in its implications. In the end, Glenda's mastectomy and its accompanying bouts of radiation and chemotherapy were a difficult ordeal, not only for her but for the whole family.

Still, life was good for many, many years afterward. Then Dave died of a heart attack just two years after his retirement, and barely over a year later Glenda developed cancer again. Her physicians were never completely sure whether this was a new disease or a recurrence of the old one. In any event, it must have lurked quietly for a while to account for its rapid development and spread after discovery. There were more tests, new diagnoses, and several rounds of unsuccessful treatment. Some of the care that Glenda required was provided in the hospital, some in one of its outpatient clinics, and some by a community home care program. A final, unproductive admission to a busy hospital eventually led to a transfer to a nearby nursing home.

Glenda liked the slower pace of the nursing home. She made some friends there, but many of the residents seemed confused and were unable to sustain a relationship. One day, one of them frightened Drew's children, and his family visited less often after that. With her daughter living far away, Glenda felt alone and overwhelmed by her problems. She became demanding and the staff seemed to have little time to really help any more.

Finally, when her pain and other symptoms became less manageable and both her physical condition and her spirits deteriorated, Glenda was transferred once again, this time to a local hospice inpatient unit. Expert care and the support of the whole hospice team helped minimize sources of distress and improve Glenda's quality of life. Glenda felt that she had almost miraculously regained control of her life.

It was a source of special delight for Glenda when Drew, his wife, and their children came to visit her in the hospice. One Sunday afternoon, they took her out for a drive (her first outing in many years). Eventually, with the support of the hospice home care team, Glenda was even able to go home to live with Drew's family for several months. In the end, Glenda was readmitted to the hospice inpatient facility, where she died. But before her death Glenda continued to marvel that people associated with the hospice program had time to just sit and be with her; this form of care seemed different because people did not spend all of their time talking about disease, treatments, and death.

Recognizing and Responding to the Needs of the Dying

"What people need most when they are dying is relief from distressing symptoms of disease, the security of a caring environment, sustained expert care, and assurance that they and their families will not be abandoned" (Craven & Wald, 1975, p. 1816). This single sentence captures the needs of those who are dying and points to that which is required from institutional programs and individual caregivers (whether they are family members, other lay persons, or professionals).

During the 1960s and 1970s, a number of sensitive caregivers began to wonder whether care provided to those who were dying was properly recognizing and responding to their needs. Subsequently, studies conducted in Great Britain (for example, Hinton, 1963, 1967; Rees, 1972), Canada (for instance, Mount, Jones, & Patterson, 1974), and the United States (such as Marks & Sachar, 1973) confirmed that the answer was no. Two points seemed to be central. First, caregivers did not always realize or acknowledge the level of pain and other forms of distress in individuals who were dying. Second, caregivers did not always have or did not believe that they had at their disposal effective resources to respond to the manifestations of terminal illness. What this meant in practice was that those who were dying were told: "Your pain cannot be as bad as you say it is"; "You can't really be feeling like that"; "You will just have to get ahold of yourself"; "We cannot offer stronger dosages of narcotic analgesics or you will risk becoming addicted"; "We have to save the really strong medications until they are truly needed"; "There is nothing more that we can do."

It is unfortunate when caregivers who want to help do not have the resources to do so. Thus, many were grateful when new forms of narcotic analgesics became available for use in terminal illness. But the real tragedy is when the needs of those who are dying are not recognized and when that is compounded by inadequate understanding or misguided fears about how to mobilize resources to meet real needs.

What all of this required was new understandings on several key points. First, a new understanding was needed of the situation of those who are coping with dying (Noyes & Clancy, 1977; Pattison, 1977). Second, the nature of pain in terminal illness needed to be better understood (LeShan, 1964; Melzack & Wall, 1989, 1991). Third, appropriate therapeutic regimes for the terminally ill needed to be established. These were first thought to depend

upon certain analgesic mixtures or the unique properties of heroin, but were later shown to involve carefully selected narcotics, other medications, and complementary therapeutic interventions (Melzack, Mount, & Gordon, 1979; Melzack, Ofiesh, & Mount, 1976; Twycross, 1977, 1979a). Fourth, the value of holistic, person-centered care and interdisciplinary teamwork needed to be recognized (Corr & Corr, 1983; Saunders, 1984). And fifth, ways in which the social organization of programs serving those coping with dying affects the care provided needed to be understood (Saunders, 1990; Sudnow, 1967). These new elements are all embodied in the hospice philosophy; many of them have been implemented in hospice and in other programs of care for those who are dying.

Hospice Philosophy and Principles

A number of attempts have been made to define the concept of hospice care (Kastenbaum, 1989e; Lack, 1977, 1979; Markel & Sinon, 1978) and to establish an overall foundation for care of those who are dying, either in the form of general principles for such care (International Work Group on Death, Dying, and Bereavement, 1979) or in terms of specific hospice standards (National Hospice Organization, 1987). For our purposes, the hospice philosophy and its central principles can be summarized by the following ten points.

1. *Hospice is a philosophy, not a facility.* In England, the hospice movement began by building its own facilities. Going outside the existing system in this way is one classic route for innovation. But it reflects the social situation and structure of the health care system in a particular country at a specific time. We know now that it is not the facility in which hospice care is delivered that is essential, but the principles that animate the services and the quality of the care itself. The point to emphasize is the outlook, attitude, or approach that is central in hospice care (Corr & Corr, 1983).
2. *The hospice philosophy affirms life, not death.* Dying is a self-limiting condition. Individuals can and will die by themselves, without assistance from others. The hard work is supporting life, not bringing about death. Helping a person to live may be especially difficult when that person is close to death and is experiencing distress in dying. The processes of dying may impose special pressures on quality in living. Still, hospice cares for and about persons who are dying because they are still living.
3. *The affirmation of life that is central to the hospice philosophy is expressed in an effort to maximize present quality in living.* Hospice is a form of palliative or symptom-oriented care that tries to minimize discomfort. That is, without abandoning interest in cure, hospice is mainly concerned with caring when cure is no longer a reasonable expectation. Thus, hospice programs focus on the alleviation of distressing symptoms, even when the underlying condition from which they arise cannot be halted or reversed.
4. *The hospice approach offers care to the patient-and-family unit.* This means that both the dying person and those whom he or she regards as family are part of the unit that receives care and that helps to give care. Hospice care seeks to provide a sense of security and the support of a caring environment for all those involved in coping with dying—not only ill persons but also families, friends, and staff.
5. *Hospice is holistic care.* It approaches the dying individual as a person, a whole human being. To do this, hospice care addresses physical, psychological, social, and spiritual needs. It seeks to enhance quality in living in each of these dimensions.
6. *Hospice offers continuing care and ongoing support to bereaved survivors after the death of someone they love.* Care for family members and friends does not cease with the death of the person they love, as we will see later in our discussions of bereaved survivors.
7. *The hospice approach seeks relevant ways to combine professional skills and human presence through interdisciplinary teamwork.* Expertise in terminal care and in the management of distressing symptoms is essential. Equally important is the availability of human companionship. Human

presence can be offered by professional caregivers, but it is often a special gift of hospice volunteers. Both expertise and presence are dependent upon being available and actively listening to understand correctly the needs of dying persons and their family members. Interdisciplinary teamwork demands respect for the skills and abilities of others, time to exchange information and insights, and a certain amount of "role blurring" in responding to the needs of those whom the hospice program is serving.

8. *Hospice programs make services available on a 24–hour-a-day, 7–day-a-week basis.* Hospice is an effort to recreate caring communities in the service of dying persons and their families. Wherever such communities already exist naturally or informally and whenever dying persons and their families are not experiencing significant distress, there may be no need for formal hospice programs. When and where a need does exist, these programs must be available around the clock, just as a caring community is.

9. *Hospice programs support their own staff and volunteers.* When its positive aims are properly understood, hospice care can be seen to be satisfying and rewarding work for those who share its values. But caring for those who are coping with dying and/or bereavement and working within the structure of an interdisciplinary team can be stressful. Thus, hospice programs also offer formal and informal programs of support for their own staff members and volunteers.

10. *The hospice philosophy can be applied to a variety of individuals and their family members who are coping with a life-threatening illness, dying, death, and/or bereavement.* In its modern usage, hospice has primarily been concerned with terminal illness (most often, cancer) and its implications, but that restriction is not intrinsic to the hospice philosophy. To derive benefit from the hospice philosophy, there must be time and opportunity to bring services to bear upon the needs of the patient-and-family unit. Thus, some advance notice that dying has begun and death is imminent (in a matter of days, weeks, or months), some willingness to accept the benefits and restrictions of hospice care, and an opportunity to mobilize services in particular circumstances are all essential. Given these conditions, the hospice philosophy can apply, in principle, in a range of circumstances (for example, International Work Group on Death, Dying, and Bereavement, 1993).

Programs That Care for the Dying

Ways in which hospice principles are put into practice can be understood better by recalling the experiences of Glenda Williams that were described at the outset of this chapter. We will examine the development, role, and functions of the caring institutions and programs that she encountered, especially during the last and most difficult parts of her life.

Hospitals

In American society, most people receive most of their medical care in hospitals, and most people (approximately 60 percent) die there. Hospitals have an ancient origin. The word *hospital* is derived from the medieval Latin *hospitale*, meaning a place of "reception and entertainment of pilgrims, travellers, and strangers" (Simpson & Weiner, 1989, VII, p. 414). *Hospitale* is the basic root of several English terms, including *hostel, hotel, hospital, hospitality,* and *hospice*. In the ancient world, the original places of reception took in pilgrims, travelers, the needy, the destitute, the infirm, the aged, and the sick or wounded. Thus, a broad range of people were served by the ancient *hospitale*. Such institutions were usually associated with some sort of religious fraternity or order.

As Western culture became more urbanized and as religious institutions were taken over by secular ones (such as the nation-state or city), hospitals began to change. Western society also became characterized by a division of labor. Specialization in carrying out tasks became the normal method of operation. No longer did one institution perform many basically different functions; instead, separate functions were now carried out by separate institutions. These changes took a long time, but they were more or less complete by the end of the 19th century.

Changes in caregiving institutions are recognizable even within the narrower historical boundaries of American culture. In particular, up to the 19th century, care of the sick and dying occurred mainly at home and was provided mainly by family members. Hospitals played virtually no role in such care. In 1800, there were only two private hospitals in the United States, one in New York and one in Philadelphia (Rosenberg, 1987).

Of course, even in that society, there were persons who were too sick to be healed at home or who had no one to take care of them. If such persons were also poor and could not afford to hire someone to come take care of them, they ended up in an almshouse. Almshouses were charitable public institutions that housed the insane, the blind, the crippled, the aged, the alcoholic, travelers, and the ordinary working man with rheumatism or bronchitis or pleurisy. These diverse types of people were all freely mixed together. Almshouses most often had large wards, which were usually crowded. Sometimes more than one person had to sleep in a single bed. Because they were usually not well funded, almshouses were typically dark, stuffy, and unpleasant places. Few people entered them voluntarily.

Modern hospitals began to be organized around the beginning of the 19th century. From the outset, they were advocated mainly as having an *educational* function, and they were not perceived as being primary agents of medical care. These early hospitals had little to offer and were avoided by anyone who could do so. They were expensive for those who could pay their way, "unnatural," and demoralizing. Thus, the physician Francis (1859, pp. 145–146) wrote just before the outbreak of the Civil War that "the people who repair to hospitals are mostly very poor, and seldom go into them until driven to do so from a severe stress of circumstances. When they cross the threshold, they are found not only suffering from disease, but in a half-starved condition, poor, broken-down wrecks of humanity, stranded on the cold bleak shores of that most forbidding of all coasts, charity."

Until the middle of the 19th century, little care could be provided inside a hospital that could not be better provided outside of it. Disease was still not well understood. Such care as was offered mainly involved the reporting of symptoms by the patient and the "treatment" of such symptoms as well as that could be done. This usually meant allowing the body to heal itself, and in particular not interfering in that process. Basically, all that a good hospital could provide was a place to rest, shelter from the elements, and decent food. By the time of the Civil War, several dozen hospitals had been founded in the United States. These were largely built by cities and counties; only the very poor entered them.

The Civil War period brought major changes. For one thing, the understanding of disease changed. Up to this time, as Rosenberg (1987, pp. 71–72) has written, the body was seen as "a system of ever-changing interactions with its environment. . . . Every part of the body was related inevitably and inextricably to every other." Health or disease were seen "as general states of the total organism. . . . The idea of specific disease entities played a relatively small role in this system of ideas and behavior." But disease now began to be seen as involving specific entities and predictable causes. In the 1860s, Pasteur and Lister contributed to the germ theory of disease. This dramatically changed Western culture's understanding of what caused disease and what could be done to treat disease. Now science with its theories and technology changed the face of modern medicine. Human bodies were seen as complex machines, disease was thought of as a breakdown in the body's machinery, and therapy involved "fixing" the "malfunctioning part"—or, as we have seen in the last 25 years, replacing that part. As Rosenberg (1987, p. 85) has written, "This new way of understanding illness necessarily underlined the hospital's importance."

The Civil War itself also taught new ideas to American medical practitioners. Cleanliness, order, and ventilation were discovered to be greatly helpful in bringing about a return to health. And for the first time in American history, people (mostly soldiers) of all social classes experienced care in (military) hospitals. Attitudes toward the hospital were changing.

Immediately after the Civil War, many new hospitals were built. In 1873 there were 178 hospitals in the United States; this number had increased to 4,359 by 1909 (Rosenberg, 1987). Health care—and as a result, dying—was moving into hospitals. The very poor and the socially isolated had died in almshouses during the 18th century and the early 19th century, but there were few of these people. (It is interesting to note as an aside that according to Rosenberg [1987, p. 31], one Philadelphia almshouse surgeon complained in 1859 that "dead bodies were often left in the wards and placed directly in coffins while the surviving patients looked on." Some persons believed that this was very hard on the surviving patients, and more or less recommended that such happenings should be hidden from public view. We see clearly here the idea that Ariès found arising in our time: the denial of death.) However, from the post–Civil War period on, more and more people would begin to die in hospitals.

This fact produced tension for health care providers and health care recipients alike. As Rosenberg (1987, p. 150) wrote, "Ordinary Americans had . . .

Technological care in a contemporary American hospital.

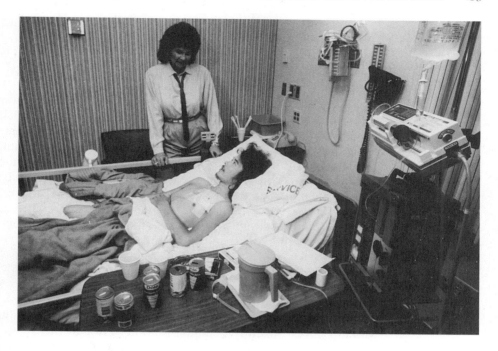

begun to accept the hospital. . . . Prospective patients were influenced not only by the hope of healing, but by the image of a new kind of medicine—precise, scientific, and effective." Consequently, hospitals were now expected to be places for the curing of specific diseases. The body's malfunctioning part was to be worked on, made functional, and then the person would get on with his or her life. In this context, death is an unhappy reminder that "scientific" medicine is not always effective—that is, if *effective* is taken to mean producing a cure. In this sort of hospital and according to this medical outlook, death is an anomaly, something abnormal. To the health care provider, death may seem to result from personal ineffectiveness. He or she was not able to "fix" the part in that body that was the problem. Thus, death is perceived to involve a kind of failure.

No wonder that by the end of the 19th century, "moribund patients were systematically transferred to special rooms" (Rosenberg, 1987, p. 292). In some places, whole wards or units were set aside for those who were not expected to recover—out of sight and, to the degree possible, out of mind. Given this development, it is perhaps not surprising that when Kübler-Ross (1969) asked to talk to dying patients in a large urban hospital in the late 1960s, she was told there were no dying patients in that hospital.

In the 1960s, specific criticisms began to be directed toward the hospital's care (or lack of care) for dying persons. The hospital in our culture is largely an acute-care, short-term facility. Its purpose is mainly to treat specific diseases and to return people to society with more or less the same functional capacity they had before they became ill. Put simply, hospitals are dominated by medical professionals who see themselves as involved in *curing* people

(Starr, 1982). This is why so many of our hospitals are now called medical centers or health centers.

In our culture, acute care is an expensive business. Diagnostic tools become ever more precise—and costly. The stethoscope is an inexpensive diagnostic tool; the CAT scanner is not. An appendectomy is a relatively inexpensive procedure; a kidney transplant is not. To permit someone to spend time in a hospital when no therapy leading to a cure is available may seem to waste bed space and the time and energy of busy caregivers who have been specially trained in the techniques of cure-oriented intervention. In its historical context, this claim seems to make sense. No wonder economists and health planners became involved in the 1980s in an attempt to make the use of the hospital's expensive services more economically efficient (Stevens, 1989). But to be humane, the care of dying persons may require additional values beyond mere economic efficiency. That was one of the concerns of Glenda Williams when she was in the hospital.

Long-Term Care Facilities

Another sort of institution in which many people die in the United States is the long-term care facility or nursing home. Prior to the 1930s, there were no nursing homes in this country (Moroney & Kurtz, 1975). They arose as the hospital became more and more an acute-care facility and as urbanization contributed to a change in the nature of the family, from an extended model or group of various relatives to a nuclear model usually restricted to husband, wife, and children. Also, by the middle of the 20th century, the average life span of Americans had increased. In an aging society, there will be a body of people with chronic diseases or other handicapping conditions who will have increasing difficulty in taking care of themselves. Such individuals will not expect to work until a matter of days or hours before their death, but will retire from work and may need assistance as they live out the remainder of their lives. This description has come to characterize the expectations of nearly the whole of our society's population.

These factors led to a situation in which long-term, chronic disability and illness increased while care for people with these conditions became less available. Nursing homes were developed to fill this gap in care (Thomas, 1969). They generally provide a place to stay, help with the routine activities of ordinary daily living, and some level of skilled nursing care. Nursing homes usually do not provide intensive physician care.

The development of funding mechanisms to offer financial assistance to those who become ill toward the end of their lives also played an important part in the development of nursing homes, especially after the passage of the Social Security Act of 1935. When financial resources are available from the personal savings of individuals, from their relatives, from government funding, and eventually from health insurance and a retirement package (most often provided as a nonsalary benefit by employers), potential providers of care will begin to think about offering services to this newly defined population. Some 16,000 nursing homes in the United States (with a total of approximately 1.6 million beds) are now certified to receive payment from Medicare and Medicaid. Another 7,000 to 8,000 state-licensed long-term care facilities do not qualify for this sort of reimbursement (Committee on Nursing Home Regulation, 1986).

A report from the Committee on Nursing Home Regulation (CNHR) of the Institute of Medicine (1986) noted that approximately 70 percent of nursing homes are operated on a for-profit basis. Until the 1980s, most hospitals did not think of themselves as profit-seeking enterprises. By contrast, nursing homes have sought both to provide a service and to be a profitable business. This puts some pressure on nursing homes, for the sort of care they provide—labor-intensive, round-the-clock care—is expensive. In practice, this has meant that most of those who work in long-term care facilities are nursing aides. Since nursing homes often experience high staff turnover, training of new persons, even when such training is minimal, must be repeated nearly constantly.

In general, long-term care facilities can be divided into several types. First, there are board and care homes or *shelter care facilities*. These are essentially residential facilities offering a place to live and to obtain one's basic meals, economies of scale in purchasing, and some companionship for those who are poor, alone, and in need of some attention on more than a short-term basis. Typically, they offer no formal nursing services.

A second sort of nursing home is the *intermediate care facility*. Care in such a facility is typically provided by nursing assistants or aides, but overall supervision of such care is often the proximate responsibility of a professional nurse, with medical guidance or consultation. This facility serves a segment of the elderly population who require nursing care, together with younger persons who have chronic illnesses or handicapping conditions. All of these individuals need assistance with activities of daily living, such as feeding, bathing, and moving around. Some individuals who are confined to a bed or wheelchair need additional help to deal with infirmities and to avoid the development of bedsores and other debilitating complications.

Finally, there are *skilled nursing care facilities* in which care is provided by professional nurses. Those being served are further compromised in their abilities to care for themselves and are in need of additional, skilled modes of assistance. For example, those in advanced stages of Alzheimer's disease may display disorientation, memory loss, combativeness, wandering, and an inability to accomplish activities of daily living.

Individuals in nursing homes can generally be divided into two groups: "short stayers," who generally come from hospitals and who either are rehabilitated and return home or who die in a relatively short period of time; and "long stayers," who are in the home for months or years until they die. The fact that these facilities discharge some 35 percent of their residents to the community each year indicates the importance of their rehabilitative role. The occupancy rate in most nursing homes is quite high. The residents in such homes are typically very dependent; they are elderly, chronically ill, confused, even emotionally disturbed. Such individuals are most often single, widowed, childless, and in general, poorer than the rest of the population. Although nursing homes

Pet therapy enriches life in long-term care.

provide services to persons needing quite different sorts of care—from those needing short-term, intensive rehabilitation to those who are incontinent, mentally impaired, seriously disabled, or very old and very frail—it is the long-term, very disabled persons who more and more occupy nursing home beds. In 1977, 70 percent of persons in these homes were over 75 years of age, and 70 percent of them were female (CNHR, 1986).

It is estimated that only 5 percent of people over 65 and 10 percent of people over 75 are in long-term care facilities. Thus, the notion that to be old in the United States means to be in a nursing home is a misperception; most elderly persons in our society are not in nursing homes. Still, the pressure on long-term care facilities is likely to grow. By the year 2000, there will be a 46% increase in the number of people over 75 in this country, and an 80% increase in those over 85 (CNHR, 1986). Most of these people will not need long-term institutional care, but many will.

The fact that overall levels of education and compensation are relatively low for staff tells us something about how our society values the increasingly important role of such facilities. Nevertheless, many people who work in long-term care facilities prefer the slower and more orderly routines of these institutions and the opportunities to develop long-term personal relationships within them, in contrast with the hectic pace and rapid patient turnover in acute-care hospitals.

Many long-term care facilities operate programs of high quality for their residents. Nevertheless, there are periodic outcries in the media, in the public, and in legislatures about the quality of care provided in nursing homes and other long-term care facilities (for example, Bennett, 1980; Mendelson, 1974; Moss & Halamanderis, 1977). Many people are dissatisfied with the quality of care in nursing homes, and we are all familiar with aged relatives who plead, "Don't send me to a nursing home."

Quality of living and dying in long-term care facilities has been described in various ways (for example, Kayser-Jones, 1981). One indicator is found in contacts between residents and those outside the institution: 13 percent of people in long-term care facilities receive *no* visitors in a year; 62 percent of them receive family or other visitors on a daily or weekly basis (CNHR, 1986). For many, this suggests disengagement from or diminishment of external social networks. Reports concerning dying in long-term care facilities have also suggested isolation and insufficient attention to bereavement needs of the institutional community, although that appears to be changing (Gubrium, 1975; Shield, 1988). Based on an average length of stay in the late 1970s of 2.6 years, approximately 30 percent of all discharges from nursing homes represented deaths (Vladeck, 1980). Many individuals are transferred from long-term care facilities to acute-care hospitals shortly before they die.

Long-term care facilities provide services that Americans apparently want or need: someone (else) to take care of long-term chronically disabled, and sometimes dying, people. This may be a choice we are comfortable making. For example, this sort of institutional program was well suited for quite some time to the needs of Glenda Williams and her family. However, an institution designed for long-term care and chronic illness may not be well suited to the demands of terminal illness.

In the case of Glenda Williams, eventually her needs required a level and type of services that her nursing home was not able to provide. Situations of this sort contribute to a stereotype often associated with the dying: alone, afraid, seriously disabled, in unrelieved distress, uncared for, and perhaps uncared about. This stereotype is probably unfair with reference to the actual care provided in many long-term care facilities, but it looms large in the minds of many who may or may not have experienced these institutions with family members or friends. In other words, like hospitals, long-term care facilities do not always provide a comfortable institutional image of dying in our society. Still, both hospitals and long-term care facilities have improved their responses to terminal illness in recent years and have in many cases associated themselves with hospice principles or programs of care (for example, Breindel, 1979).

Hospice Programs

Hospice programs are the newest social structure in our death system, one that has already become a major way of caring for those who are coping with dying. Hospice programs engage professional persons, volunteers, and the public in complex interactions. They provide information and perform both an essential service and an economic function for individuals and society. In the United States, however, hospice programs are seldom directly linked to a distinct, identifiable physical environment of the sort that characterizes some other institutions. Thus, most hospitals and nursing homes are recognizable facilities in our communities, but hospice programs usually are not identifiable in the same ways unless they are associated with those others as their parent institutions. That is because hospice is essentially a philosophy rather than a facility, and most hospice care in our society is delivered at home. As some have said, the term *hospice* may be more appropriately used as an adjective than as a noun. To understand this, we must look at how hospice programs developed.

In addition to drawing upon age-old human traditions in caring for the dying, hospice programs trace their roots back to the medieval institutions mentioned earlier that offered rest and support for weary travelers (Stoddard, 1992). In their modern sense, hospice programs emphasize care for those who are in the final stages of the journey of life. Services are designed primarily to provide care for those who are terminally ill or who have no reasonable hope of benefit from cure-oriented intervention, along with their family members.

One can trace modern hospice care to institutions run by religious orders of nuns in Ireland and England. But the great impetus clearly came from Dr. (and now also Dame) Cicely Saunders and the founding of St. Christopher's Hospice in southeast London in 1967 (DuBoulay, 1984; Hillier, 1983). Originally a nurse, Dame Cicely retrained as an almoner (social worker) after injuring her back, and then as a physician in order to pursue her conviction that better care could and should be offered to the incurably ill and dying. She worked out her theories at St. Joseph's Hospice in the East End of London during the 1950s and did research there on medications for the management of chronic pain in terminal illness. Subsequently, she went outside the National Health Service (NHS) in England to found St. Christopher's as a privately owned inpatient facility in which she could pioneer her theories of clinical practice, research, and education in the care of the dying.

At first, it was thought that innovations of this sort could only be undertaken in independent inpatient facilities built for the purpose. This was the original hospice model in England, subsequently followed by inpatient facilities built with private money and then turned over to the NHS for operation, and eventually by inpatient units within some NHS hospitals (Ford, 1979; Wilkes et al., 1980). England has also seen the development of home care teams designed to support the work of general practitioners and district nurses (Doyle, 1980), as well as hospital support teams that advise on the care of the dying in acute-care hospitals (Bates, Hoy, Clarke, & Laird, 1981) and programs of hospice day care (Wilkes, Crowther, & Greaves, 1978). These can all be better understood after noting developments in hospice care in North America.

In Canada, Dr. Balfour Mount and his colleagues developed the Palliative Care Service at the Royal Victoria Hospital in Montreal, which came into being in January of 1975. This service included an inpatient unit based in a large acute-care teaching hospital, a consultation service, a home care service, and a bereavement follow-up program (Ajemian & Mount, 1980). That structure, centered on a hospital-based inpatient unit, seems to be the dominant model for palliative care (as the Canadians prefer to call it) in Canada.

In the United States, hospice care began in September 1974, with a community-based home care program in New Haven, Connecticut (Foster, Wald, & Wald, 1978; Lack & Buckingham, 1978). Since that time, hospice care has spread across the country. (For additional information about hospice services, or to find out how to contact a local hospice program, call the Hospice Helpline at 800/658-8898, or write the National Hospice Organization, 1901 N. Moore Street, Suite 901, Arlington, VA 22209.) By 1990, it was estimated that there were nearly 1,750 hospice programs in the United States (1990 National Hospice Census; personal communication with John J. Mahoney, 9/2/92). These programs represented a wide variety of models. Many were independently based in the community, but more were organized as departments of hospitals or as a part of home health agencies. Some American hospice programs are based in other agencies, like long-term care facilities. Few have followed the early British model and built their own facility.

In 1982, a hospice benefit was approved as an aspect of Medicare reimbursement for health care. This benefit emphasized home care for the elderly. Admission criteria typically required a diagnosis of terminal illness, prognosis of less than six months to live, and the presence of a key caregiver in the home. Reimbursement rates were organized in four basic categories: a regular, daily, home care rate; an inpatient rate; a rate for short-term respite care; and a rate for continuous in-home care. Each of these rates is adjusted to take account of costs in local areas, and all have been increased to take account of rising costs since their inauguration.

Two things are worth noting about the hospice Medicare benefit. First, from the standpoint of its government funding source, it emphasizes home care and represents an effort to move reimbursement for health care from a fee-for-service basis to a flat-rate basis. For example, the hospice program will receive the amount specified in the daily home care rate for each day in which a dying person is enrolled in its care, whatever services it actually provides to that person on any given day.

Second, all monies provided under the hospice Medicare benefit (except for those paid to an attending primary physician) go directly to the hospice program. This makes the program responsible for designing and implementing each individual plan of care. No service is reimbursed unless it is included in that plan of care and approved by the hospice team. This is intended to give the hospice program an incentive to hold down costs and to provide only care that is relevant to the needs of an individual patient and family unit.

The hospice Medicare benefit, which has in significant respects become a model for private health care reimbursement in the United States, is a desirable option for those hospice programs and individuals who qualify. It is broader than other Medicare benefits and is intended to cover all of the costs of the care provided. Although it does incorporate upper limits on reimbursement to a hospice program, these are expressed in terms of program averages and total benefit days for which the program will be reimbursed, not figures that apply to any particular individual. In fact, once a person has been accepted into a Medicare-qualified hospice program, the law requires that he or she can never be involuntarily discharged—whether or not funds are still flowing for reimbursement. In 1990, more than 200,000 patients were served by the Medicare hospice benefit (mainly Caucasian Americans with cancer and over 65 years of age, almost evenly divided by gender), with an average length of stay in the hospice program of 58 days and almost all in home care (1990 National Hospice Census; personal communication with John J. Mahoney, 9/2/92).

Obviously, hospice principles have been implemented in different ways. These differences mainly concern the needs of a particular society, and especially the structure of its health care and social services systems. In the United States, hospice programs have emphasized home care in ways consistent with our society's efforts to minimize care within institutions and to encourage care in the home as more appropriate and more economical. This also led to the rapid development of hospital-based home care departments in the 1980s, alongside more traditional sorts of home care programs such as those offered by visiting nurse agencies and county or municipal health care departments. These programs are not exclusively committed to providing care for dying persons, but they usually do offer such care. Hospice programs remain exclusively dedicated to care of the dying and of their families.

Summary

The lessons of this chapter can be summarized by describing the three main programs that care for the dying in our society.

1. *Hospitals* or acute-care institutions of all sorts (general hospitals, specialized medical or psychiatric institutions, and tertiary-care trauma centers or teaching hospitals) emphasize assessment and diagnosis of illness and disease, together with cure-oriented interventions for reversible or correctable conditions. Most hospitals offer a wide variety of medical services through their own internal facilities, such as emergency departments, medical or surgical wards, and intensive care units, or through outpatient departments and clinics. Physicians also offer some types of care in their offices, in community clinics, and in various sorts of specialized centers.

Home care that is often associated with medical care may be provided by municipal or county health departments, visiting nurse programs, and home care departments of hospitals. Most of these services are not primarily designed for dying persons. Nevertheless, a very large share of hospital-based and associated forms of care is directed toward the last six months of life. Also, the largest numbers of deaths in our society occur in hospitals or are brought to these institutions for confirmation and certification of death.

2. *Long-term care facilities* emphasize long-term custodial, nursing, and rehabilitative care for individuals with chronic illnesses and other disabling conditions. It is not accurate to think of such institutions as exclusively serving the elderly, and it is incorrect to think that much more than a very small percentage of the elderly in our society are residents of such institutions at any one time. Nevertheless, approximately 6 percent of all deaths in our society occur in long-term care facilities (Lerner, 1970).

3. *Hospice programs* emphasize terminal care for dying persons and their families. In our society, that care is most likely to take place in the home, but it may also be delivered in a hospital, long-term care facility, a hospice facility under the supervision of a hospice team, or a hospice day care program (Corr & Corr, 1992a). Since their inception in the United States, hospice programs have primarily cared for elderly cancer patients, but hospice principles have also been applied to care of children (Corr & Corr, 1985a; Martin, 1989), persons with AIDS (Buckingham, 1992), individuals with motor neuron diseases like amyotrophic lateral sclerosis (ALS or Lou Gehrig's disease) (O'Gorman & O'Brien, 1990; Thompson, 1990), and others who are coping with various life-threatening conditions. Hospice programs currently care for approximately 10 percent of all deaths in our society.

This chapter has sought to describe typical programmatic responses made by our society to the demands of caring for the dying. In addition, ten principles have been identified in the hospice philosophy that can serve as a model for such care and that can be applied in a wide range of institutional and programmatic settings.

QUESTIONS FOR REVIEW AND DISCUSSION

1. This chapter discussed several programs of care for dying persons, including hospice, hospitals, and long-term care facilities. Think about being a person with a life-threatening illness (perhaps you can think about someone you knew, such as a relative or a friend). What might be the advantages and limitations of being cared for by each of these programs of care?

2. This chapter argues that modern hospitals are the products of a long historical and social development. Think about the process that led to the present

form of hospitals in American society. What were some of the turning points that led to the modern hospital? In this reflection, think about political and social changes, as well as theoretical and conceptual ones. What sorts of experiences (if any) have you had with hospitals?

3. How would you describe the essential elements in a hospice-type program of care? Why were those elements implemented (at least at first) in different ways in England, Canada, and the United States? Could hospice-type principles be implemented in other institutions (for example, hospitals or long-term care facilities) in the United States? What sorts of experiences (if any) have you had with hospice programs?

SUGGESTED READINGS

Hospice principles are set forth in numerous works, such as the following:

Ajemian, I., & Mount, B. M. (Eds.). (1980). *The R. V. H. Manual on Palliative/Hospice Care.*

Corr, C. A., & Corr, D. M. (Eds.). (1983). *Hospice Care: Principles and Practice.*

Davidson, G. W. (Ed.). (1985). *The Hospice: Development and Administration.* (2nd ed.).

National Hospice Organization. (1987). *Standards of a Hospice Program of Care.*

Saunders, C. M. (Ed.). (1984). *The Management of Terminal Malignant Disease.* (2nd ed.).

Stoddard, S. (1992). *The Hospice Movement: A Better Way of Caring for the Dying* (rev. ed.).

Hospice principles are applied to situations involving children in the following:

Corr, C. A., & Corr, D. M. (Eds.). (1985). *Hospice Approaches to Pediatric Care.*

Martin, B. B. (Ed.). (1989). *Pediatric Hospice Care: What Helps.*

Martinson, I. M., Martin, B., Lauer, M., Birenbaum, L. K., & Eng, B. (1991). *Children's Hospice/Home Care: An Implementation Manual for Nurses.*

For developments in medicine, hospitals, and long-term care facilities, consult:

Bennett, C. (1980). *Nursing Home Life: What It Is and What It Could Be.*

Gubrium, J. F. (1975). *Living and Dying at Murray Manor.*

Moss, F., & Halamanderis, V. (1977). *Too Old, Too Sick, Too Bad: Nursing Homes in America.*

Rosenberg, C. E. (1987). *The Care of Strangers: The Rise of America's Hospital System.*

Shield, R. R. (1988). *Uneasy Endings: Daily Life in an American Nursing Home.*

Starr, P. (1982). *The Social Transformation of American Medicine.*

Stevens, R. (1989). *In Sickness and in Wealth: American Hospitals in the Twentieth Century.*

PART III

BEREAVEMENT

Toynbee (1968a) has observed that "two-sidedness . . . is a fundamental feature of death . . . There are always two parties to a death; the person who dies and the survivors who are bereaved" (p. 267). In fact, as noted in Part II, the situation is even more complicated than this would suggest. Prior to death, issues in coping with dying concern not only the person who is dying but also his or her family members, friends, and care providers (whether lay persons or professionals). All of these individuals, except the dying person, are survivors-to-be. When death does occur one can rightly say that "a person's death is not only an ending; it is also a beginning—for the survivors" (Shneidman, 1973, p. 33).

What are the experiences of these survivors like? Nearly every human being who is alive has some sense of what the experience might be like because nearly everyone has survived some sort of loss in his or her own life. There are many different types of loss—not all of which are consequences of or related to death. Much language refers to experiences of bereavement, grief, and mourning. These are, in fact, fundamental experiences in human life.

Still, much remains to be learned and clarified about the experiences of those who have survived the death of someone they love. The following three chapters are devoted to analyses of the most important features of those experiences. Chapter 8 describes key elements and variables that are prominent in experiences of coping with loss and grief. Chapter 9 offers practical advice about things that can be said or done (and things that should *not* be said or done) to help those who are coping with loss. Finally, Chapter 10 provides an analysis of funeral practices and other memorial rituals in America, including a description of their principal elements and an interpretation of some of the ways in which they may or may not be helpful to those who are coping with loss.

CHAPTER 8

Coping with Loss and Grief

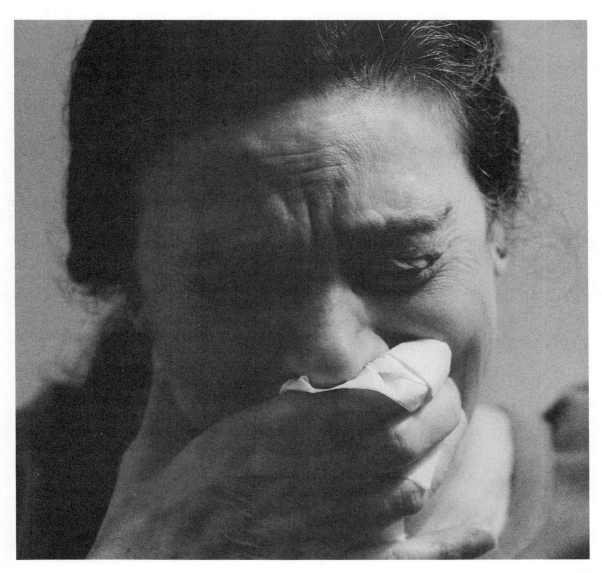

This chapter addresses the experiences of loss, grief, and bereavement encountered by those who survive a death. The goal is to clarify the nature of these experiences, the language and concepts employed to understand them, and the processes involved in coping with them.

The chapter begins with an example of a grieving person and some comments on the key concepts of loss and bereavement, which underlie all that follows. This leads to an extended analysis of the experience of grief and of the main variables that appear to be significant in grief and bereavement. Next, the related experience of mourning is considered both in terms of its normal processes (understood in the theoretical literature as phases or tasks) and its outcomes. The chapter ends with brief explorations of three variations on grief: disenfranchised grief, anticipatory grief, and pathological grief reactions or complicated mourning.

Stella Bridgman: A Grieving Person

Stella Bridgman was in her early 40s when she came to a meeting of a local chapter of the Compassionate Friends, a self-help mutual-aid group for bereaved parents. Recently, her 18-year-old son had committed suicide after a troubled history involving chemical dependency (starting with marijuana and beer, but escalating to hard liquor, cocaine, and crack) and difficulties at home, in school, and with his part-time job. It was quickly evident that Stella's pain was sharp-edged and very powerful. Her need to express her feelings dominated that night's meeting from the moment when she first spoke.

Stella had not wanted to come to the meeting. But she had no place else left to turn. So many of her relatives, neighbors, and co-workers had withdrawn or turned away from the intensity of her anger and tears. They did not know what to say to her or what to do that might help, so they said and did nothing. Finally, a friend brought her to the self-help group.

Stella talked about the shock of finding her son's body (despite his erratic behavior), the pain of losing someone who had been a part of her, the anger at him for doing this to her and to his 15-year-old sister, and the guilt in asking herself what else she might have done to prevent his death. The group acknowledged the reality and the appropriateness of her feelings. They let her talk and cry. All of them had also experienced the death of a loved person, the loneliness without that person, and the fear that in addition they would lose their memories of that person as others stopped mentioning his or her name and seemed to erase that person from their lives.

In subsequent meetings, Stella gradually told the group more about herself. We learned about earlier losses that she had experienced. Her father had died in a distant war when she was a little child; she had not really known him. Her mother, a heavy smoker, had developed early lung cancer and died after a difficult illness a little more than 20 years ago. That was the first death that had seemed to have real significance in her life. For support, she had turned to relatives and to the young man whom she later married.

The death of her husband in a fiery automobile accident eight years later was a harsh experience that left Stella with two young children, a small sum of money from insurance and savings, and no job. She had never anticipated that possibility. All the widows she had known were elderly women. Stella turned to her church, became very protective of her children, rejoined the work force, and eventually was married again to a widower whom she met at a church social activity. Her son disliked his new stepfather and the three older siblings who came with him into the new "blended" or "reconstituted" family.

One night at the Compassionate Friends meeting, Stella summed up her losses by saying that the death of her mother had seemed like the death of her past, and the death of her first husband had seemed like the end of her present life, but the suicide of her son was like the death of her hopes and the severing of her links to the future.

Stella asked over and over: What did I do? Why did this happen? How can I go on? One night, she said she felt like she was going crazy. Members of the group agreed that they had felt that way, too. She expressed amazement that other bereaved parents could speak of their dead child without breaking down. How could they get through the holidays or even find it possible to laugh once in a while? She tried to tell herself that if they had also walked "in the valley of the shadow of death" and were now able to find some way to live on, perhaps she could also. But she could not see how to do that yet.

Loss and Bereavement

To love is to give "hostages to fortune" (Bacon, 1962, p. 22). That is, everyone who experiences love or who forms an attachment to another runs the risk of losing the loved object and suffering the consequences of loss. If so, then "to grieve is to pay ransom to love" (Shneidman, 1983, p. 29).

Of course, it is in loving that a person shares with others and enriches his or her life. Stella Bridgman loved the father she had never met, her mother, her two husbands, her own children, and her second husband's children. Not to love in these ways is to cut oneself off from the rewards of human attachment—to restrict and impoverish one's life. As Brantner (in Worden, 1982, p. xi) said so aptly: "Only people who avoid love can avoid grief. The point is to learn from it and remain vulnerable to love." To learn about grief and mourning, we begin with some thoughts about loss and bereavement.

Loss

There are many sorts of losses that occur throughout human lives (Viorst, 1986). For example, my relationship with someone may break up, I may be fired or laid off from my job, I may have to leave my home and relocate, I may not be able to find a prized possession, I may not succeed in some competition, my health may deteriorate or I may experience an amputation, or someone close to me may die. What all of these losses have in common is that the individual who loses something is separated from and deprived of the lost person, object, status, or relationship. The central point is the termination of the relationship. How any individual experiences a particular loss depends upon how that person valued what was lost.

Death inevitably involves endings, separations, and losses, as is evident in the example of Stella Bridgman. What death will mean to me as a survivor depends upon the loss that I experience and the ways in which I interpret that loss. For example, death may mean the end of the time that I share with my spouse, a separation from one of my parents, or the loss of my child. However I interpret death—for example, in the framework of a possible afterlife and potential reunion with the loved one—losses through death are usually painful for those who are left behind, because death is final in this life. In addition, death-related losses may be complicated in various ways—for example, when death is sudden, unexpected, or traumatic.

Losses that are not related to death can be complicated in their own ways. Such losses may be equally as hurtful as some losses arising from death, or perhaps even more hurtful. For example, approximately 50 percent of all marriages in the United States now end in divorce. When that happens, there is often one spouse who wishes to terminate the relationship, another who does not wish to do so or who is less determined on that outcome, and perhaps a third person (such as a child) who is involved in what is happening and directly affected by its implications but not immediately able to influence what will take place. Each of these people will experience different sorts of losses in the divorce. As in death, there are elements of loss in divorce, but there are also elements of deliberate choice, guilt, and blame that are not always associated with a death, as well as theoretical opportunities for reconciliation and the inevitable implications of subsequent life decisions by all who are involved in the aftermath of a divorce.

Often, as we reflect upon our lives, we can identify the individuals or objects whose loss would mean a great deal to us. But sometimes the meaning and value of the lost person or object is only fully appreciated after the loss has taken place. In any event, to understand the ramifications of a loss, we must look back to the underlying attachments or relationships on which they are founded (Bowlby, 1982).

Bereavement

The term *bereavement* refers to the state of being bereaved or deprived of something; that is, bereavement identifies the objective situation of individuals who have experienced a loss. Both the noun *bereavement* and the adjective *bereaved* derive from a less-familiar root verb, *reave,* which means "to despoil, rob, or forcibly deprive" (Simpson & Weiner, 1989, Vol. 13, p. 295). In short, a bereaved person is one who has been deprived, robbed, plundered, or stripped of something.

In all of this language is the implication that the stolen person or object was a valued one, together with a suggestion of violence in the way in which the deprivation took place. In principle, the loss experienced by bereaved people could be of many different kinds; in fact, this language is most often used in American society to refer to the situation of those who have experienced a loss through death. In other words, our language tends to assume that death always entails a more or less brutal loss of someone or something that is important to the bereaved person.

The experience of bereavement may encompass one or more of the following central elements: (1) *grief*—which responds to loss; (2) *loneliness*—which responds to deprivation; and (3) *shame*—which responds to social stigma in certain types of loss (Parkes, 1987a). Our focus here is on the basic experience of grief and the related notion of mourning. In this context, loneliness arising from deprivation of the comforting presence of the loved object or person will be readily understandable, and social stigma leading to shame will be addressed through the notion of disenfranchised grief.

Grief

We will address three key questions about grief: (1) What is grief? (2) How does it relate to other concepts? and (3) What are its implications?

Understanding Grief

Grief is the *response to loss.* When one suffers a loss, one grieves. The word *grief* signifies one's reaction, both internally and externally, to the impact of the loss. The term arises from the grave or heavy weight that presses upon bereaved survivors (Simpson & Weiner, 1989, Vol. 6, 834–835). Not to grieve for a significant loss is an aberration, suggesting that there was no real attachment prior to the loss, that the relationship was complicated in ways that set it apart from the ordinary, or that one is suppressing or hiding one's responses to the loss.

The term *grief* is often defined as "the emotional response to loss" (for example, DeSpelder & Strickland, 1992, p. 234). But such a definition is inadequate on its own. One's response to loss is not just emotional. Grief is broader, more complex, and more deep-seated than this definition would suggest.

Grief can manifest itself in numerous ways (Worden, 1991a):

- In *feelings,* such as sadness, anger, guilt and self-reproach, anxiety, loneliness, fatigue, helplessness, shock, yearning, emancipation, relief, or numbness
- In *physical sensations,* such as hollowness in the stomach, tightness in the throat or chest, oversensitivity to noise, shortness of breath, lack of energy, a sense of depersonalization, muscle weakness, or dry mouth
- In *cognitions,* such as disbelief, confusion, preoccupation, a sense of presence of the deceased, or hallucinations
- In *behaviors,* such as sleep or appetite disturbances, absentmindedness, social withdrawal, dreams of the deceased, crying, avoiding reminders of the deceased, searching and calling out, sighing, restless overactivity, or visiting places and cherishing objects that remind one of the deceased

These are essentially physical, psychological, and behavioral manifestations of grief. To them, we should also add explicit recognition of *social* and

Grief can be an isolating experience.

spiritual manifestations of grief. These include difficulties in interpersonal relationships, problems in functioning in an organization, a search for a sense of meaning, hostility toward God, or a realization that one's value framework is inadequate to cope with this particular loss.

Thinking of grief solely as a matter of feelings risks misunderstanding and missing this full range of responsiveness to loss. For example, we do not want to risk dismissing out of hand analyses of morbidity and mortality associated with bereavement (for example, Rees & Lutkins, 1967), as well as research concerned with psychosomatic and biochemical dimensions of bereavement (Fredrick, 1971, 1977, 1983). Emotional stress arising from loss has been associated with increased risk of illness or death of the survivor (Glick, Weiss, & Parkes, 1974). An overly narrow understanding of grief will fail to establish an adequate foundation for a comprehensive appreciation of bereavement and mourning.

Appreciating the Nature of Grief

It has been noted that there are many resemblances between grief and disease (Engel, 1961). This is true in the sense that the impact of a significant loss may affect the bereaved person's ability to function, at least temporarily. Metaphors of healing are commonly employed to describe the period of time required to overcome this impaired functioning. Also, there are similarities between the sadness and other responses that are manifestations of grief and the symptoms associated with the clinical diagnosis of depression.

However, Freud (1917/1959a) long ago recognized the differences between what he called "mourning" and "melancholia." The former term pertains to normal processes associated with grief; the latter is Freud's language for the illness state of depression. Both grief and depression may involve a kind of pressing down and withdrawal from the world. But depression is a pathological form of grieving characterized by angry impulses toward the ambivalently "loved" person that are turned inward toward the self (compare Clayton, Herjanic, Murphy, & Woodruff, 1974). Normal grief reactions do not include the loss of self-esteem commonly found in most clinical depression. Other research on various forms of grief and depression confirms that they are, in principle, quite different sorts of experiences (for example, Schneider, 1980; Zisook & DeVaul, 1983, 1984, 1985). Thus, Stella Bridgman was beset by her grief, but she was not clinically depressed.

It is also useful to distinguish between grief and guilt. As has been said, *grief* is the broad term for responses to loss; *guilt* refers to thoughts and feelings that assign blame (often self-blame), fault, or culpability for the loss. Guilt in bereavement may be realistic or unrealistic. Suggestions of guilt may arise from one's role (for example, that of parent and protector) or from something that one believes he or she should or should not have done. This was the case of Stella Bridgman: even though she knew that her son had brought upon himself many of his earlier difficulties and finally his own death, she wondered whether she could not have found some way to help him.

Unrealistic guilt may be part of a process of *reality testing* in bereavement by which accepting blame is one way of confirming that there was, in fact, nothing that could have been done to prevent the death. By contrast with depression, when guilt is experienced in bereavement, "it is usually guilt associated with some specific aspect of the loss rather than a general, overall sense of culpability" (Worden, 1991a, p. 30). In other words, guilt may be part of the total grief reaction, but it may be useful to disentangle this particular strand from the larger experience and address it separately.

One can conclude from this that ordinary, uncomplicated grief is a healthy, normal, and appropriate response to loss. Bereaved persons may not be at ease with their situation or with themselves. But they are not diseased in the sense of being ill. In a society in which encounters with death, grief, and bereavement may not be very frequent for many people, it may be true that these are not very usual or ordinary experiences. But that which is unusual is scarce, infrequent, or uncommon, not necessarily strange in the way disease is foreign to health. Stella Bridgman had experienced several deaths and bereavements in her life. Each was hard in its own way, but in each case she came to realize that her grief was normal and fully warranted by her need to cope with her losses.

For these reasons, we have spoken of *signs* or *manifestations* of grief, not *symptoms*. In itself, grief is not the kind of response to loss that should lead us to speak of symptoms, since grief is not an illness or disease from which symptoms would arise.

Two qualifications should immediately be added: (1) individuals who are psychiatrically ill can experience bereavement and grief; (2) loss and grief can lead to pathological or complicated mourning.

The first of these qualifications reminds us that the appropriateness of the bereavement experience must be assessed individually in each case. That is, grief is very much an individualized phenomenon, peculiar in many ways to each particular griever and loss. Different grievers are likely to respond in different ways to the same loss; the same griever is likely to respond in different ways to different losses. One person's grief should not be construed as a standard by which others should evaluate themselves. To keep this in mind is to be sensitive and open to the very broad range of manifestations associated with loss. Thus, normal responses to loss will not be confused with the abnormalities of illness and pathology.

The second qualification is a reminder that this analysis of grief and mourning will not be complete until it addresses the subject of pathological or complicated mourning at the end of this chapter. In the meantime, the basic point of view in this chapter is that grief is a healthy, normal, and (until shown to be otherwise) appropriate response to loss.

Interpreting the Implications of Grief

Some college students express the wish that if they were to die their friends should have a party and not be sad. This misunderstands the nature both of feelings and of human attachments. It is essentially a way of telling people that they ought not to feel what they actually are feeling. Feelings are real; they cannot be turned on and off at will. All human beings have emotional responses and do not always have much control over what those responses will be when events impact upon their lives. In addition, loss always has social implications for those who go on living (Osterweis, Solomon, & Green, 1984). When I love someone, I have feelings and usually need to express them. When I lose someone whom I have loved, I also have feelings and may often need to express them.

Moreover, after a death only part of our grief is for the person who died. Perhaps for the most part, we grieve for ourselves as people who have been left behind. That is why we grieve even after a slow, lingering, or painful death when we believe that the dying person has been released from distress and is at last at rest. And it is why we grieve even when our theology assures us that the dead person has gone on to a better life. Whatever else has happened, as bereaved survivors we have experienced a real loss. It is not selfish to react to that loss with grief; it is simply a realistic human response.

As has already been noted, experiences of bereavement and grief may be more and more unusual or infrequent in a society in which average life expectancies have been greatly extended and death seems less frequently to enter into our lives. But we should not misinterpret this by thinking that bereavement and grief are *abnormal* parts of life. Loss, death, and grief are normal and natural parts of human life. Because they may be unusual in our experience and are typically associated with a feeling of being out of control, it often appears to bereaved persons that they are losing their minds. This is rarely true. Responding and adjusting to loss is a healthful process, not a morbid one. It may take a certain courage to face one's grief and to permit oneself to experience one's reactions to significant losses, but ultimately this is undertaken in the interests of one's own welfare (Tatelbaum, 1980).

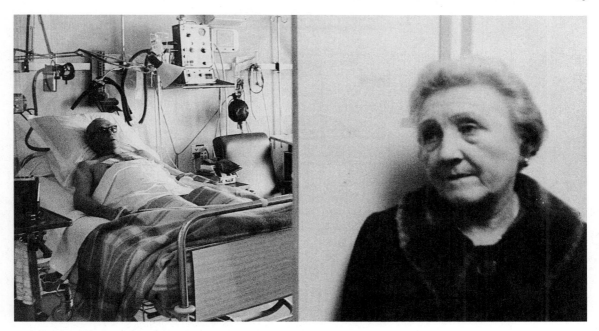

Loss breeds loneliness and powerlessness.

Mourning Can Be Very Selfish

Mourning can be very selfish. When someone you love has died, you tend to recall best those few moments and incidents that helped to clarify your sense, not of the person who has died, but of your own self. And if you loved the person a great deal . . . your sense of who you are will have been clarified many times, and so you will have many such moments to remember.

SOURCE From R. Banks, 1991.

What Makes a Difference in Bereavement and Grief?

Several scholars have undertaken to identify the principal variables that appear to make a difference in the ways in which bereavement and grief are experienced (for example, Fulton, 1970; Jackson, 1957; Parkes, 1975; Sanders, 1989). Four factors seem central: (1) the nature of the prior attachment or the perceived value that the lost person or thing has for the bereaved individual; (2) the way in which the loss occurred and the circumstances of the bereavement; (3) the coping strategies that the bereaved individual has learned to use in dealing with previous losses in his or her life; and (4) the social support that the bereaved individual receives after the loss. The first three of these factors are considered here; discussion of social support will be delayed until Chapter 9.

Prior attachments or relationships are not always what they seem to be. The full import of a relationship may not be appreciated until it is over. Some relationships are dependent, abusive, ambivalent, distorted, or complicated in many ways. Almost all relationships are multidimensional. A person whom I love is likely to be significant in my life in many ways—for example, as spouse, helpmate, homemaker, sometime enemy, lover, competitor, parent of my children, breadwinner, guide in difficult times, critic, comforter. Each of these dimensions will eventually be a part of my grief experience. Each represents a loss that will need to be grieved (Rando, 1984).

The way in which the loss takes place and the circumstances of the bereavement are also critical to the experience of grief. Some losses occur in shocking or traumatic ways (like the suicide of Stella Bridgman's son); others appear to be more gentle. Some losses can be foreseen or predicted; others cannot. Some losses occur gradually and allow time for adjustment; others are sudden. Some losses take place at a time in one's life when other burdens or challenges are heavy. Some losses are untimely in the sense that they run contrary to our expectations about the natural order of things; others seem to fit more appropriately into the overall scheme of things. As a general rule, deaths that are "off time"—that is, that occur much before or long after our expectations might have prepared us for them—are likely to be among those with which we find it most difficult to cope (Rando, 1984).

In Chapter 5, we noted that all of us throughout our lives develop *ways in which we cope with losses* of various sorts. But we may develop more or less satisfactory ways of coping. Once a significant loss or death occurs, we will likely cope in ways that make use of the repertoire of skills that we have previously acquired. That is why, despite all of the differences between death and other losses in life, it is usually a good rule of thumb to look at how someone has coped with other losses earlier in his or her life to predict how that person is likely to cope with death and bereavement (Shneidman, 1980). Developing new and more effective coping skills requires more time and energy than are usually available in the immediate aftermath of a death or other significant loss. Thus, Stella Bridgman's acquired coping skills did not seem adequate on their own to enable her to cope with the loss and grief arising from the suicide of her son.

The Family Context in Which Loss Occurs

Another important variable in the overall bereavement experience is the family context in which loss occurs. "A *family*," as Terkleson (1980, p. 23) has written, "is a small social system made up of individuals related to each other by means of strong reciprocal affections and loyalties, comprising a permanent household (or cluster of households) that persists over years and decades. Members enter by birth, adoption, or marriage, and leave only by

TABLE 8.1   The Stages of the Family Life Cycle

Family Life Cycle Stage	Emotional Process of Transition: Key Principles	Second-Order Changes in Family Status Required to Proceed Developmentally
1. Leaving home: Single young adults	Accepting emotional and financial responsibility for self	a. Differentiation of self in relation to family of origin b. Development of intimate peer relationships c. Establishment of self re: work and financial independence
2. The joining of families through marriage: The new couple	Commitment to new system	a. Formation of marital system b. Realignment of relationships with extended families and friends to include spouse.
3. Families with young children	Accepting new members into the system	a. Adjusting marital system to make space for child(ren) b. Joining in child-rearing, financial, and household tasks c. Realignment of relationships with extended family to include parenting and grandparenting roles
4. Families with adolescents	Increasing flexibility of family boundaries to include children's independence and grandparents' frailties	a. Shifting of parent-child relationships to permit adolescent(s) to move into and out of system b. Refocus on midlife marital and career issues c. Beginning shift toward joint caring for older generation
5. Launching children and moving on	Accepting a multitude of exits from and entries into the family system	a. Renegotiation of marital system as a dyad b. Development of adult-to-adult relationships between grown children and their parents c. Realignment of relationships to include in-laws and grandchildren d. Dealing with disabilities and death of parents (grandparents)
6. Families in later life	Accepting the shifting of generational roles	a. Maintaining own and/or couple functioning and interests in the face of physiological decline; exploration of new familial and social role options. b. Support for a more central role for middle generation c. Making room in the system for the wisdom and experience of the elderly, supporting the older generation without overfunctioning for them d. Dealing with loss of spouse, siblings, and other peers and preparation for own death; life review and integration

From Betty Carter and Monica McGoldrick, *The Changing Family Life Cycle: A Framework for Family Therapy,* Second Edition. Copyright © 1988 by Allyn and Bacon. Reprinted with permission.

death." Whatever our family may be historically, culturally, or in its own particularities, each of us is affected, as individuals and as members of the family group, by the lives and deaths of those who make up our family and by the family context in which we cope with loss.

In the case of a death-related loss, Walsh and McGoldrick (1991a) have argued that two major tasks confront family members and family units: (1) to share acknowledgment of the reality of death and to share the experience of loss; and (2) to reorganize the family system and to reinvest in other relationships and life pursuits. (Note that each of these combines two of Worden's [1991a] individual tasks of mourning and restates it in family systems terminology; compare Walsh & McGoldrick, 1988.) In addition to the variables noted in the previous section, these family tasks will be influenced by the family's cohesion and the differentiation of its members (for example, extremely enmeshed or disengaged families may well face complications in adapting to loss); the flexibility of the family system; whether it engages in open communication or secrecy; the availability to the family of extended family, social, and economic resources; the prior role and functioning of the deceased member in the family system; and the existence of conflicted or estranged relationships at the time of death (Walsh & McGoldrick, 1991a).

Further, McGoldrick and Walsh (1991a) have noted that it is useful to consider a life cycle perspective on family units. That is, losses occur at different points in what systems theorists portray as the three-generational family life cycle (Carter & McGoldrick, 1988; see Table 8.1): to unattached young adults who are between families (and who may experience the death of a young adult peer or sibling, a parent, or a grandparent); to young couples who are joining families and creating new family units through marriage (and who may experience the death of a spouse, an unborn child, a parent, a grandparent, or a sibling); to families with young children (who may experience the death of a spouse, a child, a parent, a grandparent, or a sibling); to families with adolescents (whose experiences may parallel those of families with young children); to families who are launching children and moving on (whose experiences may parallel those of families with adolescents); and to families in later life (who may experience the death of a peer, a spouse, or an adult child). Each of these families is coping with different challenges. Each of them may be affected in different ways and by different sorts of losses. And each of these family contexts may be complicated by untimely losses, disorders associated with recent or threatened losses, the concurrence of multiple losses or of loss with other major life cycle changes, or past traumatic loss and unresolved mourning.

Mourning: Processes and Outcomes

The term *mourning* indicates the processes of coping with loss and grief, and thus the attempt to manage those experiences by incorporating them into our ongoing lives (Siggins, 1966). Sometimes this is called "grieving" or, better yet, "grief work" (Lindemann, 1944). Mourning designates the ways in which we learn to live with loss, bereavement, and grief—to integrate them into our ongoing living.

In the Sermon on the Mount, Jesus said: "Blessed are those that mourn, for they shall be comforted." But bereavement and grief are a burden, not a blessing. If there is any blessing in the experience of bereavement, it can only be in the capacity to mourn. Only through mourning, through moving toward and working with one's grief, can one find any hope of eventual solace or comfort. Think of where Stella Bridgman would be if she had not found a support group to help her with her grief work. As Shneidman (1980, p. 179) has written: "Mourning is one of the most profound human experiences that it is possible to have. . . . The deep capacity to weep for the loss of a loved one and to continue to treasure the memory of that loss is one of our noblest human traits."

As a necessary process for those who are grieving, mourning takes two complementary forms. It is both an internal, private, or intrapersonal process—our inward struggles with the grief response; and an outward, public, or interpersonal process—the "expression" of the grief response. Our discussion of public or group processes in mourning will take place in Chapters 9 and 10; here, we concentrate on mourning as an intrapersonal or intrapsychic phenomenon, giving special attention to two primary theoretical models for interpreting mourning processes (phases versus tasks) and to the question of outcomes in mourning.

Phases in Mourning

Much attention has been paid to mourning in recent years in an effort to understand and explicate what is involved in grief work. Drawing upon work by Bowlby (1961, 1980, 1982), Parkes (1970, 1987) proposed that mourning involves four phases: (1) shock and numbness, (2) yearning and searching, (3) disorganization and despair, and (4) reorganization. These phases are said to be elements in an overall process of *realization*—that is, making real in one's inner, psychic world that which is already real in the outer, objective world.

Shock and numbness constitute an initial response to loss, although they may also recur at other times as one regrieves or works through one's grief again in different circumstances or at a later date. One is shocked or stunned at the impact of the loss. It is like being overwhelmed or being knocked off the familiar balance of one's life. One feels dazed or detached, as if one has been overloaded by news of the death and is unable to absorb or take in any further data. The effect is like being encircled by an invisible protective shield. This is similar to the "psychic numbing" or "psychic closing off" experienced by the survivors of the atomic bombing of Hiroshima (Lifton, 1967). The mourner seems to float through the next few moments or days, often unable to take care of basic needs like nutrition, hydration, or making decisions. This is a natural defense against bad news and unwanted pain. But it is almost always a temporary or transitory condition.

Yearning and searching represent an effort to return to things as they once were. As the pain of grief penetrates the dissolving barriers of shock and one realizes the magnitude of one's loss, one feels unwilling to acknowledge or relinquish that which no longer is. One yearns or pines for a time that is now gone and finds oneself falling into familiar patterns of setting his place at

A candlelight vigil in Michigan sponsored by Mothers Against Drunk Drivers (MADD).

the table or expecting her to come up the driveway at 6:00 P.M. Searching is triggered by a glimpse across a crowded room of someone who resembles him, by a passing whiff of her perfume, by the strains of "our" song (Parkes, 1970). In the objective situation, yearning and searching are doomed to failure. One can go home, but one can never go back. The past is simply no longer available as it once was. To grasp that is to realize and appreciate the depth, extent, and finality of the survivor's loss and grief.

Disorganization is an understandable reaction to the failure of efforts to reinvigorate the past. If my husband is dead, am I still a wife? If my child is dead, am I still a parent? Who am I as a survivor? These are questions of self-identity, but they are joined to practical questions of everyday living. Who will prepare dinner? How will I manage to care for our children without her? What will we do without his weekly paycheck? How can we comfort each other when we are both hurting from the death of our child? Should I sell the house and move back to the town where my family lives?

Individuals who are disorganized are often unable to concentrate on the challenges that beset them. They are easily distracted or are bewildered when it seems that everywhere they turn there are new claims made upon them. They find it difficult to focus their limited energies and to carry out or complete even small projects. It may be a real achievement to get through just a few moments, an hour, or one day at a time. Much that they had previously taken for granted has been called into question. Death has interfered with life. The effect is like walking into someone else's life—shuffling through an unfamiliar landscape, one that is unsettled, chaotic, and confused. The individual feels disoriented and unable to find his or her way.

Reorganization is initiated when one can begin to pick up the pieces of one's life again and start to shape them into some new order. Life is never the same as it once was after a significant loss or death. Once the fabric of one's life has been torn, it may be mended in one way or another, but some differences are always irrevocable. One has to find a new way of living as a person who now is no longer married or as a parent whose child now is no longer living. As each aspect of the loss is mourned, "new normals" must be developed for future living. Those who have loved us and who have died would surely want us to find constructive ways in which to reorganize our lives. But it is we, the bereaved survivors, who have to work that out in real life. Most bereaved persons do achieve some sort of reorganization in their lives. But it is a highly individual accomplishment.

The Bowlby/Parkes account of mourning is expressed in terms of four phases. Some writers have spun this out into five (Weizman & Kamm, 1985), seven (Kavanaugh, 1972), or ten (Westberg, 1971) phases. These are efforts to parse out elements in mourning in more precise ways, but it can be confusing when the proposed categories appear to overlap, are difficult to distinguish, or become impractical to apply.

This last point does not mean that the goal in a model of mourning is to have the fewest (or the most) elements. Like all theoretical explications, models of mourning arise from different concerns, serve different purposes, and should be evaluated in different ways. In general, however, the goal for a good theoretical model is to combine clarity, simplicity, and adequacy in explicating or helping to understand complex human experiences.

Many have thought that the four-phase Bowlby/Parkes model satisfies those requirements. Some have preferred a simpler account in which the two middle phases of yearning/searching and disorientation are essentially combined so as to result in a three-phase model: (1) shock, (2) a period of intense or active grieving, and (3) reestablishment of physical and mental balance (Gorer, 1965b; Miles, 1984; Tatelbaum, 1980; see Figure 8.1). The number of components in a model of this sort is not as important as its usefulness in helping us to understand the experiences of mourning.

Like stage-based models of coping with dying, phase-based models of mourning have their critics (for example, Wortman & Silver, 1989). Fundamentally, the argument is that these so-called phases are generalizations drawn from particular population groups that may not have been established with sufficient methodological rigor and that may not apply very well beyond the group from which they originated. That suggests that there is much yet to learn about the basic human experiences of grief and mourning, whether we seek to reconfirm a phase-based model or turn instead to another structure, such as the one offered by task-based models of mourning.

Tasks in Mourning

Worden (1991a) has recommended an effort to understand mourning by thinking in terms of tasks, rather than stages or phases. He has suggested

FIGURE 8.1   A model of parental grief. Adapted from M. S. Miles, 1984.

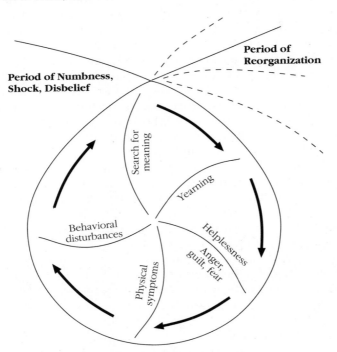

Period of Reorganization

Period of Numbness, Shock, Disbelief

Search for meaning

Yearning

Behavioral disturbances

Helplessness

Anger, guilt, fear

Physical symptoms

Period of Intense Grieving

four tasks in mourning: (1) to accept the reality of the loss, (2) to work through to the pain of grief, (3) to adjust to an environment in which the deceased is missing, and (4) to emotionally relocate the deceased and move on with life. A task-based model of this sort has the important advantage of emphasizing that mourning is an active process (Attig, 1991). This fits with the description of a task-based model for coping with dying seen earlier. Here, examining each of these four tasks in mourning provides another way of understanding the basic processes of individual mourning and their complexities.

Worden's first task involves efforts *to accept the reality of the loss.* These efforts may not be very apparent in initial grief responses, but they underlie all of the long-term work of mourning. When confronted by the death of someone we love, we often feel an immediate sense of unreality. "It can't be true," we say. Or: "This can't be happening to me." As a temporary or transitional response to a significant and perhaps abrupt change in our lives, this is wholly understandable. Nevertheless, making one's loss real and coping with one's grief involve acknowledging and accepting the reality of the death.

Failing to accept the reality of the loss is to move toward delusion and the bizarre. For example, in a fictional story by Faulkner (1924/1943) we gradually learn that the female protagonist has kept the body of her dead husband in the same bed with her in her house over a period of many years. In a real historical example, Queen Victoria of England had her husband's clothes and shaving gear laid out daily long after his death. Efforts like this to mummify or enshrine the possessions or even the body of the deceased, so that they will be ready for use when the person returns from what is imagined to be some sort of temporary absence, are really extreme attempts to suspend living at the precise moment of death in order not to face its harsh implications.

According to Worden, those who lose someone to whom they have been deeply attached are also challenged by a second task, *to work through to the pain of grief.* As Parkes (1987b, p. 192) has said, "Anything that continually allows the person to avoid or suppress this pain can be expected to prolong the course of mourning." Productive mourning acknowledges that the pain encountered in bereavement is essential and appropriate. The challenge is to find ways of experiencing the pain of grief that are not overwhelming for the individual in question. Ordinarily, the intensity of the survivor's pain and its tendency to consume the whole of the bereaved person's universe decline gradually as healthy mourning proceeds. One mother said: "It had to. You simply couldn't live with that level of pain."

Pain is hurtful, both to individuals and to those around them. Accordingly, many try to avoid their grief and pain. Some turn to drugs or alcohol to cover over their distress, but that only drives it underground in their bodies and psyches. Some people literally try to run away from grief or to erase all memory of the deceased. By obliterating all traces of the deceased's life they seek to be relieved of the task of facing the pain of grief consequent upon loss. Ultimately, all of this is futile. "Sooner or later some at least of those who avoid all conscious grieving break down—usually with some form of depression" (Bowlby, 1980, p. 158).

A society that is uncomfortable with expressions of grief may try to distract people from their loss or to assure them that the loss was not really all that significant. The wrongheaded message here is that people do not really need to grieve and that they should not "give in" to grief, which is said to be morbid and unhealthy. Sometimes, society reluctantly acknowledges that individuals need to grieve, but then gives them very unsubtle messages that they should only do so alone and in private. Prohibiting people from tasks that they need to accomplish—and may need help to learn to accomplish—is, in the end, only hurtful to the individuals in question and to society itself. Mourning is a healthy and healthful process.

The third of Worden's mourning tasks is *to adjust to an environment in which the deceased is missing.* Parkes has said, "In any bereavement it is seldom clear exactly what is lost" (1987b, p. 27). The bereaved survivor must engage in a voyage of discovery to determine the significance of the now-severed relationship, to identify each of the various roles that the deceased played in the relationship, and to adjust to the fact that the deceased is no longer available to play such roles (Rando, 1984). The burden of this task can encourage the survivor to try to ignore or withdraw from its requirements. But life calls us forward. Young children need to be changed, bathed, and fed whether or not a spouse has died. Someone must put food on the table and wash the dishes. Adopting a posture of helplessness is generally not a constructive coping technique—especially not as a permanent stance. Developing new skills and taking on roles that would have been satisfied by the deceased are productive ways of adjusting to loss and growing in the context of the postdeath environment.

Worden describes the fourth task of mourning as one that asks the bereaved person *to emotionally relocate the deceased and move on with life*. Both aspects of this task need careful attention, as Worden realizes. "Emotional relocation" does not suggest that survivors should forget the deceased person and erase his or her memory. That is neither possible nor desirable (Volkan, 1985). Similarly, "moving on with life" does not necessarily involve reinvesting in another relationship—for example, through remarriage or deciding to have another child. Options of this latter sort are not open to all bereaved persons. It may be sufficient for this task to remain open to the possibility of new relationships. Alternatively, one might soberly determine that a new, additional relationship is not required in a life that is already richly blessed and endowed with a good heritage from the past. Even when new relationships are undertaken, it is important to recognize that no two relationships are ever the same. Consequently, no new relationship, whatever it may be, will ever be identical to or play the same role in the survivor's life as the one that has now ended. Properly understood, a new relationship never supplants or takes the place of a previous relationship. A new spouse or child is just that: a new—and different—person.

Clearly, death changes relationships. To think that is not true is to delude oneself. Thus, the fourth task of mourning for the bereaved person is to modify the relationship or investment in the deceased in ways that remain satisfying but that also reflect the changed circumstances of life and death. I may continue to love my dead spouse and hold his or her memory dear in my heart, but it is probably less than helpful to pretend that he or she is still physically present and available to me in the same ways as before death. Satisfying Worden's fourth task would lead a bereaved person to readjust his or her relationship with the deceased person in the light of the loss that has taken place, to avoid becoming neurotically encumbered by the past in ways that diminish future quality in living, and to remain open to new relationships (perhaps of a different sort) and other forms of love. Stella Bridgman had successfully accomplished this task after the deaths of her mother and her first husband; now she had to find a way to go forward after the death of her son.

Like tasks in coping with dying, Worden's tasks in mourning reflect an interpretation of coping (here, mourning) as adaptation to loss. They depict mourning as a process or set of processes, not as a state. Tasks require effort, but can permit the bereaved person to regain control over his or her life. Worden indicates that the tasks of mourning "do not necessarily follow a specific order," even though "there is some ordering suggested in the definitions" (1991a, p. 10). He believes that the grieving person must accomplish these tasks before mourning can be completed. But that brings us to the question of outcomes of mourning, to which we now turn.

Outcomes of Mourning

Mourning has traditionally been described as leading to recovery, completion, or adaptation (Osterweis, Solomon, & Green, 1984, p. 52). To *recover* from one's grief seems to suggest that grief is an illness or that once one has recovered one is essentially unchanged by the experience. Like adjustment, *adaptation* seems to imply that one has made the best of an unpleasant situation. *Completion* seems to point to a fixed endpoint of the mourning process, after which there is no more grieving. Another popular term, *resolution*, seems to suggest that one has coped and is finished with one's responses to loss and bereavement. In other words, unless qualified, *resolution* appears to imply that mourning is now over and done with.

Many have tried to assign a specified time period—for example, several weeks or months, one year—as being necessary or sufficient for bringing mourning to an end. "Time heals," we are frequently told. This fits nicely with comparisons between bereavement and physical wounds. However, it is not true. Time alone does not heal. What really counts is how that time is used. The central issue is the nature of the mourning process and the outcomes to which it actually does lead.

As a rough guideline or rule of thumb, we might say that mourning has advanced satisfactorily when the survivor is able to think of the deceased person without the same intensity of pain that was previously experienced. This usually occurs when the survivor can once again take up tasks of daily living and can reinvest in life. For most people, this takes much more time than society is usually willing to concede, although for some it may not take as long. Certainly, the first year of bereavement—with all of its anniversaries, special days, and moments that repeatedly remind the survivor of the loss experienced—is a time of special challenge for the bereaved. But there is nothing magic in a single year (Clayton, 1973, 1974; Glick, Weiss, & Parkes, 1974; Parkes, 1971).

Perhaps it is better to say with Worden (1991a, p. 19): "There is a sense in which mourning can be finished, when people regain an interest in life, feel more hopeful, experience gratification again, and adapt to new roles. There is also a sense in which mourning is never finished." When bereaved persons are asked, "When did your grief end?" or "When was your mourning over?" they often respond: "Never." A bereaved person may recover from the initial impact of loss and acute grief, or from subsequent eruptions of renewed grief, while never fully completing the grief work or mourning involved in learning to live with the same loss and grief.

Bereaved families seven to nine years after the death of a child were asked how they had dealt with the "empty space" in their lives (McClowry, Davies, May, Kulenkamp, & Martinson, 1987). Three strategies were identified in the responses: (1) "getting over it," (2) "filling the emptiness," and (3) "keeping the connection." That is, some parents and other family members interpreted the mourning process as one of putting their grief behind them and getting over their responses to the loss. Others sought to fill up the empty space in their lives. Usually, this resulted in efforts at "keeping

When Is Mourning Complete?

The emotional pain caused by loss suffered does not move toward forgetfulness. It moves, rather, in the direction of enriched remembrance; the memory becomes an integral part of the mourner's personality. The work of mourning has been completed when the person (or cherished thing) no longer appears as an absence in a barren world but has come to reside securely within one's heart. Each of us must grieve in his or her own manner and at his or her own pace. For many people, one year seems to bring completion. Others require much more or much less time. Periodic waves of grief are often felt for the remainder of one's life. The mourning process must be given the freedom to find its own depth and rhythm; it cannot be artificially accelerated. A loss, like a physical wound, cannot heal overnight. There is no way to hurry the stages of tissue growth and there is no way to speed up the healing process of mourning. But when mourning has been completed, the mourner comes to feel the inner presence of the loved one, no longer an idealized hero or a maligned villain, but a presence with human dimensions. Lost irreversibly in objective time, the person is present in a new form within one's mind and heart, tenderly present in inner time without the pain and bitterness of death. And once the loved one has been accepted in this way he or she can never again be forcefully removed.

SOURCE From (with minor adaptations) R. C. Cantor, 1978.

busy'' or devoting energies to some other focus in their lives. This may be compatible with a periodic sense of the recurrence of the empty space. Still others found it important to maintain their connection to the deceased child by ensuring that he or she would remain a valued person as they went forward with their lives. Keeping the connection usually involved integrating the pain and loss into their lives, often by cherishing vivid memories and stories about the deceased child.

This research seems to suggest that mourning need not have a single outcome for all bereaved persons. As a process of coping with loss and grief, mourning is at least partly concerned with work involving "realization" (Parkes, 1987b) or "unlearning the expected presence of the deceased" (Rakoff, 1974, p. 159). But another aspect of mourning is "enriched remembrance" (Cantor, 1978), which should free the survivor to live a meaningful life in his or her new situation—without abandoning the deceased person. If this is accurate, at least for some people mourning may be a process of adjusting to the new situation created by the loss, addressing the urgent demands of acute grief, carrying forward the legacy of the relationship into the new post-death life, and continuing the work of adaptation in ways that may endure or recur for the rest of the survivor's life.

Variations on Grief

Understanding of bereavement, grief, and mourning is enhanced by considering three particular topics: disenfranchised grief; anticipatory grief; and pathological grief reactions or complicated mourning.

Disenfranchised Grief

The death system in every society usually conveys to its members—whether in formal and explicit ways or through more informal and subtle messages—its views about who can grieve which losses and in which ways. Social norms of this sort may or may not be helpful to individuals; their primary function is more likely to be to preserve what society perceives as its needs and the needs of interactions between its members. From time to time, the existence and character of social norms concerned with grieving has become the object of satire by social critics such as Mark Twain (see "At the Funeral") and of critical examination by scholars who are concerned with the implications of such norms.

For example, Doka (1989b, p. 4) has defined "disenfranchised grief" as "the grief that persons experience when they incur a loss that is not or cannot be openly acknowledged, publicly mourned, or socially supported." This is a useful concept because it recognizes the fact that grief always occurs within a particular social or cultural context and it emphasizes the many ways—constructive and unconstructive—in which that context can contribute to the experiences of the individual griever. Also, the ways in which grief is disenfranchised offer additional perspectives from which we can recognize important elements that are central to the bereavement experience (Pine et al., 1990).

According to Doka (1989b), grief can be disenfranchised in three primary ways: (1) the relationship is not recognized, (2) the loss is not recognized, or (3) the griever is not recognized. It may also be that some sorts of deaths, such as those involving suicide or AIDS, are "disenfranchising deaths" in the sense that they either are not well recognized or are associated with a high degree of social stigma (Goffman, 1963). Each of these three basic categories clarifies experiences of disenfranchisement encountered by many bereaved persons.

First, American society tends to emphasize kin-based relationships and roles. "The underlying assumption is that the 'closeness of relationship' exists only among spouses and/or immediate kin" (Folta & Deck, 1976, p. 235). But this is not correct. Thus, Folta and Deck (1976, p. 239) conclude that "rates of morbidity and mortality as a result of unresolved grief may be in fact higher for friends than for kin." Unsuspected, past, or secret relationships may simply not be publicly recognized or socially sanctioned. These could include relationships between friends, colleagues, in-laws, ex-spouses, or former lovers, and nontraditional relationships such as extra-marital affairs or homosexual relationships.

Individuals can share their grief by advocating for the social recognition of loss.

At the Funeral

Where a blood relation sobs, an intimate friend should choke up, a distant acquaintance should sigh, a stranger should merely fumble sympathetically with his handkerchief. Where the occasion is military, the emotions should be graded according to military rank, the highest officer present taking precedence in emotional violence, and the rest modifying their feelings according to their position in the service.

SOURCE From Mark Twain, *Letters from the Earth*, ed. B. DeVoto, New York: Harper & Row, 1962.

Second, the significance of some losses is not recognized by society. These might include perinatal death, losses associated with elective abortion, or the death of a pet. Similarly, advanced chronic brain syndrome or dementia may involve the loss of that individual's persona in such a manner and degree that significant others perceive the individual to be psychosocially dead, even though biological life continues.

Third, the bereaved person may not be recognized by society as one who is capable of grief or who has a need to mourn. Young children and the very old are often disenfranchised in this way, as are mentally disabled persons.

As Doka (1989b, p. 7) has observed, "The problem of disenfranchised grief can be expressed in a paradox. The very nature of disenfranchised grief creates additional problems for grief, while removing or minimizing sources of support.'' Thus, many situations of disenfranchised grief involve intensified emotional reactions (for example, anger, guilt, or powerlessness), ambivalent relationships (as in cases of abortion or among ex-spouses), and concurrent crises (such as those involving legal and financial problems) at the very time when factors that usually facilitate mourning (for instance, the existence of funeral rituals or possibilities for helping to plan and take part in such rituals) and opportunities to obtain social support (for example, through time off from work, speaking about the loss, receiving expressions of sympathy, or finding solace within some religious tradition) are unavailable. Clearly, issues associated with disenfranchised grief are becoming more prevalent in contemporary society and will require increased sensitivity from a caring community.

Anticipatory Grief

Since Lindemann's (1944) pioneering research on acute grief, there has been much interest in and controversy concerning the concept of anticipatory grief (Aldrich, 1963; Fulton & Fulton, 1971; Fulton & Gottesman, 1980; Rando, 1986c, 1988a; Schoenberg, Carr, Kutscher, Peretz, & Goldberg, 1974). This concept refers to grief experienced prior to a loss—that is, in advance of, but somehow still in relation to, impending death, such as during the dying process.

Before entering into the conceptual debates about anticipatory grief, we should set aside two misunderstandings. First, forewarning of death is not the same as anticipatory grief (Rando, 1986c; Siegel & Weinstein, 1983). Anticipatory grief may depend at least in part upon forewarning, but those who are forewarned of death may or may not enter into a process of anticipatory grieving.

Second, some comments concerning anticipatory grief reveal inadequate theoretical frameworks. That is, some people appear to think of anticipatory grief as a device for achieving predeath progress in or completion of grieving that would otherwise have been a project for the postdeath period. Here grief seems to be conceived of in terms of a "hydrological model"—that is, as a bucket of tears that must eventually be shed or poured out and that can be emptied (at least in part) either before or after a death. That is incorrect. If anticipatory grief means anything, it may affect the quality of postdeath bereavement, but it does not imply that postdeath grieving can somehow be accomplished (in whole or in part) prior to death.

The debate over anticipatory grief is properly joined by those who argue that nothing of the sort can really occur, since the task for a significant other—for example, a wife—is to support and continue to love her husband during the time when he is dying (Parkes & Weiss, 1983; Silverman, 1974). In this view, which seems to interpret grief as a process of decathexis or disattachment, grief prior to a death would involve withdrawal from and betrayal of the dying person. Obviously, if there is anything at all in human experience that can rightly be called "anticipatory grief," we will have to describe it carefully. Still, comparisons and contrasts between pre- and postdeath grief may help us to achieve one more way to understand what goes on when humans deal with loss, bereavement, grief, and mourning.

The concept of anticipatory grief depends upon two important aspects of attachment and loss: their temporality and their multidimensional nature (Rando, 1986c). As dying moves toward death, losses occur across time. At any given point in the dying process, some of these losses have already taken place, others are currently going on, and still others (including death itself) have yet to occur. For example, when a husband is in an advanced state of dying, a wife may realize that she has already lost the help that he used to give her around the house, that she is currently losing the vigorous ways in which he used to express his love for her, and that she will lose in the near future the comfort of his presence and their hope for time together in their retirement years.

Some of these losses have already occurred; they may engender grief and be mourned. Some of these losses are just now taking place. Others have yet to occur. All are compatible with efforts to maintain the loving attachments that continue to characterize the relationship between two living people. In these ways, there can be grief and mourning prior to death, although that grief and mourning are in many ways directed toward losses that have already occurred or are just now taking place. It would appear that grief and mourning directed to past or present losses are not incompatible with strengthening bonds of attachment in the face of losses that have not yet taken place.

Pathological Grief Reactions or Complicated Mourning

Is there such a thing as a pathological grief reaction—that is, grief (or mourning) that is not only unusual but also abnormal in the sense of being deviant and unhealthy? Such grieving would truly be a reflection or a species of illness. Thus far, this chapter has maintained that at least for the most part, the human experience of grief (and mourning) is normal and healthy. Still, all human processes can become distorted and unhealthy—usually when they are carried to excess. Moreover, it is obvious that loss and bereavement can happen to individuals who are already disturbed in some significant psychiatric sense. Thus, it may be useful to say something about aberrant forms of grieving, both as a contrast to healthful forms of grieving and as a guide for helpers—whose work will be discussed in Chapter 9.

The tendency among contemporary scholars is to speak of complicated grief reactions or complicated mourning, rather than pathological grief (Volkan, 1970, 1985). The language of pathology is judgmental in tone and may fail to take into account the critical distinction between grief and mourning. Complicated grief reactions are those that overwhelm the bereaved person in a persistent way, that lead the person to maladaptive behavior, or that do not move in productive ways toward satisfactory outcomes in mourning. They are, in short, excessive, distorted, or unproductive (Demi & Miles, 1987).

Worden (1991a) describes four basic types of complicated grief reactions: (1) *chronic grief reactions*, which are prolonged in duration and do not lead to an appropriate outcome; (2) *delayed grief reactions*, in which grief may be inhibited, suppressed, or postponed—here the term *unresolved* does seem appropriate; (3) *exaggerated grief reactions*, which are excessive and disabling in ways that may lead to the development of a phobia or irrational fear; and (4) *masked grief reactions*, in which individuals experience symptoms or behaviors—including the complete absence of grief (Deutsch, 1937)—that cause them difficulty but that they do not recognize as related to the loss.

Often individuals experiencing chronic grief reactions are aware that they are not making progress in getting back into living again. With delayed grief reactions, although there may have been some grieving at the time of the loss, it is likely that the grief will not surface again until later—when it will most often appear as an excessive reaction to a subsequent loss or other triggering event. Exaggerated or masked grief reactions may lead to the development of a phobia or irrational fear, to physical or psychiatric symptoms, or to aberrant or maladaptive behavior.

In general, complicated grief reactions appear to develop as a result of difficulties in the relationship with the deceased (for example, ambivalent, dependent, or narcissistic relationships); in the circumstances of the death (for instance uncertainty about or unwillingness to accept the fact of death, or a situation of multiple losses); in the survivor's own history or personality (such as a history of depressive illness, personalities that employ withdrawal to defend against extremes of emotional distress or that do not tolerate dependency feelings well, or a self-concept that includes being the "strong" one in the family); or in the social factors that surround the experience (for example, a loss that is socially unspeakable or socially negated, or when a social support network is absent). It is important for helpers to be alert to potential complications in grief and mourning, and to obtain appropriate assistance in dealing with complicated mourning.

Summary

This chapter has initiated an examination of central elements involved in the human experiences of loss, bereavement, grief, and mourning. It has focused on variables that affect those experiences, paying special attention to how one understands grief and its many manifestations, processes and interpretations of mourning (phases versus tasks), outcomes of uncomplicated and complicated mourning, ways in which grief can be disenfranchised, and the concept of anticipatory grief as a way of contrasting pre- and postdeath grieving. These topics reappear in Chapter 9 in the form of suggested principles for helping those who are coping with loss and grief, in Chapter 10 through discussion of funeral practices and other memorial rituals, and in Part 4, where loss and grief are placed in the context of a developmental perspective on death-related interactions throughout the human life cycle.

QUESTIONS FOR REVIEW AND DISCUSSION

1. Think of a time when you experienced the loss of some person or some thing that was important in your life. What elements made this an important loss for you? Would it have been different if you had lost a different person or thing, or if the loss had occurred in a different way?

2. How did you react to that loss? Try to be as complete as possible in developing this description of your reactions to the loss.

3. How did you cope with that loss? What helped you to cope with that loss or to integrate it into your ongoing living? What was not helpful? Why was it not helpful?

SUGGESTED READINGS

Introductory descriptions of loss, grief, and mourning are provided in the following:

Davidson, G. W. (1984). *Understanding Mourning: A Guide for Those Who Grieve.*
Moffat, M. J. (1982). *In the Midst of Winter: Selections from the Literature of Mourning.*
Tatelbaum, J. (1980). *The Courage to Grieve.*
Viorst, J. (1986). *Necessary Losses: The Loves, Illusions, Dependencies and Impossible Expectations That All of Us Have to Give Up in Order to Grow.*
Westberg, G. (1971). *Good Grief.*

Additional analyses of bereavement appear in the following:

Bowlby, J. (1973–82). *Attachment and Loss* (3 vols.): Vol. 1, *Attachment*; Vol. 2, *Separation: Anxiety and Anger*; Vol. 3, *Loss: Sadness and Depression.*
Freud, S. (1959). Mourning and melancholia. In J. Strachey (Ed. and Trans.), *The Standard Edition of the Complete Psychological Works of Sigmund Freud* (Vol. 14, pp. 237–258).
Jackson, E. N. (1957). *Understanding Grief: Its Roots, Dynamics, and Treatment.*
Osterweis, M., Solomon, F., & Green, M. (Eds.). (1984). *Bereavement: Reactions, Consequences, and Care.*
Parkes, C. M. (1987). *Bereavement: Studies of Grief in Adult Life* (2nd ed.).
Rando, T. A. (1984). *Grief, Dying, and Death: Clinical Interventions for Caregivers.*
Raphael, B. (1983). *The Anatomy of Bereavement.*
Sanders, C. M. (1989). *Grief: The Mourning After.*

Special topics in grief and bereavement are examined in the following:

Doka, K. J. (Ed.). (1989). *Disenfranchised Grief: Recognizing Hidden Sorrow.*
Glick, I., Weiss, R., & Parkes, C. (1974). *The First Year of Bereavement.*
Kay, W. J. (Ed.). (1984). *Pet Loss and Human Bereavement.*
Nieburg, H. A., & Fischer, A. (1982). *Pet Loss.*

Parkes, C. M., & Weiss, R. (1983). *Recovery from Bereavement.*

Pine, V. R., Margolis, O. S., Doka, K., Kutscher, A. H., Schaefer, D. J., Siegel, M-E., & Cherico, D. J. (Eds.). (1990). *Unrecognized and Unsanctioned Grief: The Nature and Counseling of Unacknowledged Loss.*

Rando, T. A. (Ed.). (1986). *Loss and Anticipatory Grief.*

Rosenblatt, P. C. (1983). *Bitter, Bitter Tears: Nineteenth-Century Diarists and Twentieth-Century Grief Theories.*

Stroebe, W., & Stroebe, M. S. (1987). *Bereavement and Health: The Psychological and Physical Consequences of Partner Loss.*

CHAPTER 9

Helping Those Who Are Coping with Loss and Grief

Important clues about helping grieving persons can be obtained by taking note of the many forms of assistance that were given to Stella Bridgman, the grieving person described at the beginning of Chapter 8. The present chapter returns to that example to introduce discussions of the needs of bereaved persons and of unhelpful messages that may be conveyed by society. After listing things not to do or say, we reformulate Worden's (1991a) tasks in mourning to demonstrate how bereaved persons can be helped with cognitive, affective, behavioral, and valuational tasks. This theme is developed through two examples of societal programs for helping the bereaved: support groups for the bereaved and hospice bereavement follow-up programs. Finally, ten principles are suggested for facilitating uncomplicated grief in counseling relationships.

Stella Bridgman: Helping a Grieving Person

When her mother died after a long, lingering illness, Stella Bridgman turned for consolation to her relatives and to the man whom she would later marry. When he died, suddenly and traumatically, she turned first to her church and her young children. Through a church activity, she met her second husband.

But when her son committed suicide, many of her friends and associates withdrew from her and were not helpful. Stella perceived this as compounding her initial loss by erasing all mention and memory of her son's life. Also, she felt hurt and set upon by these actions of individuals from whom she had expected assistance and support.

One wise friend took her to a meeting of a local Compassionate Friends chapter. Think how difficult it would be to go alone to a self-help group for the first time as a bereaved person. One might wonder: Will the group be welcoming or alien? Will it be morbid or unhelpful? What if I break down or just cannot stay? What if I am physically or emotionally unable to drive home? The presence of a caring friend who accompanied Stella to the group diminished many of these anxieties.

The group itself did not pull back when Stella expressed her pain, anger, guilt, and other strong feelings. They permitted her to give vent to such feelings, and they acknowledged the normalcy of her reactions. Members of the group recognized the appropriateness of her questions and validated her experiences as a bereaved parent. Just by being themselves, these other bereaved parents confirmed that one can survive a horrendous loss and cope with grief, that life can once again become livable. Also, just by being themselves, the members of the group served as role models and provided Stella with options that she might choose in determining how to live her own life.

Fundamental Needs of Bereaved Persons

Davidson (1984b) has written that bereaved persons need five things: social support, nutrition, hydration, exercise, and rest. Among these, social support

A hug from a special friend, Amanda the Panda.

is most frequently mentioned and is perhaps the main postdeath variable in determining high versus low grief. Recall from Chapter 8 that those variables include the nature of the prior relationship, the way in which the loss occurred, the coping strategies that the individual has learned to use in dealing with previous losses, and the nature and availability of support for the bereaved person after the loss. In practice, only the last of these is open to alteration after a death has occurred. It is, therefore, the principal subject of this chapter.

In the videotape "Pitch of Grief" (1985), a person experienced in hospice bereavement follow-up programs observes astutely that the single thing that makes a difference in bereavement is "the presence of a caring person." It is not so important what such a person says or does—although obviously there are better and worse things that one might do or say, as will be noted later in this chapter—as that the person does care and is available. This is exemplified in an unusual and appealing way by the work of Amanda the Panda in Des Moines, Iowa. JoAnn Zimmerman makes herself available to ill, dying, and grieving children as Amanda, a six-foot panda with a heart—a very special, nonjudgmental, caring friend for individual children and an inspiring presence at Camp Amanda for bereaved children.

The other factors mentioned by Davidson are often ignored in the literature on bereavement. Many bereaved persons do not have either the energy or the problem-solving ability to ensure that they obtain adequate nutrition and hydration. Individuals who are bereaved may experience a loss of appetite or disinterest in diet. That is one reason why many communities have traditions in which friends and neighbors bring food and drink to the bereaved. In addition to nourishing themselves improperly, sometimes bereaved persons willingly or unwillingly contribute to deficits in their own hydration and nutrition by consuming empty calories or dehydrating liquids like alcohol.

Similarly, exercise and rest—two factors that contribute to quality in all living—are important elements that should not be neglected by the bereaved. Bereavement disrupts normal patterns of life, including sleep and exercise cycles. An interest in pursuing the benefits of healthy exercise and an ability to obtain a good night's sleep may be signs of a productive mourning process.

How can bereaved persons be expected to cope successfully with the very challenging and difficult tasks of mourning if they do not obtain adequate nutrition, hydration, exercise, and rest? These basic survival needs that apply to all human beings are even more critical in the demanding context of bereavement and grief. They deserve careful attention by those who would help the bereaved.

Unhelpful Messages

All too often, society conveys unhelpful messages to bereaved persons. Typically, these are clustered around: (1) minimization of the loss that has been experienced; (2) admonitions not to feel (or, at least, not to express in public) the strong grief reactions that one is experiencing; and/or (3) suggestions that one should promptly get back to living and not disturb others with one's bereavement and mourning.

The first of these clusters of messages may involve the following sorts of statements:

- "Now that your baby has died, you have a little angel in heaven" (But my pregnancy was not intended as a way of making heavenly angels)
- "You can always have another baby" or "You already have other children" (How would either of these replace the baby who died?)
- "You're still young, you can get married again" (Yes, but will that bring back my first spouse or lessen the hurt of his loss in any way?)

Listening with the Whole Self

There is a way of listening which is a way of giving, and another way of listening which is a way of refusing, of refusing *oneself.* . . . The person who is at my disposal is the one who is capable of being with me with the whole of himself when I am in need; while the one who is not at my disposal seems merely to offer me a temporary loan raised on his resources. For the one I am a presence; for the other I am an object. Presence involves a reciprocity.

SOURCE From G. Marcel, 1933/1962.

- "You had a good long marriage" (Yes, but that may only make me feel all the more keenly what I have lost)
- "After all, your grandfather was a very old man" (And perhaps, for that reason, all the more dear to me)

From the standpoint of the bereaved, these messages may sound like a suggestion that the loss was really not all that momentous or that the lost one was not irreplaceable. The corresponding implication is that bereavement and grief should not be perceived by the individual as such a difficult experience. Above all, the conclusion seems to be that friends and relatives of the bereaved person, or society as a whole, should not need to be so disturbed as to be obligated to change their daily routines in order to assist the bereaved person.

The second cluster of messages that are often conveyed to the bereaved seeks to suppress the depth or intensity of the feelings that are experienced by grieving persons. For example, such individuals will be told:

- "What you need to do is to keep busy, get back to work, forget her"
- "Be strong" or "Keep a stiff upper lip"
- "You'll be fine," "Don't be so upset always," "Put a smile on your face"
- "Why are you still upset? It's been . . . [three weeks, four months, a year]"

Of course, no one can simply stop feeling what he or she is feeling. Feelings are real. They need to be lived with and lived through. They can only change in their own ways and at their own pace. The underlying theme of this second cluster of messages is that it is not good for bereaved individuals to experience some feelings or to experience them in certain (especially powerful) ways. Perhaps more important, the theme is that these ways of feeling are unacceptable reminders to those around the bereaved person of the insistent quality of his or her grief.

The third set of messages is really a variant of the first two. This set arises from the common practice in American society of what has been called "oppressive toleration," whose basic premise is that others can do or say (or, in this case, feel) whatever they wish, as long as they do not disturb me. Accordingly, it is often made clear to bereaved persons in more or less subtle ways—often in ways that are very unsubtle—that, if they insist, they can grieve as they wish, but in so doing they must take care not to bother those around them or disrupt the tranquility of society in general.

Thus, when people in contemporary American society speak of the "acceptability" of grief, they usually mean whether or not it is acceptable to the group, not to the bereaved person. When the late President Kennedy was assassinated, American society congratulated his widow on the way in which she dealt with her bereavement in public, not least because she presented a very stoic facade to the media and to the rest of us, which we could admire without having to be very disturbed. It was widely ignored that Mrs. Kennedy's example was not very relevant to or workable for most bereaved people.

Some Things Not to Do or Say

In the aftermath of the sudden and unexpected death of his 10-year-old daughter, Rachel, one father who had been an Episcopal priest for many years drew out of his experiences the following lessons for bereaved persons (Smith, 1974, pp. 35–40):

1. Don't blame yourself for what has happened.
2. Don't be brave and strong.
3. Don't try to run away.
4. Don't feel that you owe it to the dead child to spend the rest of your life tied to the place in which he or she lived.
5. Don't feel sorry for yourself.

For helpers, this person (Smith, 1974, pp. 47–52) had the following advice:

1. Immediately after a death, *do something specific to help* (for example, notify those who need to be told on the family's behalf, answer the telephone for the family, or free family members from chores that may appear meaningless to them) or make known in other practical ways your willingness to help;
2. Apart from the above, respect preferences that the family may have to be alone.
3. Assist in practical ways through the time of the funeral (for example, help with meals, cleaning, transportation).
4. In the difficult time after the funeral, do not avoid contact with the bereaved.
5. Act normally and mention the name of the deceased person in ways that would have been natural before the death.
6. Permit the bereaved to determine how or when they do or do not wish to talk about the deceased person.
7. Don't try to answer unanswerable questions or to force your religious or philosophical beliefs upon vulnerable bereaved persons.
8. Don't say, "I know how you feel"—no matter how much it may seem to be so, that is never true unless you have walked in the same path (Linn, 1986).

9. Be available, but allow the bereaved to find their own individual ways through the work of mourning.

Friends are often hesitant and may feel inadequate in approaching someone who is grieving a significant loss. Sometimes it may be enough to tell the bereaved person: "I don't know what to say to you" or "I don't know what to do to help," but also "What can I do for you right now?"

Helping Bereaved Persons with Tasks in Mourning

"For all bereaved, the central issue in any helping encounter is to learn to build a life without the deceased" (Silverman, 1978, p. 40). One value of Worden's (1991a) account of tasks of mourning discussed in Chapter 8 is that those tasks can be adopted by individuals who are helping the bereaved as ways of determining how their assistance might most usefully be offered. However, Worden's tasks are specifically formulated as projects for the bereaved. They need to be adapted in order to serve as guidelines for helpers. For that reason, we will restate Worden's tasks here in terms of cognitive, affective, behavioral, and valuational projects. That is, we will consider ways to help bereaved persons with tasks that involve what they know or believe, how they feel, how they act, and what they value.

Throughout this process, helpers need to keep one very important caution in mind. At a time when so much in the bereaved person's life is out of control and when he or she is so vulnerable to strong feelings and pain, outsiders need to be careful not to take over the bereaved person's tasks of mourning and subtly (or not so subtly) shape them in their own ways. Barring frank pathology, bereaved persons must be permitted to lead the way in their mourning. This is what Manning (1979) meant by the title of his book *Don't Take My Grief Away from Me*.

Cognitive Tasks

Everyone who is bereaved asks questions about what happened. All bereaved persons have *a need for information*. Knowing the facts about what happened is an essential step in making the event real in one's inner world. That is why many bereaved persons go over and over the details of the circumstances in which a death occurred. Outsiders become impatient with this process. They ask: "What difference does it make if the car that hit her was blue or red? Isn't she still dead?" But that misses the point. Only when a bereaved person can fill in details like this in a personal intellectual mosaic can that person also grasp the reality of its pattern. Until then, the loss seems blank, devoid of color, unlike life, unreal, and untrue. Cognitive and other tasks may be particularly difficult for bereaved persons who are themselves professionals or other individuals whose social roles make it difficult in their eyes to seek information and assistance, or to grieve openly.

The provision of prompt, accurate, and reliable information is an important role for helpers. One day, when Arthur Smith (1974) was 600 miles away from home at a chaplain's conference, he was called to the telephone. His wife's voice simply said, "Rachel died this morning." Smith later commented, "There is no other way to tell someone that a loved person has died" (p. 8). But in the circumstances, Smith's first reaction was to run over in his mind the list of sick and elderly persons in his parish who might have died. Failing to find anyone with that name, he asked, "Rachel who?" The deep silence that followed signaled the moment in which the inconceivable began to enter Rachel's father's mind.

Information is particularly important when the death is unexpected, untimely, traumatic, or self-inflicted. Anything that adds to the shocking qualities of a loss contributes to a sense of unreality. Protests quickly arise: "Surely, this cannot be happening"; "This sort of thing doesn't happen here"; "This must be some sort of bad dream." Sometimes requests for additional information really cannot be answered and are not meant to be answered. Often, they are really efforts to test reality, to obtain repeated confirmation that the death has occurred and (perhaps also) that it will not ever be adequately explained. Testing reality is an important way in which one can begin to emerge from shock and confusion into constructive processes of coping with one's grief.

For example, in cases of Sudden Infant Death Syndrome, even though the ultimate cause of the death remains unknown to us, the fact that a "syndrome" or pattern of events can be identified is an important piece of information (Corr, Fuller, Barnickol, & Corr, 1991). The exclusionary postmortem examination and associated investigation upon which an appropriate diagnosis of the syndrome rests are critical facts in assuring the bereaved parents that they did not bring about or in any way cause the death of their child and that nothing could have been done by anyone to prevent the death.

Affective Tasks

A second area in which helpers can assist bereaved persons has to do with emotional responses to the loss. Bereaved persons have *a need to express their responses* to a loss or death. To do this, they may need assistance in identifying and articulating feelings that are strange and unfamiliar to them. Informed and sensitive helpers can give names to the emotions that the bereaved are feeling. Helpers can also assist in finding appropriate ways to express strong feelings. These will need to be ways that are safe for both the bereaved person and for others who may become involved.

Often, what will be needed is the company of a caring person who can acknowledge the expression and validate the appropriateness of the feelings. Along this line, many bereaved persons have found comfort in reading the published version of the notebooks in which C. S. Lewis (1976) wrote out his feelings after the death of his wife. He wrote originally only for himself as a way of spelling out his grief, but what he felt has rung so true with other bereaved persons that his little book provides a kind of normalization and assurance that many desperately need. This model of writing out one's thoughts and feelings has been followed with good results by many bereaved persons who keep a journal or other record of their bereavement experiences (Lattanzi & Hale, 1984). There is an extensive body of writings by bereaved persons (for example, Brothers, 1990; Elmer, 1987; Graham, 1988; Start, 1968), together with literature intended to help the bereaved (for instance, Grollman, 1977; Rando, 1988b; Sanders, 1992; Simos, 1979).

Behavioral Tasks

Bereaved persons most often need to act out their responses to a loss. This is the behavioral aspect of expression of strong feelings. Often, it takes the form of commemorative activities that reflect *a need to mark or take notice of the death through some external event or action.* The goal of commemoration is to preserve the memory of the person or thing that has been lost. This may be accomplished in more or less formal or public ways, but it always involves some act or outward behavior. For example, it is common to plant a tree in memory of someone who has died. This seems to be particularly appropriate because it involves the nurturing of new life in a way that can be revisited from time to time.

Simpler forms of commemoration include attending a wake or funeral, since a prominent part of funeral ritual (to be discussed in Chapter 10) has to do with commemoration and memorialization of the deceased. Other commemorative gestures might involve putting together a scrapbook of pictures and memories, designing and executing a collage that symbolizes the life of the deceased, or tracing a family tree. The value of commemorative activities is evident in the comments of one widow about letters of condolence (see "Condolence Letters"). The point is not so much how the commemoration is accomplished as that something is done to take note of the life that has now ended.

Valuational Tasks

A fourth area for helping the bereaved has to do with their *need to make sense out of the loss.* The process of finding or making meaning seems to be essential for all human beings. In death and loss, that which had been understood as a foundation for meaning in one's life may have been severely challenged. Mourning initiates the processes of reinvigorating old value frameworks or constructing new ones.

Some people have such faith or trust in their basic values that they can incorporate a loss directly or at least be patient until meanings begin to clarify themselves. Others must ask repeatedly the ultimate question: Why? Some ways of making meaning are idiosyncratic; many are widely shared among human beings. Sometimes answers are not readily forthcoming. Almost all of us need some conviction that life truly is worth living even when death has taken someone whom we love.

Family members need each other when a death occurs.

Condolence Letters

People dread writing letters of condolence, fearing the inadequacy of their words, the pain they must address, death itself. And few people realize, until the death of someone close, what a benediction those letters are.

The arrival of letters about George was a luminous moment of each day. They made me cry. They made me feel close to him. They gave me the sense that the love he inspired in others embraced me. The best were the longer, more specific ones, the ones that mentioned something the writer cherished in George, or recounted some tale from his past that I was unaware of. Others were inexpressibly poignant. At one time I would have avoided writing any such letter, thinking it unkind to dwell on a subject that was the source of such pain, that I would be rubbing salt into a wound. But now I know that it is not unkind. There is so much joy mixed in with the pain of remembering.

SOURCE From L. Graham, 1990.

Societal Programs to Help the Bereaved

Up to this point, what has been said in this chapter about helping the bereaved has been particularly suited to lay helpers—family members, other relatives, neighbors, friends, and members of church groups or other communities. Throughout history, these are the people to whom bereaved persons have turned for support and assistance. In recent years, other programs have developed to help the bereaved, programs designed to supplement befriending and neighboring when they are not sufficient to the need, or to serve similar purposes when they are not available. These newer societal programs to help the bereaved can be illustrated by support groups for the bereaved and hospice bereavement follow-up programs.

Support Groups for the Bereaved

There are many types of support groups in the United States (Milofsky, 1980; Wasserman & Danforth, 1988). Even support groups for the bereaved take many forms. For example, one kind of support group has been established to provide assistance to a population of bereaved persons mainly through the presentation of talks and lectures by experts on a variety of practical problems. Groups of this sort try to show their members how to invest their money, complete their income tax returns, cook nourishing meals when they are alone, do small repairs around the home, and so on. Another type of support group focuses on entertainment and social activities, such as holiday parties, visits to restaurants, or bus tours to nearby attractions. Both of these types of groups, whether they concentrate upon the provision of social support or guidance in solving various types of problems, can be and are meaningful for many bereaved persons. However, because they do not take as their principal concern the work of addressing the central issues of grief and mourning, we will not say more about groups of this sort here.

Our focus is on support groups whose main concern is to help individuals cope with loss and grief. These groups offer support in the broadest sense, but their primary benefits result from the assistance that members of the group give to each other (mutual aid) and from the opportunities that these groups provide for bereaved individuals to help themselves with grief work and tasks of mourning (self-help). Many groups of this sort have sprung up throughout the United States in recent years in response to a wide variety of loss experiences (see "Selected Examples of Bereavement Support Organizations"; Lieberman & Borman, 1979; Pike & Wheeler, 1992). They may be local endeavors undertaken for a limited period of time, ongoing or open-ended projects of a community agency, or chapters of a national organization.

Principles and practices in bereavement support groups   The very existence and rapid proliferation of bereavement support groups seems to show that many bereaved persons need or are seeking assistance beyond that which is

The Serenity Prayer

*God, give us
the serenity to accept
what cannot be changed,
give us the courage to change
what should be changed,
give us the wisdom
to distinguish one from the other.*

—*Reinhold Niebuhr*

readily available to them in their own family or everyday community. By and large, however, the assistance that is being sought from these groups is not that of professional counseling or therapy. It is help from others who have shared a similar bereavement experience. Thus, the essential purpose of these groups is "to provide people in similar circumstances with an opportunity to share their experiences and to help teach one another how to cope with their problems" (Silverman, 1980, p. 40).

Groups of this sort may be time-limited or ongoing; open to new members at any time or closed once the group has been formed; available for all sorts of bereavement or organized around a specific type of loss; led by a professional facilitator or by an experienced bereaved volunteer (McNurlen, 1991; Yalom & Vinogradov, 1988). The question of leadership is important, but it will be better understood if we keep in mind the profound differences between support groups and therapy groups.

Support groups for the bereaved are not therapy groups (McNurlen, 1991). Members in support groups come together voluntarily because of the difficulties they encounter in coping with a shared life experience. Prior to their encounter with loss, such individuals were generally functioning normally in living. They do not seek to be changed, but to find assistance in coping with losses that have taxed their capacities. Although some bereavement groups do not permit leadership posts to be held by nonbereaved persons, in others leadership functions are assigned to a professional facilitator (Klass & Shinners, 1983).

In all cases, however, real, substantive expertise in bereavement groups is not perceived as hierarchical; it always reposes with the members themselves. Thus, members are encouraged to become involved with each other outside the group. Likewise, topics for discussion are those that members bring to the group and choose to share. The focus in the group is not on solving problems but on process—talking about problems, sharing experiences, and exploring situations. This emphasis is reflected in the Serenity Prayer, which is a frequent component of group ritual. It also explains why support groups for the bereaved combine elements of both self-help and mutual aid, principles that might appear to outsiders to be in conflict.

Selected Examples of Bereavement Support Organizations

Organization	Description
American Association of Suicidology 2459 South Ash Street Denver, CO 80222 (303) 692-0985	An information clearinghouse that supplies literature and local referrals to survivors of suicide
The Candlelighters Foundation 1901 Pennsylvania Ave. NW, Suite 1001 Washington, DC 20006 (301) 657-8401	An international network of support groups for parents of children who have or have had cancer
The Compassionate Friends P.O. Box 3696 Oak Brook, IL 60522 (312) 990-0010	An international support group with numerous local chapters serving bereaved parents and siblings
Make Today Count National Office Mid-America Cancer Center 1235 E. Cherokee Springfield, MO 65804 (800) 432-2273 (8:00 A.M.–4:30 P.M. Monday–Friday	A national support group for individuals who are living with life-threatening illness and for their family members
Mothers Against Drunk Driving (MADD) 1021 Southwest Blvd., Suite A Jefferson City, MO 65109 (800) 736-MADD	Support for those who have been victimized by drunken driving offenses
National Hospice Organization 1901 N. Moore Street, Suite 901 Arlington, VA 22209 (800) 658-8898; (703) 243-5900	A resource for referral to local hospice programs and related services
National Organization for Victim Assistance 1757 Park Road, NW Washington, DC 20010 (202) 232-6682; 24-hour hot line, (800) TRY-NOVA	A referral resource for local victim assistance services, plus a 24-hour telephone crisis counseling service

Support groups for the bereaved usually have more or less explicit rules or values, such as that confidentiality and a nonjudgmental attitude are to be

Selected Examples of Bereavement Support Organizations (continued)

Organization	Description
National SIDS Clearinghouse 8201 Greensboro Drive, Suite 600 McLean, VA 22102 (703) 821-8955	A national resource for information and referrals to local organizations and support groups for those affected by Sudden Infant Death Syndrome
Parents of Murdered Children 100 East Eighth Street, Suite B-41 Cincinnati, OH 45202 (513) 721-5683	Support for survivors of homicide
Parents Without Partners, Inc. 8807 Colesville Road Silver Spring, MD 20910 (301) 588-9354 (9:00 A.M.–5:00 P.M.)	Services for single parents and their children
SHARE: Pregnancy and Infant Loss Support, Inc. National Office Hospital St. Joseph Health Center 300 First Capitol Drive St. Charles, MO 63301-2893 (314) 947-6164	A national mutual-help group for parents and siblings who have experienced miscarriage, stillbirth, ectopic pregnancy, or early infant death
Sudden Infant Death Syndrome Alliance 10500 Little Patuxent Parkway, Suite 420 Columbia, MD 21044 (410) 964-8000; (800) 221-7437; (800) 638-7437	An alliance of organizations involved in research and services related to Sudden Infant Death Syndrome
THEOS (They Help Each Other Spiritually) 1301 Clark Building 717 Liberty Avenue Pittsburgh, PA 15222 (412) 471-7779	Support and education for the widowed and their families
Widowed Persons Service American Association of Retired Persons (AARP) 601 E. Street NW Washington, DC 20049 (202) 434-2260	Offers programs, literature, and other resources for the widowed

A grief support organization, THEOS (They Help Each Other Spiritually).

maintained; advice is not to be given; opportunities are made available for all to speak; side conversations are prohibited; everyone has the right to pass or remain silent; members respect each other's experiences and viewpoints; meetings start and end on time. Safety issues must be a matter of particular concern in groups for vulnerable people. Thus, such groups usually prohibit "put downs" or evangelization, and they are also sensitive to the need to refer for therapy individuals who may endanger themselves or who disrupt the work of the group.

Helping factors in bereavement support groups   The central helping factors around which most bereavement support groups are organized include identification, universality, catharsis, guidance, instillation of hope, existential issues, cohesiveness, and altruism (Luterman, 1991; McNurlen, 1991; Yalom, 1985). These are the factors that Stella Bridgman encountered in the Compassionate Friends group that she attended after the death of her son. Brief analysis of each of these helping factors will show how groups of this sort help the bereaved.

Bereavement support groups rest upon a foundation established by the shared experience of their members (Borkman, 1976). This shared experience is the basis for a bond through which group members can find *identification* with one another. In this way, bereaved individuals find that they are or need be no longer alone. Although they may feel stigmatized or marked out by their bereavement experience from so many others in the world, within the support group they discover that others share very similar experiences and that members of the group can learn from each other (Wrobleski, 1984).

Despite all of the uniqueness and individuality of the bereavement experience, there is also a degree of *universality* encountered in groups of this sort. Individuals in such groups are helped to recognize that they are not alone in their experiences and responses. For those who have been marked out by society as different, shunned, or even stigmatized because of what has happened to them, it can be helpful to know that other members of the group do not view them as "bad" or "wrong." Shared or universal elements in bereavement and in coping with loss can be a source of strength, consolation, and sustenance within the group.

Within the context of the group, long-repressed, pent-up feelings can be let out for as long as is necessary. Some people come to bereavement support groups shortly after their loss experience; others join such groups many years later. Whatever the timing, new and old members typically commend the group for permitting them to vent and share such feelings. That is, they record their need for such *catharsis* and their experience that many individuals and segments of American society conduct themselves in ways that inhibit or make unwelcome such expressions of feelings.

The group displays for its members in concrete ways that which is normal. It does this not by lectures or didactic presentations but by providing its members with a forum in which they can describe, exemplify, or live out their experiences with grief and bereavement. This may or may not validate their own individual experiences. Nevertheless, as experiences are exchanged, important information, *guidance*, and reassurance are conveyed. For example, most bereaved persons welcome information about grief and mourning processes. Many need additional information about the specific sorts of losses that they have experienced and that serve to define the nature of the group—for example, about parental bereavement, about homicide and its implications, about Sudden Infant Death Syndrome. Some may need guidance about the social stigma associated with certain kinds of death, such as suicide or AIDS.

A dimension of the group experience that is of particular significance for many bereaved persons is the inevitable interaction between new members and those who have been participants for a longer time. Coming to know people who are further along in their grief work permits newer members to witness ways in which their more experienced colleagues are managing both their grief and the rest of their lives. To the degree that this demonstrates that things can get better, hope is renewed that one's own life might also get better. This sort of *instillation of hope* must be drawn from the group processes by the individual; it cannot simply be injected or imposed from outside.

Existential issues, which involve large questions such as those concerned with the fairness of life, the benevolence of God, or the basic goodness of the universe, can be raised in bereavement support groups. Answers may not easily be found. In fact, one is likely to discover that one must work out one's own answers or ways of living with such issues, questions, and answers. Although not undertaken within the context of a bereavement support group, this is just the sort of project faced by Rabbi Harold Kushner in coping with the very unusual, progressive illness (progeria) and death of his son at a young age. Kushner's project resulted in the book *When Bad Things Happen to Good People* (1981), which has been a source of consolation to many grieving people. Within the context of a support group, one can see that these existential issues raised by loss, grief, and bereavement are legitimate and real and that different people respond to them in different ways.

The bonding among members in a bereavement support group creates a safe, caring environment in a world that—after a significant personal loss—may appear in so many ways to be unsafe and uncaring. In other words, a *cohesiveness* or basic trust develops among members in most support groups, arising from two dimensions of the group experience: the experiences that they share as bereaved persons and the discovery by hurt and vulnerable people that they can help each other simply by sharing their own great losses and pain. In fact, "sharing of experience is the fundamental concept that distinguishes the mutual help experience from other helping exchanges. . . . The essence of the process is mutuality and reciprocity" (Silverman, 1980, p. 10).

Another sort of empowerment is related to elements of *altruism* or giving to others, which is often experienced by those who remain in a bereavement support group for a long time. As they move into leadership roles or find different ways to offer to others what they have obtained from their own experiences both in bereavement and within the group, senior members also may find new rewards for themselves. This is what Klass (1985b; 1988) has called the great secret of bereavement support groups: in giving to others, one receives for oneself. Giving and receiving help reciprocally enhances one's self-esteem. Those who make the transition from intense vulnerability in an early meeting to shared ownership of the group often interpret their new-found ability to help others as an important element in finding meaning in the life and death of their loved one (Klass, 1985a).

Help outside the group   Although the main work of support groups for the bereaved occurs within their meetings, that is not the whole of what they have to offer. This point is often neglected. Well-established, ongoing bereavement support groups like The Compassionate Friends usually establish a network of referral sources for identifying potential new members. Mail or telephone contacts with such individuals may be among the early expressions of support that reach the bereaved.

Sometimes it is enough for the bereaved to know that support groups are available "in case I really need one." That may be supplemented by regular mailings of a newsletter, which is another mode of support and reassurance that additional help is within reach. Groups may also generate announcements about their activities or reports about loss and grief in the local media. Together with educational conferences and public service endeavors, these are other forms of support that reach beyond the boundaries of the group itself.

As we have noted, many bereavement support groups foster mutual aid and self-help through personal contacts outside the formal structure of a group meeting. Thus, there are many similarities between these groups and widow-to-widow programs or hospice bereavement follow-up programs, which often prepare and utilize bereaved volunteers as a resource for assisting other bereaved persons, usually on a one-to-one basis (Silverman, 1969, 1986).

Bereavement Follow-up in Hospice Programs

Hospice programs in the United States are required to provide support and counseling for the family members of those whom they serve (National Hospice Organization, 1987). This arises directly out of the hospice philosophy. If hospice affirms life and is a holistic program of care, then it must address the needs of both the dying person and his or her family members. At death, problems faced by the dying person cease, but that is only partly true for family members. In their new roles as bereaved survivors, members of the family must continue to cope with many old problems and they must also address new challenges. Consequently, hospice programs include bereavement follow-up services as an essential component of their work (Lattanzi, 1982).

Not all families need or accept bereavement follow-up from a hospice program. Some may have resources of their own that are adequate to cope with bereavement, whether or not those same resources were sufficient to cope with dying. Moreover, no hospice program would wish to disable its surviving families by making them dependent upon hospice services for the remainder of their lives (and few hospice programs would have the resources to sustain such a commitment). In fact, then, hospice bereavement follow-up is a transitional service designed to assist those family members who wish help in coping with loss and bereavement during the first 12–18 months after the death of a loved one. This is usually thought to be the most difficult period in acute bereavement. Issues that go beyond the capacities of this sort of support, either in their character or duration, would ordinarily be the subject of evaluation for referral to professional counseling or therapy.

Programs of bereavement follow-up in hospice care are commonly organized around a detailed plan of care for those who have been identified through careful assessment as key persons in bereavement (Lattanzi & Cofelt, 1979; Lindstrom, 1983). This plan of care may be initiated prior to the patient's death and usually encourages participation by family members and staff in meaningful funeral services and rituals. Subsequently, the remainder of the follow-up program is most often conducted through mail, telephone, and/or personal contacts at regular intervals. Programs of this sort offer care that is addressed to specific needs of the bereaved, such as information about typical patterns or problems in bereavement, grief, and mourning; acknowledgment and validation of feelings; suggestions about ways in which to undertake or to join in commemorative and memorialization activities; and a shared conviction that life remains worth living (Souter & Moore, 1989).

Newsletters, cards or letters, individual counseling, and social activities are familiar components of hospice bereavement follow-up. In addition, hospice programs frequently establish support groups for the bereaved or work cooperatively with community organizations that provide such services. Most of the actual services in hospice bereavement follow-up are carried out by experienced volunteers who have been selected and trained for such work and who are supported by professionals in this field (Parkes, 1979, 1980, 1981, 1987b).

Facilitating Uncomplicated Grief: Grief Counseling

What has been said thus far about helping the bereaved constitutes a set of suggestions for "walking alongside" the bereaved person as a fellow human being or fellow griever. This reflects a view that the vast bulk of grieving in bereavement is normal and uncomplicated. It is adequately served by caring and thoughtful individuals and by the social programs that have been described. Professional intervention is not normally required.

However, when professional intervention is indicated, Worden (1991a) has proposed an important distinction between *grief counseling* and *grief therapy*. The former has to do with helping or facilitating the work of bereaved persons who are coping with uncomplicated or normal grief and mourning; the latter designates more specialized techniques employed to help people with complicated or abnormal grief reactions. In helping bereaved persons, it is essential to remain alert for manifestations of complicated grief reactions. When those appear, individuals should be referred to appropriate resources for grief therapy (Rando, 1993). However, it is important not to misinterpret normal grief reactions as abnormal or pathological responses. That has the effect of overprofessionalizing the help required by most bereaved persons.

Grief counseling can be offered by those who are professionally trained for this work (for example, physicians, nurses, psychologists, social workers, or members of the clergy with appropriate preparation and qualifications), although it is important to note that not all professionals are effective as grief counselors. Grief counseling grows out of caring communities, to which it adds formal understanding of experiences in bereavement and mourning and skill in helping individuals with their own coping or problem-solving processes. For such counseling, Worden (1991a) identified the following ten principles as guidelines for facilitating uncomplicated grief reactions. Many of these principles are also relevant to nonprofessional ways of helping the bereaved.

1. Help the survivor actualize the loss.   In contrast with the sense of unreality that often accompanies bereavement, this principle recommends an effort "to come to a more complete awareness that the loss actually has occurred—the person is dead and will not return" (Worden, 1991a, p. 42). For example, one can simply assist survivors to talk about the loss. Sympathetic listening and open-ended questions encourage repeated review of the circumstances of the loss, as do visits to the grave site. Immediate family members may be familiar with these details and can often become impatient with their repetition. But, as Shakespeare wrote in *Macbeth* (IV, iii, 209), bereaved persons need to "give sorrow words." A caring helper can aid this important process of growing in awareness of the loss and in appreciation of its impact. But it is important not to push survivors too forcefully or too quickly to grasp the reality of a death if it appears that they are not yet ready to deal with it. One must follow the survivor's own cues.

2. Help the survivor identify and express feelings.   Many survivors may not recognize unpleasant feelings like guilt, anxiety, fear, helplessness, or sadness, or they may be unable to express such feelings in ways that advance the work of mourning. A helper can aid bereaved persons to recognize what they are feeling and then enable those feelings to find their appropriate focus. For example, some persons may find themselves angry at caregivers who were unable to prevent the death. Others may be angry at other survivors who appear to be insufficiently affected by the death. Still others are angry at themselves for what they have or have not done. Finally, some people are angry (and this is often very difficult to admit) at the deceased for dying and leaving the bereaved person behind with many problems to face. Thus, Caine (1975) berated her deceased husband for leaving her unprepared, as she felt, to cope with many challenges in life and to raise their children alone.

Questions like "What do you miss about him?" and "What don't you miss about him?" may help the survivor to find some balance between positive and negative feelings. Similarly, unrealistic guilt that may be experienced as part of the overall grief reaction often responds to reality testing, which may lead to the realization that "We did everything we could have done." Many (but perhaps not all) bereaved persons may need to be gently encouraged to express, rather than repress, their sadness and crying. At the same time, feelings of anxiety and helplessness can be put into perspective by identifying positive things that the bereaved person had been able to do prior to the death and is still able to do even at a time when other things are unsettled or out of control. Recognizing unpleasant feelings may be the beginning of forgiveness and moving onward from anger and blame.

3. Help the survivor live without the deceased.   The helper can assist bereaved persons to address problems or make their own decisions. Because it may be difficult to exercise good judgment during acute grief, bereaved persons are often advised not to make major life-changing decisions at such times, such as those involved in selling property, changing jobs, or relocating. Thus, a central lesson in Judy Blume's novel for young readers, *Tiger Eyes* (1981), is the emerging realization that moving from Atlantic City (where her father was killed in the holdup of his 7–11 store) to live with her aunt in Los Alamos was ultimately not a productive way of dealing with their grief and with each other for a teenage girl, her mother, and her younger brother.

Nevertheless, the role of the helper is not to take over problems and decision making for the survivor. Therefore, when issues arise concerning the making of independent decisions (such as how to deal with sexual needs in bereavement, which may range from needs to be touched or held to problems in attaining complete intimacy with a new person), the helper's main role is only to assist the survivor in the process of making decisions. Enabling survivors to acquire new and effective coping skills empowers those who may perceive themselves to be powerless in their bereavement.

4. Help the survivor emotionally relocate the deceased.   This principle does not merely emphasize encouraging the survivor to form new relationships. As time passes, that may be appropriate. But it is important not to do so too quickly in ways that inhibit adequate mourning. The central point of this principle is to "help survivors find a new place in their life for the lost loved one—a place that will [also] allow the survivor to move forward with life and form new relationships" (Worden, 1991a, p. 48). The aim is not to overthrow, supplant, or dishonor the deceased, but to encourage survivors to live as well as possible in the future and to live as well as any deceased person who loved and cared for them would have wanted them to live.

5. Provide time to grieve.   Closing doors in a rich, many-faceted relationship takes time. Intimate relationships develop on many levels and have many ramifications. Grieving and mourning, if they are to be adequate to the loss, can be no less complex. Some people return quickly to normal routines. This leads them to be impatient with a survivor who is moving more slowly or finding it more difficult to deal with his or her grief. They may not appreciate how difficult it is to deal with critical anniversaries or the time around three to six months after the death when so much support that was offered during the funeral is no longer readily available. Effective helpers may need to be available over a longer period of time than many people expect, although actual contacts may not be very frequent.

6. Interpret "normal" behavior.   Many bereaved persons feel that they are "going crazy" or "losing their minds." This is because they may be experiencing things that they usually do not experience in their lives and they may, at least temporarily, be unable to function as well as they usually have in the past. Help in normalizing grief reactions can be drawn from knowledge about or experience with bereavement. Reassurance will be appreciated that unusual experiences, such as hallucinations or a preoccupation with the deceased, are common in bereavement and are not likely to be indicators that one is going crazy. Encouragement of this sort guides and heartens the bereaved in their time of travail.

7. Allow for individual differences.   This is a critical principle for helpers. The death of a single person affects each of his or her survivors in different ways. Each survivor is a unique individual with his or her own relationship to the deceased, and with his or her own personality and coping skills. Each person grieves and mourns in his or her own ways. Help in appreciating the individuality of grief responses is especially important for families or other groups who lose a member. It is even more critical when two parents try to understand the ways in which each of them may be reacting differently to the death of their child. Just as helpers will need to respect the individuality of each bereaved person whom they seek to assist, so too bereaved persons should be guided to respect the uniqueness of grief and mourning in other individuals who have been impacted by the same loss.

For a Time of Sorrow

I share with you the agony of your grief,
> The anguish of your heart finds echo in my own.
> I know I cannot enter all you feel
> Nor bear with you the burden of your pain;
I can but offer what my love does give:
> The strength of caring,
> The warmth of one who seeks to understand
> The silent storm-swept barrenness of so great a loss.
This I do in quiet ways,
> That on your lonely path
> You may not walk alone.

SOURCE From H. Thurman, 1953.

8. Provide continuing support. Helping bereaved persons may require specific interventions during critical moments of acute stress. In general, however, mourning is more like a long-term process with peaks and valleys of grief. Thus, helping mourners may also become a long-term process in which the helper walks alongside the bereaved person, permits that person to do his or her own grief work, and upholds the faith that survival is possible and that life can be good again.

9. Examine defenses and coping styles. By drawing the attention of bereaved persons in a gentle and trusting way to their own patterns of coping, helpers may enable the bereaved to recognize, evaluate, and (where necessary) modify their behaviors. This is the gentle work of suggesting different ways of coping, not so much directly as by enabling the bereaved person (sometimes through a joint effort) to assess his or her own thoughts and behaviors. Questions such as "What seems to help get you through the day?" or "What is the most difficult thing for you to deal with?" may assist the bereaved person to understand how he or she is coping.

10. Identify pathology and refer. Most people who engage in helping the bereaved are not prepared to deal with complicated grief reactions on their own. That is, most of us do not possess the specialized skills and expertise of a qualified grief therapist (Rando, 1993). But helpers and counselors can remain alert for manifestations of complicated grief and can play a very important role in referring those who need them to appropriate resources. This is not a failure; it is a responsible recognition of one's own limitations. Such referrals are guided by the discussion of complicated grief reactions in Chapter 8 and by an informed sensitivity to that which is truly excessive in the mourning process (Sanders, 1989).

Summary

This chapter has reviewed some of the many ways in which individuals and society can act to help those who are coping with loss and grief. Examples of unhelpful messages have been noted and explained, together with helpful ways in which to assist bereaved persons with tasks in mourning. This sort of assistance essentially constitutes a program for "befriending" the bereaved. In recent years in American society, similar approaches have also been undertaken by support groups for the bereaved and hospice bereavement follow-up programs. Another form of helping the bereaved is professional counseling, which may be appropriate for those who encounter difficulties in coping with normal mourning processes. In this chapter, ten principles are sent forth for facilitating uncomplicated grieving in counseling relationships.

QUESTIONS FOR REVIEW AND DISCUSSION

1. Think of a time when you experienced the loss of some person or some thing that was important in your life. What did you want others to do with or for you at that time? What did you find unhelpful from others? What was most important: who tried to help, when they tried to help, or how they tried to help?

2. Bereaved persons often report that many other individuals were not helpful to them in their bereavement. Think of a time when you sought or at least needed help from other persons and did not receive it. Why did you not receive the help that you sought or needed? Now imagine what it would be like to be bereaved. Try to understand what it is like not to receive help when you are bereaved. Why do other individuals not understand what the lost person or object meant to the bereaved person?

3. Many bereaved persons report that they have found help in their grief from support groups or hospice bereavement follow-up programs. Why might that be so? What is it that these groups and programs offer to bereaved persons? What do you think we could learn from these groups and programs in our own efforts to help the bereaved?

SUGGESTED READINGS

For advice about helping oneself or others in grief, see:

Brothers, J. (1990). *Widowed.*
Caine, L. (1978). *Lifelines.*

Graham, L. (1990). *Rebuilding the House.*
Grollman, E. A. (1977). *Living When a Loved One Has Died.*
Grollman, E. A. (Ed.). (1981). *What Helped Me When My Loved One Died.*
Kushner, H. S. (1981). *When Bad Things Happen to Good People.*
Lewis, C. S. (1976). *A Grief Observed.*
Linn, E. (1986). *I Know Just How You Feel . . . Avoiding the Clichés of Grief.*
Manning, D. (1979). *Don't Take My Grief Away from Me: How to Walk Through Grief and Learn to Live Again.*
Rando, T. A. (1988). *Grieving: How to Go on Living When Someone You Love Dies.*
Sanders, C. M. (1992). *Surviving Grief . . . and Learning to Live Again.*
Schiff, H. S. (1986). *Living Through Mourning: Finding Comfort and Hope When a Loved One Has Died.*
Smith, A. A. (1974). *Rachel.*

Guidance for professional helpers is provided in the following:

Johnson, J., Johnson, S. M., Cunningham, J. H., & Weinfeld, I. J. (1985). *A Most Important Picture: A Very Tender Manual for Taking Pictures of Stillborn Babies and Infants Who Die.*
Johnson, S. (1987). *After a Child Dies: Counseling Bereaved Families.*
Rando, T. A. (1993). *Treatment of Complicated Mourning.*
Sanders, C. M. (1989). *Grief: The Mourning After.*
Weizman, S. G., & Kamm, P. (1985). *About Mourning: Support and Guidance for the Bereaved.*
Worden, J. W. (1991). *Grief Counseling and Grief Therapy: A Handbook for the Mental Health Practitioner* (2nd ed.).

Social implications of grief and bereavement are introduced in the following:

Carter, B., & McGoldrick, M. (Eds.). (1988). *The Changing Family Life Cycle: A Framework for Family Therapy* (2nd ed.).
Hanson, J. C., & Frantz, T. T. (Eds.). (1984). *Death and Grief in the Family.*
Magee, D. (1983). *What Murder Leaves Behind: The Victim's Family.*
Redmond, L. M. (1989). *Surviving: When Someone You Love Was Murdered.*
Walsh, F., & McGoldrick, M. (Eds.). (1991). *Living Beyond Loss: Death in the Family.*

Concerning support and self-help groups, see:

Lieberman, M. A., & Borman, L. (1979). *Self-Help Groups for Coping with Crisis.*
Silverman, P. R. (1980). *Mutual Help Groups: Organization and Development.*
Silverman, P. R. (1986). *Widow to Widow.*

CHAPTER 10

Funeral Practices and Other Memorial Rituals

This chapter examines funeral practices and other memorial rituals that are found in most communities following a death. Traditionally, such study has focused on the work of funeral directors, cemetery operators, and monument makers. In contemporary American society, this might include such elements as removal of the body from the place of death, embalming and viewing the body, a funeral service, and delivery of the body for final disposition; the role of cemeteries and crematoria in providing in-ground burial or above-ground entombment in a mausoleum or crypt; and related memorial objects, such as monuments, grave markers, and memorial photographs. People, objects, and activities of this sort are part of the social mechanisms designed to help bereaved individuals and the community begin to meet postdeath needs. Their work is an important aspect of every society's death system.

This chapter begins with a description of a Mexican-American funeral. Next are some introductory reflections on the place of ritual in dealing with crises in human life, and some general remarks on the place of funeral ritual in contemporary society. The bulk of the chapter describes funeral practices in some detail, both in themselves and in terms of the contributions they can make to the grief work of bereaved persons. To conclude, there is a brief description of some roles played by cemeteries, memorial sculpture, and memorial photographs in mourning.

A Funeral Vignette

Moore (1980, pp. 80–83) described prominent features of a Mexican-American funeral in the following way:

> After the death and its certification, the body is moved to the funeral home. . . .
> There is greater participation by all ages and degrees of involvement with the dead person than in the normal [sic] American funeral.
>
> The rosary is said in Spanish. . . . The old women wail. . . . We progress to the viewing—and touching, and kissing—of the body. . . . Condolences are then shifted from the dead person to his family and the wake moves to the home, for talking, eating and drinking.
>
> The funeral mass the next day begins to shift the focus to the whole family and community. . . . Novenas, grave visits . . . punctuate the family's life for several months after the death. . . . For a period after the burial the family lives quietly; social activities are sharply reduced. In some families, radio and television are turned off. Girls are kept from dating. . . . For several months after the death of an old person, family controls are reasserted over all members. . . . Family reintegration at the funeral depends on the sacrifices made by the large-family to be present at the ceremony.
>
> Just as the family must rally, so must the community rally. . . . The family's link to the past—its historical status in the community—is reaffirmed. . . . The funeral helps maintain ethnic cohesiveness.

Life Crises and Ritual

A funeral is a ritual, and rituals play important roles in the lives of most human beings. Ritual has been studied carefully by anthropologists and others for nearly a century. Various definitions of ritual have been used in these studies. We employ one proposed by Mitchell (1977), who described *ritual* as "a general word for corporate symbolic activity" (p. xi). The corporate or communal symbolic activity involved in ritual generally has two components: it involves *external (bodily) actions*, such as gestures, postures, and movements, which symbolize interior realities; and it is *social*—that is, usually the community is involved in ritual activity (Douglas, 1970).

One can identify ritual practices of this sort in almost all human societies. In particular, Van Gennep (1961) emphasized the links between ritual and crises in human life. That is, rituals are most often associated with a number of important turning points in human life, including childbirth, initiation into adulthood, marriage, and death. A crisis threatens the invasion of chaos into human life; ritual can order these events (to some extent), thereby making the unfamiliar more familiar by providing guidance as to how one should act in these unusual (but not unanticipated) circumstances. In other words, rituals "tame" the strange or the unusual experiences in human life to some degree.

Since death is one of the most impressive invasions of chaos and disorder into human life, it is not surprising that throughout the course of human history one can observe efforts to bring order into lives that have been affected by death (Bendann, 1930; Puckle, 1926). Thus, some of the most ancient artifacts that anthropologists and archaeologists have discovered apparently had something to do with rituals associated with death and burial. Also, as one moves forward from prehistoric to more recent times, everywhere one looks one finds societal rituals associated with death. As Mead (1973, p. 89–90) wrote: "I know of no people for whom the fact of death is not critical, and who have no ritual by which to deal with it."

Funeral Ritual in Contemporary Society

In our society, funeral and memorial practices have sometimes been severely criticized (for example, Harmer, 1963; Mitford, 1963). Some believe that funerals are useless and therefore repugnant—a form of fantasized flight from reality (Harmer, 1971). Consequently, they urge us no longer to have funerals at all and to move away from any sort of ritual activity after a death. They would prefer to use the time, energy, and money that has traditionally been invested in a funeral in some other way. Others agree in criticisms of what they perceive as lavish and expensive funeral practices (Arvio, 1974; Bowman, 1959), but favor less ostentatious memorial services conducted without the presence of the body and often held two or three weeks after the death. This latter viewpoint substitutes one form of ritual for another but is not opposed to all death-related ritual as such (Irion, 1966, 1971, 1991; Lamont, 1954; Morgan, 1990).

Of course, many in our society continue to believe that funerals can and often do serve an important role in human life. If one holds this view, one believes (at least implicitly) that some sort of funeral and burial ritual may help people to make sense of, and to bring order out of, what is potentially a very disruptive, stressful, chaotic moment in human life (for example, Jackson, 1966; Raether, 1989). That is, people holding this view recognize the role of funeral and memorial rituals in serving constructive grief work (Margolis & Schwarz, 1975; Pine, 1975; Pine et al., 1976; Rando, 1985). This view is evident in the description of the Mexican-American funeral given earlier and in the accounts of the attitudes and practices of other ethnic groups in Kalish and Reynolds (1981).

In fact, research on these topics reports both criticisms of funeral practices from certain points of view (for instance, Fulton, 1961; Kalish & Goldberg, 1978) and much satisfaction among the general public (Bolton & Camp, 1987; Fulton, 1978; Kalish & Goldberg, 1980; Marks & Calder, 1982). In the end, it seems that participation in funeral rituals and assessments of their value are matters that must be determined by specific individuals and groups. Opinions may differ in this sensitive area.

To guide those decisions, it is useful to describe some rituals that have been or are associated with death and burial in our society. The framework for this description is an analysis of three basic tasks that are involved in funeral ritual. The overall aim of this discussion is to come to a better understanding of the nature and purposes of funeral and other commemorative rituals, and to help readers determine for themselves whether or not these rituals are effective in serving significant needs in their lives. Additional information can be obtained from local sources (such as funeral homes, memorial societies, cemeteries, crematories) and from the resources listed in "Funerals and Related Matters: National Organizations."

Tasks Associated with Funeral Ritual

Some early work on funeral ritual was conducted by anthropologists and sociologists (Durkheim, 1915/1954; Fulton, 1988; Goody, 1962; Malinowski, 1954; Mandelbaum, 1959) who used the language of *functions* to explicate this ritual. In keeping with our commitment in this book to encourage proactive approaches in which bereaved and other vulnerable individuals can work to regain control over lives that have been impacted by death, we prefer to interpret funerals and other memorial rituals through a task-based approach. Accordingly, we propose that these rituals should assist bereaved persons in particular and society in general to address the following three tasks: (1) to dispose of the body in appropriate ways; (2) to contribute to realization of the implications of the death; and (3) to assist in social reintegration and meaningful ongoing living. Each of these tasks will be considered

Funerals and Related Matters: National Organizations

American Cemetery Association
3 Skyline Place, Suite 1111
5201 Leesburg Pike
Falls Church, VA 22041
(703) 379-5838

Continental Association of
Funeral and Memorial
Societies
6900 Lost Lake Road
Egg Harbor, WI 54209
(414) 868-3136

Cremation Association of North
America
401 N. Michigan Avenue
Chicago, IL 60611
(312) 644-6610

International Order of the
Golden Rule
1000 Churchill Road
Springfield, IL 62704
(217) 793-3322

Jewish Funeral Directors of
America
250 W. 57th Street, Suite 2329
New York, NY 10107
(212) 628-3465

Monument Builders of North
America
1740 Ridge Avenue
Evanston, IL 60201
(708) 869–2031

National Catholic Cemetery
Conference
710 N. River Road
Des Plaines, IL 60016
(708) 824-8131

National Funeral Directors
Association
11121 W. Oklahoma Avenue
Milwaukee, WI 53227-4096
(414) 541-2500

National Funeral Directors and
Morticians Association
1800 E. Linwood
Kansas City, MO 64109
(816) 921-1800

National Selected Morticians
5 Revere Drive, Suite 340
Northbrook, IL 60062-8009
(708) 559-9569

Telophase Cremation Society
1545 Hotel Circle S., Suite 390
San Diego, CA 92108
(619) 299-0805

in turn, as a way of describing and evaluating elements of funeral and memorial ritual.

Disposition of the Body

One unavoidable task associated with death is that the body of the deceased person must be removed from the society of the living. To fail to do so is to risk violating both social attitudes and community health. In all societies, the manner in which this removal is accomplished has required respect for the body as the remains of someone valued as a human being (Habenstein & Lamers, 1974). Thus, most human beings are uncomfortable with allowing the corpse simply to be discarded or to be left lying around. In addition, dealing with a dead body necessitates behavior in accordance with the religious or philosophical beliefs that an individual and his or her society hold about life and death (Kephart, 1950). Disrespect for either of these can result in serious conflict, as is evident in Sophocles' *Antigone*. In that play, Antigone is concerned that the body of her dead brother must be buried; by contrast, King Creon is concerned that burial of that body will show improper respect for a rebellious subject.

Disposition of the body in some traditional societies   In some societies that uphold beliefs about an afterlife, it is thought that the dead person must be assisted in his or her journey into that other life state. The ancient Egyptians were one such society that had firm beliefs about an afterlife. Apparently, part of the reason for their mummification of the bodies of the dead was to assist individuals who had been prominent persons in life as they traveled into that other world. By preserving the body and placing next to it food, utensils, or even boats for the "journey across," the ancient Egyptians appear to have been attempting to help the person accomplish the trip without mishap (Hamilton-Paterson & Andrews, 1979).

But dead bodies have also seemed frightening and dangerous to some peoples. Thus, some societies have held that the community must engage in certain actions to make certain that the dead remain dead; that is, the community must protect itself from threatening actions that the dead might take against living members of society. In this perspective, not only must the dead be assisted in their journey to the other world, but also the living must make certain that they stay there and do not return to menace us. The Navajo are one group who seem to hold beliefs of this sort (Carr & Lee, 1978). Accordingly, in Navajo tradition, great care must be taken in the ways in which dead bodies are handled, because if the body of a dead person is not handled just so, the spirit of that person may continue to threaten members of the community in this world.

Zoroastrians survive today only as a small group in India, called Parsees. In the Zoroastrian view of the world, water, fire, and the earth are all regarded as holy. In addition, Zoroastrians hold that dead bodies are contaminated and contaminating (Noss & Noss, 1990). Thus, dead bodies may not be placed in the earth or in any body of water; that would contaminate the holy. Nor may such bodies be burned; that, too, would contaminate the holy—in this case, fire. So the Parsees believe that dead bodies are to be left exposed to the air, to be consumed by vultures, bacteria, and other creatures of the air.

Early Christians believed that the afterlife would involve a resurrection of the body. Such a resurrection would require a new creative act by God. Thus, the dead body of a person was not an object about which people needed to be concerned. If God were expected to recreate the body at the moment of its resurrection, it did not matter much what might happen to the body between death and that glorious moment of new divine action. Accordingly, bodies were buried together in unmarked graves. Eventually, after the fleshy portions had decayed, the bones would be dug up and put in charnel houses, all mixed together. This reflects a different set of beliefs—and thus actions also—from those of other groups.

From these examples, we can see that rituals associated with the care of the dead body are tied to other beliefs: beliefs about the nature of persons, about whether or not there is an afterlife (and what that afterlife is like), and about the universe itself.

Disposition of the body in contemporary American society   When we turn to contemporary American society, the situation seems remarkably more complex. As a society, it would appear that Americans have few or no explicit religious or philosophical beliefs about the nature of the person, the universe, or any afterlife. For many of us, a person is either identified with our physical, material bodies, or is some combination of a body and a mind or soul. But even when there are no explicit beliefs to guide body disposition, custom and practice may continue.

For example, in contemporary American society one very common practice associated with disposition of the body is embalming (see Mayer, 1990). In the United States, embalming grew in popularity after the Civil War as a practice that made it possible to ship dead bodies back home for burial from distant battlefields. The most celebrated example of this occurred in the case of Abraham Lincoln, whose body was shipped by rail from Washington, D.C., where he was assassinated, to Springfield, Illinois, for burial. All of this took place during a warm part of the year when decomposition of the body was likely to occur more rapidly. The problem was that the funeral train made many stops along the way to accommodate the needs of grief-stricken Americans. If normal biological processes of decomposition had not been delayed, they would have transformed Mr. Lincoln's body into an object of social repugnance long before the train reached its destination.

Embalming in the modern era means the removal of blood and other bodily fluids from a corpse and their replacement with artificial preservatives that may help to retard decomposition and to color the skin. Embalming may or may not be accompanied by efforts to restore the cosmetic appearance of the corpse. (Note that no state law or federal regulation requires embalming to be done, unless certain conditions are present. For instance, embalming may be required if the body is to be transported on a common carrier, such as a train or airplane. Laws and regulations vary; consumers should check about regulations that may apply in particular situations or locations.) Embalming is not universally practiced in other parts of the world, although its use seems to be growing in some other countries now, too.

If we ask why bodies are embalmed, several answers may be offered (Raether, 1989). First, embalming supposedly prevents the spread of disease by disinfecting the corpse and neutralizing contaminants in discarded blood and bodily fluids. Second, embalming slows decay in the bodily tissues of the corpse. One could achieve these first two goals by disposing of the body promptly or by refrigerating the body. It has also been claimed that embalming in our society today is done in order to permit viewing of the body during a wake or a funeral with an open casket. If such viewing is not held to be an important social function, embalming may have little apparent significance as a general practice.

One could also argue that embalming has an important *psychological* significance. That is, embalming may help mourners to evade thoughts of the decay of the body of the person who has died. In this way, embalming may play a role in death denial, or at least in permitting mourners to turn their attention away from the full implications of death. But unless one insists upon full and immediate confrontation with all of the consequences of death, this sort of behavior is not in itself undesirable—at least temporarily or for some persons.

In the United States today, disposal of bodies is typically carried out in one of the following ways: burial in the ground or in some sort of crypt, vault, or mausoleum above the ground; cremation; donation to a medical or other institution for dissection or other similar purposes, such as scientific research or professional education (Habenstein & Lamers, 1962).

Burial in the ground is still the most common form of body disposal in the United States ("Cremations," 1992). Generally, the body is buried within several days of the death; for some groups, it may be accomplished prior to sundown on the day of the death or within 24 hours. The amount of time between death and burial in our society is usually related to the time needed to prepare the body, make necessary arrangements, and—above all—gather together family members and other important persons from distant parts of the country.

Cremation involves placing the body in some sort of container and reducing its size through the application of intense heat (Irion, 1968). The container need not be a casket; crematories typically only require that the body be turned over to them in a container in which it can be handled easily and safely. The body and its container are then heated to approximately 1800 degrees Fahrenheit. Since most of the human body is water, the water evaporates. At the high temperatures reached during cremation, the rest of the soft tissues are consumed by spontaneous combustion. The effect of this process is to reduce the size of bodily remains in a rapid and significant fashion. The residue is primarily ash and those fragments of dense bone that have not been vaporized by heat. When these remains have cooled, they are collected and then usually ground up or pulverized into a coarse powder. Subsequently, the person responsible for the "cremains" may choose what to do with this residue. For example, it may be scattered over water (as practiced by the Neptune Society in California), enclosed in an urn or permanent container, buried, or placed in a crypt or niche in a mausoleum. In 1991, cremation was the outcome in approximately 17 percent of the more than two million deaths in the United States ("Cremations," 1992). Cremation may be an alternative to embalming, viewing, and a funeral, or it may follow those activities as a step between them and final disposition.

Some persons prefer to have their bodies put to some constructive use after death. If one wishes to *donate one's body for teaching or research purposes*, arrangements must be made well ahead of time. Careful preservation of the body is important under these circumstances, and the techniques required to prevent decay are considerably more stringent than those used in the typical embalming procedure. Thus, the receiving institution will require access to the body soon after death. Following use of the body for scientific or educational purposes, those elements that remain may be cremated or buried by the institution or returned to next of kin for similar disposition.

Making Real the Implications of Death

A second task addressed by funeral and memorial ritual is the recognition and acceptance—the "making real"—by survivors of the implications of death. (Some have called this "separation" from the deceased.) This is a difficult task for many persons. If a person is unable to accomplish this task, that person's life may be disrupted in more serious ways than if the task is accomplished. Thus, it may be helpful to engage in actions that assist in the process of recognizing the permanent separation of the dead from the living.

The funeral can be of assistance in this process of psychological separation of survivors from the deceased (Mandelbaum, 1959; Turner & Edgley, 1976). Some have argued that seeing the dead body helps to make the death real. Observing the behavior of people at wakes lends some credence to this claim. During a wake, survivors often return again and again to the casket. Often, they will stare at, touch, or kiss the dead body. They seem to be saying final farewells and impressing a last image into their minds, even as the cold, rigid, and nonlifelike features of the corpse convey to them in a silent but forceful way the realities of its differences from a living body.

If in fact the ritual of the funeral is to help with separation, then presumably some of the actions and events associated with it should point to the permanence of the separation. Criticisms have been directed to some contemporary funeral practices as failing to assist the bereaved in this task. For example, it has been argued that the use of cosmetics and the expensive linings of caskets both seem to promote an image of life, rather than of death (Harmer, 1963, 1971; Mitford, 1963). If it is important to help survivors make the death real for themselves, then contributing to the appearance that the dead person is "asleep," head on a pillow, lying on a mattress, surrounded by beautiful bed linens, may be counterproductive. At least, some critics have urged this.

At the same time, other critics have argued that this process draws too much attention to the body itself (Morgan, 1990). After all, issues involved in making real the implications of death are concerned primarily with taking leave of the *person*. In this sense, the body is not the primary concern, although it is certainly important. The death is a fact. Funeral and memorial rituals are intended to contribute to the recognition of that fact in the subjective world of individual and social psyches.

Issues involved in realization and separation also arise at the place of burial. Sometimes mourners are encouraged to leave the grave site before the body is lowered into the grave. In other cases, cemeteries have built chapels and prefer that the last rite be performed there, rather than at the grave site. These practices appear to have to do mainly with allocation of work load among the cemetery's personnel and a desire not to risk upsetting mourners in the course of a process that usually involves enclosing the casket within a vault or grave liner, lowering it into the grave, and refilling the grave. But these practices also tend to distance mourners from the realities of the death and may in that way run counter to the desired work of making real the implications of the death.

These issues stand out when one thinks about practices at an earlier time in the history of our society that are continued even today in some ethnic or religious groups (for example, among the Amish, as mentioned in Chapter 2). According to such practices, the family might bathe and dress the body, hold the wake in the home, perhaps make the coffin with their own hands, dig the grave, lower the body into the grave, and throw the first shovelfuls of dirt and/or fill in the grave with dirt (see, for example, Faulkner, 1930). These were seen as loving acts of respect for the person who had died. It may be easier to understand how acts of this type contribute to realization and separation than how some other practices found in contemporary society do so. This suggests the importance of connecting ritual practice with its symbolic or functional meaning and associated tasks.

A second set of criticisms has been directed toward costs involved in much contemporary funeral practice (Arvio, 1974; Bowman, 1959). Airtight or watertight metal caskets are expensive objects. Critics have asked: What real purposes are served by such elaborate merchandise? Even if they prevent the body from decaying—and they almost certainly do not—why is that important?

The answers to some of these questions seem to reside at the psychological level of mourning. Some persons have argued that spending money for a funeral and burial allows mourners to feel satisfaction in having shown respect and love for the person who has died. After all, it is often said that the expenditures involved in buying a casket and paying the associated costs of a funeral and burial are the third highest financial outlay that most people will make during their lives, exceeded only by the purchase of a house and an automobile. In this sense, the expenses associated with a funeral can be seen as a kind of "going-away" present. At least indirectly, this may support the realization that the dead person *is* going away.

In addition, the purchases associated with the funeral represent to some people the last gift or service that they can make to the person who has died. And the conviction that the body will be "protected from the elements" may provide some psychological satisfaction to the survivor. Note that this may be true whether or not the merchandise or services actually do accomplish what the buyer thinks they will accomplish. That is, much of what is going on here—especially in its psychological components—is really designed to serve the needs of the living (Jackson, 1963). As consumers, individuals must themselves determine whether the costs of funeral practices and other associated items are justified by the services they purchase (Consumer Reports, 1977; Nelson, 1983).

Reintegration and Ongoing Living

Death involves disintegration, so a third task facing survivors is to achieve a new integration. Funeral practices and other ways in which persons conduct themselves after a death can assist in beginning this process (Malinowski, 1954).

Death and disintegration   The death of someone whom one loves leads to disintegration, a breaking apart of the world as it has been known. This sort of disintegration occurs at many levels. For purposes of this discussion, individual, familial, and social levels of disintegration can be distinguished.

People who experience the death of an important person in their lives often experience various kinds of disintegration at *the individual level*. That is, they feel a loss of integrity or unity within themselves. For example, some mourners have the sense that they are "going crazy." Sleep patterns, eating patterns, and health concerns all may be disrupted by the death of a loved person. In short, the customary ways in which individuals live in the world and their familiar sense of who they are can be shredded by a death.

The impact of death is also evident at *the familial level*. The death of a person has many meanings for those closest to that person. It has economic repercussions, such as the loss of income, the loss of an owner of property, or the loss of the person who may typically have handled certain financial transactions. Death also has consequences for the ways in which those closest to the person relate to the rest of the world. They may, in some important respects, no longer have the social identity that they previously had—for example, as the spouse of the dead person. Also, death can exacerbate old tensions within a family, just as it may create new tensions. All of these are forms of familial disintegration associated with death. They impose upon members the task of reintegrating the family unit (Friedman, 1980; Goldberg, 1973).

Finally, almost all deaths have an impact at *the social level* to some degree or other. This is most obvious when someone of great social standing, such as a president or a pope, dies. But the death of any one person is likely to cause some measure of social disintegration. Someone else will have to make the decisions that that person used to make. Someone else will have to take over the work associated with that person's job. Someone else will have to drive more often in the car pool.

Achieving a new integration   In our society, perhaps the most noticeable sign of renewed integration after a death is the physical or geographical drawing together of persons who ordinarily see little of each other in their everyday lives. Our families are often scattered among several towns or states. A funeral is one moment when families are reintegrated.

Ritual and support for a mother who has lost her son.

In doing this, a funeral can help to make clear that the disintegration brought about by this death can be overcome. The mourners need not see themselves as *alone*. The work they need to perform *can* be accomplished, in part through the aid of persons drawn to their sides by the funeral. Although mourners may feel overwhelmed by the grief and disorientation that they experience, they are not simply powerless or adrift on wholly uncharted seas. They cannot change the fact that a death has occurred. But they can, with the assistance of relatives, friends, and other helpers, determine how to respond to that fact and how to regain control over the course of their lives.

In some cultural groups, the funeral and other rituals associated with a death go on for months or even years (at different levels of activity during these periods of time). A good example of this is the Jewish tradition of rending one's clothes (*Keriah*), reciting the prayer for the dead (*Kaddish*), and organizing activities in specified ways for particular periods of time. As Gordon (1974, p. 101) has written: "Judaism recognizes that there are levels and stages of grief and so it organizes the year of mourning into three days of deep grief, seven days of mourning [*shivah*], thirty days of gradual readjustment [*Shloshim*], and eleven months of remembrance and healing." In practices such as these, the support system is there, again and again, to assist survivors in finding their way through this period of crisis and into the new world that they are entering—a world without the dead person in it. By contrast, for most individuals in our society, the funeral takes place usually, at most, a matter of days after the death. After that, the participants scatter again, and for many people there is no agreed-upon or designated path through the wilderness of grief and mourning. Integration may be hard to achieve under such circumstances. The most important considerations in this situation are how individuals make use of funeral ritual and how they follow up on the beginnings represented by that ritual.

At the social level, funeral rituals can help to provide a sense that the society is not going to fall apart because of this death. Clear examples of this have been provided by the funerals of national leaders, such as John Kennedy or Martin Luther King, Jr. The public ritual of their funerals gave testimony to the ongoing viability of the community and provided opportunities for individuals to rededicate themselves to working on behalf of a better society in the future (Greenberg & Parker, 1965; Wolfenstein & Kliman, 1965).

A funeral, then, can help to pull together a family, a society, or an individual disrupted and disintegrated by a death. Integration of this sort may take a long time. With the brief rituals that we call funerals in our society, this process can usually only be begun. A funeral, as we typically know it in the United States today, may not go very far toward accomplishing this task, but it can be a beginning. Perhaps it is in recognition of the limitations of contemporary funeral practices in many segments of our society that many funeral directors have recently developed "aftercare" programs of support and counseling for the bereaved (Raether, 1989). All of these activities help to initiate the process of grief work and make plain that integration is possible.

Cemeteries and Memorialization

Social activities following a death usually include three components: (1) a wake or visitation (that is, a viewing of the body and/or coming together of survivors) and the funeral (some sort of more or less formal service); (2) burial or some other form of disposition of the remains; and (3) other elements of memorialization. The wake, funeral, and burial contribute toward the commemoration of a life that has now ended. Other memorial activities are represented by the development of cemeteries, memorial sculpture, and memorial photography.

Activities following a death in America have gradually evolved into what has been called a distinctively American way of death (Coffin, 1976; Fales, 1964; Farrell, 1980). To begin with, *cemeteries* in America have evolved from frontier graves, domestic homestead graveyards, churchyards, potter's fields, and town or city cemeteries (such as the New Haven Burying Ground in Connecticut) especially typical of the 17th and 18th centuries, through what were originally 19th-century rural cemeteries (like Mount Auburn in the Boston area) and lawn-park cemeteries (like Spring Grove in Cincinnati), to memorial parks in the 20th century (like Forest Lawn in the Los Angeles area) (Kastenbaum, 1989b; Sloane, 1991). Recently, our society has also witnessed rapid growth in the development of animal cemeteries for beloved pets (Spiegelman & Kastenbaum, 1990).

Most American cemeteries were and are privately owned, although there also are national cemeteries (such as those for veterans) and cemeteries with public or religious ownership. In the last 100 to 150 years, many cemeteries have stressed an aesthetic layout, even a picturesque or pastoral landscape. Some have become major tourist attractions—for example, Forest Lawn Memorial Park in Glendale, California, which has been the object of both literary satire (Huxley, 1939; Waugh, 1948) and scholarly study (French, 1975; Rubin, Carlton, & Rubin, 1979; Zanger, 1980). For our purposes, the diversity and changing character of cemeteries in our society give testimony to the fact that death and the place of final disposition for the body have aroused quite different attitudes in Americans over the history of our country.

Beyond this, "the most remarkable changes in the American cemetery industry in the last forty years have been the resurgence of entombment as an important method of disposal and the steady, recently spectacular, rise of cremation" (Sloane, 1991, p. 220). These two developments, both alternatives to earth burial, reflect different, although not necessarily wholly disconnected, historical phenomena. Also, the mausoleum in which entombment is accomplished is an aspect of a larger history of *memorial sculpture.*

This history is associated with the evolution of cemeteries, in which wooden or stone markers have given way to marble, granite, and bronze (Forbes, 1927; Gillon, 1972). Some of these markers have been quite plain (providing, for example, only the name and dates of birth/death for the deceased). Others have included artistic icons and three-dimensional markers or pieces of sculpture. In times past, grave markers often displayed elaborate epitaphs (Coffin, 1976; Mann & Greene, 1962, 1968). Recently, for aesthetic reasons and in light of costs associated with maintenance, memorial sculpture in American cemeteries has mainly taken the form of religious or abstract objects of art as centerpieces in the landscape, together with flush-to-the-ground markers at individual grave sites. Again, many factors enter into American attitudes toward death and contribute to a changing view of the tasks that fall upon bereaved survivors.

A third area of memorialization is seen in the practice of *memorial photography,* which has developed since the invention and ready availability of photographic technology in the 19th century. Memorial photographs have been used in our society as a means of retaining for survivors a tangible memento of the person and funeral of the deceased (Burns, 1990; Jury & Jury, 1978). They include snapshots taken by relatives, as well as images created and preserved by professional photographers. More recently, for some people these practices have come to include the use of videotaping.

Although it has been claimed that postmortem photography is a morbid or unhealthy custom (Lesy, 1973), the extent of this practice and its many variations testify to the fact that it must serve some needs of those involved.

*A cemetery in
San Juan,
Puerto Rico.*

In fact, this sort of photography is a striking example of the related needs of survivors to distance themselves from the dead, to acknowledge the implications of their loss, and to carry with them an image of the deceased as they move on in their own lives (Ruby, 1984, 1987, 1991, in press). This directly parallels the three tasks described earlier in this chapter as associated with funeral ritual. In addition, differences in attitudes toward memorial photographs illustrate tensions in our society between practices that individuals perceive as helping them meet the requirements of their grief work and public lack of understanding or discomfort with such practices. Efforts to achieve a new understanding of funeral and memorial ritual may help to ease these tensions in our society.

The National Cemetery in San Francisco.

Benjamin Franklin's Epitaph

The body of Benjamin Franklin, Printer
(Like the cover of an old book
Its contents worn out
And stripped of its lettering and golding)
Lies here, food for the worms.
Yet the work shall not be lost,
For it shall (as he believed) appear once more
In a new and most beautiful edition
Corrected and Revised
By the Author.

Summary

Funeral and memorial ritual can help survivors and society dispose of the body in appropriate ways, realize the implications of a death, and begin social reintegration and meaningful ongoing living. The issue is whether these tasks are accomplished well or poorly. That is, the basic question that emerges from this chapter is whether and how any specific funeral practice or associated ritual serves the needs of bereaved individuals and their social groups.

Because there are many possible choices concerning such practices and rituals, individuals and communities have available to them important options following a death.

In planning or taking part in a funeral or other memorial ritual, it is always appropriate to ask: What do these gestures, these actions, or these words mean or suggest? This sort of question may be difficult to pose when a person is in the throes of grief. A better moment to think through the rationale for what one might desire in funeral and other forms of postdeath ritual is *before* the ritual is needed. Preplanning can be helpful in providing a funeral that successfully meets individual, familial, and societal needs. Such preplanning should take account of the individual and social tasks to which funeral and memorial ritual can contribute.

QUESTIONS FOR REVIEW AND DISCUSSION

1. This chapter has argued that ritual can play an important role in human life. Think about rituals (activities involving symbolic external or bodily actions by a community) that you have attended. What purpose(s) do you think they were intended to serve? Why did the persons involved engage in the ritual at all? And why did they choose to engage in the specific (symbolic) actions they performed?

2. Suppose someone whom you love has died. What sorts of activities would you want to have performed at his or her funeral or memorial service? What might be helpful for you at such a moment? What might not be helpful? Reflect carefully on your answers here and compare them to an actual funeral or memorial service that you have attended (or, if you have not attended such an event, think about what you have heard others say about such events).

3. If you were to die, what would you want done with your body? After you answer this question, ask yourself why you gave that answer. Can you relate it to other beliefs, attitudes, and encounters that you have had concerning death?

SUGGESTED READINGS

Criticisms of American funeral practices can be found in the following:

Arvio, R. P. (1974). *The Cost of Dying and What You Can Do About It.*
Bowman, L. E. (1959). *The American Funeral: A Study in Guilt, Extravagance and Sublimity.*

Harmer, R. M. (1963). *The High Cost of Dying.*
Mitford, J. (1963). *The American Way of Death.*
Waugh, E. (1948). *The Loved One.*

More favorable analyses of funeral practices are provided by the following:

Habenstein, R. W., & Lamers, W. M. (1962). *The History of American Funeral Directing* (rev. ed.).
Habenstein, R. W., & Lamers, W. M. (1974). *Funeral Customs the World Over* (rev. ed.).
Irion, P. E. (1966). *The Funeral: Vestige or Value?*
Jackson, E. N. (1963). *For the Living.*
Jackson, E. N. (1966). *The Christian Funeral: Its Meaning, Its Purpose, and Its Modern Practice.*
Margolis, O., & Schwarz, O. (Eds.). (1975). *Grief and the Meaning of the Funeral.*
Pine, V. R. (1975). *Caretaker of the Dead: The American Funeral Director.*
Pine, V. R., Kutscher, A. H., Peretz, D., Slater, R. C., DeBellis, R., Volk, A. I., & Cherico, D. J. (Eds.). (1976). *Acute Grief and the Funeral.*

Alternatives to traditional funeral practices are described in the following:

Irion, P. E. (1968). *Cremation.*
Irion, P. E. (1971). *A Manual and Guide for Those Who Conduct a Humanist Funeral Service.*
Lamont, C. (1954). *A Humanist Funeral Service.*
Morgan, E. (1990). *Dealing Creatively with Death: A Manual of Death Education and Simple Burial* (12th ed.).

The history and roles of cemeteries, photography, and other memorial practices are described in the following:

Burns, S. B. (1990). *Sleeping Beauty: Memorial Photography in America.*
Forbes, H. (1927). *Gravestones of Early New England and the Men Who Made Them, 1653–1800.*
Gillon, E. (1972). *Victorian Cemetery Sculpture.*
Ruby, J. (in press). *Secure the Shadow ere the Substance Fade: Death and Photography in America.*
Sloane, D. C. (1991). *The Last Great Necessity: Cemeteries in American History.*

PART IV

LIFE CYCLE PERSPECTIVES

Each human being who is alive is a member both of a common human community and of a distinctive developmental cohort. Much of this book describes that which is widespread or common in contemporary North American experiences of death—changing encounters with death and attitudes toward death that affect everyone in society, and the experiences of dying or bereavement that many or all share, regardless of age or developmental status. In addition, a variety of cultural differences have been identified in ways in which individuals and groups interact with death. The four chapters that follow consider another point of view, that of development across the life span. We examine aspects of death-related experiences that are more or less unique to specific eras in the human life cycle.

To take up a developmental point of view is not to abandon but to complement the social, cultural, historical, and universal contexts that have been described thus far. In other words, a developmental perspective adds to these situational factors elements arising from the special tasks and projects associated with human maturation.

Originally, the merit of a developmental perspective was most evident in the explication of childhood. Subsequently, it came to be recognized that developmental processes continue throughout the human life cycle. It cannot yet be claimed that we have a full or final understanding of the implications of a developmental perspective. A richer appreciation of what is involved in human development is available at some stages of the life cycle than at others, just as more is known about developmental implications in some subject areas than in others. Nevertheless, the value of a developmental perspective in overall comprehension of human life and experiences is unmistakable.

Many thinkers, such as Freud (1933/1959b), Jung (1933/1970), Havighurst (1953), Bühler (1968), and Neugarten and Datan (1973), have contributed to our understanding of the human life cycle. Among such thinkers, Erikson (1963, 1968) is especially well known for his articulation of eight stages or eras in human development. These stages are set forth in Table IV.1, along with the polarities or tensions and the ego qualities that Erikson believed are characteristic of each stage.

Erikson's model is meant to describe the normal and healthy development of an individual ego (which may be, but is not necessarily, correlated with chronological age) as it pursues the establishment of its own identity. Each stage in development is characterized by a basic issue or task. That issue,

TABLE IV.1   Erikson's Stages in the Human Life Cycle

Stage	Age	Predominant Issue	Virtue
Infancy	0–1	Basic trust vs. mistrust	Hope
Early childhood	1–3	Autonomy vs. shame and doubt	Will or self-control
Play age	4–5	Initiative vs. guilt	Purpose or direction
School age	6–11	Industry vs. inferiority	Competency
Adolescence	12–21	Identity vs. role confusion	Fidelity
Young adulthood	21–45	Intimacy vs. isolation	Love
Middle age	45–65	Generativity vs. stagnation and self-absorption	Production and care
Maturity	65+	Ego integrity vs. despair	Renunciation and wisdom

From Erickson, 1963, 1968.

in turn, is conceptualized as a pair of alternative orientations or "attitudes" toward life, the self, and other people. These alternative attitudes represent opposed tendencies or dialectical polarities. The way in which each of these basic issues is resolved by the developing person leads to a "virtue"—that is, a strength or quality of ego functioning.

Erikson's point is that each basic issue or task has a time of special ascendancy in the life cycle that is critical for the overall development of the ego. The way in which an individual resolves a given polarity or tension and establishes its corresponding ego quality or virtue is likely to be relatively persistent or enduring. According to Erikson, failure to resolve the tasks of one era leaves unfinished work for subsequent eras. In other words, Erikson maintains that (1) developing individuals strive to integrate aspects of their inner lives and their relationships with the social world around them; (2) the tasks undertaken in this effort toward integration depend upon the stimulus of different crises or turning points that unfold as development proceeds; and (3) the way in which the integration is or is not managed determines the individual's present quality of life, potential for future growth, and residual or unresolved work yet to be achieved.

Erikson's model is not the only theoretical framework that might be significant for a developmental portrait of death, dying, and bereavement, and it is not without its limitations (see, for example, Miller, 1983). It has limitations in the ways in which it is relevant to different cultural groups; it may apply equally to both sexes only in societies that give equal options to men and women (Gilligan, 1982); and it tends to describe individuals outside familial or other systemic contexts (McGoldrick, 1988). Nevertheless, Erikson's work does provide a paradigm from which to begin to investigate the developmental implications of death-related experiences. The point to emphasize in this section is not so much the details of developmental theory as the fact that "death is one of the central themes in human development throughout the life span. Death is not just our destination; it is a part of our 'getting there' as well" (Kastenbaum, 1977b, p. 43). The question to ask is: How or in what ways is death a distinctive part of our "getting there" during the principal eras of the human life cycle? In the following chapters, answers to that question are organized around four main developmental cohorts: children, adolescents, adults, and the elderly.

One other concept from Erikson that is useful for a developmental discussion is the idea of "triple bookkeeping." By this, Erikson means that an adequate account of human development must bring together three sets of factors: social context, ego process or identity, and somatic process or constitution (Erikson, 1963). These three factors represent "history, personality, and anatomy" (Erikson, 1975, p. 228) or the arenas of the humanities, social sciences, and biology. What a developmental account of death-related experiences in our society calls for is a sensitivity to the many dimensions of human interactions with death at different stages in the life cycle.

The four chapters that follow highlight both the shared and the unique aspects of a developmental perspective on death-related experience through a common general structure consisting of a short introductory paragraph and vignette or case example; a brief description of the particular era in the life cycle and its associated Eriksonian tasks; and individual sections on encounters with death, attitudes toward death, issues in dying, issues in bereavement, and issues that have special prominence in the era at hand.

CHAPTER 11

Children

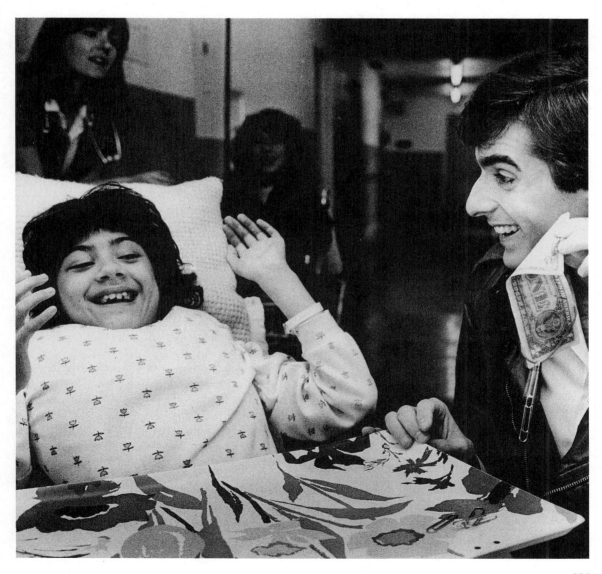

This chapter examines interactions with death during childhood. This is the period from birth to adolescence, roughly through age 11, which developmental theorists like Erikson (1963, 1968) have further divided into four distinguishable stages: infancy, early childhood, preschool or play age, and school age or the latency period. Some believe that more is known about death-related experiences during childhood than in any other period in the human life cycle. Still, much remains to be learned about this period in relationship to the subject matter of this book. Partly for that reason, it is useful here to discuss the whole of childhood in a single chapter. Also, this approach permits us to identify developmental changes and continuities that run throughout the period.

After a brief vignette designed to illustrate some of the issues that may arise for children in relationship to death in contemporary American society, this chapter considers in turn additional comments about children and their distinctive developmental tasks; typical encounters with death in American society during childhood; the development of death-related concepts and attitudes toward death during this period; issues related to dying children; issues related to bereaved and grieving children; and principles for helping children cope with death.

One Child and Death

In the film *And We Were Sad, Remember?* (1979), a young girl named Allison who is about 7 years old is awakened during the night by a telephone call from her father to her mother. He is calling from a hospital in another town where Allison's grandmother has just died.

After the call, Allison's mother explains to her that Grammie's heart has just stopped. She says that she will drive to the other town tomorrow, and asks whether Allison and her younger brother, Christopher, would like to go with her to Grammie's funeral. She explains what a funeral is and Allison says that she wants to attend. When Christopher wakes up, Allison asks him if he would also like to go with her to the "fumeral."

A day or two later, Allison's father tells her that he has arranged for her and Christopher to stay with an adult friend during the funeral and to have a fun adventure. Allison replies that her mother had told her that she could go to the funeral. She insists that she wants to attend and begs him to let her do so. He is quite reluctant, finally agreeing only that he will think about it and decide later. Allison observes that whenever he says things like that, it usually means no.

When the family and friends are all gathered at the home, Allison and her cousin get into an argument. They are playing with their dolls and acting out a scene of illness and death. Allison wants to cover the doll who has "died" with a blanket. Her cousin replies that she has been told that dying is like going to sleep. If so, the doll will still need to breathe and it cannot do so if the blanket covers its face. The children take their dispute to Allison's father, who orders them to stop fighting, to put the dolls away, and to get ready for bed. When

Allison insists that he settle their disagreement, he replies in exasperation: "Little girl, you don't have to worry about that for a hundred years."

Children, Developmental Tasks, and Death

At one time, children were mainly thought of as miniature adults (Ariès, 1962). After infancy, when they became able to move about more or less independently, their clothing and much of their behavior was expected to be modeled along adult lines (the Amish still follow many of these practices). More recently, with greater sensitivity to developmental differences, that viewpoint has largely been abandoned. Now distinctions are drawn between childhood and all other stages in the human life cycle, and discriminations are made between different eras within childhood itself. Thus, developmental theorists trace a succession of tasks throughout the specific stages of childhood—from the development of *trust* and *autonomy* in infants and young children, through the establishment of *initiative* and *industry* in preschool and school-age children (Erikson, 1963; see Table IV.1). Adults are able to correlate that account with their own appreciation of children, who can be evaluated as confident and hopeful infants, as relatively independent and sometimes willful agents in early childhood (think of the "terrible twos"), as becoming more purposeful during their preschool years, and as developing specific competencies throughout their primary school years.

Some youngsters advance in these developmental processes more rapidly than others. Some are delayed by various physical or psychosocial factors. Others are influenced by the social, cultural, or historical contexts in which they find themselves. Often, a child's development is defined and evaluated in relationship to chronological markers, which are relatively easy to determine and which appear to be objective. However, this is not primarily a matter of chronology but one of psychosocial development. Thus, some individuals who are adult in body and size remain at the developmental level of a young child and must in many (but perhaps not all) ways be treated with the latter perspective in mind.

Sensitivity to the special status and characteristics of children, coupled with a heightened awareness of the roles of adults as their comforters and protectors, has led many in American society to adopt a policy that assumes that children are unaware of and must be sheltered from all death-related events. For example, like Allison's father, many adults in the United States today hold the view that it is inappropriate for children to attend or take part in funerals. In support of such a viewpoint, it is claimed that children under some stipulated age would not be able to cope with the emotionally charged experience of a funeral and, more generally, would be traumatized by encounters with the realities of death. Thus, Grollman's (1967, p. 24) suggestion that "from approximately the age of seven, a child should be encouraged to attend" has been misinterpreted to support the view that children under the age of 7 should be prohibited from attending funerals. Is that true? If chronological age is not, on its own, a sufficient criterion for determining what is or is not appropriate for children in their interactions with death, why should the age of 7 be taken as a magic threshold in deciding whether or not children should attend funerals?

At this point, it is not important to belabor questions about children and funerals or issues involving the responsibilities of adults as authoritative guides for the constructive socialization of children. We will return to such topics later in this chapter after we have considered more fully the typical sorts of encounters, understandings, and attitudes that many children have in relationship to death.

Encounters with Death

" 'The kingdom where nobody dies,' as Edna St. Vincent Millay once described childhood, is the fantasy of grown-ups" (Kastenbaum, 1973, p. 37). The realities of life during childhood include both deaths *of* children and deaths experienced *by* children. *Deaths of children* are especially prominent in infancy and early childhood. Approximately 39,000 children die each year during their first year of life in the United States. More than half of these deaths are the result of four principal causes: congenital anomalies, Sudden Infant Death Syndrome (SIDS), disorders related to short gestation and low birth weight, and Respiratory Distress Syndrome (RDS; a pattern of events most often associated with premature birth and inadequate respiratory development) (National Center for Health Statistics, 1993). Approximately 7,000 children die each year in the United States during early childhood (the next three years of life), mainly as a result of accidents and congenital anomalies. In fact, after the first year of life, accidents are the leading cause of death throughout the remainder of childhood (and on through adolescence and early adulthood) (National Safety Council, 1991). Moreover, by 1990 human immunodeficiency virus (HIV) infection had become the eighth leading cause of death for children 1–4 years of age and the tenth leading cause of death for those 5–14 years of age (National Center for Health Statistics, 1993). Often, for young children this represents an infection transmitted from their mothers during pregnancy, at birth, or shortly thereafter (Kübler-Ross, 1987).

Given its special features, we discuss SIDS—the leading cause of infant deaths in the period from one month to one year of age, which caused some 5,400 deaths in the United States in 1990 (National Center for Health Statistics, 1993)—in Chapter 13 in relationship to parental bereavement, along with miscarriage, spontaneous abortion, and stillbirth.

One wit has said that "being born is hazardous to life." This is evident in the congenital anomalies and inadequate fetal development that result in so many deaths during infancy and the years of early childhood. It is also evident in the remaining years of childhood, even though childhood has the lowest of all death rates for all age groups in the United States (just over 30 per 100,000). During this developmental period (normally corresponding to the time from 4 through 11 years of age), American society records a yearly average of approximately 1,000 deaths for each year of age.

It is true that both the rates and numbers of deaths in later childhood are much lower than those in the first three years of life and in all subsequent years; nevertheless, preschool and school-age children *do* die in the United States from communicable diseases, cancers, other natural causes, and homicide. Because these latter deaths are relatively infrequent in American society, they are often perceived as especially tragic by survivors.

Deaths experienced by children are also a reality of life in the United States today, though American society and many of its members appear to undervalue their prevalence and importance for children. Death may come to grandparents, parents, friends, neighbors, siblings, peers, pets, and other animals while an individual is a child. The pattern of these experiences will very likely differ for individual children and may vary according to ethnic, cultural, or other social groupings. Around the globe, children may experience deaths from combat or starvation; these are not so likely in American society, although some urban, Appalachian, and Native-American children are not unfamiliar with violent deaths of various sorts.

The point to emphasize is that living in the world even as a child exposes one to these and other death-related events, whether or not adults or society recognizes that fact (Papadatou & Papadatos, 1991). The inquisitive curiosity of children makes it unlikely that such events would be completely ignored, although the ways in which they are acknowledged and dealt with by a child may not be obvious to a casual observer. To appreciate the ways in which children experience death, two large topics associated with children's encounters with death must be examined: the development of death-related concepts and the development of death-related attitudes in childhood.

The Development of Death-Related Concepts in Childhood

One of the best-known studies of the development of death-related concepts in childhood is the work of Maria Nagy (1948). Nagy examined 378 children who were 3–10 years of age in Budapest just before World War II. Her methods were as follows: children in the 7–10-year-old range were asked to "write down everything that comes into your mind about death" (p. 4); children in the 6–10-year-old range were asked to make drawings about death (many of the older children also wrote explanations of their creations); and discussions were held with *all* of the children, either about their compositions and drawings, or (in the case of 3–5 year olds) to get them to talk about their ideas and feelings about death.

According to Nagy (1948, p. 7), the results suggested three major developmental stages: (1) "The child of less than five years does not recognize death as an irreversible fact. In death it sees life"; (2) "Between the ages of five and nine death is most often personified and thought of as a contingency"; and (3) "In general only after the age of nine is it recognized that death is a process happening in us according to certain laws." Brief descriptions of each of these stages, using Nagy's own characterizations, will permit evaluation of her account.

Stage 1: There Is No Definitive Death

In this stage of children's conceptual development, Nagy believes that *death is not seen as final.* That is, life and consciousness are attributed to the dead. Thus, death is understood either as a departure or a sleep, or as gradual or temporary. In the first pair of alternatives, death is interpreted in terms of continued life elsewhere (departure) or as a diminished form of life (sleep). For Nagy, this denies death entirely. Note, however, that even when death is interpreted as the deceased living on in altered circumstances, changes in one's life that are brought about by this separation may still be painful. One does not have to have what some would call a "mature" or "adequate" concept of death in order to experience strong feelings.

There is another point to notice about the notion that death is a kind of continuation of life: since most children are not satisfied with the simple fact of death as disappearance, they will usually want to know where and how the deceased person continues to live. This may lead children to fanciful speculations about the nature of life in the grave. Because these speculations are based upon a limited fund of life experiences, they may generate misinterpretations or ill feelings on the part of the child.

As a result of her study, Nagy believes that there is also a second set of alternatives within this first stage of conceptual development. In these alternative concepts Nagy says that children "no longer deny death, but . . . are still unable to accept it as a definitive fact" (p. 13). That is, children who hold these views cannot completely separate death from life. Hence, death is seen as a gradual, transitional process (between dying and being buried or arriving in heaven) or as a temporary situation in which links with life have not yet been completely severed. To Nagy, this means that life and death are either held in simultaneous relation or they are interpreted as being able to change places with one another repeatedly. In short, although death exists, it is not absolutely final or definitive.

Stage 2: Personification of Death

According to Nagy, in this stage *death is imagined as a separate person* (such as a skeleton, grim reaper, bogey man, ghost, or death angel), or else *death is identified with the dead themselves.* For Nagy, this means that the definitiveness or finality of death has been accepted. However, in her view children have a strong aversion to the thought of death. As a result, they interpret death as a reality outside or remote from us. In this way, death is conceived of as final, but avoidable or not inevitable. Those whom the external force catches do die; those who escape or get away from the clutches of that force do not die. It may be important to note here that later researchers (for example, Anthony, 1972; Gartley & Bernasconi, 1967) have emphasized the theme of death's avoidability in this stage, rather than its personification (which may only be a child's concrete way of emphasizing the avoidability of death through the device of an external figure).

Stage 3: The Cessation of Bodily Activities

In this stage, Nagy believes that children recognize that *death is the cessation of corporeal life*. That is, death is final. It is also universal and inevitable—that is, no longer avoidable. The reason for this is that death is now understood to be a process operating within human beings. In other words, death is a part of life; it applies to everyone. Death applies to me; it is personal.

Nagy's concluding remarks (1948, p. 27) are good advice for everyone: "To conceal death from the child is not possible and is also not permissible. Natural behavior in the child's surroundings can greatly diminish the shock of its acquaintance with death."

Some Thoughts About Stage-Based Models of Cognitive Development

There is much to be said on behalf of Nagy's investigation of the development of death-related concepts in childhood. It was thoughtful and well organized. Key elements in the concept of death are exposed, such as finality, avoidability versus inevitability, external versus internal forces, and universality (Lonetto, 1980).

Nagy's work also had the great advantage of fitting easily within the larger framework of Jean Piaget's overall system of developmental psychology (Wass, 1984; see Table 11.1). Because of that, Nagy's work was readily accepted and perhaps not adequately subjected to critical challenge in light of other views on this subject. Nagy's characterization of the earliest stages in her account of children's concepts of death accorded with Piaget's observations about an egocentric orientation and several other characteristics of what he calls "preoperational thought"—for example, magical thinking (in which all events are explained by the causal influence of various commands, intentions, and forces), animism (in which life and consciousness are attributed to inanimate objects), and artificialism (in which it is believed that all objects and events in the world have been manufactured to serve people, a belief that directly opposes animism). Similarly, the universality and inevitability that characterize Nagy's final stage conform to Piaget's account of objectivity, generality, and propositional thinking in what he calls the "period of formal operations." Both Piaget and Nagy essentially view childhood as involving a maturation in the capacity to form more or less abstract concepts of subjects such as death.

TABLE 11.1   *Piaget's System of Cognitive Development*

Period and Stage[a]	Life Period[b]	Some Major Characteristics
I. Period of sensori-motor intelligence	Infancy (0–2)	"Intelligence" consists of sensory and motor actions. No conscious thinking. Limited language.[c] No concept of reality.
II. Period of preparation and organization of concrete operations		
1. Stage of preoperational thought	Early childhood (2–7)	Egocentric orientation. Magical, animistic, and artificialistic thinking. Thinking is irreversible. Reality is subjective.
2. Stage of concrete operations	Middle childhood/preadolescence (7–11/12)	Orientation ego-decentered. Thinking is bound to concrete. Naturalistic thinking. Recognizes laws of conservation and reversibility.
III. Period of formal operations	Adolescence and adulthood (12+)	Propositional and hypodeductive thinking. Generality of thinking. Reality is objective.

[a]Each stage includes an initial period of preparation and a final period of attainment; thus, whatever characterizes a stage is in the process of formation.

[b]There are individual differences in chronological ages.

[c]By the end of age 2, children have attained a vocabulary of approximately 250–300 words, on the average. From H. Wass, 1984. *Concepts of Death.*

To some extent, Nagy's model has suffered at the hands of followers who simplify it, make it more rigid than was originally suggested, and apply it uncritically. Thus, Nagy's stages have been generalized to all children, without taking into account methodological problems with her work and historical or cultural variables in different populations of children. Many who write about children have also been insufficiently attentive to the impact of socialization upon human development and to the difference between developmental stages and chronological age. Only by ignoring this last distinction could we continually assert that children under (or over) some specific age are or are not able to think in particular conceptual ways about death. When children are screened for their developmental level, as in research by Koocher (1973), it becomes obvious that the most significant variable in children's concepts of death is not age but level of cognitive development. Even that variable should not be framed in overly rigid stages that permit only one direction of movement and do not allow for conceptual "retrogression" in certain circumstances (for example, in challenging crises). In addition, broad concepts of death also should be examined in terms of their significant subconcepts, such as irreversibility, cessation, causality, and inevitability (Lazar & Torney-Purta, 1991).

As adults strive to explain the ways in which children understand death, it should be noted again that cognitive development is not the only relevant factor. In the first place, maturation is a multidimensional process that applies to all aspects of a child's life; it is not confined solely to cognition. Moreover, there are at least three other significant variables that affect children's interactions with death: life experiences, individual personality, and patterns of communication and support (Kastenbaum, 1977b). More broadly, socialization processes across the life span draw upon multiple components, such as personality, culture, and social institutions. Those who seek to enter into the world of children in responsible ways must see beyond chronological age on its own in order to be sensitive to the many differences that make each child unique.

For example, quite different challenges are presented to a child when he or she is asked to comprehend the two following sentences: "You are dead" and "I will die" (Kastenbaum, 1992; Kastenbaum & Aisenberg, 1972). The first sentence applies to another person at the present time; the second is valid for me at some unspecified time in the future. Thus, the issues involved are partly conceptual, but they are also directly related to the way in which the second sentence is or is not seen to have personal relevance for the individual child in question. Therefore, when it comes to efforts to understand death, children who are able to draw upon a fund of personal experience, whose self-concept is stable and well formed, who communicate openly, and who have adequate support from the adults around them are in a different position from children who do not have these resources.

It is also important to keep in mind that development in all respects, whether in childhood or in other parts of life, is a complex and ongoing process. It may only conform in very broad and general ways to theoretical depictions of sharply defined phases and stages. Obviously, children do not develop at the same pace, in the same ways, or with the same outcomes. Adults who draw sharp chronological lines across the fluid processes of human development may primarily be satisfying their own needs for conceptual neatness.

Moreover, it is incorrect to believe that children who have not achieved a certain developmental stage will necessarily have no conceptual or other cognitive interpretation of death. More likely, if the subject of death has arisen for them in some form, they will have their own concepts and interpretations, different from the concepts of adults and/or of other children. Children who think of death as sleep are not without any concept of death. They have *an* understanding—however undifferentiated it may be from other concepts and however inadequate it may seem in the light of some adult standard—with which they will try to make sense of new experiences. The fundamental lesson of Nagy's study is that children do make an active effort to grasp or understand death.

To communicate effectively with children, adults need to try to appreciate the concepts and the language used by children. Children are not blank tablets until (at some arbitrary age) adults first write upon them. To enter into the thinking of children, adults must listen to them, determine what and how they are able to understand, and decide whether a particular cognitive interpretation of death should or should not be reinforced. In other words, adults must learn how to shape messages so as to serve their own needs and the needs of children simultaneously. This is a lesson that Allison's father in our opening vignette has not yet learned.

The Development of Death-Related Attitudes in Childhood

Children in the United States today receive many messages about death. The primary sources of those messages are the societal death system that surrounds them and that expresses itself, in particular, through the media; their parents, family members, and others with whom they come into contact; and their own experiences in life.

Many messages from society, parents, and other adults tell children that death is not an acceptable topic for discussion and that death-related events are not open to participation by children. These messages have not been shared with children in all societies at all times. For example, in some subgroups in colonial America (Stannard, 1977) and in contemporary Amish society (Hostetler, 1980), children were or are expected to take part in both the happy and the sad events in a family's life. Anything other than that would have seemed or would still seem undesirable and impracticable.

Death-related situations and experiences may be new to children in American society, as are many other situations in life. But new experiences need not be overwhelming until children have been taught to view them that way. Just because something is new, it need not be out of bounds from the inquiring mind of a child. When one is told that "the child is so recently of the quick that there is little need in his spring-green world for an understanding of the dead" (Ross, 1967, p. 250), it is likely that one is listening either to someone who is really unfamiliar with the authentic lives of children or to an adult who himself or herself finds it difficult to cope with death and who is projecting his or her anxieties upon the children around him or her. In fact, there is ample evidence in everyday interactions with children and in the scholarly literature (going back as far as the 1920s and 1930s, for example, Childers & Wimmer, 1971; Hall, 1922; Koocher, O'Malley, Foster, & Gogan, 1976; Schilder & Wechsler, 1934) that normal, healthy children do have thoughts and feelings about death.

The specific form of any particular child's attitudes toward death, as toward any other significant subject, will relate to the nature of the child's involvement with that subject and to the developmental, personal, and societal resources that help to shape the child's interpretation and response to a given experience. For example, very young infants who have little experience or conceptual capacity give very clear evidence of separation anxiety. Older children who had no role in a parent's death may nevertheless blame themselves if they believe that something they said or did was magically related to the death. In short, attitudes toward death are complex, even in childhood, and may derive from many sources. Contrasting explanations have focused on different aspects of children's feelings, perceptions, and behavior (Wass & Cason, 1984). Rather than speculate about the origins of death-related attitudes in childhood, it will be more profitable here simply to describe two arenas in which death-related attitudes are manifested during childhood.

Death-Related Games

Maurer (1966) suggested that the game of peek-a-boo is a paradigm of a death-related game in childhood. From the child's egocentric perspective, what happens in this game is that the external world vanishes and then suddenly reappears. As a child focuses on the (apparent) disappearance of the world, he or she may become fearful; its reappearance will often produce delight. What have we learned here? In childhood, one can easily identify attitudes related to experiences that are (at least) very much like death.

Further, Rochlin (1967) reported research with children and their play activities that demonstrated "that at a very early age well-developed mental faculties are functioning to defend oneself against the realization that life may end" (p. 61). Thus, children appear to recognize that their lives might be changed in important ways by death and act upon that recognition in the fantasy world of their play. Rochlin's research focused especially upon children's games that are concerned with action, violence, and at least the potential for death. From this, he concluded that "death is a matter of deep consideration to the very young child . . . thoughts of dying are commonplace . . . behavior is influenced by such thoughts" (p. 54). This is not a point to dismiss lightly, since play is the main work of a child's life.

Rhymes, Songs, Humor, and Fairy Tales

Death frequently appears in children's rhymes and humor. For example, many have sung a little ditty in which "the worms crawl in, the worms crawl out." Others will be familiar with "Ring Around the Rosie," but may not have realized that it is an English song arising from a plague and describing the roseate skin pustules of smallpox, as a result of which "we all fall down." Even lullabies, like "Rock-a-Bye Baby," are suffused with falling cradle themes (Achté, Fagerström, Pentikäinen, & Farberow, 1990).

Children's fairy tales, whether oral or written, are also full of references to death. Little Red Riding Hood and her grandmother were eaten by the wicked wolf in the original version of the story, not saved by a passing woodsman or hunter before or after they found themselves in the wolf's stomach (Bertman, 1984; Dundes, 1989; Zipes, 1983). The Big Bad Wolf who pursued the three little pigs with threats to huff and puff and blow their houses down, died in a scalding pot of hot water when he fell down the last chimney. Hansel and Gretel (who had been left to die in the forest by their parents because there was not enough food) tricked the wicked witch and shut her up in the hot oven where she had planned to cook them. The wicked stepmother ordered the death of Snow White and demanded her heart as proof. A gentle kiss may have awakened Sleeping Beauty from a state of coma, but the false bride in "The Goose Girl" was put into a barrel lined with sharp nails and rolled until she was dead (Lang, 1889/1975).

It is not correct to think that death-related humor and stories of this sort are necessarily morbid or unhealthful for children. Bettelheim (1977) has argued forcefully that they are, in fact, wholesome experiences in which children can work through fears and anxieties related to death in safe and distanced ways. Death is not absent from the fantasy world of childhood. Its familiar presence gives the lie to the view that children are simply unfamiliar with death-related thoughts and feelings. Indeed, in the United States today the very powerful force of television repeatedly suggests that the way in which people usually come to be dead is by being killed, that only "bad" guys really die, and that death itself is not permanent.

Children Coping with Life-Threatening Illness and Dying

Children who are coping with life-threatening illness and dying are likely to experience a great deal of anxiety. As they acquire information about their condition, their self-concept is likely to change in discernible ways. And they are likely to share an identifiable set of specific concerns associated with dying.

Anxiety in Ill and Dying Children

When Vernick and Karon (1965) so aptly asked, "Who's afraid of death on a leukemia ward?" their answer was *everyone*—children, family members, and professional caregivers. This is important, because it suggests a basis for coming together and sharing with children.

By contrast, when Waechter (1971) first began to study ill and dying children, she found herself working in a context in which parents and caregivers did not share with such children accurate information about their diagnoses and prognoses. Waechter investigated the attitudes of these children by creating four matched groups of 6- to 10-year-olds: children with chronic disease for which death was predicted; children with chronic disease with a good prognosis; children with brief illness; and nonhospitalized, well children. In the course of an interview, each child was given a projective test (a set of pictures for which the child was to develop a story in each case) and a test designed to measure general anxiety.

This study demonstrated that anxiety levels in fatally ill children were much higher than those for either of the other two groups of hospitalized children or for the well children, and that the fatally ill children expressed significantly more anxiety specifically related to death, mutilation, and loneliness than did other ill children. This was true even though the fatally ill children had not formally been informed of their prognosis. Other studies of ill and dying children have confirmed similar findings (for example, Spinetta & Maloney, 1975; Spinetta, Rigler, & Karon, 1973; and Waechter, 1984, in the United States; and Lee, Lieh-Mak, Hung, & Luk, 1984, in China).

Acquiring Information and Changing Concepts of Self

A different sort of study was conducted by Bluebond-Langner (1977, 1978; see Table 11.2) using the techniques of cultural anthropology with hospitalized, terminally ill children with leukemia. This study revealed the children's keen awareness of their situation. According to Bluebond-Langner, five stages could be identified in the children's process of acquiring information. The sobering—and really not very surprising—lesson from this portion of Bluebond-Langner's study is that children pay attention to important experiences in their lives, and acquire information from people and events that impact very closely upon them.

Bluebond-Langner's research went one step further. She noted that acquisition of information was coordinated with parallel shifts in the child's self-concept. That is, as the children obtained information, they applied it to a changing understanding of themselves. According to Bluebond-Langner, changes in self-concept were associated with events in the illness process and the information that presented to the children. There are two significant elements here: the timing of these changes in relationship to external events and the ability of the children to integrate and synthesize information arising from their experiences in order to form new self-concepts.

Children learn from their experiences, from other children, and from the ways in which they are treated by adults around them. How could it be otherwise? What they learn is not just abstract information; it comes to have meaning and significance for them. As suggested in a seminal article by Alexander and Adlerstein (1958), the central point may be not so much the *content* of death conceptions, as their *significance* for the individuals in question. This is a point that will be pursued in Chapter 12. Here it is enough to suggest that children's concepts of death will be intimately associated with ways they feel about and interpret both themselves and the world around them.

Issues for Ill and Dying Children

Various authors have described the needs of ill and dying children in slightly different ways. For example, Adams (1979, 1984) has written about the importance of love and security with freedom from pain, freedom from deep-seated feelings of guilt, a sense of belonging, a feeling of self-respect, and understanding of self. Waechter (1984) added a developmental perspective in her description of children with life-threatening illness. According to Waechter, preschool children are likely to have principal concerns about the causality of their illness, threats to body image, treatment procedures, and fears of dying, while school-aged children have concerns about communicating about the future, education and social relationships, body image, and additional issues related to hospitalization and procedures. Not surprisingly, much of this is about safety (pain or other forms of distress, intervention procedures, bodily assault) and security (both within oneself and in relationship to family members, peers, and other important persons).

TABLE 11.2   *The Private Worlds of Dying Children*

Stages in the Process of Acquiring Information	Changes in Self-Concept
1. I have a serious illness	1. From diagnosis (prior to which I had thought of myself as well) to awareness that I am seriously ill
2. I know the drugs that I am receiving, when and how they are being used, and their side effects	2. At the first remission, to the view that I am seriously ill—but will get better
3. I know the purposes of treatments and procedures	3. At the first relapse, to the view that I am always ill—but will get better
4. I understand that these treatments, procedures, and symptoms fit together to identify a disease in which there is a cycle of relapses and remissions (that is, the medicines do not always last as long or work as well as they are supposed to) (does not include death)	4. After several more remissions and relapses, to the view that I am always ill—but will never get better
5. I understand that the cycle of disease is finite, it has an end, and that end is death—there are only a limited number of drugs and when they stop working, I will die soon	5. After the death of a leukemic peer, to the realization that I am dying

From M. Bluebond-Langner, 1978. *The Private Worlds of Dying Children.*

Many of the concerns of dying children emphasize quality in living and the immediate or present-tense implications of various sorts of threats to quality in living (Krementz, 1989; Pendleton, 1980). This is not surprising when one considers the tendency of many children to live in the moment. It is reinforced by the fact that cure rates for many illnesses that were once highly lethal for children have changed so dramatically in recent years that the challenge has largely changed from coping with dying to living with a serious or life-threatening illness (Adams & Deveau, 1987; Koocher & O'Malley, 1981; Spinetta & Deasy-Spinetta, 1981).

Children Coping with Bereavement and Grief

At one point in the scholarly literature, there was a debate about whether or not children are able to grieve after a death (see, for example, Furman, 1973). This debate appears to rest upon a failure to distinguish between grief and mourning and upon an absence of adequate models for childhood mourning. Surely, children grieve (that is, react to loss). They may cry, get angry, become depressed, have trouble sleeping, regress in their behavior, or respond in other ways to loss.

However, children do not always react to loss in the same ways that adults do, and they may not always express their reactions in the same ways that adults do (Wolfenstein, 1966). For example, grieving children may not display their feelings as openly as many adults do, they may not withdraw into preoccupation with thoughts of the deceased person, and they may immerse them-

Those who have AIDS need love and care as do all living persons.

selves in activities of everyday life (Romond, 1989). In short, there may be significant differences between adult and child grievers, a point that should not be very surprising when we think about the differences between children and adults.

The real issue for grieving children is not so much whether they can grieve but what their grief and mourning are like. That is, what are the central concerns that are likely to preoccupy grieving children? And what are the tasks of mourning that children face in coping with loss and grief?

Issues for Grieving Children

Three central issues are likely to be prominent in the grief experiences of bereaved children and may apply to the perceived or real termination of any relationship for children: (1) Did I cause it (death or some other form of loss) to happen?; (2) Is it going to happen to me?; and (3) Who is going to take care of me? (Worden, 1991b). The egocentricity of these issues is obvious. When a child does not rightly understand the causality involved in a loss, perhaps because of ignorance or magical thinking, it is not surprising that issues of origin and endangerment would present themselves.

The death of a parent or other caring adult may be especially significant for the first and third of the issues identified by Worden (1991b). For example, if Mommy says in exasperation one day, "You'll be the death of me," and is later killed in a car accident, a child may indeed wonder whether the latter event fulfilled the promise of the former statement. Similarly, when children are dependent upon parents and other adults in so many ways for their safety and welfare, it is not surprising that a child who observes the death of an important person in his or her life might begin to wonder who will provide the care that he or she needs when that person is gone (Donnelly, 1987; Furman, 1974; Krementz, 1981).

If someone dies in the family and a child perceives that that sad event was not prevented by Daddy (or by the doctor or others), then the child may think that he or she could experience the same unhappy fate. Here, the death of a sibling or other child may be especially difficult since it seems to strike so close to the child's own peer group. A sibling or playmate is simultaneously companion, competitor, and alter ego; loss and ongoing deprivation of that person may have long-term effects through the individual's childhood and later life (Donnelly, 1988; Rosen, 1986).

Children respond to bereavement experiences in ways that suit the characteristics of their particular developmental situation (Fleming, 1985; Furman, 1974; Silverman, Nickman, & Worden, 1992; Silverman & Worden, 1992). For example, children who do not appreciate the finality of death may wonder what sort of activities are undertaken by the deceased, who is understood to be alive in a different way or in a different place. By contrast, children who do appreciate the finality of death may ask very concrete questions about what happens to one's body when it stops working.

In their actions, grieving children sometimes simply turn away—for example, to watch television or to go off to school. To adults, this appears to display lack of awareness, comprehension, or feeling. In fact, it may involve a short attention span or a temporary defense against being overwhelmed by the loss and its implications. Strong feelings of anger and fears of abandonment or death may be evident in the behaviors of grieving children. Also, as noted earlier, it appears that children often play death games as a way of working out their feelings and anxieties in a relatively safe setting. After all, games are a familiar part of the lives of children and in games the child can stand safely aside from the harm that comes to the toys or imaginary figures.

In American society, many adults withdraw into themselves and limit communication when they are grieving. By contrast, children may talk to those around them, even to strangers, as a way of watching for reactions and seeking clues to guide their own responses. Similarly, children often ask questions over and over again—"I know that Grandpa died, but when will he come home?"—as a way of testing reality and confirming that the story about what happened has not changed. Some questions from children baffle adults: "Where is dead?"; "When you die and go to heaven, do you have to do home-

A child's depiction of her grief.

work, too?''; ''If Grammie died and went *up* to heaven, why is she buried *down* in the ground?'' When viewed from the developmental and experiential perspective of a child, these are quite logical efforts to interpret the meaning of what has happened.

Tasks in Mourning for Grieving Children

Ill children, dying children, and children who are bereaved may all be grieving children. As such, they are children who are responding to the events and the losses that have occurred in their lives. Mourning is the process of coping or learning to live with loss and grief. In childhood, mourning is a situational response that overlays basic developmental tasks. Therefore, the work of mourning in childhood may need to be addressed again and again in appropriate ways at different developmental levels. Thus, an individual child may grieve and mourn the death of his or her mother, her absence in months and years that follow, what that subsequently means for being different from schoolmates who have a living mother, and his or her inability to draw upon the absent mother's support or to share achievements with her in later school years. Reworking losses and grief responses in this way is quite consistent with maturational processes. Healthy mourning integrates losses in ways that shake off unhealthy encumbrances and facilitate ongoing living (E. Furman, 1984; R. A. Furman, 1973).

Fox (1988) identified four tasks that are central to productive mourning in grieving children: (1) to understand and make sense out of what is happening or has happened; (2) to grieve or express emotional responses to the present or anticipated loss; (3) to commemorate the loss through some formal or informal remembrance; and (4) to learn how to go on with living and loving. One way to interpret Fox's model is to see the first of these as a cognitive task; it involves assembling information and seeking to interpret its meaning. Then, the second task has to do with affect or emotion; for children, it may involve the identification and validation of feelings, as well as their appropriate expression. The third task has to do with behavior or acting out some form of memorializing or remembering the life that was lived. The fourth task looks to values; it concerns the framework and perhaps the permission that a child may need in order to know that it is appropriate to find ways to go on with healthy living in the aftermath of a significant loss. It is important to keep in mind that these and similar mourning tasks may shift in focus and relative significance as the bereaved child proceeds in his or her grief work (Baker, Sedney, & Gross, 1992).

Helping Children Cope with Death

The basic principle in helping children to cope with death is more a matter of attitude than one of technique or easily definable skills. As Erikson (1963, p. 269) has written: "Healthy children will not fear life if their elders have integrity enough not to fear death." All too often, adults adopt tactics that attempt to insulate children from death-related events, avoid such topics, and deny the finality of death (Becker & Margolin, 1967). If so, children's efforts to acquire information, to get answers to their questions, to express their feelings, and to obtain support will all be blocked. In all of this, helpers should assist children in their coping and help to empower the adults in a child's life (parents or other family members, teachers, or other significant persons) to assist that child.

At the very least, children deserve the support and assistance of their elders in dealing with challenges presented by death. These challenges *will* arise and children *will* attempt to deal with them. The only real option open to adults is to choose whether or not to make available their experience, insights, and emotional resources to children. The more responsible course is to help our children, not more or less deliberately to hinder them.

"Part of each child's adventure into life is his discovery of loss, separation, non-being, death. No one can have this adventure for him, nor can death be locked in another room until a child comes of age" (Kastenbaum, 1972, p. 37). Although we cannot live life for our children or face death on their behalf, we can prepare them to do this for themselves and we can often walk alongside, at least part of the way. This really applies to all children, not just to those who are dying or bereaved (Schaefer & Lyons, 1986).

Helping children to cope with death is an ongoing process, not a unique event that occurs only at one specific point in time. Children often repeat over and over again questions or insights that interest them. Important issues will need to be readdressed as children confront different developmental and situational challenges. This is part of the continuing maturation and socialization

Being a Child and Being Alone

Do you know the sensation of being a child and being alone? Children can adapt wonderfully to specific fears, like a pain, a sickness, or a death. It is the unknown which is truly terrifying for them. They have no fund of knowledge in how the world operates, and so they feel completely vulnerable.

SOURCE From J. Katzenbach, 1986.

of children. It will be conducted in a natural and effective manner when it draws upon ordinary events in living, together with questions and initiatives posed by children. That does not preclude opportunities that adults might help to create for constructive dialogue. For example, summer camps for children who share an illness experience (such as cancer) have been shown to help establish relationships between such children that last beyond the camp sessions and supplement relationships with healthy peers in constructive ways (Bluebond-Langner, Perkel, & Goertzel, 1991).

In a society that has less experience with natural human death and whose death system all too often tends to inhibit constructive interactions between children and death, adults may need to make special efforts to help children cope with death. This entails accepting certain related responsibilities, such as undertaking preparation—by initiating a reflective analysis (which no mortal ever fully completes) of their own thoughts and feelings about death, and by becoming familiar with basic principles in the body of knowledge that has developed in this area; responding to real needs in children; communicating effectively; and working cooperatively—with children, with other adults, and with relevant institutions in American society (Corr, 1984a).

Effective Communication with Children

When adults seek to enter into the world of children in helpful ways, the central guideline is "take your cues from the children, answer what they want to know, what they are asking about, in their terms" (Bluebond-Langner, 1977, p. 64). By listening carefully, adults put themselves in a position to grasp the concerns of a child and to avoid responding with unnecessary or misleading information. By responding in language that is meaningful to children, one can minimize confusion of the sort generated by the adults in Agee's *A Death in the Family* (1969), who carefully explained that God had taken the children's father because he had had an "accident." The adults were using this word to mean a fatal automobile mishap, but the children understood it in terms of a loss of bladder control and the adults never realized how foolish their careful explanation seemed to the children.

Effective communication avoids euphemisms and inconsistent or incomplete answers because they so easily lead children into misunderstandings

that may be more disturbing than the real facts. More important, effective communication is dependable: the child must be able to rely upon what is said, even if it is not the whole of the available truth. Candor of this sort can encourage trust, the basis of all comforting relationships. That is why it is better to admit what one does not know rather than to tell stories in which one does not believe. After all, even good communication is limited, fallible, and subject to error, as in the case of the children who were eager to attend a funeral in order to see the "polarbears" who would, so they had heard, carry the casket (Corley, 1973; see also Brent, 1978). Although one may take delight in this particular malapropism, adults should generally seek (to the best of their abilities) to minimize miscommunication with children in topics related to death (Wolfelt, 1983). Thus, effective communication also involves checking for verification by asking children to clarify what they understood from the message.

Adults must also consider that children communicate in many ways and at many levels (Kübler-Ross, 1983). At least three modes of communication are possible: (1) symbolic, nonverbal communication—which might, for example, take place through artwork of various sorts; (2) symbolic, verbal communication—in which discussions of imaginary friends or anthropomorphized figures may really have to do with the child's own concerns; and (3) nonsymbolic, verbal communication—which most resembles ordinary interchanges between adults. Especially for young children who have not yet acquired much verbal skill, symbolic communications through art or other media may be particularly important vehicles for deep-seated or emotionally charged concerns (Furth, 1988). This was evident in one 6-year-old child who, while he was dying, drew a series of pictures of ships—darker and smaller ships on a progressively darker background as the illness advanced (Grove, 1978).

The Value of Prior Preparation

Whenever possible, one helps children best by preparing them ahead of time to deal with issues associated with sadness and loss (Crase & Crase, 1976). This can be done by making use of relatively safe encounters with death, such as a dead bird found in the woods (Brown, 1958) or a dead fish from the school aquarium. (Note that a child's beloved pet may present quite a different and much less "safe" situation than that arising from a strange, wild animal; see Balk, 1990.) Children can explore such "teachable moments" with adults and with each other in ways that are not highly charged with personal feelings (Carson, 1984). They can also "try out" adult rituals by acting out various sorts of memorializing practices, as in the case of a group of classmates who planted a tree in memory of their teacher's dead son (Simon, 1979).

There is now available an extensive body of literature designed to be read with or by children at all developmental and reading levels (for an annotated list of selected examples, see Appendix A; see also Corr, 1986, 1993b). In addition, there is also available a body of literature for parents and educators who are helping children cope with death, and in some areas there may be workshops or college courses on issues related to children and death (Corr, 1980, 1984b, 1992b). From this, it is evident that adults are not without resources for helping children cope with death. Suggestions on how to use these resources are set out in "Some Guidelines for Adults in Using Death-Related Resources with Children." The underlying principle is that "any subject can be taught effectively in some intellectually honest form to any child at any stage of development" (Bruner, 1962, p. 33).

Helping Ill or Dying Children

Specific examples of ways in which to help ill and dying children include programs like the Ronald MacDonald Houses, home care for dying children, and other forms of pediatric hospice care. *Ronald MacDonald Houses* provide economical, convenient, and hospitable places where families can stay while a child is receiving treatment in a pediatric medical facility. This minimizes family disruption, reduces financial and logistical burdens (such as those involving travel, finding lodgings, preparing food, and doing laundry), and

Selected Literature for Children About Death, Dying, and Bereavement

Picture and Coloring Books for Preschoolers and Beginning Readers

About the deaths of pets and other animals:

Brown, M. W. (1958). *The Dead Bird.*

Dodge, N. C. (1984). *Thumpy's Story: A Story of Love and Grief Shared by Thumpy, the Bunny.*

Kantrowitz, M. (1973). *When Violet Died.*

Stickney, D. (1985). *Water Bugs and Dragonflies.*

Stull, E. G. (1964). *My Turtle Died Today.*

Viorst, J. (1971). *The Tenth Good Thing about Barney.*

Warburg, S. S. (1969). *Growing Time.*

Wilhelm, H. (1985). *I'll Always Love You.*

About the deaths of grandparents, parents, and other adults:

Bartoli, J. (1975). *Nonna.*

De Paola, T. (1973). *Nana Upstairs and Nana Downstairs.*

Fassler, J. (1971). *My Grandpa Died Today.*

Hazen, B. S. (1985). *Why Did Grandpa Die? A Book About Death.*

Zolotow, C. (1974). *My Grandson Lew.*

About the deaths of siblings, peers, and other children:

Clardy, A. F. (1984). *Dusty Was My Friend: Coming to Terms with Loss.*

Cohn, J. (1987). *I Had a Friend Named Peter: Talking to Children About the Death of a Friend.*

Weir, A. B. (1992). *Am I Still a Big Sister?*

About other sorts of death-related events:

Boulden, J. (1989). *Saying Goodbye.*

Heegaard, M. E. (1988). *When Someone Very Special Dies.*

Jordan, M. K. (1989). *Losing Uncle Tim.*

Newman, K. S. (1988). *Hospice Coloring Book.*

Storybooks and Other Texts for Primary School Readers

About the deaths of pets and other animals:

Carrick, C. (1976). *The Accident.*

White, E. B. (1952). *Charlotte's Web.*

permits constructive interactions (if not formal counseling) both within and among families who are facing difficult challenges in childhood illness.

Programs of *home care for dying children* and their families were pioneered by Ida Martinson (1976) and her colleagues (Martinson, Martin, Lauer, Birenbaum, & Eng, 1991) in Minnesota. Careful research in this project demonstrated that for some children and families it was both feasible and desir-

Selected Literature for Children About Death, Dying, and Bereavement (continued)

About the deaths of grandparents, parents, and other adults:
Buck, P. S. (1948). *The Big Wave.*
Bunting, E. (1982). *The Happy Funeral.*
Donnelly, E. (1981). *So Long, Grandpa.*
Goodman, M. B. (1990). *Vanishing Cookies: Doing OK When a Parent Has Cancer.*
Krementz, J. (1981). *How It Feels When a Parent Dies.*
Miles, M. (1971). *Annie and the Old One.*
Powell, E. S. (1990). *Geranium Morning.*
Simon, N. (1979). *We Remember Philip.*
Whitehead, R. (1971). *The Mother Tree.*

About the deaths of siblings, peers, and other children:
Chin-Yee, F. (1988). *Sam's Story: A Story for Families Surviving Sudden Infant Death Syndrome.*
Coburn, J. B. (1964). *Annie and the Sand Dobbies: A Story About Death for Children and Their Parents.*
Coerr, E. (1977). *Sadako and the Thousand Paper Cranes.*
Greene, C. C. (1976). *Beat the Turtle Drum.*
Krementz, J. (1989). *How It Feels to Fight for Your Life.*
Smith, D. B. (1973). *A Taste of Blackberries.*

About postdeath events:
Arnold, C. (1987). *What We Do When Someone Dies.*
Corley, E. A. (1973). *Tell Me About Death, Tell Me About Funerals.*
Johnson, J., & Johnson, M. (1978). *Tell Me, Papa: A Family Book for Children's Questions About Death and Funerals.*

Annotated descriptions of these books and complete bibliographical information are available in Appendix A.

SOURCE Based on C. A. Corr, 1993.

able to take a child home to die. Such families typically needed preparation, guidance, and support to mobilize their own resources, as well as supplementary assistance to provide needed services. In similar ways, other programs of *pediatric hospice care* have applied hospice principles to various situations involving children (Corr & Corr, 1985a, 1985b, 1985c, 1988, 1992b). This has been accomplished in various ways (for example, at home, through respite care, in a medical facility) and with various types of staffing (for instance, based in a hospital, hospice, or home care program) (Martin, 1989). The implementation of these principles in a neonatal intensive care unit (Siegel, 1982; Whitfield et al., 1982) demonstrates that it is not the setting that is critical but the focus on holistic care for the ill child and family-centered care for parents, siblings, and others who are involved (Rosen, 1990).

Selected Literature for Adults About Children and Death

Bernstein, J. E., & Rudman, M. K. (1989). *Books to Help Children Cope with Separation and Loss*, Vol. 3. (By Bernstein alone: Vol. 1, 1977; Vol. 2, 1983.) New York: R. R. Bowker. Informed and sensitive descriptions of hundreds of books for children. Broad topical range and keen evaluations, plus guidance concerning the use of books to help children cope with loss and grief.

Gordon, A. K., & Klass, D. (1979). *They Need to Know: How to Teach Children About Death*. Englewood Cliffs, NJ: Prentice-Hall. Provides a rationale and goals for educating children about death, plus suggested curricula, activities, and resources laid out by grade level from preschool through high school.

Grollman, E. A. (1990). *Talking About Death: A Dialogue Between Parent and Child* (3rd ed.). Boston: Beacon. Principles for helping children to cope with death; a passage to be read with a child; guides for responding to questions arising from the read-along section; and a guide to helpful resources.

Jackson, E. N. (1965). *Telling a Child About Death*. New York: Hawthorn. An older resource, with a strong tendency to link developmental level to chronological age. Otherwise, clear, simple, and useful recommendations from an experienced clergyperson and grief counselor.

Jewett, C. L. (1982). *Helping Children Cope with Separation and Loss*. Boston: Harvard Common Press. Suggested techniques from a child-and-family therapist built around a phase theory of grief and mourning.

Schaefer, D. & Lyons, C. (1986). *How Do We Tell the Children?* New York: Newmarket. Helpful advice for parents from a funeral director and his colleague.

Wass, H., & Corr, C. A. (1984). *Childhood and Death*. Washington, DC: Hemisphere. Sections on death, dying, bereavement, suicide, and helping children, plus selected, annotated resources (books for adults, books for children, organizations, and audiovisuals).

Wass, H., & Corr, C. A. (1984). *Helping Children Cope with Death: Guidelines and Resources* (2nd ed.). Washington, DC: Hemisphere. Guidelines for parents and other adults, plus annotated resources (printed materials, audiovisuals, and organizations).

Wass, H., et al. (1980 & 1985). *Death Education: An Annotated Resource Guide*, Vols. 1 and 2. Washington, DC: Hemisphere. Annotated bibliographies of various sorts of resources, including children's literature in Vol. 2.

Wolfelt, A. (1983). *Helping Children Cope with Grief*. Muncie, IN: Accelerated Development. Advice, suggested activities, and resources for helping grieving children from a clinical psychologist.

Helping Grieving Children

Fox's (1988) task-based model provides a natural agenda for adults who are helping grieving children: provide accurate information and frameworks for interpreting what has happened; help children to identify, feel secure in, and bring to

Some Guidelines for Adults in Using Death-Related Resources with Children

1. *Evaluate the book or other resource yourself before attempting to use it with a child.* No resource suits every reader or every purpose.
2. *Select resources, topics, and approaches that suit the needs of the individual child.* To be useful, any resource must meet the needs of a particular child.
3. *Be prepared to cope with limitations.* Every resource is likely to have both strengths and limitations. Adapt existing resources to individual purposes.
4. *Match materials to the capacities of the individual child.* Stories, pictures, music, play, drawing, and other options must suit the child's abilities. For example, in using literature, determine the child's reading or interest level. Direct a precocious child to more advanced materials; direct some older children to less challenging titles or invite them to join in partnership with an adult to assess the suitability of simpler materials for younger readers (Lamers, 1986) so that their abilities are not directly challenged by materials that are too difficult.
5. *Read or work along with children.* Seize opportunities for rewarding interactions and valuable "teachable moments" from which all can profit (Carson, 1984). Show interest in the child, provide interpretations as needed, and learn from the child.

expression their feelings of grief; suggest ways to commemorate the life of the deceased; and give permission to go on with living and loving. This agenda can be implemented in various ways for grievers both before and after a death.

Good memories are as important to bereaved children as they are to adults (Bartoli, 1975; Jewett, 1982; Zolotow, 1974). When possible, one should strive to lay down a fund of such memories before loss or death occur. Even when that is not possible, as in cases of unanticipated death, an adult might work with a child after a death to develop and articulate the elements of a legacy that the child can carry forward into the future—for example, by examining a scrapbook or photo album depicting the dead person's life, or by sharing events from that life in which the child might not have participated. Helping grieving children after a death has occurred might also include assembling a memorial collage, donating to a worthy cause, or planting a living memorial.

After a death, commemoration and memorialization most often are expressed in funeral and burial practices. In recent years many people in the United States have raised questions about whether children should take part in such practices (Corr, 1991). A basic rule is that no child should be forced to take part in any experience that will be harmful. But that need not occur when adults follow a course of action involving prior preparation, support during the event, and follow-up afterward. That is, the child should be told ahead of

Activities enhance the lives of ill and disabled children.

time what will occur at the wake, funeral, or burial, why we engage in these activities, and what his or her options are for participation. If the child chooses to take part in some or all of these activities, a caring adult should be present to attend to his or her needs, an adult not wholly absorbed in his or her own grief and one who could accompany a child who might need to arrive late or leave early. After the event, adults should discuss with the child his or her reactions or feelings, answer any questions that might arise, and share their own responses to what has taken place.

Concerns about disruptive behavior by children are no more unique to funerals and burials than they are to graduations and weddings. They can be addressed by providing a special time for children to come to the funeral home when the main body of adults is not present or by limiting the role of the children at the funeral service or at the burial to one appropriate to the individuals in question and to their tolerance for public ritual. Crase and Crase (1976, p. 25) have offered good advice for those helping grieving children: "The wise management of grief in children revolves around the encouragement and facilitation of the normal mourning process while preventing delayed and/or distorted grief responses."

Normal mourning processes after a death can also be assisted by support groups for grieving children (Zambelli & DeRosa, 1992). The Dougy Center (3909 S.E. 52nd Avenue, Portland, OR 97286; (503) 775-5683), founded in December, 1982, by Beverly Chappell, is a fine model for this sort of work. Four principles underlie the work of the center: (1) Grief is a natural reaction to loss for children as well as for adults; (2) within each individual is the natural capacity to heal oneself; (3) the duration and intensity of grief is unique for each individual; and (4) caring and acceptance assist in the healing process (Corr et al., 1991; Knope, 1989). The Dougy Center operates groups

*Grieving
children express
their feelings
through art.*

for children as young as ages 3–5 (Smith, 1991) and as old as 19. It distinguishes between groups for those who have experienced a death of a parent or caregiver; of a brother, sister, or close friend; through suicide; or through murder. And it offers groups for parents or other adult caregivers that meet concurrently with each of the children's groups.

Individuals who facilitate groups at the Dougy Center are regarded not as counselors or therapists but as fellow grievers. Their roles are to honor and be available for each child, trust his or her mourning processes, remain alert for signs of complicated mourning processes, walk alongside, and uphold the vision that each grieving person will once again be able to feel his or her life. Other support groups for grieving children regard facilitators in a more traditional counseling role and adopt a more structured, time-limited agenda for group meetings (for example, Harper, Royer, & Humphrey, 1988; Hassl & Marnocha, 1990; Reynolds, 1992). An approach of this sort may also apply to short-term camps for bereaved children. Like many similar programs (for example, Braza & Bright, 1991), the Dougy Center has developed a manual of activities (Whitney, 1991) and other resources for grieving youngsters.

Summary

This chapter has explored many aspects of interactions between children and death in contemporary American society. The distinctive developmental tasks of childhood—striving to achieve trust versus mistrust in infancy, autonomy versus shame and doubt in early childhood, initiative versus guilt in the preschool years, and industry versus inferiority in the early school years—have a direct bearing on how children relate to death. These tasks influence encounters with death among children (we noted that in infancy and early childhood, death rates are high, mainly arising from congenital anomalies, SIDS, RDS, and accidents; in preschool and school-age children, death rates are low and result from communicable diseases, natural causes, and homicide) and the development of death-related concepts and attitudes toward death in childhood. For children coping with life-threatening illness and dying, it is especially important to maintain trust and security, to minimize separation and threats to body image, and to foster normal routines and social contacts. For children coping with bereavement and grief, it is important to acknowledge that children do grieve in their own distinctive ways; that they will principally be concerned about what caused the death, whether or not it will happen to them, and who is going to take care of them; and that they face four central tasks in productive mourning. We have also mentioned strategies and resources for helping children cope with death.

QUESTIONS FOR REVIEW AND DISCUSSION

1. What sorts of death-related losses do you think are most typical in childhood and what do you think such losses usually mean to children? What sorts of death-related losses did you experience in your own childhood and what did they mean to you?

2. Try to remember a time in your life when you were a child and you were seriously ill or you experienced an important loss. What were your most significant concerns about that illness or loss? Or perhaps you know a child who has been in such a situation. If so, what were his or her most significant concerns?

3. If you were asked to recommend to adults how they could help children cope with death, what would you recommend? How would the following make a difference in your recommendations: the age or developmental status of the children who are to be helped; the home or family situation of the children who are to be helped; the ethnic or cultural background of the children who are to be helped; the nature of the death-related loss that the children are experiencing; the cultural background or social role (such as parent, teacher, counselor, or health care provider) of the adults to whom you are speaking?

SUGGESTED READINGS

For developmental perspectives on the life cycle (with or without special reference to death), consult:

Cook, A. S., & Oltjenbruns, K. A. (1989). *Dying and Grieving: Lifespan and Family Perspectives.*
Erikson, E. H. (1963). *Childhood and Society* (2nd ed.).
Erikson, E. H. (1968). *Identity: Youth and Crisis.*
Levinson, D. J. (1978). *The Seasons of a Man's Life.*

On children and their development, see:

Anthony, S. (1972). *The Discovery of Death in Childhood and After.*
Ariès, P. (1962). *Centuries of Childhood: A Social History of Family Life.*
Lonetto, R. (1980). *Children's Conceptions of Death.*

General resources on children and death include:

Grollman, E. A. (Ed.). (1967). *Explaining Death to Children.*
Papadatou, D., & Papadatos, C. (Eds.). (1991). *Children and Death.*
Sahler, O.J.Z. (Ed.). (1978). *The Child and Death.*
Wass, H., & Corr, C. A. (Eds.) (1984). *Childhood and Death.*

Concerning life-threatening illness in childhood, consult:

Adams, D. W. (1979). *Childhood Malignancy: The Psychosocial Care of the Child and His Family.*
Adams, D. W., & Deveau, E. J. (1987). *Coping with Childhood Cancer: Where Do We Go from Here?* (rev. ed.).
Bluebond-Langner, M. (1978). *The Private Worlds of Dying Children.*
Koocher, G. P., & O'Malley, J. E. (1981). *The Damocles Syndrome: Psychosocial Consequences of Surviving Childhood Cancer.*
Spinetta, J. J., & Deasy-Spinetta, P. (1981). *Living with Childhood Cancer.*

Bereavement and grief in childhood are explored in the following:

Furman, E. (Ed.). (1974). *A Child's Parent Dies: Studies in Childhood Bereavement.*
Krementz, J. (1981). *How It Feels When a Parent Dies.*
LeShan, E. (1976). *Learning to Say Good-by: When a Parent Dies.*

Rosen, H. (1986). *Unspoken Grief: Coping with Childhood Sibling Loss.*

For teaching children about death or helping them to cope with death, see:

Agee, J. (1969). *A Death in the Family.*
Gordon, A. K., & Klass, D. (1979). *They Need to Know: How to Teach Children About Death.*
Grollman, E. A. (1990). *Talking About Death: A Dialogue Between Parent and Child* (3rd ed.).
Jackson, E. N. (1965). *Telling a Child About Death.*
Jewett, C. L. (1982). *Helping Children Cope with Separation and Loss.*
Rudolph, M. (1978). *Should the Children Know?: Encounters with Death in the Lives of Children.*
Schaefer, D., & Lyons, C. (1986). *How Do We Tell the Children?*
Smilansky, S. (1987). *On Death: Helping Children Understand and Cope.*
Wass, H., & Corr, C. A. (Eds.). (1984). *Helping Children Cope with Death: Guidelines and Resources* (2nd ed.).

Some special situations or subjects are explored in the following:

Balk, D. E. (1990). *Children and the Death of a Pet.*
Bettelheim, B. (1977). *The Uses of Enchantment—The Meaning and Importance of Fairy Tales.*

CHAPTER 12

Adolescents

This chapter examines interactions with death during adolescence. Adolescence is a transitional period in the human life cycle between childhood and adulthood. At one time in American society—and in many other societies or cultural groups today—there was no such "in between" period. "Coming of age" rituals marked a rather direct and relatively abrupt division between the era of the child and the reality of adult responsibilities (Ariès, 1962). By contrast, contemporary American society has evolved a complex, extended, and rather special developmental stage between the primary school years and the complete recognition of adult status.

Adolescence deserves attention in this chapter in its own right as well as for what it adds retrospectively to an account of childhood and prospectively to what will be said about adulthood. After a brief vignette designed to illustrate some of the issues concerning adolescents and death in the United States today, the chapter will consider developmental tasks, boundaries, and interpretations of adolescence; typical encounters with death in American society during the adolescent years; attitudes toward death during this period; issues related to dying and bereaved adolescents; and special issues concerning pregnancy and suicide.

The Death of Dean Thomas

The death of Dean Thomas was a shock to his family, his friends at school, and his co-workers at the service station. At 17, Dean was the oldest of three children in his family. Dean was an above-average athlete who was a running back on the football team, a small forward in basketball, and a combination outfielder and third baseman on the baseball team.

Dean's girlfriend, Susie, tutored him in mathematics and other difficult subjects, and she always urged him to work harder at academics. Susie had won a place on the school cheerleading squad so that she could travel with Dean to various athletic events. But she was mostly determined to get both Dean and herself admitted to the nearby state university, where she wanted to prepare for a career in business and fashion marketing, and where Dean hoped to win a ROTC scholarship leading to a commission as an Air Force officer.

Dean's father worked for the city in a job that offered security but not a very high salary. As Dean approached his 17th birthday, the family had been able to buy a new car at the end of the model year and decided to give their old car to him. That enabled Dean to take the transfer that he had been offered at work to a new job near the outskirts of the city.

Ever since he had become a teenager, Dean had worked to earn his own pocket money, first at odd jobs around the neighborhood and then at the service station. When Dean left work that first Saturday evening with his new paycheck, he felt that everything was really going right for him.

Unfortunately, Dean never got home that night. A drunken driver hit him broadside at an intersection just two miles from his home. Dean was thrown from the car and killed instantly. He had not been wearing his seat belt. The other driver was pulled from his car with only minor bruises.

When the police officer came to their home that night, Dean's parents were stunned to learn of the death of their healthy, happy, easygoing son. They huddled together with their other two children, alternately crying and expressing disbelief. It was hard for them to notify the family's relatives and to call Susie, who became hysterical when she learned what had happened.

At school on Monday, an announcement was made about Dean's death, but most of the students already knew about it. The athletic department dedicated the remainder of its season to Dean's memory, and a small display with Dean's picture was set up near the school office.

On Tuesday, many students were let out of school early to attend the visitation at a nearby funeral home. Some older adults were upset by the large crowd of adolescents who were crying, hugging each other, and moving in and out of the funeral home. But both Dean's parents and Susie were heartened by this outpouring of love for Dean and support for them. On the next morning, the funeral itself was a somber affair, but Dean's parents invited the mourners back to their home where there was food and more crying that gradually turned to stories about Dean's practical jokes, memories of his life, and some smiles and laughter.

Adolescence: Developmental Tasks, Boundaries, and Interpretations

In American society, adolescence is an era when an individual is no longer simply to be treated as a child. That is, adolescence is a period when one gradually takes on more advanced responsibilities of a sort not generally assigned to children. Thus, adolescents are usually accorded special privileges of various sorts that are not open to children, even though adolescents are not yet accorded full status as adults. This common social view of adolescence in American society is supported by the work of developmental psychologists and others who have drawn attention to the distinctive qualities and tasks of adolescence.

Developmental Tasks in Adolescence

Developmental studies and theoretical models, such as those of Erikson (1963), have described adolescence as an era particularly devoted to the establishment of a relatively stable sense of personal identity. When that task is not effectively accomplished, the maturing adolescent may experience a diffuse or confused sense of his or her identity, with unfinished work in this area carrying over into young adulthood. According to Erikson, the characteristic virtue to be pursued during the adolescent era is fidelity, or faithfulness to self, to ideals, and to others.

Many scholars agree with this description of adolescence. For example, Kohlberg and Gilligan (1971) suggested that adolescents should be understood as incipient philosophers who seek to link change and adventure with an evolving sense of self. That is, adolescents undergo significant physical and psychosocial changes in their development; confront an evolving future with horizons broadened far beyond the limits of childhood; live intensely in the present; and reflect upon what their experiences mean for their own self-concept and sense of self-esteem.

Fleming and Adolph (1986) have carried this further by proposing a more detailed account of tasks and conflicts in normal adolescent development, organized around three maturational phases (see Table 12.1). As part of the overall developmental project of determining one's identity in adolescence, these tasks involve, in succession, work to emancipate oneself from the security and predictability of a child's family life; to develop one's own competencies in the new arena of freedom; and to achieve a new synthesis of personal and social identity within which one can initiate new and renewed relationships. According to this account, a number of core issues will be encountered at each of these three maturational levels in adolescence, each of which will provoke cognitive, behavioral, and affective responses. A developmental framework of this sort is the context within which adolescents encounter and cope with death-related issues.

Boundaries and Interpretations of Adolescence

In the literature on adolescence, there are significant disagreements about the boundaries of the adolescent era and the character of the adolescent experience (Bandura, 1980; Marcia, 1980). For example, the boundaries of the adolescent era are subject to some lack of precision and disagreement. They have been described in various ways: chronologically, usually with some rough correspondence to the teenage years, but many statistical reports use data for ages 15–24, which mix adolescents with young adults; biologically, originating from the marker provided by puberty; or socially, beginning with secondary school and ending at the quite individual and variable point at which one leaves home and family of origin. None of these descriptions is definitive; each might be challenged in one way or another. The difficulty is that they all define adolescence in ways that depend upon different and inconsistent interfaces with adjacent periods.

Issues relating to the "external" boundaries of adolescence have been complicated by suggestions that attention should also be paid to "internal" boundaries or subdivisions. Here, we have already seen a tripartite schema in the work of Fleming and Adolph (1986). Some draw a simpler division between early and later adolescence (Kagan & Coles, 1972; Schiamberg, 1985). Essentially, this latter distinction is one between individuals who are 12–16 years of age and those who are 17 to early or mid-20s. Early adolescents are still in the period that American society assigns to secondary education (although they may have dropped out of school). Later adolescents are at the

TABLE 12.1   *Tasks and Conflicts for Adolescents by Maturational Phase*

Phase I	Age:	11–14
	Task:	Emotional separation from parents
	Conflict:	Separation vs. reunion
		(Abandonment vs. safety)
Phase II	Age:	14–17
	Task:	Competency/mastery/control
	Conflict:	Independence vs. dependence
Phase III	Age:	17–21
	Task:	Intimacy and commitment
	Conflict:	Closeness vs. distance

From S. J. Fleming, & R. Adolph, 1986.

point when most young people in the United States enter college or the working world.

Roughly speaking, later adolescents are less sheltered by neighborhood schools and proximity to home than their younger counterparts. Later adolescents are also increasingly distinguished by society's willingness to permit them to obtain an automobile driver's license, volunteer for military service, drink alcoholic beverages, and exercise the right to vote. These observations suggest that boundaries within and at the edges of the adolescent era may be better conceived of as more or less extended periods in their own right, rather than as sharp lines of demarcation.

Interpretations of adolescence have ranged from accounts that emphasize "storm and stress"—change, turbulence, and difficulties in adolescent life (for example, Freud, 1958)—to reports from the empirical work of Offer, Ostrov, and Howard (1981) in which large numbers of adolescents from different cultures appear to describe themselves as relatively untroubled, happy, and self-satisfied. A transitional and changing period in the life span such as adolescence clearly presents challenges to its interpreters; responses to these challenges color much that is said about the adolescent era.

Encounters with Death

However one interprets adolescence either in itself or in the overall schema of the human life cycle, typical encounters with death are unambiguous during the second and part of the third decade of life. In terms of deaths of adolescents, during the period from 15–24 years of age, the three leading causes of death in 1990 were accidents (rate = 43.9 per 100,000; the vast majority of which involved motor vehicles), homicide (rate = 19.9), and suicide (rate = 13.2) (National Center for Health Statistics, 1993). This is unique in comparison to other age periods. All of these are human-induced deaths; together they add up to approximately 77 percent of all deaths during the adolescent era. Adolescence is the only period in the whole of the human life span during which some form of natural death is not included among the three leading causes of death. The fourth (malignant neoplasms or cancer; rate = 4.9), fifth (diseases of the heart; rate = 2.5), and sixth (human immunodeficiency virus

Automobile accidents are the leading cause of death among adolescents.

[HIV] infection; rate = 1.5) leading causes of death during the adolescent era *taken together* add up to a death rate that is less than that of adolescent deaths from suicide.

What this reveals is that adolescents in contemporary American society are, for the most part, healthy young persons. As a group, adolescents enjoy a very low death rate. They have escaped the dangers of natural death in childhood, but they have not lived long enough to succumb to the dominant degenerative diseases of later adulthood. As a result, most adolescents will live on into adulthood unless they bring about their own deaths or others kill them.

In the meantime, there are other important implications of adolescent encounters with death. In the first place, the appearance and rising significance of infection from the HIV as a leading cause of death in the adolescent years is deeply troubling. It draws attention to sexual behavior, as well as to the use of alcohol and other drugs, as contributors to morbidity and mortality among adolescents. Even in the face of education and knowledge about these behaviors, many adolescents in the United States do not appear to be altering behaviors that leave them vulnerable to illness and death.

Second, human-induced deaths typically take place in a sudden and unexpected manner and are often associated with trauma or violence. This means that the typical death of an adolescent both is, and is usually perceived as, shocking and untimely.

Third, if one gathers or examines mortality data in a slightly different way, the picture changes somewhat for adolescents. For example, the second leading cause of death in the United States among individuals who are 15–19 years of age is suicide, not homicide. And it is suspected that deaths of some teens in solo car wrecks should really be described as suicides rather than as auto accidents. None of this changes the fact that an adolescent is dead, nor does it alter the importance of the role of human behavior in deaths among adolescents. But it may alter emphases or approaches in preventative efforts.

Adolescents also experience the *deaths of others* in various forms (Ewalt & Perkins, 1979). Statistically, the most likely of these are the deaths of grandparents and/or parents. Such deaths may be especially significant for their impact on the developmental work of adolescents. For example, an early adolescent who is defining his or her identity in terms of emancipation from a dominant parent may suddenly feel abandoned without a reference point if that parent dies. Similarly, a later adolescent who is "promoted" into a protective role for a surviving parent may experience problems in working out his or her own bereavement when he or she has to be "strong" or serve as a surrogate protector for that parent.

Adolescents are also confronted with a number of large-scale perils, many of which appear to depend upon what their elders have done, such as global tensions and the threat or reality of war; dangers associated with the nuclear era, which began in 1945 with the atomic bombing of Hiroshima and Nagasaki; and problems facing the environment, such as acid rain, the destruction of the world's rain forests, the depletion of the ozone layer in the atmosphere, the so-called "greenhouse effect" involving climatic warming, population growth, and waste disposal. Dangers associated with nuclear weaponry may seem to have declined with the dissolution of the Soviet Union in 1991, but nuclear weapons are still in the hands of several countries around the world. A peacetime threat is posed by incidents at nuclear power plants like those that took place at Three Mile Island in the United States in 1979 and at Chernobyl in Ukraine in 1986.

Finally, adolescents encounter references to death and death-related themes in a significant portion of the music that is so much a part of their lives. Music is a common idiom in adolescent life, one that is shared across national, cultural, and political boundaries. Although adolescent music is a diverse and fast-changing phenomenon that has not been well cataloged with regard to what it has to say about death, dying, and bereavement, initial studies (Attig, 1986; Thrush & Paulus, 1970) have identified a rich variety of death-related themes. These can be illustrated in the following examples from the period of the late 1960s through the early 1990s:

- *Late 1960s through early 1970s:* "Will the Circle Be Unbroken?" (Joan Baez, 1969); "But I Might Die Tonight" (Cat Stevens, 1970); the theme from M*A*S*H, "Suicide Is Painless" (1970); "Bridge over Troubled Water" (Paul Simon and Art Garfunkel, 1970); "Daniel" (Elton John, 1970); and "I Think I'm Gonna Kill Myself" (Elton John, 1972).
- *Late 1970s through mid-1980s:* "Die Young, Stay Pretty" (Blondie, 1979); "Suicide Solution" (Ozzie Osbourne, 1981); "You're Only Human (Second Wind)" (Billy Joel, 1985).
- *Late 1980s:* "You're All I Need" (Mottely Crue, 1987); "Operation Mind-crime" (Queensryche, 1988); and "The Living Years" (Mike and the Mechanics, 1988).
- *Early 1990s:* "For My Broken Heart" (Reba McEntire, 1991); and "Tears in Heaven" (Eric Clapton, 1992).

It is very difficult to remain current with this dynamic and varied musical milieu. But nearly all adolescents in American society are familiar with music of this type. Those who are acquainted with such music are often willing to join in a project of identifying death-related lyrics in various types of popular music. It is indisputable that death-related lyrics are widespread in this musical genre. The significance of these lyrics is less clear, although some studies (Wass, Miller, & Stevenson, 1989a; Wass et al., 1989b) have suggested that certain sorts of music are listened to more frequently by certain sorts of adolescents.

Attitudes Toward Death

Considering the seriousness of the problems that face American society, perhaps it should not surprise us that research reveals a significant degree of concern about the future in many adolescents (Austin & Mack, 1986; Beardslee & Mack, 1982; Blackwell & Gessner, 1983; Gould, Moon, & Van Hoorn, 1986; Stillion, 1986), especially as related to war and the nuclear threat. However, it is difficult to say with precision what adolescents as a group think and feel about death itself. We must consider several factors in order to begin a sketch of this subject.

For instance, it is generally accepted that by the beginning of the adolescent era individuals with normal cognitive development are capable of understanding death as final, universal, and inevitable (see Chapter 11). Adolescents in Western society are well into what Piaget and Inhelder (1958) called the period of formal operations, which is characterized by propositional and hypothetical-deductive thinking, generality of concepts, and an objective view of reality.

However, it is not enough simply to note that adolescents are capable of thinking on an adult level. How adolescents actually think about death can be affected by several factors (Noppe & Noppe, 1991). For example, the rapid physical maturation and sexual development of adolescents may be associated with an awareness of inevitable biological decline and ultimate death. Some adolescents may at times wish to return to an earlier, safer, less sexual era. Similarly, newly developed cognitive capacities may embrace both optimistic and pessimistic thoughts about the future. In addition, changing social relationships with family members and peers carry potential for enrichment and for isolation or social deaths of various sorts. Finally, adolescent feelings about death are likely to be closely associated with a sense of self-esteem, purpose in life, and whether or not one's real self matches one's ideals.

Early adolescents, in particular, may carry over with them from their childhood the "tattered cloak of immortality" (Gordon, 1986). That is, although they know better in principle, they may still wish to think of death as not directly relevant to their own personal lives. This is supported by what Elkind (1967) has called "the personal fable," a kind of egocentrism that leads some adolescents to believe that they can enter into rebellious or risk-taking activities without real personal danger.

A central element in the adolescent's sense of vulnerability or invulnerability has to do with lessons that may or may not have been learned from life experiences. The inability or unwillingness of many adolescents to recognize the personal implications of mortality may have much to do with the limits of adolescent experience and the perspectives that dominate much of adolescent life. This is confirmed by an analysis of factors that enter into well-known driving patterns in later adolescence (Jonah, 1986). There are two elements that are significant here: (1) adolescent drivers may simply not perceive risks that are inherent in their behavior (such as the likelihood that an accident might occur or that it might result in serious consequences) and thus may inadvertently put themselves into situations fraught with danger; and (2) adolescent drivers may perceive positive utility or value in taking certain risks, such as seizing control over one's life by acting independently, expressing opposition to adult authority and conventional society, coping with anxiety or frustration, or gaining acceptance from a peer group. This is why "death is a very remote event for most young people" (Jonah, 1986, p. 268).

Something like this appears in Tolstoy's (1884/1960, p. 131) celebrated novella *The Death of Ivan Ilych*. Tolstoy wrote the following about Ivan as he was dying: "The syllogism he had learnt from Kiezewetter's Logic: 'Caius is a man, men are mortal, therefore Caius is mortal,' had always seemed to him correct as applied to Caius, but certainly not as applied to himself." In other words, mortality for the young Ivan Ilych was an abstraction, whose personal force and relevance to his own life came home to him only many years later as he was dying.

This is supported by the work of Alexander and Adlerstein (1958), who conducted an empirical study in which participants were asked to say the first word that came into their minds in response to a series of stimulus words that included death-related words. Responses were measured in two ways: in terms of the speed with which they were offered and by association with decreased galvanic skin resistance (increased perspiration or sweating). Resulting scores from boys who were 5–8 years old and 13–16 years old contrasted with those from 9–12 year olds. This was taken to mean that the younger children and adolescents displayed more death-related anxiety than did those in the middle age grouping. In other words, death has "a greater emotional significance for people with less stable ego self-pictures" (p. 175).

This seems to suggest that death-related threats have greatest personal significance at times of transition in the life span and, within adolescence, at times of decreased stability and self-confidence. For many, early adolescence is a time of little sense of futurity and a high degree of egocentrism (Elkind, 1967). Thus, a key variable in adolescent attitudes toward death may be the level of maturity that the adolescent has achieved (Maurer, 1964), with greater maturity being associated both with "greater sophistication and acknowledgement of the inevitability of death as well as with enjoyment of life and altruistic concerns" (Raphael, 1983, p. 147).

In short, what emerges for many adolescents is a tendency to live in the moment and not to appreciate personal threats associated with death. Thus, the key issue for adolescents may not be so much related to their capacity to think about death but to ways in which the significance of death-related concepts is or is not related to their personal lives. There is a kind of paradox here in what is required of adolescents in order for them to grasp the personal significance of death. That is, adolescents must *simultaneously* move away from the intensity of their lived experience so as to put their feelings into perspective *and* move toward applying apparently abstract concepts of death in ways that have personal reference and meaning.

Adolescents Coping with Life-Threatening Illness and Dying

Because dying and adolescence are both transitional experiences, Papadatou (1989, p. 28) has wisely noted that "it could be argued that seriously ill adolescents experience a double crisis owing to their imminent death and their developmental age." Like others who are coping with dying, adolescents face a need to find meaning and purpose both in their lives and in their deaths. That is, adolescents attach great importance to living in the present and being oriented toward the immediate future (Farrell & Hutter, 1980; Pendleton, 1980).

This is reflected in all of the ways in which those who have worked with dying adolescents articulate their needs. For example, Adams and Deveau (1986) have reported that dying adolescents need to maintain a sense of identity; to be treated with honesty; to pursue independence; to control what is happening to them; to have opportunities for privacy; to pursue an orientation to the future; and to experience love, comfort, reassurance, and freedom from pain. Similarly, Waechter (1984) described dying adolescents as being concerned with isolation, body deterioration, the future, and the threat of premature death. And Papadatou (1989) emphasized that dying adolescents desire to strive for independence, need to control some aspect of their lives, and struggle to maintain a sense of identity, dignity, and pride.

Cancer is the most common natural or disease-related cause of death in adolescence (National Center for Health Statistics, 1993). Happily, cancer is much less lethal now than it was in the 1950s or 1960s. Only a small number of adolescents now die each year from cancer, or from heart disease and other lethal illnesses. But this changing demographic pattern provides little comfort to the individuals and families who are directly affected. Indeed, as society becomes less accustomed to encounters with natural death during adolescence, it may also become less helpful to those who are coping with that sort of dying.

Some adolescents and young adults also die from long-term genetic diseases that usually do not result in death during childhood, such as cystic fibrosis, sickle cell anemia, muscular dystrophy, and chronic kidney disease (Blum, 1984). Such diseases are very demanding, both for the ill person and for others who are involved. For example, Bluebond-Langner (1991) has chronicled the path of disease progression in cystic fibrosis with special attention to its import for the views of well siblings (see Table 12.2). Similar examinations could be made of other long-term, progressive diseases and their various influences on children, adolescents, and adults.

Adolescents who are coping with progressive, chronic diseases of this sort are challenged to learn how to live with a life-threatening condition (Koocher & O'Malley, 1981; Spinetta & Deasy-Spinetta, 1981). This will place great emphasis upon individual and familial resources, and upon processes of communication within the family (Adams & Deveau, 1987; Spinetta, 1978). And all of these issues are likely to be compounded as AIDS becomes a more lethal presence among adolescents in the immediate future (DiClemente, 1990).

Adolescents who are coping with dying can be helped by honest and effective communication; good symptom control (Plumb & Holland, 1974); and responsiveness to the needs outlined earlier. This enables such adolescents to live out their lives in their own ways, which will often include valued involvements with peers, school, and families—the ordinary milieu of adolescent life. Papadatou (1989, p. 31) suggested the following perspective for helpers who wish to enter into the world of adolescents and their families who are coping with life-threatening illness: "We must also believe that we are not helpless or hopeless, but have something valuable to offer: an honest and meaningful relationship that provides the adolescent with a feeling that we are willing to share his journey through the remainder of his life."

Adolescents Coping with Bereavement and Grief

One study of more than 1,000 high school juniors and seniors disclosed that 90 percent of those students had experienced the death of someone whom they loved (Ewalt & Perkins, 1979). In nearly 40 percent of this sample, the loss involved the death of a friend or peer who was roughly their own age. In 20 percent of the sample, the students had actually witnessed a death. Clearly, it is not correct to think that contemporary adolescents have no experience with death and bereavement.

When adolescents experience the death of a family member, friend, personal acquaintance, or figure in popular culture (such as Elvis Presley or John

TABLE 12.2   Well Siblings' Views of Cystic Fibrosis and Their Own Sibling's Condition

Disease Trajectory	Well Siblings' Views
Diagnosis First year following diagnosis First annual examination	A serious illness
	A condition one does things for
Months/years following first annual examination (without a major exacerbation)	
First major exacerbation	A disease, not merely a condition
Succeeding exacerbations and other illnesses, with periodic hospitalizations	A series of episodes of acute illness and recovery
Frequent exacerbations, episodes of other diseases, and hospitalizations	Questions emerge about cure, course of the disease, control of it, and efficacy of treatment
Development and increase in complications	Chronic, progressive, incurable disease that shortens the life span (*N.B.* This view does not apply to one's own sibling—at least not in the near future.)
Increased deterioration	Chronic, progressive, incurable disease that shortens the life span (*N.B.* In some cases this view now applies to one's own sibling.)
Terminal phases	Chronic, progressive, incurable disease that shortens the life span (*N.B.* In all cases this view now applies to one's own sibling.)

From: M. Bluebond-Langner, 1991.

Lennon), like all human beings they respond by grieving. Not surprisingly, adolescent grief often manifests itself in confusion, crying, depression, feelings of emptiness and/or loneliness, disturbances in patterns of sleep and eating, and exhaustion (Balk, 1983; LaGrand, 1981, 1986). However, as Jackson (1984, p. 42) has written, "Adolescents are apt to think that they are the discoverers of deep and powerful feelings and that no one has ever loved as they love." If so, adolescents may assume that their grief is similarly unique and incomprehensible—to themselves and to others. Consequently, expressions of adolescent grief may be limited to brief outbursts or may be actively suppressed because adolescents may fear loss of emotional control and often put great weight upon how they will be perceived by others.

What is most important to note in bereaved adolescents, as in bereaved children, is that their mourning processes are likely to conform to the characteristics of their distinctive developmental stage and thus may not exactly parallel those of adults. As one example, although adolescent mourning may involve grieving that comes and goes, the overall process may extend over a long period of time (Hogan & DeSantis, 1992). In other words, adolescent mourning is paradoxically both continuous and intermittent (Raphael, 1983).

Several factors are influential in shaping mourning processes in adolescence. These include closeness in some interpersonal relationships (such as with a grandparent), as well as ambivalence in other relationships (for example, with a parent or sibling) (Krementz, 1981); the tendency of adolescents

A gang-related shooting of a friend leads to grief in Minnesota.

to idealize the deceased, which may complicate mourning with guilt and self-blame; a possibility that the relationship or the grief may be unacknowledged or disenfranchised by society (Doka, 1989a); the intense, if sometimes relatively transitory, quality of adolescent feelings; and the availability or non-availability of support from peers and adults, which facilitates healthy mourning.

In particular, research by Hogan and DeSantis (in press) has shown that grieving adolescents appear to be helped in coping with their bereavement by activities that reduce stress (playing a musical instrument, keeping busy, or releasing pent-up emotions); their own personal belief system; support from parents, other relatives, or friends; professionals or mutual support groups who could normalize grief reactions; and the passage of time. Grief in adolescents is hindered by intrusive thoughts and images; parental discord and grief; insensitivity of people; rumors and gossip; and beliefs that the world is an unfair place.

Mourning in adolescence poses situational tasks that overlay normal developmental tasks. Especially in adolescence, typical developmental tasks of establishing emotional separation, achieving competency or mastery, and developing intimacy (Fleming & Adolph, 1986) echo in significant ways processes in normal adolescent mourning, which Sugar (1968) has described as involving protest/searching, disorganization, and reorganization. Parsing out these processes is a challenging assignment that has only recently been recognized and undertaken (Balk, 1991; Garber, 1983). There is much yet to learn about adolescent bereavement that involves different sorts of relationships (for example, with a parent, sibling, peer, pet, or other significant person), different modes of death, and different types of support. In particular, issues involving family dynamics and long-term consequences of death on adolescent development should be explored further (Hogan & Balk, 1990; Hogan & Greenfield, 1991; Martinson, Davies, & McClowry, 1987; McClowry et al., 1987).

Adolescents, Pregnancy, and Suicide

Many adolescents in American society confront challenges from losses that were not even possible for younger children and that have not yet been well studied or understood. Many of these losses relate to sexual activity. For example, the epidemic of teenage pregnancies that is a well-known and distinctive feature of American society (Bolton, 1980) involves many losses for young people and may challenge their sense of invulnerability ("It can't happen to me"). Moreover, sexual and other forms of behavior put adolescents in jeopardy of acquiring sexually transmitted diseases, such as herpes and HIV infection. Pregnancies among young and disadvantaged teenagers put their own lives and the lives of their offspring in jeopardy. Issues of pregnancy and elective abortion may confront adolescents for the first time with life-and-death decisions and with interrelated loss experiences (Joralemon, 1986). And the potential for early deaths (for instance, perinatal or neonatal deaths and Sudden Infant Death Syndrome) may place adolescents in the situation of becoming bereaved parents (Barnickol, Fuller, & Shinners, 1986; Schodt, 1982).

Suicidal behavior among adolescents has attracted much attention in recent years (for example, Alcohol, Drug Abuse, and Mental Health Administration, 1989; Giovacchini, 1981; Klagsbrun, 1976; Peck, Farberow, & Litman, 1985), for two primary reasons: (1) to many, adolescence seems to be a healthy and productive era during which the individual evolves from child to adult, and from which arise important openings to the future; and (2) during the period between 1960 and 1990, suicide rates among adolescents increased more rapidly than similar rates for any other age cohort (Maris, 1985). It has seemed paradoxical that self-inflicted death (which is always underreported; see Chapter 17) should leap forward to become the third leading cause of death among adolescents, who are in an era of the life span that is perceived by many to be satisfying and promising. In fact, of course, suicide is an option that is often chosen by individuals who do not share the rosy view of their situation that may be held by others, who are unable to identify constructive options to resolve their problems, and who are depressed that life is good and auspicious for others (Mack & Hickler, 1981). Attention to life-threatening behavior in adolescents has also led to concern about similar behavior in preadolescents (Orbach, 1988; Pfeffer, 1986, 1989).

Suicidal behavior is usually complex and multidetermined (see Chapter 17). Oversimplifying the situation of those who attempt or complete actions that may end their lives is not helpful (Tishler, McHenry, & Morgan, 1981). Important factors in this behavior among adolescents have to do with inadequacies or alterations in relationships between adolescents and significant others, such as parents and family members, peers, schoolmates, or co-workers; strong pressures among adolescents to conform with peers; inexperience in coping with problems; and suicide as a response to dysfunction. All of these are associated with ineffective communication and coping skills. In other words, some adolescents may be unable to express their needs, solve their problems, or obtain assistance that they require.

Adolescents who can neither resolve their problems nor put them into a larger perspective can become isolated and depressed. Since depression is frequently associated with feelings of helplessness and hopelessness, such adolescents may become desperate. That is, they may be prone to tunnel vision in which self-destruction may appear to be the only available option. Most often, this does not reflect a wish to be dead. In fact, many suicidal individuals are ambivalent in their feelings about life and death. But for suicidal adolescents, in particular, what may be most significant is an overpowering wish to *escape* from the stressful life situation (Berman, 1986).

Individuals who are ambivalent about ending their lives often communicate their need for help in some way or other. For example, they may begin to give away cherished possessions or speak vaguely about how things would be better if they were no longer around. However, these may not be very effective ways of getting across the desired message. After all, the ability to achieve effective communication is usually directly related to an ability to resolve problems. In addition, those to whom the adolescent's needs are poorly communicated may not recognize such messages as cries for assistance, partly because the messages may be obscure in themselves and partly because those who are living healthful lives may be unable or unwilling to grasp the desperation that is associated with such messages.

Adolescents cannot really be prevented from attempting or completing suicides, although much can be done to minimize the likelihood of such behaviors. Efforts to increase self-esteem, foster the ability to make sound decisions, and enhance constructive coping skills in adolescents are all desirable. School-based education and intervention programs for teachers, counselors, parents, and adolescents are designed to teach about warning signs of suicide and practical strategies for offering help, such as peer counseling and crisis intervention (Berkovitz, 1985; Leenaars & Wenckstern, 1991; Poland, 1989; Ross, 1980, 1985). The important thing about such programs is that the individuals to whom they are addressed are ideally positioned to identify and

*Depression in a
17 year old.*

assist adolescents who might engage in suicidal behavior. With suitable adaptation, programs of this sort may also be appropriate for college students and for preadolescents.

Some have been concerned that education about suicide may produce the very behaviors it is designed to minimize. This is one version of the so-called contagion theory, according to which it is thought that mentioning suicide is likely to infect the hearer with a tendency to engage in such behavior. Such a concern has been associated in recent years with "cluster suicides," or situations in which the example of others and/or reports in the media seem to have established models for troubled youth. In fact, no reliable evidence supports these views (Ross, 1985).

It is not exposure to knowledge about suicide or even to the suicidal behavior of others that is crucial in itself, but actions that are perceived to legitimize life-threatening behavior. This is precisely what is absent in education that is frank about the negative consequences of suicidal behavior. Especially for adolescents, such education insists that suicide is a permanent solution to a temporary problem. It mobilizes resources for resolving problems in other ways and directs attention to the great pain that is always a widespread legacy of suicide. Talking about suicide in a constructive educational format is far more likely to clear the air and minimize suicidal behavior than to suggest or encourage such behavior.

Crisis intervention programs offer another useful model of intervention designed to minimize suicidal behaviors in adolescents and others (Fairchild, 1986; Hatton & Valente, 1984). Such programs are directed precisely at those who are sufficiently ambivalent about ending their lives as to initiate telephone contact with the helping agency. Many of the volunteers who respond to such contacts are themselves adolescents who have been selected for such work and who are trained, supervised, and supported in what they do (Valente & Saunders, 1987). Such volunteers offer a caring presence, an attentive companion during what is most often a rather limited period of crisis, an ability to evaluate needs, a helper who can aid in the identification of alternative strategies for resolving problems, and a guide to additional resources for further assistance.

One area that is not well understood regarding adolescent suicide has to do with survivors of suicide attempts and the aftereffects of such behavior (Valente & Sellers, 1986). It is clear that grief following the suicide of an adolescent is likely to be intense. This applies to all who are so bereaved but especially to adolescent peers: "Adolescent suicide is a particularly toxic form of death for peers who are left behind" (Mauk & Weber, 1991, p. 115). The bereavement of adolescents who survive the suicide of a peer is frequently complicated by feelings of guilt, rejection, frustration, and failure. Quite often, it is also overlaid by societal disapproval, labeling, and stigma—all of which add to the burdens of grief and mourning. Adolescents who must endure such experiences deserve sensitivity, care, and support in their bereavement. They should also be helped to celebrate and commemorate not the manner of death but the life of their deceased friend.

Helping Adolescents Cope with Death

Adolescents can be helped in their efforts to cope with death through education and preparation prior to the fact and through support and constructive intervention at the time of and after a death.

Education and Prior Preparation

Parents and other adults influence adolescent coping with death through the foundation they lay down in childhood and the environment they create for

*Adolescence,
guns, and
violence: a lethal
mixture.*

adolescents to function in (Larson, 1972). Open lines of communication, sharing of thoughts and feelings, role modeling, and other constructive socialization processes enable adolescents to feel secure in themselves and to find satisfaction in the rewards of living, even as they also take account of issues related to loss and death.

McNeil (1986) has suggested the following guidelines for adults in family and other forms of communication with adolescents about death:

1. Take the lead in heightened awareness of an adolescent's concerns about death and in openness to discussing whatever he or she wishes to explore.
2. Listen actively and perceptively, with special attention to the feelings that appear to underlie what the adolescent is saying.
3. Accept the adolescent's feelings as real, important, and normal.
4. Use supportive responses that reflect acceptance and understanding of what the adolescent is trying to say.

5. Project a belief in the worth of the adolescent by resisting the temptation to solve his or her problems and by conveying an effort to help the adolescent find his or her own solutions.
6. Take time to enjoy the company of the adolescent and to provide frequent opportunities for talking together.

Communications of this sort can be supplemented by proactive programs of death education in secondary schools (for example, Crase & Crase, 1984; Rosenthal, 1986) and at the college level (for example, Corr, 1978). An extensive body of death-related literature is directed toward and can be helpful to middle school, high school, and other young readers (see Appendix B; see also Lamers, 1986). Also, principles set forth in literature for adults about children and death (as suggested in Chapter 11) may be relevant to adolescents, with suitable modifications, and there is literature for adults that deals directly with adolescents and death (for example, Corr & McNeil, 1986). In all programs of education and support for adolescents, careful attention must be paid to the goals that one seeks to achieve and to the needs and experiences of adolescents. In her account of processes in designing a course on death, dying, and bereavement for adolescents, Rosenthal (1986) advised educators to make decisions about possible topics, objectives, materials, methods, and evaluation procedures in terms of three primary aspects of death-related education for adolescents: information, self-awareness, and skills for helping. The important thing is to reach out and make constructive contacts with vulnerable adolescents before they become isolated and alienated.

Support and Assistance After a Death

After a death, much can be done to help bereaved adolescents. In terms of the task-based model proposed by Fox (1988) for grieving children and adolescents (see Chapter 11), bereaved adolescents can be helped to obtain accurate information about a loss and begin the process of interpreting and integrating that loss into their ongoing lives; identify affective responses to a death, express their feelings in safe and manageable ways, and find their own ways of coping; take active roles in funeral practices and commemorate losses in constructive ways; and find ways to go on with healthy and productive living.

Counseling interventions with adolescents should be guided by two principles: (1) provide a safe environment in which the adolescent can explore difficulties; and (2) assist with the process of addressing the developmental and situational tasks that are often closely interrelated in adolescent bereavement (Calvin & Smith, 1986). This latter principle means that it must be the adolescent, not the counselor, who works out acceptable solutions to challenges in his or her own life. More detailed guidance for counselors is provided by a number of authors (Balk, 1984; Floerchinger, 1991; Gray, 1988; Jones, 1977; McNeil, Silliman, & Swihart, 1991; Zinner, 1985).

Adolescents who are unwilling to talk to parents, counselors, or other adults may find it more congenial to address their death-related concerns in

Selected Literature for Adolescent About Death, Dying, and Bereavement

Literature for Middle School Readers

About the death of a parent or grandparent:
Blume, J. (1981). *Tiger Eyes.*
Cleaver, V., & Cleaver, B. (1970). *Grover.*
Farley, C. (1975). *The Garden Is Doing Fine.*
LeShan E. (1976). *Learning to Say Good-by: When a Parent Dies.*
Little, J. (1984). *Mama's Going to Buy You a Mockingbird.*
Mann, P. (1977). *There Are Two Kinds of Terrible.*

About dying and/or death in adolescence:
Grollman, S. (1988). *Shira: A Legacy of Courage.*
Jampolsky, G. G., & Murray, G. (Eds.). (1982). *Straight from the Siblings: Another Look at the Rainbow.*
Jampolsky, G. G., & Taylor, P. (Eds.). (1978). *There Is a Rainbow Behind Every Dark Cloud.*
Paterson, K. (1977). *Bridge to Terabithia.*
Richter, E. (1986). *Losing Someone You Love: When a Brother or Sister Dies.*

About suicide in adolescence:
Arrick, F. (1980). *Tunnel Vision.*
Geller, N. (1987). *The Last Teenage Suicide.*

About loss, coping, and death-related education for adolescents:
Bernstein, J. E. (1977). *Loss: And How to Cope with It.*
Heegaard, M. E. (1990). *Coping with Death and Grief.*
Rofes, E. E. (Ed.), and the Unit at Fayerweather Street School. (1985). *The Kids' Book About Death and Dying, by and for Kids.*
Romond, J. L. (1989). *Children Facing Grief: Letters from Bereaved Brothers and Sisters.*
Shura, M. F. (1988). *The Sunday Doll.*
Sternberg, F., & Sternberg, B. (1980). *If I Die and When I Do: Exploring Death with Young People.*

the context of a support group populated by peers with similar experiences (Baxter, Bennett, & Stuart, 1989). Groups of this sort dispel the stigma of being "different" or marked out by a death and confirm the fundamental lesson that it is natural to grieve the experience of a significant loss.

Many adolescents recognize that there can be positive outcomes even in the wake of intense tragedy, such as a deeper appreciation of life, greater caring for and stronger emotional bonds with others, and greater emotional strength (Oltjenbruns, 1991). Adults can help to encourage such outcomes in adolescents and can learn important lessons from them in their own lives.

Selected Literature for Adolescent About Death, Dying, and Bereavement (continued)

Literature for High School Readers

About the dying and/or death of a parent, grandparent, or other adult:

Agee, J. (1969). *A Death in the Family.*
Craven, M. (1973). *I Heard the Owl Call My Name.*
Greenberg, J. (1979). *A Season In-between.*
Lewis, C. S. (1976). *A Grief Observed.*
Martin, A.M. (1986). *With You and Without You.*
Tolstoy, L. (1960). *The Death of Ivan Ilych and Other Stories.*

About confronting death as an adolescent:

Deaver, J. R. (1988). *Say Goodnight, Gracie.*
Gunther, J. (1949). *Death Be Not Proud: A Memoir.*
Hughes, M. (1984). *Hunter in the Dark.*
Pendleton, E. (Comp.). (1980). *Too Old to Cry, Too Young to Die.*

About suicide in adolescence:

Colman, W. (1990). *Understanding and Preventing Teen Suicide.*
Francis, D. B. (1989). *Suicide: A Preventable Tragedy.*
Gardner, S. & Rosenberg, G. (1985). *Teenage Suicide.*
Hyde, M. O., & Forsyth, E. H. (1986). *Suicide: The Hidden Epidemic.*
Klagsbrun, F. (1976). *Too Young to Die: Youth and Suicide.*
Kolehmainen, J., & Handwerk, S. (1986). *Teen Suicide: A Book for Friends, Family, and Classmates.*
Langone, J. (1986). *Dead End: A Book About Suicide.*
Leder, J. M. (1987). *Dead Serious: A Book for Teenagers About Teenage Suicide.*
Schleifer, J. (1991). *Everything You Need to Know About Teen Suicide* (rev. ed.).

About loss, death, and coping in American society.

Langone, J. (1972). *Death Is a Noun: A View of the End of Life.*
Langone, J. (1974). *Vital Signs: The Way We Die in America.*

Annotated descriptions of these books and complete bibliographical information are available in Appendix B.

SOURCE Based on C. A. Corr, 1993.

Summary

This chapter has explored many aspects of interactions between adolescents and death in contemporary American society. The distinctive developmental tasks of adolescence—striving to achieve a stable sense of identity versus role confusion—have a direct bearing on how adolescents relate to death. These tasks influence encounters with death among adolescents (we noted that adolescence is an era characterized by low death rates and involving deaths mainly from accidents, homicide, and suicide) and attitudes of adolescents toward death (which generally combine a strong emphasis upon the present and a tendency to resist recognition of the personal significance of death). In coping with life-threatening illness and dying, it is especially important for adolescents to maintain privacy; a positive body image; an ability to express individuality, independence and control; and peer interaction. Adolescents coping with bereavement and grief are doing so at a time in life when grief may seem unique, incomprehensible, and overpowering and when developmental tasks are similar to mourning tasks. This chapter has also discussed issues related to pregnancy and suicide in adolescents and has suggested some guidelines for helping adolescents cope with death.

QUESTIONS FOR REVIEW AND DISCUSSION

1. What sorts of death-related losses are most typical in adolescence and what do such losses usually mean to adolescents? What sorts of death-related losses have you experienced in your own adolescence and what did they mean to you?

2. During your own adolescence, have you been seriously ill or have you experienced an important loss? If so, what were your most significant concerns about that illness or loss? Or perhaps you know an adolescent who has been in such a situation. If so, what were his or her most significant concerns?

3. If you were asked to recommend to adults how they could help adolescents cope with death, what would you recommend? How would the following make a difference in your recommendations: the home or family situation of the adolescents who are to be helped; the ethnic or cultural background of the adolescents who are to be helped; the nature of the death-related loss the adolescents are experiencing; the cultural background or social role (such as parent, teacher, counselor, or health care provider) of the adults to whom you are speaking?

SUGGESTED READINGS

General resources on adolescents, their development, and death include:

Corr, C. A., & McNeil, J. N. (Eds.). (1986). *Adolescence and Death.*

Offer, D., Ostrov, E., & Howard, K. I. (1981). *The Adolescent: A Psychological Self-Portrait.*

Concerning life-threatening illness in adolescence, consult:

Krementz, J. (1989). *How It Feels to Fight for Your Life.*
Pendleton, E. (Comp.). (1980). *Too Old to Cry, Too Young to Die.*

Bereavement and grief in adolescence are explored in the following:

Baxter, G., Bennett, L., & Stuart, W. (1989). *Adolescents and Death: Bereavement Support Groups for Secondary School Students* (2nd ed.).
Fairchild, T. N. (Ed.). (1986). *Crisis Intervention Strategies for School-Based Helpers.*
Grollman, E. A. (1993). *Straight Talk about Death for Teenagers: How to Cope with Losing Someone You Love.*
LaGrand, L. (1986). *Coping with Separation and Loss as a Young Adult: Theoretical and Practical Realities.*

Teaching adolescents about death or helping them to cope with death is a topic examined in the following:

Sternberg, F., & Sternberg, B. (1980). *If I Die and When I Do: Exploring Death with Young People.*

Suicide and life-threatening behavior among adolescents and younger children are explored in the following:

Alcohol, Drug Abuse, and Mental Health Administration. (1989). *Report of the secretary's task force on youth suicide* (4 vols.).
Giovacchini, P. (1981). *The Urge to Die: Why Young People Commit Suicide.*
Klagsbrun, F. (1976). *Too Young to Die: Youth and Suicide.*
Mack, J. E., & Hickler, H. (1981). *Vivienne: The Life and Suicide of an Adolescent Girl.*
Orbach, I. (1988). *Children Who Don't Want to Live: Understanding and Treating the Suicidal Child.*
Peck, M. L., Farberow, N. L., & Litman, R. E. (Eds.). (1985). *Youth Suicide.*
Pfeffer, C. R. (1986). *The Suicidal Child.*

CHAPTER 13

Adults

This chapter examines interactions with death during adulthood. Adulthood is the so-called "prime of life," extending from the end of adolescence until the beginning of a new developmental era designated by some as the period of "maturity" or "old age." Because adulthood is such a long period in the life cycle, because many variables impact upon the lives of adults, and because the developmental aspects of adulthood have not been as well studied as those of some other periods, one must be cautious in making generalizations about adult humans and their experiences.

We can begin by thinking of human adults as "middle-escents," individuals situated in terms of developmental processes between their younger counterparts (children and adolescents), on the one hand, and those who precede them (the elderly), on the other hand. Despite notable differences among themselves, such individuals have much to share—for example, issues arising from new elements in family relationships, work roles, and an evolving set of death-related concerns.

After a brief vignette designed to illustrate some of the characteristic issues that may arise for adults in relationship to death in the United States today, this chapter considers in turn the distinctive developmental tasks of young and middle-aged adults; typical encounters with death in American society during the adult years; attitudes toward death during this period; issues related to dying as an adult; issues related to bereavement and grief in adults; and special issues concerning AIDS.

One Man at Midlife

George Anderson was 43. Until recently, things had been going quite well for him. He had a good family, a nice home in the suburbs, and a satisfying job. George had read some things about the "midlife crisis" that men, especially, were supposed to experience around the age of 40. But he had been offered a major promotion at the age of 41 to a much more significant position at the firm where he worked. For George, it seemed that there would be interesting challenges in the years ahead, along with very tangible rewards for the years of work that he had invested to get to his present situation in life.

The first shadow that appeared in George's life took the form of what was later diagnosed as Alzheimer's disease in his mother. George's parents had been very independent people all their lives. Although they lived in the same city and were willing to help out with babysitting and similar chores, George's parents had been determined to let their children live their own lives. They enjoyed good relations, marked by warmth and mutual respect.

Later, George realized that his father had been covering for his mother over several years as her early memory lapses gradually became more serious and developed into confusion and dementia. All of this was suddenly exposed when George's father suffered a cerebral hemorrhage one night and died the next day. Suddenly, George's mother could no longer cope on her own. George and his younger sister had to find a nursing home that would admit

Alzheimer's patients, relocate his mother, dispose of unneeded possessions, and sell the family home. Suddenly, it seemed to George that there was no longer anyone in the older generation out there "ahead" of him whose mere presence seemed to serve as a kind of shield or protection against the challenges of illness, aging, and death.

Next, George suddenly felt himself to be besieged by new challenges from his own children. Until that point, George would have said that he and Mary had been "blessed" with four children: 16-year-old Edward, 12-year-old Lucy, and his "bonus babies," Harry and Holly, their 5-year-old twins. But with the death of his favorite grandfather, Edward just seemed to switch off from the family. He was always away at school, driving around with his friends, coming and going at odd times, or locked in his room playing computer games.

By contrast, Lucy kept dragging her father to the nursing home, where he was depressed (and perhaps a bit scared in case any of this was hereditary) to witness his mother's present condition. Lucy would hold her grandmother's hand, feed her soft foods, wipe away drool, and chatter on lovingly, while George wished they could leave and tried not to look at the other residents.

The twins just kept asking blunt questions that George did not know how to answer: "Is Grandpa cold lying there in the ground?"; "What do you do when you're dead?"; "Where is dead?"; "What is Grandma thinking?"; "Why can't she recognize us?"; "Will you die, too, or get like Grandma?"

The final straw for George was when his friend Andy had a heart attack. George and Andy had gone to school together when they were kids and had lived in the same town all their lives. When the season was right, they hunted and fished together. The year they were both 40, George and Andy and their wives flew to the Virgin Islands for two weeks of swimming, sailing, and good food. George realized that he and Andy had gained a little weight since high school and were losing some of their hair. But he had been just about ready to start that new exercise and diet program when Andy keeled over on the way to church one Sunday morning. Andy's death almost paralyzed his wife and six children. George had to step in and make all of the arrangements for this second funeral, just at a time when he himself was finding it so hard to deal with the death of his friend.

Adults, Developmental Tasks, and Death

Adulthood is the longest single period in the human life span, extending from the third decade of life through at least the seventh decade. Roughly, this includes the period from age 20 or 21 until age 65, although statistical data are often expressed in terms of ten-year periods from ages 25 to 65.

Those who occupy the 40–plus years of adult life in American society actually make up two roughly 20–year generational cohorts. Thus, in Erikson's (1963) schema, the period of adulthood encompasses two distinguishable eras in the life span: young adulthood (roughly ages 21 or 25 to 45) and middle age (ages 45 to 65). For Erikson, the major task in young adulthood is the achievement of intimacy (versus the danger of isolation), with a principal theme of affiliation and love. By contrast, the major task of middle age in Erikson's schema is generativity (versus the danger of stagnation), with a principal theme of productivity and care.

We might put this another way by saying that adulthood is a period of exploiting and exploring the identity established in earlier stages of development through choices about one's lifestyle, relationships, and work (Stevens-Long, 1988). That is, the decisions made in the vitality of young adulthood chart much of the course of our lives in terms of relationships, vocation, and lifestyle and enable us to know ourselves in much fuller ways than were possible during adolescence. In middle age, one typically conserves and draws on an endowment of personal, social, and vocational resources that one established earlier. The celebrated midlife transition can be focused on that which is past and gone (youth and its distinctive opportunities), or it can lead to a renewed appreciation of life as one achieves a new self-concept and determines how to live out the remainder of one's life.

Levinson (1978) drew a distinction between early or young adulthood (roughly ages 17–45) and middle adulthood (roughly ages 40–65). On that basis, Levinson distinguished several "seasons" or qualitatively distinct eras in the life cycle, with boundary zones, periods of transition, and characteristic issues. Within young adulthood, this involves an early adult transition from preadulthood; a novice phase in which one enters the adult world and is involved in "forming a dream"; an internal transition at about age 30; and a period of "settling down." Similarly, according to Levinson, middle adulthood can be depicted in terms of another novice or introductory period; an internal transition around age 50; and a concluding period; followed by a transition into old age or late adulthood. The boundary between young and middle adulthood for Levinson is the celebrated midlife transition, within which the individual reappraises the past and terminates young adulthood, modifies the life structure and initiates middle adulthood, and seeks to resolve four principal polarities (young/old; destruction/creation; masculine/feminine; and attachment/separateness).

In discussions of adulthood, it is fair to keep in mind that much of the work undertaken by researchers like Levinson has been accomplished with male subjects. Patterns of adult maturation for females have not been as thoroughly or as clearly studied. Gilligan (1982) is one of the most prominent researchers to have noted that developmental patterns in females are very likely to differ in significant ways from those of their male counterparts. For example, both male and female adults are part of the so-called "sandwich generation," caught between the competing pressures of older and younger cohorts, even as they struggle to cope with issues involving themselves and their peers. But responses to issues that face the sandwich generation should be expected to differ in important ways for males and females.

For example, when care was required for an elderly relative or an ill child, at one point in American social history the adult male would have been expected to provide economic support while society would have turned to the adult female for nurturing and practical hands-on care. For many, that might still be the case. If so, differences between male and female roles in adulthood are clear. But these traditional divisions of roles are no longer accurate for many people in American society. Nevertheless, even when or where gender roles are changing rapidly, significant differences are still likely to remain between men and women. The point is that *common* aspects in adult development may coexist with *differences* arising from gender and other factors, as will be seen in the following survey of death-related interactions.

Encounters with Death

Overall Mortality Rates During Adulthood

In the United States in 1990, overall mortality rates were at a level of 109.9 per 100,000 for individuals in the 20- to 24-year-old age group. By contrast, death rates for the 60- to 64-year-old group were 1,457.2 (National Center for Health Statistics, 1993). Obviously, that sort of major difference in mortality rates reflects very significant changes in mortality patterns during the 45-year period of adult life. These changes can be highlighted in a number of ways.

The first point to note is simply the accelerating increase in death rates with age. Death rates of approximately 110 per 100,000 for ages 20–24 more than doubled to 252.8 per 100,000 for ages 40–44. An even sharper increase is noted in the next 20 years, when death rates of just over 377 per 100,000 for ages 45–49 nearly quadrupled to 1,457 per 100,000 for ages 60–64. This figure for the 60- to 64-year-old cohort is the first in the life span to exceed the very high mortality rates of infancy (National Center for Health Statistics, 1993).

To put this another way, in 1990 the total number of deaths in the United States was 143,653 in the 25- to 44-year-old age group and 371,304 in the 45- to 64-year-old age group (National Center for Health Statistics, 1993). That is, in 1990 nearly 2.6 times as many Americans died in middle age as in young adulthood. That occurred in a middle-aged population that was nearly 25 percent smaller than the group of young adults.

Leading Causes of Death During Adulthood

There are significant changes also in the leading causes of death throughout the adult era in the life span. For ages 25–44, the three leading causes of death are accidents (27,663 deaths), malignant neoplasms (cancer; 21,650 deaths), and human immunodeficiency virus (HIV) infection (18,748 deaths), followed fairly closely by diseases of the heart (15,045 deaths), suicide (12,267 deaths), and homicide and legal intervention (12,060 deaths) (National Center for Health Statistics, 1993). Accidents are well ahead of the second and third causes on this list. This reflects ongoing vigor and excitement in the lifestyle of many young adults in contemporary American society.

Comparing adolescence to young adulthood reveals that rates for accidental death (especially as related to motor vehicles) have declined significantly (from 43.9 to 34.3 per 100,000) from the former to the latter period. Death rates for homicide slightly decrease during young adulthood by comparison with adolescence, whereas those from suicide slightly increase.

For ages 45–64, the two leading causes of death are malignant neoplasms (134,742 deaths for a rate of 291.8 per 100,000) and diseases of the heart (107,750 deaths for a rate of 233.4) (National Center for Health Statistics, 1993). The combined death rates for these two causes are approximately three times the total rates for the next eight leading causes of death in middle age (cerebrovascular diseases, accidents, chronic obstructive pulmonary diseases and allied conditions, chronic liver disease and cirrhosis, diabetes mellitus, suicide, pneumonia and influenza, and HIV infection) and nearly twice the total rates for these and all other causes of death in this period of life. Among cancer deaths, leading causes for both sexes are cancer of the respiratory and intrathoracic organs, followed by prostate and colon/rectum cancer for males and by breast and colon/rectum cancer for females.

Accidental death rates decrease slightly during middle adulthood by contrast with young adulthood, and deaths related to motor vehicles continue to decline throughout middle age, eventually to reach their lowest levels since childhood and a lower level than will be seen in subsequent years. Homicide rates also decline during this era, whereas suicide rates creep upward. In general, these patterns reflect the growing prominence of the degenerative diseases as leading causes of death during the middle and later segments of the life span.

HIV Infection and AIDS During Adulthood

During the 1980s, a new factor entered into encounters with death, a factor that was especially significant during young adulthood and middle age. This factor is the human immunodeficiency virus (HIV) and acquired immune deficiency syndrome (AIDS). The HIV attacks the immune system, which defends the body against a variety of natural assaults (see Chapter 19). In this way, infected persons develop an acquired immune deficiency. Such individuals do not die of AIDS itself, but from a broad range of opportunistic diseases (such as Kaposi's sarcoma or *Pneumocystis carinii* pneumonia) and their side effects (such as severe diarrhea or wasting syndrome). Many of these opportunistic diseases had been quite rare or specialized in their influence until the advent of the HIV.

The impact of HIV infection in the United States is evident in data on deaths and death rates for 1990. In that year, HIV infection was the sixth leading cause of death in adolescence (with a death rate of only 1.5 per 100,000, representing 541 deaths), the sixth leading cause of death in young adulthood (with a death rate of 15.0, representing 12,060 deaths), and the tenth leading cause of death in middle adulthood (with a death rate of 11.1, representing 5,126 deaths) (National Center for Health Statistics, 1993). More specifically,

HIV infection is the leading cause of death among young adult males in their 20s and 30s. This is a population group in the prime of life that generally enjoys a very low mortality rate. For such a group, it is both a particular difficulty and a special irony that a new communicable disease should have risen to infamy in this unfortunate way in recent years. HIV infection is also becoming increasingly prevalent among young adult women, particularly African Americans and Hispanic Americans.

Attitudes Toward Death

Some features of adult encounters with death are particularly significant in shaping attitudes toward death—especially during middle adulthood. The years of the late 20s and early 30s often are times of greater ego stability than adolescence. As a result, anxiety about one's own personal death seems to be a less prominent feature of young adulthood than of adolescence. Of course, this will be altered where newly emerging encounters with HIV infection and AIDS generate new threats and anxieties. But for many persons in American society, these general sets of attitudes begin to alter as one moves more firmly into the middle years of adulthood.

For example, as we have seen in the experiences of George Anderson, typical encounters with death during adulthood are likely to increase as the next-older generation begins to encounter higher death rates. The death of George's father and the illness and institutionalization of his mother are examples of events that are all too likely to confront a middle-aged adult in the United States today. This, together with issues arising from their developing children, is what is meant when one speaks of the "sandwich generation," a group that feels trapped by new and different pressures from both the older and younger generations that surround it. The worries and concerns that characterize young adults in relation to death are most likely to concern the deaths of others.

However, as one progresses in the life cycle and/or, more significantly, as one learns from one's own life experiences, like George Anderson one encounters the appearance of a newly personalized sense of mortality (Doka, 1988). This occurs particularly in two ways: through encounters with the deaths of peers, parents, and spouses, often for the first time in the life cycle and especially as a result of natural causes; and through one's own newly emerging realization of oneself as a mortal creature who will die someday.

Peers or a spouse can die at any time during the life span, but adulthood is an era when it is more likely that they will die of natural causes (such as heart attack, cancer, or stroke). When that happens, their surviving peers can no longer effectively dismiss death as the result of ill fortune or external forces. Similarly, when one begins to sense the limits of one's bodily capacities or to recognize problems associated with aging or lifestyle, one's personal sense of invulnerability must diminish. As students of the midlife crisis often report, this is a time when one begins to make a retrospective assessment of one's achievements, to realize that one has already passed through half or two-thirds of average life expectancy, to appreciate that the future does not stretch end-lessly before one, and to entertain prospective thoughts of retirement and impending death. This can lead to a reappraisal of one's values and priorities, which may result in an enriched capacity for love and enjoyment, and a richer, more philosophical sense of meaning in one's life—or it may have less posi-tive results (Jacques, 1965). In short, the implications of death play a promi-nent role in the reevaluation of life and self that characterizes middle age.

As young and middle-aged adults turn to thoughts of their own personal death, they are likely to think of what that will mean for their children, family members, or significant others as well as for the vocational and other projects that are likely to have occupied so much of their time and energy.

To all of this, HIV infection and AIDS have added a somewhat mysterious and very lethal specter of an infectious disease. Someone said to us recently: "There was a world before the discovery of AIDS, and there is a world after the discovery of AIDS. But things will never be the same after the discovery of AIDS."

Also, the Desert Storm war in Kuwait and Iraq in 1991 had a special impact on many mature adults. Undoubtedly, everyone who took part in that war experienced the hazards of a combat theater. But the older reservists who were called up for the war because of their specialized skills were perhaps in a rather different situation from many younger volunteers who were already serving on active duty. These reservists were often mature adults who would not otherwise have faced such a situation short of a global conflict.

There are, in other words, a number of new death-related perils for young and middle adults near the end of the 20th century. Some (such as issues related to the nuclear threat or to the environment) are shared with all of those who inhabit this planet. Others (such as those involving starvation or war) apply mainly to individuals in specific localities or roles. Still others are particularly relevant to those in the long middle years of the life span. In general, however, one might say that "the issue of death in the young adult is one of frustration and disappointment," and "the issue of death in the middle years is more likely to take on an interpersonal tone" (Pattison, 1977, pp. 24–25).

Adults Coping with Life-Threatening Illness and Dying

When one has a life-threatening illness or is dying, situational challenges of the illness/dying processes are superimposed upon the developmental tasks of human maturation. This section considers what that means in terms of implications for young and middle-aged adults.

Coping as a Young Adult

According to Erikson, the basic developmental task in young adulthood is that of achieving intimacy. With this in mind, Cook and Oltjenbruns (1989) have suggested that life-threatening illness and dying challenge the needs of young adults to develop intimate relationships, express their sexuality, and obtain realistic support of their goals and future plans.

"Intimacy involves the ability to experience an open, supportive, and close relationship with another person, without fear of losing oneself in the process. The establishment of intimacy with a significant other implies the capacity for mutual empathy, the ability to help meet each other's needs, the acceptance of each other's limitations, and the commitment to care deeply for each other" (Cook & Oltjenbruns, 1989, p. 270). In short, intimacy depends upon a sense of one's own identity and trust in the other.

To achieve quality in living, young adults who are seriously ill or dying need to maintain and pursue intimacy. According to Erikson (1963), an inability to develop intimate relationships results in isolation, or a loss of affiliation and love, which might be expressed in superficial relationships with others and preoccupation with oneself. As observed in Chapter 5, isolation is precisely the leading problem faced by most individuals who are coping with dying. Thus, developmental tasks of young adulthood are subject to particularly sharp challenge by life-threatening illness and dying during that period of life.

Young adults pursue the development of an intimate relationship with others primarily through reciprocal self-disclosure (Derlega & Chaikin, 1975; Lowenthal & Weiss, 1976). This process may, but need not, be compromised when young adults are ill or dying. Through intimate relationships of various sorts, concerns and fears are shared, the value and worth of the human beings who are involved is affirmed, and a foundation of trust is established upon which hope and compliance can be based. Thus, intimacy is a critical element in the lives of young adults who are seriously ill or dying—for themselves, for their family members and friends, and for their professional caregivers. When there is difficulty in achieving or maintaining intimacy, it will be important for all concerned to reexamine barriers (such as fear or lack of information) and to consider what can be gained by renewed efforts to risk sharing in a pressured and precious time.

Sexuality is not an element in all intimate relationships, but it is a natural expression of intimacy in many couples. Sexuality expresses itself in a broad range of thoughts, feelings, and behaviors; it is not confined to intercourse alone. As such, the expression of sexuality in appropriate ways is to be fostered in the lives of seriously ill and dying adults (Gideon & Taylor, 1981; Leviton, 1978). This may involve decisions about grooming or dressing, a gentle touch or caress, open discussion of physical and psychological needs, and other aspects of feeling positive about oneself. Nonjudgmental attitudes, privacy, and efforts to adapt to changes brought about by disease and treatment (for example, mastectomy or colostomy) can all be helpful in this area.

For young adults, a life-threatening illness may threaten *goals and future plans* in many areas, such as getting married, having children, and pursuing educational or vocational aspirations. Such individuals are obliged to evaluate their plans and to determine what may be appropriate in their new situation. They will appreciate assistance from those who can draw their attention to the realities of the situation, while also supporting their autonomy and their own decision-making processes. In this way, one respects efforts to satisfy important personal and developmental needs, while also recognizing constraints on former hopes and dreams.

Coping as a Middle-Aged Adult

According to Erikson, the principal task for middle-aged adults is the pursuit of generativity. In relationship to life-threatening illness and dying, this means that the "needs of the dying at midlife . . . include (1) the need for reevaluation of one's life, (2) the need for continuation of roles, and (3) the need to put affairs in order" (Cook & Oltjenbruns, 1989, p. 330). Reassessment, conservation, and preparation are characteristic activities of all middle-aged adults. In turn, they involve "stock-taking" (Butler & Lewis, 1982), efforts to sustain generativity as an alternative to self-indulgence and stagnation (Erikson, 1963), and a need to prepare for the future and to carry out one's responsibilities for others.

Awareness of a life-threatening illness or situational challenges involved in coping with dying are likely to heighten, rather than to overthrow, these developmental processes. Thus, the characteristic question of *reevaluation*— "What is the meaning of my life?"—is one that becomes more, not less, poignant and urgent, under the dual stimuli of illness and maturation. Answers to such a question may generate more intense pursuit of projects established in young adulthood in view of the pressures that may now appear to work against their completion. Alternatively, a midlife adult may decide to make changes in his or her earlier projects and to strike out in new directions or relationships. Either of these orientations may involve some degree of grieving for that which has not been attained, together with some overshadowing awareness concerning losses yet to come.

However they choose to look toward a future that may now be perceived as less unclouded and extensive than it was before, middle-aged adults who are coping with life-threatening illness or dying can be expected to consider the prospects for *continuation* or enduring value in the legacies that they have been establishing for the future. Again, they may strive more diligently to achieve such goals, alter their form in ways that appear more satisfying or more achievable, or choose to settle for that which has already been achieved. Insofar as possible, it would be desirable to support constructive processes of generativity in ill and dying midlife adults by enabling them to continue to take part in meaningful roles and relationships in suitable ways.

Similarly, midlife adults are often greatly concerned with what they perceive to be their responsibilities to those whom they love. Looking to the future in light of such maturational tasks involves efforts to *put one's affairs in order*—that is, to continue to meet such obligations and to ensure that they are met after the individual dies. Life-threatening illness and dying threaten one's ability to meet such responsibilities but need not render that completely impossible. With support, one can strive to influence the future to the degree possible or to arrange for others to assume specific responsibilities on one's behalf. This can take the form of making a will, disposing of property, or conveying important wishes and messages. In this perspective, activities such as those involved in planning one's own funeral and burial arrangements represent not a morbid surrender to impending death but a healthy vitality in continuing to fulfill prized roles and an ability to minimize postdeath disruptions or burdens on others.

*A**dults Coping with Bereavement and Grief*

An aging, sandwich generation is beset with potential death-related losses on all sides. Young and middle-aged adults may suffer a full range of significant deaths: their parents and grandparents; their spouses, siblings, and peers; their children; and themselves. This is itself distinctive in some respects: youngsters do not experience the deaths of their own children, and the elderly are at low risk of experiencing the deaths of their own parents. What is most characteristic of bereavement in young and middle adults is the very real potential for so many kinds of death-related losses. Even the birth of a child who is impaired in some way may present adult parents with both opportunities and challenges that they must meet. (See "Welcome to Holland" on page 303.)

The meaning of any loss or death can only be evaluated by those who are most closely affected. Each will be difficult in its own way; none can rightly be dismissed by outsiders. As a general rule, however, research by Sanders (1979) has shown that adult bereavement is usually impacted most significantly by the death of a child, a spouse, and a parent—in that order. This is consistent with a familiar saying among bereaved adults, who report that "the death of my parent is the death of my past; the death of my spouse is the death of my present; the death of my child is the death of my future." As is universally true, it is the meaning of the relationship terminated by death that is the principal fact for the survivor.

Death of a Child

Fetal death   Like adolescent parents, many adults experience the death of a child in the uterus or in the birthing process. These are properly called "fetal deaths" rather than "miscarriage" (which may carry the usually unjustified assumption of responsibility by the mother for the loss) or "spontaneous abortion" (Davidson, 1984a). Fetal deaths may take place at various times during gestation and are usually distinguished from elective abortion. Fetal deaths may also include perinatal deaths that take place during the birthing process.

There are approximately 40,000 documented cases of late fetal death in the United States each year (Davidson, 1984a). At one point, it was thought that such experiences had minimal psychosocial impact upon the parents and did not generate a significant grief reaction. Parents were offered false conso-

Welcome to Holland

by Emily Perl Kingsley

I am often asked to describe the experience of raising a child with a disability—to try to help people who have not shared that unique experience to understand it, to imagine how it would feel. It's like this . . .

When you're going to have a baby, it's like planning a fabulous vacation trip—to Italy. You buy a bunch of guidebooks and make your wonderful plans. The Coliseum. The Michelangelo David. The gondolas in Venice. You may learn some handy phrases in Italian. It's all very exciting.

After months of eager anticipation, the day finally arrives. You pack your bags and off you go. Several hours later, the plane lands. The stewardess comes in and says, "Welcome to Holland."

"Holland?!?" you say. "What do you mean, Holland?? I signed up for Italy! I'm supposed to be in Italy. All my life I've dreamed of going to Italy."

But there's been a change in the flight plan. They've landed in Holland and there you must stay.

The important thing is that they haven't taken you to a horrible, disgusting, filthy place, full of pestilence, famine and disease. It's just a different place.

So you must go out and buy new guidebooks. And you must learn a whole new language. And you will meet a whole new group of people you would never have met.

It's just a *different* place. It's slower-paced than Italy, less flashy than Italy. But after you've been there for a while and you catch your breath, you look around . . . and you begin to notice that Holland has windmills . . . Holland has tulips. Holland even has Rembrandts.

But everyone you know is busy coming and going from Italy . . . and they're all bragging about what a wonderful time they had there. And for the rest of your life, you will say, "Yes, that's where I was supposed to go. That's what I had planned."

The pain of that will never, ever, ever go away . . . because the loss of that dream is a very, very significant loss.

But . . . if you spend your life mourning the fact that you didn't get to Italy, you may never be free to enjoy the very special, the very lovely things . . . about Holland.

lation: "Now you have a little angel in heaven" (But I was not engaged in generating angels); "You can always have another child" (But no individual child ever is or should be a replacement for another child).

This sort of easy dismissal of the import of the loss reflects ignorance and the discomfort of outsiders. It was bolstered by an erroneous claim that there could not be much grief when there had not been real bonding with the infant. Such a claim ignores the active ways in which most parents begin to reshape their lives and self-concepts during pregnancy to accommodate the anticipated baby (Klaus & Kennell, 1976). Such parents observe the movements of the fetus in the womb (now with the aid of new imaging technologies), explore potential names for the baby, plan accommodations, and develop dreams. When the outcome of all of this is the death of the infant, one must *complete* a process of bonding that has already been under way in order to enhance opportunities for productive grief and mourning (Lamb, 1988). There is now ample evidence that parental grief associated with fetal or infant death is a reality that is related not to the length of a baby's life but to the nature of the attachment (Borg & Lasker, 1981; DeFrain, Martens, Story, & Stork, 1986; Jimenez, 1982; Kennell, Slyter, & Klaus, 1970; Peppers & Knapp, 1980; Wolff, Nielson, & Schiller, 1970).

That is why in recent years programs have emerged in which parents and other family members are permitted (if they wish to do so) to see and hold their dead infant, give it a name, take pictures (Johnson et al., 1985; Reddin, 1987; Siegel et al., 1985), retain other mementos (such as a blanket, name tag, or lock of hair), obtain information from an autopsy, and take part in rituals that validate the life and the loss. Practices of this sort provide opportunities to interact with the baby, to facilitate shared experiences, and to strengthen a realistic foundation for mourning. Implementing such practices requires attention to detail and sensitivity to individual preferences. The aim is to affirm the value of the child and his or her abbreviated life and to respect the need of survivors to know that this child was real, that this was not all just some horrible nightmare.

Even in cases of elective abortion, when the parents feel unable or unwilling to bring the baby to term, or in cases of infant adoption, when the child is given over shortly after birth to be raised by others, there is usually a lingering sense of loss and grief (Doane & Quigley, 1981; Peppers, 1987). To choose (however deliberately or ambivalently) to abort, even with the conviction that the fetus is not yet a human child, is seldom to put aside all feelings associated with the ending of a life. To opt for adoption, even with the conviction that one is not able to rear this child, usually leaves one with feelings of pain or regret. Neither abortion nor adoption need result in grief that incapacitates. But it is wrong to assume that these are easy, painless decisions and to dismiss out of hand the implications for parents of events and decisions that close off opportunities involving what is or would become their offspring.

Neonatal and other infant deaths   After birth, the principal causes of death during infancy are congenital anomalies, Sudden Infant Death Syndrome (SIDS), disorders related to short gestation and low birth weight, and Respiratory Distress Syndrome (RDS). These present contrasting scenarios for parents and significant others. On the one hand, congenital anomalies, disorders related to short gestation and low birth weight, and RDS in American society may involve a struggle for life, the intervention of professionals and advanced technology prior to the death, and lingering implications of genetic etiology and responsibility. In such circumstances, the death of the infant is likely to occur in an institutional context and when the parents are not present. On the other hand, SIDS may involve none of these, since it is the prototype of a death from an unknown cause whose first symptom is a dead infant (Corr, Fuller, Barnickol, & Corr, 1991; DeFrain, Ernst, Jakub, & Taylor, 1991).

For survivors, neonatal and other infant deaths have in common the untimely and perhaps unheralded death of a vulnerable individual (Delgadillo & Davis, 1990). Even though pregnancy, the birthing process, and infancy are known to be times of risk for the offspring, a common societal image is that tiny babies should not die. Thus, it is often said in the wake of such a death that "it's just not fair." The hard fact is that "none of us is guaranteed long life, only a lifetime" (Showalter, 1983, p. x).

The specific impact of various sorts of infant deaths will depend upon diverse factors that enter into the mode of death and the situation of survivors. For example, the death of an infant in a neonatal intensive care unit can be an excruciating experience for professionals and parents alike. The experience may be even more difficult if there is conflict between professional care providers and family members (or between family members themselves) about care goals (Stinson & Stinson, 1983). Some bereaved mothers may prefer to remain on a maternity ward because of the staff's expertise in postpartum care, whereas others may wish to be relocated in order not to be confronted with happy parents interacting with newborn babies.

The death of a child and the uniqueness of each individual's experiences in bereavement may also add significantly to existing strains upon parental relationships in American society. That most bereaved parents can find ways in which to go on with productive living, even after a difficult infant death such as SIDS with its sudden, unanticipated, and (ultimately) unexplained cause, is testimony to the very great resilience of bereaved survivors (Knapp, 1986; Miles, n.d.). Such parents deserve the best that we can provide them in terms of information (for example, about the realities of the "syndrome" or recognized pattern that is SIDS), professional support, and contact with those who have had similar experiences (Donnelly, 1982; Johnson, 1987; Klass, 1988; Schiff, 1977; Schwiebert & Kirk, 1986). In many cases, one key area of decision making will involve whether or not (and, if so, when) to consider undertaking a subsequent pregnancy and how to help subsequent children relate to their older sibling who died before they were born (Schwiebert & Kirk, 1986).

Deaths during childhood and adolescence   Parental bereavement occasioned by the death of a child or adolescent may come about in a number of ways—for example, through some sort of accident (often involving a motor vehicle), as a result of homicide or suicide, through natural causes, even through war or some sort of societal conflict. Typically, these deaths take place suddenly and without much warning or opportunity for preparation. In all cases, they involve multiple dimensions: loss of the life of the child, loss of that which was or is a part of the self, and loss of the hopes and dreams that the child represents. When the death has come about by some form of more or less deliberate behavior (for example, suicide or homicide), by inadvertence

*A grieving
mother holds
her dead child.*

(for instance, accidents), or by irresponsible behavior (such as drunken driving), elements of responsibility, guilt, or blame may enter into the bereavement experience. Such elements can be expected to add to the burdens of parental grief and mourning (Bolton, 1989; Chance, 1992).

Guilt in parental bereavement   Guilt is the conviction that one has done wrong by violating some principle or responsibility. The principle may originate in moral, religious, or other convictions; the responsibility may be imposed by society or assumed by oneself. Guilt may be realistic and well founded or unrealistic and unjustified. Typically associated with guilt are lowered self-esteem, heightened self-blame, and a feeling that one should expiate or make retribution for the supposed wrong. Guilt is by no means exclusive to parental bereavement, but it is almost always—at least initially—a significant part of such bereavement.

A Letter to My Family and Friends

Thank you for not expecting too much from me this holiday season.

It will be our first Christmas without our child and I have all I can do coping with the "spirit" of the holiday on the radio, TV, in the newspapers and stores. We do not feel joyous, and trying to pretend this Christmas is going to be like the last one will be impossible because we are missing one.

Please allow me to talk about my child if I feel the need. Don't be uncomfortable with my tears. My heart is breaking and the tears are a way of letting out my sadness.

I plan to do something special in memory of my child. Please recognize my need to do this in order to keep our memories alive. My fear is not that I'll forget, but that you will.

Please don't criticize me if I do something that you don't think is normal. I'm a different person now and it may take a long time before this different person reaches an acceptance of my child's death.

As I survive the stages of grief, I will need your patience and support, especially during these holiday times and the "special" days throughout the year.

Thank you for not expecting too much from me this holiday season. Love,

A bereaved parent

SOURCE From M. Cleckley, E. Estes, & P. Norton, (Eds.). 1992.

Miles and Demi (1984, 1986) have suggested that guilt in parental bereavement arises from feelings of helplessness and responsibility. These feelings lead parents to ask how their past and present actions and feelings might have contributed to the child's death. Inevitable discrepancies between ideal standards and actual performance, along with perceived violations of self-expectations, culminate in guilt feelings, although how that will work itself out in individual cases will depend upon parental, situational, personal, and societal variables. For bereaved parents, there are at least six potential sources of guilt:

1. *Death causation guilt*, related to the belief that the parent either contributed to or failed to protect the child from the death
2. *Illness-related guilt*, related to perceived deficiencies in the parental role during the child's illness or at the time of death
3. *Parental role guilt*, related to the belief that the parent failed to live up to self-expectations or societal expectations in the overall parental role
4. *Moral guilt*, related to the belief that the child's death was punishment or retribution for violating a moral or religious standard
5. *Survival guilt*, related to violating the standard that a child should outlive his or her parents

6. *Grief guilt*, related to the behavioral and emotional reactions at the time of or following the child's death—that is, feeling guilt about how one acted at or after the time of the child's death

To understand correctly the bereavement experience of any particular parent, one must identify those elements of grief and guilt that appear in the overall experience. Each will need to be addressed in the mourning process.

Gender and role differences in parental bereavement   Fathers and mothers are different; married, unmarried, and divorced parents are different. Before being impacted by the death of a child, each survivor is distinguished by his or her gender, role(s), and individual characteristics. Each of these distinguishing factors may influence the bereavement experience. For example, according to traditional gender-based roles in American society, expression of strong feelings was sanctioned for females but discouraged for males. Similarly, wives were expected to remain at home, while husbands went out to work. These two factors alone are likely to encourage different types of grief experiences in mothers and fathers. Thus, one might expect that such spouses would be in different places in their grief work at any given point and might not be available to support each other as they usually do in healthy marital relationships (Schatz, 1986; Simonds & Rothman, 1992; Staudacher, 1991).

As gender expectations are altered, as social roles change, and as individual differences are permitted freer expression, responses to bereavement will be affected. Traditional models will change or cease to apply. A single parent will be alone in new ways after the death of a child, a divorced or widowed parent whose child dies may face competing demands from grief and surviving children, a young parent and a grandparent may or may not be able to help each other in mourning. The point is not to lay down a limited number of dominant models, but to appreciate the many factors that enter into each individual experience of parental bereavement during adulthood.

Death of a Spouse or Peer

Bereavement and grief in pair relationships   During the period of adulthood in human life, pair relationships can be very important. They may be relationships established and carried over from childhood or adolescence, or they may be newly formed during the adult years. Such relationships may be of many types; those involving marital ties are a dominant but not exclusive model. One may have special bonds with many other adults, such as a sibling, relative, friend, co-worker, or lover (heterosexual, gay, or lesbian). The relationship may be overt or hidden, continuous or intermittent, satisfying or complicated, healthy or abusive. There are perhaps as many variables in adult-to-adult relationships as there are in the individuals involved and in their modes of interaction.

The dimensions of an adult's bereavement occasioned by the death of someone who is also an adult will depend, in the first place, upon the intimacy and significance of the roles that the deceased played in the survivor's

Thoughts on the Death of a Spouse

Agony is socially unacceptable. One is not supposed to weep. Particularly is one not supposed to weep when one is moderately presentable and thirty-two. When one's wife has been dead six months and everyone else has done grieving.

Ah well, they say: he'll get over it. There's always another pretty lady. Time's a great healer, they say. He'll marry again one day, they say.

No doubt they're right.

But oh dear God . . . the emptiness in my house. The devastating, weary, ultimate loneliness. The silence where there used to be laughter, the cold hearth that used to leap with fire for my return, the permanent blank in my bed.

Six months into unremitting ache I felt that my own immediate death would be no great disaster. Half of myself had gone; the fulfilled joyful investment of six years' loving, gone into darkness. What was left simply suffered . . . and looked normal.

Habit kept me checking both ways when I crossed the road; and meanwhile I tended my shop and sold my wines, and smiled and smiled and smiled at the customers.

[Later, at a picnic] . . . I talked, as one does, to a succession of familiar half-known people, seen once a year or less, with whom one took on as one had left off, as if time hadn't existed in between. It was one of those, with best intentions, who said inevitably, "And how's Emma? How's your pretty wife?"

I thought I would never get used to it, that jab like a spike thrust into a jumpy nerve, that positively physical pain. Emma . . . dear God.

"She's dead," I said, shaking my head slightly, breaking it to him gently, absolving him from embarrassment. I'd had to say it like that often: far too often. I knew how to do it now without causing discomfort. Bitter, extraordinary skill of the widowed, taking the distress away from others, hiding one's own.

"I'm so sorry," he said, meaning it intensely for the moment, as they do. "I'd no idea. None at all. Er . . . when?"

"Six months ago," I said.

"Oh." He adjusted his sympathy level suitably. "I'm really very sorry."

I nodded. He sighed. The world went on. Transaction over, until next time. Always a next time. And at least he hadn't asked "How?" and I hadn't had to tell him, hadn't had to think of the pain and the coma and the child who had died with her, unborn.

SOURCE From D. Francis, 1984.

life (Brothers, 1990; Elmer, 1987; Graham, 1988). In spousal relationships, for example, it is typical that two individuals have distinguished themselves from their families of origin to join together in a new relationship that gradually

Grief is expressed in different ways in a multigenerational family.

becomes an important and enduring part of their identity. When one member of such a relationship dies, the other experiences the loss not only of another person but also of a portion of his or her own identity. The beloved individual is no longer alive to receive love, the many different contributions that he or she made to the relationship go unmade, the comforting presence to which one formerly turned for love and solace is no longer available, and plans that the couple had made for the future may now go unrealized.

Death of a spouse or peer changes the world, the other, and the self for a bereaved adult. The death of just one person in this sort of relationship can entail many emotional, social, financial, spiritual, and other losses. It can also precipitate renewed struggles with identity (DiGiulio, 1989; Golan, 1975). Just as the death of a spouse is experienced in different ways by widows and widowers (Campbell & Silverman, 1987; Kohn & Kohn, 1978; Lopata, 1973; Stillion, 1985), loss of a former spouse (Doka, 1986) and other situations in which deaths of adults impact upon adults each has its own peculiar dynamics. Nevertheless, anger—including anger at the deceased for contributing to the death or for abandoning the survivor—and loneliness are common experiences in such bereavement.

Bereavement and grief associated with HIV infection and AIDS in adults

Individuals who are infected with HIV will likely at some point find themselves coping with a life-threatening illness as well as its immediate situational and developmental implications, its acute and chronic challenges, and the social stigma often attached to this diagnosis. The immediate implications of HIV infection and AIDS during adulthood may be of many sorts; they may bear upon intimate relationships, expressions of sexuality, personal and financial security, or one's vocation and health insurance. Grief over losses experienced as one copes with the illness and concerns about the future may be overlaid with social disapprobation and withdrawal of support. Alienation and isolation challenge critical developmental needs in adults for intimacy and generativity at a time when energies may be diminished and concentration diverted.

During the dying process or following the death of an adult with AIDS, his or her peers face grief and bereavement that is complicated by similar psychosocial factors. The disease may have led to disclosure of hitherto unknown lifestyle choices that are difficult for survivors to accept. A person who was emotionally and existentially tied to the deceased (the man's homosexual mate, for example) may be shunned by the family of origin and not permitted to take part in providing care or in funeral ritual (Fuller, Geis, & Rush, 1988; Geis, Fuller, & Rush, 1986). All of this is a classic pattern of rejection, stigmatization, and isolation associated with disenfranchised relationships, losses, and grievers (Doka, 1989a), manifesting itself in new forms generated largely by ignorance and fear associated with HIV infection and AIDS.

Death of a Parent or Grandparent

As adolescents develop into adults, they emancipate themselves in some measure from parental and family bonds. For example, they may move away from parental influences, either geographically or psychosocially. In healthy maturation, they also reestablish new relationships with parents, grandparents, and other family members to replace the relationships that characterized their childhood. In a number of cases, this may not occur. In any case, many adults have special relationships—simple, ambivalent, or complicated though they may be—with their own parents and grandparents throughout their adult lives. These members of an older generation often are sources of advice, support, and assistance to their adult children and grandchildren.

In the United States today, death is increasingly associated with the elderly—a group that experienced more than 1.5 million of the 2.1 million deaths in the United States in 1990 (National Center for Health Statistics, 1993). This means that most adults expect their parents and grandparents to precede them in death. Nevertheless, when such deaths occur, they often are difficult experiences for survivors (Horowitz et al., 1984; Moss & Moss, 1983; Myers, 1986). They involve the loss of a lifelong relationship, full of shared (playful and sorrowful) experiences. The surviving adult may also perceive such a death as the removal of a "buffer" or source of generational "protection" against his or her own personal death (Angel, 1987). The death may present itself as the completion of a long, full life or as a release from suffering. Just as easily, it may involve lost opportunities and a failure to experience certain developmental or situational milestones on the part of the deceased, the adult survivor, or the survivor's children. For example, following the death of a parent or grandparent the adult child will no longer have an opportunity to renew or extend relationships with the deceased person on an adult-to-adult basis. Almost inevitably, the death of a parent will give his or her adult children a "developmental push" (Osterweis, Solomon, & Green, 1984) in which they will feel with additional force their own finitude and the weight of their own responsibility as members of the now-oldest living generation.

Summary

This chapter has explored many aspects of interactions between young and middle-aged adults and death in contemporary American society. The distinctive developmental tasks of younger adulthood (striving to achieve intimacy versus isolation) and middle age (striving to achieve generativity versus stagnation) have a direct bearing on how adults relate to death. These tasks influence encounters with death among young and middle-aged adults (we noted an accelerating increase in death rates mainly brought about by accidents, on the one hand, and diseases of the heart and cancer, on the other hand) and attitudes of adults toward death (concern about the deaths of others in young adults and the appearance of a newly personalized sense of mortality in middle adults). In coping with life-threatening illness and dying, it is especially important for young adults to continue to pursue intimacy, to avoid isolation, to express their sexuality, and to cultivate realistic plans and goals; and for middle-aged adults to carry on with reevaluation of their lives, to maintain continuity of roles, and to put their affairs in order. Adults must cope with bereavement and grief arising most often from the death of a child at various points in that child's development, the death of a spouse or peer, or the death of a parent or grandparent. This chapter has also discussed issues related to HIV infection and AIDS.

QUESTIONS FOR REVIEW AND DISCUSSION

1. What sorts of death-related losses do you think are most typical in adulthood and what do you think such losses usually mean to adults?

2. Do you know an adult who has experienced significant death-related losses? What were those losses like for that person?

SUGGESTED READINGS

Concerning life-threatening illness in adulthood, consult:

Cousins, N. (1979). *Anatomy of an Illness as Perceived by the Patient.*
Frank, A. W. (1991). *At the Will of the Body.*

Bereavement and grief in adulthood are explored in several ways:
1. In terms of the death of one's child:

Bolton, I. (1989). *My Son, My Son: A Guide to Healing After a Suicide in the Family* (11th ed.).

Borg, S., & Lasker, J. (1981). *When Pregnancy Fails: Families Coping with Miscarriage, Stillbirth, and Infant Death.*

Chance, S. (1992). *Stronger than Death.*

Corr, C. A., Fuller, H., Barnickol, C. A., & Corr, D. M. (Eds.). (1991). *Sudden Infant Death Syndrome: Who Can Help and How.*

DeFrain, J., Ernst, L., Jakub, D., & Taylor, J. (1991). *Sudden Infant Death: Enduring the Loss.*

DeFrain, J., Martens, L., Story, J., & Stork, W. (1986). *Stillborn: The Invisible Death.*

Donnelly, K. F. (1982). *Recovering from the Loss of a Child.*

Jimenez, S. L. M. (1982). *The Other Side of Pregnancy: Coping with Miscarriage and Stillbirth.*

Klass, D. (1988). *Parental Grief: Solace and Resolution.*

Knapp, R. J. (1986). *Beyond Endurance: When a Child Dies.*

Leach, C. (1981). *Letter to a Younger Son.*

Miles, M. S. (n.d.). *The Grief of Parents When a Child Dies.*

Osmont, K., & McFarlane, M. (1986). *Parting is Not Goodbye.*

Peppers, L. G., & Knapp, R. J. (1980). *Motherhood and Mourning: Perinatal Death.*

Rando, T. A. (Ed.). (1986). *Parental Loss of a Child.*

Schiff, H. S. (1977). *The Bereaved Parent.*

Simonds, W., & Rothman, B. K. (Eds.). (1992). *Centuries of Solace: Expressions of Maternal Grief in Popular Literature.*

Stinson, R., & Stinson, P. (1983). *The Long Dying of Baby Andrew.*

2. In terms of the death of one's spouse or peer:

Brothers, J. (1990). *Widowed.*

Caine, L. (1975). *Widow.*

Campbell, S., & Silverman, P. (1987). *Widower: What Happens When Men Are Left Alone.*

Elmer, L. (1987). *Why Her, Why Now: A Man's Journey Through Love and Death and Grief.*

Graham, V. (1988). *Life After Harry: My Adventures in Widowhood.*

Kohn, J. B., & Kohn, W. K. (1978). *The Widower.*

Lewis, C. S. (1976). *A Grief Observed.*

Lopata, H. Z. (1973). *Widowhood in an American City.*

Stroebe, W., & Stroebe, M. S. (1987). *Bereavement and Health: The Psychological and Physical Consequences of Partner Loss.*

3. In terms of the death of the adult's parent or grandparent:

Angel, M. D. (1987). *The Orphaned Adult.*

Myers, E. (1986). *When Parents Die: A Guide for Adults.*

CHAPTER 14

The Elderly

This chapter examines interactions with death during that portion of the life cycle inhabited by those who are 65 years of age or older. These "golden-agers" or "senior citizens," according to the American Association of Retired Persons (AARP, 1991), represented some 12.6 percent of the total population in the United States in 1990. Because the elderly are a growing portion of America's population, some have spoken of the "graying" of America. In many societies, these elders would be thought of as the repository of social wisdom, but that does not always seem to be the case in America's youth-oriented society.

With the emergence of a body of gerontological and geriatric knowledge about these individuals, much has been learned about the developmental tasks and other issues that distinguish older adults from other members of American society. In particular, it has been recognized that aging is not identical with pathology. Becoming an older adult is often marked by a variety of biological, psychological, and social changes. But many elderly persons in the United States are living vigorous, productive, and satisfying lives.

Nevertheless, many in American society give evidence of what Butler (1969) called "ageism," which he later (1975, p. 12) defined as "a process of systematic stereotyping of and discrimination against people because they are old." The elderly are unfairly stereotyped and treated when they are casually lumped together, when their lives are devalued, and when appreciation is lacking for what they have in common with all other human beings. Against this, it is desirable to acknowledge the shared humanity, the significant human values, and the great diversity to be found in this portion of the population. If it is true that "human beings are more alike at birth than they will ever be again" (Stillion, 1985, p. 56), then it should also be true that human beings are most unalike in older adulthood, in view of the many years in which each has had to work out his or her long story.

Research on late adulthood has demonstrated that it is not appropriate to speak of "old age" without qualification, since we know that the elderly can legitimately be divided into a number of subgroups, such as the "young-old" and the "old-old" (Neugarten, 1974; compare Erikson, Erikson, & Kivnick, 1986; Havighurst, 1972). This suggests that the elderly are neither a static nor a monolithic segment of the population. As people are more careful in what they say about the elderly and as the elderly come to exert growing influence in society, more can be learned about older adults, about their interactions with death, dying, and bereavement, and about inadequacies and elements of bias in ageist outlooks.

After a brief vignette designed to illustrate some of the characteristic issues that may arise for the elderly in relationship to death in contemporary American society, this chapter will consider the distinctive developmental tasks of the elderly; typical encounters with death in the United States during the later adult years; attitudes toward death during this period; issues related to dying for the elderly; issues related to bereavement and grief for the elderly; and special issues concerning suicide.

Warning

I shall wear purple
With a red hat which doesn't go, and doesn't suit me.
And I shall spend my pension on brandy and summer gloves
And satin sandals, and say we've no money for butter.
I shall sit down on the pavement when I'm tired
And gobble up samples in shops and press alarm bells
And run my stick along the public railings
And make up for the sobriety of my youth.
I shall go out in my slippers in the rain
And pick the flowers in other people's gardens
And learn to spit.
You can wear terrible shirts and grow more fat
And eat three pounds of sausages at a go
Or only bread and a pickle for a week
And hoard pens and pencils and beermats and things in boxes.
But now we must have clothes that keep us dry
And pay our rent and not swear in the street
And set a good example for the children.
We will have friends to dinner and read the papers.
But maybe I ought to practice a little now?
So people who know me are not too shocked and surprised
When suddenly I am old and start to wear purple.

SOURCE From J. Joseph, 1992.

An Elderly Woman

Helen Longworth had really enjoyed living in a retirement center for the elderly for the first five years. Helen was 87 and her husband had died eight years ago. She had tried to go on by herself in their house, but it was just too much for her. It seemed to Helen as if there was always something: a faucet would start to leak, the pilot light on the water heater would blow out, or the yard would need work. Once a tree fell and brought down the power lines. Another time, Helen forgot to shut off the gas and left the stove burning all night. That really scared her. And everything seemed to cost so much more each month.

Just over a year before his father's death, Helen's son had moved to Europe with his family, where he had a good job in the foreign branch of a major American corporation. When he suggested that she think about selling her house, at first Helen had been upset and anxious about the idea of leaving the home that she had shared for so many years with her husband. But gradually she reconciled herself. She would just have to do it.

In fact, after just a month or so Helen had fallen in love with her new living arrangements. She made some new friends among the other residents.

One person would talk to her about the interests that they shared in knitting and crocheting. Another individual seemed to take special interest in Helen and often asked her for advice about family matters. Unfortunately, these two new friends moved away a little while later for different reasons, but Helen still took delight in many of the activities offered to the residents. For a while, she even went on some of the center's social outings. But best of all, there was Helen's next door neighbor, Bessie. They hit it off so well and just talked all day long about the old times.

During her last year and a half in the retirement center, most of Helen's friends from the old neighborhood and from her church had died. Helen felt these losses keenly. She found herself looking at the obituary notices in the newspaper each day. Gradually, a blanket of sadness descended over her, like a fog. Helen had no other children and there was no one really left to visit her, except her younger brother who lived in the next state. Letters from her son and her grandchildren gradually dwindled to a few lines once in a while or a card at holidays and birthday anniversaries.

One March, things got much harder. Early that month, Helen's neighbor, Bessie, developed a persistent infection that settled in her lungs. At first, Bessie was moved to a nearby long-term care facility and then she was taken to a hospital. In the end, the head nurse at the hospital told Helen that Bessie had just had too many problems to survive. Bessie's body was shipped far away for burial alongside her first husband.

Helen's life was then disrupted almost immediately by the death of her brother. After the death of his wife, Helen's brother had visited once or twice to pour out his troubles. Then his own failing health made that impossible. Two weeks after Bessie's death, he took his own life. In his last letter to Helen, which arrived the day after his death, he apologized but said that life no longer held any joy for him. He said that he could not face living alone any longer and that he would not enter an institution.

The Elderly, Developmental Tasks, and Death

In Erikson's (1959) original schematization of the life cycle, the concluding period was named "senescence." This term had been used earlier by Hall (1922) to designate the last half of human life. The word itself identifies the process of "growing old," and thus by transference designates the old or the elderly themselves. Unfortunately, *senescence* is etymologically linked to the terms *senile* and *senility,* which now often designate not only the condition of being old but also the presence of weaknesses or infirmities associated with old age. For those who wish to distinguish between normal developmental stages and pathology, this linkage is undesirable. Perhaps to avoid such implications, at a later point Erikson (1963) spoke about this period in life as the era of "maturity."

However the final stage in the human life cycle is named, for Erikson its tasks involve the achievement of ego integrity versus despair or disgust. That is, the principal developmental work of old age involves the attainment of an inner sense of wholeness. Thus Maslow (1968) spoke of "self-actualization" and Birren (1964) of "reconciliation." The balance and harmony in this wholeness are achieved by successfully resolving earlier developmental tasks and coming to terms with one's past. That emerges from a process of introspection, self-reflection, and reminiscence, which Butler (1963) called "life review" (compare Woodward, 1986).

In this process of heightened interiority, past experiences are spontaneously brought to consciousness, reviewed and assessed, and perhaps reinterpreted or reintegrated. The aim is to resolve old conflicts and to achieve a new sense of meaning, both as an accounting to oneself of one's past life and as a preparation for death. If this process is carried out successfully, it eventuates in integrity and wisdom (Erikson & Erikson, 1981). If the process is unsuccessful, it results in a sense of despair because one is not satisfied with what one has done with one's life and does not feel that sufficient time or energy remains to alter directions and compensate for the ways in which one has lived.

Within that general framework, it has been customary in the United States to think of the elderly as those individuals who are 65 years of age or older. The social marker defining the beginning of this period used to be retirement, once mandatory for many persons at age 65. However, for most individuals the requirement to retire at some stipulated age no longer exists. Others increasingly opt to take early retirement before the age of 65. Furthermore, in 1990 persons reaching age 65 had an average life expectancy of an additional 17.2 years (18.6 years for females; 14.8 years for males) (AARP, 1991). However, these are average figures, with the very oldest segment of the population growing the most rapidly.

In short, with healthier lifestyles, better health care, and overall improvements in wellness, many—at least in the age group between 55 and 75—possess relatively good health, education, purchasing power, and free time, and are politically active (Neugarten, 1974). These observations also suggest the need to draw an important distinction within the elderly between the "young-old" (those who are between 55 and 75 years of age) and the "old-old" (those who are age 75 and over). If so, there may be different social cohorts among the elderly and distinctive developmental tasks in this evolving population.

Encounters with Death

Overall death rates rise rapidly in old age: from a rate of 2,159.1 per 100,000 in 1990 for those 65–69 years of age; through 4,933.9 per 100,000 for those 75–79 years of age; to 15,327.4 per 100,000 for those 85 years of age and older (National Center for Health Statistics, 1993). For the elderly in the United States as a whole, the overall death rate is 4,963.2 per 100,000. All of these figures are significantly in excess of the overall mortality rate in the United States, which is 863.8 per 100,000.

Deaths among the elderly in 1990 in the United States numbered approximately 1.5 million. This included 477,949 deaths in the 65- to 74-year-old age group, 601,439 deaths in the 75- to 84-year-old age group, and 463,105 deaths among those 85 years old and over (National Center for Health Statistics, 1993). These deaths occurred in a population of some 25 million elderly persons and represented some 72 percent of all deaths in 1990 in the United States.

Leading causes of death among the elderly are diseases of the heart (1,914.0 deaths per 100,000, representing a total of 594,858 deaths in 1990); malignant neoplasms or cancer (1,111.3 deaths per 100,000, representing a total of 345,387 deaths); and cerebrovascular diseases (403.5 deaths per 100,000, representing a total of 125,409 deaths) (National Center for Health Statistics, 1993). In order, other significant causes of death and death rates among the elderly are chronic obstructive pulmonary diseases and allied conditions (234.1); pneumonia and influenza (226.8); diabetes mellitus (114.3); accidents (84.3); nephritis (55.7); atherosclerosis, or blocking of the blood vessels of the heart (55.2); and septicemia (49.4). Except for pneumonia, influenza, accidents, and septicemia, all of these are degenerative diseases, associated with long-term cumulative influences of lifestyle and environment.

The rate of accidental death is greatly increased in the elderly by contrast with middle-aged adults. However, the relative importance of accidents as a cause of death among the elderly is overshadowed by several other conditions. Also, the highest rate of suicide (24.9) in the whole of American society is found among the elderly persons aged 75–84. Finally, homicide rates have declined to fewer than 5 per 100,000 among the elderly, a lower rate than at any other time in the life span except ages 1–14.

Only 5 percent of those who are 65 years of age or older are residents of nursing homes and other long-term care facilities (AARP, 1991). Nevertheless, the vast majority of individuals who enter such facilities die either there or after transfer to some acute-care facility (Butler & Lewis, 1982). In short, many older adults are living longer in the United States today. Of these, many are living much healthier lives; others are living with one or more major health problems. Often, those who die do so in ways that require institutional care, frequently on a long-term basis.

Attitudes Toward Death

There is general agreement in the research literature that the elderly are significantly less fearful of death than younger persons (for example, Bengston, Cuellar, & Ragan, 1977; Kalish & Johnson, 1972). Of course, "fear of death" is not an uncomplicated notion, and older adults may differ among themselves in this regard. Also, it appears that variables that tend to reduce or threaten quality of life in the elderly, such as poor physical and mental health, being widowed, or being institutionalized, are likely to be inversely associated with

*An elderly
woman seeks
comfort in her
faith.*

fear of death (Marshall, 1975; Swenson, 1961; Templer, 1971). Nevertheless, many studies (such as Kastenbaum, 1967; Matse, 1975; Saul & Saul, 1973) have shown that elderly persons make frequent references to and talk about death, even within fairly restrictive institutional environments that may not encourage such discussions.

Kalish (1985a) proposed three explanations for the relatively low level of fear of death among older adults: (1) older persons may accept death more easily than others because they have been able to live a long, full life; (2) older persons may have come to accept their own deaths through a socialization process through which they repeatedly experience the deaths of others; and (3) older persons may have come to view their lives as having less value than the lives of younger persons and thus may not object so strenuously to that which is involved in giving up their lives. For any of these reasons, death may seem to an elderly person to represent less of a threat than, for example, debility, isolation, or dependence.

*E*lders Coping with Life-Threatening Illness and Dying

Four specific needs of older adults who are coping with life-threatening illness or dying have been identified by Cook and Oltjenbruns (1989, p. 384): "(1) maintaining a sense of self, (2) participating in decisions regarding their lives, (3) being reassured that their lives still have value, and (4) receiving appropriate and adequate health care services."

Maintaining a Sense of Self

Preserving the identity that one established in adolescence or in subsequent developmental work is an important task for all human beings, but this is particularly true for individuals involved in transitions and reassessments such as those that characterize maturational work in older adulthood. One's sense of integrity is founded upon one's self-concept and self-esteem. As already noted, in the elderly this is typically pursued through the processes of life review—reflection, reminiscence, and reevaluation.

For elderly persons who are coping with life-threatening illness or dying, these processes need not be eliminated, although they may be curtailed by distress, lack of energy or ability to concentrate, and absence of social support. Against these inhibiting factors, family and professional caregivers can encourage life review activities in a number of ways. For example, they can directly participate by listening and serving as sounding boards or by providing stimuli such as photographs and prized mementos. Enabling ill or dying elders to remain at home or to retain and express their individuality within an institution is another way of affirming the person's uniqueness and value. Hospice programs often encourage ill or dying elders to identify achievable goals in craft work or other ways of making tangible gifts to give to others. Passing on such gifts or valued personal items can be a cherished activity in itself and a way of leaving behind an enduring legacy. Accepting such gifts with warmth and appreciation is not an expression of a wish for the death of an elder, but rather an act of affection.

Participating in Decisions Regarding Their Lives

In Western society, autonomy or the ability to be in charge of one's own life is a prized value for many individuals. This may be particularly true for elderly persons, who may already have experienced a number of losses and who are often concerned with issues related to dependence. Continuing to take part in decisions regarding their own lives, insofar as that is possible, is often seen as desirable by older adults. They may have a very broad and active role in such decision making, or that role might be quite constrained and largely symbolic. Nevertheless, it will usually be regarded as important and should be sustained as much as possible.

Fostering autonomy may require delicate negotiations between the individual elder, his or her family members, and professional care providers. For example, many older adults in the United States desire to and, in fact, do remain in their own homes. For such individuals, the decision to enter a long-term care facility may become a matter of contention and has been shown in some cases to lead to a kind of learned helplessness (Solomon, 1982).

Lately, American society has gradually come to realize—in theory, at least—the need for autonomy and the values that it represents. Thus, according to the Patient Information Act, which went into effect in 1991, individuals who enter a health care facility must be informed of their rights to fill out a living will, grant someone their durable power of attorney in health care matters, or otherwise have their wishes concerning treatment recorded and respected. A "patient's bill of rights" and similar documents are intended to respect the autonomy of each individual and to permit persons to take responsibility for at least part of their care. This contributes to positive mental health (Seligman, 1975) and general satisfaction with life (Rodin & Langer, 1977). In other words, it works against premature psychosocial and even physical decline—and death—in elders who have felt beset by loss of control and other external or internal pressures that undermine autonomy and quality of life and that foster hopelessness, helplessness, and "giving up" (Maizler, Solomon, & Almquist, 1983; Schulz, 1976; Verwoerdt, 1976).

Being Reassured That Their Lives Still Have Value

As already noted, in a youth-oriented society ageism fosters discrimination against and devaluation of the lives of older adults. When combined with losses that such elders may have experienced, such as those involved in retirement or in bodily functioning, this may encourage older persons to depreciate their own value and sense of worth. Life-threatening illness or dying may compound this process of devaluation by self and others. Reduced contacts with significant others may lead to isolation and justified or unjustified concerns about social death even when physical death is not imminent. At least for some elders, an ongoing dimension of quality of life involves the possibility or impossibility of ongoing expression of sexuality and sexual needs (Verwoerdt, Pfeiffer, & Wang, 1969; Weinberg, 1969)—which may often involve no more than simple touching or hugging, as described in Chapter 13.

The hospice philosophy, with its emphasis upon life and maximizing present quality in living, points the way to an antidote to this sort of devaluation of the lives of elderly persons. Conveying to older adults, even those who are coping with life-threatening illness and dying, that their lives are still valued and appreciated, that they are important to others, and that they can still find satisfaction in living can enhance their sense of self-worth. Showing family members how to be involved in constructive ways in the life and care of an ill or dying elder can improve present quality in living for all concerned and diminish feelings of guilt or frustration (for example, York & Calsyn, 1977).

Receiving Appropriate and Adequate Health Care Services

Studies conducted some time ago in both the United States (Sudnow, 1967) and Great Britain (Simpson, 1976) demonstrated that older adults who were brought to hospital emergency rooms in critical condition were likely to receive care that was not as thorough or vigorous as that provided to younger persons. This raises questions of equity, particularly for those who are critically ill, dying, and vulnerable. Constructive lessons drawn from the life-affirming orientation of hospice programs, as well as positive developments in geriatric medicine and in gerontological specializations in other fields such as nursing and social work, can do much to change this. Older adults who are coping with life-threatening illness or dying have helped to create and support societal health care and welfare systems. Accordingly, such systems should address their health care needs. Through political action and organizations such as the American Association of Retired Persons, elders are mobilizing to try to ensure that these needs are addressed.

Elders Coping with Bereavement and Grief

There are many occasions for bereavement in older adulthood: the deaths of spouses and peers; the deaths of "old-old" parents who may have lived to such advanced old age that their children have now reached "young-old" status; the deaths of adult children; and the deaths of grandchildren or great-grandchildren. In addition, there is the special poignance of the death of a companion animal when its owner is an older adult, and the impact of physical disability or psychosocial impoverishment. In fact, as Kastenbaum (1969) has noted, the elderly are likely to experience losses in greater number, variety, and rapidity than any other age group. Consequently, the elderly are often exposed to "bereavement overload," a situation in which they do not have the time or other resources needed to grieve and mourn one significant loss effectively before another occurs. For such older persons, grief is a constant companion. Some of its many manifestations are explored in the following pages.

Illness, Disability, and Loss

Older adults may be grieving as a result of the many "little deaths" that they have experienced throughout life or in later adulthood. Among these are losses associated with illness of various sorts. Not every elderly person is experiencing such losses, but many are living with one or more illness-related burdens. For example, high blood pressure and constriction or obstruction in the arteries are common in many elderly persons, as are certain forms of cancer (lung and prostate cancer in males; lung and breast cancer in females). Even when these conditions are not fatal, they may restrict quality of life. Chronic health problems, such as those involved in rheumatism or arthritis, have similar effects.

Some long-term degenerative diseases, such as Alzheimer's and Parkinson's diseases or amyotrophic lateral sclerosis (ALS, often called "Lou Gehrig's disease" in the United States), have special import for losses in the elderly. These diseases may manifest themselves in ways that are physical (for example, through pain or loss of muscle control), psychological (for instance, through confusion), social (for example, through institutionalization or loss of mobility and capacity for social intercourse), and/or spiritual (as in questions about the meaning of one's life and the goodness of a universe in which these losses occur). They affect both the individual person—for example, the elder with Alzheimer's disease who may be aware of his or her declining mental function—and those who love and must care for a person who may become unable to perform even the most basic activities of daily living (Kapust, 1982; Mace & Rabins, 1991). Often, they generate the very special problems of complicated or "ambiguous" loss (Boss, 1988) involved in what Toynbee (1968a, p. 266) has termed "the premature death of the spirit in a human body that still remains physically alive." These issues stand alongside very difficult problems of decision making, appropriate modes of care, and costs.

Less dramatic, but still significant in terms of well-being, are the accumulated losses of disability that elders often experience in effective functioning. These can include sensory and cognitive impairments, oral and dental problems, loss of energy, reduced muscle strength, diminished sense of balance, and problems related to osteoporosis or arthritis. Specific losses of this sort and their combined effect upon an individual elder can reduce quality in living and generate regret on the part of the individual, his or her family members, and his or her care providers for that which has been lost.

The Death of a Spouse or Other Significant Peer

Surviving the death of a spouse, partner, or other significant peer is a common experience in older adulthood. The individual who has died may be a marriage partner, an individual of the same or opposite sex with whom one has lived for some time and formed a stable relationship, or a peer who possesses some other sort of special significance. Especially in spousal relationships, the elderly person who survives is most often a female. This is not surprising in a society in which women outlive men on the average and in which women most often marry men who are their own age or older.

When the relationship with the partner is such that their lives are closely interwoven, "the loss of one partner may cut across the very meaning of the other's existence" (Raphael, 1983, p. 177). Not all relationships with a partner are ideal or uncomplicated, and the bereavement experience may be influenced by several variables, including age, mode of death, and the availability of social support (Ball, 1977; Sanders, 1980). Nevertheless, every survivor experiences multiple losses in the death of such a person, and it appears that those who have experienced the death of a spouse are at higher risk during the following year for increased morbidity and mortality (from illness or suicide, for example) (Glick, Weiss, & Parkes, 1974). Sustaining roles and relationships appears to be crucial to these individuals. For elders, the most important of these roles and relationships may include companionship, someone with whom one can talk or argue, someone with whom to share burdens, pleasures, and sexual gratification, and someone to offer presence and care in the future as one's own needs increase (Lund, 1989).

The death of a spouse in late adulthood often generates experiences of separation and deprivation—grief (including yearning, pain, and anger), isolation, and loneliness (Clayton, 1979). Widowers are more likely than widows to remarry (Carey, 1979). This reflects many factors, including the relative availability of potential spouses for the elderly male, the opposite situation for the elderly female, and social encouragement for women to view the marital role as an important part of their identity. However, emotional ties to the deceased are likely to persist and memories may be cherished by both sexes (Moss & Moss, 1984). Thus, it may not so much be the experience of bereavement as its expression that is influenced by sex roles (Raphael, 1983).

Both in place of or as a supplement to other forms of social support, self-help groups (Lieberman & Borman, 1979; Lund, Dimond, & Juretich, 1985; Yalom & Vinogradov, 1988) and widow-to-widow programs (Silverman, 1969, 1986) have been found to be very helpful for bereaved elders. Such groups and programs typically serve the full range of bereaved persons who have experienced certain kinds of losses (not just those evaluated as "high risk") and do so on a foundation of shared experience. Through these groups and programs, individuals who have had similar bereavement experiences can share feelings and problems and can encourage each other to regain control in living by evaluating options and alternatives represented in the lives of the others. Through these resources, the bereaved can also obtain helpful information about loss, grief, and living.

The Death of an Adult Child

To a parent, one's offspring always remains one's child in some important senses despite his or her age. In the United States, as average life expectancy increases, it becomes increasingly likely that middle-aged and elderly parents may experience the deaths of their adult children. For example, when young adults in their 20s and 30s die in accidents or from communicable diseases, and when individuals in their 40s, 50s, and 60s die of degenerative diseases, many of these people may leave behind a surviving parent (Rando, 1986b). In fact, one study (Moss, Lesher, & Moss, 1986) reported that as many as 10 percent of elderly persons with children had experienced the death of a child when the parent was 60 years of age or older.

For such a parent, the grief felt at a death-related loss may be combined with special developmental complications (Brubaker, 1985; Moss, Lesher, & Moss, 1986). For example, surviving parents may feel that the death of an adult child is an untimely violation of the "natural" order of things in which the older generation is expected to die before the younger. Such parents may experience "survivor guilt" and may wish to have died in place of their child. In addition, there may be special hardships in the loss if the adult child had assumed certain responsibilities as helper or care provider for the parent. How will these needs be satisfied after the death? Does the parent now face an increased likelihood of institutionalization or of diminished social contacts? How will family legacies be carried forward? The parent may also join to his or her own sense of loss added regret and grief for the pain that the spouse or children of the adult child are experiencing. And, in some cases, the elderly survivor may be obliged to take over the care of surviving grandchildren.

The Death of a Grandchild or Great-Grandchild

If it is more likely that children and adolescents will have living grandparents and great-grandparents because of increased life expectancy among older adults, then it is also more likely that these older adults may experience the death of one of their grandchildren or great-grandchildren. This is not a well-studied area of bereavement, even though it is recognized that cross-generational relationships between grandchildren and grandparents can involve special bonds of intimacy (Wilcoxon, 1986).

Grandparents have been described as "forgotten grievers" (Gyulay, 1975), both connected to and distanced from events involving the fatal illness, death, or bereavement of a grandchild. The grief of such grandparents responds to their own losses, to the losses experienced by their son or daughter, and to the losses experienced by the grandchild. Such grief may contain elements of hurt over such an "out of sequence" death, anger at parents who perhaps did not seem to take adequate care of the grandchild, guilt at their own presumed failure to prevent the loss or death, and resentment at God for letting such tragic events occur (Hamilton, 1978). All of this may be compli-

Pets, too, may be memorialized.

cated in situations in which there is unwillingness to acknowledge certain causes of death (such as suicide) or discuss openly the circumstances of the death. Finally, there may be conflicts between grandparents and surviving parents—for example, when one blames the other for a perceived failure to prevent the death.

Loss of a Pet

Loss of a pet is often described as a typical experience of childhood. It is that, but it can also be of similar importance in the lives of older adults. In addition to serving as sources of unconditional love, companion animals are objects of care and affection in the lives of many elderly persons. Companion animals protect and aid the handicapped and have in recent years become familiar mascots or welcome visitors in many nursing homes, long-term care facilities, and other sorts of institutions. In all of these roles, pets can relieve loneliness, contribute to a sense of purpose, and enhance self-esteem (Rynearson, 1978).

The death of a pet confirms that it is the relationship that is most important, not the intrinsic value of its animal object (Kay, 1984; Nieburg & Fischer, 1982). Although such a loss is often dismissed by insensitive remarks, it can represent a major bereavement for an elderly person who may otherwise have only limited social contacts (Quackenbush, 1985; Shirley & Mercier, 1983). Similar losses and grief may occur when an older adult is no longer able to care for a pet, cannot pay for expensive veterinary services that it would need, must give up the pet in relocating to new living quarters or to an institution, or must have a sick, older animal euthanized, or "put to sleep" (Kay et al., 1988). Evidence of significant mourning following the death of a pet is clear in the growth of pet cemeteries in the United States (Spiegelman & Kastenbaum, 1990). Older adults may also be concerned about what will happen to a prized pet if they should die.

Suicide Among the Elderly

The highest rates of suicide in the United States are found among the elderly, reaching 24.9 per 100,000 in the 75- to 84-year-old age group and 22.2 in the group that is 85 years old and older (National Center for Health Statistics, 1993). Among other elderly persons, white males are most likely to end their own lives in this way. In general, older adults are far more deliberate in suicidal behavior than their younger counterparts: they are unlikely to ask for help that might redirect the course of their behavior and they are unlikely to fail to complete the suicidal act once they have undertaken the attempt (Butler & Lewis, 1982; Farberow & Moriwaki, 1975; McIntosh, 1985a). Clearly, any indicators of suicidal tendencies on the part of elderly persons should be taken seriously and evaluated carefully.

The single most significant factor associated with suicidal behavior in the elderly is depression. When the life review process results in a sense of despair about one's life, when one experiences physical or mental debility, or when the individual experiences the death of a spouse or other significant person (especially one upon whom the individual had been dependent for care and support), then a willingness may arise to consider suicide as an alternative to continued living under what now appear to be unsatisfactory conditions. Factors of this sort—such as the impact of retirement upon males whose identity had hitherto been greatly dependent upon their vocational roles, previous dependency upon a now-deceased female caretaker, or social isolation—appear to account for much higher rates (rising with age) of male over female suicides among the elderly (Miller, 1979).

In American society, there are a number of obstacles to interventions designed to minimize the likelihood of suicidal behavior among the elderly. For example, claims that suicide is a permanent solution to a temporary problem apply more aptly to impulsive decisions by adolescents than to decisions arising from long deliberation in the elderly. Similarly, advice to concentrate upon a promising future or to consider interpersonal obligations to others seems better suited to younger persons than to many elders with less rosy expectations and diminished social relationships. Again, the argument that suicide terminates the life cycle prematurely and cuts short a full life is less obviously relevant to a person in advanced old age. In addition, one could argue that efforts intended to thwart suicidal behavior in the elderly are inappropriate assaults upon the autonomy of older adults (Moody, 1984).

In short, suicidal behavior among the elderly appears to arise from the broad psychosocial situation of older adults in American society, such as those noted earlier involving ageism, devaluation, and unresponsiveness to needs. If so, then significant changes in social attitudes would be required to alter suicidal behavior in the elderly.

Summary

This chapter has explored many aspects of interactions between elderly persons and death in contemporary American society. The distinctive developmental tasks of older adulthood (striving to achieve ego integrity versus despair) have a direct bearing on how elders relate to death. These tasks influence encounters with death among the elderly (we noted high death rates mainly brought about by long-term degenerative diseases) and attitudes of older adults toward death (in general, manifesting less fear and anxiety than are displayed by younger persons). It is especially important for elders coping with life-threatening illness and dying to maintain a sense of self, participate in decisions regarding their lives, be reassured that their lives still have value, and receive appropriate and adequate health care services. The need to cope with bereavement and grief is most likely to arise from illness, disability, and loss; the death of a spouse or other significant peer; the death of an adult child; the death of a grandchild or great-grandchild, or the loss of a pet. High rates of suicide among the elderly are strongly associated with depression.

QUESTIONS FOR REVIEW AND DISCUSSION

1. What sorts of death-related losses do you think are most typical among elderly persons and what do you think such losses usually mean to elders?

2. Do you know an elderly person who has experienced significant death-related losses? What were those losses like for that person?

SUGGESTED READINGS

On aging and the elderly, consult:

Butler, R. N. (1975). *Why Survive? Being Old in America.*
Cole, T. R., & Gadow, S. A. (Eds.). (1986). *What Does It Mean to Grow Old? Reflections from the Humanities.*
Erikson, E. H., Erikson, J. M., & Kivnick, H. (1986). *Vital Involvement in Old Age.*
Nouwen, H. (1974). *Aging: The Fulfillment of Life.*
Van Tassel, D. (Ed.). (1979). *Aging, Death, and the Completion of Being.*

On death and the elderly, consult:

Callahan, D. (1987). *Setting Limits: Medical Goals in an Aging Society.*
Lund, D. A. (1989). *Older Bereaved Spouses: Research with Practical Applications.*
Miller, M. (1979). *Suicide After Sixty: The Final Alternative.*
Osgood, N. J. (1985). *Suicide in the Elderly: A Practitioner's Guide to Diagnosis and Mental Health Intervention.*

PART V

LEGAL, CONCEPTUAL, AND MORAL ISSUES

The four chapters that follow address legal, conceptual, moral, and religious or philosophical issues directly related to dying, death, and bereavement. This discussion begins with legal issues in Chapter 15 because the law is the most explicit framework of rules and procedures that a society establishes within its death system. Any legal system, at least in part, grows out of a society's historical encounters with death-related issues and expresses the attitudes or postures that the society wishes to adopt regarding those issues. With its powers of regulation, enforcement, and sanction, the law does or can address itself to many important death-related issues, such as definition of death, prior directives for treatment of the dying, certification of death, investigation of sudden or suspicious deaths, and disposition of both the body and property of the individual who has died.

However, many aspects of death-related encounters and attitudes are not directly addressed by the law. These include a number of individual behaviors (for example, the decision whether to visit a dying relative), ethnic and religious practices (dictating, for instance, what is appropriate in matters of ritual or public ceremony following a death), and social custom (governing matters such as how one talks to children about death or offers support to the bereaved). Also, particularly in connection with advances in medical technology, new questions arise from time to time that may not have been anticipated by the existing legal system. Such issues may require adjustments to the legal system or may remain essentially outside its scope.

Two important social issues that are essentially of this latter sort are euthanasia and suicide, the subjects of Chapters 16 and 17. In today's society, *euthanasia* (which means literally "good" [*eu*] + "death" [*thanatos*], from the Greek) seems to designate situations in which one withholds, withdraws, or undertakes interventions that might have a bearing upon ending or failing to sustain the life of another. Similarly, *suicide* (which means literally "self" [*sui*] + "killing" [*cide*], from the Latin) identifies situations in which one deliberately ends one's own life. Neither of these is addressed as such in the American legal system, although in some jurisdictions there are prohibitions and sanctions against assisting suicide. Generally, however, when situations involving euthanasia or suicide are put before the law, they are addressed in terms of other categories, such as homicide.

Finally, Chapter 18 considers what are simultaneously the broadest and the most personal frameworks within which individuals and societies approach and respond to death-related experiences. These are the frameworks of religion and philosophy, which interpret death in terms of ultimate values. In another language, these frameworks represent the deepest commitments of the human spirit, which guide its efforts to articulate the meaning and place of death in human life.

Issues related to the law, to euthanasia, to suicide, and to questions of ultimate meaning are brought together here in Part V because they pose challenges on both conceptual and moral levels. In the other parts of this book, it is less difficult to distinguish conceptual and moral dimensions of the topics raised. For example, in some cases one understands what a topic (such as grief) means, but may be unsure how one should respond morally. In other cases, moral obligations may be grasped quite clearly (for example, obligations to help children cope with life), but one may be unsure what that requires in practice. The issues addressed in the following four chapters challenge us simply to understand or make sense out of them and to develop a personal and societal position that draws upon basic values and enables individuals and groups to decide whether and/or how to act.

CHAPTER 15

Legal Issues

Every society develops a more or less formal system on behalf of its own interests as a community as well as to promote the welfare of its individual members. Such a system may consist of written or unwritten rules and procedures. These rules and procedures reflect values that are upheld within a particular society as well as ways in which it organizes itself to implement those values. In contemporary America, a formal set of rules and procedures governing social conduct is embodied in our legal system.

Any system of societal rules and procedures is likely to function most effectively when social values are well established and when it is called upon to respond to familiar events. It may be less responsive when social values are in disagreement, when they are in flux, or when progress (for example, in the form of new medical procedures or technology) poses new problems that are not easily evaluated by existing legal frameworks. In contemporary American society, challenges to the legal system have arisen in recent years from all three of these circumstances: there is disagreement over some social values as they apply to our heterogeneous population, other social values appear to be in transition, and new challenges have arisen from new circumstances and technology.

This chapter discusses ways in which American society has organized itself through its legal system to deal with issues relating to death, dying, and bereavement. The discussion begins with a short case history and some brief comments on various aspects of the American legal system. Thereafter, three important clusters of legal issues are examined: (1) those that are principally concerned with matters of importance prior to death, such as advance directives for treatment of the dying; (2) those that arise at death itself, such as definition and determination of death; and (3) those that may have been initiated prior to death but whose real force is exerted in the aftermath of death, such as disposition of one's body and estate. This division of topics is similar, but not identical, to Bernstein's (1980) list of three basic ways in which lawyers can provide expert legal advice to terminally ill persons: in long-range planning, immediately prior to death, and when death arrives.

Judith Ann Debro

On October 16, 1975, Judith Ann Debro was involved in a head-on automobile collision in Jefferson County, Missouri, just outside the St. Louis metropolitan area ("Woman in Machine," 1975; "Fenton Man Asks for Court Order," 1975). At the time of the accident, Mrs. Debro was 33 years old. She and her husband, Gary, had been married for three months. From the site of the accident, Mrs. Debro was taken to Saint Anthony's Medical Center in southern St. Louis County, where emergency efforts were undertaken to stabilize and evaluate her condition.

Within a day or two of her accident, Mrs. Debro's physician (a neurosurgeon) reported to her husband that in his judgment she was dead. That is, she was unable to sustain essential bodily functions spontaneously. She met the criteria for irreversible coma that had been developed by an ad hoc committee at the Harvard Medical School and that had been published in the *Journal of the American Medical Association* in August of 1968 (Ad hoc Committee, 1968). By 1975, those criteria had come to have significant influence within the medical community, but they did not yet have statutory legal force in the state of Missouri. In fact, in Missouri in 1975, not much clear legal guidance existed for a case of this kind.

For example, in Mrs. Debro's case, common law might have suggested a definition of death as something like a total stoppage of the circulation of the blood and cessation of respiration, pulsation, and so on. Since she was attached to life-support machinery, one might have argued that circulation and respiration were continuing. Of course, the key question was whether these were assisted functions of a living body (such as respiration) or merely machine-induced mimicry (such as ventilation) in a dead body.

Without clear legal guidance, Mrs. Debro's physician offered to resolve the situation by removing her life-support machinery. However, he said that he would do so only on the condition that her husband and other members of her family agreed with this decision. Her husband agreed; other family members did not. In light of this disagreement, Mrs. Debro's husband petitioned the courts for authority to remove her life-support machinery. The first state court to respond to this petition refused to act, on the grounds that no legal basis was available for making a decision. Additional legal proceedings were in process when, on November 9, 1975, Mrs. Debro's body ceased to cooperate with the life-support machinery to which it was still connected.

One might want to say that Mrs. Debro "died" on November 9, 1975. But that is precisely the point in question. When did she die?

In view of the circumstances of this case, the medical examiner in St. Louis County conducted a postmortem examination. As a result, it was possible to determine the moment of her death with some precision. This is because brain cells do not regenerate when they have been damaged or destroyed. Thus, one can determine from the condition of the brain on autopsy when it had begun to deteriorate and how long it had been undergoing that process. The medical examiner indicated that, in his opinion, Judith Ann Debro had died on October 18, 1975. As her husband said on November 9th, "she had been dead a long time" ("Judith Ann Debro Pronounced Dead," 1975, p. 5A).

In this case, sophisticated and expensive medical interventions had been applied for roughly three weeks to (what many would perceive to be) a corpse.

American Society and Its Laws

In the United States, our federal system assigns certain responsibilities (such as foreign relations and defense) to the national government and reserves most other responsibilities to the authority or jurisdiction of the individual states and their subordinate entities. For most issues that have to do with death, dying, and bereavement, state law governs what is to be done and how it is to be done. Given the diversity that is cherished by our states, different laws and procedures apply in different states. Some states may have enacted no legislation on a particular subject. That is one reason why this chapter can only address legal issues and structures in a general way and why individuals should seek competent legal advice that is appropriate to their particular circumstances.

The establishment of legislation is often a slow and complicated process subject to political pressures, competing interests, and social circumstances. When values in a society are changing or when it has not been possible to achieve a consensus on social values, the process of embodying and codifying those values in legislation may not go forward very easily. Difficult cases may frustrate a society in its process of determining how to implement its values. This is particularly true in cases that involve fast-moving advances in medical technology and procedures.

When there is no specific legislation addressing a particular subject, judges are pressed to make decisions in the circumstances of actual cases. One way in which they do so is by searching out relevant precedents set by prior court decisions. Such prior decisions and precedents constitute what is called *case law*.

In matters that have not been addressed either by a legislature or by the courts in their prior determinations, the legal system turns to *common law*. Originally, this was a set of shared values and views drawn from English and early American legal and social history. In practice, it is typically represented in a more formal way by the definitions contained in standard legal dictionaries. In its many editions, *Black's Law Dictionary* (Black, 1979) is a well-known example of this sort of organized expression of common law.

It is important to be clear about which sort(s) of legal rules and procedures apply to any given issue. The principles set forth here constitute the broad, general legal framework within which a larger spectrum of moral, social, and human issues are addressed in American society. This legal framework is an important part of the contemporary American death system, but only one such component. There are issues related to death that the legal system does not address, such as cemetery regulations and cultural or religious rituals. Also, there are issues that the legal system has not found itself able to address very effectively, such as euthanasia and suicide (see Chapters 16 and 17), which remain wholly or partially outside its framework.

Before Death

The phrase ''prior directives'' or ''advance directives'' is applicable to a wide range of instructions that one might make orally or set down in writing concerning actions that one would want or not want to be taken if one were somehow incapacitated and unable to participate in decision making. Of course, the degree to which any advance directives are made depends upon an individual's willingness to address ahead of time the implications of death for his or her life and for the lives of his or her family members and friends. Many people are reluctant to consider issues of this sort, perhaps because they involve contemplating the implications of one's own mortality. Nevertheless, since the end of 1991, federal legislation in the form of the Patient Information Act has required that individuals being admitted to a health care institution must be informed of their right to execute an advance directive and also about the options available to implement that right (Cate & Gill, 1991).

Some advance directives are intended to come into force upon the fact of one's death—for example, directives concerning organ donations, the disposition of one's body, or the distribution of one's estate. Directives of that sort will be discussed in subsequent sections of this chapter. First, however, advance directives that bear upon decisions about treatment before death will be considered. Advance directives of this sort are most prominent in the form of living wills or durable powers of attorney in health care matters.

Living Wills

Living wills were developed in the early 1970s as a means whereby persons who were competent decision makers could express their wishes to professional care providers, family members, and friends about interventions that they might or might not wish to permit in the event of a terminal illness. In particular, living wills are intended to convey a set of prior instructions in situations in which a terminal illness has rendered an individual unable to make or express such decisions.

When they were originally formulated, living wills had no legal standing. As such, they could take any form. That is, the term *living will* simply designated any sort of document through which a variety of individual wishes could be expressed about treatment prior to death. The common threads of living wills were (1) a concern about the possibility or likelihood of finding oneself in a situation in which the mode of dying would leave one unable to take part in the making of important decisions; and (2) a concern about the context of dying in which one might be in an unfamiliar or alien environment, among acquaintances or even strangers who might have their own individual or professional views of what should or should not be done, and who might not understand, appreciate, or agree with the wishes of the person who wrote the living will.

In response to concerns of this sort, early living wills usually combined a recommendation made by those who composed and signed them; a request that the recommendation be given serious consideration by those who might be providing care to the signers; and an effort to share responsibility for certain decisions made in specified situations. In terms of this last point, living wills could be understood as an effort on the part of those who composed them to protect health care providers from accusations of malpractice, as well as from civil liability or criminal prosecution. That is, in the early 1970s living

The family of Nancy Cruzan meets with reporters during their legal fight to withdraw her artificial feeding.

wills were a formalized way of offering in advance the kind of consent that the physician in the Debro case could only seek after the fact of Mrs. Debro's accident.

Some people think it is unfortunate that the modern American death system has created a situation in which these concerns have become—or at least have seemed to become—so pressing for so many people. Others argue that it is desirable for individuals to share with other relevant persons their own views about interventions that intimately affect their lives and deaths. However one interprets their context, living wills originally represented and still represent a desire to think ahead about issues of life and death, to formulate one's views concerning important decisions, and to communicate them to others (Alexander, 1988).

In the absence of legal standing or requirements, individuals and organizations were free to formulate living wills in any manner that they wished. One well-known early effort to standardize the form and language of living wills was undertaken by an organization whose current name is Choice in Dying (formerly known as the Euthanasia Educational Council, then as the Concern for Dying/Society for the Right to Die; currently at 200 Varick Street, New York, NY 10014; 212-366-5540). This organization produced a document (see Figure 15.1), hundreds of thousands of copies of which have been distributed. The key passages in this document are the directive to withhold or withdraw treatment that merely prolongs dying when one is in an incurable or irreversible condition with no reasonable expectation of recovery, and the directive to limit intervention in such circumstances to that which is designed to provide comfort and to relieve pain.

FIGURE 15.1 *Living will form distributed by Choice in Dying (formerly the Society for the Right to Die).*

ADVANCE DIRECTIVE
Living Will and Health Care Proxy

*D*eath is a part of life. It is a reality like birth, growth and aging. I am using this advance directive to convey my wishes about medical care to my doctors and other people looking after me at the end of my life. It is called an advance directive because it gives instructions in advance about what I want to happen to me in the future. It expresses my wishes about medical treatment that might keep me alive. I want this to be legally binding.

If I cannot make or communicate decisions about my medical care, those around me should rely on this document for instructions about measures that could keep me alive.

I do not want medical treatment (including feeding and water by tube) that will keep me alive if:
- I am unconscious and there is no reasonable prospect that I will ever be conscious again (even if I am not going to die soon in my medical condition), <u>or</u>
- I am near death from an illness or injury with no reasonable prospect of recovery.

I do want medicine and other care to make me more comfortable and to take care of pain and suffering. I want this even if the pain medicine makes me die sooner.

I want to give some extra instructions: *[Here list any special instructions, e.g., some people fear being kept alive after a debilitating stroke. If you have wishes about this, or any other conditions, please write them here.]*

**The legal language in the box that follows is a health care proxy.
It gives another person the power to make medical decisions for me.**

I name _____ , who lives at _____

_____ , phone number _____ ,

to make medical decisions for me if I cannot make them myself. This person is called a health care "surrogate," "agent," "proxy," or "attorney in fact." This power of attorney shall become effective when I become incapable of making or communicating decisions about my medical care. This means that this document stays legal when and if I lose the power to speak for myself, for instance, if I am in a coma or have Alzheimer's disease.

My health care proxy has power to tell others what my advance directive means. This person also has power to make decisions for me, based either on what I would have wanted, or, if this is not known, on what he or she thinks is best for me.

If my first choice health care proxy cannot or decides not to act for me, I name _____

_____ , address _____

phone number _____ , as my second choice.

(over, please)

LWGEN

FIGURE 15.1 (*continued*)

I have discussed my wishes with my health care proxy, and with my second choice if I have chosen to appoint a second person. My proxy(ies) has(have) agreed to act for me.

I have thought about this advance directive carefully. I know what it means and want to sign it. I have chosen two witnesses, neither of whom is a member of my family, nor will inherit from me when I die. My witnesses are not the same people as those I named as my health care proxies. I understand that this form should be notarized if I use the box to name (a) health care proxy(ies).

Signature _____

Date _____

Address _____

Witness' signature _____

Witness' printed name _____

Address _____

Witness' signature _____

Witness' printed name _____

Address _____

Notary [to be used if proxy is appointed]_____

Drafted and Distributed by Choice In Dying, Inc.—the National Council for the right to Die. Choice In Dying is a National not-for-profit organization which works for the rights of patients at the end of life. In addition to this generic advance directive, Choice In Dying distributes advance directives that conform to each state's specific legal requirements and maintains a national Living Will Registry for completed documents.

CHOICE IN DYING INC.—
the national council for the right to die
(formerly Concern for Dying/Society for the Right to Die)
200 Varick Street, New York, NY 10014 (212) 366-5540

5/92

It should be noted that this document does not call for active or direct killing. Indeed, one early version of a living will contained the following line: "I am not asking that my life be directly taken, but that my dying be not unreasonably prolonged." All of this language is primarily intended to refuse certain kinds of cure-oriented interventions ("artificial means" and "heroic measures") when they are no longer relevant, to request that dying be permitted to take its own natural course, and to ask that suffering associated with terminal illness be mitigated with effective palliative care, even if such palliative care should have a collateral or side effect of hastening the actual moment of death.

The larger context of living wills is the widely recognized right of competent decision makers to give or withhold informed consent to those who propose to intrude upon their bodies (Katz, 1978; President's Commission, 1982, 1983a, 1983b; Rozovsky, 1990). All advance directives assume that the right of informed consent includes the right to refuse unwanted interventions. Accordingly, living wills specify a particular set of circumstances and focus upon a certain sort of refusal of or request for treatment, even when such refusal or request might affect the timing of the requester's death.

To the degree that this sort of approach and these general principles were acceptable to them, other organizations formulated their own statements of living wills. For example, the Catholic Hospital Association approved a "Christian Affirmation of Life" in June 1974 and Eden Publishing House of the United Church of Christ published a "Christian Living Will" in 1975. These documents have been bypassed by subsequent events and are now out of print, but they illustrate the fact that some religious groups found it possible to support their own versions of living wills.

In 1976, the legislature of the state of California enacted the first "natural death" or "living will" legislation. Since that time, similar legislation has been passed in all of the 50 states (Society for the Right to Die, 1991). Typically, such legislation (1) specifies the conditions under which a competent adult is authorized to sign a document of this sort; (2) stipulates the form that such a document must take in order to have legal force; (3) defines what sorts of interventions can or cannot be refused—for example, interventions undertaken with a view toward cure, which may or may not include hydration or nutrition; (4) authorizes oral or written repudiation of the signed document by the signer at any time; (5) requires that professional care providers must either cooperate with the document's directives or withdraw from the case and arrange for alternative care providers (consenting to do so is thus legally protected, while failure to do so is usually subject not merely to potential malpractice liability but also to penalties that theoretically extend to loss of professional licensure); and (6) stipulates that death resulting from actions authorized by the legislation is not to be construed as suicide for insurance purposes.

Model legislation on this subject (intended to supplement existing legislation in the various states or to guide future legislative action) has been proposed by a presidential commission (President's Commission, 1982) and by the Legal Advisors Committee of Concern for Dying (reprinted in Wass, Berardo, & Neimeyer, 1988, pp. 429–437). The latter proposal has the following important features: (1) it applies to all competent adults and mature minors— that is, it is not restricted to the terminally ill; (2) it applies to all medical interventions—that is, it does not limit the types of interventions that may be refused; (3) it permits the designation of a surrogate or substitute decision maker in a manner similar to that described in the following section; (4) it requires health care providers to follow the directives of the individual and incorporates sanctions for those who do not do so; and (5) it requires that palliative care be continued for those who refuse other interventions.

Durable Power of Attorney in Health Care Matters

Living wills are not without their limitations or potential difficulties (Culver & Gert, 1990; Robertson, 1991). Like any documents that are written down in advance of a complex and life-threatening situation, living wills may not have anticipated every relevant feature of the future situation. In part for this reason, their significance and force may be subject to interpretation and/or dispute among the very family members and professional care providers whom they seek to guide (Colen, 1991; Flynn, 1992).

Because of these limitations and potential difficulties, some have preferred an alternative approach to advance directives. This alternative takes the form of state legislation that would authorize a durable power of attorney for the making of decisions in health care matters. "Power of attorney" refers to an authorization that one individual gives to another individual (or group of individuals) that empowers the individual so designated to make decisions and take actions on behalf of the person authorizing the designation in specific circumstances or for a specified period of time, while that person remains competent. For example, a power of attorney might authorize an individual to sign a contract on my behalf at a time when I am out of the country. A "durable" power of attorney is one that endures until it is revoked; that is, it continues in force even (or especially) when the individual who authorized the designation is no longer able to act as a competent decision maker. A durable power of attorney in health care matters is one that applies in that subject area.

Advocates argue that durable powers of attorney have two significant advantages over written directives, such as living wills. First, although the authorization for the durable power of attorney is itself a written document, its effect is to empower a surrogate or substitute decision maker to take part in the making of decisions in any circumstances that might arise and to speak in all authorized arenas on behalf of the individual who signs the durable power of attorney. Second, the surrogate decision maker can be instructed to refuse all interventions, to insist upon all interventions, or to approve some interventions and reject others. The first of these advantages attempts to minimize problems arising from changing circumstances and competing interpretations of written documents; the second seeks to maximize opportunities for individualizing expressions of favor or disfavor for differing interventions.

Durable powers of attorney in health care matters were first authorized in the state of California in 1985. Similar legislation has been approved since that time or is under consideration in a number of other (but not all) states (Society for the Right to Die, 1991). A booklet explaining powers of attorney in health care matters and providing a sample document is available from the American Bar Association and the American Association of Retired Persons (Sabatino, 1990). An example of a durable power of attorney for health care is given in Figure 15.2 in the format prepared by the Catholic Health Association (formerly the Catholic Hospital Association) of the United States, but it is important to note that an effective document of this sort must satisfy the legislative requirements of the particular legal jurisdiction within which it is to be enforced.

In September of 1991, this type of legislation was taken one step further in the state of Illinois. The state legislature enacted and the governor signed a bill empowering specified individuals to function as surrogate decision makers in health care matters even in the absence of a living will, durable power of attorney, or other formal indicator of intent on the part of an individual who cannot now participate in health care decision making.

In the absence of legislation based on the Illinois model, many (for example, Williams, 1991) have suggested that where it is possible, it might be useful for individuals to complete both a state-authorized living will (providing general guidance to decision makers) and to establish a durable power of attorney (authorizing discretion within those guidelines).

At Death

Death Certificates, Coroners, and Medical Examiners

Most people in North America and in other developed countries die in health care institutions (such as hospitals or long-term care facilities), in organized programs of hospice or home care, or while they are under the care of a physician. In such circumstances, a physician or other authorized person usually determines the time and cause of death, together with other significant conditions. That information is recorded on a form called a *death certificate*, which is then signed or certified by the physician or other authorized person.

Death certificates are the principal documents on which determinations of death are recorded (Shneidman, 1973). They are also the basis for much of the record keeping and statistical data concerning mortality and health in modern societies. Death certificates are or may be the basis for claiming life insurance and other death benefits, disposition of property rights, and the investigation of crime. Death certificates are fundamental documents in any modern death system, serving a broad range of public and private functions.

Most state certificates of death (see Figure 15.3) are a single-page form containing the following categories of information: personal information about the deceased and the location of his or her death; the names of his or

FIGURE 15.2   *Durable power of attorney for health care form distributed by the Catholic Health Association.*

DURABLE POWER OF ATTORNEY FOR HEALTHCARE*

1. CREATION OF A DURABLE POWER OF ATTORNEY FOR HEALTHCARE

To my family, doctors, and all those concerned with my care:

I, _____ (name), residing at _____ (street address) in _____ (city or county), _____ (state), being of sound mind, intend by this document to create a durable power of attorney for healthcare. My executing this durable power of attorney for healthcare is voluntary. I expect, despite the creation of this durable power of attorney for healthcare, to be fully informed about and to make any healthcare decision for myself whenever I am able to do so. For purposes of this document, "healthcare decision" means an informed decision in the exercise of my right to accept, maintain, discontinue, or refuse any care, treatment, service, or procedure to maintain, diagnose, or treat my physical or mental condition.

2. DESIGNATION OF HEALTHCARE AGENT

If I am unable to make healthcare decisions for myself, due to my incapacity, I hereby designate my _____ (relationship), _____ (name), residing at _____ (street address) in _____ (city or county), _____ (state) (home telephone: _____ - _____), to be my healthcare agent for the purpose of making healthcare decisions on my behalf. If she/he is ever unable or unwilling to do so, I hereby designate my _____ (relationship) _____ (name) to be my first alternate healthcare agent for the purpose of making healthcare decisions on my behalf. In the event that neither the person named to be my healthcare agent nor the person named as first alternate healthcare agent is able or willing to be my healthcare agent, I then designate my _____ (relationship) _____ (name) to be my second alternate healthcare agent for the purpose of making healthcare decisions on my behalf.

3. GENERAL STATEMENT OF AUTHORITY GRANTED

Unless I have specified otherwise in this document, if I ever am unable to receive and evaluate information effectively or to communicate decisions to such an extent that I lack capacity to manage my healthcare decisions, I instruct my healthcare provider to obtain the healthcare decision of my healthcare agent for all my healthcare. I have discussed my desires thoroughly with my healthcare agent as well as those named as alternates and believe that they understand my philosophy regarding the healthcare decisions I would make if I were able to do so. I desire that my wishes be carried out through the authority given to my healthcare agent under this document.

My healthcare agent is instructed that if I am unable, due to my incapacity, to make a healthcare decision she/he shall make a healthcare decision for me. My healthcare agent shall base her/his healthcare decision on any healthcare choices that I have expressed prior to the time of the decision. If I have not expressed a healthcare choice about the healthcare in question, my healthcare agent shall base her/his healthcare decision on what she/he believes to be in my best interest.

_____

*CHA believes that if you sign this document you do not need a living will. CHA prepared this document to be applicable in most states, but does not assure that it includes every state's technical requirements.

FIGURE 15.2 (continued)

4. ADMISSION TO NURSING HOMES OR LONG TERM CARE FACILITIES

My healthcare agent may admit me to a nursing home or other long term care facility as she/he may deem appropriate.

5. PROVISION OF NON-ORALLY INGESTED NUTRITION AND HYDRATION

My healthcare agent may have non-orally ingested nutrition and hydration withheld or withdrawn from me. This includes nutrition and hydration supplied through tubes entering anywhere in my body.

_____Yes, my agent has specific authority regarding non-orally ingested nutrition and hydration.
(initials)

IF I HAVE NOT INITIALED "YES," MY AGENT DOES NOT HAVE AUTHORITY TO WITHHOLD NON-ORALLY INGESTED NUTRITION AND HYDRATION.

6. STATEMENT OF DESIRES, SPECIAL PROVISIONS, OR LIMITATIONS

In exercising authority under this document, my healthcare agent shall act consistently with my following stated desires, if any, and is subject to any special provisions or limitations that I specify.

_____

_____

_____

_____

_____

_____

_____

_____

7. INSPECTION AND DISCLOSURE OF INFORMATION RELATING TO MY PHYSICAL OR MENTAL HEALTH

Subject to any limitations in this document, my healthcare agent has the authority to do all of the following:

(a) Request, review, and receive any information, verbal or written, regarding my physical or mental health, including medical and hospital records.
(b) Execute on my behalf any documents that may be required to obtain this information.
(c) Consent to the disclosure of this information.

8. SIGNING DOCUMENTS, WAIVERS AND RELEASES

Where necessary to implement the healthcare decisions that my healthcare agent is authorized by this document to make, my healthcare agent has the authority to execute on my behalf any of the following:

(a) Documents titled or purported to be a "consent to permit treatment," "refusal to permit treatment," or "leaving hospital against medical advice"
(b) A waiver or release from liability required by a hospital or physician

_____ Dated: _____, 199__
SIGNATURE

FIGURE 15.2 (continued)

STATEMENT OF WITNESSES

The foregoing document was declared by _____ (name) to be her/his grant of a Durable Power of Attorney for Healthcare and was signed in our presence, all being present at the same time, and we, at her/his request and in her/his presence and in the presence of each other, have subscribed our names as witnesses on the date above written.

_____ (name)
                                 residing at

_____
                                 (street address)

_____
                                 (city or county, state, ZIP)

_____ (name)
                                 residing at

_____
                                 (street address)

_____
                                 (city or county, state, ZIP)

(Notary affidavit is optional in most states but is recommended)

AFFIDAVIT

STATE OF _____   )
) SS.
COUNTY OF _____   )

I, the undersigned, an officer authorized to administer oaths, certify that _____ _____ and the witnesses, whose names are subscribed to the attached or foregoing instrument, having appeared together before me and first having been duly sworn, each then declared to me that _____ signed and executed the instrument as her/his grant of a Durable Power of Attorney for Healthcare, and that she/he had willingly made and executed it as her/his free and voluntary act and deed for the purposes therein expressed; and that each of the witnesses, in the presence and hearing of the said _____ and each other, signed the document as witnesses; and to the best of their knowledge _____ was at the time at least eighteen years of age, and was of sound mind and under no constraint, duress, fraud,or undue influence; and that each of said witnesses was then at least eighteen years of age.

   IN WITNESS WHEREOF, I have hereunto subscribed my name and official seal this _____ day of _____, 199____.

_____
Notary Public

My commission expires on _____

FIGURE 15.3   An example of a death certificate.

DECEDENT'S BIRTH NO.	REGISTRATION DISTRICT NO.	STATE OF ILLINOIS		STATE FILE NUMBER
	REGISTERED NUMBER	**MEDICAL CERTIFICATE OF DEATH**		

Type or Print in PERMANENT INK See Funeral Directors, Hospital, or Physicians Handbook for INSTRUCTIONS

A . . . .

DECEASED

B . . . .
C . . . .
D . . . .
E . . . .

PARENTS

1 . . . .
2 . . . .
3 . . . .
. . . .
. . . .

CAUSE

4 . . . .
5 . . . .
N . . . .
P . . . .
. . . .

CERTIFIER

DISPOSITION

DECEASED–NAME   FIRST   MIDDLE   LAST   SEX   DATE OF DEATH (MONTH, DAY, YEAR)
1.   2.   3.

COUNTY OF DEATH   AGE–LAST BIRTHDAY (YRS)   UNDER 1 YEAR MOS. DAYS   UNDER 1 DAY HOURS MIN.   DATE OF BIRTH (MONTH, DAY, YEAR)
4.   5a.   5b.   5c.   5d.

CITY, TOWN, TWP, OR ROAD DISTRICT NUMBER   HOSPITAL OR OTHER INSTITUTION–NAME (IF NOT IN EITHER, GIVE STREET AND NUMBER)   IF HOSP. OR INST. INDICATE D.O.A. OP/EMER. RM, INPATIENT (SPECIFY)
6a.   6b.   6c.

BIRTHPLACE (CITY AND STATE OR FOREIGN COUNTRY)   MARRIED, NEVER MARRIED, WIDOWED, DIVORCED (SPECIFY)   NAME OF SURVIVING SPOUSE (MAIDEN NAME, IF WIFE)   WAS DECEASED EVER IN U.S. ARMED FORCES? (YES/NO)
7.   8a.   8b.   9.

SOCIAL SECURITY NUMBER   USUAL OCCUPATION   KIND OF BUSINESS OR INDUSTRY   EDUCATION (SPECIFY ONLY HIGHEST GRADE COMPLETED) Elementary/Secondary (0-12)   College (1-4 or 5 +)
10.   11a.   11b.   12.

RESIDENCE (STREET AND NUMBER)   CITY, TOWN, TWP, OR ROAD DISTRICT NO.   INSIDE CITY (YES/NO)   COUNTY
13a.   13b.   13c.   13d.

STATE   ZIP CODE   RACE (WHITE, BLACK, AMERICAN INDIAN, etc.) (SPECIFY)   OF HISPANIC ORIGIN? (SPECIFY NO OR YES–IF YES, SPECIFY CUBAN, MEXICAN, PUERTO RICAN, etc.)
13e.   13f.   14a.   14b. ☐ NO   ☐ YES   SPECIFY:

FATHER–NAME   FIRST   MIDDLE   LAST   MOTHER–NAME   FIRST   MIDDLE   (MAIDEN) LAST
15.   16.

INFORMANT'S NAME (TYPE OR PRINT)   RELATIONSHIP   MAILING ADDRESS (STREET AND NO. OR R.F.D., CITY OR TOWN, STATE, ZIP)
17a.   17b.   17c.

18. PART I.   Enter the diseases, or complications that caused the death. Do not enter the mode of dying, such as cardiac or respiratory arrest, shock, or heart failure. List only one cause on each line.   APPROXIMATE INTERVAL BETWEEN ONSET AND DEATH

Immediate Cause (Final disease or condition resulting in death)   (a)
DUE TO, OR AS A CONSEQUENCE OF

CONDITIONS, IF ANY WHICH GIVE RISE TO IMMEDIATE CAUSE (a) STATING THE UNDERLYING CAUSE LAST.   (b)
DUE TO, OR AS A CONSEQUENCE OF
(c)

PART II.   Other significant conditions contributing to death but not resulting in the underlying cause given in PART I.   AUTOPSY (YES/NO)   WERE AUTOPSY FINDINGS AVAILABLE PRIOR TO COMPLETION OF CAUSE OF DEATH? (YES/NO)
19a.   19b.

DATE OF OPERATION, IF ANY   MAJOR FINDINGS OF OPERATION   IF FEMALE, WAS THERE A PREGNANCY IN PAST THREE MONTHS?
20a.   20b.   20c.   YES ☐   NO ☐

I (DID) (DID NOT) ATTEND THE DECEASED AND LAST SAW HIM/HER ALIVE ON   (MONTH, DAY, YEAR)   WAS CORONER OR MEDICAL EXAMINER NOTIFIED? (YES/NO)   HOUR OF DEATH
21a.   21b.   21c.   M.

TO THE BEST OF MY KNOWLEDGE, DEATH OCCURRED AT THE TIME, DATE AND PLACE AND DUE TO THE CAUSE(S) STATED.   DATE SIGNED (MONTH, DAY, YEAR)
22a. SIGNATURE ▶   22b.

NAME AND ADDRESS OF CERTIFIER   (TYPE OR PRINT)   ILLINOIS LICENSE NUMBER
22c.   22d.

NAME OF ATTENDING PHYSICIAN IF OTHER THAN CERTIFIER   (TYPE OR PRINT)   NOTE: IF AN INJURY WAS INVOLVED IN THIS DEATH THE CORONER OR MEDICAL EXAMINER MUST BE NOTIFIED.
23.

BURIAL, CREMATION, REMOVAL (SPECIFY)   CEMETERY OR CREMATORY–NAME   LOCATION   CITY OR TOWN   STATE   DATE (MONTH, DAY, YEAR)
24a.   24b.   24c.   24d.

FUNERAL HOME   NAME   STREET AND NUMBER OR R.F.D.   CITY OR TOWN   STATE   ZIP
25a.

FUNERAL DIRECTOR'S SIGNATURE   FUNERAL DIRECTOR'S ILLINOIS LICENSE NUMBER
25b. ▶   25c.

LOCAL REGISTRAR'S SIGNATURE   DATE FILED BY LOCAL REGISTRAR (MONTH, DAY, YEAR)
26a. ▶   26b.

VR200 (Rev. 5/89)   Illinois Department of Public Health—Division of Vital Records   (BASED ON 1989 U.S. STANDARD CERTIFICATE)

her parents, together with the name and address of the person who provided this and the previous information; cause and conditions of death; certification of death and information about the certifier; and information about disposition of the body (whether by burial, cremation, removal), together with the signature of a funeral director. When completed, a death certificate is delivered to a local (usually county) registrar, who signs the form, records it, and provides a permit for disposition of the body.

Medical technology makes possible interventions that raise new social issues.

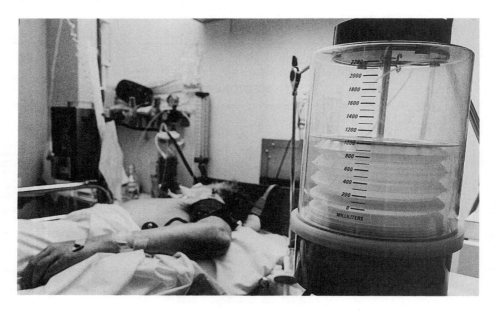

Every death certificate classifies the mode of death in four basic categories: natural, accidental, suicide, or homicide. Collectively, these are known by their first initials as the NASH system. Some deaths may also be categorized as "undetermined."

Deaths come under the jurisdiction of a *coroner* or *medical examiner* if the person who died was not under the care of a physician, if the death occurred suddenly, if there is reason to suspect foul play, and in all cases of accidents, suicide, or homicide (Wecht, 1974). The function of a coroner or medical examiner is to conduct an investigation into the circumstances and causes of such deaths. Coroners and medical examiners are empowered to take possession of the body, to conduct various kinds of investigations, and to hold an inquest or coroner's jury, which is a quasijudicial proceeding designed to determine the cause of a death.

The term *coroner* goes back to medieval times in England, where it identified the representative of the crown (*corona* in Latin). Originally, the coroner's function was to determine whether the property of the crown—that is, the deceased—had been unlawfully appropriated or killed. In modern societies, coroners are usually political officials who have been elected to office. They are not normally required to have any special qualifications other than being adult citizens of their elective jurisdiction. Many—but not all—coroners or deputy coroners in the United States, particularly in rural areas, are funeral directors. By contrast, medical examiners are appointed to their positions and are required to be qualified medical doctors (usually forensic pathologists). Some states have eliminated the office of coroner and have replaced it with the medical examiner. Other states continue to maintain a coroner system, often with medical examiners in large, urban centers.

Determination of Death

Determination of death has to do with deciding whether or not death has actually occurred, establishing the conditions under which it took place, evaluating the nature of the death, and confirming whether or not further investigation is required. These functions that enter into determination of death are analogous to the roles of umpires or referees in sports. That is, the individuals who fill these roles are expected to bring to them expertise in what they know about the subject and good judgment in applying their expertise to individual cases. Like umpires or referees, those who determine that death has occurred do not make the rules in their area of interest. Their role is to apply tests or criteria in an expert manner to arrive at the best decisions possible. They may also help to develop new and better ways of determining death.

The tests that have traditionally been applied to determine whether or not someone has died are well known. For example, in times past one might have held a feather under an individual's nostrils and observed whether it moved when he or she exhaled or inhaled. Sometimes a mirror was used in a similar way; one observed whether moisture contained in exhalations from a warm body condensed on its cool surface. One could also place one's ear on the chest to listen for a heartbeat, or touch the body at certain points to feel for arterial pulsation. Over time, more sensitive and discriminating tests have been developed (Molinari, 1978). For example, stethoscopes make possible a more refined way of listening for internal bodily sounds.

In all cases, the tests used to determine death depend upon established procedures and available technology. This varies from place to place and from time to time (Shrock, 1835). The complex testing procedures of a highly developed society are not likely to be available in the rudimentary health care system of an impoverished country, just as the advanced technology of a major urban medical center is not likely to be found in a sparsely populated rural area. Determination of death is closely related to the state of the art or prevailing community practices in a particular setting. Although they can vary, procedures to determine death in American society are clearly adequate for the vast majority of deaths. But as can be expected, determination of death is inevitably subject to human limitations and fallibility.

In the case of Judith Ann Debro, advanced life-support systems made it unclear for a number of days if death had actually occurred. The issue was whether or not the support systems were sustaining life itself or some limited bodily functions. More to the point, were they sustaining or merely imitating vital bodily functioning? When a respirator forces air into a body and then withdraws it, is that body breathing or merely being ventilated? Is that body alive, or does it merely present the appearance of being alive?

Concern over questions of this sort led an ad hoc committee of the Harvard Medical School (Ad Hoc Committee, 1968) to develop the following criteria for irreversible coma as a basis for certifying that death has occurred:

1. *Unreceptivity and unresponsivity.* Neither externally applied stimuli nor inner need evokes awareness or response.
2. *No movements or breathing.* Observation over a period of at least one hour does not disclose spontaneous muscular movement, respiration, or response to stimuli. For individuals on respirators, one must turn off the machine for a period of three minutes and observe for any effort to breathe spontaneously.
3. *No reflexes.* A number of reflexes that can normally be elicited are absent. For example, pupils of the eye will be fixed, dilated, and not responsive to a direct source of light. Similarly, ocular movement (which normally occurs when the head is turned or when ice water is poured into the ear) and blinking are absent.
4. *Flat electroencephalogram.* The electroencephalograph (EEG) is a sophisticated machine that monitors minute electrical activity in the upper brain (cerebrum). A flat EEG reading suggests the absence of such activity. The Harvard Committee indicated that the EEG has its primary value in confirming the determination that follows from the previous three criteria.

One other important point in the Harvard Committee's report is that "all of the above tests shall be repeated at least 24 hours later with no change" (p. 338).

To apply the Harvard criteria properly, one must exclude two special conditions: hypothermia, in which the temperature of the body has fallen below 90 degrees Fahrenheit; and the presence of central nervous system depressants, such as barbiturates. In both of these special conditions, the ability of the body to function may be masked or suppressed in such a way as to yield a false negative on the Harvard Committee's tests.

It is useful to pay careful attention to the achievements and the limitations of the Harvard Committee's report. The first three of the committee's criteria are essentially sophisticated and modernized restatements of tests that have traditionally been employed in determination of death. The fourth criterion adds a new test but depicts it as confirming the others—that is, not as an independent test in its own right. The requirement to repeat all four tests after a 24-hour interval indicates the committee's desire to proceed with great care in this important matter.

The limits of the committee's work are clear in its own stipulation: "We are concerned here only with those comatose individuals who have no discernible central nervous system activity" (p. 337). In other words, these criteria are not intended to be applied to all determinations of death. Rather, they represent an effort to define "irreversible coma." That is, a negative outcome resulting from a careful application of the Harvard criteria (two sets of four tests each, separated by a 24-hour period) is intended to demonstrate the presence of irreversible coma, and irreversible coma is to be understood as a new indicator that death has occurred.

It has been observed (President's Commission, 1981, p. 25) that the phrase "irreversible coma" may be misleading here since any coma is a condition of a living person, while "a body without any brain functions is dead and thus *beyond* any coma." This observation reminds us of the difficulty of maintaining linguistic and conceptual clarity in matters of this sort.

There would have been no need for criteria of the kind proposed by the Harvard Committee if irreversible coma had not become an object of some puzzlement in modern society. In times past, individuals in irreversible coma would simply have begun to deteriorate. There would have been no way to sustain even the limited functioning that they seemed to have. That is, interventions resulting from advances in modern medical technology have made it possible to sustain the reality or the appearance of vital bodily functioning. The Harvard criteria are intended to identify situations in which life only appears to continue and to equate such situations with death.

Definition of Death

Definition of death reflects the fundamental human and social understanding of the difference between life and death. This underlies all that has previously been said about determination of death. That is, determination of death is intended to identify whether or not the condition exists that society has defined as death. This determination must be based upon a definition that discriminates between real and only apparent death. There are many reasons why it is important to be as clear and accurate as possible in one's definition of death. Some of these reasons will be discussed in later sections of this chapter. But the most basic reason is the need to be as clear as possible as to who is to be included among those who are alive or dead. It is just as wrong to treat the dead as if they were living as it is to treat those who are alive as if they were already dead. The dead are no longer alive; the living are not yet dead.

No difference is more fundamental than that between being alive and being dead. Aristotle called death a kind of destruction or perishing that involves a change from being to nonbeing (see *Physics*, Bk. V, Ch. 1; *Metaphysics*, Bk. XI, Ch. 11). That is, death involves a change in the very substance of the being. When a human being dies, two important consequences follow: (1) there is no longer a human being present—instead, there is a body or a corpse; and (2) there is no longer a person present—there is only that person's remains. The corpse or remains that are left behind after a death are objects deserving honor and respect. Therefore, corpses are not simply discarded in a cavalier or thoughtless manner. But it is also important not to confuse the remains with a living human person (Nabe, 1981). That is why two distinct things can be said after, for example, the death of a spouse: "These are the hands that held and caressed me" and "Everything that was the person whom I knew and loved is no longer here."

How can we define the condition that we call death, the condition that is the opposite of life? A presidential commission (President's Commission, 1981) has proposed the following definition of death: "An individual who has sustained either (1) irreversible cessation of circulatory and respiratory functions, or (2) irreversible cessation of all functions of the entire brain, including the brain stem, is dead" (p. 73). The commission added: "A determination of death must be made in accordance with accepted medical standards." This last point has already been discussed in the preceding section.

Several points in the commission's proposed definition are essential: (1) it speaks of "an individual," not "a person," because whether or not a person is present is precisely the issue; (2) it requires *irreversible* cessation of the designated functions, not merely a temporary or reversible halt; (3) it speaks to situations in which, for example, a respirator masks the precise status of respiratory and circulatory functions—that is, in which it may be unclear whether they are being maintained by the individual or by the machinery; (4) in such circumstances, the proposed definition requires evaluation of the capacities of the central nervous system—which is the body's command and control center—because the definition recognizes that under normal circumstances, the life of the central nervous system ends shortly (a matter of a few minutes) after respiratory and circulatory functions are brought to a halt; and finally and most important, (5) in such circumstances, it concludes that irreversible cessation of all functions of the brain and brain stem (which controls autonomic activities, such as respiration and circulation) is the condition that we understand to be death.

Some have proposed that the irreversible loss of the capacity for bodily integration and social interaction is sufficient to define the death of a human being (Veatch, 1975, 1976). This proposal focuses upon neocortical or upper brain activity as definitive of the presence or absence of human life, to the exclusion of lower brain or brain stem activity. That is, it contends that the human person may be dead even when bodily or vegetative functioning remains. In other words, this proposal would regard the presence of a "persistent vegetative state" as the equivalent of death (Gervais, 1986).

Critics have charged that this proposal could lead, in the extreme, to a situation in which society would be asked to bury a body that demonstrated no upper brain function but in which there was spontaneous respiratory and circulatory function (Ramsey, 1970; Walton, 1979, 1982). In practice, the realistic situation would call not for immediate burial but for the removal of artificial support, including artificial means of providing nutrition and hydration, on the grounds that the individual was no longer alive as a human being. Note that this depends upon a concept or definition of death; if one conceded that the individual was alive and still proposed to remove artificial support, then the discussion would fall in the realm of euthanasia (discussed in Chapter 16).

After Death

Following a death, there are two broad areas of legal concern: the first has to do with advance directives that bear upon the donation of specific organs or the donation and disposition of one's body; the second has to do with the disposition of one's property or estate.

Organ and Body Donation

The modern era of organ donations began in the 1950s when a combination of advances in knowledge, technology, pharmacology, and practice made it possible for biomedical scientists and clinicians to transplant specific organs from one human body to another (Fox & Swazey, 1974). The aim is to sustain or to improve the quality of life of the recipient. To do so without harm to the donor, there are only two possibilities for donation: the organ in question is not uniquely vital to the donor's health; or the donor is already legally dead. Living donors are appropriate for replaceable materials (such as blood, blood products, or skin tissue) or in cases of twinned organs (such as kidneys) when close tissue matching is established. Cadaver donors are suitable for a variety of other purposes (such as heart transplant), when tissue matching is established, and when conditions preceding, at the time of, or immediately following the death do not damage the organ or otherwise render it unsuitable for transplantation. In the case of cadaver donors, this usually means that suitable organs must be retrieved shortly after the death of an otherwise healthy donor (for example, someone who has died as a result of external trauma) before the cadaver has begun to deteriorate.

Two points are especially critical for organ donation from cadavers. The first is determination of the time and circumstances of death, a matter addressed earlier in this chapter. Just as one would not wish to declare an individual to be dead prematurely (in his or her own interests), so one would not wish to wait any longer than necessary for an appropriate determination of death (in the interests of the organ recipient). The second critical point is the matter of permission to invade one body in order to take from it an organ to transplant to a second body. Following general principles of informed consent (Rozovsky, 1990), living donors can speak for themselves in this sort of matter. Obviously, cadavers cannot. Furthermore, it is a generally accepted principle in law that once a person has died, he or she no longer owns his or her body—for the very good reason that he or she is no longer a living person who can exercise such ownership. And no one would wish to repeat a celebrated case that occurred in Virginia on May 25, 1968 (Veatch, 1972), in which it seems that no permission was sought—from anyone—to transplant a heart and kidney from a man who had suffered a massive brain injury in a fall the day before.

To authorize and regularize organ donations, a Uniform Anatomical Gift Act (UAGA) was drafted and approved in 1968 by the National Conference of Commissioners on Uniform State Laws (Dukeminier, 1978; Kastenbaum, 1989f). It has since been passed by all of the state legislatures in the United States with only slight variations. The key provisions in the UAGA determine who may execute an anatomical gift; who may receive such donations and for what purposes; how such an anatomical gift may be authorized, amended, or revoked; and the rights and duties at death of a donee—that is, an individual or organization to whom such a gift is made. In brief, under the provisions of the UAGA an individual who is of sound mind and 18 years of age or older can donate all or any part of his or her body, the gift to take

A young athlete is encouraged by Kendall Barnes, a kidney transplant recipient and the Outstanding Male Athlete at the 1992 U.S. Transplant Games.

effect upon his or her death and to be made for the purposes of health care education, research, therapy, or transplantation. Great care is taken by the UAGA to ensure an absence of conflict of interest, in that the same care provider is precluded from serving both the potential donor and the potential recipient.

A gift of this sort can be made through one's will, although wills are generally not officially read for some time after a death and thus may not be a good vehicle for this time-significant purpose. Nevertheless, the UAGA authorizes donation even through a will that has not been probated or that may be declared invalid for testamentary purposes. Still, it would seem that a better vehicle for donation would be some other document or card that is signed

At the 1992 U.S. Transplant Games, honorary co-chair Victoria Principal presents an award to Outstanding Female Athlete Sandra Pridham.

both by the donor and by two witnesses and that is likely to be readily available at the time of death. Such documents are found on the reverse side of many state automobile driver's licenses in the United States.

In the absence of actual notice of contrary indications by the decedent, under the UAGA the following persons may authorize an organ or body donation at the time of death: the spouse; an adult son or daughter; either parent; an adult brother or sister; a legal guardian of the person of the decedent at the time of his or her death; and any other person authorized or under obligation to dispose of the body. The order of priority in this list of persons is important; actual notice of opposition on the part of an individual of the same or a prior class would prevent a donation. In other words, an adult child may give consent to donate organs from the body of his or her dead parent, but such consent would not be valid if objections were lodged by that parent's spouse or by one of the child's adult siblings.

In practice, it is probably unlikely that an anatomical gift of any sort would be accepted if there were objections from any of the individuals listed in the previous paragraph. Donees would be reluctant to enter into conflicts between family decision makers, and only a relatively short period of time is usually available for the resolution of such matters.

For those who might wish to donate their organs or bodies after death, one implication of this is that they should prepare the way ahead of time. Such preparation has two aspects. First, there was a time when American society experienced a shortage of donated bodies for medical education and research.

That is no longer true for whole bodies, although there is a very urgent need for many specific organs. Those who wish to make a gift of their body or organs at death should determine in advance that such a gift will be welcomed by its intended recipients. This can usually be done by contacting a local hospital, medical or dental school, organ bank, or transplant center. Second, one should discuss this matter with one's next of kin, since it is likely that they may make some key decisions in this matter, regardless of any written or oral expression of wishes that an individual might make (Williams, 1989).

In view of the critical need for organs on the part of potential recipients, Congress enacted the National Organ Transplant Act in 1984 to establish a national network to facilitate organ transplantation through the matching of donated organs with potential recipients. In addition, several states and the federal government have required that acute care hospitals must in all appropriate circumstances offer to surviving family members an opportunity to donate needed organs from the body of a relative who has just died. These requirements call for the development of a protocol for identifying potential organ and tissue donors, training of staff to implement that protocol, and close cooperation with organ procurement centers.

It may not seem to be an easy task to approach survivors and raise the matter of organ donation immediately after the death of a loved one. This is compounded by the fact that the most suitable potential cadaver donors are often relatively young persons who had been healthy until they experienced a sudden and traumatic death. Nevertheless, the need for most organs is critical and the opportunity to help other individuals is great. In addition, the opportunity to make a vital human gift may be seen by survivors as a constructive outcome of a tragic situation. Extending such opportunities must be accomplished in a sensitive and caring way and should be accompanied by a suitable program of bereavement follow-up for the survivors who have been asked to make such donation decisions.

A wide range of bodily organs are suitable for donation and transplantation, including blood and blood components; kidneys; hearts; eyes and ocular components; lungs; pancreases; skin tissue; and bones. The expanding range of transplantable organs is welcome news to potential recipients and further testimony to advances in medical progress.

Disposition of the Body

It is often thought that almost all aspects of the disposition of bodies following death are tightly controlled by legislation. This is not really true. In fact, state and local regulations provide a general framework that is principally concerned with recording vital statistics, giving formal permission for the burial or disposition of a body, preventing bodies or institutions that handle bodies from becoming a source of contamination or a threat to the health of the living, protecting the uses of cemetery land, and governing processes of disinterment or exhumation. Beyond that, regulation of body disposition is essentially a matter of professional practice, social custom, and good taste.

For example, as indicated in Chapter 10, there is no general legal requirement that bodies be embalmed following a death, although this is common practice among many in the United States. Embalming is legally required when bodies are to be transported via common carrier in interstate commerce. It may also be mandated when disposition of a body does not occur promptly and when refrigeration is not available. In other circumstances, the practice of embalming is essentially undertaken to permit viewing of the body in funeral ceremonies. Similarly, concrete grave liners and other forms of individual vaults that are used as the outer liners for caskets in the graves at many cemeteries are typically required not by the law but by the cemeteries themselves to prevent settling of the ground.

Disposition of Property: Probate

Upon a death, a variety of matters deserve attention: disposition of the body in an appropriate manner, with particular attention to the needs of survivors; payment of debts, taxes, funeral costs, and other expenses; and distribution to others of property that the individual owned at the time of death. As a general rule, disposition of body and property is governed by the laws of the state where a person lived at the time of death, whereas disposition of real estate (land and the structures built upon it) is governed by the laws of the state where the real estate is located. The process of administering and executing these functions is called *probate*, a term deriving from a Latin word (*probare* = "to prove") that has to do with proving or verifying the legitimacy of a will.

In the American death system, the probate court supervises the work of a decedent's personal representative who is charged to carry out necessary post-death duties (Manning, 1991; Prestopino, 1989). That representative is called an "executor" or "executrix" if he or she has been named by the decedent in a will; "administrator" or "administratrix" if appointed by the court. The responsibilities of such a representative are to make an inventory and collect assets of the estate; notify parties who may have claims against the estate of the individual's death; pay debts, expenses, and taxes; wind up business affairs; arrange for the preparation of necessary documents; manage the estate during the process; distribute the decedent's remaining property to those entitled to receive it; and close the estate (Dukeminier & Johanson, 1990). Charges levied against the estate may include a commission for the personal representative, fees charged by attorneys, accountants, or others who assist in administering the estate, and court costs. Many individuals seek to reduce these costs, along with the time consumed by the probate process, by arranging their affairs in ways that minimize involvements with or complexities for the probate process.

Wills and Intestacy

Individuals who die without a valid will are said to have died "intestate"—that is, without a testament stating their wishes. In every state, there are laws governing how the estate of an intestate individual will be distributed. These rules vary from state to state but are generally based upon assumptions made by state legislators as to how a typical person would wish to distribute his or her property (Atkinson, 1953). For example, a surviving spouse and children are likely to be regarded as preferred heirs, and the decedent's descendants are likely to be given precedence over parents, other ancestors, or their descendants. In the case of an intestate individual who leaves behind no one who qualifies as an heir under the intestacy statute, the estate "escheats" or passes to the state.

Individuals gain some measure of control over the distribution of their property through estate planning and a formal statement of their wishes, commonly called a *will* (Bernstein, 1977a). Each state has regulations as to how a will must be prepared and submitted to the probate process. Such regulations are intended to communicate the importance that the state attaches to the process of drawing up a will and to provide an evidential basis for proving during the probate process that the document really is the individual's will and does actually represent his or her intentions. For example, wills are to be drawn up, signed, and dated by adults ("testators") who are of "sound mind," who are not subject to undue influence, and whose action is witnessed by the requisite number (as provided by state law) of individuals who do not have a personal interest in the will in the sense that they would benefit from the disposition of the estate for which it provides. In general, through their wills individuals are free to dispose of their property as they wish, subject to exceptions, such as community property law relating to marriages, that have been enacted by most states to protect certain close family members from total disinheritance.

"Holographic" wills—those that are handwritten and unwitnessed—are acceptable in many states. However, state law varies significantly on this matter, and wills of this sort may be unreliable if they do not include specific, required language, or if the meaning of their language is ambiguous.

In general, professional legal assistance is usually recommended to draw up and execute a formal, written will in order to ensure that the document does convey its intended meaning and will have legal effect, notwithstanding changes in the testator's circumstances (Manning, 1991; Prestopino, 1989).

Wills can be changed at any time before the testator's death, assuming that the individual remains of sound mind and gives evidence of intent to make the change. This may be accomplished through a supplementary document called a "codicil," which leaves the previous document intact while altering one or more of its provisions; through a new will that revokes the previous document either explicitly or implicitly; through a formal revocation process that does not establish a new will; or through some physical act, such as divorce, subsequent marriage, or marriage followed by the birth of a child. The most recent valid will is the document that governs disposition of the decedent's estate. The particular relevance of many of these matters for the terminally ill and the role of lawyers in teams that serve such individuals have been discussed by Bernstein (1976, 1977b, 1979) in a series of articles. A number of handbooks (for example, Clifford, 1989; Esperti & Peterson, 1988; Hughes & Klein, 1987) are also available to guide lay readers in this area.

Trusts and Other Will Substitutes

It is both possible and legal to seek to avoid the expense and delay of a probate process by transferring assets during one's life. Also, one can make transfers that convey possession and complete ownership rights to another person upon the death of the current owner of the property, even though the current owner retains many benefits from and control over the property until his or her death. For example, with the exception of certain limited circumstances in which death is imminent, one can simply make an irrevocable and unconditional *gift* of property in which full control of the gift is conveyed to the recipient at the time the gift is made (Brown, 1975). Such gifts can now be made by individuals in amounts as high as $10,000 per year per donee (the receiver of such a gift) without incurring any federal tax liability. Similarly, ownership of real estate (land and the structures built upon it) can be directly and immediately transferred through a written *deed*. Both gifts and deeds surrender ownership and benefit of the object of the gift or deed, although some states permit *revocable deeds* or other conditions under which the transfer is not as absolute. Gifts and deeds may reduce the size of an estate that is presented for probate or considered for tax purposes.

Joint tenancy with right of survivorship amounts to an arrangement for transfer of property at death through a form of co-ownership. That is, under this arrangement, two or more parties possess equal rights to the property during their mutual lifetimes. When one party dies, his or her rights dissolve. In other words, upon the death of one joint owner the rights of the survivor(s) automatically expand to include that person's previous ownership rights. This process can continue until the last survivor acquires full and complete ownership of the entire property interest. At each stage in the process nothing is left unowned by a living person and nothing is therefore available to pass through the probate process. Thus, joint tenancy with right of survivorship usually saves delay in getting assets to survivors, but it does not necessarily reduce tax liability.

Many will be surprised to realize that *life insurance policies* are another common social vehicle through which assets are transferred from one person to another at the time of the first person's death. But this is certainly the case. That is, life insurance policies depend upon a contractual agreement in which premium payments made by the policyholder result in a payment of benefits to a specified beneficiary by an insurance company upon the death of the insured (Scheible, 1988). Many life insurance policies provide considerable flexibility to the insured as to how the monetary value of the policy can be employed during his or her lifetime, including the power to change beneficiaries before death. Benefits from life insurance policies are not included as taxable assets in the estate of the insured, although they clearly contribute to the property or estate of the beneficiary.

Establishing a *trust* is "probably the most effective and flexible method of avoiding probate" (Scheible, 1988, p. 308). One makes a trust by transferring property to a trustee (usually a third party, such as an officer of a corporation or a bank), with instructions regarding its management and distribution (Abts, 1989; Haskell, 1987; Lynn, 1992). Trustees are legally bound to use the trust property for the benefit of the beneficiaries and only under the terms provided in the trust instrument or imposed by the law. Typically, the maker of the trust retains extensive use and control over the property during his or her life.

Usually, upon the death of the person who established the trust (the "settlor"), the property is distributed to designated beneficiaries without becoming part of the estate in probate. However, a trust can be established that stipulates other circumstances for distribution of property. For example, a trust might stipulate that the settlor's surviving spouse receives a life estate in the income from the trust assets, with the principal to be distributed to the children upon the death of the spouse. Rights to amend or revoke the trust can be retained by the person who established the trust. In addition to these *testamentary trusts*, one can also establish *living trusts*, which are essentially set up for the benefit of the trustor—for example, in case he or she is incapacitated and unable to act on his or her own behalf. Living trusts of this sort are especially useful for single adults with no dependents and with minimal assets.

Taxes

Two basic forms of taxes relate to death: estate taxes and inheritance taxes. Although both are postdeath taxes, each has its own unique bearing. *Estate taxes* are imposed upon and paid from the decedent's estate. To be precise, estate taxes could be described as taxes not on property itself but on the transfer of property from a decedent to his or her beneficiaries. This occurs before all remaining assets in the estate are distributed to heirs or beneficiaries. By contrast, *inheritance taxes* are imposed upon individuals who receive property through inheritance.

Federal estate tax law applies uniformly throughout the United States. This tax exempts the first $600,000 worth of property in the estate, together with an unlimited amount of property that is donated to charity. Also, one can transfer an unlimited amount of property to a surviving spouse without estate taxes. Note that this may only have the effect of postponing or deferring rather than avoiding taxes, since property that is transferred in this way and that remains in the possession of the spouse at the time of his or her death will become part of that individual's estate.

There is no longer a federal income tax on gifts and inheritances. However, most states have estate and/or inheritance taxes. These taxes vary from state to state, and they may impose different rates upon those who are more closely or more distantly related to the decedent. Thus, it is simply sound and prudent advice to recommend that "expert tax advice should be obtained in order to maximize tax savings" (Scheible, 1988, p. 309).

Summary

This chapter has surveyed legal issues that arise before, at, and after the death of a human being in the United States. Its purpose has been to describe how legal aspects of the American death system impinge upon death-related events. Thus, it has considered issues involved in advance directives for health care (represented by living wills and durable powers of attorney in health care matters), definition and determination of death, organ and body donation, disposition of one's body and property, and wills, trusts, and taxes.

QUESTIONS FOR REVIEW AND DISCUSSION

1. Which of the available alternatives (living wills or durable powers of attorney) discussed in this chapter seem to you most desirable to cover situations where you could not make a decision as to whether or not medical treatment was to be continued for you? What advantages do you see to each of these options? What disadvantages?

2. Think about the role that technology plays in producing the need for new laws in the determination of when someone has died. Why is it difficult in some cases in contemporary American society to decide whether someone is dead? Why is it important to make such a decision? Using the Debro case as an example, who needed a decision made as to whether or not she was dead? What are the consequences of making or not making such a decision? What do you see as the important difference(s) between a live person and a person who has died?

3. How do you respond to the notion of donating your organs for use after your death? How do you respond to the idea of donating the organs of someone you care about? Try to describe why you respond as you do. What feelings, beliefs, and values are called up when you reflect on these questions?

4. What have you already done or what should/might you do about disposition of your body and/or disposition of your property if you should die? If you have already done something about these matters, what did you do and why? If you think you should or might do something about these matters, what do you think you should/might do and why? If you have done nothing yet about these matters, why is that the case?

5. Why is it desirable for anyone who has property (such as a car or a computer) to have a will? What are the consequences of not having a will? Who benefits from your not having a will, and who benefits if you do have one?

SUGGESTED READINGS

Concerning informed consent and advance directives, see:

Alexander, G. J. (1988). *Writing a Living Will: Using a Durable Power-of-Attorney.*
Cate, F. H., & Gill, B. A. (1991). *The Patient Self-Determination Act: Implementation Issues and Opportunities.*
Flynn, E. P. (1992). *Your Living Will: Why, When, and How to Write One.*
Rozovsky, F. A. (1990). *Consent to Treatment: A Practical Guide* (2nd ed.).
Sabatino, C. P. (1990). *Health Care Powers of Attorney: An Introduction and Sample Form.*
Society for the Right to Die. (1991). *Refusal of Treatment Legislation: A State by State Compilation of Enacted and Model Statutes.*
Williams, P. G. (1991). *The Living Will and the Durable Power of Attorney for Health Care Book, with Forms* (rev. ed.).

On the topic of defining death, see:

Cantor, N. (1987). *Legal Frontiers of Death and Dying.*
Gervais, K. G. (1986). *Redefining Death.*
Veatch, R. M. (1976). *Death, Dying, and the Biological Revolution: Our Last Quest for Responsibility.*
Walton, D. N. (1979). *On Defining Death: An Analytic Study of the Concept of Death in Philosophy and Medical Ethics.*

On the topic of organ donation, see:

Williams, P. G. (1989). *Life from Death: The Organ and Tissue Donation and Transplantation Source Book, with Forms.*

Concerning personal estate planning and disposition of property, consult:

Abts, H. W. (1989). *The Living Trust: The Fail-Proof Way to Pass Along Your Estate to Your Heirs Without Lawyers, Courts, or the Probate System.*
Clifford, D. (1989). *Plan Your Estate.*
Esperti, R. A., & Peterson, R. L. (1988). *The Handbook of Estate Planning* (2nd ed.).
Hughes, T. E., & Klein, D. (1987). *A Family Guide to Wills, Funerals, and Probate: How to Protect Yourself and Your Survivors.*

On professional estate planning and disposition of property, consult:

Atkinson, T. E. (1953). *Handbook of the Law of Wills and Other Principles of Succession.*
Brown, R. A. (1975). *The Law of Personal Property* (3rd ed., by W. B. Rauschenbush).
Dukeminier, J., & Johanson, S. M. (1990). *Wills, Trusts, and Estates* (4th ed.).
Haskell, P. G. (1987). *Preface to Wills, Trusts, and Administration.*
Lynn, R. J. (1992). *Introduction to Estate Planning in a Nutshell* (4th ed.).
Manning, J. A. (1991). *Estate Planning* (4th ed.)
Prestopino, D. J. (1989). *Introduction to Estate Planning* (2nd ed.).

CHAPTER 16

Euthanasia

Decisions to sustain or not sustain human life are at the heart of some of the most difficult moral, conceptual, and legal dilemmas that face individuals and society near the end of the 20th century. In this chapter, issues surrounding such decisions are addressed in four primary ways. First, the example of Nancy Cruzan introduces some reflections on ways in which moral dilemmas arise in modern society. Second, a review of key concepts and distinctions reveals ways in which efforts have been made to define the notion of euthanasia and to set out boundaries between acceptable and unacceptable actions in this area. Third, arguments for and against euthanasia are shown to depend upon basic values and principles. Fourth, examples from the recent past suggest prospects for the immediate future, both for individual decision making and for public practice and policy.

Nancy Cruzan

In January of 1983, 26-year-old Nancy Cruzan was in an automobile accident ("The court and Nancy Cruzan," 1990). When she was found by the side of the road, she appeared to be dead. Nancy lay in the snow in a field for some time until paramedics arrived and restarted her heart. In the meantime, she had suffered severe brain damage from lack of oxygen. She never regained consciousness. By 1989, Nancy was in a state-run rehabilitation center, curled up in a fetal position. She was not on a respirator, but she was fed through a tube that had been implanted directly into her stomach shortly after her accident. According to one report, her doctors suggested that she might continue to live this way for 30 more years.

Nancy's parents maintained that she would not want to live in this condition. In 1987, they began legal proceedings to have the feeding tube removed. The state in which Nancy was being cared for (Missouri) had a "living will" statute, enacted in 1985. According to that statute, persons living in Missouri may draw up a living will, which is to provide clear and convincing evidence of their wishes as to whether they want their lives to be prolonged by certain forms of medical treatment if they have a fatal illness and become incompetent. Nancy had not signed such a document. Nor would such a document (according to Missouri's law at that time) allow for the removal of feeding tubes.

A circuit judge ordered Nancy's feeding tube removed. That ruling was appealed by the state to the Missouri Supreme Court, where it was overturned by a margin of one vote. The opinion accompanying the ruling of the Missouri Supreme Court indicated that the state had an interest in preserving the lives of its citizens *without regard to their quality*. The Cruzans appealed to the United States Supreme Court, which heard the case in 1989. The decision of the Court was that states can establish within their jurisdictions the conditions that apply to the removal of interventions that support life.

In 1990, the Cruzans returned to state court with testimony from Nancy's co-workers that had not previously been offered. That testimony stated that

*Nancy Cruzan
shortly before
her automobile
accident.*

prior to her accident Nancy had said that she would not want to be maintained by medical technology in a persistent vegetative state. The court ruled that this met Missouri's requirements for a clear and explicit statement of Nancy's wishes. Consequently, the court authorized removal of her feeding tube. That took place and Nancy Cruzan died on December 28, 1990.

Moral Dilemmas in Modern Society

The issues raised in cases like that of Nancy Cruzan represent difficult moral dilemmas that are, for the most part, unique to our time. Modern technology has allowed caregivers to maintain certain functions such as ventilation or circulation and to provide nutrition and hydration to persons who before the intervention of such caregivers with their special knowledge and equipment would have promptly died. In many respects, that is one of the blessings of living in the latter half of the 20th century. But the situation of Nancy Cruzan—and hundreds of others who are or have been in similar situations—makes plain that this can sometimes become a mixed blessing (Beauchamp & Perlin, 1978; Ladd, 1979; Veatch, 1976). The issues involved in cases such as this present themselves at the bedside (Gorovitz, 1991), in legal debate (Cantor, 1987; Rhoden, 1989), in efforts to establish professional and public policy (Veatch, 1978), and in individual decision making (Baird & Rosenbaum, 1989; President's Commission, 1983a).

In most situations, keeping someone alive is a good that all can celebrate. But for some persons in some situations, it is less obvious that one should celebrate the caregivers' intervention (Amundsen, 1989). Did those who attempted to bring to bear the resources of modern medical technology on behalf of Nancy Cruzan actually "help" this young woman? Or were their interventions merely the impetus that sent her on a journey without meaning? Would it have been appropriate not to have intervened, presumably thus assuring Nancy's death at an earlier time? Can death ever be appropriate? Is Cicely Saunders correct when she urges that sometimes allowing death to occur is the *caring* thing to do? These difficult and disturbing questions lead to the topic of this chapter: euthanasia.

Euthanasia literally means "good death." There are those for whom that phrase is an oxymoron—a contradiction in terms. Such persons believe that death is always and everywhere evil. Persons who hold this view will easily resolve questions about euthanasia. If death is always evil, then it must always be resisted, presumably with every means at one's disposal.

Actually, to make this position as clear as possible, it is necessary to go one step further. To maintain that death must always be resisted with every available means, one must believe that death is the *most profound* evil known to human beings. After all, for most persons, death *is* something to be resisted; it is something to be avoided—*if possible*. But for someone to resolve the questions associated with euthanasia easily, that individual must believe that nothing is *more* evil than death. Thus, every other value must be sacrificed if the alternative is death. When stated this way, however, few might be willing to go along with the claim. That is, for most persons, death is not the most profound evil that they know. Some things are worse than death.

It is important to note the qualification in the second-to-last sentence: for *most* persons. It has already been suggested that there are *some* who do find death to be the most horrible evil imaginable. So there is disagreement at this level. But there is even more disagreement among those who do not find death to be the worst evil of all. That is, people disagree among themselves about just *which* things are worse than death. And this reveals in another way that euthanasia is a difficult subject. In a pluralistic society, there may be little agreement about the values that are held to be most dear. Americans value many things: freedom, privacy, persons, religious traditions, life, self-respect, justice, a good life, and so on. Euthanasia calls into question just what one values, why it is valued, and to what extent it is valued. An adequate discussion of euthanasia will require *care*.

Concepts and Distinctions

A "Good Death"?

Thus far, an attempt has been made to show how questions about euthanasia arise in fact and why those questions can be so disturbing. Now, a further effort must be made to try to draw some order into these reflections. Some content can be suggested for the notion of what a "good death" might mean by pointing to a related notion introduced by Weisman (1972): what he called an "appropriate death." Weisman defined an appropriate death as a death one might choose for oneself, if one could choose. He believed that for most people the sort of death they would choose for themselves includes several facets: (1) it would be relatively pain free, (2) suffering would be reduced, and (3) emotional and social impoverishment would be kept to a minimum.

This certainly is reinforced by the authors' experience. We have asked thousands of college students to describe the sorts of deaths they would want for themselves or for persons they loved. Repeatedly, and by large percentages, they describe deaths that are pain-free, sudden (unexpected), and in one's sleep. These are deaths that do not involve much dying. That is, an appropriate death for many people in American society today is one that finds them at the time of their death operating fairly much as they always have done (that is, as socially and emotionally effective and comfortable), and cognitively unaware of any discomfort—emotional, physical, or social—associated with their death.

Thus, if a "good death" can be associated with Weisman's notion of an appropriate death, then a "good death" is one that is pain-free, free of suffering, and that limits social and psychological impairment as much as possible. Return now to the situation of Nancy Cruzan. When her feeding tube was removed, what happened? Essentially, she starved to death. Some experts claimed that she felt nothing. If they were right, there was no pain and no suffering. Nor did removing the tube bring about an inappropriate form of social or psychological impairment. Nancy's brain injury had already reduced her social and psychological functioning to a minimal level—if they even existed at all any longer. Her death then might have been a "good" one, on the criteria Weisman suggested for an appropriate death.

But this discussion does not get us very far. Even if people could agree that Cruzan's death was an appropriate one in Weisman's sense, they might be less confident that this alone could have been employed as the criterion to decide whether her feeding tube should have been removed. More precision is required here.

A Definition of Euthanasia

To get closer to the question of what should or should not be done, it will be useful to become clearer about just what is meant by euthanasia. Even at this level, there is disagreement (Cole, 1989). That is, there are debates about precisely what is meant by the term *euthanasia*. Several definitions have been proposed.

Here, a modified form of a definition of euthanasia proposed by Beauchamp and Davidson (1979) may be helpful. According to these authors, for there to be an instance of euthanasia, the following four criteria must be met:

1. The person's death must be intended by at least one other person, and the cause of death must involve either something this second person does or does not do.
2. The person who dies must either be acutely suffering or irreversibly comatose (and there must be sufficient *evidence* that this is the case); or there must be sufficient evidence to believe that the person who dies *will be* acutely suffering or irreversibly comatose.
3. The person whose action or nonaction contributes to the death of the other person must have as his or her primary intention the ending of the suffering or of the comatose state.
4. There must be sufficient evidence that the means used to end the person's life will not produce more suffering than if no intervention occurred.

This definition makes plain that someone other than the person who dies is always involved in a case of euthanasia. In particular, the death occurs because of some action that second person either does or does not perform. This distinguishes euthanasia from suicide. In suicide, the death is the result of the actions (or nonactions) of the person who dies. Furthermore, in cases of euthanasia, the second person must intentionally contribute to the death of the other. That is, the intention of the second person is that the other person die. Thus, an accidental death will not be an instance of euthanasia.

If euthanasia is thought of in this way, it can be distinguished from instances of "assisted suicide," in which individuals end their own lives through the use of information, drugs, or equipment provided to them by others. At least in the present definition, this would not be euthanasia because the second person does not directly contribute to or cause the death. Note that if this sort of case were to be described as a form of euthanasia, then anyone who provided the means (for example, a physician or druggist who provided drugs that are potentially lethal) could be said to be engaging in euthanasia. This is an unworkable view, so it does not appear to be desirable to include "assisted suicide" under the concept of euthanasia.

Second, an event will be called an instance of euthanasia only if the person who dies is acutely suffering or irreversibly comatose. Notice that it has not been said that the person need be terminally ill. That is, someone may be suffering without having a condition that will in itself lead to death. Also, "suffering" may refer to experiencing physical pain or it may refer to experiencing some other form of great discomfort, such as emotional trauma. Nor do persons have to be undergoing such suffering or be in an irreversible coma now; it might be foreseeable that they will enter such a condition in the future (for example, as a consequence of the disease with which they are diagnosed). This is a more controversial part of this definition, perhaps. It at least demands great care in making such prognoses. (We will return to this problem later.) But it is understandable that some people with diseases that lead to great suffering might want their lives to end before that happens.

Third, for an event to be called euthanasia, the primary intention of the persons involved must be to end the suffering or comatose state. No other intentions can be used to justify calling some event euthanasia.

Using these criteria, could the removal of the feeding tube from Nancy Cruzan be described as an instance of euthanasia?

1. It certainly involved people other than Nancy. And anyone removing such an intervention would expect (and thus might be held to intend) that Nancy would die because of the removal of the feeding tube. So the case of Nancy Cruzan meets the first criterion.
2. Nancy was believed by her caregivers to be in an irreversibly comatose state. This seems to meet the second criterion.
3. The reasons given for removing the intervention relate to Nancy's desire "not to live this way." This might be taken to mean that she believed that living in this way would cause suffering. Thus, to end this life would end her suffering. We will return to this point later.
4. If (as some of her caregivers argued) Nancy would experience no (hunger) pain as her interventions were removed, then the means used to bring about her death would not produce more suffering for her than if no intervention had occurred.

Basically, it appears that the situation of Nancy Cruzan did meet the four proposed criteria. If so, removing the feeding tube from Nancy was an instance of euthanasia, *according to this definition*. If someone disagreed with this definition—for example, by rejecting the second criterion—and believed that euthanasia can only properly refer to situations of life-threatening illness, a different conclusion might be reached. Nancy was not "terminally ill." She had no condition that would have led inevitably to her dying in the near future. If *euthanasia* is to be used to refer only to cases where life-threatening illness is present, the case of Nancy Cruzan was not an instance of euthanasia.

So far, this discussion has concerned one definition of euthanasia. No attempt has yet been made to determine whether or not euthanasia—even in this definition—is morally acceptable. To know what something is, is not to know whether or not it is morally appropriate.

Some Proposed Distinctions

There are other ways of thinking about euthanasia or understanding the concept that it represents. Many discussions of this topic point to distinctions that might be drawn around supposed instances of euthanasia (for example, Behnke & Bok, 1975; Bok, 1978). For instance, such cases might be distinguished on the basis of whether the person who dies contributes to the decision, whether the action leading to the death is one that is committed or omitted, and whether the means of treatment provided are ordinary or extraordinary.

Voluntary versus nonvoluntary euthanasia   If the person who dies asks for or assents to his or her death, this would be called "voluntary euthanasia" (Downing, 1974; Gruman, 1973). The will of the person who dies is known. Persons who plead with others to kill them or to let them die are contributing to instances of voluntary euthanasia. If the will of the person who dies regarding his or her own death remains unknown, then it would be called "nonvoluntary euthanasia." For example, the person might be unconscious or unable to make plain his or her choice for some other reason (think of a person who has had a severe stroke). Or the person might be incompetent to make such a decision, as in the case of a child or someone intellectually or emotionally disabled. If a second person somehow contributes to the death of this sort of person, then it would be called an example of nonvoluntary euthanasia.

A third sort of case is one in which the wishes of the person are known— he or she wants to be kept alive—but someone else decides to end that life. Perhaps this could be called "involuntary euthanasia." But this is more like homicide than like a "good death," so one might not wish to associate it with the term *euthanasia* in any way.

Using the distinctions discussed here, the case of Nancy Cruzan is puzzling. Because she could not communicate her wishes when she was in a comatose state, her situation seems to present an example of nonvoluntary euthanasia. Nevertheless, in this case, parents, other relatives, and friends argued on behalf of allowing Nancy to die precisely because this young woman would not have wanted "to live like this." That is, they claimed to be abiding by wishes of this woman that were expressed before she became comatose. In this indirect sense, then, Nancy might present a case of voluntary euthanasia.

This points up one of the uncertainties associated with euthanasia. It is sometimes argued that someone who is acutely suffering, by the very fact of that suffering, has diminished capacity to make difficult decisions. Thus, one might be uncomfortable following the directions offered by someone in severe physical or emotional pain. Choosing to cooperate in someone's death is an *irreversible* decision; in the face of that irrevocability, one would want to be as certain as possible that that person's own choice was clearly before one.

Active versus passive euthanasia   Another distinction often employed in these discussions is that between active and passive euthanasia. Active euthanasia is described as a death that occurs through an action that the second party *commits*. That is, the person who contributes to the death of the person who dies actually does something or performs some act that directly produces the death. The death is caused by what this person does. In passive euthanasia, the second person *omits* an action, and that omission allows or permits death to occur.

At the extremes, this distinction is easy enough to understand. Shooting someone in order for their death to result is the commission of an act that directly produces death. Withholding or not giving the antibiotics needed to end a life-threatening case of pneumonia is the omission of an act that will result indirectly in death. The death is said to result indirectly because it is the direct product of the underlying condition (here, pneumonia) that brings it about.

One problem with this distinction is that a large number of situations do not clearly and recognizably involve commissions or omissions. Quite often, these involve not withholding an intervention but *withdrawing* one that has already been initiated. For example, it is unclear whether withdrawing or removing a respirator from a person who needs it to breathe is the commission of an act (*doing* something, such as lifting the respirator from the person's face or turning off the flow of air) or the omission of an act (*not doing* something, such as no longer providing the necessary means of respiration).

The reason that this lack of clarity is important is that some (such as Beauchamp, 1989) argue that passive euthanasia (allowing someone to die in certain circumstances) is morally more acceptable than is active euthanasia (directly causing someone's death). Others believe that this is not the case, either because they do not accept the relevance or utility of the active/passive distinction or because they do not necessarily concede the moral inferiority of active euthanasia (Foot, 1977; Rachels, 1975). If one were to accept the claim of the moral superiority of passive euthanasia, it would become essential to be able to identify with some degree of clarity the differences between an instance of passive euthanasia and an instance of active euthanasia. If one could not decide whether a particular behavior was passive or active, the distinction would not be helpful.

Ordinary versus extraordinary means   A third distinction often introduced into discussions about euthanasia is that between ordinary and extraordinary means of treatment. The point of this distinction is to argue that there is no *moral* obligation to provide extraordinary means of treatment. This claim has been made by many; for instance, the Roman Catholic tradition has long argued that care providers have no such moral obligation (McCormick, 1974).

The helpfulness of this distinction depends on one's ability to distinguish *ordinary* means of health care from *extraordinary* means of health care. Several criteria are offered to help implement this distinction. Ordinary means of therapy are those that (1) have outcomes that are predictable and well known; (2) offer no unusual risk, suffering, or burden for either the person who is being treated or for others; and (3) are effective.

Extraordinary means of treatment fail to meet one or more of these criteria. That is, extraordinary means of treatment have outcomes that are not predictable or well known. Often, one might be thinking of some sort of experimental procedure here. If so, the procedure will not have been widely used or studied, so that one cannot be certain what will happen when one embarks on its use in a particular case. Or it may be that the procedure itself puts the patient at risk or imposes undue burdens on those who would assist the patient. That is, the procedure may have a broad range of outcomes, some of which make the person worse off than he or she was before. The side effects, for instance, of a treatment might produce more suffering than the person is undergoing before the treatment begins. An extraordinary means of treatment might indeed produce effects that are worse than the disease. Since the outcome of the use of these means of therapy is unpredictable, one might have little confidence that they will in fact be helpful in dealing either with the person's symptoms or disease. That is, the actual effectiveness of an extraordinary means of treatment is uncertain, too.

If the therapy proposed for use or already in use is an extraordinary means of treatment *according to the criteria listed here*, then most moralists agree that there is no moral obligation to use it. Individuals may choose not to begin the use of such a therapy, or they may choose to terminate its use with no moral culpability being attached to that decision.

Return again to the case of Nancy Cruzan. Was the use of the stomach tube to feed her an ordinary or extraordinary means of treatment? The outcome of its use was predictable and well known. Such tubes had been used widely to feed people who could not feed themselves. The food supplied through the tube provided nourishment for her bodily cells and tissues. There was little or no risk in using such a tube, and no suffering was known to be caused when it was used with a comatose person. Furthermore, the use of a feeding tube was effective therapy; it kept the body alive. On these criteria, it appears that the use of the feeding tube in Nancy Cruzan's case was an *ordinary* means of treatment. However, the feeding tube was not a cure-oriented intervention. It stabilized Nancy in her condition, but it did not act to reverse that condition and to restore her to a more healthful form of living.

What Cruzan's case demonstrates again is that this distinction is not as simple as it might appear to be on first glance. What counts as ordinary and extraordinary is not determinable independent of an individual person's context. That is, what might be ordinary treatment in one situation could be extraordinary in another. There is no list of treatments that can—purely on their own—be determined to be ordinary, and another list of treatments that can be determined to be extraordinary. Whether a specific treatment is ordinary or extraordinary must be decided in terms of a particular person's situation.

This brings the discussion back up against questions of euthanasia. The distinction between ordinary and extraordinary means is employed in the following way. Not to begin to use or to stop using extraordinary means of treatment is *not* to be engaged in decisions about euthanasia. Questions about euthanasia arise only when one is trying to decide whether or not to use ordinary means of treatment. Those who argue in favor of euthanasia will suggest that in some situations there is no moral requirement to use ordinary means of treatment. Those who argue against euthanasia will suggest that in *this* situation (or in all situations) one morally must use the ordinary means of treatment under discussion.

In short, the discussion so far has sought to make clear what euthanasia is and how one might begin to think with some clarity about this topic. Now, it is important to try to become clearer about the *morality* of euthanasia. That is, suppose that we agree that the removal of the feeding tube from Nancy Cruzan's body was an instance of euthanasia. The question now is, *Should* this have been done? What are the *moral* questions associated with this decision?

Values and Principles

To raise *moral* questions is to be concerned with *values* and *principles* that affect human lives (Kluge, 1975). That is, in the first place such questions are concerned with what persons, objects, attitudes, and behaviors are to be regarded as having positive or negative value. Second, through such questions an effort is made to try to uncover what rules or laws or principles are relevant to the governing of behavior when humans move toward those things they value or move away from (or against) those things they disvalue. In laying out the values and principles that are relevant to moral beliefs, arguments are offered in the form of attempts to show *why* one holds the particular values and principles that one does. These arguments are of various sorts and they appeal to different types of foundations (Kamisar, 1958; Williams, 1958). Here, several of the best-known moral arguments that have been marshaled on behalf of positions that are relevant to euthanasia are summarized.

Arguments Against Euthanasia

Preservation of life   One argument used to show that euthanasia is morally inappropriate is that it violates the caregiver's (and society's) commitment to the preservation of life. According to this argument, it is part of the caregiver's role as a provider of care to preserve life. Thus, if a caregiver deliberately behaves in such a way that the death of the person for whom he or she has been caring will result, then that caregiver has behaved immorally. That is, the person has not fulfilled in an appropriate manner his or her role as a provider of care.

This argument holds that life is good and that, therefore, we ought to preserve and support life whenever we can. Schindler (1990) reported, for instance, that Jewish thought values life as supreme, so the "preservation of human life is paramount and one is obligated to do all, even if life is extended for only a short period" (p. 83). But a qualified form of this view might be held. In this latter view, life *is* valuable, but it is not the *preeminent* value. That is, it does not take precedence over *all* other values in *all* instances. If this is the view one holds, it will not be possible to resolve whether or not euthanasia is morally acceptable (or even desirable) in some instances merely by appealing to the sanctity of life.

"Slippery slope" arguments   Another argument used against the morality of euthanasia is a "slippery slope" argument. It contends that once a decision is made to end someone's life for whatever reason, then one will have moved onto a slippery slope upon which it is all too easy to slide toward ending other people's lives for other reasons. If it is too difficult to stop once one has begun to act in these ways, it is better not to begin at all, at least until some way of knowing where to stop has been established.

Additional arguments   Other issues associated with the implementation of euthanasia raise questions about the wisdom of engaging in this practice. For example, medicine is at best an uncertain science. Wrong diagnoses and prognoses are made. Also, medicine moves quickly sometimes and nearly always with some degree of unpredictability. New therapies and new cures are discovered at unknown moments. So when one considers ending a person's life, there is always the possibility of a misdiagnosis or of the appearance of a new cure or therapy that would ease or even end that person's suffering.

These arguments have some weight. Whether or not they are persuasive in showing that one ought never to engage in euthanasia depends on how much weight one gives to them. Human wisdom is always imperfect; if one waits for complete certainty in any moral matter, one will seldom act at all. But not to decide is to decide. If one chooses not to engage in euthanasia, one allows the suffering to continue. There is a danger here too. If a person's suffering is allowed to continue because of moral uncertainty or unclarity, there is a risk of becoming inured to suffering.

And although it is true that at any moment a new therapy or cure may come along, it is not certain that such a discovery will help all persons with the particular disease at issue. They may have progressed too far in the course of the disease, or it may have brought other problems in its wake that the new therapy or cure can do nothing about. So these issues are relevant but not necessarily decisive.

Arguments for Euthanasia

Prevention of suffering   An argument to support euthanasia's moral acceptability is that pain and suffering are evil. Therefore, one function of caregivers is to prevent and, if possible, end pain and suffering. Hence, actions involving euthanasia to achieve such a goal would be permissible. Again, one could take this argument to its extreme and urge that *all* pain and suffering are evil, and therefore that one ought *always* to strive to end *any* pain or suffering. But again, probably few would hold this view. From slogans supporting physical exercise as a means to health ("no pain, no gain"), to the realization that success in most valued endeavors (such as intellectual growth, emotional maturity, artistic creativity) involves some pain and suffering, the conclusion seems to follow that some pain and suffering have consequences that are good. So, at least as a means to some desired good end, pain and suffering cannot automatically be taken to be things to be eliminated altogether. Once more, one is forced to evaluate particular instances of pain and suffering, rather than to issue blanket condemnations (Cassell, 1991). This conclusion, of course, may again leave us uncertain about what to do in a particular instance.

Enhancement of liberty   Another argument sometimes used to support euthanasia depends upon a view of the value of human liberty. Most Americans believe that liberty is good. That is, they value being free from external coercion when making decisions about themselves and their lives. Another way to say this is to say that many people value autonomy—a word that literally means being able to make law (*nomos*) for oneself (*auto*) (Childress, 1990). Such individuals disvalue interference from others in matters that they believe to be their own affair. This value supports the rights of individuals to decide what to do about their own pain and suffering. And someone might so disvalue the pain and/or suffering that he or she is experiencing, that that individual may prefer that his or her life end. In short, those who value autonomy must seriously consider the view that it is the suffering person's right as an autonomous agent to make that decision, and others ought not to interfere with it.

However, there are two difficulties with accepting this argument as definitive. One is that it presupposes that one can tell when someone is acting autonomously. But someone who is experiencing severe pain or emotional trauma may not be completely free of coercion. That is, the pain or emotional suffering itself may be so affecting the person that any decision made under its influence is *not*, in fact, autonomous. It is not always easy to decide about this. On the other hand, one position to guard against is the belief that such pain or trauma *always* is a coercive factor in someone's ability to make rational decisions. That is, even with severe pain or suffering, it is possible that the person is still an autonomous agent. Individuals involved in the lives of people who are experiencing severe pain or suffering must find ways—*really* listening to such a person is a step in this direction—to decide what is happening in this particular instance that they are confronting.

But even if the person *is* autonomous, that does not automatically decide what others ought to do in the face of his or her autonomy. Really difficult moral dilemmas often involve conflicts between autonomous persons. Individuals may decide autonomously that they want their lives to end, but that may come into conflict with the autonomous decisions of others. Remember that according to the definition being used in this chapter, euthanasia always involves (at least) *two* persons. One person's autonomous decision to have his or her life ended may conflict with another person's autonomous decision not to participate in that sort of event. Furthermore, a decision to engage in euthanasia seldom involves only the persons who are directly associated with the particular event of this one death. Typically, euthanasia has broader social effects. So even if one's decision to end one's life is autonomous, the acting out of that decision will inevitably affect others, and that, too, must be taken into account.

Quality of life   Another argument relevant to this discussion depends upon the value assigned to quality of life. This argument holds that it is not *life as such* that is good, but rather *a certain form of life*. Most Americans do not concern themselves with life as such; for example, they are perfectly willing to kill bacteria, viruses, pesky mosquitoes, and so forth. Rather, this argument maintains that we are properly concerned primarily with particular forms of life. To be specific, some urge that human beings ought to be especially concerned with *human* life.

In this argument, it becomes compelling to clarify what counts as human life. Some people today suggest that life in a comatose state is inhuman or undignified and is therefore not worth living. Others have argued that certain levels of physical pain or disability are so inhuman that death is preferable. Examples of such situations are usually taken from very advanced and progressively debilitating diseases such as muscular dystrophy or Lou Gehrig's disease (amyotrophic lateral sclerosis), where individuals may be mentally alert but physically unable to say or do anything for themselves. Similarly, persons with certain forms of mental impairment, such as advanced stages of Alzheimer's disease or the condition of those who are in a "persistent vegetative state," also are sometimes used as examples of those whose quality of life is so low that death is preferable. It is situations like these that may lead someone to say, at one time or another, "I wouldn't want to live like that," when that person is thinking of some particular form of life as repulsive.

This argument depends upon asserting that some form of life is so disvalued that it is less valuable than death. Widespread agreement about this is unlikely. For example, a powerful videotape ("Please Let Me Die," 1974; compare Kliever, 1989; Platt, 1975; White & Engelhardt, 1975) depicts a young man who was burned over 67 percent of his body and was subjected to excruciatingly painful baths each day to prevent infection. The young man requested that his treatments be discontinued and that he be allowed to die. Some might argue that the young man had a great deal to learn about the value of suffering; others have insisted that he was clearly competent and should have had the right to reject unwanted and painful interventions. Clearly, what one person counts as unbearable, someone else may not.

Summing Up These Arguments

This section has examined arguments for and against the moral acceptability of euthanasia. As is often the case in moral dilemmas, most people can see the reasonableness—and the difficulty—of each of these arguments. The conclusions that any particular individual or society as a whole reaches on this issue will have something to do with the *priority* given to the associated values and how they are applied in particular circumstances (Arras, 1984; Brody, 1988). Is quality of life more important than life itself? Is life more important than autonomy? Is pain more of a disvalue than death? Each individual is likely to rank these in his or her own way, and each person may rank them differently in different particular circumstances.

Euthanasia is not an easy problem for most people to resolve. Perhaps it is wisest to recognize this truth about the inherent difficulty of the moral dilemmas involved in euthanasia and so to be wary of those who offer all-too-easy solutions. Also, perhaps it would be desirable to think about one's own values *before* one might be confronted with such dilemmas in one's own life.

Individual Decisions and Societal Policy: Recent Examples and Future Prospects

In the future, euthanasia is likely to become a more (not less) pressing question in American society. That will be true both for individual decision makers and for society as a whole (especially in terms of public practices and policies). The difficulties to be confronted are evident in examples from the recent past and some thoughts about the immediate future.

Karen Ann Quinlan

On the evening of April 14, 1975, a 21–year-old woman named Karen Ann Quinlan went to a party with some friends (Colen, 1976; Quinlan, Quinlan, & Battelle, 1977). The precise events that took place are unclear, although they appear to have involved the ingestion of alcohol (gin and tonic) and tranquilizers (such as Valium and Librium). In any event, Karen passed out and was taken to her home by her friends. Feeling some anxiety about her condition, the friends returned and took her to a local hospital. Efforts at resuscitation failed and by the next morning Karen had slipped into a comatose state, supported by liquid feeding through a nasogastric tube and by a respirator to assist her breathing.

Karen never regained consciousness, although she displayed faint signs of residual electrical activity in her upper brain and occasional blinking of her eyelids. After three months, with no prospect of recovery and with the advice of their parish priest, Karen's adoptive parents, Joseph and Julia Quinlan, asked her doctors to remove her from the respirator, which they had come to regard as noncurative and an extraordinary means of support. The physicians refused. The Quinlans then applied to state courts in New Jersey to appoint her father as her guardian for the purpose of removing her from the respirator. The superior court rejected their request, saying: "There is no constitutional right to die that can be asserted by a parent for his incompetent child."

Many points of view were heard during the debates between lawyers representing Karen, the Quinlans, her physicians, the nursing home, and the state. It was generally agreed that she was in a persistent vegetative state from which she could not be expected to recover. Eventually, the New Jersey Supreme Court ruled in March of 1976 in favor of the Quinlans' petition, with the proviso that an institutional ethics committee must examine Karen's situation and also agree. In its unanimous vote, the court said: "No compelling interest of the state could compel Karen to endure the unendurable." The basis for the ruling was Karen's right to privacy—that is, she had a right to be left alone unless those offering an intervention could forecast some expectation that cure might result. An ethics committee was established and it did agree with the Quinlans' petition.

By the time she was removed from the respirator on May 22, 1976, Karen had lost nearly half of her body weight and was curled into a rigid fetal position in a state-owned nursing home in New Jersey. But she did not die until June 11, 1985. Intravenous feeding was maintained throughout this long period, and her parents visited her frequently and regularly until her death.

Euthanasia Practices in the Netherlands and Proposed Policy in Washington State

In the Netherlands euthanasia is technically illegal when it is understood as the active termination by a physician of a patient's life at his or her request (De Wachter, 1989, 1992). However, physicians who engage in such practices in the Netherlands have not been subject to criminal sanctions since 1985 (Gomez, 1991; Van der Maas, Van Delden, Pijnenborg, & Looman, 1991).

According to De Wachter (1992), three conditions are considered to be essential in the Dutch situation: (1) voluntariness—that is, "the patient's request must be persistent, conscious, and freely made" (p. 23); (2) unbearable suffering, including (but not limited to) physical pain that cannot be relieved by any other means in a patient whose condition is considered to be beyond recovery or amelioration; and (3) consultation, whereby "the attending physician must consult with a colleague regarding the patient's condition and the genuineness and appropriateness of the request for euthanasia" (p. 23).

In 1991, a proposal was offered in a legislative referendum (initiative 119) in the state of Washington to legalize practices similar to those in the Netherlands (Carson, 1992). The initiative failed, but the proposal is significant for what might happen in the future. It sought to establish a legal right to "death with dignity" or "physician aid-in-dying," understood as "voluntary active euthanasia." The aid in question was to have been provided by physicians who would end the lives of competent, terminally ill adults who requested that their lives be terminated. The initiative would have applied to patients with as long as six months to live and to individuals in irreversible comas or persistent vegetative states.

The main themes of practices in the Netherlands and the campaign on behalf of the Washington State initiative are quality in living and personal choice. Opponents generally describe such practices and policies as rife with danger and not possessed of adequate safeguards. One commentator (Callahan, 1992) has suggested that such practices and policies are not sound and are improperly founded on an overemphasis on self-determination.

Prospects for the Future

As medical technology advances, it is likely that more and more people will find themselves in situations wherein they seriously question the quality of life offered by continued medical interventions, either for themselves or for others about whom they care. And health care providers may find themselves in situations in which those for whom they are caring ask for assistance in ending their lives. Especially difficult challenges are likely to appear in cases involving individuals who are not competent (such as infants, children, the mentally ill, and those in an irreversible coma or persistent vegetative state) and when the issues involve removal not just of external support (for example, a respirator), but also of artificially assisted nutrition and hydration (Lynn, 1986).

In addition, it is also likely that issues related to euthanasia will be presented to society, either when some individuals seek to have their views prevail over others in individual situations (as in the cases of Karen Quinlan and Nancy Cruzan) or when efforts are made to legitimize widespread practice in some form of public policy (as in the cases of the Netherlands and the Washington State initiative).

Whether or not American society adopts policies or practices that favor voluntary active euthanasia, decisions about euthanasia *will* be made in individual circumstances (Gorovitz, 1991). That is, individuals will decide whether to help to end the life of another. These decisions cannot be evaded. This means, also, that *someone* will decide. Some are most concerned about this latter point—*who* will or ought to decide whether euthanasia is to be provided. It has seemed to many that the *grounds* for making moral decisions are the most fundamental matter, but certainly the question of identifying appropriate decision makers is also significant.

Summary

This chapter has surveyed some of the issues involved in achieving a good death in American society. It has especially emphasized the moral dilemmas that must be faced in decision making related to the topic of euthanasia. Special attention has been paid to concepts and distinctions that are often employed to explain the meaning of euthanasia, to values and principles that are frequently introduced to argue for or against instances of euthanasia, and to implications for individual decisions and social policy. The primary concern of this discussion has been to help individuals think about this subject before they are forced to confront it in their own lives. No effort has been made to advocate a particular view of euthanasia.

QUESTIONS FOR REVIEW AND DISCUSSION

1. This chapter suggested that human beings put value on such things as freedom, privacy, persons, religious traditions, life, self-respect, justice, and a good life. Which of these are most important to you? Why? Which of these would you be willing to sacrifice in order to preserve some other more

important value(s)? Why? Relate your responses to these questions to the issue of deciding whether to allow someone who is incurably ill to die.

2. This chapter offered a definition of euthanasia that would clearly distinguish euthanasia from suicide or homicide. What value is there in making such distinctions? What practical consequences might result from failing to make such distinctions?

3. Would you be willing to assist someone who was thinking about ending his or her life if (a) that person was not terminally ill (that is any disease condition that the person had would not cause his or her death), (b) that person was suffering great emotional distress, and (c) that person was in great pain that could not be relieved? Why do you respond as you do to these questions? What are the values that you hold that lead you to these responses?

4. This chapter offered several arguments used to support the moral appropriateness of euthanasia, and several arguments used against its moral appropriateness. Which of these arguments do you find most compelling? Which are least persuasive to you?

5. Would you support a law allowing physicians to assist in ending someone's life if that person requested such assistance? Why or why not?

SUGGESTED READINGS

General works concerning ethical issues in death and dying include the following:

Beauchamp, T., & Perlin, S. (1978). *Ethical Issues in Death and Dying.*
Brody, B. (1988). *Life and Death Decision Making.*
Gorovitz, S. (1991). *Drawing the Line: Life, Death, and Ethical Choices in an American Hospital.*
Kluge, E-H. W. (1975). *The Practice of Death.*
Ladd, J. (1979). *Ethical Issues Relating to Life and Death.*
Pojman, L. P. (1992). *Life and Death: Grappling with the Moral Dilemmas of Our Time.*
Reich, W. (Ed.). (1978). *Encyclopedia of Bioethics* (4 vols.).
Veatch, R. M. (1976). *Death, Dying, and the Biological Revolution: Our Last Quest for Responsibility.*

Resources that are specifically concerned with issues of euthanasia include the following:

Baird, R. M., & Rosenbaum, S. E. (Ed.). (1989). *Euthanasia: The Moral Issues.*
Behnke, J., & Bok, S. (Eds.). (1975). *The Dilemmas of Euthanasia.*
Downing, A. B. (Ed.). (1974). *Euthanasia and the Right to Death: The Case for Voluntary Euthanasia.*
Gomez, C. F. (1991). *Regulating Death: Euthanasia and the Case of the Netherlands.*
Kliever, L. D. (Ed.). (1989). *Dax's Case: Essays in Medical Ethics and Human Meaning.*

CHAPTER 17

Suicide and Life-Threatening Behavior

For many people, behavior that puts one's life at risk or that appears to involve a deliberate intention to end one's life is puzzling. Such behavior seems to challenge values that are widely held, although perhaps not often or not effectively articulated by many. The motivations or intentions behind suicidal behavior appear enigmatic or incomprehensible. Perhaps for that reason, when a death occurs by suicide there is often a desperate search for a note, an explanation, or some elusive meaning that must have been involved in the act. But perhaps there is no single explanation or meaning in all of the individuality and complexities that typify suicidal and life-threatening behavior. As Alvarez (1970, p. xiv) has written: "Suicide means different things to different people at different times." And that may be the most tantalizing aspect of it all.

This chapter explores the subject of suicide in a series of sections that, in effect, respond to the following questions: What is suicide? How (if at all) can one explain suicidal behavior? Or, more precisely, what sorts of factors might enter into an effort to understand such behavior? What are the demographic data about suicide in contemporary American society? What impact does suicide have upon survivors? And what sorts of interventions can individuals and social groups undertake to prevent or at least to minimize suicidal behavior? The suicides of two well-known writers are briefly considered in order to introduce these issues.

Two Completed Suicides

Ernest Hemingway

At the time of his death on July 1, 1961, Ernest Hemingway was 62 years old and an extremely successful journalist, writer of short stories, and novelist. Perhaps best known for his longer works of fiction, such as *The Sun Also Rises* (1926), *A Farewell to Arms* (1929), and *For Whom the Bell Tolls* (1940), Hemingway won the Pulitzer Prize for his novella *The Old Man and the Sea* (1952), and two years later he was awarded the Nobel Prize for literature. The image that he presented to the public was that of a writer, hunter, and sportsman characterized by courage and stoicism—the classic macho male. In his private life, Hemingway was subject to severe depression and paranoia, like his father. In the end (also like his father), he committed suicide, using a shotgun to blow away the upper half of his head (Lynn, 1987). This is a notoriously deliberate, lethal, and effective means of committing suicide. Perhaps it was foreshadowed in the words of a character in *For Whom the Bell Tolls* (1940, p. 468), who said, "Dying is only bad when it takes a long time and hurts so much that it humiliates you."

Sylvia Plath

Sylvia Plath (1932–1963) was an American poet and novelist, perhaps best known for her novel *The Bell Jar* (1971), which was first published in England

*Ernest
Hemingway
(1899–1961).*

under an assumed name in January of 1963, just a month before her death. This book has a strongly autobiographical quality in its description of a woman caught up in a severe crisis who attempts suicide. Like the author's poetry, *The Bell Jar* emphasizes conflicts that result from family tensions and rebellion against the constricting forces of society.

The death of Plath's father when she was 8 years old was an extremely significant event in her life, as was what Alvarez (1970, p. 7) called her "desperately serious suicide attempt" in 1953 (in which she used stolen sleeping pills, left a misleading note to cover her tracks, and hid behind firewood in a dark, unused corner of a cellar). Also, Plath survived a serious car wreck during the summer of 1962, in which she apparently ran off the road deliberately. In one of her own very penetrating poems, Plath (1964) seems to describe these events in the following way:

Sylvia Plath
(1932–1963).

I have done it again.
One year in every ten
I manage it—

A sort of walking miracle . . .
I am only thirty.
And like the cat I have nine times to die.

This is Number Three. . . .

Plath separated from her husband—the British poet Ted Hughes, whom she had married in June 1956—and moved from Devon to London with her two children (Freda and Nicholas) in December of 1962. Early on the morning of February 11, 1963, Plath died.

In the days before her death, Plath's friends and her doctor had been quite concerned about her mental state. Her doctor had prescribed sedatives and had tried to arrange an appointment for her with a psychotherapist. But Plath convinced them that she had improved and could return to her apartment to stay alone with her children during the night of February 10–11. That winter was the coldest in Britain since 1813–14. But a new Australian *au pair* girl was due to arrive at 9:00 A.M. on the morning of Monday, February 11, to help with the children and housework, so that Plath could get on with her writing.

When the *au pair* girl arrived and could raise no response at the door of the building, she went to search for a telephone. No telephone had yet been installed in Plath's apartment, but the girl wanted to call the agency that employed her in order to confirm that she had the right address. After returning and trying the door again, and then calling her employer a second time, the girl came back to the house at about 11:00 A.M. and was finally able to get into the building with the aid of some workmen. Smelling gas, they forced the door of the apartment and found Plath's body still warm, together with a note asking that her doctor be called and giving his telephone number. The children were asleep in an upstairs room, wrapped snugly in blankets and furnished with a plate of bread and butter and mugs of milk in case they should wake up hungry before the *au pair* girl arrived—but their bedroom window was wide open to protect them from the effects of the gas.

Apparently, about 6:00 A.M. Plath had arranged the children and the note about calling her doctor, sealed herself in the kitchen with towels around the door and window, placed her head in the oven, and turned on the gas (Stevenson, 1989). A deaf neighbor downstairs slept without his hearing aid, but was also knocked out by seeping gas and thus was not awake to let the *au pair* girl into the building when she arrived.

Alvarez (1970, p. 34) had this to say about Plath's death: "I am convinced by what I know of the facts that this time she did not intend to die."

What Is Suicide?

There is no completely satisfactory, single definition of suicide (McIntosh, 1985b). The *Oxford Universal Dictionary* (Simpson & Weiner, 1989, Vol. 17, pp. 144–145) traces the word *suicide* back to Latin roots (*suicidium*). That word literally means "of oneself" (*sui*) + "killing" (*cidium*) or "killing of oneself." Thus, this dictionary defines suicide as "the or an act of taking one's own life, self-murder." By contrast, the *Random House Dictionary* (1987, p. 1902) defines suicide as "the intentional taking of one's own life." The differences between these two dictionary definitions reveal some of the problems involved in investigating and understanding suicide.

"An act of taking one's own life" is quite vague. It seems to include the instance of someone who plays (and loses) Russian roulette by pulling the trigger on a revolver that has only one loaded chamber, while pressing the barrel of the gun to his or her head. This is an *act*. Also, if the one chamber containing a bullet is struck by the hammer, one may very well end up taking one's own life. According to the *Oxford Universal Dictionary*, then, we would have to say this person committed suicide.

But is that true? If the person playing this dangerous game truly believed that luck was on his or her side and held no belief that death would result from these actions, many of us would be unclear whether or not this really was an instance of suicide.

What is lacking in the first definition, then, is the notion of intention. That is, for many people, an act that *accidentally* or *unintentionally* results in "taking one's own life" (that is, merely acting in such a way that one ends up dead) does not count as a suicide. The *Random House Dictionary* definition may thus appear to get closer to the usual meaning of suicide, since it indicates that an act of suicide must include a particular intention.

One might assume that suicidal behavior involves the intention to end up dead. If so, one might form a definition that reads like this: "Suicide is an act—motivated by the intention to end up dead—that results in the death of the agent."

But years of study by suicidologists suggest that this definition also does not always successfully describe suicide. Suicide often turns out to involve a peculiarly ambiguous and ambivalent sort of behavior. In the first place, the intentions of those who engage in suicidal behavior are varied. Not every such action involves a specific intention. Also, the intentions that any individual has for many of his or her actions are unknown to others, and even often to the person in question. So if suicide is to be defined (and thus recognized) in terms of particular intentions, one will often end up uncertain about whether a particular act is a suicide.

Moreover, it is not clear, in fact, that any *action* needs to be involved in suicide. Some suicidologists have argued that people who *refrain* from certain sorts of action (for example, those who fail to take their insulin, or who fail to give up smoking even in the face of developing respiratory symptoms) are actually also engaging in suicidal action.

Uncertainty about just what constitutes suicide has important consequences for anyone studying this subject. First, if one thinks of or defines suicide too narrowly, one may fail to include certain examples of this sort of behavior. This can complicate already existing problems. For example, statistical data on the number of deaths that are the result of suicidal behavior will at best be inaccurate (Evans & Farberow, 1988).

But of course, data concerning suicide may also be inaccurate for other reasons. For example, since suicide often carries a high degree of social stigma, family members and others concerned about their welfare may resist attempts to label a particular death as a suicide. In other words, even when the definition of suicide is clear, there might be questions concerning its application in particular situations. Thus, sociologists have suggested that the number of deaths due to suicide might be at least twice the number actually recorded (Neuringer, 1962; O'Carroll, 1989). If this is the case, the impact of suicide on individual lives and on society may be seriously misunderstood.

Second, when one is uncertain about just what suicide is, one may fail to recognize suicidal behavior when confronted by it. For instance, if one believes that suicide always involves the intention to end up dead, one may pay less attention to someone who does not express or even denies such an intention. Thus, certain forms of life-threatening behavior are sometimes discounted on the grounds that they are *only* a "cry for help" (Farberow & Shneidman, 1965). But even a cry for help can have lethal consequences.

Third, the lack of clarity about just what constitutes suicide makes it difficult to understand this behavior. A variety of interpretations of what is involved in suicide have been developed. Sociologists have developed sociological interpretations of suicide and psychologists have developed psychological interpretations. In each case, part of the work of these interpretations has been to try to elucidate the *causes* of (or, perhaps better, contributing factors to) suicide.

Sociological Explanations of Suicide

The best-known sociological explanation of suicide comes from a book by a French sociologist, Emile Durkheim (1897/1951; Selkin, 1983), originally published in France at the end of the 19th century. Durkheim argued that no psychological condition *by itself* invariably produces suicidal behavior. Instead, he believed that suicide can be understood as an outcome of the relationship of the individual to his or her society, with special emphasis on ways in which individuals are or are not integrated and regulated in their relationships with society. Durkheim's analysis has been criticized (for example, by Douglas, 1967; Maris, 1969), but his book remains a classic in the literature on suicide. In it, he identified three primary sorts of relationships between individuals and society as conducive to suicidal behavior, and he made brief reference to the possibility of a fourth basic type of suicide.

Egoistic Suicide

The first of these relationships may result in what Durkheim called "egoistic suicide," or suicide involving more-or-less isolated individuals. In the presence of a social group that provides some integration for the individual (especially in terms of meaning for his or her life), the risk of suicide is diminished. But when such integration is absent, loses its force, or is somehow removed (especially abruptly), suicide becomes more of a possibility. Durkheim argued for this thesis in the case of three sorts of "societies"—religious society, domestic society, and political society.

According to Durkheim, to the extent that a *religious society* has a unified, strong creed, it provides integration (meaning) for its members. To the extent that it has a weaker creed and encourages a spirit of free inquiry (thus providing fewer definitive answers for its adherents), it is a less integrated society, and thereby leaves its adherents in a less integrated (more uncertain) state. They must find their *own* meaning for their lives; in so doing, they must rely more on themselves (their own egos). When this is difficult for individuals to accomplish, they may be at greater risk for meaninglessness and suicidal behavior.

Entering into marriage or a *domestic society* also seems to be a factor that tends to reduce suicidal behavior. In addition to the fact of marriage, Durkheim noted that the more members of the family there are, the less significant the risk of suicide becomes. He accounted for this in part as follows: "In a family of small numbers, common sentiments and memories cannot be very intense; for there are not enough consciences in which they can be represented and reinforced by sharing them" (1897/1951, p. 202). Thus, a life shared intimately with others provides integration; when this sort of intimacy and its consequent integration into a meaningful pattern is not present, again the individual is forced to fall back upon his or her own ego resources.

Last, Durkheim argued that as a *political society* disintegrates, it fails to provide the integration that a strong, healthy political unit can provide. Once more, the individual loses the necessary integration into a meaning larger than just himself or herself—and, to that extent, becomes relatively more disintegrated or isolated.

Thus, whenever an individual—for whatever reason, in whatever context—is disintegrated from society, egoistic suicidal behavior can result. Such behavior typically occurs in those who are apathetic about life—that is, tired of living or bored by the world.

Altruistic Suicide

The second form of relationship between the individual and his or her society that is related to suicide involves an *over*involvement. In this situation, the ties that produce the integration between the individual and the social group are too strong. This may result in "altruistic suicide" or suicide undertaken on behalf of the group. By contrast with the apathy of egoistic suicide, altruistic suicide is characterized by energy and activity, whether one acts out of a sense of obligation or from a kind of enthusiasm leading to self-sacrifice. That is, personal identity gives way to identification with the welfare of the group and the individual finds the meaning of his or her life (completely) outside of himself or herself. For example, in some strongly integrated societies, there are contexts in which suicide may be seen as a duty. In other words, the surrender of the individual's life may be demanded on behalf of what is perceived to be the society's welfare.

Durkheim listed several examples found in various historical cultures that involve relationships of strong integration or involvement and that lead to suicidal behavior: persons who are aged or ill (the Eskimo); women whose husbands have died (the practice of *suttee* in India before the English came); servants of social chiefs who have died (many ancient societies). One might think also of persons who have failed in their civic or religious duties so as to bring shame on themselves, their families, and/or their societies—for example, the samurai warrior in Japanese society who commits ritual *seppuku* or *hara-kiri*.

Durkheim wrote: "Whereas [egoistic suicide] is due to excessive individuation, [altruistic suicide] is caused by too rudimentary individuation" (1897/ 1951, p. 221). These two sorts of suicide are related to how a society does or does not integrate its members into a community that provides meaning for their individual lives. When it fails to integrate them and throws them back onto their individual egos, then if they are unable to develop their own individual meanings for life, that may bring about a situation leading to suicide. But if a society integrates its members so fully into the tightly bound community that their individual egos are not allowed to develop enough strength even to be self-protective, that, too, can result in a situation in which suicide becomes a real possibility.

Anomic Suicide

Durkheim called the third form of suicide that he discussed "anomic suicide." This he described not in terms of integration of the individual into society but rather in terms of how the society *regulates* its members. Durkheim pointed out that all human beings need to regulate their desires (for material goods, for sexual activity, and so forth). To the extent that a society assists individuals in this regulation, it helps keep such desires under control. When a society is unable or unwilling to help its members in the regulation of their desires—for example, because the society is undergoing rapid change and its regulations are in a state of flux—a condition of anomie is the result. (The term *anomie* comes from the Greek *anomia* = *a* [without] + *nomoi* [laws or norms], and means "lawlessness" or "normlessness.")

Anomie can be conducive to suicide, especially when it thrusts an individual suddenly into what he or she perceives to be a chaotic and intolerable situation. In contemporary American society, examples of this sort of suicide might involve adolescents who have been suddenly rejected by their former peer group or middle-aged employees who have developed specialized work skills and who have devoted themselves for years to their employer only to be thrown out of their jobs and economically dislocated.

Fatalistic Suicide

A fourth type of suicide in Durkheim's schema is called "fatalistic suicide." It is only mentioned by Durkheim in a footnote in his book (1897/1951, p. 276), where it is described as the opposite of anomic suicide. That is, fatalistic suicide derives from excessive regulation of individuals by society. This might happen when one becomes a prisoner or a slave. These are the circumstances of "persons with futures pitilessly blocked and passions violently choked by oppressive discipline" (1897/1951, p. 276). Durkheim did not think that this type of suicide was very common in his own society, but it may be useful as an illustration of social forces that lead an individual to seek to escape from an overcontrolling social context.

Psychological Explanations of Suicide

Sigmund Freud introduced the best-known psychological account of suicide, the psychoanalytical theory (Litman, 1967). Freud argued that suicide is murder turned around 180 degrees. Karl Menninger (1938) provided a good, extensive account of this theory in *Man Against Himself.* Its psychological character is clear in the following statement: "Behavior is never determined only by external forces; there are impulses from within, the adjustment of which to external reality necessarily brings about stresses and strains which may be highly painful, but endurable except to a very few" (Menninger, 1938, p. 18). Menninger identified three separate psychological motives that may be associated with a suicidal act and that govern the behavior of those who are unable to adjust successfully to external reality: (1) the wish to kill, (2) the wish to be killed, and (3) the wish to die. This analysis is important because it begins to make plain the complexities and disparities within the motivations involved in suicide.

The Wish to Kill

Suicide often involves hostility, aggression, and violence. But, as Menninger argued, everyone has such impulses. These impulses are usually directed toward whatever lies outside of ourselves that thwarts us in our activity and desire. However, in some situations the directing of these destructive impulses away from ourselves cannot be accomplished and we become frustrated. Then they may be turned back upon the self. Now, one extreme way in which our destructive impulses (our hostility, aggression, and violence) can be directed is toward killing whatever is in our way. Thus, one way in which these impulses can be directed when turned back upon the self is the wish to kill one's self. This leads to a kind of displaced murder.

The Wish to Be Killed

According to Menninger, suicide also involves a wish to be killed. This is a variation not on *aggression* but on *submission*. Part of being human involves recognition of and submission to authority. Eventually, individuals take over the role of external authority (parents, teachers, and so forth) and internalize it into their consciences. With conscience comes guilt. And because (according to Freudian theories) a part of everyone's conscience is unconscious, guilt may play a role in our lives without our being aware of what it is we feel guilty about. Because we feel guilty, a part of us demands to be punished. When the crime we feel guilty about is serious enough, we may wish for a *serious* punishment. Being killed is an ultimate form of punishment. So, many suicides may exhibit the person's unconscious desire to be punished in an extreme form—that is, the wish to be killed.

What is interesting about this discussion so far is that neither of these two wishes (to kill and to be killed) obviously involves the wish to be dead. The wish to kill is a form of the impulse to act destructively. The wish to be killed is a form of the impulse to submit to authority and to be punished. In fact, there is often a curious lack of clarity in what it is a person who engages in life-threatening behavior is seeking to accomplish (Shneidman, 1980).

The Wish to Die

Menninger suggested that suicide may also involve a third wish, the wish to die. This third component may help to make an important distinction. Some suicidologists have argued that there are two classes of people who engage in suicidal behavior: attempters and completers (Dorpat & Boswell, 1973; Dorpat & Ripley, 1967; Stengel, 1964). Those who are *suicide attempters* often engage in suicide attempts more than once. In addition, they frequently choose means that are not particularly effective or lethal. Menninger (1938) discussed such cases and described them as situations in which the self-destructive impulses carrying obviously aggressive and punitive components are thwarted by a weakness of the wish to die. That is, such persons may have strong impulses toward both aggression and submission, but they have a weak (or no) impulse toward being dead. These are the situations in which the suicidal behavior looks very much like a "cry for help" or a desperate search for attention. Note that even in these cases, the attempter may miscalculate. The means chosen may turn out to be more effective than expected, and death may result.

Those who are *suicide completers* may be people in whom the third component (the wish to die) is strong enough to result in behavior actually leading to death. Such a wish seems obvious in the behavior of Ernest Hemingway; it does not seem to be as clear in the behavior of Sylvia Plath. Menninger traced this wish to what Freud called a "death instinct." Menninger was tentative about this view, and it remains a controversial part of Freudian theory. However, it does help to make sense of persons who engage in a suicidal act of high deliberateness and lethality, especially on the first attempt.

Suicide: A Multidetermined, Multivalenced Act

Durkheim argued that suicidal behavior cannot be understood solely by studying the psychology of those who engage in such behavior; Menninger agreed with this. As Menninger (1938, p. 23) wrote, "Suicide is a very complex act, and not a simple, incidental, isolated act of impulsion, either logical or inexplicable." That is, these two theorists saw the completed suicide as an outcome of *many* causes, not just one. Shneidman (1980), Douglas (1967), and others (such as Breed, 1972) also have suggested that a variety of elements may enter into suicidal behavior.

One popular way to depict this concept is to think of suicidal behavior as involving three elements: haplessness (being ill-fated or unlucky), helplessness, and hopelessness. Shneidman (1980) proposed a more precise account than this in terms of three main components and a triggering process: (1) *inimicality* or an unsettled life pattern in which one acts against one's own best interests; (2) *perturbation* or an increased psychological disturbance in the person's life; (3) *constriction*, which appears in "tunnel vision" and "either/or" thinking, and which represents a narrowing of the range of perception, opinions, and options that occur to the person's mind; and (4) the

Depression and suicidal behavior are often linked.

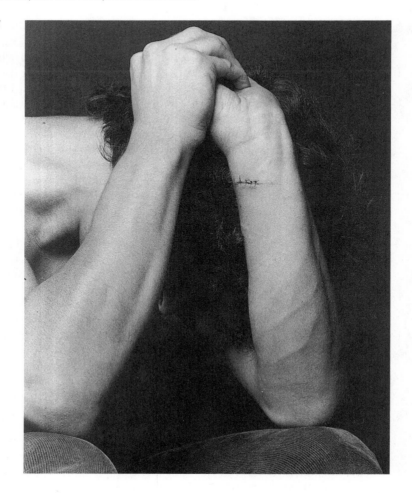

idea of *cessation*, of resolving the unbearable pain of disturbance and isolation by simply stopping or being out of it.

A still more complex effort to identify ten common characteristics of suicide has been provided by Shneidman (1985, pp. 119–149):

Situational aspects
1. The common *stimulus* in suicide is unendurable psychological *pain*.
2. The common *stressor* in suicide is frustrated psychological *needs*.

Conative aspects
3. The common *purpose* of suicide is to seek a *solution*.
4. The common *goal* of suicide is *cessation* of consciousness.

Affective aspects
5. The common *emotion* in suicide is *hopelessness-helplessness*.
6. The common *internal attitude* toward suicide is *ambivalence*.

Cognitive aspect
7. The common *cognitive state* in suicide is *constriction*.

Relational aspects

8. The common *interpersonal act* in suicide is *communication of intention.*
9. The common *action* in suicide is *egression.*

Serial aspect

10. The common *consistency* in suicide is with *lifelong coping patterns.*

On the basis of these characteristics, Shneidman (1985, p. 203) defined suicide in the following way: "Currently in the Western world, suicide is a conscious act of self-induced annihilation, best understood as a multidimensional malaise in a needful individual who defines an issue for which the suicide is perceived as the best solution."

These characterizations of suicide can lead to an important conclusion in the search for an understanding of suicidal behavior. There often is a natural impulse among students of suicidal behavior and bereaved family members to look for *the* cause of a suicide. This can perhaps best be illustrated by noting the efforts of many survivors to find a suicide note that might explain what has happened. But in fact, there usually is no such *single* cause. Suicide is most often a multidetermined and multivalenced act. It arises from a context of many sorts of causes, among which social and psychological factors are surely prominent (Lester, 1983, 1990; Maris, 1981, 1988; Maris, Berman, Maltsberger, & Yufit, 1992). In fact, the preeminent expert on suicide notes has written that "in order to commit suicide, one cannot write a meaningful suicide note; conversely, if one could write a meaningful note, one would not have to commit suicide" (Shneidman, 1980, p. 58).

*R*ational Suicide

In much of the suicidal behavior that has been discussed thus far, depression, ambivalence, and other strong feelings are central elements. For many, these are precisely the elements that justify intervention in an effort to prevent a fatal outcome arising from unsuitable foundations. There is, however, another sort of suicidal behavior in which it is maintained that the central motives are lucid, rational, and appropriate. In the words of Betty Rollin in the foreword to a book by Humphry (1991, p. 14), the issues involved are these: "The real question is, does a person have a right to depart from life when he or she is nearing the end and has nothing but horror ahead? And, if necessary, should a physician be permitted to help?" In other words, this is a view of suicide as "self-deliverance" and an argument on behalf of assisting such behavior, both of which are portrayed as responsible exercises of individual rights to self-determination in certain circumstances.

There really are three strands in this web of argumentation: (1) a claim that the right to end one's own life should be recognized in certain circumstances; (2) a claim that others should have the right to assist someone to end his or her own life in certain circumstances; and (3) a claim that one should have the right to request physician aid-in-dying—that is, to request that one's life be terminated in certain circumstances.

The first of these strands is really an assertion that the legitimate scope of individual autonomy and self-determination should include the right to end one's life. Whether or not that is so, it is certainly very difficult to prevent someone who wishes to end his or her life from doing so, if the individual is both deliberate and determined. The second strand is an effort to protect those who help others to end their lives. At the moment, in the United States it is not illegal to commit suicide, but it may be illegal in some jurisdictions to assist in such behavior, or helping may lay one open to legal charges of other sorts (such as manslaughter or conspiracy). The last strand in the argument is really a request for euthanasia and has already been addressed as such in Chapter 16.

In general, the circumstances that are most prominently mentioned as examples of situations in which "rational suicide" might be thought to be appropriate involve terminal illness and unendurable pain or suffering. It may be conceded that hospice-type care can relieve this sort of distress in most cases. But proponents argue that options for suicide should remain open for individuals whose distress cannot be relieved by care in the hospice mode as well as for individuals experiencing other forms of suffering that, in their view, render life undesirable (Humphry, 1991).

At one point, this argument was advanced by individuals like Rollin (1985), who recounted stories of great suffering in the lives of persons whom they loved, or by individuals like Roman (1980) who spoke of the importance of taking action to control the ending of their lives and of doing so before circumstances made that impossible. With the founding of organizations like the Hemlock Society in the United States and EXIT (the British Voluntary Euthanasia Society) in Great Britain, and with the publication of *Final Exit: The Practicalities of Self-Deliverance and Assisted Suicide for the Dying* (Humphry, 1991), deliberate efforts have been made to provide information to individuals who might wish to end their lives. In addition, those who wish to help in such actions are advised how to do so in ways that are least likely to render them open to adverse legal action. For example, in 1990 Jack Kevorkian, a retired physician in Michigan, began to provide a "machine" to persons who wanted to end their lives (Humphry, 1991). These persons used the equipment provided; once instructed in its use, the person did not have to have Kevorkian present or actively involved when he or she committed suicide. Much controversy remains in this area.

The Impact of Suicide

Thus far, this chapter has examined theoretical, conceptual issues focused around the idea of suicide. Next, it is useful to consider the impact of suicide, first in terms of its importance as a cause of death, and then in terms of how it affects survivors.

Dr. Jack Kevorkian and his "suicide machine."

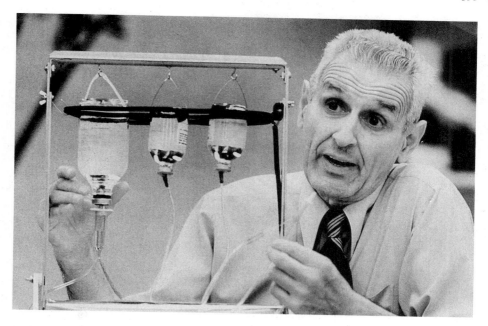

Demographic Data

To study suicide as a cause of death, one really needs to have accurate statistics. But, as suggested earlier, accurate counts of completed suicides, much less of attempted (but uncompleted) suicides, may simply not be available (Neuringer, 1962; O'Carroll, 1989). One reason for this arises from difficulties in identifying a suicide attempt, whether it is completed or not. For instance, it has been suggested that someone who has respiratory difficulties, knows the statistical evidence relating cigarette smoking to lung cancer, and who nevertheless continues to smoke is really engaging in suicidal—or, at least, life-threatening or indirectly self-destructive—behavior (Farberow, 1980). How can one determine with any precision the "count" of such persons? Similarly, if someone dies while driving an automobile that runs into a bridge abutment on a familiar road on a day when the pavement is dry and the weather is clear, and there are no skid marks, and the person had not previously been abusing alcohol or other drugs, it may not be clear whether this death was the result of an accident (Tabachnick, 1973).

Another difficulty with collecting accurate data on the number of deaths attributable to suicide is that for many personal and social reasons people are often reluctant to admit that a suicide has occurred. Police, coroners, and physicians may be unwilling to record a death as a suicide because of concern for, or pressure from, family members and friends of the deceased. Americans are often made very uncomfortable by suicide. Although suicide—along with attempted suicide—is no longer a crime in any of the 50 states, it is still regarded with moral and social revulsion by many persons. To discuss the morality of suicide would take more space than is available here. But it is certain that at least some persons believe that to take one's own life is an immoral act. Thus, one common impact of suicide involves social stigma (Goffman, 1963). That stigma may adhere to the act, the agent, the surviving family and friends, and perhaps even to the broader society as well. This will be discussed further in the next section.

For all of these reasons, the collected data about suicide must be regarded with some wariness. One of the few safe generalizations is that there are likely to be more deaths from suicide than those recorded as such. But even within an uncertain or understated body of data, certain patterns can be discerned (Allen, 1984; Diggory, 1976; Frederick, 1978). In 1990, suicide ranked as the eighth leading cause of death in the United States, accounting for 1.4 percent of all deaths that year or a total of 30,906 deaths (National Center for Health Statistics, 1993).

If one compares data from the United States with data from other countries, one finds that many other nations have much higher suicide rates. For example, Hungary, Denmark, Finland, and Austria all have suicide rates at least twice as high as those for the United States. Of course, this ought not to make Americans complacent. If each individual who died by suicide in 1990 had just ten close family members or friends (a very conservative estimate), more than 309,000 people in the United States were directly affected by suicide in 1990. In addition, it is estimated that ten suicides are attempted for every suicide that is completed. Clearly, suicide is an important social reality.

In 1990, the highest rate of completed suicides (24.9 per 100,000) in the United States occurred among persons in the 75- to 84-year-old age group, followed closely (22.2 per 100,000) by the group that is 85 and older (National Center for Health Statistics, 1993). Because the population is aging in the United States, and because suicide is a problem of great statistical significance among the aged, suicide may become an even more pressing problem in this society in the near future (Osgood, 1985). It is also clear that suicide is statistically more significant among Americans of European descent than among those of African descent, and it is more prevalent in some Native American populations than in other non-Anglo groups (McIntosh, 1989b; McIntosh & Santos, 1982).

In terms of gender, completed suicides are more prevalent (by a ratio of approximately 3:1) among American males than among females, even though females attempt suicide approximately three times more frequently than males (Ellis & Range, 1989; Wilson, 1981). Some of this has to do with the tendency of males to select more lethal—and often more disfiguring—means of attempting suicide (Card, 1974; Lester & Beck, 1981).

Suicide is the third leading cause of death (behind accidents and homicide) among persons 15–24 years of age—that is, in the group composed of older adolescents and young adults (National Center for Health Statistics, 1993). For individuals in the 15- to 19-year-old age group, suicide is the second leading cause of death. In addition, although many may find this surprising, suicide can be listed as a cause of death for children and adolescents under the age of 15 (Orbach, 1988; Pfeffer, 1986). Clearly, suicide can become a reality in nearly any age group, although some age groups are more vulnerable than others. Many (for example, Peck, Farberow, & Litman, 1985) have been especially concerned with the rapid increase in recent years in rates of suicide among adolescents and young adults, whereas others (such as, Stillion, McDowell, & May, 1989) have sought to show how patterns of suicidal behavior differ in important ways across the life cycle.

In any case, the data make plain that suicide has a large impact on American society. Many lives are lost to this form of death each year. And this form of death seems peculiarly tragic, since it is often felt that a life lost to suicide was an unnecessary loss.

Survivors

Someone who completes a suicide never dies alone. Survivors of the person who has died from suicide almost always have a difficult time dealing with that death. Many deaths leave survivors struggling with complex feelings: anger, sadness, and guilt almost always play some role in mourning. But with suicide these feelings may be increased in intensity (Cain, 1972; Dunne, McIntosh, & Dunne-Maxim, 1987; Wallace, 1973). Stone (1972) studied suicide and nonsuicide survivors. He found, perhaps not unexpectedly, that the spouses of individuals who had completed suicide had a more difficult mourning; suicide survivors had more physical complaints; suicide survivors had more thoughts of suicide themselves; and the spouses of individuals who had completed suicide experienced more anger toward the spouse who had died. Lum (1974, pp. 147–148) listed the following problems associated with surviving the suicide of someone who was loved: "a marred memory of the deceased person, the social taboo of suicide, the implication of insanity, the potential acting-out of further suicidal and self-destructive impulses among family members, unresolved grief, social isolation and withdrawal, and the effect upon children."

These factors can be grouped into two general sets of variables that help to make the mourning of the survivors of a suicide difficult. One set could be called *external* factors. These are related to the responses of society to a suicide. For instance, the initial persons who deal with a death by suicide and with the survivors of that death are likely to be law enforcement personnel. Since it is their job to determine just what happened and to be alert for possible acts of homicide, the period of investigation can include direct accusations or indirect suggestions that survivors might somehow have taken part in the death. For example, the question may be: Was this a suicide or a murder? Once past this initial phase, society's responses may continue to add to the implication of guilt on the part of the survivors. Others may imply that the family members (or friends, or associates—the field of possibly guilty persons may be large) could have contributed to the motivation for the act, or at least might not have done something that could have prevented the act. All of this loads on external sources of guilt.

There also are *internal* factors that may aggravate bereavement following a death by suicide. Most persons close to the dead person will question themselves about their possible responsibility for the death. What did I say or do that might have contributed to this tragic outcome? What was it that I did not say or do that might have helped? Why couldn't I see or realize what he (or she) was planning to do? The potential questions are many. A completed suicide is a self-clarifying act that may, in retrospect, alter our view of events that transpired prior to the event. Nevertheless, questions of this sort are usually unanswerable. The time before the death can no longer be relived after the death.

One way to deal with the guilt arising in this context is to direct it outward. For example, Resnik (1972) recorded an instance in which a father thought about suing the persons who owned a building from which his daughter had jumped to her death. A more frequent way of dealing with the guilt is not to discuss the death at all. The survivors may simply not communicate with anyone about the death, attempting to wall themselves off from the event, from those who refer to it, and from the very great pain that they associate with it. Since suicide makes many members of society uncomfortable, others may be content with this sort of self-isolation on the part of survivors and may thus encourage it.

Denial, too, is a frequently encountered response. "He was drunk at the time and did not realize the gun was loaded." Such denial may prevent a working through of the feelings associated with the death. In fact, the mourning of survivors of suicide is often inadequately handled. This is in part due to their isolating of themselves, as well as to society's withdrawal from them. So Lindemann and Greer (1972, p. 67) wrote: "The survivors of a suicide are likely to get 'stuck' in their grieving and to go on for years in a state of cold isolation, unable to feel close to others and carrying always with them the feeling that they are set apart or under the threat of doom."

But as seen earlier, mourning is a process in which people need a support system. If one is to cope adequately with mourning a suicide, communication, or at least the nonjudgmental presence of others, can be helpful (Bolton, 1989; Chance, 1992).

Many persons have noted that the rate of suicide attempts—whether or not they lead to the completion of the act in the form of death—is high among suicide survivors. Although there is little evidence to support the view that "suicidal tendencies" can be inherited, there is evidence to show that survivors often find themselves thinking about suicide and identifying with the action of the person who committed suicide (Cain, 1972). This implies that suicide, like other coping strategies, is essentially learned behavior that may be influenced by conduct that one has observed in others (Frederick & Resnik, 1971). This may help to explain so-called "copycat behavior" or "cluster suicides" that sometimes appear to be triggered by media reports and efforts to model the behavior of others (Coleman, 1987).

All of this suggests that there is an important need for support by friends and family members of those who survive the death by suicide of a loved person. Suggestions concerning ways in which to help the bereaved apply here, except that in cases of suicide, human presence and good will are often even more needed.

Suicide Intervention

This section focuses attention on suicide prevention. But because one cannot really prevent very determined acts of suicide, it is better to speak here of intervention on behalf of reducing the likelihood of a completed suicide

(Shneidman, 1971). Many programs have been developed throughout the United States and in other countries to work toward this goal. They are usually described as programs of crisis intervention. Such programs minister to the needs of persons who feel themselves to be in crisis or who sense a propensity toward suicide. Over decades of work, much has been learned about how many persons of this sort behave. In turn, much has been learned about how others can assist such people—that is, about how to intervene constructively in cases of suicidal or life-threatening behavior (Seiden, 1977).

First of all, mistaken impressions about suicidal behavior must be confronted. For instance, many people believe that suicidal persons do not talk about their intentions, that suicide is the result of a sudden impulse, and that mentioning suicide to someone who is emotionally upset may make a suggestion to that person that he or she had not previously entertained. These are all erroneous beliefs (Maris, 1981).

People who are thinking about killing themselves most often *do* talk about this. One estimate claims that 80 percent of persons who are inclined toward suicide communicate their plans to family members, friends, authority figures (such as physicians or clergy), or telephone intervention programs (Hewett, 1980, p. 23).

Suicide seldom occurs without warning. It is not an action that erupts from nowhere. It is often thought out well in advance and planned for. Frequently, a suicidal person gives many clues about his or her intentions. These clues may or may not be verbal. They might include giving away beloved objects, making changes in eating or sleeping habits, or even displaying a sense of calmness after a period of agitation (calmness because a *decision* has finally been made as to what to do).

Asking someone if he or she is thinking about attempting suicide is *not* planting an idea that would otherwise not have occurred to the person. Individuals who are depressed (and suicide is highly correlated with depression), or who are severely agitated, most likely have already thought about killing themselves. In fact, many suicidologists believe that almost all human beings think about the possibility of suicide at one time or another. Thus, suicide is not an infrequently encountered idea. If the person is thinking about suicide, and if someone else is to intervene in helpful and productive ways, it is important to know what the first person is thinking. The simplest way to discover this, if the person does not volunteer it, is to ask.

Once suicidal intentions are noticed, several different actions can be taken to intervene (Hatton & Valente, 1984). To begin with, one should note that many suicidal intentions are not long lasting. A primary goal may be to get the person past a relatively short-term crisis period. That is one basic strategy employed by all crisis intervention programs.

As has often been the case in earlier discussions about how to help persons in crisis, a principal recommendation in helping suicidal persons is to listen. Paying attention to and being present to someone who is suffering is a first, essential step toward helping that person. Others really must hear the feelings being expressed in order to try to understand what is needed by this person. Part of the listening involved in this case is to hear suicidal remarks for

Facts and Fables About Suicide

These statements are NOT true	These statements ARE true
Fable: People who talk about suicide don't commit suicide.	*Fact:* Of any ten persons who kill themselves, eight have given definite warnings of their suicidal intentions. Suicide threats and attempts *must* be taken seriously.
Fable: Suicide happens without warning.	*Fact:* Studies reveal that the suicidal person gives many clues and warnings regarding his or her suicidal intentions. Alertness to these cries for help may prevent suicidal behavior.
Fable: Suicidal people are fully intent on dying.	*Fact:* Most suicidal people are undecided about living or dying, and they "gamble with death," leaving it to others to save them. Almost no one commits suicide without letting others know how he or she is feeling. Often this "cry for help" is given in "code." These distress signals can be used to save lives.
Fable: Once a person is suicidal, he or she is suicidal forever.	*Fact:* Happily, individuals who wish to kill themselves are "suicidal" only for a limited period of time. If they are saved from self-destruction, they can go on to lead useful lives.
Fable: Improvement following a suicidal crisis means that the suicide risk is over.	*Fact:* Most suicides occur within about three months following the beginning of "improvement," when the individual has the energy to put his morbid thoughts and feelings into effect. Relatives and physicians should be especially vigilant during this period.
Fable: Suicide strikes more often among the rich—or, conversely, it occurs more	*Fact:* Suicide is neither the rich man's disease nor the poor man's curse. Suicide is very "democratic" and is represented

(continued)

(continued)

frequently among the poor.	proportionately among all levels of society.
Fable: Suicide is inherited or "runs in a family."	*Fact:* Suicide does *not* run in families. It is an individual matter and can be prevented.
Fable: All suicidal individuals are mentally ill, and suicide always is the act of a psychotic person.	*Fact:* Studies of hundreds of genuine suicide notes indicate that although the suicidal person is extremely unhappy, he or she is not necessarily mentally ill. His or her overpowering unhappiness may result from a temporary emotional upset, a long and painful illness, or a complete loss of hope. It is circular reasoning to say that "suicide is an insane act," and therefore all suicidal people are psychotic.

SOURCE From Shneidman & Farberow, "Some Facts About Suicide" (1961).

what they are and to recognize the several levels or dimensions that each remark may contain. Most crisis intervention workers insist that *every* suicidal remark must be taken seriously.

Once such a remark is heard, the actual intentions and plans should be evaluated. The more the person has thought about suicide, and the more he or she has worked out actual plans for suicide, the more seriously must the remarks be taken. A remark like "Sometimes I just feel like killing myself" with no follow-up is less serious than remarks that indicate someone's having thought out when and how he or she intends to accomplish the act.

In general, changes in affect are significant. If someone has been depressed but now seems suddenly much lighter in emotional tone, this is not necessarily a time for reduced concern (Farberow, 1983). Suicidal actions actually increase when people are coming out of depression. In such circumstances, they may finally have the requisite energy to act. Similarly, a change toward agitation can signal a crisis.

In listening, attention must be paid to what the person says. This usually means that one should not engage in the process of evaluating in a judgmental way (from one's own point of view) what the person believes or feels. What looks like a problem from the suicidal person's point of view *is* a problem for that person. Telling such individuals that their problems are insignificant is not likely to be of much help. It is more likely to sound as though we are not really hearing them or are unwilling to appreciate the magnitude of the problems that they believe themselves to be facing. Not surprisingly, they may then turn away from us.

For many suicidal persons, there is a narrowing of focus on possibilities for resolving the crisis. Some suicidologists call this "tunnel vision." A person with tunnel vision perceives a very narrow range of possible solutions: one of the few solutions that seem to be available may be suicide itself. One way to help is to point out other, constructive options for resolving the crisis. One such option is to draw on inner resources; another is to turn to external resources available in the community that will help with the crisis (whether it is emotional, physical, financial, or whatever).

Finally, specific action is called for. Getting some particular agreement ("Will you agree *not* to do anything until I get there?" or "Will you go with me to talk to a counselor?" or "Will you promise not to commit suicide until after you next see your therapist?") can be helpful. It is also usually important not to let the person be alone nor to have access to the means intended to be used to commit suicide.

If we accept the ten-point characterization of suicidal behavior formulated by Shneidman (1985) and listed earlier, then much of what has been said here about intervention can be summed up by Shneidman's corresponding list of practical measures for helping suicidal persons (1985, pp. 231–232):

1. *Stimulus (unbearable pain):* Reduce the pain.
2. *Stressor (frustrated needs):* Fill the frustrated needs.
3. *Purpose (to seek a solution):* Provide a viable answer.
4. *Goal (cessation of consciousness):* Indicate alternatives.
5. *Emotion (hopelessness-helplessness):* Give transfusions of hope.
6. *Internal attitude (ambivalence):* Play for time.
7. *Cognitive state (constriction):* Increase the options.
8. *Interpersonal act (communication of intention):* Listen to the cry, involve others.
9. *Action (egression):* Block the exit.
10. *Consistency (with lifelong patterns):* Invoke previous positive patterns of successful coping.

One last word: some crisis intervention workers have pointed out that in the end no one can really take responsibility for someone else's life. If a person is seriously determined to end his or her life, someone else cannot ordinarily prevent that, short of essentially "jailing" him or her. Although guilt is a frequently encountered response to suicide, suicide is finally an action over which others have little control. It is an option for human beings.

Summary

This chapter has explored some of the many dimensions and implications of suicide and life-threatening behavior. Its focus has been on clarifying the concept of suicide and emphasizing the many elements that may enter into a completed suicide. Social and psychological factors of various sorts that contribute to explanations of suicidal behavior have been examined. In addition, this chapter has considered what suicidal behavior means both for protagonists (those who attempt or complete a suicide) and for survivors. Finally, attention has also been given to interventions that individuals and society might initiate to minimize suicidal behavior.

QUESTIONS FOR REVIEW AND DISCUSSION

1. This chapter began with two examples of individuals who took their own lives: Ernest Hemingway and Sylvia Plath. Using what you have learned about suicide, what similarities and differences do you see in these two actions?

2. Why are statistical data on suicide unreliable? Why is it important to have reliable data about suicide?

3. Have you ever thought about ending your life? Has anyone you know and care about thought about ending his or her life? What sorts of factors contributed to such thoughts? What was going on in your life (or in the other person's life) that led to such thoughts? How did you (or the other person) get past that point? What might you (or someone else) have done to help a person with such thoughts get past that point?

4. Have you ever known someone who ended his or her life by suicide? What was your response to that action? Think about how other people reacted to that action. How were these responses like what we learned about grief and mourning in Chapter 8? How were they different?

SUGGESTED READINGS

The following are introductions to the subject of suicide:

Evans, G., & Farberow, N. L. (Eds.). (1988). *The Encyclopedia of Suicide.*
Farberow, N. L., & Shneidman, E. S. (Eds.). (1965). *The Cry for Help.*
Hatton, C. L., & Valente, S. M. (Eds.). (1984). *Suicide: Assessment and Intervention* (2nd ed.).
Leenaars, A. A., & Wenckstern, S. (Eds.). (1991). *Suicide Prevention in the Schools.*
Lester, D. (1983). *Why People Kill Themselves* (2nd ed.).
Lester, D. (1990). *Understanding and Preventing Suicide: New Perspectives.*
Maris, R. W. (1981). *Pathways to Suicide: A Survey of Self-Destructive Behaviors.*
Maris, R. W. (Ed.). (1988). *Understanding and Preventing Suicide.*
McIntosh, J. L. (1985). *Research on Suicide: A Bibliography.*
Plath, S. (1971). *The Bell Jar.*

Poland, S. (1989). *Suicide Intervention in the Schools.*
Shneidman, E. S. (1980). *Voices of Death.*
Stone, H. (1972). *Suicide and Grief.*

More detailed theoretical analyses include the following:

Alvarez, A. (1970). *The Savage God: A Study of Suicide.*
Durkheim, E. (1951). *Suicide: A Study in Sociology.*
Menninger, K. (1938). *Man Against Himself.*
Resnik, H.L.P. (Ed.). (1968). *Suicidal Behaviors: Diagnosis and Management.*
Shneidman, E. S. (1985). *Definition of Suicide.*
Stengel, E. (1964). *Suicide and Attempted Suicide.*

Survivors and the aftermath of suicide are the focus in the following:

Cain, A. (Ed.). (1972). *Survivors of Suicide.*
Douglas, J. D. (1967). *The Social Meanings of Suicide.*
Dunne, E. J., McIntosh, J. L., & Dunne-Maxim, K. (Eds.). (1987). *Suicide and Its Aftermath.*
Hewett, J. (1980). *After Suicide.*
Wallace, S. E. (1973). *After Suicide.*

An important, specialized topic is considered in the following:

Farberow, N. L. (Ed.). (1980). *The Many Faces of Suicide: Indirect Self-Destructive Behavior.*

On ethical and philosophical aspects of suicide, as well as the practicalities of "rational suicide" or "self-deliverance," consult:

Battin, M. P. (1982). *Ethical Issues in Suicide.*
Battin, M. P., & Mayo, D. J. (Eds.). (1980). *Suicide: The Philosophical Issues.*
Humphry, D. (1991). *Final Exit: The Practicalities of Self-Deliverance and Assisted Suicide for the Dying.*
Rollin, B. (1985). *Last Wish.*
Roman, J. (1980). *Exit House: Choosing Suicide as an Alternative.*

CHAPTER 18

The Meaning and Place of Death in Life

This chapter explores issues that in a sense underlie everything that has been considered throughout this book. These are issues relating to the human attempt to determine the meaning and place of death in life. This chapter addresses these issues through the example of some things that Socrates had to say when he was facing his own death; by considering some of the many questions that death raises for human beings; through an examination of a series of alternative images of the meaning of death that have been proposed by major religious and philosophical perspectives from around the world; by identifying in a brief transitional section a common concern in religious images of the meaning of death; through a discussion of near-death experiences—their content and interpretations; and by returning to the basic issue that faces all human beings—the place of death in human life.

The Death of Socrates

More than 400 years before the birth of Christ, Socrates was a well-known figure in the city-state of Athens. In the eyes of his critics, Socrates was a person who challenged their beliefs and disrupted the social order. In the eyes of his supporters—especially those of his student Plato, who provided the most extended descriptions of what is known about Socrates—Socrates was "of all those whom we knew in our time, the bravest and also the wisest and most upright man" (Plato, 1961, p. 98; *Phaedo*, 119b).

When Socrates was 70 years old, some of his critics brought charges against him for not believing in the gods in whom the state believed and for corrupting the youth (by teaching them to challenge the beliefs of their elders). Socrates defended himself as a person engaged in a divine mission, an intellectual midwife who would help people to recognize their own ignorance. He argued that this would ultimately benefit individuals and society, since "an unexamined life is not worth living" (Plato, 1948, p. 45; *Apology*, 38a). In other words, the overthrow of false beliefs could be the beginning of the search for true wisdom.

Despite his arguments, Socrates was found guilty of the charges. In a separate vote the jury accepted the penalty proposed by his accusers and Socrates was condemned to death. In response, Socrates offered the following comments about the meaning of death (Plato, 1948, pp. 47–48; *Apology*, 40b–41a):

> This thing that has come upon me must be a good; and those of us who think that death is an evil must needs be mistaken. . . . For the state of death is one of two things: either the dead man wholly ceases to be and loses all consciousness or, . . . it is a change and a migration of the soul to another place. And if death is the absence of all consciousness, and like the sleep of one whose slumbers are unbroken by any dreams, it will be a wonderful gain. . . . For it appears that all time is nothing more than a single night. But if death is a journey to another place, and what we are told is true—that all who have died are there—what good could be greater than this? . . . What would you not give to converse with Orpheus and

Socrates accepts his death sentence and calmly drinks poison while his friends weep.

Musaeus and Hesiod and Homer? . . . It would be an inexpressible happiness to converse with [heroes such as these] and to live with them and to examine them.

Questions Raised by Death and Some Preliminary Responses
Questions Raised by Death

To study death, dying, and bereavement is to look into some of the most profound questions confronting human beings. Human beings everywhere and always eventually come up against an inescapable fact about themselves: they are mortal. For many persons, such a moment raises questions of meaning: Why was I born? What is the meaning of my having lived? What is the impact of the fact of my death on the value and significance of my life? In short, what is the relationship of life and death? Are they simple contraries? That is, where there is death, is there no life?

To raise questions such as these is to recognize what is distinctive about human forms of living. The fact of eventual death is common to human, animal, and plant forms of life. What is unique about human beings is that they can think about or reflect upon this fact and its implications ahead of time. As Feifel (1969, p. 292) has written, "It is man's excelling capacity to conceptualize a future—and inevitable death—which distinguishes him from other species."

Some Preliminary Responses

As human beings have reflected on questions raised by death, they have responded in many different ways (for example, Becker, 1973; Grof & Halifax, 1978). One can sample such responses by concentrating on attempts to understand what happens after death (Toynbee, Koestler, et al., 1976). These responses are addressed to the question of the relationship of life and death after *biological* death has occurred. These responses have appeared in all of the basic modalities of human expression, such as art and popular culture (Bertman, 1991), anthropology (Reynolds & Waugh, 1977), literature (Enright, 1983; Weir, 1980), philosophy (Carse, 1980; Choron, 1963, 1964), and theology (Gatch, 1969; Mills, 1969; Rahner, 1973). Indeed, some of the best thinking ever done by human beings has focused on such issues. Socrates and Camus, Paul of Tarsus and Muhammad, the writer of Ecclesiastes and the writer of the Bhagavad Gita: in the work of such people can be found examples of attempts to address the disturbing implications of death in human life.

Some—for instance, Socrates, who is reported (Plato, 1961, p. 46; *Phaedo*, 64a) to have said that "those who really apply themselves in the right way to philosophy are directly and of their own accord preparing themselves for dying and death"—have argued that everything humans do in life is finally to be evaluated by testing it against the fact of their mortality. If this is so, then everything presented earlier in this book about how to treat dying persons and survivors, about the place of euthanasia and suicide in human life, in fact about responses to death and dying in all their varied forms, finds its origins in more basic questions about the meaning of mortality. To say that people should care for dying persons in one way rather than in another way eventually finds part of its justification in beliefs about death. For instance, if one believes that death is always and everywhere to be disvalued, if one thinks of death as irremediably evil, and if one holds that death is the greatest evil known, then this will affect how one treats dying persons.

How death is evaluated is ultimately dependent on what can reasonably be called philosophical or theological beliefs (Congdon, 1977; Momeyer, 1988). That is, evaluations of death are linked in perhaps inescapable ways to how the nature and the meaning of death are understood. Probably everyone has such beliefs, although everyone may not explicitly formulate or consciously reflect upon them.

Death: A Door or a Wall?

Feifel (1977a) simplified (perhaps overly so) how humans are likely to think of death when he wrote that death can be portrayed as either a door or a wall.

That is, when one looks at death, one can ask oneself what one sees. Is death simply the cessation of life? Is it the case that where death intrudes, life is irrevocably lost? Then death is something up against which all will come, and it will mean the end of everything that one does or can know. It is a wall into which one crashes and through which one cannot pass.

But some people believe that death is a stage along life's way. It is a river to cross, a stair to climb, a door through which to pass. If this is one's view, then death may be seen not as the irrevocable opposite to life but rather as a passage from one sort (or stage) of life to another sort (or stage) of life.

Probably all people come to have one or the other of these beliefs at one point or another in their lives. In a way, one's concept of the meaning of death cannot be evaded. If one's evaluation of death is dependent on one's philosophical beliefs about death, then whenever some value judgment is made some belief about the status and meaning of death in a philosophical sense is presupposed, at least implicitly (and perhaps unconsciously). For example, "Grandmother is better off dead" presupposes that death is not the worst evil that could happen in Grandmother's (and perhaps our own) life.

It is also the case that the evaluation one makes of death is not tied in any *obvious* way to whether one sees it as a door or as a wall (Nabe, 1982). One can think of death as a wall and evaluate that as good: for example, at least all suffering is over. One can see death as a door and evaluate that as evil: for example, it will bring eternal torment or a shadowy, shallow form of life. And, of course, some would see death as a wall as evil, and death as a door as good. The point is only that how one thinks of death philosophically is tied in *some* important way to one's evaluation of it.

Alternative Images of an Afterlife

At this point, it will be helpful to consider some of the principal religious or philosophical images that human beings have employed to try to understand how death and life are related. That is, this section examines responses to the questions: Is *this* life all there is? and Is death the irrevocable loss of any sort of life? Human beings have tried to respond to questions of this sort in quite an astonishing array of ways (Toynbee, 1968b). Here, several of the best-known and most influential of these ways are considered.

Greek Concepts of the Afterlife

Before Socrates spoke about death to his judges, he had earlier made it plain to his hearers that he believed that humans cannot really *know* what death is. That is, according to Socrates, everyone is left with *beliefs* about death. This is one of the poignant aspects of any study of death-related issues. It is unlikely that humans can know for certain just what death means for their continued existence. On this most pressing point, a choice must be made on less than demonstrative proof.

Socrates was content not to decide finally just what death is. Perhaps that was in part due to the options he believed death might involve. If death is either a permanent sleep (unconsciousness) or a form of life in which one meets old friends and can make new ones (as Socrates suggested in the passage quoted earlier), then death does not appear to be frightening or threatening.

But these do not exhaust the possibilities. Another description is provided by Socrates' beloved Homer. At one point in Homer's *Odyssey*, Odysseus calls up another Greek hero (Achilles) from the afterlife in Hades. Achilles says about that life, "Don't bepraise death to me . . . I would rather be plowman to a yeoman farmer on a small holding than lord paramount in the kingdom of the dead" (Homer, 1937, p. 125). Achilles says this because Hades is described as a very unhappy place; the dead have no sense or feeling and are mere "phantoms."

Another view found in ancient Greek sources is that of the "immortality of the soul." This view is presented in the writings of Plato, who sometimes represented the human being as made up of two parts, a body (earthly, mortal) and a soul (immortal). Plato even offered arguments intended to prove the inherent immortality of the soul. That is, in his view, souls are essentially immortal—they are deathless by their very nature. Nothing can cause a soul not to be; thus it must exist forever. Because human beings (and all bodies that move "of themselves"—that is, animals) are in part souls, death must mean only the separation of the body and the soul. It does not mean the end of the soul.

Greek thought provided one major strand of Western beliefs about the philosophical questions we are studying. But another major strand came from the Judeo-Christian tradition. Much of the basis for that tradition is found in the Bible.

Some Western Religious Beliefs

Many different beliefs about an afterlife are expressed in the Old and New Testaments. Bailey (1978) found the following notions associated with an afterlife in those texts:

1. "Immortality" is sometimes associated only with divine beings (Eccles. 17:30; 1 Tim. 6:16).
2. Sometimes "deathlessness" is seen as being given by the gods to particular human beings (for example, Enoch in Gen. 5:24, and Elijah in 2 Kings 2:1–12).
3. An afterlife might be related to a phantomlike existence, a sort of "diminished life." (Compare Achilles' description of Hades noted earlier.) Some people have found this view present in Saul's consultations with a witch, who calls up Samuel from the afterworld (see 1 Sam. 28).

4. Ongoing life after death is often related to what one leaves behind at one's death, such as one's children.

Actually, in the Jewish scriptures, the notion of the individual surviving death is only rarely encountered. If there is a notion of ongoing life after death, it is found in the community and in one's specific descendants. I may die, but my community will go on. I may die, but my children and my children's children will go on. It is the community's life that is important, and it is the ongoing life of the familial line that is significant.

In fact, it is even uncertain whether the Greek notion of a soul discussed earlier is found in the Old Testament. The Hebrew word often translated as "soul" (*nepesh*) means most simply "life." It is necessarily tied up with a body. Thus, at death, the *nepesh* ceases to exist, since it is no longer bound up with a particular body. Eichrodt (1967) reports that various images are used: at death, the *nepesh* "dies; at the same time it is . . . feasible to think of it leaving a man at death, though this does not mean that one can ask where it has gone! . . . It is described as having been taken or swept away" (p. 135). He continues: "In no instance does there underlie the use of *nepeš* [a] conception of an immortal *alter ego*. . . . Equally remote from the concept . . . is the signification of a numinous substance in Man who survives death" (p. 140). If this is correct, then the notion of an immortal soul is not part of the original Judaic tradition. In fact, Eichrodt (1967) holds that this idea entered Judaic thought much later, under the influence of Hellenic culture.

None of the meanings found in the Judaic scriptures that have been discussed so far is clearly related to another biblical image of an afterlife—the image of resurrection. This image grows out of the Judaic belief that the human being is not a combination of two different sorts of entities, a body and a soul. Instead, the belief is that the human being is an integrated whole. To be human is not to be a soul entombed in a body, it is to be a living-body. Life in this view cannot be understood *except* as embodied. (Islam sometimes teaches this, too; see Muwahidi, 1989, pp. 40–41). Thus, if there is to be a life after death, it must be an embodied life. And that is what *resurrection* means: it refers to the "raising-up" of a human being as a living-body. This raising up would require some new action by God. It would demand a recreation of the human being by God.

Western religion also has often associated an afterlife with the concepts of heaven and hell. These concepts are remarkably fully developed in Islam. According to Islam, at a Last Judgment each individual's behavior while living in this world will be judged. If a person behaved in ways acceptable to Allah, rewards will be waiting after death. If a person behaved in unacceptable ways, punishments will be waiting. These rewards or punishments are often described vividly, and in ways that are "materialistic" (Smart, 1976, p. 400):

> The inmates of hell would be covered with fire . . . the sinners would eat the fruit of a strange tree which rose up from the bottom of hell, and it would boil up like oil in their bellies . . . the righteous would enter a region where there were gardens and fountains, and they would be clothed in beautiful raiment. Delicious

Mary holds the dead body of her son, Jesus, in Michelangelo's "Pieta."

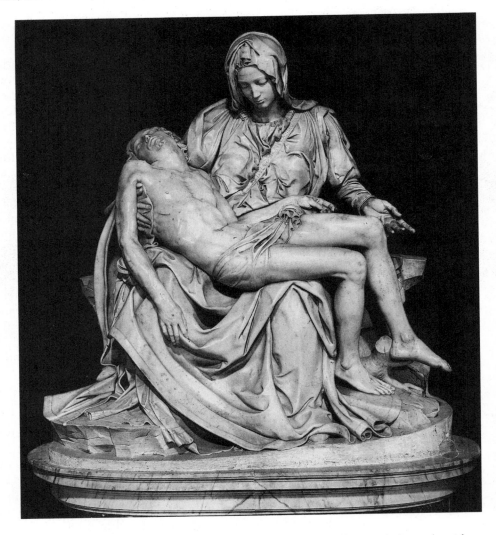

food and wine would be served to them by celestial youths . . . dark-eyed maidens . . . would wait on their commands.

Some Muslims take such descriptions literally; others see them as metaphoric—that is, as attempts to describe something that it is difficult if not impossible to describe.

Similar concepts are found in other religious cultures, too: they can be found in Christianity, in Hinduism, and in some forms of Buddhism. But one of their earliest historical appearances is in an ancient religion that today has only a few adherents in India. That religion is Zoroastrianism.

Zarathustra, the founder of this religion, taught that after death came the awful judgment. . . . The dead one would approach the Chinvat Bridge, which crosses to . . . paradise. Below it hell would yawn. If a man's good deeds outweighed his bad ones, he would be beckoned onward and could cross the bridge with ease. But the wicked would find it impossible and topple over into the regions of punishment. (Smart, 1976, p. 263)

Zarathustra lived in ancient Persia no later than the fifth century B.C. Some have argued that his ideas were picked up by the Jews while they were in exile in Babylon and that the concepts of a heaven and a hell thus returned to Palestine with the returning Jews. Such ideas were present in Palestine when Jesus taught, and he presented them in some of his teachings. In any case, much of Western thought—Jewish, Christian, and Islamic—has made use of such ideas.

But there are other cultures, with quite different beliefs.

Some African Beliefs

The continent of Africa contains many cultures, and the philosophical and theological beliefs of the people in these various cultures have not been extensively described or studied. But some preliminary generalizations have been made (Mbiti, 1970).

In general, for many of these people, the human being is seen as part of the world, not as separate from it. The power that makes life possible is everywhere the same—in plants, in animals, and in human beings (Opoku, 1978, 1987). So human life is part of nature, and it is a constant cyclic process of becoming (as is nature). This process does have certain distinguishing moments or turning points in it: birth, adolescence, marriage, death. But each of these crises only marks a particular point in the process of becoming. Those in the community who are alive are in one stage; those who are the "living-dead" (that is, those who are not living as we are here) are simply in a further stage. The community contains both the living and the "living-dead." The "living-dead" are not thought of as being in another world; they are just in a different part of this world. The transition to this other part of the world is sometimes symbolized as a land journey, often including the crossing of a river, perhaps because rivers form natural boundaries between one part of the natural world and another part.

The "living-dead," in this view, are quasi-material beings, and as ancestors they are prized and respected. Their lives are ones of serenity and dignity, given over to concern for the well-being of the living wing of their families and clans. No notion of a heaven (a life of bliss) nor of a hell (a life of torment) is mentioned.

These are images drawn from a people living in close contact with nature. There is no notion of a pale, empty afterlife, as seen in Homer. Nor is there a notion of resurrection or of heaven or hell. The afterlife as it is portrayed here is a simple, natural continuation of the life we know. There *are* differences, just as living in the desert on this side of the river is different from living in the forest on the other side of the river. But the life of the "living-dead" is not a wholly foreign existence, and it is not a threatening one.

Hindu and Buddhist Beliefs

When one thinks about the philosophical and theological beliefs of the people of the Indian subcontinent, perhaps the notion that most often springs to mind is reincarnation. (A variety of terms are associated with this idea: *transmigration of souls, metempsychosis, rebirth.* These terms are treated here as if they are interchangeable.) It is a very ancient idea. Indeed, it can be found in Western thought, too. For example, ideas like this are found in some of Plato's dialogues, although how literally he meant his readers to take his myths about reincarnation is uncertain. In any case, the idea is certainly older than Plato's writings (the fourth century B.C.).

The first writings that discuss this idea of reincarnation go back at least to the seventh century B.C. In one of the Hindu scriptures (the "Katha Upanishad") one finds the following passage (Radhakrishnan & Moore, 1957, pp. 45–46):

> The wise one . . . is not born, nor dies.
> This one has not come from anywhere, has not become anyone.
> Unborn, constant, eternal, primeval, this one
> Is not slain when the body is slain.
> If the slayer think to slay,
> If the slain think himself slain,
> Both these understand not.
> Know thou the self (*atman*) as riding in a chariot,
> The body as the chariot. . . .
> He . . . who has not understanding,
> Who is unmindful and ever impure,
> Reaches not the goal,
> But goes on to transmigration. . . .
> He . . . who has understanding,
> Who is mindful and ever pure,
> Reaches the goal
> From which he is born no more . . .

This passage marks out many of the most important and unique characteristics of the Hindu view of the human being. Humans are essentially an unborn, undying soul (*atman*). This soul is repeatedly incarnated in bodies (and not necessarily always in human bodies, but also in "lower" forms). What body the soul is incarnated into is dependent on what one has done in previous lives. "Unmindfulness," "impurity," and a lack of understanding about the nature of reality will lead to transmigration of the soul from one body or one sort of body to another. But transmigration necessarily brings with it suffering. So the goal is to end transmigration, or rebirth. In Hinduism, such rebirths are undesirable.

Perhaps one of the clearest statements of this view is found in the *Bhagavad Gita.* It contains the teachings of the lord Krishna (a god) to a human being (Arjuna). Arjuna is agonized about the killing that occurs in war. But Krishna tells him:

Wise men do not grieve for the dead or for the living. . . . Never was there a time when I was not, nor thou . . . nor will there ever be a time hereafter when we shall cease to be. . . . Just as a person casts off worn-out garments and puts on others that are new, even so does the embodied soul cast off worn-out bodies and take on others that are new. (Radhakrishnan, 1948, pp. 102–108)

If this is so, then what does this tell people about how to live their lives here? Krishna answers:

Endowed with a pure understanding, firmly restraining oneself, turning away from sound and other objects of sense and casting aside attraction, and aversion. . . . Dwelling in solitude, eating but little, controlling speech, body, and mind . . . taking refuge in dispassion . . . casting aside self-sense, force, arrogance, desire, anger, possession, egoless, and tranquil in mind, he becomes worthy of becoming one with *Brahman.* (Radhakrishnan, 1948, p. 370)

That is, right living can lead to an end of the rebirths and to complete peace or union with God.

Prashad (1989) reported that these beliefs affect Hindu actions at the time of death. What one is thinking at the moment of death sums up all of one's life experience and can determine what the next rebirth will be. One should thus die with the name of God on one's lips, because this helps to produce a favorable outcome after death.

After death, three possibilities exist: (1) the *atman* may be in one of the heavens, awaiting rebirth; (2) the *atman* is immediately reborn; or (3) the *atman* is in a state of eternal bliss with God, having achieved liberation from the cycle of rebirths.

Buddhism is a sort of reform movement of Hinduism. Its founder (Siddhartha Gautama) was raised as a Hindu but eventually found current practices and beliefs unacceptable. One of the teachings in Hinduism with which he took issue was the notion of the *atman* (soul). He taught that there is no soul. Still, he retained notions of reincarnation (or rebirth). This is a puzzling and quite unique feature of Buddhism. Rebirth occurs, but it is not rebirth of the soul.

Thus, at death there are two possibilities for Buddhism: (1) some aspect of the human being is reborn; or (2) *nirvana* is achieved. One image used by Buddhists to explain these possibilities is the following. If one begins with a single flame, it can be passed from one candle to another candle, then to another candle, and so forth. Although there is *continuity* from one flame to the next, it is unclear that there is *identity*—that is, it is not obvious that the same flame is present at the end of the process as was there at the beginning. Some sort of (causal) influence is passed along; and that is what rebirth is like. At some point, one might blow out the flame (and *nirvana* literally means "blowing out"); then there would be nothing to pass along from that sequence. Rebirths would have ceased.

Again, in this view, the "total balance sheet of good and evil deeds performed during a given lifetime is summarized in the state of mind held by the dying person" (Becker, 1989, p. 114). This influences rebirth. If the person clings to life, energy is sent forth that becomes associated with some child in the womb.

But for Buddha, a fundamental fact about human life is that it involves suffering. Consequently, rebirths involve suffering, and so they are undesirable. One must strive to end all desire and to become detached. If this is achieved, nirvana is the result and the chain of rebirths is ended.

Nirvana is not heaven. In fact, it is a condition impossible to describe verbally. But it involves serenity and peace (Radhakrishnan & Moore, 1957). It is also absolute quiescence (Chan, 1963).

A Common Concern in Images of an Afterlife

The various notions described thus far about what happens after death range from a permanent sleep (unconsciousness) through recreation in an embodied form (resurrection) and on to a "blowing out" or a condition of absolute stillness. Some of these pictures seem threatening: a hell involving punishment or a Hades as it is described in Homer. Some seem attractive: meeting old companions or eternal joy in a heavenly state. Some provide a sense of peace: a surcease from a constant round of suffering. Each notion is likely to affect how one lives one's life here and now, and how one evaluates death.

In the United States in the 1990s, it would appear that many persons no longer hold the typical religious beliefs of earlier centuries. The modern, scientific world view has convinced many people that they are simply natural bodies. On that basis, it seems to many that when our bodies no longer function, then we simply are no more. Death means extinction.

It is not wholly clear how this view is likely to affect one's evaluation of death. In a sense, this is an unthreatening view because there is no suffering after death. But of course, death means the loss of everything one has valued and loved. If this life is seen as basically good, then its loss is likely to be held to be an unhappy event. Death may then be only feared and hated . . . and denied. This may be one source of death denial.

In the face of uncertainty, people seek evidence. They would like to know what death means in terms of ongoing existence. And yet, Socrates seems to have been correct; we cannot *know*. We must choose some picture of what death means and make do with it. For all of us, religious and nonreligious alike, faith here is the only possible route.

Near-Death Experiences

Or is faith the only possible route? In the last few years, some have claimed that they have evidence to show what happens after death. They claim that having been close to death, they "saw" what the afterlife is. That is, they have had a near-death experience (NDE). This is a notion that needs some clarification.

What Are NDEs and What Do They Suggest?

Some people have claimed to have been dead and then to have returned to life. It may be that they were "clinically dead"—that they met some criteria used by medical personnel to decide when death has occurred. But the relationship between "clinical death" and death itself is unclear; the two need not be identical. So it is not obvious that such persons were in fact dead.

Accordingly, one might revise the claim and say that these people have been near to death but not in fact dead. But to be "near to death" is not the same as "being dead." I may be near to Chicago but not there. What I experience when I am near to Chicago need not be at all like what I would experience if I were there. So it is not certain that near-death experiences tell us anything about what happens after death.

Of course, this analogy might not be accurate. Perhaps an NDE is more like being by a window or a door and looking through it into another room. The difficulty with this analogy is that we know how to mark the difference between this room and the next when we stand in a doorway; we have had this sort of experience before. We know what is happening when we look through a doorway from one room to another room.

But an NDE is not like this, in the interpretation that it reveals an afterlife. In the ordinary course of experience, when one perceives *another* room through a window or door, one has prior experiences of perceiving a room. But in the case of an NDE, no *perception* is involved (dead eyes do not see, dead ears do not hear). Therefore, the person is not doing the same sort of thing as the analogy suggests. There is no earlier experience to which this one (the NDE) can be properly compared. So any understanding of it is more uncertain. Thus, whether it discloses anything about an afterlife (which is what is at issue) remains uncertain.

Another problem about associating these experiences with an afterlife is that people who are not near to death have similar experiences to those who claim to have had near-death experiences. For instance, people who are anoxic for a period of time, or who are undergoing anesthesia, often make claims about what they "saw" and "heard" that are similar to the claims of those who say they have had an NDE. So it is unclear again whether NDEs reveal anything about what there is after death.

More Formal Claims

Several writers (such as Moody, 1975; Osis & Haraldsson, 1977; Ring, 1980, 1984, 1989; Sabom, 1982) have made other claims about such experiences. For instance, it is said that after being revived, persons who were clinically dead have told stories that have been quite similar to each other. And Grosso (1989, pp. 238–239) claimed that a poll revealed that "millions of Americans had the archetypal NDE."

Cockburn (1989, p. 244) wrote this about NDEs: "To have a near-death experience is to have thoughts, feelings, visual sensations . . . while in a state in which one shows . . . no external behavioral or physiological signs of life."

Ring (1980) conducted what he called scientific studies of such experiences. He began with 102 cases, obtained by referrals. His work led to classifying five stages of what he took to be the core of near-death experiences. The first of these stages he characterized as peace and a sense of well-being; 60 percent of his cases mentioned this. The second stage involved "a sense of detachment from one's physical body" (p. 45); 37 percent of his sample reported this. Third, 23 percent of the sample reported "entering the darkness" (p. 53). The fourth stage was marked by the appearance of light; 16 percent of Ring's sample reported this. Last, 10 percent of his sample reported "entering the light" (p. 60).

Similarly, Sabom (1982) looked at 116 cases. He used Moody's table of ten characteristics of an NDE to classify his data (see Moody, 1975). Frequently reported aspects included a sense of calm and peace, a sense of bodily separation, a sense of being dead, and a sense of "returning" to life.

Lorimer (1989) reported that such experiences have common components, at least in the United States, the United Kingdom, and France. Of course, the United States, the United Kingdom, and France share important cultural backgrounds. Cross-cultural studies would be of great interest in this subject area. But very little work of this type has been done. This does not show that NDEs are no more than a cultural artifact, but it leaves uncertainty as to whether they represent a universal human phenomenon. If, in fact, such experiences portray an afterlife, it would seem that people everywhere ought to have the same sort of experiences.

Evaluating the Claims

All of this work needs careful study and analysis. And there are large questions about what these experiences mean (Grosso, 1981; Vicchio, 1979, 1981). For instance, because someone shows no external signs of consciousness does not mean that that person is having no experiences. "Unconscious" in this context means little more than "not showing signs of consciousness"; it does not mean no consciousness is present. And to sense separation from one's body is a fascinating experience, but how such experience is or is not related to death is uncertain. This sort of experience in itself reveals nothing about what happens after death unless one makes other assumptions. For example, one would have to assume that NDEs provide evidence that human beings are not just bodies and that this "other part" of the human can live separated from the body, perhaps for long periods of time. Neither of these assumptions is obvious.

There may be other lines of evidence that support beliefs about an afterlife. But they have not been studied extensively, and when they have been studied, the evidence is at best ambiguous (Kastenbaum, 1977a). Socrates' dictum seems to stand: we do not, and perhaps cannot, know what happens after death. We must take a stand—even those who are agnostic are under the same practical compulsion—on less than complete proof. This central fact of our humanness—our mortality—remains a mystery.

The Place of Death in Human Life

Afterlife Images and Life Here and Now

Having considered several images of what happens after death, it is now useful to ask a question of some immediacy and practicality: What conclusions can we draw from these images for the meanings(s) of our lives as we live them in this temporal, physical world?

It might be argued that what we do here in this life influences what will happen to us after death. This becomes an argument meant to persuade us to behave in one way rather than another in order to "reap benefits" in an afterlife. Certain forms of Christianity, Islam, Hinduism, and Buddhism make suggestions like this. They contend that what we do here and now has desirable or undesirable consequences (for us) after death.

But even if one holds no such ideas, one can still make ties between what happens after death and life in the world now. For instance, if death is permanent extinction, then perhaps humans ought to live life to the fullest and seek to get as much experience as they can. Or, again, if death means extinction, one might hold that that eliminates the value of everything that we know and do in our lives: all is vanity. And death can mean an end to suffering, as Hindus and Buddhists claim; it eliminates "the heartache and the thousand natural shocks that flesh is heir to" (*Hamlet*, III, i, 62). In this sense, death might be courted, even welcomed.

Some have gone beyond this to maintain the "conviction that in the last analysis all human behavior of consequence is a response to the problem of death" (Feifel, 1977a, p. xiii). If that seems too bold or too broad a thesis, then at least it can be said that we human beings are able to make of death an important steering force in the way we interpret its place in our lives. Consequently, "appreciation of finiteness can serve not only to enrich self-knowledge but to provide the impulse to propel us forward toward achievement and creativity" (Feifel, 1977a, p. 11).

Efforts to Circumvent or Transcend Death

Many people have tried to circumvent death and have done this in a variety of ways. Another way to say this is that people have sought to find a way to continue after they die what they have found valuable in their lives. Lifton (1979) pointed to several such forms of what he called "symbolic immortality." The main varieties that he described are biological, social, natural, and theological immortality. That is, one's life (and the values one finds in life) might be continued in one's biological descendants. Or it could be continued

*Revisiting
memories of a
family's life.*

in what one has created: a painting, a garden, a book; perhaps in the lives of others one has touched: students, patients, clients, friends. People have also looked for a continuation of their lives after their own deaths in the natural world around them. In this view, one's body returns to the ground (dust to dust), wherein its components dissolve and are reorganized into new life. And people have looked for immortality in the form of an afterlife and reunion with or absorption into the divine (as described in an earlier section).

The attempt to circumvent death reveals a meaning for that irrevocable, unavoidable moment: it produces suffering. If anything is valued in this life, death threatens that value. It means the loss (at least for now) of persons we have loved, places we have enjoyed, music, sunrise, the feeling of material (soil, paper and ink, the bow on the strings) coming into form through our labor.

If this is the meaning we find for death, inevitably it will influence how we live and how we treat each other. It teaches us that life is precious. So we have given to this book the title *Death and Dying, Life and Living*. It seems to the authors that whatever meaning we find for death, to look at death leads us to realize the fragility and the value of life. Indeed, perhaps death makes possible the value of life. A life (as we know life here) that went on indefinitely might become unbearable. Why do anything today, when there are endless tomorrows in which to do it (see, for example, Fowles, 1964)?

Ultimately, the meaning any individual finds for death will be his or her own. In this sense, *each individual is alone in facing his or her own death*. But there is a history—thousands of years long—and a cultural diversity—of other persons with whom one can enter into dialogue. Each person can enter into this dialogue in order to gain help in choosing how to live his or her own life and how to make sense of his or her own death and the deaths of those whom he or she cares for and about. Each individual can also contribute to the history of human debate about the meaning and place of death in human life. This book is but one voice in that ongoing dialogue.

Summary

This chapter has engaged in a reflection on the meaning and place of death in human life. It has considered questions raised for human beings by death and responses offered, on the one hand, by religious and philosophical perspectives, and, on the other hand, by students of near-death experiences. The lesson from all of this is that each person is free to determine for himself or herself the stand that he or she will take in the face of death.

QUESTIONS FOR REVIEW AND DISCUSSION

1. This chapter reviewed several notions of what happens after death. These included (a) immortality of the soul; (b) resurrection of the body; (c) life continued in a place of bliss (heaven) or torture (hell) or exceeding boredom (the Greek Hades); (d) rebirth (transmigration or reincarnation of the soul); (e) a life much like this one only somewhere else; (f) permanent peace and stillness (nirvana, extinction). Which of these views are you inclined toward? How might your response to this question affect how you live your life? How might it influence how you treat someone else who is dying?

2. This chapter discussed near-death experiences. What is your assessment of what such experiences can or do tell us about what happens to us after we die?

SUGGESTED READINGS

For religious perspectives on death-related issues, consult:

Badham, P., & Badham, L. (Eds.). (1987). *Death and Immortality in the Religions of the World.*

Bailey, L. (1978). *Biblical Perspectives on death.*

Frazer, J. G. (1977). *The Fear of the Dead in Primitive Religion.*

Gatch, M. McC. (1969). *Death: Meaning and Mortality in Christian Thought and Contemporary Culture.*

Hatchett, M. (1976). *Sanctifying Life, Time and Space.*

Mills, L. O. (Ed.). (1969). *Perspectives on Death.*

Opoku, K. A. (1978). *West African Traditional Religion.*

Radin, P. (1973). *The Road of Life and Death: A Ritual Drama of the American Indians.*

Rahner, K. (1973). *On the Theology of Death.*

Reynolds, F. E., & Waugh, E. H. (Eds.). (1977). *Religious Encounters with Death: Insights from the History and Anthropology of Religion.*

For philosophical and conceptual perspectives on death-related issues, see:

Berger, A., Badham, P., Kutscher, A. H., Berger, J., Perry, M., & Beloff, J. (Eds.). (1989). *Perspectives on Death and Dying: Cross-Cultural and Multi-Disciplinary Views.*

Carse, J. P. (1980). *Death and Existence: A Conceptual History of Mortality.*

Chan, W.-T. (1963). *A Sourcebook in Chinese Philosophy.*

Choron, J. (1963). *Death and Western Thought.*

Choron, J. (1964). *Death and Modern Man.*

Congdon, H. K. (1977). *The Pursuit of Death.*

Doka, K. J., with Morgan, J. D. (Eds.). (1993). *Death and Spirituality.*

Durkheim, E. (1954). *The Elementary Forms of Religious Life.*

Frankl, V. (1984). *Man's Search for Meaning.*

Grof, S., & Halifax, J. (1978). *The Human Encounter with Death.*

Mbiti, J. S. (1970). *African Religion and Philosophy.*

Momeyer, R. W. (1988). *Confronting Death.*

Radhakrishnan, S., & Moore, C. (1957). *A Sourcebook in Indian Philosophy.*

Toynbee, A., Koestler, A., & others. (1976). *Life After Death.*

Toynbee, A., Mant, A. K., Smart, N., Hinton, J., Yudkin, S., Rhode, E., Heywood, R., & Price, H. H. (1968). *Man's Concern with Death.*

Issues related to near-death experiences are examined in the following:

Kastenbaum, R. (1977). *Between Life and Death.*

Moody, R. A. (1975). *Life After Life.*

Osis, K., & Haraldsson, E. (1977). *At the Hour of Death.*

Ring, K. (1980). *Life at Death: A Scientific Investigation of the Near-Death Experience.*

Ring, K. (1984). *Heading Toward Omega: In Search of the Meaning of the Near-Death Experience.*

Sabom, M. B. (1982). *Recollections of Death: A Medical Investigation.*

PART VI

NEW CHALLENGES AND NEW OPPORTUNITIES

As the end of the 20th century approaches, new challenges and new opportunities have arisen for human beings in their interactions with death, dying, and bereavement. Perhaps the most complex and significant of these new challenges and opportunities are associated with infection by the human immunodeficiency virus (HIV) and its end state, Acquired Immunodeficiency Syndrome (AIDS). Together, these raise new questions and illustrate issues seen throughout this book.

The HIV and AIDS are a fresh beginning because they constitute a new sort of infection. Just when many in the United States had almost come to believe that communicable diseases were less and less significant as agents of mortality, AIDS arrived on the world scene as a mysterious, frightening, and extremely lethal cause of death. Nevertheless, despite all of the many novel features of HIV infection and AIDS, the social attitudes and coping problems that they have generated are familiar in their broad outlines to those who are knowledgeable about previous epidemics and elements that enter into human interactions with death. Chapter 19 describes HIV infection and AIDS in themselves, as characteristics of the death-related environment in which we shall live for the foreseeable future and as additional examples of many of the central topics and themes of this book.

Research, caring, and support are three essential elements in responding to HIV infection and AIDS, just as they are in coping with any sort of life-threatening illness, dying, or death. These subjects have been addressed in various ways throughout this book. Chapter 20 makes explicit a fourth essential element: education about death, dying, and bereavement. At present, education is, in fact, the major weapon in coping with the spread of HIV infection and AIDS. It is also a preparation for the rest of our lives—as individuals, as fellow human beings, and as members of society. A discussion of education in the field of death, dying, and bereavement is, therefore, both a summary and a reflective analysis of the project undertaken in this book. To give explicit attention to different goals, functions, and other aspects of this sort of education is to think about ways to empower oneself, to benefit from social discussion, and to shape one's search for a better life in the future.

CHAPTER 19

HIV Infection and AIDS

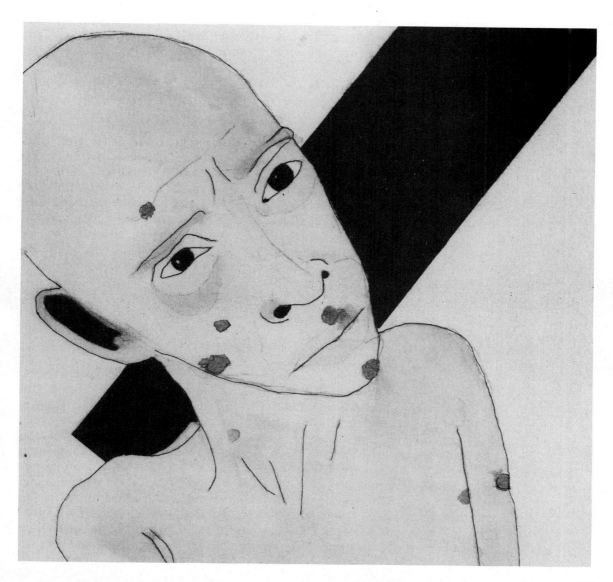

This chapter examines HIV infection and AIDS as an important subject in its own right and also as an example designed to summarize and draw together the many themes of this book. Thus, this chapter takes up two related concerns: (1) an analysis of dying, death, and bereavement as they are related to a new disease phenomenon that first appeared among human beings during the last two decades of the 20th century—infection with the human immunodeficiency virus (HIV) and Acquired Immunodeficiency Syndrome (AIDS); and (2) an effort to employ the perspectives provided by HIV infection and AIDS to bring together and illustrate in a new way the central themes of this book.

For the first of these concerns, some background information is provided about the HIV and its resulting disease states. This includes consideration of the history and manifestations of the virus, its discovery, epidemiology, and transmission. Individual and social responses to HIV infection and AIDS are also discussed. Of course, whatever is or can be said on these matters at any one point in time is subject to revision.

For the sake of this chapter, however, current experiences with HIV infection and AIDS can help us to learn important lessons about death, dying, and bereavement. In part, this is because these experiences constitute in some ways a unique phenomenon for persons living in the United States at this point in its history. HIV infection is a communicable disease that often leads to death in young persons. Many Americans in the late 20th century find these aspects of this experience with death to be surprising and discomforting.

In another sense, however, HIV infection and AIDS are also typical phenomena. Many of the difficulites, much of the emotion, the work of the coping—indeed, the whole of the living out of their effects—are similar to other experiences of death, dying, and bereavement discussed in this book. For these reasons, HIV infection and AIDS—however they might develop in the future—provide a significant window through which to reconsider the subjects of this book.

Three Persons with HIV or AIDS

Many (but not all) of the issues associated with HIV infection and AIDS can be introduced through the examples of Ryan White, Elizabeth Glaser, and "Magic" Johnson. No limited set of real-life examples can completely represent the great diversity and many ramifications of HIV infection and AIDS, whether in the United States or around the world. For example, data from the Centers for Disease Control (1989a, 1991 b–d, 1992a) report that homosexual males and intravenous (IV) drug users were and are the population groups with the highest numbers of individuals affected by the HIV/AIDS epidemic in the United States at the present moment. Also, in contrast to two of the following examples, it is expected that transfusion-related infection with HIV will be extremely rare after 1985. Nevertheless, the three examples given here have been chosen because of their prominence in the public eye and because of what they may (at least partly) represent for the future: HIV infection and

AIDS in a child, a woman, and a heterosexual man, as well as HIV infection and AIDS both in the heterosexual white community and in a member of a minority group in American society.

Ryan White

Ryan White (1971–1990) was a hemophiliac living in Kokomo, Indiana, in the early 1980s (White & Cunningham, 1991). Hemophilia is a genetically transmitted blood disorder that most often appears in young males. It manifests itself in an inability of the blood to clot when one experiences an external cut or an internal bruise. Hemophiliacs must be careful not to subject themselves to bleeding and must take regular treatments with a blood factor or product in order to enhance the clotting qualities of their blood.

When Ryan became ill with a mysterious and changing set of symptoms, he was tested for a variety of problems. After much testing, Ryan was diagnosed with AIDS in 1984. Apparently, he had become infected as a result of contaminated blood products at a time when the supply of blood and blood products was not safe from the HIV. The tragic irony in the case of Ryan White is that treatments that he took to ward off one life-threatening disease became the source of a second life-threatening illness.

Ryan had to fight in court to be readmitted to junior high school after being diagnosed with AIDS. His school district perceived him as a potential threat to other students because of his HIV status. Many parents and others fought against his readmission to school, and some students treated him badly when he did return to school. At one point, it was proposed that Ryan be taught in a separate facility and attempts were made to link him to his class through a telephone and computer hookup. All of this proved unsatisfactory. In any event, the courts eventually ruled that he must be admitted to school. Actually, Ryan was less of a threat to the health of other students than they were to his health, because of his hemophilia and his high risk of acquiring opportunistic infections.

Ryan White died in 1990 at the age of 18. A major, federal AIDS care funding bill was named in his honor, a movie and audio cassette have been made about his experiences, and an educational foundation has been established in his name.

Elizabeth Glaser

Elizabeth (Betsy) Glaser is the wife of actor Paul Michael Glaser, who (three months after their marriage) became well known to the public for his work as co-star in the television series "Starsky and Hutch." Elizabeth acquired the HIV from a transfusion of seven pints of blood in 1981 when she hemorrhaged after the delivery of her first child, Ariel (Glaser & Palmer, 1991). In hindsight, it appears now that Elizabeth unknowingly transmitted the HIV to Ariel through breast-feeding.

Elizabeth, Ariel, and Paul Michael Glazer.

Several years later, Ariel became sick at a time when very little was known about HIV infection and AIDS in children. Only when Ariel was eventually diagnosed in 1986 did the Glasers learn that Ariel had AIDS and that both her mother and her brother, Jake (who was born in 1984), were infected with the HIV. Jake apparently became infected in the uterus before his birth and before Elizabeth learned of her HIV status. At the time of diagnosis, the Glasers were told by a physician that "the world is not ready for your family" (Glaser & Palmer, 1991, p. 48).

Subsequently, Elizabeth cofounded the Pediatric AIDS Foundation, an organization dedicated to raising funds and encouraging research on pediatric AIDS and maternal transmission issues. Her aim in founding this organization was to stimulate scientists and the government—and to supplement their funding efforts—to support research on HIV infection and AIDS that is needed to prevent the deaths of other children and pregnant women. After years of fighting to maintain secrecy about their HIV status in order to protect their children, their family, and Paul's career from discrimination and stigma, Elizabeth and Paul Glaser revealed their situation to the public in 1988. Later, they appeared on the television program "60 Minutes" and in 1992 Elizabeth spoke about AIDS at the Democratic National Convention.

Earvin "Magic" Johnson

In November of 1991, at the age of 32, Earvin "Magic" Johnson, a popular and highly regarded American basketball player, disclosed in a news conference that he was HIV positive as a result of nonmonogamous heterosexual behavior and was retiring from his basketball career. Johnson discovered his status during a routine blood test required as part of his application for a life insurance policy. He sought that insurance as part of his preparations for marrying his childhood sweetheart, Cookie Kelly, his wife of two months at the time of the announcement. Happily, after testing, neither Johnson's wife nor their unborn child were found to be infected with the HIV.

Johnson played in the NBA All-Star Game in February of 1992 and on the American team that won the gold medal at the Olympics in the summer of 1992. In September of 1992, he announced that he would resume his basketball career at least on a limited basis, but in November these plans were canceled as a result of (unwarranted) fears over the potential spread of HIV infection if Johnson were to "bleed on another player." Off the basketball court, Johnson (1992) has published a book for young readers about HIV infection and AIDS, and has undertaken an educational campaign to help people avoid this disease. President Bush appointed Johnson to the National Commission on AIDS, but Johnson resigned in September of 1992 with the comment that he could not continue to serve on a commission that, in his judgment, was being ignored by the administration. This is reminiscent of other complaints made by AIDS activists and observers about government inactivity and lethargy—perhaps the best known of which is the book *And the Band Played On* (Shilts, 1987).

HIV Infection and AIDS: Background Information

How did HIV infection and AIDS first come to the attention of the medical community, and what has been learned about it since then? This section addresses these questions, discussing the history, manifestations, epidemiology, and transmission of HIV infection and AIDS.

First Manifestations of a New Syndrome: 1981–1983

On June 5, 1981, the *Morbidity and Mortality Weekly Report* of the U. S. Centers for Disease Control (CDC, 1981a) published a report regarding five young men who had been admitted to three different hospitals in the Los Angeles area with an unusual type of pneumonia. The report noted that its "observations suggest the possibility of a cellular-immune dysfunction related to a common exposure that predisposes individuals to opportunistic infections such as pneumocystosis and candidiasis" (p. 251).

With the advantage of hindsight, some researchers have been able to identify cases of HIV infection and/or AIDS that occurred prior to 1981 (Grmek, 1990). But 1981 is generally accepted as the chronological marker for the many important differences between the world before HIV infection and AIDS, and the world in which we now must live with HIV infection and AIDS.

The manifestations that first drew the attention of the Centers for Disease Control (CDC) had to do with a pneumonia caused by a commonly occurring protozoan, *Pneumocystis carinii* (CDC, 1981a; compare Gottlieb, M. S., et al., 1981). Prior to that time, serious cases of *Pneumocystis carinii* pneumonia (PCP) had mainly been seen in individuals with immune system deficiencies (for example, in newborns or in adults treated with immunosuppressive drugs). In addition, at roughly the same time in New York City, a number of severe cases of a hitherto rare form of cancer (Kaposi's sarcoma) were observed in a group of young men (CDC, 1981b; Gottlieb, G. J., et al., 1981; Hymes et al., 1981). Kaposi's sarcoma (KS) is a tumor of blood vessel tissue in the skin and/or internal organs. Up to that time, this disease had been found in relatively benign forms and only among elderly Italian and Jewish men of Mediterranean descent.

By late August of 1981, the CDC (1981c) reported that the total of these unusual cases had exceeded 110. All of the individuals in whom these diseases were observed were otherwise healthy. All were homosexual. They ranged in age from 15–52 years old. Several had other serious infections. But the most important factor that distinguished them was that they all gave evidence of immune deficiency—that is, of a reduction in the effectiveness of the body's natural defense systems. In their cases, this deficiency was not related to any known cause. Thus, they were eventually assigned a diagnosis of Acquired (not genetic or natural) Immunodeficiency Syndrome—*syndrome* being the term that identifies a clinical entity or recognizable pattern of manifestations that arise from an unknown cause.

Although AIDS was first recognized in homosexual men, it soon became apparent that it was not confined nor unique to that group of people. Quite early on in the United States, AIDS was also recognized in IV drug users, Haitian immigrants (who were later recognized to be HIV positive because of IV drug use and/or specific sexual behaviors), and prostitutes. That is, AIDS was initially observed in groups that are seen by many in American society as somehow marginalized or stigmatized. Additional experience identified the syndrome in a number of other population groups, especially including individuals who had received transfusions of blood or blood components, children in families in which one or both parents were infected with the HIV (that is, who were HIV positive), and heterosexual partners of those who either had or were at risk for AIDS. Thus, in 1982 the CDC defined AIDS as "a disease, at least moderately predictive of a defect in cell-mediated immunity, occurring in a person with no known cause for diminished resistance to that disease" (CDC, 1982b, p. 508; compare CDC, 1983, 1985a, 1985b).

A greatly magnified photograph of the human immunodeficiency virus (HIV).

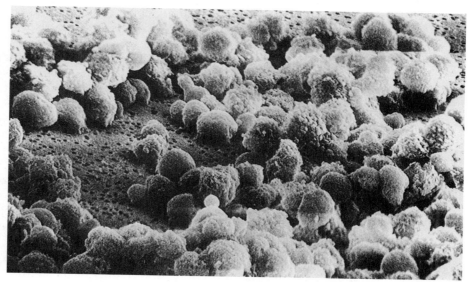

Discovery of the HIV and Its Implications: 1983–1986

By the summer of 1982, the appearance of AIDS in hemophiliacs who had received filtered blood products confirmed that the cause of this disease was a virus (CDC, 1982a; Francis, Curran, & Essex, 1983; Grmek, 1990). Such blood products were not ordinarily heat-treated for sterilization, but they were filtered to remove bacteria, fungi, and protozoa. An infectious agent that passed through such filtration had to be a virus. This set off an intense competition to discover and determine the nature of this virus (Connor & Kingman, 1988; Grmek, 1990).

In 1983 and 1984, French and American researchers discovered almost simultaneously the viral agent that is the cause of AIDS (CDC, 1984). French researchers named their virus "lymphadenopathy associated virus" (Barré-Sinoussi et al., 1983); one group of Americans named their virus "human T-cell lymphotrophic virus type III" (Gallo et al., 1984); a second group of Americans named their virus "AIDS-associated retrovirus" (Levy et al., 1984). In 1986, the virus was renamed "human immunodeficiency virus" by an international committee on nomenclature (Coffin et al., 1986).

Discovery of the HIV is the basis for an important distinction between the virus and the state of infection that it produces, on the one hand, and the disease state of AIDS, on the other hand. That is, although everyone who has AIDS has been infected by the HIV, it is not the case that all who are infected (and thus are HIV positive) have AIDS. Authoritative estimates place the proportion of those who have AIDS at about 20 percent of those who are HIV positive (CDC, 1992a). AIDS is the pathologic end-stage manifestation of HIV infection, a stage characterized by unusual opportunistic infections and rare malignancies in otherwise healthy individuals with no other reason for immune system compromise. In fact, with the discovery of its underlying etiology, AIDS is no longer (to speak properly) a syndrome but a retroviral infectious disease.

The HIV is a member of a class of viruses discovered in the late 1970s. Because these "retroviruses" have only recently been recognized, their nature and action is not yet fully understood. Nevertheless, retroviruses appear to be distinguished by their ability to transcribe their genetic material (RNA or ribonucleic acid) into DNA (deoxyribonucleic acid) and then to insert that DNA into the DNA of the host cell (Grmek, 1990; Roth, 1989). In this process, the virus "retrofits" the original program of the host cell so that it will now produce more viruses. That is, the HIV first attaches itself to the outer membrane of a cell at what is known as the CD4 receptor molecule. Subsequently, the HIV enters the host cell, integrates itself or retrofits the host cell, and apparently remains dormant or latent for a long period of time. In this dormant state, the virus is transmitted to each offspring at every cellular division.

The action of the HIV within the body is complicated and multifaceted. In particular, the HIV appears to attack a special kind of white blood cell called a helper T4 lymphocyte. This is a type of white blood cell that organizes the body's immune response to a large variety of infections, disease organisms, and other foreign matter. Under normal circumstances, the T4 is precisely the sort of cell that would be among the principal enemies of the HIV. The HIV also appears to attack macrophages, another form of white cells that migrate to all parts of the body in order to provide protection from disease. Infected macrophages may spread the HIV to cells of the central nervous system, brain, and spinal cord, thereby producing dementia and other sorts of mental disorders that are often seen in AIDS.

Manifestations of HIV Infection

Shortly after the HIV enters the body, some people experience a mild fever, similar to that arising from mononucleosis. Thereafter, infected individuals may have no further symptoms and feel completely well for quite a long time. Nevertheless, they are infected and infectious; they can communicate that infection to others without awareness of what is happening.

By 1985, reliable tests had been developed to detect whether the body has been exposed to the HIV. Among these, the best known are the ELISA (enzyme-linked immunosorbent assay) and Western blot tests (CDC, 1984). These tests do not indicate the presence of the HIV directly; what they show is the body's reaction to the HIV by identifying the presence of specific antibodies in the blood that the body manufactures in an attempt to fight off HIV infection. To have "seroconverted" and to be "seropositive" is to be carrying these antibodies in one's blood. Because the process of seroconversion may take several weeks or months after infection, this sort of testing may need to be repeated (usually after six months) to confirm that initial testing that may have followed infection did not precede the development of antibodies.

In 1992, a procedure used earlier for other purposes—the polymerase chain reaction test—began to be used to identify HIV proviral DNA. From this procedure the possibility arises of a quicker diagnosis because the procedure does not just test for antibodies but also for the activity of the virus itself, and because it tests for very small quantities of the agent (Bush, DiMichele, Peterson, Sherman, & Godsen, 1992). Nevertheless, a positive test either for antibodies or for HIV itself is not diagnostic for AIDS and does not mean that the person has AIDS. Instead, it means that he or she is infected with the HIV virus and may be at risk of developing AIDS.

During a long and relatively benign latency period that can average ten or more years after initial infection, there may be persistent generalized lymphadenopathy (PGL) or swelling of the lymph nodes or glands in those who are HIV positive, which may or may not be apparent to the individual. Subsequently, the development of a set of identifiable symptoms, such as night sweats, fatigue, excessive weight loss, or persistent diarrhea, was the basis for what used to be called "AIDS-related complex" or ARC. In 1986, however, additional experience, data, and research led to abandonment of the term "AIDS-related complex" and adoption of a more complex classification system for individuals diagnosed with HIV infection based on clinical manifestations of their disease. The CDC classification system for HIV infection is as follows (CDC, 1986; revised slightly in CDC, 1987a):

Group I. Acute infection. Seroconversion plus a mononucleosis-like syndrome.

Group II. Asymptomatic infection. No manifestations of HIV infection.

Group III. Persistent generalized lymphadenopathy (PGL). Enlargement of lymph nodes persisting for more than three months without explanation other than HIV infection.

Group IV. Other disease. One or more of the following, with or without PGL.

  Subgroup A. Constitutional disease. One or more of the following: fever persisting more than one month, involuntary weight loss greater than 10 percent of baseline, or diarrhea persisting more than 1 month—without explanation other than HIV infection.

  Subgroup B. Neurologic disease. Dementia, myelopathy, or peripheral neuropathy—without explanation other than HIV infection.

  Subgroup C. Secondary infectious diseases. Diagnosis of an infectious disease associated with HIV infection and/or at least moderately indicative of a defect in cell-mediated immunity.

    Category C-1. Specified secondary infectious diseases listed in the CDC surveillance definition for AIDS. One of 12 invasive diseases, such as *Pneumocystis carinii* pneumonia.

    Category C-2. Other specified secondary infectious diseases. One of 6 specified diseases, such as oral hairy leukoplakia or multidermatomal herpes zoster.

  Subgroup D. Secondary cancers. Diagnosis of one or more kinds of cancer (for example, Kaposi's sarcoma, non-Hodgkin's lymphoma, or primary lymphoma of the brain) associated with HIV infection and/or at least moderately indicative of a defect in cell-mediated immunity.

  Subgroup E. Other conditions. The presence of other clinical findings or diseases, not classifiable above, that may be attributed to HIV infection and/or may be indicative of a defect in cell-mediated immunity, such as chronic lymphoid interstitial pneumonitis.

AIDS itself was originally understood as that stage of HIV infection in which the body has been attacked by at least one life-threatening opportunistic disease or tumor. That is, to speak of AIDS is to represent a situation in which vulnerability to opportunistic infection has become greater, in part as a result of a more severe compromise of the immune system. But much of this involved classifications based upon external or clinical manifestations. Accordingly, as of January 1, 1993, the CDC (1992b) implemented a revised classification system for HIV infection and an expanded surveillance case definition for AIDS among adolescents and adults. This new definition of AIDS adds three clinical conditions—pulmonary tuberculosis, recurrent pneumonia, and invasive cervical cancer—to the 23 clinical conditions employed in the earlier surveillance case definition. This expanded definition also includes (in addition to those previously classified as having AIDS) all HIV-positive individuals who have a CD4 lymphocyte blood cell count of 200 or less per cubic millimeter even if no overt symptoms are present.

Two features of the expanded surveillance case definition are of special significance. First, it adds a biological or quantitative laboratory measure to existing clinical standards for the diagnosis of AIDS. Second, it is expected to enlarge the number of those who are understood to have AIDS. This will have special relevance for women and children, who have not always displayed recognized clinical manifestations of opportunistic disease that have hitherto been associated with AIDS and who have, therefore, not always been diagnosed or entered into treatment as early as others.

Because of the very long period of dormancy of the HIV in the body, one can be a carrier of the virus without knowing it. That is, one can be infected but asymptomatic. Consequently, many people who are HIV positive may not be aware of their infection status. Obviously, it is difficult for an individual who is infected with the HIV to recognize that fact when he or she is unaware of any indicators or manifestations resulting from that infection. Thus, an infected person may transmit the HIV to other individuals without anyone realizing what is happening. This increases uncertainty about vulnerability to HIV infection. In practical terms, it would appear to require that individuals must conduct themselves as if all others around them were HIV positive, whether or not that is actually the case.

Antiviral drugs, such as zidovudine (originally known as azidothymidine or AZT, and marketed as Retrovir), appear to have had some success in slowing the progress of HIV infection (Arno & Feiden, 1992). They are, however, expensive and are often associated with distressing side effects. Drugs of this sort are a form of palliative care that seeks to prolong the lives of infected people with minimal side effects. Any attempt to "cure" HIV infection is likely to be much more difficult since it would appear to require an ability to prevent or reduce the likelihood of acquiring the HIV; and/or to limit the expression of an already-acquired HIV; and/or to reverse established disease; and perhaps even to remove the HIV genetic material from the human genetic material in the cells of an infected person and restore immune function. In each of these cases, the curative agent would need to be responsive to various strains or mutations of the HIV.

Epidemiology

Recognition that HIV infection originates from the transmission of a virus coincided with epidemiological reports and confirmed their basic lesson. A disease that results from a virus is not confined to any specific population groups. *Anyone* can be infected with the HIV. Thus, a disease that was first associated with certain clusters of people in the United States has now been shown to appear in both women and men, Caucasians, African Americans, Asian Americans, and Hispanics, infants, children, and adolescents, the poor and the rich, and those who are educated and uneducated. In fact, in some parts of Africa where HIV infection is far more widespread than in the United States, it is the heterosexual population that is most at risk for HIV infection and AIDS (and among this group, persons especially at risk are those who patronize prostitutes and those who live along major trucking routes) (Connor & Kingman, 1988; Quinn, Mann, Curran, & Piot, 1986).

Throughout the 1980s, the Centers for Disease Control (CDC, 1991b, 1991d) provided estimates of the number of individuals who were affected by the HIV/AIDS epidemic during its first ten years. One can get a sense of the spread of this epidemic by noting the fact that it took just over eight years to record the first 100,000 cases of AIDS in the United States, but only a little more than two additional years to record the second 100,000 cases (CDC, 1989a, 1992a). By 1988, HIV infection was already the third leading cause of death among men 25–44 years of age and the eighth leading cause of death among women 25–44 years of age. By 1990, HIV infection and deaths associated with AIDS had become the tenth leading cause of death in the population as a whole, representing 25,188 deaths in that year alone. In addition, HIV infection and AIDS have been recognized as matters of significance among the elderly in the United States (Hinkle, 1991; Riley, Ory, & Zablotsky, 1989).

In 1990, 43,449 cases of AIDS were reported to the Centers for Disease Control—up by 23 percent from 1989. In the same year, 31,196 deaths were reported as associated with HIV infection and AIDS. Over the first ten years of the HIV epidemic in the United States, the largest *number* of deaths associated with HIV infection and AIDS has occurred among white males. However, in 1990 much higher death *rates* from this cause have been reported for African Americans (29.3 per 100,000) and Hispanic Americans (22.2 per 100,000), as compared to non-Hispanic Caucasian Americans (8.7 per 100,000) (CDC, 1991b). As a cause of death, HIV infection and AIDS is rising rapidly in influence among African Americans, Hispanic Americans, women, children, and adolescents. Heterosexual and perinatal transmission of HIV infection are rising more rapidly than other modes (Richardson, 1988).

From a global standpoint, a global report (Mann, Tarantola, & Netter, 1992) offered sophisticated analyses of estimates as of January 1, 1992 (see

TABLE 19.1   Estimates of HIV Infection, AIDS Cases, and AIDS-Related Deaths, North America and Worldwide, as of January 1, 1992

	North America (US and Canada)	Worldwide
HIV infection	1.2 million total	12.9 million total
	1.039 million men	7.1 million men
	128,500 women	4.7 million women
	16,000 children	1.1 million children
AIDS cases	266,500 total	2.6 million total
	257,500 adults	2.0 million adults
	9,000 children	574,000 children
AIDS-related deaths	223,500 total	2.5 million
	214,500 adults	1.9 million adults
	9,000 children	562,500 children

SOURCE: Mann, Tarantola, & Netter, 1992.

Table 19.1), and projections to 1995 (see Table 19.2) for HIV infection, AIDS cases, and AIDS-related deaths in both North America and the world. From these data, it is evident that "AIDS will remain a major public health challenge worldwide in the 21st century" (CDC, 1991c, p. 357). Resources for reliable information and/or assistance related to the HIV/AIDS epidemic are listed in the box on page 438.

In addition to its lethality, the potential universality of HIV infection may help to explain why so much of the response to this infectious disease has been nearly hysterical. We are *all* vulnerable to it, at least insofar as we engage in the behaviors through which the virus is transmitted.

Transmission

Curiously, the human vulnerability to HIV infection and AIDS is not nearly as threatening as vulnerability to many other forms of contagious disease, such as hepatitis, tuberculosis, cholera, or measles. The HIV itself does not appear to be very hardy or long-lived outside the human body. It is susceptible to heat and can be killed by a number of common disinfecting agents, such as bleach or chlorine (Douglas & Pinsky, 1992). In addition, although it can be communicated from one human being to another, the HIV is not contagious in the same ready manner in which airborne cold or flu viruses are transmitted.

That is, by contrast with most other communicable diseases, the HIV is relatively difficult to "catch." For example, apart from situations in which the individuals engage in the specific risk behaviors associated with transmission, there are no known cases of HIV infection through casual contacts or among family members who are caring for individuals who are HIV positive or who have AIDS (Sande, 1986). Furthermore, there is no evidence that infection has been spread under normal living conditions that do not involve exchange of bodily fluids, apparently because the virus is unable to penetrate normal skin.

TABLE 19.2   Projections of HIV Infection, AIDS Cases, and AIDS-Related Deaths, North America and Worldwide, as of 1995

	North America (US and Canada)	Worldwide
HIV infection	1.524 million cases	19.8 million cases
	1.495 million adults	17.5 million adults
	29,000 children	2.3 million children
AIDS cases	555,000 cases	6.4 million cases
	534,000 adults	4.9 million adults
	21,000 children	1.5 million children
AIDS-related deaths	496,000 deaths	6.2 million deaths
	475,500 adults	4.7 million adults
	20,500 children	1.5 million children

SOURCE: Mann, Tarantola, & Netter, 1992.

It has been noted that "the epidemic of HIV infection and AIDS is a composite of many individual, though overlapping, smaller epidemics, each of which has its own dynamics and time course" (CDC, 1987b, p. 13). That is, although infection stems from basically the same biological organism, it can have different manifestations and different consequences. Thus, one must understand and address the dynamics of each of these smaller epidemics in order to develop an adequate response to each of them (Turner, Miller, & Moses, 1989).

HIV infection is transmitted through direct contact between the bloodstream of the recipient, and the blood, semen, or vaginal or cervical secretions of the carrier. Consequently, although the HIV has been isolated in various organs and bodily fluids, there are only four primary routes of HIV transmission: (1) sexual activity that involves the exchange of bodily fluids; (2) sharing unsterilized needles; (3) contact with infected blood; and (4) perinatal transmission from mother to fetus or infant. We will look at each of these in turn.

Sexual activity that involves the exchange of bodily fluids   The most common route of transmission for HIV infection is by way of sexual intercourse or intimate sexual behavior that permits the virus to enter the bloodstream through tiny breaks in genital, rectal, or oral membranes—traditional barriers to infection (Grmek, 1990). The primary mode of this sort of infection around the globe has involved heterosexual intercourse, and this appears to be the route of transmission through which "Magic" Johnson acquired the HIV. During intimate sexual behavior, men can spread the virus to women, and women can spread it to men. Recent studies in the United States have shown that in heterosexual intercourse the HIV is 20 times more likely to be spread from men to women than the other way around. Thus, HIV infection is spreading most rapidly in sexually active adolescents and young adults.

In the United States, AIDS was first recognized in homosexual and bisexual men. However, the rate of HIV infection among such individuals has

National Resources for Information and Assistance Concerning HIV and AIDS, Unites States and Canada

In the United States

The Centers for Disease Control
National AIDS Hotline
(800) 342-AIDS
24 hours a day, 7 days a week

  La Linea Nacional de SIDA
  (800) 344-SIDA (Spanish
  language)
  8:00 A.M.–2:00 A.M. EST, 7 days
  a week

  (800) 243-7889
  TDD, hearing impaired
  Monday through Friday,
  10:00 A.M.–10:00 P.M. EST

AIDS Hotline for Teens
(800) 234-TEEN
Monday through Friday, 4:00–
8:00 P.M.

American Civil Liberties Union
  (ACLU)
  AIDS and Civil Liberties Project
(215) 592-1513

American Foundation for AIDS
  Research (AmFAR)
(212) 682-7440

American National Red Cross
(800) 26-BLOOD

Centers for Disease Control
  AIDS Information Office
(404) 329-2891

Gay Men's Health Crisis
(212) 807-6655

IGY Gay/Lesbian Youth Hotline
(800) 347-TEEN
Thursday through Sunday,
7:00 P.M.–11:45 P.M. EST

National AIDS Information
  Clearinghouse
(800) 458-5231

National Association of People
  with AIDS
(800) 338-AIDS

National Institute of Allergy and
  Infectious Diseases (NIAID)
(800) TRIALS-A

AIDS Clinical Trials Information
  Service
  (800) 243-7012
  TTY-DD, hearing impaired
  (301) 217-0023
  International number

National Institute of Drug Abuse
  (NIDA) Hotline
(800) 662-HELP

National Minority AIDS Council
(800) 669-5052

National Native American AIDS
  Prevention Center
(800) 283-AIDS

National Runaway Switchboard
(800) 621-4000

National Sexually Transmitted
  Disease Hotline
(800) 227-8922

National Youth Crisis Hotline
(800) 448-4663

The Pediatric AIDS Foundation
(800) 488-5000; (310) 395-9051

Pediatric and Pregnancy AIDS
  Hotline
(212) 430-3333
Monday through Friday,
  9:00 A.M.–5:00 P.M. EST

(continued)

(continued)

In Canada

Canadian AIDS Society
(613) 230-3580

National AIDS Secretariat
(613) 952-5258

Canadian Hemophilia Society
(514) 848-0503

National AIDS Clearinghouse
(613) 725-3769

decreased in recent years. This appears to result from significant changes in intimate sexual behavior among homosexual men and increased efforts at education concerning "safer sex" practices (CDC, 1991c; Douglas & Pinsky, 1992).

Because HIV infection is transmitted by sexual intercourse, it carries enormous emotional power. It invades human lives just when persons are often at their most open, most intimate, and most loving. And because much of American society is uncomfortable with homosexuality, HIV infection has carried more symbolic power than many other diseases (Sontag, 1989). Attitudes toward certain forms of intimate sexual behavior have played an important role in the HIV epidemic (Shilts, 1987; Turner, Miller, & Moses, 1989). They have interfered with attempts at education designed to modify or prevent such behaviors, perhaps the most notable of which was a pamphlet mailed by the government to every household in the United States in June 1988 (Koop, 1988). Two years earlier, in releasing "The Surgeon General's Report on AIDS," Dr. Koop had said: "Education about AIDS should start at an early age so that children can grow up knowing the behaviors to avoid to protect themselves from exposure to the AIDS virus" (Koop & Samuels, 1988, p. 8). In addition, attitudes concerning sexuality have interfered with attempts at prevention itself (for example, efforts to provide condoms or instruction concerning sexual practices that would minimize the likelihood of HIV infection).

Simple abstinence from sexual intercourse and other forms of intimate sexual behavior would make it impossible for one to acquire the HIV in this way (Johnson, 1992). Nevertheless, this is often ineffective advice and an unhelpful guideline for many individuals. In the case of HIV infection, a more attainable goal than total abstinence from sexual intercourse might be for an individual to limit sexual activity to a long-term, mutually monogamous relationship with a single person who is not otherwise and was not previously at risk for HIV infection. That this is not done testifies to the power of human sexuality, even in the face of the great threat of HIV infection and AIDS.

Although the ways in which the HIV is sexually transmitted seem now to be relatively clear, they also include some discomforting elements of uncertainty. It appears that sexual intercourse with an infected person can be relatively safe, as long as no transfer of blood, semen, or vaginal or cervical secretions occurs. In general, it is thought that latex condoms when appropriately used (that is, in conjunction with spermicides containing nonoxynol-9) are quite effective in preventing the exchange of these fluids, and thus in preventing the transfer of the virus from one person to another (Feldblum & Fortney, 1988). But many people apparently find the use of condoms to be awkward and/or embarrassing. In the passion of the moment, caution can appear to be an undesirable or unnecessary impedance.

For example, there is good research (for example, Catania et al., 1992) that shows that many in high-risk groups continue to have unprotected, multipartner sexual encounters, despite their awareness and general knowledge of the AIDS epidemic. Even when such individuals protect themselves against pregnancy, they often leave themselves vulnerable to HIV and other sexually transmitted infections. Thus, on its own, education about the facts of HIV infection and the risks of AIDS does not seem to be wholly effective in changing people's behaviors. Sex is so powerful a force in human life that even vulnerability to a lethal disease does not always interfere with its power. Even though individuals may have an intellectual understanding of the connections between risk-taking behaviors and the likelihood of acquiring the infection, they may not act upon that understanding as they conduct their lives.

Sharing unsterilized needles   In addition to sexual transmission, there are other means of exchanging bodily fluids. One of the most important of these in the transmission of HIV is the sharing of unsterilized needles. Such needles may carry blood and the HIV from one person to another. This may occur in a number of ways. In poor countries, it might involve the reuse of expensive needles in health care without adequate sterilization procedures. Among athletes, it might have to do with sharing needles in the administration of steroids. In the United States, it has most often involved the illicit use of intravenous drugs, which has come to be one of the main routes of HIV infection (CDC, 1991c; Turner, Miller, & Moses, 1989). It is a particularly insidious route.

This is true because of issues associated with intravenous drug use in American society. Those who engage in such behaviors are already acting in ways that are not socially approved. They are, in many ways, resistant to social pressures and educational efforts that warned of the dangers of such behavior long before the HIV epidemic appeared on the scene. Nevertheless, risk-reduction efforts have taken various forms and have had some impact on intravenous drug users (Friedman, Des Jarlais, & Goldsmith, 1989).

Many Americans are as uncomfortable about the nonmedical use of intravenous drugs as they are about intimate sexual behavior. Thus, many are unwilling to support programs that provide sterilized needles to intravenous drug users as a public health measure. Consequently, in many segments of American society, education and preventive actions designed to minimize the use of unsterilized needles may be even less effective than education about safer sex practices.

Moreover, once a person has been infected with the HIV virus, he or she can spread the virus to others in any exchange of infected bodily fluids. Thus, someone who was infected from sharing an unsterilized needle may spread the virus to a sexual partner. When this occurs, a person who was not directly involved in the use of unsterilized needles may acquire the virus.

Contact with infected blood   A third route of transmission of the HIV is related to a group of behaviors involving contact with infected blood, bodily tissues, or organs. Statistically, the most significant of these has involved persons with hemophilia and other individuals who have acquired the HIV as a result of receiving transfusions of contaminated blood or concentrated blood products. This was the way in which both Ryan White and Elizabeth Glaser acquired the HIV. Similarly, when the former tennis champion Arthur Ashe (who died in February of 1993) announced in April of 1992 that he had AIDS and that he had known since 1988 that he was infected with the HIV, he attributed his infection to a transfusion of infected blood during surgery in 1983.

These transfusion-related infections came about in the early 1980s when the infectious agent had not yet been identified, when its mode or route of action was not clear, and when screening tests were not yet available to detect whether it was present in the supply of blood available for transfusion (Pindyck, 1988; Stehr-Green, Holman, Jason, & Evatt, 1988).

By 1985, however, effective screening tests for donors of blood, bodily tissues, and organs had been developed. There is no evidence that any transmissions of the HIV virus through this route have occurred since that time, and apparently there is no longer any significant risk of this sort of transmission occurring in the United States.

Thus, reported cases of HIV infection in the United States involving transfusion of blood or blood products stabilized at around 1,300 per year in 1988 (involving persons infected *before* 1985) and have gradually declined since that time. Of course, even if this sort of transmission of the virus has been completely eliminated, the long dormancy period between infection and manifestation in the form of external signs or symptoms will mean that transfusion-related cases of AIDS may continue to be reported for a number of years after 1985.

Contact with an infected person's blood has also resulted in acquisition of the HIV by a small number of health care workers (McCray, 1986). For example, the health care worker might have been accidentally stuck with a needle containing the blood of an infected person in such a way as to transmit the virus to the worker's bloodstream. However, careful surveillance of health care workers with AIDS has revealed that their share (5 percent) of all AIDS cases in the United States is less than their share (6 percent) of the U.S. labor force, and that "most health care workers with AIDS have reported nonoccupational risk factors for HIV infection" (Chamberland et al., 1991, p. 3461).

Furthermore, in the occupational transmission of disease from patient to health care worker there is a much higher risk of acquiring a serious or even lethal infection from the hepatitis B virus (HBV) than from HIV. For example, it has been estimated that some 12,000 U.S. health care workers are infected with HBV each year through exposure at work and that approximately 250 of them will die (CDC, 1989b). In addition, "because the hepatitis B virus is also bloodborne and is both hardier and more infectious than HTLV-III/LAV [that is, HIV], recommendations that would prevent transmission of hepatitis B will also prevent transmission of AIDS" (CDC, 1985d, p. 681). The likelihood of acquiring either of these infections is greatly reduced by scrupulous adherence to the principles of "universal precautions" in the workplace, which are meant to insist upon careful clinical practice in all instances and to minimize the possibility of accidents (CDC, 1985d; Brown & Turner, 1989).

There is also the theoretical possibility of transmission of HIV infection from a health care worker to a person who is receiving care. That is, concern has been expressed that a person receiving care might acquire the HIV virus through contact with an infected health care worker. However, throughout the entire first decade of the HIV epidemic there appears to have been only one health care worker in the whole of the United States who transmitted the HIV virus to patients. This is the case of Dr. David Acer, a dentist in Florida who died in 1990, who appears to have infected six of his patients with the HIV virus (CDC, 1990, 1991a, 1991e; Ciesielski et al., 1992), although the actual method of transmission even in this case is uncertain. This suggests only an extremely small risk of transmission of HIV from health care workers to patients, one that can be minimized by adherence to authoritative recommendations (CDC, 1991f).

Perinatal transmission from mother to fetus or infant   Finally, there is a significant risk that pregnant women who have been infected with the HIV may transmit the virus to their fetus perinatally—that is, either in the uterus, at birth, or shortly after birth. It is generally accepted that this sort of transmission mainly takes place across the placental barrier or in breast-feeding. However, exact mechanisms, conditions, and timing are not thoroughly understood (Minkoff, 1989). Not all infants acquire the HIV from an infected mother; not all infants who test positive for HIV antibodies continue to do so over time. Nevertheless, 80 percent of women with HIV infection are of child-bearing age (Smeltzer & Whipple, 1991b).

Two principal areas of concern are related to this route of transmission. The first involves women. Here, the Centers for Disease Control (1985e) have developed a set of recommendations to guide uninfected women in learning how to avoid becoming infected, to counsel infected women concerning decisions to become pregnant, and to help infected women to manage their pregnancies and care for their children. However, various cultural, social, and psychological factors influence decisions related to pregnancy. Many women may not have the power in various social and sexual relationships (for example, in male-dominated societies, in abusive or highly dependent relationships, in circumstances of poverty) to negotiate changes concerning avoidance of intravenous drug use or unprotected intimate sexual behavior. Thus, HIV infection may bear upon women and children in distinctive ways (Chin, 1990; Lester, 1989; Rogers, 1985).

The second area of concern arising from perinatal transmission of the HIV has to do with infants and children. As has been noted, this is how both of the children of Elizabeth Glaser acquired the HIV. As cofounder of the Pediatric AIDS Foundation, Glaser has worked to raise funds and to encourage research on pediatric AIDS and maternal transmission issues.

Clearly, issues involving HIV infection in women and children need more study in their own right. There is much yet to be learned about the vulnerability of women (Corea, 1992; Rieder & Ruppelt, 1988; Smeltzer & Whipple, 1991a, 1991b) and children (Boland & Rizzi, 1986; Krasinski, Borkowsky, & Holzman, 1989; Qtoby, 1990; Scott, Hutto, & Makuch, 1989) to HIV infection and about the course of the disease in such individuals. Issues deserving additional study include questions related to transmission of the virus; determinations about appropriate and distinctive manifestations of AIDS in women and children (which may be different from clinical markers in adult males); and principles underlying care of those who are infected. In the meantime, women and children increasingly are the persons who are becoming infected with the HIV virus (CDC, 1991d; National Research Council, 1990).

*I*ndividual and Social Responses to HIV Infection and AIDS

Individual and social responses to HIV infection and to AIDS are not wholly unlike human responses to some other epidemic diseases. Whenever a society has been threatened by a "plague" (a contagious disease that reaches epidemic proportions) or a "pandemic" (a worldwide epidemic), both historical and literary analysis have shown that people react in quite similar ways (Black, 1985; Camus, 1947/1972; McNeill, 1976). Contagious diseases frighten us. This is especially true when we are uncertain about their causes, unclear about or unwilling to acknowledge their modes of transmission, and aware that they are life-threatening and that there is no immediate means of preventing death.

In the case of AIDS, there is agreement that HIV infection is a necessary cause (that is, it must be present to get this disease), but there is uncertainty that it is (always) enough by itself to cause the AIDS disease (that is, it may not be sufficient). As has been noted, the length of the latency period (the time between infection with the virus and the onset of disease symptoms) can be up to ten years or more. That is, there appears to be a very long period during which the HIV lurks within the body without being active. This is very puzzling. It leaves us unclear as to whether the HIV is actually inactive or dormant, or whether it is at work during this period in some very slow or hitherto undiscovered way.

In any case, it is not yet fully understood what triggers the virus to become (more) active at some point or whether there are conditions or cofactors that move one from being infected with the virus (but not yet having AIDS) to actually having the disease and showing the symptoms associated with AIDS (Piel, 1989). Some have even wondered whether everyone who is infected with the HIV will develop AIDS. The short history of experience with the HIV and its unusually long latency period in the body have not thus far permitted definitive answers to questions of this sort.

Another matter to consider in responses to HIV infection and AIDS is that human beings do not like uncertainty, especially about matters of life and death. Still, life is full of uncertainties and uncertain facts. For example, individuals in the United States are much more likely to die in motor vehicle

accidents than from becoming infected by the HIV. Thus, it is curious that there appears to be much less concern among many Americans about the epidemic of deaths associated with motor vehicle accidents in the United States (the cause of 46,814 deaths in 1990) than about AIDS-related deaths (25,188 deaths in the same year) (National Center for Health Statistics, 1993).

And why is AIDS regarded as so much more threatening to health care workers than, for example, hepatitis B? Hepatitis is more infectious than is HIV and results in many more deaths of health care workers in a single year (Heeg & Coleman, 1992; McCray, 1986). Yet we hear much less about hepatitis, and health care workers appear to feel less threatened by it. Nor has there been much public discussion in the early 1990s of threats arising from new drug-resistant strains of tuberculosis—threats that could become very significant to anyone who enters or works in health care institutions.

Perhaps the response to AIDS has much to do with its being perceived as a new, rapidly spreading disease that involves sex and blood and that leads inexorably to death. The swift dissemination of HIV infection has been startling, but some have noted that the question of its inevitable lethality needs to be carefully explored. Of the 179,136 cases of AIDS reported during the first ten years of the HIV epidemic in the United States, more than 113,000 or some 63 percent have died. Thus, Douglas and Pinsky (1992, p. 6) wrote:

> AIDS is often described as "invariably fatal," but this contradicts the facts . . . many people have had AIDS for a number of years and are still alive. One study . . . found that 15% of people with AIDS survive at least five years . . . increasing medical knowledge and better treatment improve the life expectancy of people with AIDS.

Perhaps in time, AIDS will be seen as a chronic disease rather than a life-threatening one. But for now, that is not the usual perception.

Lessons from HIV Infection and AIDS

With this background about HIV infection and AIDS in mind, it can now be asked how AIDS fits into the central topics and themes of this book. In some ways, this new epidemic is a particularly striking exemplar for many of the issues that are discussed here. That can be illustrated by focusing on four central issues as they are related to HIV infection and AIDS: encounters with death; attitudes toward death; dying; and grief and bereavement.

Encounters with Death

Chapter 1 noted how encounters with death in late 20th-century America are different from those of many other cultures. That discussion included such matters as *who* dies, *what* they die from, and *where* they die. Typical death-related patterns in American society involve an old(er) person, dying in a lengthy process of a degenerative disease, in a hospital. HIV infection and AIDS provide forceful contrasts with this image of dying and death.

First noticed in young (often in their 20s) men, HIV infection and AIDS continue to affect young adults—both female and male—and children, including newborns. HIV infection is a communicable disease that has appeared at a time when modern society has had spectacular successes in diminishing or eradicating the lethal threat of many communicable diseases. For example, some have claimed that smallpox has essentially been eliminated in the modern world, and this is true as well for some other communicable diseases (such as measles and cholera), at least in many of the industrial nations. Notwithstanding outbreaks of cholera in other parts of the world and the apparent development of drug-resistant strains of tuberculosis in developed countries, HIV infection and AIDS dramatically challenge the belief that modern society can eliminate or even radically control contagious diseases.

Furthermore, many persons with AIDS have deliberately chosen (or been forced) to die in places other than hospitals. In these and many other ways, AIDS undercuts popular images associated with dying and death in American society. Death is suddenly perceived again to be not just (or mainly) a concern of the old; it can strike anyone. In recent years, humans have learned once again the hard lessons that a communicable disease can still savage a community. Also, once more it has been recognized that the health care establishment is less than omnipotent—at stopping infection, at successfully treating (that is, curing) disease, and even at preventing death. These lessons reveal how naive earlier faith in the omnipotence of modern medicine was.

Attitudes Toward Death

As experiences change, attitudes are bound to be affected. One of the striking outcomes of the HIV epidemic has been that many people have learned to face their own death and/or the deaths of loved ones with courage and even equanimity (for example, Monette, 1988; Peabody, 1986; Whitmore, 1988). Death is still perceived to be an enemy, an unwanted intruder, but compared to the dying sometimes associated with the last stages of AIDS, it is often almost welcome.

AIDS may reinforce the belief that death is not the worst thing that can happen to humans. It may help people to recognize the value in and to strive for what Weisman (1972) called an "appropriate death." And it may do this not solely among those who were formerly most vulnerable to death (the poor and the old), but also among those who up to now had thought of themselves as less vulnerable to death—young adults, the middle-aged, and those who are economically better off.

HIV infection and AIDS are also instructive about attitudes toward death by demonstrating how clearly such attitudes affect behavior. People have beliefs, feelings, and values relating to some behaviors that can lead to transmission of the HIV infection, and they have beliefs, feelings, and values related to the disease process itself and to associated processes of dying. Attitudes of this sort are often expressed in metaphors used to discuss disease; they are superimposed upon the disease entity itself and upon those who are associated with it (Ross, 1988; Sontag, 1978, 1989). Such attitudes directly affect behavior: in the case of HIV infection and AIDS they have all too often led to social and psychological isolation for infected persons (Herek & Glunt, 1988). A notable example of this isolation in the history of the AIDS epidemic in the United States occurred at one point when Haitian immigrants—who were poor, black, and spoke French—seemed to provide a convenient scapegoat for at least part of what was happening (Grmek, 1990).

To our greater communal shame, in some instances individual and societal attitudes have led to violence against such persons. This is what happened to Ryan White in 1984 in his fight to be readmitted to junior high school in Indiana after his diagnosis with AIDS. A similar tragedy befell the family of Clifford and Louise Ray on August 28, 1987, when they found their home set afire and burned to the ground in Arcadia, Florida. The Ray family had three hemophiliac children who had acquired HIV infection through transfused blood products and who had won a legal battle to be able to return to school. (The oldest of the Ray children, Ricky, died of AIDS-related complications in

December of 1992 at age 15.) Events like these occurred despite early and authoritative statements favoring school attendance and unrestricted foster care for most youngsters who are HIV positive (for example, American Academy of Pediatrics, 1986; CDC, 1985c). Ironically, youngsters with compromised immune systems are far more likely to be at risk of acquiring a lethal infection from their peers than they are of communicating such an infection to peers (Kirp, 1989).

Many individuals who have been diagnosed with the HIV have lost their jobs, have experienced the loss of work-related health insurance, have been abandoned by former friends, and may even have found themselves without a place to live. These would be difficult experiences for a healthy person to endure; they are infinitely more burdensome for someone made ill by a virus that undermines bodily defenses and energies, renders the individual subject to the unpredictable ravages of opportunistic diseases, and may directly attack the individual's mental capacities to ensure care for personal needs and safety. Nevertheless, feelings run high with this disease. All too often, HIV infection and AIDS have been characterized by extreme threat, uncertainty, and stigmatization (Joseph & Ostrow, 1987). This has occurred despite clear evidence that such people are not a significant threat to others. In addition, American society has long-standing legal prohibitions against discrimination on the basis of health status (Dalton & Burris, 1987; Hunter & Rubenstein, 1992) and the Americans with Disabilities Act (which became effective in 1991) encompasses protection for persons with HIV infection or AIDS within its scope.

Attitudes related to HIV infection and AIDS also reveal themselves in other ways. Because of the nature of the main routes of HIV infection so far in American society, to announce that one has the virus or has AIDS is often to arouse suspicion about one's past behavior. That is, accusations (overt or silent) of "unacceptable" behavior may accompany such an announcement. Many persons diagnosed with this disease have had to reveal at once not only their illness but also their sexual orientation—as in the case of the actor Rock Hudson, who died of AIDS in 1985. Since homosexuality is so poorly understood and often is judged negatively in American society, many persons resist "coming out" to friends and family members (Monette, 1992). Many have suffered rejection upon doing so. This becomes very difficult when one is also suffering from AIDS or from the many evident sources of distress associated with HIV infection (for example, the lesions of Kaposi's sarcoma). Just when one most needs support, others may turn away because of their moral disapprobation of one's behavior. So to tell is to risk rejection and isolation in dying. And not to tell is also to risk isolation, because if the people to whom we are closest do not know we are ill, they cannot be with us when we are in extreme peril.

Today, HIV infection and AIDS are still so closely associated in many people's minds with homosexuality or use of illicit drugs that to be diagnosed with the disease is to be looked at with suspicion. Again, there is a catch-22 here; to tell or not to tell? Either way, there is a risk. Despite all of the media discussion of HIV infection and AIDS, the examples of individu-

A man comforts a friend at an exhibition of the AIDS quilt.

als who were or became public figures associated with HIV infection and AIDS (such as Ryan White, Arthur Ashe, Rock Hudson, Liberace, Elizabeth Glaser, and "Magic" Johnson), and extensive efforts at professional and community education (such as the Names Project, in which traveling displays of three-by-six-foot patches for a quilt commemorating individuals who have died of AIDS are set up in public arenas), it is not yet clear whether and exactly how some aspects of attitudes toward AIDS may be changing in the United States.

Coping with Dying

Not surprisingly, all of this affects experiences associated with dying and the care provided for persons with HIV infection or AIDS (and their families). The trajectory of the disease is complicated, multidimensional, and often lengthy.

One does not die of HIV infection or AIDS itself; one dies of the opportunistic infections that AIDS renders one unable to fight off. As a result, an infected person is likely to encounter a series of infections, interventions, and repeated infection. Each infection represents its own relatively unpredictable assault from one or more of a variety of possible sources; each counterattack may represent a mobilization of one's remaining natural defenses, along with whatever resources are available from modern medicine. In the short run, this process is likely to resemble a roller coaster ride of relapse and remission; in the long run, it is typically an experience of gradual decline—more and more severe losses of healthy functions over a period of weeks, months, or years.

Thus, dying associated with AIDS is rightly perceived as particularly difficult for many individuals. Being vulnerable to infectious organisms (which is what "immune deficiency" of any sort makes one), persons with AIDS are peculiarly exposed to their environments. This means that persons with AIDS are vulnerable to opportunistic diseases for which both they and most other persons are carriers, because nearly everyone is a carrier of organisms that can produce disease in ourselves or in those to whom we may transmit the organisms.

A person with a normal or uncompromised immune system is ordinarily able to keep such organisms in check, both in his or her own body and as a result of transmission from others. Furthermore, even HIV infection does not compromise all of the elements in the body's natural immune system. Thus, much of the work of modern medicine (when it is not able to directly attack the disease-producing organism) is devoted to efforts to encourage the mobilization of an individual's own internal defense system and palliation of distressing symptoms. But persons who have a natural or acquired immune deficiency are not able to mobilize all of these natural bodily defenses. As a result, they sometimes suffer one disease after another, and the associated pathogens may affect various parts of their bodies, such as lungs, gastrointestinal tract, or brain. Severe weight loss, diarrhea, and even dementia are possible symptomatic responses to invading organisms.

Furthermore, American society has displayed in many ways a tendency to distance itself from death. This can frequently lead to isolation of those who are dying. Such isolation is often magnified in the case of HIV infection and AIDS (although, paradoxically enough, personal contact with an infected individual may help to humanize the situation and to generate tolerance and compassion). Just as the first hospice in Connecticut encountered opposition from some parts of the community to its initial plans to build an inpatient facility, resistance has also been shown in many areas in more recent years to building or maintaining residences for persons with AIDS. And there have been problems in adapting established programs of hospital and hospice care to the needs of those with HIV infection and AIDS.

Both hospital and hospice programs that had dealt with dying persons and their family members for many years have had to learn new lessons in coping with HIV infection and AIDS (Buckingham, 1992). These lessons have involved problems in caring for new sorts of distressing symptoms (such as persistent fever or diarrhea associated with constitutional disease in a person with AIDS), issues concerning the confusion and dementia that are often associated with AIDS (Fenton, 1987), and challenges related to psychosocial reactions to HIV infection and AIDS (Lyons, Larson, Anderson, & Bilheimer, 1989; Nichols, 1985). Some groups and some communities have formed programs of care and support for persons with AIDS, thereby encouraging hospitals, hospice programs, and other social institutions to find their roles in this work (International Work Group on Death, Dying, and Bereavement, 1992b).

Along with the usual discomfort of caring for persons who are dying, caring for persons who are dying with AIDS includes a fear of contagion. Nevertheless, the American Medical Association's Council on Ethical and Judicial Affairs (1988) has made clear that "a physician may not ethically refuse to treat a patient whose condition is within the physician's current realm of competence solely because the patient is seropositive. . . . Neither those who have the disease [AIDS] nor those who have been infected with the virus should be subject to discrimination based on fear or prejudice, least of all by members of the health care community" (p. 1360). Most other organizations of health care providers have adopted similar policies insisting that persons with HIV or AIDS are not to be rejected for care, and there is clear consensus in support of this view from an ethical standpoint (for example, Arras, 1988; Jonsen, 1990; Pellegrino, 1988).

The proper human response to those who have HIV infection and/or AIDS is clear, as Shenson (1988, p. 48) has suggested:

> In all its horror AIDS, like leprosy, is another disease—no more no less. It is not symbolic of anything. There are no "victims," because there is no crime. There are no "innocents," because there are no "guilty," and there is no blame, because there has been no intention to cause harm. There are only sick men, women and children, all of whom need our help.

Coping with Grief and Bereavement

Loss and grief associated with HIV infection begin with the realization that the world of the late 20th century has changed and will never again be the same as it was prior to the appearance of the HIV. New risks have been introduced and old risks have been reinforced. Old ways of behavior may need to be abandoned or modified. Thousands upon thousands of people have become ill and died, a much larger number is infected, and many, many more are affected. Hard lessons have once again been learned about human limitation.

Those who are infected, as well as those who care about and for such individuals, experience many losses during the course of the very unpredictable trajectory associated with immune deficiency. Physical distress may take numerous forms, such as diarrhea and pain. Psychological distress may arise from threats to security, self-image, and competence. Social relationships may be challenged, along with one's vocational role as a contributor to the community and one's confidence that society will return the support that is needed. And spiritual issues may be especially poignant when life is threatened in its prime or shortly after birth by a new and unanticipated disease.

These challenges may begin with diagnosis of HIV infection and extend throughout much of the illness; they are also likely to continue after death for survivors. Thus, a sense of loss and grief may be present at many levels for many individuals both prior to and after death. It may express itself, for example, in problems associated with social stigma both for the ill person and for the families of persons with HIV infection (Goffman, 1963). The announcement that someone who is loved is HIV positive or has AIDS has led to ostracism and isolation for many individuals. Almost from the moment they know the diagnosis, these people fall into the category of "disenfranchised grievers" (Doka, 1989a), both in terms of who is grieving and what they are grieving about.

In the case of a homosexual couple, the person closest to the infected individual may be pushed aside, ignored, or treated cruelly because that individual's relationship with the ill person is not approved. This is further complicated in those cases wherein the person who has been shunted aside in this way may not only be grieving the dying and imminent death of the ill person but may also be concerned about his or her own health. Families often believe that they cannot tell close friends what is really wrong for fear that they will be rejected. Consequently, their grieving must be done in isolation—and, even then, perhaps under a cloud of suspicion. The specter of HIV infection and AIDS can make even worse an already-difficult situation of loss, grief, and bereavement.

Summary

The HIV/AIDS epidemic simultaneously reflects many of the patterns that have been discussed throughout this book and creates new patterns of its own. It challenges us as individuals and as members of a society to look again at our beliefs, feelings, values, and behaviors. Information must replace ignorance and reasoned judgment must replace irrational decisions in all aspects of public policy, interpersonal relations, research, the provision of care, and education (Institute of Medicine, 1986, 1988). The reason for this is that a person who is living with HIV infection or dying with AIDS is, in the end, like all of the rest of us: most fundamentally, he or she is a person. And he or she is a person living with suffering.

In an address presented to a joint session on AIDS of the California legislature on March 6, 1987, former Surgeon General C. Everett Koop quoted the last sentence of Thornton Wilder's 1927 novel *The Bridge of San Luis Rey*: "There is a land of the living and a land of the dead and the bridge is love, the only survival, the only meaning" (Koop & Samuels, 1988, p. 18). As health care providers, as spiritual guides, as members of social communities, as friends, as family members, and, finally, just as fellow human beings, we must care about and for persons with HIV infection and AIDS. Not to do so is to risk the loss of our own best selves, our humanness. In caring for others, we care for ourselves—as individuals and as a community. That is, we become fully who we are—human beings.

QUESTIONS FOR REVIEW AND DISCUSSION

1. This chapter described the history of the HIV/AIDS epidemic, the discovery of the virus, and how it acts to lead to AIDS and death. All of this involves a great deal of information. In your judgment, what are the main facts that we should retain from all of this information and what are the main lessons that we should learn?

2. Many (perhaps most) people in the United States report that they know how the HIV is transmitted and what should be done to prevent acquiring that virus. Many people in American society also report that they are not doing what is necessary to prevent transmission and acquisition of the HIV. Do you know what is involved in transmission/acquisition of the HIV? Are you doing what is necessary to prevent transmission/acquisition of the HIV? Why or why not?

3. In your judgment, what is the most important thing that each of us as individuals should do to help individuals who are already infected with the HIV and/or who have AIDS? In your judgment, what is the most important thing that society should do to help individuals who are already infected with the HIV and/or who have AIDS? Are you doing such things? Is society doing such things? Why or why not?

SUGGESTED READINGS

Historical and personal accounts can be found in the following:

Black, D. (1985). *The Plague Years: A Chronicle of AIDS, the Epidemic of Our Times*.
Monette, P. (1988). *Borrowed Time: An AIDS Memoir*.

Peabody, B. (1986). *The Screaming Room: A Mother's Journal of Her Son's Struggle with AIDS.*

Shilts, R. (1987). *And the Band Played On: Politics, People, and the AIDS Epidemic.*

Whitmore, G. (1988). *Someone Was Here: Profiles in the AIDS Epidemic.*

For general introductions to HIV infection and AIDS, consult:

Douglas, P. H., & Pinsky, L. (1992). *The Essential AIDS Fact Book* (rev. ed.).

Koop, C. E. (1988). *Understanding AIDS.*

Kübler-Ross, E. (1987). *AIDS: The Ultimate Challenge.*

Pinsky, L., & Douglas, P. H. (1992). *The Essential HIV Treatment Fact Book.*

Roth, J. S. (1989). *All About AIDS.*

More detailed analyses are available in the following:

Cohen, P. T., Sande, M. A., & Volberding, P. A. (Eds.). (1990). *The AIDS Knowledge Base: A Textbook in HIV Disease from the University of California, San Francisco, and the San Francisco General Hospital.*

Corless, I. B., & Pittman-Lindeman, M. (Eds.). (1988). *AIDS: Principles, Practices, and Politics.*

Gostin, L. O. (Ed.). (1990). *AIDS and the Health Care System.*

Grmek, M. D. (1990). *History of AIDS: Emergence and Origin of a Modern Pandemic.*

Mann, J. M., Tarantola, D.J.M., & Netter, T. W. (Eds.). (1992). *AIDS in the World: A Global Report.*

National Research Council. (1990). *AIDS: The Second Decade.*

Piel, J. (Ed.). (1989). *The Science of AIDS.*

Sontag, S. (1989). *AIDS and Its Metaphors.*

Special issues concerning women, the workplace, and other policy matters are considered in the following:

Brown, K. C., & Turner, J. G. (1989). *AIDS: Policies and Programs for the Workplace.*

Corea, G. (1992). *The Invisible Epidemic: The Story of Women and AIDS.*

Dalton, H. L., & Burris, S. (Eds.). (1987). *AIDS and the Law: A Guide for the Public.*

Hunter, N. D., & Rubenstein, W. B. (Eds.). (1992). *AIDS Agenda: Emerging Issues in Civil Rights.*

Lester, B. (1989). *Women and AIDS: A Practical Guide for Those Who Help Others.*

Richardson, D. (1988). *Women and AIDS.*

Rieder, I., & Ruppelt, P. (Eds.). (1988). *AIDS: The Women.*

CHAPTER 20

Education About Death, Dying, and Bereavement

This chapter offers an analysis of the nature and role of education about death, dying, and bereavement—sometimes called "death education." Following two short concrete examples, each of which describes a student who is enrolled in a college course on death and dying, the central portions of this chapter respond to questions like the following: What is education about death, dying, and bereavement? What might lead someone to become interested in this sort of education? In what forms might this sort of education be presented? What are some of its different dimensions, goals, functions, and basic lessons?

Two Students

Mary Jones

Mary Jones was a bit older than the typical undergraduate college student. When Mary enrolled in a death and dying course, her children were 5 and 7 years old. The death and dying course supported Mary's career objectives in nursing, but she also chose this course as a means to address her own special personal concerns. These related especially to her two young children and their grandparents. Two years earlier, Mary's father-in-law had died rather suddenly of a heart attack. Mary, her husband, and their children were shocked and stunned by this death. They had not previously had any experience with a significant death in their lives and they were bewildered by all the things that had to be dealt with afterward.

Mary had not known what to say to her children when her father-in-law died. She had heard from a friend that young children would not be able to cope with the feelings expressed at a funeral, so she had not permitted them to attend. Later, she regretted that decision. The children asked many questions about their grandfather, about what had happened, and about when he would come to visit them again. Mary did not know how to answer such questions or how to help her husband and mother-in-law in their grief.

Recently, Mary's own father had died after a long and very difficult period of physical and mental debilitation arising from Alzheimer's disease. His early episodes of mild confusion had seemed odd and sometimes even a bit humorous to his children and grandchildren. But when he began to wander off alone, act in an irritable way, and even become abusive to those around him, life became difficult. Placing her father in a nursing home was a hard decision for Mary and her mother. It did help to reduce some of their worries about his difficult behavior, but it was hard to visit and witness his ongoing decline. His funeral was a sad but quiet experience.

The family's experiences with the illness and death of Mary's own father were quite different, but still difficult and baffling. This time, Mary allowed the children to visit her father when he was still at home and in the nursing home, and they did attend the funeral. But what could one say about this awful, progressive disease? The children wanted to know if the same thing could happen to their father and Mary or to themselves. They did not understand why their two grandmothers seemed to behave so differently after the deaths of their husbands—one dissolving into tears, sadness, and depression, while the other joined a group for widows and entered into new activities and relationships.

Mary hoped that the course in death education would teach her how to cope with the dying persons for whom she would care as a nurse and that it would help her to guide her own children in dealing with past and future losses.

Tom Smith

Tom was a 19-year-old business student when he enrolled in a death and dying course. When Tom came to the first meeting of the class, he was disappointed to learn that he would be expected to undertake a research or interview project. Tom did not contribute much to class discussions. He was happy just to get through the term.

Eight months later, Tom's fiancée—a bright young woman whom he had dated on a steady basis since their sophomore year in high school—was killed in a fiery automobile accident. Tom was devastated. He did not know what to say to his fiancée's parents or to her brothers and sisters. He wanted to run away from the funeral or to hit some of the people who kept saying to him that they were "so sorry." Tom tried to keep busy and not think about his feelings. He stayed away from places and people that reminded him of his fiancée, but he also realized that some of his friends had changed their behaviors with regard to him. They avoided or drew back from him for a while, and they tried not to mention his fiancée's name in his presence.

One day as he walked across campus, Tom ran into one of the instructors from the death and dying course. Suddenly, he realized that many of the things that had been discussed in that course were now happening to him.

Forms of Education

Education occurs in various contexts and is conducted in many different ways. For example, *formal education* is typically associated with programs of organized instruction (elementary and secondary education; college and university curricula; professional and postgraduate education; training and inservice programs for those who work as care providers; workshops and presentations for members of support groups and for the general public).

Informal education usually begins at an earlier point in time in the arms of a parent or guardian and in the interactions within a family or similar social group. It includes the many lessons that individuals learn from their own experiences, from the people whom they meet throughout their lives, and from the events in which they take part. Travel, the media, and many other

*Two young
children learn
about death
during a visit to
a cemetery.*

sources contribute raw materials and insights to a lifelong process of informal education that may go on almost without one's notice.

Opportunities for informal education emerge naturally from teachable moments, although such moments can also be used to good advantage by flexible programs of formal education. The phrase "teachable moments" refers to unanticipated events in life that offer potential for developing useful educational insights and lessons, as well as for personal growth. In a simple picture book for young readers, Brown (1958) describes one such moment when some children find a dead bird in the woods. As the children touch the cold and stiff body of the bird, they begin to realize the difference between a living and a dead animal. As they bury the bird, mark its grave, and return for several days to revisit the site, they try out adult ritual and learn something about death and sadness.

Teachable moments thrust themselves into the middle of life in different ways. Some illustrate in concrete ways lessons that had already somehow been taught. Others, such as near-miss auto accidents, remind individuals that they are not as immune to life-threatening danger as they might have wished to believe. Still others, like the explosion of the Challenger shuttle in 1986 and the deaths of its astronauts, combine a need to provide support to grieving persons with opportunities for useful education about life and death.

The Emergence of Death Education

During the 1960s and early 1970s, it was common for people to say that death was a taboo topic in American society, a subject that was somehow out of bounds for scholarly research and education (for example, Feifel, 1963). This did not mean that there had never been discussion of issues related to death, dying, and bereavement. On the contrary, research by Choron (1963, 1964) revealed a rich tradition of human interest in death-related topics.

Nevertheless, it was undeniably true that in the United States around the middle of the 20th century, research and writing on death, dying, and bereavement were limited, and there were few educational opportunities in this field. An important, fundamental, and constitutive dimension of human life had been set apart from many forms of critical study and investigation. It was as if death needed to be quarantined in order not to infect the way in which people wished to view the remainder of their lives.

As one might expect, these sorts of barriers to study and prohibitions against curiosity were not likely to endure—particularly when they concerned an area of human life that is crucial to human welfare. A reaction of some sort was almost inevitable. It emerged in several ways.

Early work by a number of isolated scholars began to achieve broader recognition. New initiatives by modern pioneers like Feifel (1959) encouraged behavioral scientists, clinicians, and humanists to direct attention to these topics, to study how people were behaving in this area, to develop new programs of care for the dying and the bereaved, and to undertake research on attitudes toward death. This was the beginning of the modern death awareness movement (Pine, 1977, 1986). It was soon followed and paralleled by a desire to convey the results of this new awareness. This expressed itself in a wide range of articles, books, and literature of all sorts, in the establishment of organizations and journals in this field, and eventually in countless programs of all sorts of death-related education. In terms of education, this new movement realized that throughout human life everyone receives educational messages about death, dying, and bereavement in a variety of informal and formal ways. For that reason, death-related education has concentrated on an examination of the validity and value of educational messages in this field.

Concerns That Lead to an Interest in Death Education

Kalish (1989, p. 75) described expressions of interest in education in the field of death, dying, and bereavement in terms of four basic types of concern: "(1) personal concern because of some previous experience that has not been resolved; (2) personal concern because of some ongoing experience, such as the critical illness or very recent death of a close family member; (3) involvement with a relevant form of work, such as nursing, medicine, social work, the ministry, or volunteer service through a hospice organization; or (4) a wish to understand better what death means or how to cope more effectively with one's own death or the death or grief of others."

People with each of these types of concern can readily be identified in classes, workshops, or presentations on death, dying, or bereavement. Those who are dealing with *the aftermath of an unresolved death-related experience* or with *a current death-related experience* deserve special sensitivity. They may be very tender in their feelings and vulnerable to added pain. Many (like Mary Jones, who was mentioned at the outset of this chapter) have chosen to come to an educational forum in order to use the information and other resources that it provides in coping with their own experiences. When education takes on personal relevance in this way, it can be productive and rewarding for all who are involved.

Concerns of this sort remind educators in the field of death, dying, and bereavement that their role includes an important dimension of providing care for their students (Attig, 1981). But it is important to keep in mind that there is a difference between offering education and/or support to an individual, on the one hand, and personal counseling or therapy, on the other hand. That is, educators must be alert to those individuals who are unable to deal with their experiences on their own. For such individuals, education on its own may not be sufficient to address their fears, anxieties, and/or grief reactions. In such situations, referral for personal counseling or therapy may be appropriate. In addition, some students should be encouraged not to take a course in death and dying if they have recently experienced a significant death-related loss, are struggling to cope with that loss, and will have their coping complicated by the work of the course. This is not a failure of education but a recognition that the classroom context may not meet all needs.

Individuals who enroll in death-related educational offerings for *vocational reasons* usually express a desire to improve their competencies to help those whom they serve as patients or clients. For example, this was also one of the motivations that led Mary Jones to enroll in a death and dying class, and it was nurses who first flocked to seminars in this field offered by Dr. Elisabeth Kübler-Ross (1969), because they had the courage to acknowledge their limitations in this area. Such nurses recognized that they were likely to find themselves alone in the middle of the night with a dying person or a grieving family. Consequently, they were eager to expand their competencies to help such persons.

Some who link death education to a vocational concern tend to emphasize what the education will mean for their clients. Others realize that it also applies to them, both as professionals in coping with their work-related responsibilities and as persons in their own right. With Kübler-Ross (1969), death education seeks to show its relevance in all of these ways: to the client who is coping with dying or bereavement; to the helper in his or her work-related role; and to the helper as a person in his or her own right. As Shneidman (1978) has noted, death-related interactions are unique in being the only ones in which it is always the case that the problems being faced by the client are also problems to be faced by the helper.

A fourth type of concern that leads individuals to seek out education in the field of death, dying, and bereavement is somewhat different in character. It does not arise from the immediate pressure of a past or present experience, nor from work-related concerns. Rather, it is motivated by *curiosity about the subject*, which may be combined with *a desire to prepare for personal experiences that might arise in the future*. Sometimes, people with this concern will say, "No important person in my life has yet died. But my grandparents are getting pretty old." These are individuals who are proactive, who prefer to act ahead of time in order (insofar as possible) to prepare themselves and not just wait until events demand some response under pressure. Individuals of this sort have benefited from the longer average life expectancies of what Fulton (1976, p. 85) has called the "death-free generation," but they are sufficiently alert to realize that their advantage cannot be endless. No human life is ever completely "death-free."

Four Dimensions of Death Education

Four dimensions are present in almost all forms of education in the field of death, dying, and bereavement. These dimensions have to do with what people know, how they feel, how they behave, and what they value. In other words, there are cognitive, affective, behavioral, and valuational dimensions of death education. Specific educational programs in this field may emphasize one or more of these dimensions. But it is more common to find that all four dimensions are present, in some degree or other, in the overall educational enterprise. These dimensions are described here as interrelated but distinguishable aspects of death education.

Death education is a *cognitive* or intellectual enterprise in the sense that it provides information about death-related experiences and aids in understanding those experiences. Information of this sort takes many forms. For example, it is important to know that toward the end of the 1980s lung cancer surpassed breast cancer as the leading cancer cause of death for women. This tragic fact is clearly related to changing patterns of smoking (Retherford, 1975) and is, in part, an ironic outcome of cigarette advertising that tells women, "You've come a long way, baby." Similarly, during the early 1980s it was the recognition of an unusually high incidence in young males of a relatively rare form of skin cancer, Kaposi's sarcoma, which had hitherto been confined largely to elderly males of Mediterranean descent, that helped to identify a new disease and cause of death, Acquired Immune Deficiency Syndrome (AIDS) (Shilts, 1987).

The cognitive dimensions of death education are similar to the intellectual dimensions in all academic or classroom education, although these are not the only ways in which such dimensions can be addressed. In addition to presenting facts, this dimension of education includes new ways of organizing or interpreting the data of human experience. In the field of thanatology (a term employed by some to designate the study of death and death-related phenomena), for example, Elisabeth Kübler-Ross (1969) and Maria Nagy (1948) are both well known for stage-based models that they advanced to explicate coping with dying (in the case of Kübler-Ross) and the development of death-related concepts in children (in the case of Nagy). Each of these theoretical models, along with many others, has been described at appropriate points in this book. In so doing, it has been noted that nearly every theoretical insight or model has its limitations and its critics. But insofar as a theoretical model has helped to attract attention and to illuminate an important aspect of human life and experience, it deserves appropriate attention in its particular subject area.

The *affective* dimensions of death education have to do with feelings and emotions about death, dying, and bereavement. For example, a wide range of feelings are involved in experiences of loss and bereavement. Consequently, it is appropriate for education in this area to try to sensitize the nonbereaved to the depth, intensity, duration, and complexities of grief following a death. Much of this has not been communicated effectively to the public at large, who may still wrongly tend to think that a few days or weeks may be more than adequate to "forget" or "get over" the death of an important person in one's life (Osterweis, Solomon, & Green, 1984). In fact, mourning is far more like ongoing adaptation or learning to live with one's loss than it is like ending a process or solving a problem, and research has shown that it is important, at least for some bereaved persons, to maintain the "empty space" and not "finish grieving" (McClowry et al., 1987). Sharing and discussing grief responses is an important part of the affective dimension of education in the field of death, dying, and bereavement.

In addition, as an aspect of its affective dimensions, death education seeks to appreciate the feelings of those who have not yet encountered death in any personal form. For example, it has been noted that it is usually unhelpful for someone who has not been bereaved to say to a bereaved person, "I know how you feel." No one can ever experience the feelings of another person. Many bereaved persons have reported how arrogant it appears to them for someone else to claim to know how they feel, and how it seems to diminish the uniqueness and poignancy of their loss.

Similarly, instead of dismissing grief associated with miscarriage or still-birth, good pediatric care now recognizes and validates the legitimacy of parental grief in such cases. This has led to recognition in professional pediatric circles of the value of permitting parents to see and hold the dead infant as a means of completing the bonding process and laying the foundation for healthy mourning. In the light of realistic education about the affective dimensions of death-related experiences, what might have seemed to the uninformed to be repugnant can instead be seen as part of a healthy process.

The third important dimension of death education has to do with *behavioral* considerations. Why do people act as they do in death-related situations? How should or could people act in such situations? Behavior is the outward expression of what people feel and believe. In contemporary American society, much behavior, both public and private, seeks to avoid contact with death, dying, and bereavement. Often, that is because people do not know what to say or what to do in such situations. They pull back from contact with the dying or the bereaved in the way that Tom Smith's friends did. This leaves grievers alone, without support or companionship at a time when sharing and solace may be most needed. Similarly, many people even hesitate to mention the name of a deceased person to those who loved that person. For survivors, this can feel like a double loss: the deceased person is no longer present and others seem to be trying to erase the very memory of that person.

In contrast to all of this, the hospice movement in recent years has demonstrated how very much can be done to help those who are coping with dying (Corr & Corr, 1983). Similarly, research on funeral rituals (Fulton, 1988) and on self-help groups (Lieberman & Borman, 1979) has shown how to assist those who are coping with bereavement. Such education affirms the very great value to be found in the presence of a caring person and it directs helpers not so much to talk to grieving persons as to *listen* to them. It can also lead to the development of skills in interacting with those who are experiencing a significant loss. Sometimes, death education teaches that it is appropriate to be comfortable with one's discomfort—that is, to be present, sit quietly, and do nothing else when that is all there really is to do. None of this eliminates the sadness of death, but it can help to recreate the caring communities that all vulnerable people need but that seem too frequently to have atrophied or disappeared in many modern societies.

The fourth or *valuational* dimension of death education concerns its role in helping to identify, articulate, and affirm the basic values that govern human lives. The only life that is known in this world is inextricably bound up with death. We would not have *this* life if death were not one of its essential parts. In fact, it involves quite an imaginative struggle to try to conceive what any sort of life without death might be like. Life and death, living and dying, happiness and sadness, attachments and loss—neither pole in these and many other similar dyads stands alone in human experience. For this reason, the perspective of death is an essential one (but not the only one) in helping humans to achieve an adequate understanding of life.

Many of the points that have already been mentioned direct attention to that which is valued: courage, endurance, resilience, concern for others, love, and community. But perhaps values come to the fore most sharply when adults are asked what they will tell children about death and how they will respond to the moral problems of our time. Shall death be hidden from children? Should they be beguiled with descriptions of this life as an unending journey without shadows or tears? Can such a charade be sustained for very long? Will such an approach really enable children to cope with life on their own when adults are gone (dead) or unavailable? Or should adults introduce children to the realities of death in ways that are appropriate to their developmental level and capacities, and with the support of mature values that will enable them to live life wisely and to cope with death in constructive ways (Corr, 1991; Wass & Corr, 1984a, 1984b)?

Death-related values are intimately associated with many of the moral problems of the late 20th century: nuclear warfare, epidemics, famine and malnutrition, dislocation of populations, capital punishment, abortion, euthanasia, and all of the quandaries posed by modern medicine and its complex technologies. For example, is life the ultimate value? Many might say yes; others would say no. Certainly, human life is a value; for the most part, it is an important value. This is part of what is meant by saying that life is sacred. But that is not the same as the assertion that life is an absolute value. One person might sacrifice his or her life for the sake of the lives of others or perhaps for some transcendent value.

Goals of Death Education

Any sort of education about death, dying, and bereavement has three basic goals. The first concerns individuals themselves in their own right; the second involves individuals in their personal transactions with society; and the third relates to individuals in their public roles as citizens.

In the first place, education about death, dying, and bereavement is intended to *enrich the personal lives* of those to whom it is directed. It tries to help them to understand themselves, to appreciate their strengths and their limitations as finite human beings. For example, they may wish to control every aspect of their lives. However, that is not a wish they can expect to fulfill completely. Instead, humans can only realistically hope to influence those aspects of their lives that fall within the scope of their self-governing autonomy. Thus, for instance, although accidents (mostly involving automobiles) are the fourth leading cause of death in American society and even though no one can completely prevent his or her death in an accident, it is nevertheless important for one to fasten one's seat belt and to drive defensively whenever one is out on the road.

There is a self-help group called Make Today Count (Kelly, 1975) for those who have a life-threatening illness. Its members are living under the threat of death. Is that not true in some larger sense for everyone? In response to this realization, members of Make Today Count chapters seek to find meaning and fulfillment in each day that they are alive. Against this, think about

New Jersey high school students and their depictions of death.

people who are merely "killing time." Death education encourages every individual to make each day of his or her life as satisfying and meaningful as it can be. This is not a hedonism of the moment, which gives no thought to the consequences of one's actions. That sort of hedonism is blind to the future, in just the way that too much living for the future is blind to the passing present. When one acts to "make today count" one does not exclude memories from the past or hopes for the future, but one emphasizes that the past is gone, the future may not come, and the present is what one has right now to treasure and enjoy. One can draw upon the past and plan for the future, but it is only in the present that one actually lives and is able to create new value and contribute to the lives of those whom one loves.

The second goal of death education is to *inform and guide individuals in their personal transactions with society.* This goal can be illustrated by considering transactions with two major components of the American death system: health care services and the funeral industry. From birth to death, everyone is a consumer of health care, but statistics show that such services are drawn upon most during the last six months of life. Care for those who have far-advanced illnesses, who are chronically ill and unable to care for themselves, or who are terminally ill is big business in modern societies.

In recent years, the death-awareness movement has drawn attention to the fact that even those who are within days or hours of death are alive. In other words, it is important to realize that dying patients are living human beings. As such, dying persons and their family members need to be informed about services that are available to them and options that they might or might not select. Are there moments in the progress of a disease when further attempts to cure are too unlikely to be successful or too burdensome to bear? Does it ever become appropriate to place greater emphasis upon the management of distressing symptoms? Who should provide such services and where should they be provided—at home or in an institution? Education describes alternatives and enables individuals to select for themselves those that best satisfy the needs, preferences, and values of the persons involved.

Similarly, education reveals the importance of funeral ritual as a means to help survivors with significant tasks: disposal of the body in appropriate ways; realization of the implications of the death; and assistance in social reintegration and meaningful ongoing living (see Chapter 10). But different societies and individuals address these tasks in different ways. For example, in the United States today, there are several options for disposal of the body. Each of these options has served the needs of some people at some time; any one of them may be unsatisfactory to a particular person or group. Thus, education in this area is intended to inform people about alternatives that are available and to assist them to choose those that best serve their needs.

It is frequently said that a funeral represents the third largest expenditure (after the costs of a house and an automobile) that most individuals will make in their lives. Especially toward the end of life, health care is also a major expense, although its burden may be reduced by federal funding and/or private insurance. If death education only resulted in an informed consumer with respect to health care and the funeral industry, it would have done much to improve the ways in which individuals relate to the society in which they live.

The third goal of death education is to *prepare individuals for their public roles as citizens and professionals within a society.* Once upon a time, when questions were raised about the legal meaning of death, society turned to common law, the common body of knowledge and wisdom about any subject. For example, death was once defined as "cessation of the flow of vital bodily fluids" (Black, 1979). New technology seemed to raise challenges as to whether this conventional definition was adequate for all of the situations that might arise. Whether in civil litigation or in criminal proceedings, how should judges and juries determine whether mechanically assisted ventilation is life itself or merely the counterfeit imitation of vital functioning? And how should legislatures codify new standards for definition and determination of death in their legal statutes? Decisions of this sort must take into account the views of experts in the field, but ultimately they reflect the fundamental convictions of ordinary citizens and those who represent them about the meaning and significance of life and death.

Clearly, when the populace and its representatives are informed and articulate, a better foundation exists for sound public policy. The task of education is to contribute to policymaking on issues like definition of death, natural death or "living wills," durable powers of attorney in health care matters, organ transplantation, euthanasia, capital punishment, and a variety of other matters. No one can expect a democratic system to function effectively when its educational underpinnings are inadequate.

Functions of Death Education

Education in the field of death, dying, and bereavement serves four basic functions: (1) to promote understanding of death-related dimensions of human life (and thus, indirectly, to promote understanding of life itself); (2) to foster empowerment for those who are coping with death-related problems; (3) to emphasize participation or the shared aspects of coping with dying, death, and bereavement; and (4) to provide guidance for caregivers and helpers, whether they are professionals, volunteers, family members, or friends (Corr, 1992c).

In terms of *understanding*, death education communicates the insights and the interpretative perspectives that individuals need in order to comprehend the facts and the significance of death-related events. It reveals what people have in common with all other human beings (and perhaps also with other living creatures), what they share only with some other persons, and what is unique to each of them as individuals.

In terms of *empowerment*, death education helps to establish a foundation that is indispensable for making decisions about the conduct of one's life. That is, death education discloses and differentiates between that which is beyond one's control and that which remains within one's control. In this way, death education liberates human beings to live meaningful and productive lives.

With respect to *participation*, death education reaffirms in a sharp and unmistakable way the fundamental fact that human beings are social creatures who live out their lives in communities. It also suggests ways to recreate caring communities where they may have atrophied—for example, in coping with dying or bereavement and in interacting with children. Thus, in everything that it undertakes and seeks to accomplish, death education affirms the value of life and living. It suggests that individuals will achieve a better appreciation of themselves and of many of their interactions with other human beings if they pay attention—at least sometimes—to the perspective of death.

Finally, when people think of *helping one another*, death education illuminates reliable principles that can guide them in coping with some of the most difficult situations in human life. Effective helping attends to all of the needs of the person being helped and is animated by a constructive and nonjudgmental posture. Most people do want to help others who are in need. Death education encourages and guides their efforts to render assistance by fostering awareness of the individual and of the interactive processes that are involved in coping with death, dying, and bereavement. Here again, death education emphasizes the dynamic tension between individual and community that is characteristic of human existence.

On the basis of these principles, one can develop practical programs of education in the field of death, dying, and bereavement that can benefit the general public as well as professionals, nonprofessionals, and volunteers who work with persons coping with life-threatening illness, death, dying, and bereavement (International Work Group on Death, Dying, and Bereavement, 1991a, 1991b, 1992a).

Summary

This chapter has reflected on education about death, dying, and bereavement—its multiple dimensions, goals, and functions. From the outset of this book, it has been noted that human beings cannot magically make death, loss, and sadness disappear from their lives, but they can study these subjects and share insights with each other as a way of learning to live richer, fuller, and more realistic lives. In so doing, as noted in Chapter 3, human beings face issues of coping with limitation and control, problems in learning how to be both individuals and members of social communities, confrontations that involve both human vulnerability and resilience, and challenges in achieving quality and meaningfulness in their lives. The study of death, dying, and bereavement can contribute much to these understandings about human life and living, as Ted Rosenthal indicates in the epilogue that follows this chapter.

QUESTIONS FOR REVIEW AND DISCUSSION

1. This is a book about death, dying, and bereavement. What has it been like to read this book? Have you found it easy or difficult? What would have made this book more helpful to you? (If you wish to share such suggestions with the authors of this book, we would be happy to receive them; write to us c/o Box 1433, Southern Illinois University, Edwardsville, IL 62026.)

2. This book is part of an effort to improve what is sometimes called "death education"—that is, education about death, dying, and bereavement. In your judgment, is it useful for people to engage in this sort of education? Why or why not? Would you recommend this sort of education to a friend or relative? Why or why not?

3. If you read this book along with others or as part of a course on death, dying, and bereavement, what did you learn from sharing some of its contents with other people? What do you think are the main lessons that you learned from this book or that you would want other people to learn, either from your experience of reading this book or from their own reading of this book?

4. The prologue to this book is "The Horse on the Dining-Room Table" by Richard A. Kalish. The epilogue is an extract from "How Could I Not Be Among You?" by Ted Rosenthal. Read the epilogue now. What did you learn from each of these short pieces? What similarities and differences do you see in the lessons that these two authors want to teach us?

SUGGESTED READINGS

Two early leaders in this field have published important and still-influential volumes that would be worth consulting here:

Feifel, H. (Ed.). (1959). *The Meaning of Death.*

Feifel, H. (Ed.). (1977b). *New Meanings of Death.*

Shneidman, E. S. (1973). *Deaths of Man.*

Shneidman, E. S. (1980). *Voices of Death.*

General resources in the field of death, dying, and bereavement include:

Kastenbaum, R. (1992). *The Psychology of Death* (2nd ed.).

Kastenbaum, R., & Aisenberg, R. (1972). *The Psychology of Death.*

Kastenbaum, R., & Kastenbaum, B. (Eds.). (1989). *Encyclopedia of Death.*

Wass, H., Corr, C. A., Pacholski, R. A., & Forfar, C. S. (1985). *Death Education II: An Annotated Resource Guide.*

Wass, H., Corr, C. A., Pacholski, R. A., & Sanders, C. M. (1980). *Death Education: An Annotated Resource Guide.*

Zalaznik, P. H. (1992). *Dimensions of Loss and Death Education* (3rd ed.).

How Could I Not Be Among You?

Ted Rosenthal

My name is Ted Rosenthal.
I am 31.
I live in Berkeley where I have
Lived for the last 10 years.
I was born and raised in New York City.
So I am 31.
I lived well into my thirties.
I can always say that.

Though you may find me picking flowers
Or washing my body in a river, or kicking rocks,
Don't think my eyes don't hold yours.
And look hard upon them
and drop tears as long as you stay before me
Because I live as a man who knows death
and I speak the truth
to those who will listen.

Never yield a minute to despair, sloth, fantasy.
I say to you, you will face pain in your life
You may lose your limbs, bleed to death
Shriek for hours on into weeks in unimaginable agony.
It is not aimed at anyone
but it will come your way.
This wind sweeps over everyone.

You will feel so all alone, abandoned,
come to see that life is brief.
And you will cry, "No, it cannot be so,"
but nothing will avail you.
I tell you never to yearn for the past.
Speak certain knowledge.
Your childhood is worthless.
Seek not ritual. There is no escape in Christmas.
Santa Claus will not ease your pain.
No fantasy will soothe you.

You must bare your heart and expect nothing in return.
You must respond totally to nature.
You must return to your simple self.
I do not fool you. There lies no other path.
I have not forsaken you, but I cannot be among you all.
You are not alone
so long as you love your own true simple selves
Your natural hair, your skin, your graceful bodies
your knowing eyes and your tears and tongues.

I stand before you all aching with truth
Trembling with desire to make you know.
Eat, sleep, and be serious about life.
To be serious is to be simple;
to be simple is to love.
Don't wait another minute, make tracks, go home.
Admit you have some place to return to.
The bugs are crawling over the earth, the sun shining over everyone
The rains are pounding, the winds driving
The breeze is gentle and the grass burns.
The earth is dusty. Go ankle deep in mud.

Get tickled by the tall cattails.
Kick crazily into the burrs and prickles.
Rub your back against the bark, and go ahead, peel it.
Adore the sun.
O people, you are dying! Live while you can.
What can I say?
The blackbirds blow the bush.
Get glass in your feet if you must, but take off the shoes.
O heed me. There is pain all over!
There is continual suffering, puking and coughing.
Don't wait on it. It is stalking you.
Tear ass up the mountainside, duck into the mist . . .

. . . Roll among the wet daisies. Blow out your lungs
among the dead dandelion fields.
But don't delay, time is not on your side.
Soon you will be crying for the hurt, make speed.
Splash in the Ocean,
leap in the snow.
Come on everybody! Love your neighbor
Love your mother, love your lover,
love the man who just stands there staring.
But first, that's alright, go ahead and cry.
Cry, cry, cry your heart out.
It's love. It's your only path.

O people, I am so sorry.
Nothing can be hid.
It's a circle in the round.
It's group theater,
no wings, no backstage, no leading act.
O, I am weeping, but it's stage center for all of us.
Hide in the weeds but come out naked.
Dance in the sand while lightning bands all around us.

Step lightly, we're walking home now.
The clouds take every shape.
We climb up the boulders; there is no plateau.
We cross the stream and walk up the slope.
See, the hawk is diving.
The plain stretches out ahead, then the hills, the valleys, the meadows.
Keep moving people. How could I not be among you?

Selected Literature for Children: Annotated Descriptions

Picture and Coloring Books for Preschoolers and Beginning Readers

Bartoli, J. (1975). *Nonna*. New York: Harvey House. A boy and his younger sister, with good memories of their grandmother, are permitted to participate in her funeral, burial, and the division of her property among family members so that each receives some memento of her life.

Boulden, J. (1989). *Saying Goodbye*. Available from P.O. Box 9358, Santa Rosa, CA 95405; (707) 538-3797. A story about death as a natural part of life, the feelings that are involved in saying goodbye, and the conviction that love is forever. Activity book format allows the child-reader to draw pictures, color images, or insert thoughts on its pages.

Brown, M. W. (1958). *The Dead Bird*. Reading, MA: Addison-Wesley. Some children find a wild bird that is dead. They touch the bird, bury it in a simple ceremony, and return to the site each day to mourn ("until they forgot"). Sadness need not last forever; life can go on again. An early classic for the youngest readers.

Clardy, A. F. (1984). *Dusty Was My Friend: Coming to Terms with Loss*. New York: Human Sciences. An 8-year-old boy remembers his friend Dusty (10), who was killed in an automobile accident. Benjamin struggles to understand his feelings about losing a friend in this way. Benjamin's parents give him permission to articulate his thoughts and feelings, to grieve for his loss, to remember the good times that he shared with Dusty, and to go on with his own life.

Cohn, J. (1987). *I Had a Friend Named Peter: Talking to Children About the Death of a Friend*. New York: Morrow. One section of this book is intended to prepare adults for the work of assisting children in coping with death. The children's section describes Beth's reactions when her friend Peter is killed by a car. Beth's parents and her teacher are attentive and helpful in responding to Beth's needs, the needs of her classmates, and the needs of Peter's parents.

De Paola, T. (1973). *Nana Upstairs and Nana Downstairs*. New York: Putnam's. Tommy likes to visit his grandmother and his great-grandmother, the two nanas in the book's title. Tommy and his great-grandmother are especially close; they share candy, play with toys and imaginary beings, and both are restrained in their chairs in one picture. One morning, Tommy is told that Nana Upstairs is dead. He does not believe this until he sees her empty bed. A few nights later, Tommy sees a falling star and accepts his mother's explanation that it represents a kiss from the older Nana who is now "upstairs" in a new way. Later, an older Tommy repeats the experience and interpretation after the death of Nana Downstairs. A charming story about relationships, whose interpretations should be addressed with caution.

Dodge, N. C. (1984). *Thumpy's Story: A Story of Love and Grief Shared by Thumpy, the Bunny.* Springfield, IL: Prairie Lark Press (P.O. Box 699–B, Springfield, IL 62705). Through text and pictures, a rabbit tells about the death of his sister, Bun, and its effect upon their family. Also available in Spanish, as a coloring book, and with a workbook that allows children to draw and write about their own family and loss experiences.

Fassler, J. (1971). *My Grandpa Died Today.* New York: Human Sciences. David's grandfather tries to prepare the boy for his impending death. Among other things, he tells David that he does not fear death because he knows that David is not afraid to live. When he dies, David still needs to grieve. Nevertheless, David finds comfort in a legacy of many good memories from his relationship with his grandfather. And he is able to play again in a while because he knows that his grandfather would want him to do so.

Hazen, B. S. (1985). *Why Did Grandpa Die? A Book About Death.* New York: Golden. Young Molly and her grandfather have much in common. When Grandpa dies suddenly, Molly cannot accept that harsh fact. She feels awful and frightened, but she cannot cry. Molly's father reminds her that he also loved and lost Grandpa (his father). Many things remind Molly of how much she misses Grandpa. After a long time she finally acknowledges that Grandpa will not come back and she cries over his death. Grandpa remains available to Molly through pictures, in her memories, and in stories shared with her family.

Heegaard, M. E. (1988). *When Someone Very Special Dies.* Minneapolis, MN: Woodland Press (99 Woodland Circle, Minneapolis, MN 55424; (612) 926-2665). A story line about loss and death provides inspiration and opportunity for children to illustrate or color. A useful vehicle for encouraging children to share thoughts and feelings.

Jordan, M. K. (1989). *Losing Uncle Tim.* Niles, IL: Albert Whitman & Co. An attractive and sensitive story about the friendship between a young boy and his Uncle Tim. Unfortunately, Uncle Tim becomes infected with the human immunodeficiency virus (HIV), develops AIDS (Acquired Immunodeficiency Syndrome), and dies. With the help of caring parents, the boy seeks solace through an idea that he had once discussed with his uncle: "Maybe Uncle Tim is like the sun, just shining somewhere else."

Kantrowitz, M. (1973). *When Violet Died.* New York: Parents' Magazine Press. After the death of Amy and Eva's pet bird, they have a funeral involving their young friends. The funeral includes poems, songs, punch, and even humor. Realizing that nothing lasts forever makes everyone sad. But then Eva realizes that life can go on in another way through an ever-changing chain of life involving the family cat, Blanche, and its kittens.

Newman, K. S. (1988). *Hospice Coloring Book.* Orlando, FL: Hospice of Central Florida (2500 Maitland Center Parkway, Suite 300, Orlando, FL 32751; (407) 875-0028). Just what the title says it is.

Stickney, D. (1985). *Water Bugs and Dragonflies.* New York: Pilgrim Press. A happy colony of water bugs notices that every once in a while, one of their members seems to lose interest in their activities, climbs out of sight on the stem of a pond lily, and is seen no more. They wonder what is happening. None of those who leave ever returns. So they agree among themselves that the next to go will come back to explain where he or she had gone and why. The next climber broke through the surface of the water, fell onto a broad lily pad, and found himself transformed in the warmth of the sun into a dragonfly. One day the new dragonfly remembered his promise and tried to return, only to bounce off the surface of the water. He realizes that the members of the old colony might not recognize him in his new body, and he concludes that they will just have to wait for their own transformation in order to understand what happens.

Stull, E. G. (1964). *My Turtle Died Today*. New York: Holt, Rinehart & Winston. A boy seeks help for his sick turtle. His father suggests giving it some food, his teacher admits that she does not know what to do, and the pet shop owner says that the turtle will die. It does die and is buried. The boy and his friends discuss what all of this means and conclude that life can go on in another way through the newborn kittens of their cat, Patty. Much of this is sound, but the book also poses two questions that need to be addressed with care: Can you get a new pet in the way that one child has a new mother? and Do you have to live—a long time—before you die?

Viorst, J. (1971). *The Tenth Good Thing About Barney*. New York: Atheneum. Barney, the boy's cat, dies, is buried, and is mourned. The boy's mother suggests that he might compose a list of ten good things about Barney to recite at the funeral. Among the items that the boy includes are these facts about Barney: he was brave and smart and funny and clean; he was cuddly and handsome and he only once ate a bird; it was sweet to hear him purr in my ear; and sometimes he slept on my belly and kept it warm. But that's only nine. Later, the boy argues with a friend about whether or not cats are in heaven. Eventually, the tenth good thing is learned in the garden: "Barney is in the ground and he's helping grow flowers."

Warburg, S. S. (1969). *Growing Time*. Boston: Houghton Mifflin. When Jamie's aging Collie, King, dies, Jamie's father produces a new puppy. At first, Jamie is not ready for the new dog; premature replacement is a mistake. But after Jamie is allowed to express his grief, he finds it possible to accept the new relationship. Healthy grieving has its appropriate role in the lives of children and adults; it should not be suppressed.

Weir, A. B. (1992). *Am I Still a Big Sister?* Newtown, PA: Fallen Leaf Press (P.O. Box 942, Newtown, PA 18940). This simple story follows the concerns of a young girl through the illness, hospitalization, death, and funeral of her baby sister, and the subsequent birth of a new brother.

Wilhelm, H. (1985). *I'll Always Love You*. New York: Crown. A boy and his dog, Elfie, grow up together. But Elfie grows old and dies while her master is still young. Afterward, members of the family express regret that they did not tell her that they loved her. But the boy did so every night and he realizes that his love for her will continue even after her death. He is not ready for a new puppy just now, even though he knows that Elfie will not come back and that there may come a time in the future when he will be ready for a new pet.

Zolotow, C. (1974). *My Grandson Lew*. New York: Harper. One night, 6-year-old Lewis wakes up and wonders why his grandfather has not visited lately. His mother says that Lewis had not been told that his grandfather had died four years ago because he had never asked. The boy says that he hadn't needed to ask; his grandfather just came. Son and mother share warm memories of someone they both miss: Lewis says, "he gave me eye hugs"; his mother says, "Now we will remember him together and neither of us will be so lonely as we would be if we had to remember him alone.''

Storybooks and Other Texts for Primary School Readers

Arnold, C. (1987). *What We Do When Someone Dies.* New York: Franklin Watts. Combines a picture book format with informational content at about the level of primary school readers. Its scope covers feelings, concepts, and beliefs about death, but greatest attention is given to disposition of the body, funeral customs, and memorial practices.

Buck, P. S. (1948). *The Big Wave.* New York: Scholastic. Two Chinese boys are friends, Jiya the son of fishing people and Kino the offspring of poor farmers. After a tidal wave kills all the fishing people on the shore, Jiya mourns the loss of his family and chooses to live with Kino's warm and understanding family (versus adoption by a rich man). Years later, Jiya marries Kino's sister and chooses to move back to the seaside with his new bride. Loss is universal and inevitable, but life is stronger than death.

Bunting, E. (1982). *The Happy Funeral.* New York: Harper & Row. Can there be a ''happy funeral''? Two young Chinese-American girls prepare for their grandfather's funeral. Food is provided for the journey to the other side, paper play money is burned, people cry and give speeches, a marching band plays, and a small candy is provided after the ceremony to sweeten the sorrow of the mourners. In the end, the children realize that although they were not happy to have their grandfather die, his good life and everyone's fond memories of him did make for a happy funeral.

Carrick, C. (1976). *The Accident.* New York: Seabury Press. Christopher's dog, Bodger, is accidentally killed when he runs in front of a truck. The boy examines every detail of these events in an effort to overturn the loss. Christopher is angry at the driver, at his father for not getting mad at the driver, and at himself for not paying attention and allowing Bodger to wander to the other side of the road as they walked. Christopher's parents bury Bodger too quickly the next morning, before he can take part. But when he and his father are able to join together to erect a marker at Bodger's grave, anger dissolves into tears.

Chin-Yee, F. (1988). *Sam's Story: A Story for Families Surviving Sudden Infant Death Syndrome.* Available from the Canadian Foundation for the Study of Infant Deaths, 586 Eglinton Ave. E., Suite 308, Toronto, Ontario, Canada M4P 1P2; (416) 488-3260, (800) END-SIDS. A rare book that tells a story (with pictures) about the confusing experiences of a child in a family that has experienced the sudden death of his infant brother.

Coburn, J. B. (1964). *Annie and the Sand Dobbies: A Story About Death for Children and Their Parents.* New York: Seabury Press. Young Danny encounters death in two forms in this book: his toddler sister dies in her sleep of a respiratory infection and his dog runs away to be found frozen to death. A neighbor uses imaginary characters to suggest that the deceased are safe with God. A gentle, deeply spiritual book for primary school readers.

Coerr, E. (1977). *Sadako and the Thousand Paper Cranes.* New York: Putnam's. This book is based on a true story about a Japanese girl who died of leukemia in 1955 as one of the long-term results of the atomic bombing of Hiroshima (which occurred when Sadako was two years old). While in the hospital, a friend reminded Sadako of the legend that the crane is supposed to live for a thousand years and that good health will be granted to a person who folds 1,000 origami paper cranes. With family members and friends, they began folding. Sadako died before the project was finished, but her classmates completed the work and children all over Japan have since contributed money to erect a statue in her memory.

Corley, E. A. (1973). *Tell Me About Death, Tell Me About Funerals*. Santa Clara, CA: Grammatical Sciences. A funeral director describes a conversation between a young girl whose grandfather has recently died and her father. Topics include guilt, abandonment, and choices about funerals, burial, cemeteries, mausoleums, and so on. Children are curious about such topics and will welcome this clear, noneuphemistic response. At one point, we are introduced to a child's delightful misunderstanding about the "polarbears" who carry the casket.

Donnelly, E. (1981). *So Long, Grandpa*. New York: Crown. Michael at 10 witnesses the deterioration and eventual death from cancer of his grandfather. The book portrays Michael's reactions and those of others. The way in which Michael's grandfather had helped to prepare the boy by taking him to an elderly friend's funeral is especially significant.

Goodman, M. B. (1990). *Vanishing Cookies: Doing OK When a Parent Has Cancer*. Available from the Benjamin Family Foundation, 2401 Steeles Avenue West, Downsview, Canada M3J 2P1. Brightly colored illustrations alternate with text by a Canadian psychologist in this book for 7–12 year olds. The goal is to bridge the gap between adults and children and to help them share feelings in situations when an adult is coping with cancer. Children are encouraged to ask questions and are offered information about cancer, treatments, coping with feelings, friends and school, and death. The title refers to the vanishing cookies that some children shared with their mother when they visited her in the hospital.

Greene, C. C. (1976). *Beat the Turtle Drum*. New York: Viking. Mostly, this book describes a loving, warm family that includes 13-year-old Kate and 11-year-old Joss. When Joss is abruptly and unexpectedly killed in a fall from a tree, the family is flooded with grief. Conveying this sense of the many dimensions of bereavement is the book's strong point.

Johnson, J., & Johnson, M. (1978). *Tell Me, Papa: A Family Book for Children's Questions About Death and Funerals*. Available (along with other helpful resources) from the Centering Corporation, P.O. Box 3367, Omaha, NE 68103; (402) 553-1200. Using the format of a discussion between children and a grandparent, this slim book provides an explanation of death, funerals, and saying good-bye.

Krementz, J. *How It Feels When a Parent Dies* (1981) and *How It Feels to Fight for Your Life* (1989). Boston: Little, Brown; paperback by Simon & Schuster, 1991. Short essays by children and adolescents (7–16 years old) describe their individual reactions to the death of a parent and to a variety of life-threatening illnesses. Each essay is accompanied by a photograph of its author. Authentic and concrete.

Miles, M. (1971). *Annie and the Old One*. Boston: Little, Brown. A 10-year-old Navajo girl is told that it will be time for grandmother to return to Mother Earth when her mother finishes weaving a rug. Annie tries to unravel the weaving in secret and to distract her mother from weaving, until the adults realize what is going on and her grandmother explains that we are all part of a natural cycle. When Annie realizes that she cannot hold back time, she is ready herself to learn to weave. Death is a natural part of life that need not be feared.

Powell, E. S. (1990). *Geranium Morning.* Minneapolis: CarolRhoda Books. Two young children—Timothy, whose father died suddenly in an accident, and Frannie, whose mother is dying—struggle with strong feelings, memories, guilt ("if onlys"), and some unhelpful adult actions. In sharing their losses, the children help each other; Frannie's father and her mother (before she dies) also are helpful.

Simon, N. (1979). *We Remember Philip.* Chicago: Whitman. When the adult son of a male elementary school teacher dies in a mountain climbing accident, Sam and other members of his class can observe how Mr. Hall is affected by his grief. In time, Mr. Hall shares with the children a scrapbook and other memories of his son. Eventually, they plant a tree as a class memorial. An afterword addresses the fact that children often feel a sense of personal threat when death touches their lives or the lives of people close to them. They need opportunities to talk about their concerns, to share sadness, to gain reassurance, and to express compassion to those who care for them.

Smith, D. B. (1973). *A Taste of Blackberries.* New York: Scholastic. After the death of Jamie as a result of an allergic reaction to a bee sting, his best friend (the book's unnamed narrator) reflects on this unexpected event: Did it really happen or is it just another of Jamie's pranks? Could it have been prevented? Is it disloyal to go on eating and living when Jamie is dead? He concludes that no one could have prevented this death, "some questions just don't have answers," and life can go on.

White, E. B. (1952). *Charlotte's Web.* New York: Harper. When this classic story was first published, the author was criticized for including death in a book for children. But he knew his audience better than his critics did. The story is mainly about friendship, on two levels: first, a young girl named Fern who lives on a farm saves Wilbur, the runt of the pig litter; later, Charlotte, the spider, spins fabulous webs that save an older and fatter Wilbur from the butcher's knife. In the end, Charlotte dies of natural causes, but her achievements and her offspring live on. Charlotte's death and threats to Wilbur's life do not traumatize young readers; instead, they are charmed and delighted.

Whitehead, R. (1971). *The Mother Tree.* New York: Seabury Press. Where do 11-year-old Tempe and her 4-year-old sister, Laura, turn for comfort in the early 1900s when their mother dies and Tempe is made to assume her duties? To a temporary spiritual refuge in the large, backyard tree of the book's title and eventually to good memories of their mother that endure within them.

Based on Corr, "Children's Literature on Death" (1993b).

Selected Literature for Adolescents: Annotated Descriptions

Literature for Middle School Readers

Arrick, F. (1980). *Tunnel Vision*. Scarsdale, NY: Bradbury. After Anthony hanged himself at 15, his family, friends, and teacher cope with feelings of bewilderment and guilt. There is no easy resolution for such feelings, but important questions are posed: What should be done in the face of serious problems? Where should one turn for help?

Bernstein, J. E. (1977). *Loss: And How to Cope with It*. New York: Clarion. Knowledgeable advice for young readers about how to cope with loss through death. Topics include what happens when someone dies; children's concepts of death; feelings in bereavement; living with survivors; handling feelings; deaths of specific sorts (for example, parents, grandparents, friends, pets); traumatic deaths (such as suicide or murder); and the legacy of survivors.

Blume, J. (1981). *Tiger Eyes*. Scarsdale, NY: Bradbury. Davey's father is killed at the age of 34 during a holdup of his 7–11 store in Atlantic City. Davey (15), her mother, and her younger brother all react differently and are unable to help each other in their grief. Seeking a change of scene, they move to Los Alamos, the "bomb city," to visit Davey's aunt. It takes almost a year to find better ways to mourn and to decide to move back to New Jersey to rebuild their lives. Important issues of safety and security, sharing with others and being alone, are explored in an insightful manner.

Cleaver, V., & Cleaver, B. (1970). *Grover*. Philadelphia: Lippincott. When Grover was 11 his mother became terminally ill and took her own life in order (she thought) to "spare" herself and her family the ravages of her illness. The adults around Grover surround his mother's illness in mystery. Because his father cannot face the fact of her suicide or the depth of his grief, he tries to hold his feelings inside and to convince his son that the death was an accident. Issues posed include whether one must endure life no matter what suffering it holds; Is religion a comfort?; and How should one deal with grief?

Farley, C. (1975). *The Garden Is Doing Fine*. New York: Atheneum. While he is dying of cancer, Corrie's father inquires about his beloved garden. Corrie can neither tell him that the garden is dead nor can she lie. Instead, she searches for reasons that would explain why a good person like her father would die. She also tries to bargain with herself and with God to preserve her father's life. A wise neighbor helps Corrie see that even though there may be no reasons for her father's death, she and her brothers are her father's real garden. The seeds that he has planted in them will live on and she can let go without betraying him.

Geller, N. (1987). *The Last Teenage Suicide*. Auburn, ME: Norman Geller Publishing (P.O. Box 3217, Auburn, ME 04210). Text and pen-and-ink drawings describe the death by suicide of a high school senior, together with reactions from his family, friends, and acquaintances. In response to this tragedy, the community develops a program to identify and respond to the needs of those who are potentially suicidal or hurting emotionally. Their goal is to make this death the last teenage suicide in their community.

Grollman, S. (1988). *Shira: A Legacy of Courage*. New York: Doubleday. Shira Putter died at the age of 9 in 1983 from a rare form of diabetes. Here the author tells Shira's story on the basis of her own writings and personal accounts from family members and friends. The effect is a celebration of life in which one finds hardship, courage, love, and hope.

Heegaard, M. E. (1990). *Coping with Death and Grief*. Minneapolis: Lerner Publications. Marge Heegaard experienced the death of her first husband when her children were 8, 10, and 12 years old. During the last 15 years she has worked as a grief and loss counselor with children and adults. This book describes change, loss, and death as natural parts of life, provides information and advice about coping with feelings, and suggests ways to help oneself and others who are grieving.

Jampolsky, G. G., & Murray, G. (Eds.) (1982). *Straight from the Siblings: Another Look at the Rainbow*. Berkeley, CA: Celestial Arts. Brothers and sisters of children who have a life-threatening illness write about the feelings of the siblings and ways to help all of the children who are involved in such difficult situations. From the Center for Attitudinal Healing.

Jampolsky, G. G., & Taylor, P. (Eds.) (1978). *There Is a Rainbow Behind Every Dark Cloud*. Berkeley, CA: Celestial Arts. Eleven children, 8–19 years old, explain what it is like to have a life-threatening illness and the choices that youngsters have in helping themselves (for example, when one is first told about one's illness, in going back to school, in coping with feelings, and in talking about death). From the Center for Attitudinal Healing.

LeShan E. (1976). *Learning to Say Good-by: When a Parent Dies*. New York: Macmillan. The author describes experiences of grief following the death of a parent and ways in which adults often respond to children's mourning. Topics include overprotection; the importance of honesty; trust; sharing; funerals; fear of abandonment; anticipatory grief; and guilt. Also recovering from grief; accepting the loss of the deceased; maintaining a capacity for love; and meeting future changes. Helpful for both young readers and adults.

Little, J. (1984). *Mama's Going to Buy You a Mockingbird*. New York: Viking Kestrel. Jeremy and his younger sister, Sarah, learn that their father is dying from cancer by overhearing people talk about it. Lack of information and limited contacts when he is in the hospital leave the children confused and angry. After the death, the children are permitted to attend the funeral, but it does not seem to have been a very helpful experience for them. Also, they must take on new responsibilities resulting from a relocation and their mother's return to school. All of this illustrates the many losses, large and small, that accompany dying and death. The need for support from others is evident in the relationships within the family and in Jeremy's new friendship with Tess, a girl who has been deserted by her mother and is treated as an outcast at school.

Mann, P. (1977). *There Are Two Kinds of Terrible*. New York: Doubleday/Avon. Robbie breaks his arm, is hospitalized, and has an operation—but it ends. His mother develops cancer and dies—but for Robbie and his "cold fish" father the experience seems to have no conclusion. They are together, but each grieves alone until they begin to find ways to share their suffering and their memories. Good vignettes—for example, a substitute teacher threatens to call Robbie's mother when he misbehaves.

Paterson, K. (1977). *Bridge to Terabithia.* New York: Crowell. Eleven-year-old Jess and Leslie have a special, secret meeting place in the woods, called Terabithia. But when Leslie is killed one day in an accidental fall on her way to visit Terabithia alone, the magic of their play and friendship is disrupted. Jess grieves the loss of this special relationship and is supported by his family. Eventually, he is able to initiate new relationships that will share friendship in a similar way with others.

Richter, E. (1986). *Losing Someone You Love: When a Brother or Sister Dies.* New York: Putnam's. Fifteen adolescents describe in their own words how they are feeling in response to a wide variety of experiences of sibling death. Many young people will identify with what these teen contributors have to say and will find it important to know that they are not alone in their feelings of grief.

Rofes, E. E. (Ed.), and the Unit at Fayerweather Street School. (1985). *The Kids' Book About Death and Dying, by and for Kids.* Boston: Little, Brown. This book resulted from a class project involving a teacher and a group of his 11- to 14-year-old students. It describes what these young authors have learned about a wide range of death-related topics: what is involved in a death; funeral customs; thoughts about the death of a pet, an older relative or parent, or a child; violent deaths; and whether there is life after death. The book makes clear what children want to know about these subjects and how they want adults to talk to them. The opening and closing chapters reflect on what has been learned concerning talk about death. One main lesson is that "a lot of the mystery and fear surrounding death has been brought about by ignorance and avoidance" (p. 111). Another lesson is expressed in the hope "that children can lead the way in dealing with death and dying with a healthier and happier approach" (p. 114).

Romond, J. L. (1989). *Children Facing Grief: Letters from Bereaved Brothers and Sisters.* St. Meinrad, IN: Abbey Press. After the death of Mark, her 7-year-old son, the author found herself obliged to help John, her 3-year-old surviving son, cope with his brother's death. In listening to John's questions and comments, she began to record other observations of surviving siblings. In this slim book, the observations of 18 children (ages 6–15) are organized in the form of letters to a friend. Helpful comments from young people who have been there in grief.

Shura, M. F. (1988). *The Sunday Doll.* New York: Dodd, Mead. At the time of her 13th birthday, Emily is shut out by her parents from something terrible that is going on and that somehow involves her older sister, Jayne. Emily is sent to visit Aunt Harriet in Missouri, who had previously given Emily an Amish doll without a face. Eventually, Emily learns that Jayne's boyfriend has been missing; later he is found to have taken his life. Meanwhile, Aunt Harriet suffers one of her "spells" (transient ischemia attacks) and comes close to death, but she also shows Emily her own strengths. Lesson: like the Sunday doll, one can choose which face to present to the world. A richly textured story.

Sternberg, F., & Sternberg, B. (1980). *If I Die and When I Do: Exploring Death with Young People.* Englewood Cliffs, NJ: Prentice-Hall. This book is the product of a nine-week middle-school course on death and dying taught by the first author for three years in Colorado. The text mainly consists of drawings, poems, and statements by the students on various death-related topics, plus a closing chapter of 25 suggested activities.

Literature for High School Readers

Agee, J. (1969). *A death in the family*. New York: Bantam. This Pulitzer Prize–winning novel unerringly depicts the point of view of two children in Knoxville, Tennessee, in 1915. When Rufus and his younger sister, Catherine, are told of the accidental death of their father, they struggle to understand what has happened and to grapple with its implications. Some questions are acceptable: Is death like waking up in heaven where the people on earth can no longer see you? Do animals go to heaven, too? Other questions seem less appropriate to adults: What did it mean to say that God took their father to heaven because he had "an accident" ("Not in his *pants*," Rufus wanted to tell Catherine)? And if their father was dead and they would never see him again, did that mean he would not be home for supper? When Rufus asks if they were "orphans," so that he could mention this one day in school to the other children, Catherine wonders what it is to be "a norphan." Agee skillfully portrays ways in which the children experience unusual events, sense strange tensions within the family, and strive to work out their implications.

Craven, M. (1973). *I Heard the Owl Call My Name*. New York: Dell. This novel describes a young Episcopal priest with a terminal illness who is sent by his bishop to live with Indians in British Columbia. The Indians recognize that death will come when the owl calls someone's name. From them, the bishop hopes that the young priest will learn to face his own forthcoming death.

Deaver, J. R. (1988). *Say Goodnight, Gracie*. New York: Harper & Row. Jimmy and Morgan have been close friends since birth. When Jimmy is killed by a drunken driver in an automobile accident, Morgan is disoriented by the extent of her loss. She is unable to face her feelings, attend Jimmy's funeral, or speak to his parents. Her own parents offer support and tolerate Morgan's withdrawal from the world. Eventually, a wise aunt helps Morgan confront her feelings in a way that leads her to more constructive coping and to decide to go on with living.

Greenberg, J. (1979). *A Season In-Between*. New York: Farrar. Carrie Singer, a seventh grader, copes with the diagnosis of her father's cancer in spring and his death that summer. Rabbinical moral: turn scratches on a jewel into a beautiful design.

Gunther, J. (1949). *Death Be Not Proud: A Memoir*. New York: Harper. One of the earliest books of its type; a moving account of a 15-month struggle with a brain tumor by the author's 15-year-old son.

Hughes, M. (1984). *Hunter in the Dark*. New York: Atheneum. Mike Rankin is going hunting in the Canadian woods for the first time. He has leukemia (and overprotective parents) and needs to face life and death on his own. Thus, this novel is about one adolescent's efforts to confront threats at different levels in his life.

Klagsbrun, F. (1976). *Too Young to Die: Youth and Suicide*. New York: Houghton Mifflin; paperback edition by Pocket Books, 1977. A simple, clear, informed, and readable introduction to the myths and realities surrounding youth suicide, with useful advice for helpers. Other books for young readers about suicide include W. Colman, *Understanding and Preventing Teen Suicide* (Chicago, Children's Press, 1990); D. B. Francis, *Suicide: A Preventable Tragedy* (New York: E. P. Dutton, 1989); S. Gardner & G. Rosenberg, *Teenage Suicide* (New York: Messner, 1985);

M. O. Hyde & E. H. Forsyth, *Suicide: The Hidden Epidemic* (New York: Franklin Watts, 1986); J. Kolehmainen & S. Handwerk, *Teen Suicide: A Book for Friends, Family, and Classmates* (Minneapolis: Lerner, 1986); J. M. Leder, *Dead Serious: A Book for Teenagers About Teenage Suicide* (New York: Atheneum, 1987); and J. Schleifer, *Everything You Need to Know About Teen Suicide* (rev. ed.; New York: The Rosen Publishing Group, 1991).

Langone, J. (1986). *Dead End: A Book About Suicide.* Boston: Little, Brown. John Langone is a medical reporter who has published other books (*Death Is a Noun: A View of the End of Life*, 1972; *Vital Signs: The Way We Die in America*, 1974) for mature young readers about death in our society. Langone's work on suicide is current, thoughtful, detailed, and particularly well suited for the education of teenage readers.

Lewis, C. S. (1976). *A Grief Observed.* New York: Bantam. The author, a celebrated British writer and lay theologian, married rather late in life an American woman who soon developed cancer and died. In this book, he records his own experiences of grief on notebooks that were lying around the house. The result is an unusual and extraordinary document, a direct and honest expression of one individual's grief that has helped innumerable readers by normalizing their own experiences in bereavement.

Martin, A. M. (1986). *With You and Without You.* New York: Holiday House; paperback by Scholastic. This story describes the reactions of parents and four children in a family when the father is told that he will die in the next 6–12 months as a result of an inoperable heart condition. Each member of the family tries to make the father's remaining time as good as possible. After his death, they struggle to cope with their losses. One important lesson is that no one is ever completely prepared for a death; another is that each individual must cope in his or her own way.

Pendleton, E. (Comp.). (1980). *Too Old to Cry, Too Young to Die.* Nashville: Thomas Nelson. Thirty-five teenagers describe their experiences in living with cancer. The voices of these adolescent authors ring with truth about such topics as treatments, side effects, hospitals, parents, siblings, and friends.

Tolstoy, L. (1960). *The Death of Ivan Ilych and Other Stories.* New York: New American Library. The title story is an exceptional piece of world literature, first published in 1886. Ivan Ilych is a Russian magistrate who drifts into marriage (mainly for social reasons), enjoys playing cards with his friends, and in all else prefers to confine himself to what might be written down on letterhead stationery. In the prime of life, Ivan is afflicted with a grave illness that becomes steadily more serious. As his health deteriorates, Ivan suddenly realizes that glib talk in college about mortality does not just apply to other people or to humanity in general. Those around Ivan gradually withdraw and become more guarded in what they say to him, except for one servant and his young son. A masterful portrait of the experience of dying.

Based on Corr, A. "Children's Literature on Death" (1993b).

References

Ablon, J. (1970). The Samoan funeral in urban America. *Ethnology, 9,* 209–227.

Abts, H. W. (1989). *The living trust: The fail-proof way to pass along your estate to your heirs without lawyers, courts, or the probate system.* Chicago: Contemporary Books.

Abrahamson, H. (1977). *The origin of death: Studies in African mythology.* New York: Arno Press.

Achté, K., Fagerström, R., Pentikäinen, J., & Farberow, N. L. (1990). Themes of death and violence in lullabies of different countries. *Omega, 20,* 193–204.

Achté, K. A., & Vauhkonen, M. L. (1971). Cancer and the psyche. *Omega, 2,* 46–56.

Ad hoc Committee of the Harvard Medical School to Examine the Definition of Brain Death. (1968). A definition of irreversible coma. *Journal of the American Medical Association, 205,* 337–340.

Adams, D. W. (1979). *Childhood malignancy: The psychosocial care of the child and his family.* Springfield, IL: Charles C Thomas.

Adams, D. W. (1984). Helping the dying child: Practical approaches for non-physicians. In H. Wass & C. A. Corr (Eds.), *Childhood and death* (pp. 95–112). Washington, DC: Hemisphere.

Adams, D. W., & Deveau, E. J. (1986). Helping dying adolescents: Needs and responses. In C. A. Corr & J. N. McNeil (Eds.), *Adolescence and death* (pp. 79–96). New York: Springer.

Adams, D. W., & Deveau, E. J. (1987). *Coping with childhood cancer: Where do we go from here?* (rev. ed.). Hamilton, Ontario: Kinbridge.

Adler, B. (1979, March). You don't have to do homework in heaven! *Good Housekeeping,* p. 46.

Agee, J. (1969). *A death in the family.* New York: Bantam.

Ajemian, I., & Mount, B. M. (Eds.). (1980). *The R. V. H. manual on palliative/hospice care.* New York: Arno Press.

Alcohol, Drug Abuse, and Mental Health Administration. (1989). *Report of the secretary's task force on youth suicide* (4 vols.). Washington, DC: U.S. Government Printing Office.

Aldrich, C. K. (1963). The dying patient's grief. *Journal of the American Medical Association, 184,* 329–331.

Alexander, G. J. (1988). *Writing a living will: Using a durable power-of-attorney.* New York: Praeger.

Alexander, I. E., & Adlerstein, A. M. (1958). Affective responses to the concept of death in a population of children and early adolescents. *Journal of Genetic Psychology, 93,* 167–177.

Allen, N. (1984). Suicide statistics. In C. L. Hatton & S. M. Valente (Eds.), *Suicide: Assessment and intervention* (2nd ed., pp. 17–31). Norwalk, CT: Appleton-Century-Crofts.

Alsop, S. (1973). *A stay of execution.* Philadelphia: Lippincott.

Alvarez, A. (1970). *The savage god: A study of suicide.* New York: Random House.

American Academy of Pediatrics. (1986). School attendance of children and adolescents with human T lymphotropic virus III/lymphadenopathy-associated virus infection. *Pediatrics, 77,* 430–431.

American Association of Retired Persons (AARP). (1991). *A profile of older Americans: 1991.* Washington, DC: Author.

American Medical Association, Council on Ethical and Judicial Affairs. (1988). Ethical issues involved in the growing AIDS crisis. *Journal of the American Medical Association, 259,* 1360–1361.

Amundsen, D. (1989). The physician's obligation to prolong life: A medical duty without classical roots. In R. M. Veatch (Ed.), *Cross-cultural perspectives in medical ethics: Readings* (pp. 248–263). Boston: Jones & Bartlett.

And we were sad, remember? [Film]. (1979). Northern Virginia Educational Telecommunications Association. (Available from the National Audiovisual Center, Reference Department, National Archives and Records Service, Washington, DC 20409)

Angel, M. D. (1987). *The orphaned adult.* New York: Human Sciences.

Anthony, S. (1972). *The discovery of death in childhood and after.* New York: Basic Books. (Revision of *The child's discovery of death.* New York: Harcourt Brace & World, 1940.)

Antonovsky, A. (1967). Social class, life expectancy and overall mortality. *The Milbank Memorial Fund Quarterly, 45,* 31–73.

Ariès, P. (1962). *Centuries of childhood: A social history of family life.* Trans. R. Baldick. New York: Random House.

Ariès, P. (1974a). The reversal of death: Changes in attitudes toward death in Western societies. Trans. V. M. Stannard. *American Quarterly, 26,* 55–82.

Ariès, P. (1974b). *Western attitudes toward death: From the middle ages to the present.* Trans. P. M. Ranum. Baltimore: Johns Hopkins University Press.

Ariès, P. (1981). *The hour of our death.* Trans. H. Weaver. New York: Knopf.

Ariès, P. (1985). *Images of man and death.* Trans. J. Lloyd. Cambridge, MA: Harvard University Press.

Arkin, W., & Fieldhouse, R. (1985). *Nuclear battlefields.* Cambridge, MA: Ballinger.

Arno, P. S., & Feiden, K. L. (1992). *Against the odds: The story of AIDS drug development, politics and profits.* New York: HarperCollins.

Arras, J. D. (1984). Toward an ethic of ambiguity. *Hastings Center Report, 14*(2), 25–33.

Arras, J. D. (1988). The fragile web of responsibility: AIDS and the duty to treat. *Hastings Center Report, 18*(2), Special Supplement, pp. 10–20.

Arvio, R. P. (1974). *The cost of dying and what you can do about it.* New York: Harper & Row.

Atkinson, T. E. (1953). *Handbook of the law of wills and other principles of succession, including intestacy and administration of decedents' estates* (2nd ed.). St. Paul, MN: West.

Attig, T. (1981). Death education as care of the dying. In R. A. Pacholski & C. A. Corr (Eds.), *New directions in death education and counseling* (pp. 168–175). Arlington, VA: Forum for Death Education and Counseling.

Attig, T. (1986). Death themes in adolescent music: The classic years. In C. A. Corr & J. N. McNeil (Eds.), *Adolescence and death* (pp. 32–56). New York: Springer.

Attig, T. (1991). The importance of conceiving of grief as an active process. *Death Studies, 15,* 385–393.

Austin, D. A., & Mack, J. E. (1986). The adolescent philosopher in a nuclear world. In C. A. Corr & J. N. McNeil (Eds.), *Adolescence and death* (pp. 57–75). New York: Springer.

Bacon, F. (1962). Of marriage and single life. In *Francis Bacon's Essays.* New York: Dutton. (Original work published 1625.)

Badham, P., & Badham, L. (Eds.). (1987). *Death and immortality in the religions of the world.* New York: Paragon House.

Baez, J. (1969). Will the circle be unbroken? *David's album.* New York: Vanguard Records.

Bailey, L. (1978). *Biblical perspectives on death.* Philadelphia: Fortress Press.

Bailey, S. S., Bridgman, M. M., Faulkner, D., Kitahata, C. M., Marks, E., Melendez, B. B., & Mitchell, H. (1990). *Creativity and the close of life.* Branford, CT: The Connecticut Hospice.

Baines, M. (Ed.). (1981). Drug control of common symptoms. *World Medicine, 17,* 47–60.

Baird, R. M., & Rosenbaum, S. E. (Ed.). (1989). *Euthanasia: The moral issues.* New York: Prometheus.

Baker, J. E., Sedney, M. A., & Gross, E. (1992). Psychological tasks for bereaved children. *American Journal of Orthopsychiatry, 62,* 105–116.

Balk, D. (1983). Adolescents' grief reactions and self-concept perceptions following sibling death: A study of 33 teenagers. *Journal of Youth and Adolescence, 12,* 137–161.

Balk, D. (1984). How teenagers cope with sibling death: Some implications for school counselors. *The School Counselor, 32,* 150–158.

Balk, D. E. (1990). *Children and the death of a pet.* Manhattan, KS: Cooperative Extension Service, Kansas State University.

Balk, D. (Ed.). (1991). Death and adolescent bereavement. *Journal of Adolescent Research, 6*(1).

Ball, J. F. (1977). Widow's grief: The impact of age and mode of death. *Omega, 7,* 307–333.

Bandura, A. (1980). The stormy decade: Fact or fiction? In R. E. Muuss (Ed.), *Adolescent behavior and society: A book of readings* (3rd ed., pp. 22–31). New York: Random House.

Banks, R. (1991). *The sweet hereafter.* New York: HarperCollins.

Barnickol, C. A., Fuller, H., & Shinners, B. (1986). Helping bereaved adolescent parents. In C. A. Corr & J. N. McNeil (Eds.), *Adolescence and death* (pp. 132–147). New York: Springer.

Barré-Sinoussi, F., Chermann, J.-C., Rey, F., Nugeyre, M.T., Chamaret, S., Gruest, J., Dauguet, C., Exler-Blin, C., Vézinet-Brun, F., Rouzioux, C., Rozenbaum, W., & Montagnier, L. (1983). Isolation of a T-lymphotropic retrovirus from a patient at risk for acquired immune deficiency syndrome (AIDS). *Science, 220,* 868–871.

Barron, A. (1969). Death [Film]. New York: Filmmakers Library.

Bartoli, J. (1975). *Nonna.* New York: Harvey House.

Bates, T., Hoy, A.M., Clarke, D. G., & Laird, P. P. (1981). The St. Thomas's Hospital terminal care support team: A new concept of hospice care. *Lancet, 30,* 1201–1203.

Battin, M. P. (1982). *Ethical issues in suicide.* Englewood Cliffs, NJ: Prentice-Hall.

Battin, M. P., & Mayo, D. J. (Eds.). (1980). *Suicide: The philosophical issues.* New York: St. Martin's Press.

Bauer, Y. (1982). *A history of the Holocaust.* New York: Franklin Watts.

Bauer, Y. (1986). Introduction. In E. Kulka, *Escape from Auschwitz* (pp. xiii–xvii). South Hadley, MA: Bergin & Garvey.

Baxter, G., Bennett, L., & Stuart, W. (1989). *Adolescents and death: Bereavement support groups for secondary school students* (2nd ed.). Etobicoke, Ontario: Canadian Centre for Death Education and Bereavement at Humber College.

Beaglehole, E., & Beaglehole, P. (1935). Hopi of the second mesa. *American Anthropological Association, Memoirs, 44.*

Beardslee, W. R., & Mack, J. E. (1982). The impact on children and adolescents of nuclear developments. In R. Rogers (Ed.), *Psychosocial aspects of nuclear developments* (Task Force Report #20) (pp. 64–93). Washington, DC: American Psychiatric Association.

Beaty, N. L. (1970). *The craft of dying.* New Haven, CT: Yale University Press.

Beauchamp, T. (1989). A reply to Rachels on active and passive euthanasia. In R. M. Veatch (Ed.), *Cross-cultural perspectives in medical ethics: Readings* (pp. 263–274). Boston: Jones & Bartlett.

Beauchamp, T., & Davidson, A. (1979). The definition of euthanasia. *Journal of Medicine and Philosophy, 4,* 294–312.

Beauchamp, T., & Perlin, S. (1978). *Ethical issues in death and dying.* Englewood Cliffs, NJ: Prentice-Hall.

Becker, C. B. (1989). Rebirth and afterlife in Buddhism. In A. Berger, P. Badham, A. H. Kutscher, J. Berger, M. Perry, & J. Beloff (Eds.), *Perspectives on death and dying: Cross-cultural and multi-disciplinary views* (pp. 108–125). Philadelphia: Charles Press.

Becker, D., & Margolin, F. (1967). How surviving parents handled their young children's adaptations to the crisis of loss. *American Journal of Orthopsychiatry, 37,* 753–757.

Becker, E. (1973). *The denial of death.* New York: Free Press.

Behnke, J., & Bok, S. (Eds.). (1975). *The dilemmas of euthanasia.* Garden City, NY: Doubleday Anchor.

Bendann, E. (1930). *Death customs: An analytical study of burial rites.* New York: Knopf.

Bengston, V. L., Cuellar, J. B., & Ragan, P. K. (1977). Stratum contrasts and similarities in attitudes toward death. *Journal of Gerontology, 32,* 76–88.

Benjamin, B. (1965). *Social and economic factors affecting mortality.* The Hague: Mouton & Co.

Bennett, C. (1980). *Nursing home life: What it is and what it could be.* New York: Tiresias Press.

Benoliel, J. Q., & Crowley, D. M. (1974). The patient in pain: New concepts. In *Proceedings of the national conference on cancer nursing* (pp. 70–78). New York: American Cancer Society.

Berger, A., Badham, P., Kutscher, A. H., Berger, J., Perry, M., & Beloff, J. (Eds.). (1989). *Perspectives on death and dying: Cross-cultural and multi-disciplinary views.* Philadelphia: Charles Press.

Berkman, L., Singer, B., & Manton, K. (1989). Black/white differences in health status and mortality among the elderly. *Demography, 26,* 661–678.

Berkovitz, I. H. (1985). The role of schools in child, adolescent, and youth suicide prevention. In M. L. Peck, N. L. Farberow, & R. E. Litman (Eds.), *Youth suicide* (pp. 170–190). New York: Springer.

Berman, A. L. (1986). Helping suicidal adolescents: Needs and responses. In C. A. Corr & J. N. McNeil (Eds.), *Adolescence and death* (pp. 151–166). New York: Springer.

Bernstein, B. E. (1976). Lawyer and counselor as an interdisciplinary team: The timely referral. *Journal of Marriage and Family Counseling, 2*(4), 347–354.

Bernstein, B. E. (1977a). Lawyer and counselor as an interdisciplinary team: Interfacing for the terminally ill. *Death Education, 1,* 277–291.

Bernstein, B. E. (1977b). Lawyer and social worker as collaborators in the medical setting. *Health and Social Work, 2,* 148–155.

Bernstein, B. E. (1979). Lawyer and therapist as an interdisciplinary team: Serving the terminally ill. *Death Education, 3,* 11–19.

Bernstein, B. E. (1980). Lawyer and therapist as an interdisciplinary team: Serving the survivors. *Death Education, 4,* 179–188.

Bernstein, J. E., & Rudman, M. K. (1989). *Books to help children cope with separation and loss,* Vol. 3. New York: R. R. Bowker. (By the first author alone: Vol. 1, 1977; Vol. 2, 1983)

Bertman, S. L. (1984). Children's and others' thoughts and expressions about death. In H. Wass & C. A. Corr (Eds.), *Helping children cope with death: Guidelines and resources* (2nd ed., pp. 11–31). Washington, DC: Hemisphere.

Bertman, S. L. (1991). *Facing death: Images, insights, and interventions.* Washington, DC: Hemisphere.

Bettelheim, B. (1977). *The uses of enchantment—The meaning and importance of fairy tales.* New York: Vintage Books.

Birren, J. E. (1964). *The psychology of aging.* Englewood Cliffs, NJ: Prentice-Hall.

Black, D. (1985). *The plague years: A chronicle of AIDS, the epidemic of our times.* New York: Simon & Schuster.

Black, H. C. (1979). *Black's law dictionary* (5th ed.). St. Paul: West.

Blackwell, P. L., & Gessner, J. C. (1983). Fear and trembling: An inquiry into adolescent perceptions of living in the nuclear age. *Youth and Society, 15,* 237–255.

Blauner, R. (1966). Death and social structure. *Psychiatry, 29,* 378–394.

Blondie. (1979). Die young, stay pretty. *Eat to the beat.* Los Angeles: Chrysalis Records.

Bluebond-Langner, M. (1977). Meanings of death to children. In H. Feifel (Ed.), *New meanings of death* (pp. 47–66). New York: McGraw-Hill.

Bluebond-Langner, M. (1978). *The private worlds of dying children.* Princeton, NJ: Princeton University Press.

Bluebond-Langner, M. (1991). Living with cystic fibrosis: The well sibling's perspective. *Medical Anthropology Quarterly, 5*(2), 133–152.

Bluebond-Langner, M., Perkel, D., & Goertzel, T. (1991). Pediatric cancer patients' peer relationships: The impact of an oncology camp experience. *Journal of Psychosocial Oncology, 9*(2), 67–80.

Blum, R. W. (1984). The dying adolescent. In R. W. Blum (Ed.), *Chronic illness and disabilities in childhood and adolescence* (pp. 159–176). Orlando, FL: Grune & Stratton.

Blume, J. (1981). *Tiger eyes.* Scarsdale, NY: Bradbury.

Boase, T.S.R. (1972). *Death in the middle ages: Mortality, judgment and remembrance.* New York: McGraw-Hill.

Bok, S. (1978). Death and dying: Euthanasia and sustaining life: Ethical views. In W. Reich (Ed.), *Encyclopedia of bioethics* (pp. 268–278). New York: Free Press.

Boland, M., & Rizzi, D. (1986). *The child with AIDS (human immunodeficiency virus): A guide for the family.* Newark, NJ: United Hospitals Medical Center, Children's Hospital of New Jersey.

Bolton, C., & Camp, D. J. (1987). Funeral rituals and the facilitation of grief work. *Omega, 17,* 343–352.

Bolton, F. G. (1980). *The pregnant adolescent.* Newbury Park, CA: Sage.

Bolton, I. (1989). *My son, my son: A guide to healing after a suicide in the family* (11th ed.). Belmore Way, GA: Bolton Press.

Borg, S., & Lasker, J. (1981). *When pregnancy fails: Families coping with miscarriage, stillbirth, and infant death.* Boston: Beacon Press.

Borkman, T. (1976). Experiential knowledge: A new concept for the analysis of self-help groups. *Social Service Review, 50,* 445–456.

Boss, P. (1988). *Family stress management.* Newbury Park, CA: Sage.

Boulden, J. (1989). *Saying goodbye.* Available from P.O. Box 9358, Santa Rosa, CA 95405; (707) 538-3797.

Bowlby, J. (1961). Processes of mourning. *International Journal of Psychoanalysis, 42,* 317–340.

Bowlby, J. (1973). *Attachment and loss: Separation—Anxiety and anger* (Vol. 2, with additional notes by the author). New York: Basic Books.

Bowlby, J. (1980). *Attachment and loss: Loss—Sadness and depression* (Vol. 3). New York: Basic Books.

Bowlby, J. (1982). *Attachment and loss: Attachment* (Vol. 1; 2nd ed.). New York: Basic Books.

Bowman, L. E. (1959). *The American funeral: A study in guilt, extravagance and sublimity.* Washington, DC: Public Affairs Press.

Brady, E. M. (1979). Telling the story: Ethics and dying. *Hospital Progress, 60,* 57–62.

Braza, K., & Bright, B. (1991). *Memory book: For bereaved children.* Salt Lake City, UT: Holy Cross Hospital Grief Center.

Breed, W. (1972). Five components of a basic suicide syndrome. *Life-Threatening Behavior, 2,* 3–18.

Breindel, C. L. (1979). Issues with the provision of care to the terminally ill patient in nursing homes. *The Journal of Long-Term Care Administration, 7,* 47–55.

Brent, S. (1978). Puns, metaphors, and misunderstandings in a two-year-old's conception of death. *Omega, 8,* 285–294.

Brim, O., Freeman, H., Levine, S., & Scotch, N. (Eds.). (1970). *The dying patient.* New York: Russell Sage Foundation.

Brodman, B. (1976). *The Mexican cult of death in myth and literature.* Gainesville: University of Florida Press.

Brody, B. (1988). *Life and death decision making.* New York: Oxford University Press.

Brothers, J. (1990). *Widowed.* New York: Simon & Schuster.

Brown, J. A. (1990). Social work practice with the terminally ill in the Black community. In J. K. Parry (Ed.), *Social work practice with the terminally ill: A transcultural perspective* (pp. 67–82). Springfield, IL: Charles C Thomas.

Brown, J. E. (1987). *The spiritual legacy of the American Indian.* New York: Crossroad.

Brown, J. H., Henteleff, P., Barakat, S., & Rowe, C. J. (1986). Is it normal for terminally ill patients to desire death? *American Journal of Psychiatry, 143,* 208–211.

Brown, K. C., & Turner, J. G. (1989). *AIDS: Policies and programs for the workplace.* New York: Van Nostrand Reinhold.

Brown, M. W. (1958). *The dead bird.* Reading, MA: Addison-Wesley.

Brown, R. A. (1975). *The law of personal property* (3rd ed., by W. B. Rauschenbush). Chicago: Callaghan.

Broyard, A. (1992). *Intoxicated by my illness, and other writings on life and death.* Comp. and Ed. A. Broyard. New York: Clarkson Potter.

Brubaker, E. (1985). Older parents' reactions to the death of adult children: Implications for practice. *Journal of Gerontological Social Work, 9,* 35–48.

Bruner, J. S. (1962). *The process of education.* Cambridge: Harvard University Press.

Bryer, K. B. (1979). The Amish way of death: A study of family support systems. *American Psychologist, 34*(3), 255–261.

Buckingham, R. W. (1992). *Among friends: Hospice care for the person with AIDS.* Buffalo, NY: Prometheus.

Buckman, R. (1988). *I don't know what to say: How to help and support someone who is dying.* Toronto: Key Porter Books.

Buckman, R. (1992). *How to break bad news: A guide for health care professionals.* Toronto: University of Toronto Press.

Bühler, C. (1968). The general structure of the human life cycle. In C. Bühler & F. Massarik (Eds.), *The course of human life: A study of goals in the humanistic perspective.* (pp. 12–26). New York: Springer.

Bunting, E. (1982). *The happy funeral.* New York: Harper & Row.

Burns, S. B. (1990). *Sleeping beauty: Memorial photography in America.* Altadena, CA: Twelvetrees Press.

Bush, C. E., DiMichele, L. J., Peterson, W. R., Sherman, D. G., & Godsen, J. H. (1992). Solid-phase, time-resolved fluorescence detection of human immunodeficiency virus: Polymerase chain reaction amplification products. *Analytical Biochemistry, 202,* 146–151.

Butler, R. N. (1963). The life review: An interpretation of reminiscence in the aged. *Psychiatry, 26,* 65–76.

Butler, R. N. (1969). Age-ism: Another form of bigotry. *The Gerontologist, 9,* 243–246.

Butler, R. N. (1975). *Why survive? Being old in America.* New York: Harper & Row.

Butler, R. N., & Lewis, M. I. (1982). *Aging and mental health* (3rd ed.). St. Louis: C. V. Mosby.

Cade, S. (1963). Cancer: The patient's viewpoint and the clinician's problems. *Proceedings of the Royal Society of Medicine, 56,* 1–8.

Cain, A. (Ed.). (1972). *Survivors of suicide.* Springfield: Bannerstone House.

Caine, L. (1975). *Widow.* New York: Bantam Books.

Caine, L. (1978). *Lifelines.* New York: Doubleday.

Callahan, D. (1987). *Setting limits: Medical goals in an aging society.* New York: Simon & Schuster.

Callahan, D. (1992). When self-determination runs amok. *Hastings Center Report, 22*(2), 52–55.

Callanan, M., & Kelley, P. (1992). *Final gifts: Understanding the special awareness, needs, and communications of the dying.* New York: Poseidon.

Calvin, S., & Smith, I. M. (1986). Counseling adolescents in death-related situations. In C. A. Corr & J. N. McNeil (Eds.), *Adolescence and death* (pp. 215–230). New York: Springer.

Campbell, G. R. (1989). The political epidemiology of infant mortality: A health crisis among Montana American Indians. *American Indian Culture and Research Journal, 13,* 105–148.

Campbell, S., & Silverman, P. (1987). *Widower: What happens when men are left alone.* New York: Prentice-Hall Press.

Campos, A. P. (1990). Social work practice with Puerto Rican terminally ill clients and their families. In J. K. Parry (Ed.), *Social work practice with the terminally ill: A transcultural perspective* (pp. 129–143). Springfield, IL: Charles C Thomas.

Camus, A. (1972). *The plague.* Trans. S. Gilbert. New York: Vintage Books. (Original work published 1947)

Cantor, N. (1987). *Legal frontiers of death and dying.* Bloomington, IN: Indiana University Press.

Cantor, R. C. (1978). *And a time to live: Toward emotional well-being during the crisis of cancer.* New York: Harper & Row.

Card, J. J. (1974). Lethality of suicidal methods and suicide risk: Two distinct concepts. *Omega, 5,* 37–45.

Carey, R. G. (1979). Weathering widowhood: Problems and adjustment of the widowed during the first year. *Omega, 10,* 263–274.

Carr, B. A., & Lee, E. S. (1978). Navajo tribal mortality: A life table analysis of the leading causes of death. *Social Biology, 25,* 279–287.

Carse, J. P. (1980). *Death and existence: A conceptual history of mortality.* New York: Wiley.

Carson, R. (1992). Washington's I-119. *Hastings Center Report, 22*(2), 7–9.

Carson, U. (1984). Teachable moments occasioned by "small deaths." In H. Wass & C. A. Corr (Eds.), *Childhood and death* (pp. 315–343). Washington, DC: Hemisphere.

Carter, B., & McGoldrick, M. (Eds.). (1988). *The changing family life cycle: A framework for family therapy* (2nd ed.). New York: Gardner.

Cartwright, T. (1574). *A replye to an answere made of Master Doctor Whitgifte agaynste the admonition to the Parliament.* London.

Cassell, E. (1991). *The nature of suffering and the goals of medicine.* New York: Oxford University Press.

Catania, J. A., Coates, T. J., Stall, R., Turner, H., Peterson, J., Hearst, N., Dolcini, M. M., Hudes, E., Gagnon, J., Wiley, J., & Groves, R. (1992). Prevalence of AIDS-related risk factors and condom use in the United States. *Science, 258,* 1101–1106.

Cate, F. H., & Gill, B. A. (1991). *The patient self-determination act: Implementation issues and opportunities.* Washington, DC: The Annenberg Washington Program.

Centers for Disease Control. (1981a). *Pneumocystis* pneumonia—Los Angeles. *Morbidity and Mortality Weekly Report, 30,* 250–252.

Centers for Disease Control. (1981b). Kaposi's sarcoma and *Pneumocystis* pneumonia among homosexual men—New York City and California. *Morbidity and Mortality Weekly Report, 30,* 305–308.

Centers for Disease Control. (1981c). Follow-up on Kaposi's sarcoma and *Pneumocystis* pneumonia. *Morbidity and Mortality Weekly Report, 30,* 409–410.

Centers for Disease Control. (1982a). *Pneumocystis carinii* pneumonia among persons with hemophilia A. *Morbidity and Mortality Weekly Report, 31,* 365–367.

Centers for Disease Control. (1982b). Update on Acquired Immune Deficiency Syndrome (AIDS). *Morbidity and Mortality Weekly Report, 31,* 507–508, 513–514.

Centers for Disease Control. (1983). *Case definitions of AIDS used by CDC for epidemiology surveillance.* Atlanta: Author.

Centers for Disease Control. (1984). Antibodies to a retrovirus etiologically associated with Acquired Immunodeficiency Syndrome (AIDS) in populations with increased incidences of the syndrome. *Morbidity and Mortality Weekly Report, 33,* 377–379.

Centers for Disease Control. (1985a). *The case definition of AIDS used by the CDC for national reporting (CDC-Reportable AIDS)* (Document No. 0312S). Atlanta, GA: Author.

Centers for Disease Control. (1985b). Revision of the case definition of Acquired Immunodeficiency Syndrome for national reporting—United States. *Morbidity and Mortality Weekly Report, 34,* 373–375.

Centers for Disease Control. (1985c). Education and foster care of children infected with human T-lymphotropic virus Type III/lymphadenopathy-associated virus. *Morbidity and Mortality Weekly Report, 34,* 517–521.

Centers for Disease Control. (1985d). Recommendations for preventing transmission of infection with human T-lymphotropic virus Type III/lymphadenopathy-associated virus in the workplace. *Morbidity and Mortality Weekly Report, 34,* 681–695.

Centers for Disease Control. (1985e). Recommendations for assisting in the prevention of perinatal transmission of human T-lymphotropic virus Type III/lymphadenopathy-associated virus and Acquired Immunodeficiency Syndrome. *Morbidity and Mortality Weekly Report, 34,* 721–726, 731–732.

Centers for Disease Control. (1986). Classification system for human T-lymphotropic virus type III/lymphadenopathy-associated virus infections. *Morbidity and Mortality Weekly Report, 35,* 334–339.

Centers for Disease Control. (1987a). Revision of the CDC surveillance case definition for Acquired Immunodeficiency Syndrome. *Morbidity and Mortality Weekly Report, 36,* 1–S.

Centers for Disease Control. (1987b). Human immunodeficiency virus infection in the United States: A review of current knowledge. *Morbidity and Mortality Weekly Report, 36* (Suppl. No. S-6).

Centers for Disease Control. (1989a). First 100,000 cases of Acquired Immunodeficiency Syndrome—United States, 1989. *Morbidity and Mortality Weekly Report, 38,* 561–563.

Centers for Disease Control. (1989b). Guidelines for prevention of transmission of human immunodeficiency virus and hepatitis B virus to health-care and public-safety workers. *Morbidity and Mortality Weekly Report, 38,* S-6.

Centers for Disease Control. (1990). Possible transmission of human immunodeficiency virus to a patient during an invasive dental procedure. *Morbidity and Mortality Weekly Report, 39,* 489–493.

Centers for Disease Control. (1991a). Update: Transmission of HIV infection during an invasive dental procedure—Florida. *Morbidity and Mortality Weekly Report, 40,* 21–27, 33.

Centers for Disease Control. (1991b). Mortality attributable to HIV infection/AIDS—United States, 1981–1990. *Morbidity and Mortality Weekly Report, 40,* 41–44.

Centers for Disease Control. (1991c). The HIV/AIDS epidemic: The first 10 years. *Morbidity and Mortality Weekly Report, 40,* 357.

Centers for Disease Control. (1991d). Update: Acquired Immunodeficiency Syndrome—United States, 1981–1990. *Morbidity and Mortality Weekly Report, 40,* 358–363 & 369.

Centers for Disease Control. (1991e). Update: Transmission of HIV infection during invasive dental procedures—Florida. *Morbidity and Mortality Weekly Report, 40*, 377–381.

Centers for Disease Control. (1991f). Recommendations for preventing transmission of human immunodeficiency virus and hepatitis B virus to patients during exposure-prone invasive procedures. *Morbidity and Mortality Weekly Report, 40*, No. RR-8.

Centers for Disease Control. (1992a). The second 100,000 cases of Acquired Immunodeficiency Syndrome—United States, June 1981–December 1991. *Morbidity and Mortality Weekly Report, 41*, 28–29.

Centers for Disease Control. (1992b). 1993 revised classification system for HIV infection and expanded surveillance case definition for AIDS among adolescents and adults. *Morbidity and Mortality Weekly Report, 41*, No. RR-17.

Chamberland, M. E., Conley, L. J., Bush, T. J., Ciesielski, C. A., Hammett, T. A., & Jaffe, H. W. (1991). Health care workers with AIDS: National surveillance update. *Journal of the American Medical Association, 266*, 3459–3462.

Chan, W.-T. (1963). *A sourcebook in Chinese philosophy*. Princeton, NJ: Princeton University Press.

Chance, S. (1992). *Stronger than death*. New York: Norton.

Charmaz, K. (1980). *The social reality of death: Death in contemporary America*. Reading, MA: Addison-Wesley.

Childers, P., & Wimmer, M. (1971). The concept of death in early childhood. *Child Development, 42*, 1299–1301.

Childress, J. F. (1990). The place of autonomy in bioethics. *Hastings Center Report, 20*(1), 12–17.

Chin, J. (1990). Current and future dimensions of the HIV/AIDS pandemic in women and children. *Lancet, 336*, 221–224.

Choron, J. (1963). *Death and Western thought*. New York: Collier.

Choron, J. (1964). *Death and modern man*. New York: Collier.

Ciesielski, C., Marianos, D., Ou, C-Y., Dumbaugh, R., Witte, J., Berkelman, R., Gooch, B., Myers, G., Luo, C-C., Schochetman, G., Howell, J., Lasch, A., Bell, K., Economou, N., Scott, B., Furman, L., Curran, J., & Jaffe, H. (1992). Transmission of human immunodeficiency virus in a dental practice. *Annals of Internal Medicine, 116*, 798–805.

Clapton, E. (1992). Tears in heaven. *Unplugged*. Burbank, CA: Reprise Records/Warner Bros.

Clayton, P. J. (1973). The clinical morbidity of the first year of bereavement: A review. *Comprehensive Psychiatry, 14*, 151–157.

Clayton, P. J. (1974). Mortality and morbidity in the first year of widowhood. *Archives of General Psychiatry, 30*, 747–750.

Clayton, P. J. (1979). The sequelae and nonsequelae of conjugal bereavement. *American Journal of Psychiatry, 136*, 1530–1534.

Clayton, P. J., Herjanic, M., Murphy, G. E., & Woodruff, R. A. (1974). Mourning and depression: Their similarities and differences. *Canadian Psychiatric Association Journal, 19*, 309–312.

Cleckley, M., Estes, E., & Norton, P. (Eds.). (1992). *We need not walk alone: After the death of a child* (2nd ed.). Oak Brook, IL: The Compassionate Friends.

Clifford, D. (1989). *Plan your estate.* Berkeley, CA: Nolo Press.

Cockburn, D. (1989). People and the paranormal. In A. Berger, P. Badham, A. H. Kutscher, J. Berger, M. Perry, & J. Beloff (Eds.), *Perspectives on death and dying: Cross-cultural and multi-disciplinary views* (pp. 244–255). Philadelphia: Charles Press.

Coffin, J., Haase, A., Levy, J. A., Montagnier, L., Oroszian, S., Teich, N., Temin, H., Toyoshima, K., Varmus, H., Vogt, P., & Weiss, R. (1986). Human immunodeficiency viruses. *Science, 232,* 697.

Coffin, M. M. (1976). *Death in early America: The history and folklore of customs and superstitions of early medicine, burial and mourning.* Nashville: Thomas Nelson.

Cohen, M. N. (1989). *Health and the rise of civilization.* New Haven, CT: Yale University Press.

Cohen, P. T., Sande, M. A., & Volberding, P. A. (Eds.). (1990). *The AIDS knowledge base: A textbook in HIV disease from the University of California, San Francisco, and the San Francisco General Hospital.* Waltham, MA: The Medical Publishing Group, a Division of the Massachusetts Medical Society.

Cole, J. J. (1989). Moral dilemma: To kill or allow to die? *Death Studies, 13,* 393–406.

Cole, T. R., & Gadow, S. A. (Eds.). (1986). *What does it mean to grow old? Reflections from the humanities.* Durham, NC: Duke University Press.

Coleman, L. (1987). *Suicide clusters.* Boston and London: Faber & Faber.

Colen, B. D. (1976). *Karen Ann Quinlan: Dying in the age of eternal life.* New York: Nash.

Colen, B. D. (1991). *The essential guide to a living will: How to protect your right to refuse medical treatment.* New York: Prentice-Hall Press.

Committee on Nursing Home Regulation, Institute of Medicine. (1986). *Improving the quality of care in nursing homes.* Washington, DC: National Academy Press.

Congdon, H. K. (1977). *The pursuit of death.* Nashville: Abingdon.

Connor, S., & Kingman, S. (1988). *The search for the virus.* London: Penguin Books.

Consumer Reports. (1977). *Funerals: Consumers' last rights. The Consumers Union report on conventional funerals and burial . . . and some alternatives, including cremation, direct cremation, direct burial, and body donation.* New York: Pantheon.

Cook, A. S., & Oltjenbruns, K. A. (1989). *Dying and grieving: Lifespan and family perspectives.* New York: Holt, Reinhart & Winston.

Corea, G. (1992). *The invisible epidemic: The story of women and AIDS.* New York: HarperCollins.

Corless, I. B., & Pittman-Lindeman, M. (Eds.). (1988). *AIDS: Principles, practices, and politics.*

Corley, E. A. (1973). *Tell me about death, tell me about funerals.* Santa Clara, CA: Grammatical Sciences.

Corr, C. A. (1978). A model syllabus for death and dying courses. *Death Education, 1,* 433–457.

Corr, C. A. (1980). Workshops on children and death. *Essence, 4,* 5–18.

Corr, C. A. (1981). Hospices, dying persons, and hope. In R. A. Pacholski & C. A. Corr (Eds.), *New directions in death education and counseling: Enhancing the quality of life in the nuclear age* (pp. 14–20). Arlington, VA: Forum for Death Education and Counseling.

Corr, C. A. (1984a). Helping with death education. In H. Wass & C. A. Corr (Eds.), *Helping children cope with death: Guidelines and resources* (2nd ed., pp. 49–73). Washington, DC: Hemisphere.

Corr, C. A. (1984b). A model syllabus for children and death courses. *Death Education, 8,* 11–28.

Corr, C. A. (1986). Educational resources for children and death. In G. R. Paterson (Ed.), *Children and death: Proceedings of the 1985 King's College conference* (pp. 231–248). London, Ontario: King's College.

Corr, C. A. (1991). Should young children attend funerals? What constitutes reliable advice? *Thanatos, 16*(4), 19–21.

Corr, C. A. (1992a). A task-based approach to coping with dying. *Omega, 24,* 81–94.

Corr, C. A. (1992b). Teaching a college course on children and death: A 13-year report. *Death Studies, 16,* 343–356.

Corr, C. A. (1992c). *Someone you love is dying: How do you cope?* Houston, TX: Service Corporation International.

Corr, C. A. (1993a). Coping with dying: Lessons that we should and should not learn from the work of Elisabeth Kübler-Ross. *Death Studies, 17,* 69–83.

Corr, C. A. (1993b). Children's literature on death. In S. Z. Goltzer & A. Armstrong-Dailey (Eds.), *Hospice care for children* (pp. 266–284). New York: Oxford University Press.

Corr, C. A. (1993c). The day we went to Auschwitz. *Omega, 27,* 105–113.

Corr, C. A., & Corr, D. M. (Eds.). (1983). *Hospice care: Principles and practice.* New York: Springer.

Corr, C. A., & Corr, D. M. (Eds.). (1985a). *Hospice approaches to pediatric care.* New York: Springer.

Corr, C. A., & Corr, D. M. (1985b). Situations involving children: A challenge for the hospice movement. *The Hospice Journal, 1,* 63–77.

Corr, C. A., & Corr, D. M. (1985c). Pediatric hospice care. *Pediatrics, 76,* 774–780.

Corr, C. A., & Corr, D. M. (1988). What is pediatric hospice care? *Children's Health Care, 17,* 4–11.

Corr, C. A., & Corr, D. M. (1992a). Adult hospice day care. *Death Studies, 16,* 155–171.

Corr, C. A., & Corr, D. M. (1992b). Children's hospice care. *Death Studies, 16,* 431–449.

Corr, C. A., Fuller, H., Barnickol, C. A., & Corr, D. M. (Eds.). (1991). *Sudden Infant Death Syndrome: Who can help and how.* New York: Springer.

Corr, C. A., & McNeil, J. N. (Eds.). (1986). *Adolescence and death.* New York: Springer.

Corr, C. A., & the staff of the Dougy Center. (1991). Support for grieving children: The Dougy Center and the hospice philosophy. *The American Journal of Hospice and Palliative Care, 8*(4), 23–27.

Cousins, N. (1979). *Anatomy of an illness as perceived by the patient: Reflections on healing and regeneration.* New York: Norton.

Counts, D. R., & Counts, D. A. (Eds.). (1991). *Coping with the final tragedy: Cultural variation in dying and grieving.* Amityville, NY: Baywood.

The court and Nancy Cruzan. (1990). *Hastings Center Report, 20*(1), 38–50.

Crase, D., & Crase, D. (1976). Helping children understand death. *Young Children, 32*(1), 21–25

Crase, D. R., & Crase, D. (1984). Death education in the schools for older children. In H. Wass & C. A. Corr (Eds.), *Childhood and death* (pp. 345–363). Washington, DC: Hemisphere.

Craven, J., & Wald, F. S. (1975). Hospice care for dying patients. *American Journal of Nursing, 75,* 1816–1822.

Craven, M. (1973). *I heard the owl call my name.* New York: Dell.

Cremations and % of death. (1992). *Cremationist, 28*(3), 4.

Crue, M. (1987). You're all I need. *Girls, girls, girls.* New York: Elektra/Asylum Records, Warner Communications.

Culver, C. M., & Gert, B. (1990). Beyond the Living Will: Making advance directives more useful. *Omega, 21,* 253–258.

Czarnecki, J. P. (1989). *Last traces: The lost art of Auschwitz.* New York: Atheneum.

Dalton, H. L., & Burris, S. (Eds.). (1987). *AIDS and the law: A guide for the public.* New Haven, CT: Yale University Press.

Danforth, L. M. (1982). *The death rituals of rural Greece.* Princeton, NJ: Princeton University Press.

Davidson, G. W. (1975). *Living with dying.* Minneapolis: Augsburg.

Davidson, G. W. (1979). Hospice care for the dying. In H. Wass (Ed.), *Dying: Facing the facts* (pp. 158–181). New York: McGraw-Hill/Hemisphere.

Davidson, G. W. (1984a). Stillbirth, neonatal death, and Sudden Infant Death Syndrome. In H. Wass & C. A. Corr (Eds.), *Childhood and death* (pp. 243–257). Washington, DC: Hemisphere.

Davidson, G. W. (1984b). *Understanding mourning: A guide for those who grieve.* Minneapolis: Augsburg.

Davidson, G. W. (Ed.). (1985). *The hospice: Development and administration* (2nd ed.). Washington, DC: Hemisphere.

Davidson, M. N., & Devney, P. (1991). Attitudinal barriers to organ donation among Black Americans. *Transplantation Proceedings, 23,* 2531–2532.

Dawidowicz, L. S. (1975). *The war against the Jews 1933–1945.* New York: Holt, Rinehart & Winston.

De Beauvoir, S. (1973). *A very easy death.* Trans. P. O'Brian. New York: Warner. (Original work published 1964)

DeFrain, J., Ernst, L., Jakub, D., & Taylor, J. (1991). *Sudden infant death: Enduring the loss.* Lexington, MA: Lexington Books.

DeFrain, J., Martens, L., Story, J., & Stork, W. (1986). *Stillborn: The invisible death.* Lexington, MA: Lexington Books.

Delgadillo, D., & Davis, P. (1990). *When the bough breaks.* San Diego, CA: San Diego County Guild for Infant Survival.

Demi, A. S., & Miles, M. S. (1987). Parameters of normal grief: A Delphi study. *Death Studies, 11,* 397–412.

Derlega, V. J., & Chaikin, A. L. (1975). *Sharing intimacy.* Englewood Cliffs, NJ: Prentice-Hall.

DeSpelder, L. A., & Strickland, A. L. (1992). *The last dance: Encountering death and dying* (3rd ed.). Mountain View, CA: Mayfield.

Deutsch, H. (1937). Absence of grief. *Psychoanalytic Quarterly, 6,* 12–22.

Devore, W. (1990). The experience of death: A Black perspective. In J. K. Parry (Ed.), *Social work practice with the terminally ill: A transcultural perspective* (pp. 47–66). Springfield, IL: Charles C Thomas.

De Wachter, M.A.M. (1989). Active euthanasia in the Netherlands. *Journal of the American Medical Association, 262,* 3315–3319.

De Wachter, M.A.M. (1992). Euthanasia in the Netherlands. *Hastings Center Report, 22*(2), 23–30.

DiClemente, R. J. (1990). The emergence of adolescents as a risk group for human immunodeficiency virus infection. *Journal of Adolescent Research, 5,* 7–17.

Diggory, J. C. (1976). United States suicide rates, 1933–1968: An analysis of some trends. In E. S. Shneidman (Ed.), *Suicidology: Contemporary developments* (pp. 30–69). New York: Grune & Stratton.

DiGiulio, R. C. (1989). *Beyond widowhood: From bereavement to emergence and hope.* New York: Free Press.

Dixon, M. I., & Clearwater, H. E. (1991). Accidents. In D. Leviton, *Horrendous death, health, and well-being* (pp. 219–237). Washington, DC: Hemisphere.

Doane, B. K., & Quigley, B. Q. (1981). Psychiatric aspects of therapeutic abortion. *Canadian Medical Association Journal, 125,* 427–432.

Doka, K. J. (1986). Loss upon loss: The impact of death after divorce. *Death Studies, 10,* 441–449.

Doka, K. J. (1988). The awareness of mortality in midlife: Implications for later life. *Gerontology Review, 2,* 1–10.

Doka, K. J. (Ed.). (1989a). *Disenfranchised grief: Recognizing hidden sorrow.* Lexington, MA: Lexington Books.

Doka, K. J. (1989b). Disenfranchised grief. In K. J. Doka (Ed.), *Disenfranchised grief: Recognizing hidden sorrow* (pp. 3–11). Lexington, MA: Lexington Books.

Doka, K. J. (1993). *Living with life-threatening illness: A guide for parents, families, and caregivers.* Lexington, MA: Lexington Books.

Doka, K. J., with Morgan, J. D. (Eds.). (1993). *Death and spirituality.* Amityville, NY: Baywood.

Donne, J. (1952). Devotions upon emergent occasions. VI. Meditation. In C. M. Coffin (Ed.). The Complete poetry and selected prose of John Donne (pp. 1181–1184). New York: Modern Library. (Original work published 1624.)

Donnelly, K. F. (1982). *Recovering from the loss of a child.* New York: Macmillan.

Donnelly, K. F. (1987). *Recovering from the loss of a parent.* New York: Dodd, Mead.

Donnelly, K. F. (1988). *Recovering from the loss of a sibling.* New York: Dodd, Mead.

Dorpat, T. L., & Boswell, J. W. (1973). An evaluation of suicidal intent in suicide attempts. *Comprehensive Psychiatry, 4,* 117–125.

Dorpat, T. L., & Ripley, H. S. (1967). The relationship between attempted suicide and completed suicide. *Comprehensive Psychiatry, 8,* 74–89.

Douglas, J. D. (1967). *The social meanings of suicide.* Princeton, NJ: Princeton University Press.

Douglas, M. (1970). *Natural symbols.* New York: Random House.

Douglas, P. H., & Pinsky, L. (1992). *The essential AIDS fact book* (rev. ed.). New York: Pocket Books.

Downing, A. B. (Ed.). (1974). *Euthanasia and the right to death: The case for voluntary euthanasia.* London: Peter Owen.

Doyle, D. (1980). Domiciliary terminal care. *Practitioner, 224,* 575–582.

DuBoulay, S. (1984). *Cicely Saunders: The founder of the modern hospice movement.* London: Hodder & Stoughton.

Dukeminier, J. (1978). Organ donation: II. Legal aspects. In W. T. Reich (Ed.), *Encyclopedia of bioethics* (pp. 1157–1160). New York: Free Press.

Dukeminier, J., & Johanson, S. M. (1990). *Wills, trusts, and estates* (4th ed.). Boston: Little, Brown.

Dumont, R., & Foss, D. (1972). *The American view of death: Acceptance or denial?* Cambridge, MA: Schenkman.

Dundes, A. (1989). *Little Red Riding Hood: A casebook.* Madison, WI: University of Wisconsin Press.

Dunne, E. J., McIntosh, J. L., & Dunne-Maxim, K. (Eds.). (1987). *Suicide and its aftermath.* New York: Norton.

Durkheim, E. (1951). *Suicide: A study in sociology.* Trans. J. A. Spaulding & G. Simpson. Glencoe, IL: Free Press. (Original work published 1897).

Durkheim, E. (1954). *The elementary forms of religious life.* Trans. J. W. Swaine. London: Allen & Unwin. (Original work published 1915)

Eichrodt, W. (1967). *Theology of the Old Testament, Vol. 2.* Trans. J. A. Baker. Philadelphia: Westminster.

Eisenbruch, M. (1984). Cross-cultural aspects of bereavement. II: Ethnic and cultural variations in the development of bereavement practices. *Culture, Medicine & Psychiatry, 8,* 315–347.

Elkind, D. (1967). Egocentrism in adolescence. *Child Development, 38,* 1025–1034.

Elliot, G. (1972). *The twentieth century book of the dead.* New York: Random House.

Ellis, J. B., & Range, L. M. (1989). Characteristics of suicidal individuals: A review. *Death Studies, 13,* 485–500.

Elmer, L. (1987). *Why her, why now: A man's journey through love and death and grief.* Seattle, WA: Signal Elm Press.

Engel, G. L. (1961). Is grief a disease? A challenge for medical research. *Psychosomatic Medicine, 23,* 18–22.

Enright, D. J. (Ed.). (1983). *The Oxford book of death*. New York: Oxford University Press.

Erikson, E. H. (1959). Identity and the life cycle: Selected papers. *Psychological Issues, 1*, 1–171.

Erikson, E. H. (1963). *Childhood and society* (2nd ed.). New York: Norton. (Original edition, 1950)

Erikson, E. H. (1968). *Identity: Youth and crisis*. London: Faber & Faber.

Erikson, E. H. (1975). *Life history and the historical moment*. New York: Norton.

Erikson, E. H., & Erikson, J. M. (1981). On generativity and identity: From a conversation with Erik and Joan Erikson. *Harvard Educational Review, 51*, 249–269.

Erikson, E. H., Erikson, J. M., & Kivnick, H. (1986). *Vital involvement in old age*. New York: Norton.

Esperti, R. A., & Peterson, R. L. (1988). *The handbook of estate planning* (2nd ed.). New York: McGraw-Hill.

Evans, G., & Farberow, N. L. (Eds.). (1988). *The encyclopedia of suicide*. New York: Facts on File.

Evans, J. (1971). *Living with a man who is dying: A personal memoir*. New York: Taplinger.

Ewalt, P. L., & Perkins, L. (1979). The real experience of death among adolescents: An empirical study. *Social Casework, 60*, 547–551.

Ewing, C. P. (1990). *Kids who kill*. New York: Free Press.

Fairchild, T. N. (Ed.). (1986). *Crisis intervention strategies for school-based helpers*. Springfield, IL: Charles C Thomas.

Fales, M. (1964). The early American way of death. *Essex Institution Historical Collection, 100*(2), 75–84.

Farberow, N. L. (Ed.). (1980). *The many faces of suicide: Indirect self-destructive behavior*. New York: McGraw-Hill.

Farberow, N. L. (1983). Relationships between suicide and depression: An overview. *Psychiatria Fennica Supplementum, 14*, 9–19.

Farberow, N. L., & Moriwaki, S. Y. (1975). Self-destructive crises in the older person. *The Gerontologist, 15*, 333–337.

Farberow, N. L., & Shneidman, E. S. (Eds.). (1965). *The cry for help*. New York: McGraw-Hill.

Farrell, F., & Hutter, J. J. (1980). Living until death: Adolescents with cancer. *Health and Social Work, 5*, 35–38.

Farrell, J. J. (1980). *Inventing the American way of death: 1830–1920*. Philadelphia: Temple University Press.

Faulkner, W. (1930). *As I lay dying*. New York: Random House.

Faulkner, W. (1943). A rose for Emily. In *Collected stories of William Faulkner* (pp. 119–130). New York: Random House. (Original work published 1924)

Fee, E., & Fox, D. M. (Eds.). (1992). *AIDS: The making of a chronic disease*. Berkeley & Los Angeles: University of California Press.

Feifel, H. (Ed.). (1959). *The meaning of death*. New York: McGraw-Hill.

Feifel, H. (1963). Death. In N. L. Farberow (Ed.), *Taboo topics* (pp. 8–21). New York: Atherton.

Feifel, H. (1969). Attitudes toward death. *Journal of Consulting and Clinical Psychology, 33*, 292–295.

Feifel, H. (1977a). Preface and introduction: Death in contemporary America. In H. Feifel (Ed.), *New meanings of death* (pp. xiii–xiv, 4–12). New York: McGraw-Hill.

Feifel, H. (Ed.). (1977b). *New meanings of death.* New York: McGraw-Hill.

Feigenberg, L. (1980). *Terminal care: Friendship contracts with dying cancer patients.* Trans. P. Hort. New York: Brunner/Mazel.

Feldblum, P. J., & Fortney, J. A. (1988). Condoms, spermicides, and the transmission of human immunodeficiency virus: A review of the literature. *American Journal of Public Health, 78*, 52–53.

Fenton man asks for court order to allow comatose wife to die. (1975, October 26). *St. Louis Post-Dispatch*, pp. 1A, 23A.

Fenton, T. W. (1987). AIDS-related psychiatric disorder. *British Journal of Psychiatry, 151*, 579–588.

Fingerhut, L. A., Ingram, D. A., & Feldman, J. J. (1992). Firearm homicide among Black teenage males in metropolitan counties. *Journal of the American Medical Association, 267*, 3054–3058.

Fleming, S. J. (1985). Children's grief: Individual and family dynamics. In C. A. Corr & D. M. Corr (Eds.), *Hospice approaches to pediatric care* (pp. 197–218). New York: Springer.

Fleming, S. J., & Adolph, R. (1986). Helping bereaved adolescents: Needs and responses. In C. A. Corr & J. N. McNeil (Eds.), *Adolescence and death* (pp. 97–118). New York: Springer.

Floerchinger, D. S. (1991). Bereavement in late adolescence; Interventions on college campuses. *Journal of Adolescent Research, 6*, 146–156.

Flynn, E. P. (1992). *Your living will: Why, when, and how to write one.* New York: Citadel Press.

Folta, J. R., & Deck, E. S. (1976). Grief, the funeral, and the friend. In V. R. Pine, A. H. Kutscher, D. Peretz, R. C. Slater, R. DeBellis, R. J. Volk, & D. J. Cherico (Eds.), *Acute grief and the funeral* (pp. 231–240). Springfield, IL: Charles C Thomas.

Foot, P. (1977). Euthanasia. *Philosophy and Public Affairs, 6*, 85–112.

Forbes, H. (1927). *Gravestones of early New England and the men who made them, 1653–1800.* Boston: Houghton Mifflin.

Ford, G. (1979). Terminal care from the viewpoint of the National Health Service. In J. J. Bonica & V. Ventafridda (Eds.), *International symposium on pain of advanced cancer: Advances in pain research and therapy, Vol. 2* (pp. 653–661). New York: Raven Press.

Foster, Z., Wald, F. S., & Wald, H. J. (1978). The hospice movement: A backward glance at its first two decades. *New Physician, 27*, 21–24.

Fowles, J. (1964). *The aristos.* Boston: Little, Brown.

Fox, R. C., & Swazey, J. P. (1974). *The courage to fail: A social view of organ transplants and dialysis.* Chicago: University of Chicago Press.

Fox, S. S. (1988, August). Helping child deal with death teaches valuable skills. *The Psychiatric Times*, pp. 10–11.

Francis, D. (1985). *Proof.* New York: Ballantine Books.

Francis, D. P., Curran, J. W., & Essex, M. (1983). Epidemic acquired immune deficiency syndrome: Epidemiologic evidence for a transmissible agent. *Journal of the National Cancer Institutes, 71,* 1–4.

Francis, V. M. (1859). *A thesis on hospital hygiene.* New York: J. F. Trow.

Frank, A. W. (1991). *At the will of the body: Reflections on illness.* Boston: Houghton Mifflin.

Frankl, V. (1984). *Man's search for meaning.* New York: Simon & Schuster.

Frazer, J. G. (1977). *The fear of the dead in primitive religion.* New York: Arno Press.

Frederick, C. J. (1978). Current trends in suicidal behavior in the United States. *American Journal of Psychotherapy, 32,* 172–200.

Frederick, C. J., & Resnik, J.L.P. (1971). How suicidal behaviors are learned. *American Journal of Psychotherapy, 25,* 37–55.

Fredrick, J. F. (1971). Physiological reactions induced by grief. *Omega, 2,* 71–75.

Fredrick, J. F. (1977). Grief as a disease process. *Omega, 7,* 297–305.

Fredrick, J. F. (1983). The biochemistry of bereavement: Possible basis for chemotherapy? *Omega, 13,* 295–303.

French, S. (1975). The cemetery as cultural institution: The establishment of Mount Auburn and the "rural cemetery" movement. In D. E. Stannard (Ed.), *Death in America* (pp. 69–91). Philadelphia: University of Pennsylvania Press.

Freud, A. (1958). Adolescence. *Psychoanalytic Study of the Child, 13,* 255–268.

Freud, S. (1959a). Mourning and melancholia. In J. Strachey (Ed. and Trans.), *The standard edition of the complete psychological works of Sigmund Freud* (Vol. 14, pp. 237–258). London: Hogarth Press. (Original work published 1917)

Freud, S. (1959b). *New introductory lectures on psycho-analysis.* In J. Strachey (Ed. and Trans.), *The standard edition of the complete psychological works of Sigmund Freud* (Vol. 22, pp. 1–182). London: Hogarth Press. (Original work published 1933)

Friedman, E. H. (1980). Systems and ceremonies: A family view of rites of passage. In E. A. Carter & M. McGoldrick (Eds.), *The family life cycle: A framework for family therapy* (pp. 429–460). New York: Gardner.

Friedman, S. R., Des Jarlais, D. C., & Goldsmith, D. S. (1989). An overview of AIDS prevention efforts aimed at intravenous drug users circa 1987. *Journal of Drug Issues, 19*(1), 93–112.

Friel, M., & Tehan, C. B. (1980). Counteracting burn-out for the hospice caregiver. *Cancer Nursing, 3,* 285–293.

Fuller, R. L., Geis, S. B., & Rush, J. (1988). Lovers of AIDS victims: A minority group experience. *Death Studies, 12,* 1–7.

Fulton, R. (1961). The clergyman and the funeral director: A study in role conflict. *Social Forces, 39,* 317–323.

Fulton, R. (1970). Death, grief, and social recuperation. *Omega, 1,* 23–28.

Fulton, R. (1976). *Death and identity* (rev. ed.). Bowie, MD: Charles Press.

Fulton, R. (1978). The sacred and the secular: Attitudes of the American public toward death, funerals, and funeral directors. In R. Fulton & R. Bendiksen

(Eds.), *Death and identity* (rev. ed., pp. 158–172). Bowie, MD: Charles Press.

Fulton, R. (1988). The funeral in contemporary society. In H. Wass, F. M. Berardo, & R. A. Neimeyer (Eds.), *Dying: Facing the facts* (2nd ed., pp. 257–277). Washington, DC: Hemisphere.

Fulton, R., & Fulton, J. (1971). A psychosocial aspect of terminal care: Anticipatory grief. *Omega, 2,* 91–100.

Fulton, R., & Gottesman, D. J. (1980). Anticipatory grief: A psychosocial concept reconsidered. *British Journal of Psychiatry, 137,* 45–54.

Furman, E. (Ed.). (1974). *A child's parent dies: Studies in childhood bereavement.* New Haven, CT: Yale University Press.

Furman, E. (1984). Children's patterns in mourning the death of a loved one. In H. Wass & C. A. Corr (Eds.), *Childhood and death* (pp. 185–203). Washington, DC: Hemisphere.

Furman, R. A. (1973). A child's capacity for mourning. In E. J. Anthony & C. Koupernik (Eds.), *The child in his family: The impact of disease and death* (pp. 225–231). New York: Wiley.

Furth, G. M. (1988). *The secret world of drawings: Healing through art.* Boston: Sigo.

Gallo, R. C., Salahuddin, S. Z., Popovic, M., Shearer, G. M., Kaplan, M., Haynes, B. F., Palker, T. J., Redfield, R., Oleske, J., Safai, B., White, G., Foster, P., & Markham, P. (1984). Frequent detection and isolation of cytopathic retroviruses (HTLV-III) from patients with AIDS and at risk for AIDS. *Science, 224,* 500–503.

Garber, B. (1983). Some thoughts on normal adolescents who lost a parent by death. *Journal of Youth and Adolescence, 12,* 175–183.

Garcia-Preto, N. (1986). Puerto Rican families. In M. McGoldrick, P. Hines, E. Lee, & N. Garcia-Preto, Mourning rituals: How cultures shape the experience of loss. *The Family Therapy Networker, 10*(6), 33–34.

Garfield, C. A. (1976). Foundations of psychosocial oncology: The terminal phase. In J. M. Vaeth (Ed.), *Breast cancer: Its impact on the patient, family, and community* (pp. 180–212). Basel: Karger.

Gartley, W., & Bernasconi, M. (1967). The concept of death in children. *Journal of Genetic Psychology, 110,* 71–85.

Gatch, M. McC. (1969). *Death: Meaning and mortality in Christian thought and contemporary culture.* New York: Seabury Press.

Gee, E. M., & Veevers, J. E. (1985). Increasing sex mortality differentials among Black Americans, 1950–1978. *Phylon, 46*(2), 162–175.

Geis, S. B., Fuller, R. L., & Rush, J. (1986). Lovers of AIDS victims. *Death Studies, 10,* 43–53.

Gervais, K. G. (1986). *Redefining death.* New Haven, CT: Yale University Press.

Gideon, M. A., & Taylor, P. B. (1981). A sexual bill of rights for dying persons. *Death Education, 4,* 303–314.

Gill, D. L. (1980). *Quest: The life of Elisabeth Kübler-Ross.* New York: Harper & Row.

Gilligan, C. (1982). *In a different voice: Psychological theory and women's development.* Cambridge, MA: Harvard University Press.

Gillon, E. (1972). *Victorian cemetery sculpture.* New York: Dover.

Giovacchini, P. (1981). *The urge to die: Why young people commit suicide.* New York: Macmillan.

Glaser, B., & Strauss, A. (1965). *Awareness of dying.* Chicago: Aldine.

Glaser, B., & Strauss, A. (1968). *Time for dying.* Chicago: Aldine.

Glaser, E., & Palmer, L. (1991). *In the absence of angels: A Hollywood family's courageous story.* New York: Putnam's.

Glick, I., Weiss, R., & Parkes, C. (1974). *The first year of bereavement.* New York: Wiley.

Goffman, E. (1963). *Stigma: Notes on the management of spoiled identity.* Englewood Cliffs, NJ: Prentice-Hall.

Golan, N. (1975). Wife to widow to woman. *Social Work, 20,* 369–374.

Goldberg, S. B. (1973). Family tasks and reactions in the crisis of death. *Social Casework, 54,* 398–405.

Goldscheider, C. (1971). *Population, modernization, and social structure.* Boston: Little, Brown.

Gomez, C. F. (1991). *Regulating death: Euthanasia and the case of the Netherlands.* New York: Free Press.

Goody, J. (1962). *Death, property, and the ancestors: A study of the mortuary customs of the LoDagaa of West Africa.* Stanford, CA: Stanford University Press.

Gordon, A. K. (1974). The psychological wisdom of the Law. In J. Riemer (Ed.), *Jewish reflections on death* (pp. 95–104). New York: Schocken.

Gordon, A. K. (1986). The tattered cloak of immortality. In C. A. Corr & J. N. McNeil (Eds.), *Adolescence and death* (pp. 16–31). New York: Springer.

Gordon, A. K., & Klass, D. (1979). *They need to know: How to teach children about death.* Englewood Cliffs, NJ: Prentice-Hall.

Gorer, G. (1965a). The pornography of death. In G. Gorer, *Death, grief, and mourning* (pp. 192–199). Garden City, NY: Doubleday.

Gorer, G. (1965b). *Death, grief, and mourning.* Garden City, NY: Doubleday.

Gorovitz, S. (1991). *Drawing the line: Life, death, and ethical choices in an American hospital.* New York: Oxford University Press.

Gostin, L. O. (Ed.). (1990). *AIDS and the health care system.* New Haven, CT: Yale University Press.

Gottfried, R. S. (1983). *The black death: Natural and human disaster in medieval Europe.* New York: Free Press.

Gottlieb, G. J., Ragaz, A., Vogel, J. V., Friedman-Kien, A., Rywkin, A. M., Weiner, E. A., & Ackerman, A. B. (1981). A preliminary communication on extensively disseminated Kaposi's sarcoma in young homosexual men. *American Journal of Dermatopathology, 3,* 111–114.

Gottlieb, M. S., Schroff, R., Schanker, H. M., Weisman, J. D., Fan, P. T., Wolf, R. A., & Saxon, A. (1981). *Pneumocystic carinii* pneumonia and mucosal candidiasis in previously healthy homosexual men: Evidence of a new acquired cellular immunodeficiency. *New England Journal of Medicine, 305,* 1425–1431.

Gould, B. B., Moon, S., & Van Hoorn, J. (Eds.). (1986). *Growing up scared? The psychological effect of the nuclear threat on children.* Berkeley: Open Books.

Gove, W. R. (1973). Sex, marital status, and mortality. *American Journal of Sociology, 79,* 45–67.

Graham, L. (1990). *Rebuilding the house.* New York: Viking.

Graham, V. (1988). *Life after Harry: My adventures in widowhood.* New York: Simon & Schuster.

Gray, R. E. (1988). The role of school counselors with bereaved teenagers: With and without peer support groups. *The School Counselor, 35,* 188–193.

Greenberg, B. S., & Parker, E. B. (Eds.). (1965). *The Kennedy assassination and the American public: Social communication in crisis.* Stanford, CA: Stanford University Press.

Grmek, M. D. (1990). *History of AIDS: Emergence and origin of a modern pandemic.* Trans. R. C. Maulitz & J. Duffin. Princeton, NJ: Princeton University Press.

Grof, S., & Halifax, J. (1978). *The human encounter with death.* New York: Dutton.

Grollman, E. A. (1967). Prologue: Explaining death to children. In E. A. Grollman (Ed.), *Explaining death to children* (pp. 3–27). Boston: Beacon Press.

Grollman, E. A. (1977). *Living when a loved one has died.* Boston: Beacon Press.

Grollman, E. A. (1980). *When your loved one is dying.* Boston: Beacon Press.

Grollman, E. A. (Ed.). (1981). *What helped me when my loved one died.* Boston: Beacon Press.

Grollman, E. A. (1990). *Talking about death: A dialogue between parent and child* (3rd ed.). Boston: Beacon Press.

Grollman, E. A. (1993). Straight talk about death for teenagers: How to cope with losing someone you love. Boston: Beacon Press.

Grosso, M. (1981). Toward an explanation of near-death phenomena. *Journal of the American Society for Psychical Research, 75,* 37–60.

Grosso, M. (1989). A postmodern mythology of death. In A. Berger, P. Badham, A. H. Kutscher, J. Berger, M. Perry, & J. Beloff (Eds.), *Perspectives on death and dying: Cross-cultural and multi-disciplinary views* (pp. 232–243). Philadelphia: Charles Press.

Grove, S. (1978). I am a yellow ship. *American Journal of Nursing, 78,* 414.

Gruman, G. J. (1973). An historical introduction to ideas about voluntary euthanasia, with a bibliographic survey and guide for interdisciplinary studies. *Omega, 4,* 87–138.

Gubrium, J. F. (1975). *Living and dying at Murray Manor.* New York: St. Martin's Press.

Gunther, J. (1949). *Death be not proud.* New York: Harper.

Gyulay, J. E. (1975). The forgotten grievers. *American Journal of Nursing, 75,* 1476–1479.

Habenstein, R. W., & Lamers, W. M. (1962). *The history of American funeral directing* (rev. ed.). Milwaukee: Bulfin.

Habenstein, R. W., & Lamers, W. M. (1974). *Funeral customs the world over* (rev. ed.). Milwaukee: Bulfin.

Hall, G. S. (1922). *Senescence: The last half of life.* New York: D. Appleton.

Hamilton, J. (1978). Grandparents as grievers. In O.J.Z. Sahler (Ed.), *The child and death* (pp. 219–225). St. Louis: C. V. Mosby.

Hamilton-Paterson, J., & Andrews, C. (1979). *Mummies: Death and life in ancient Egypt.* New York: Penguin.

Hanlan, A. (1979). *Autobiography of dying.* Garden City, NY: Doubleday.

Hanson, J. C., & Frantz, T. T. (Eds.). (1984). *Death and grief in the family.* Rockville, MD: Aspen Systems Corp.

Hanson, W. (1978). Grief counseling with Native Americans. *White Cloud Journal of American Indian/Alaska Native Mental Health, 1*(2), 19–21.

Harmer, R. M. (1963). *The high cost of dying.* New York: Collier.

Harmer, R. M. (1971). Funerals, fantasy and flight. *Omega, 2,* 127–135.

Harper, B. C. (1977). *Death: The coping mechanism of the health professional.* Greenville, SC: Southeastern University Press.

Harper, C. D., Royer, R. H., & Humphrey, G. M. (1988). *The special needs of grieving children: A seven-week structured support group with resource section and bibliography,* Vol. 1, No. 1. North Canton, OH: The Grief Support and Education Center.

Harrison, W. (1989). *Three hunters.* New York: Random House.

Haskell, P. G. (1987). *Preface to wills, trusts, and administration.* Mineola, NY: Foundation Press.

Hassl, B., & Marnocha, J. (1990). *Bereavement support group program for children.* Muncie, IN: Accelerated Development.

Hatchett, M. (1976). *Sanctifying life, time and space.* New York: Seabury Press.

Hatton, C. L., & Valente, S. M. (Eds.). (1984). *Suicide: Assessment and intervention* (2nd ed.). Norwalk, CT: Appleton-Century-Crofts.

Havighurst, R. J. (1953). *Human development and education.* New York: Longmans, Green.

Havighurst, R. J. (1972). *Developmental tasks and education* (3rd ed.). New York: McKay.

Heacock, D. R. (1990). Suicidal behavior in Black and Hispanic youth. *Psychiatric Annals, 20*(3), 134–142.

The Heart of the New Age Hospice [videotape]. (1987). The University of Texas at Houston, Health Sciences Center.

Heeg, J. M., & Coleman, D. A. (1992). Hepatitis kills. *RN, 55*(4), 60–66.

Hemingway, E. S. (1926). *The sun also rises.* New York: Scribner's.

Hemingway, E. S. (1929). *A farewell to arms.* New York: Scribner's.

Hemingway, E. S. (1940). *For whom the bell tolls.* New York: Scribner's.

Hemingway, E. S. (1952). *The old man and the sea.* New York: Scribner's.

Herek, G. M., & Glunt, E. K. (1988). An epidemic of stigma. Public reactions to AIDS. *American Psychologist, 43,* 886–891.

Hersey, J. (1948). *Hiroshima.* New York: Bantam.

Herz, F. M., & Rosen, E. J. (1982). Jewish families. In M. McGoldrick, J. K. Pearce, & J. Giordano (Eds.), *Ethnicity and family therapy* (pp. 364–392). New York: Guilford.

Hewett, J. (1980). *After suicide.* Philadelphia: Westminster Press.

Hillier, E. R. (1983). Terminal care in the United Kingdom. In C. A. Corr & D. M. Corr (Eds.), *Hospice care: Principles and practice* (pp. 319–334). New York: Springer.

Hines, P. (1986). Afro American families. In M. McGoldrick, P. Hines, E. Lee, & N. Garcia-Preto, Mourning rituals: How cultures shape the experience of loss. *The Family Therapy Networker, 10*(6), 32–33.

Hinkle, K. L. (1991). A literature review: HIV seropositivity in the elderly. *Journal of Gerontological Nursing, 17*(10), 12–17.

Hinton, J. (1963). The physical and mental distress of the dying. *Quarterly Journal of Medicine*, New Series, *32*, 1–21.

Hinton, J. (1967). *Dying*. New York: Penguin.

Hinton, J. (1984). Coping with terminal illness. In R. Fitzpatrick, J. Hinton, S. Newman, G. Scambler, & J. Thompson (Eds.), *The experience of illness* (pp. 227–245). London: Tavistock Publications.

Hirayama, K. K. (1990). Death and dying in Japanese culture. In J. K. Parry (Ed.), *Social work practice with the terminally ill: A transcultural perspective* (pp. 159–174). Springfield, IL: Charles C Thomas.

Hoess, R. (1959). *Commandant of Auschwitz: The autobiography of Rudolf Hoess*. Trans. C. FitzGibbon. Cleveland: World Publishing.

Hogan, N. S., & Balk, D. E. (1990). Adolescent reactions to sibling death: Perceptions of mothers, fathers, and teenagers. *Nursing Research, 39*, 103–106.

Hogan, N. S., & DeSantis, L. (1992). Adolescent sibling bereavement: An ongoing attachment. *Qualitative Health Research, 2*, 159–177.

Hogan, N. S., & DeSantis, L. (in press). Things that help and hinder adolescent sibling bereavement. *Western Journal of Nursing Research*.

Hogan, N. S., & Greenfield, D. B. (1991). Adolescent sibling bereavement symptomatology in a large community sample. *Journal of Adolescent Research, 6*, 97–112.

Homer. (1937). *Odyssey*. Trans. W.H.D. Rouse. New York: New American Library.

Hoppe, S. K., & Martin, H. W. (1986). Patterns of suicide among Mexican Americans and Anglos, 1960–1980. *Social Psychiatry, 21*, 83–88.

Horowitz, M. J., Weiss, D. S., Kaltreider, N., Krupnick, J., Marmar, C., Wilner, N., & DeWitt, K. (1984). Reactions to the death of a parent. *Journal of Nervous and Mental Disease, 172*, 383–392.

Hostetler, J. A. (1980). *Amish society* (3rd ed.). Baltimore: Johns Hopkins University Press.

Hughes, T. E., & Klein, D. (1987). *A family guide to wills, funerals, and probate: How to protect yourself and your survivors*. New York: Scribner's.

Hultkrantz, A. (1979). *The religions of the American Indians*. Trans. M. Setterwall. Berkeley: University of California Press.

Humphry, D. (1991). *Final exit: The practicalities of self-deliverance and assisted suicide for the dying*. Eugene, OR: Hemlock Society.

Hunter, N. D., & Rubenstein, W. B. (Eds.). (1992). *AIDS agenda: Emerging issues in civil rights*. New York: New Press.

Huxley, A. (1939). *After many a summer dies the swan*. New York: Harper & Brothers.

Hymes, K. B., Greene, J. B., Marcus, A., et al. (1981). Kaposi's sarcoma in homosexual men: A report of eight cases. *Lancet, 2*, 598–600.

Ingles, T. (1974). St. Christopher's Hospice. *Nursing Outlook, 22*, 759–763.

Institute of Medicine. (1986). *Confronting AIDS: Directions for public health, health care, and research.* Washington, DC: National Academy Press.

Institute of Medicine. (1988). *Confronting AIDS: Update 1988.* Washington, DC: National Academy Press.

International Work Group on Death, Dying, and Bereavement. (1979). Assumptions and principles underlying standards for terminal care. *American Journal of Nursing, 79*, 296–297. (Also published in the same year in *Health and Social Work, 4*, 117–128; and *Canadian Medical Association Journal, 120*, 1280–1281.)

International Work Group on Death, Dying, and Bereavement. (1990). Assumptions and principles of spiritual care. *Death Studies, 14*, 75–81.

International Work Group on Death, Dying, and Bereavement. (1991a). A statement of assumptions and principles concerning education about life-threatening illness, death, dying, and bereavement for volunteers and non-professionals. *American Journal of Hospice and Palliative Care, 7*(2), 26–27.

International Work Group on Death, Dying, and Bereavement. (1991b). A statement of assumptions and principles concerning education about death, dying, and bereavement for professionals in health care and human services. *Omega, 23*, 235–239.

International Work Group on Death, Dying, and Bereavement. (1992a). A statement of assumptions and principles concerning education about death, dying, and bereavement. *Death Studies, 16*, 59–65.

International Work Group on Death, Dying, and Bereavement. (1992b). Assumptions and principles concerning care for persons affected by HIV disease. *AIDS and Public Policy Journal, 7*, 28–31.

International Work Group on Death, Dying, and Bereavement. (1993). Position statement: Palliative care for children. *Death Studies, 17*, 277–280.

Irion, P. E. (1966). *The funeral: Vestige or value?* Nashville: Abingdon.

Irion, P. E. (1968). *Cremation.* Philadelphia: Fortress Press.

Irion, P. E. (1971). *A manual and guide for those who conduct a humanist funeral service.* Baltimore: Waverly Press.

Irion, P. E. (1991). Changing patterns of ritual response to death. *Omega, 22*, 159–172.

Irish, D. P., Lundquist, K. F., & Nelson, V. J. (Eds.). (1993). *Ethnic variations in dying, death, and grief: Diversity in Universality.* Washington, DC: Taylor & Francis.

Jackson, E. N. (1957). *Understanding grief: Its roots, dynamics, and treatment.* Nashville, TN: Abingdon.

Jackson, E. N. (1963). *For the living.* Des Moines, IA: Channel Press.

Jackson, E. N. (1965). *Telling a child about death.* New York: Hawthorn.

Jackson, E. N. (1966). *The Christian funeral: Its meaning, its purpose, and its modern practice.* New York: Channel Press.

Jackson, E. N. (1984). The pastoral counselor and the child encountering death. In H. Wass & C. A. Corr (Eds.), *Helping children cope with death:*

Guidelines and resources (2nd ed., pp. 33–47). Washington, DC: Hemisphere.

Jackson, M. (1980). The Black experience with death: A brief analysis through Black writings. In R. A. Kalish (Ed.), *Death and dying: Views from many cultures* (pp. 92–98). Farmingdale, NY: Baywood.

Jacques, E. (1965). Death and the mid-life crisis. *International Journal of Psychoanalysis, 46*, 502–514.

Jewett, C. L. (1982). *Helping children cope with separation and loss.* Harvard, MA: Harvard Common Press.

Jimenez, S.L.M. (1982). *The other side of pregnancy: Coping with miscarriage and stillbirth.* Englewood Cliffs, NJ: Prentice-Hall.

Joel, B. (1985). You're only human (Second wind). *Billy Joel's greatest hits: Vol. 2, 1978–85.* New York and Los Angeles: Columbia Records.

John, E. (1970). Daniel. *Don't shoot me, I'm only the piano player.* Universal City, CA: MCA Records International.

John, E. (1972). I think I'm gonna kill myself. *Honky chateau.* Universal City, CA: MCA Records International.

Johnson, E. (1992). *What you can do to avoid AIDS.* New York: Times Books.

Johnson, J., Johnson, S. M., Cunningham, J. H., & Weinfeld, I. J. (1985). *A most important picture: A very tender manual for taking pictures of stillborn babies and infants who die.* Omaha, NE: Centering Corporation.

Johnson, S. (1987). *After a child dies: Counseling bereaved families.* New York: Springer.

Jonah, B. A. (1986). Accident risk and risk-taking behaviour among young drivers. *Accident Analysis and Prevention, 18*(4), 255–271.

Jones, W. H. (1977). Death-related grief counseling: The school counselor's responsibility. *The School Counselor, 24*, 315–320.

Jonsen, A. R. (1990). The duty to treat patients with AIDS and HIV infection. In L. O. Gostin (Ed.), *AIDS and the health care system* (pp. 155–168). New Haven, CT: Yale University Press.

Jonsen, A. R., & Helleghers, A. E. (1974). Conceptual foundations for an ethics of medical care. In L. R. Tancredi (Ed.), *Ethics of health care* (pp. 3–20). Washington, DC: National Academy of Science.

Joralemon, B. G. (1986). Terminating an adolescent pregnancy: Choice and loss. In C. A. Corr & J. N. McNeil (Eds.), *Adolescence and death* (pp. 119–131). New York: Springer.

Joseph, J. (1992). *Selected poems.* Newcastle-upon-Tyne, England: Bloodaxe Books.

Joseph, J., & Ostrow, D. G. (1987). Biobehavioral aspects of AIDS: Implications for healthcare providers. In D. G. Ostrow (Ed.), *Biobehavioral control of AIDS* (pp. 197–203). New York: Irvington.

Judith Ann Debro pronounced dead. (1975, November 10). *St. Louis Post-Dispatch,* pp. 1A, 5A.

Jung C. G. (1970). The stages of life. In H. Read, M. Fordham, & G. Adler (Eds.), *Collected works of Carl G. Jung* (2nd ed., Vol. 8). Princeton, NJ: Princeton University Press. (Original work published 1933)

Jury, M., & Jury, D. (1978). *Gramps: A man ages and dies.* Baltimore: Penguin.

Kagan, J., & Coles, R. (Eds.). (1972). *Twelve to sixteen: Early adolescence.* New York: Norton.

Kain, E. L. (1988). Trends in the demography of death. In H. Wass, F. M. Berardo, & R. A. Neimeyer (Eds.), *Dying: Facing the facts* (2nd ed., pp. 79–96). Washington, DC: Hemisphere.

Kalish, R. A. (Ed.). (1980). *Death and dying: Views from many cultures.* Farmingdale, NY: Baywood.

Kalish, R. A. (1985a). Death and dying in a social context. In R. H. Binstock & E. Shanas (Eds.), *Handbook of aging and the social sciences* (2nd ed., pp. 149–170). New York: Van Nostrand.

Kalish, R. A. (1985b). The horse on the dining-room table. In *Death, grief, and caring relationships* (2nd ed., pp. 2–4). Pacific Grove, CA: Brooks/Cole.

Kalish, R. A. (1989). Death education. In R. Kastenbaum & B. Kastenbaum (Eds.), *Encyclopedia of death* (pp. 75–79). Phoenix, AZ: Oryx Press.

Kalish, R. A., & Goldberg, H. (1978). Clergy attitudes toward funeral directors. *Death Education, 2,* 247–260.

Kalish, R. A., & Goldberg, H. (1980). Community attitudes toward funeral directors. *Omega, 10,* 335–346.

Kalish, R. A., & Johnson, A. I. (1972). Value similarities and differences in three generations of women. *Journal of Marriage and the Family, 34,* 49–54.

Kalish, R. A., & Reynolds, D. K. (1981). *Death and ethnicity: A psychocultural study.* Farmingdale, NY: Baywood. (Originally, Los Angeles: Andrus Gerontology Center, 1976)

Kamisar, Y. (1958). Some non-religious views against proposed "mercy-killing" legislation. *Minnesota Law Review, 42,* 969–1042.

Kapust, L. R. (1982). Living with dementia: The ongoing funeral. *Social Work in Health Care, 7*(4), 79–91.

Kastenbaum, R. (1967). The mental life of dying geriatric patients. *The Gerontologist, 7*(2), Pt. 1, 97–100.

Kastenbaum, R. (1969). Death and bereavement in later life. In A. H. Kutscher (Ed.), *Death and bereavement* (pp. 28–54). Springfield, IL: Charles C Thomas.

Kastenbaum, R. (1972). On the future of death: Some images and options. *Omega, 3,* 306–318.

Kastenbaum, R. (1973, January). The kingdom where nobody dies. *Saturday Review, 56,* 33–38.

Kastenbaum, R. (1977a). *Between life and death.* New York: Springer.

Kastenbaum, R. (1977b). Death and development through the lifespan. In H. Feifel (Ed.), *New meanings of death* (pp. 17–45). New York: McGraw-Hill.

Kastenbaum, R. (1989a). Ars moriendi. In R. Kastenbaum & B. Kastenbaum (Eds.), *Encyclopedia of death* (pp. 17–19). Phoenix, AZ: Oryx Press.

Kastenbaum, R. (1989b). Cemeteries. In R. Kastenbaum & B. Kastenbaum (Eds.), *Encyclopedia of death* (pp. 41–45). Phoenix, AZ: Oryx Press.

Kastenbaum, R. (1989c). Dance of death (*danse macabre*). In R. Kastenbaum & B. Kastenbaum (Eds.), *Encyclopedia of death* (pp. 67–70). Phoenix, AZ: Oryx Press.

Kastenbaum, R. (1989d). Dying. In R. Kastenbaum & B. Kastenbaum (Eds.), *Encyclopedia of death* (pp. 101–107). Phoenix, AZ: Oryx Press.

Kastenbaum, R. (1989e). Hospice: Philosophy and practice. In R. Kastenbaum & B. Kastenbaum (Eds.), *Encyclopedia of death* (pp. 143–146). Phoenix: AZ: Oryx Press.

Kastenbaum, R. (1939f). Uniform anatomical act. In R. Kastenbaum & B. Kastenbaum (Eds.), *Encyclopedia of death* (pp. 279–280). Phoenix, AZ: Oryx Press.

Kastenbaum, R. (1991). *Death, society, and human experience* (4th ed.). New York: Macmillan.

Kastenbaum, R. (1992). *The psychology of death* (2nd ed.). New York: Springer.

Kastenbaum, R., & Aisenberg, R. (1972). *The psychology of death.* New York: Springer.

Kastenbaum, R., & Kastenbaum, B. (Eds.). (1989). *Encyclopedia of death.* Phoenix, AZ: Oryx Press.

Katz, J. (1978). Informed consent in the therapeutic relationship: II. Legal and ethical aspects. In W. T. Reich (Ed.), *Encyclopedia of bioethics* (pp. 770–778). New York: Free Press.

Katzenbach, J. (1986). *The traveler.* New York: Putnam's.

Kaufert, J. M., & O'Neil, J. D. (1991). Cultural mediation of dying and grieving among Native Canadian patients in urban hospitals. In D. R. Counts & D. A. Counts (Eds.), *Coping with the final tragedy: Cultural variation in dying and grieving* (pp. 231–251). Amityville, NY: Baywood.

Kavanaugh, R. E. (1972). *Facing death.* Los Angeles: Nash.

Kay, W. J. (Ed.). (1984). *Pet loss and human bereavement.* Ames, IA: Iowa State University Press.

Kay, W. J., Cohen, S. P., Nieburg, H. A., Fudin, C. E., Grey, R. E., Kutscher, A. H., & Osman, M. M. (Eds.). (1988). *Euthanasia of the companion animal: The impact on pet owners, veterinarians, and society.* Philadelphia: Charles Press.

Kayser-Jones, J. S. (1981). *Old, alone, and neglected: Care of the aged in Scotland and the United States.* Berkeley: University of California Press.

Kelly, O. (1975). *Make today count.* New York: Delacorte Press.

Kelly, O. (1977). Make today count. In H. Feifel (Ed.), *New meanings of death* (pp. 182–193). New York: McGraw-Hill.

Kennard, E. A. (1932). Hopi reactions to death. *American Anthropologist, New Series, 39,* 491–496.

Kennell, J., Slyter, H., & Klaus, M. (1970). The mourning response of parents to the death of a newborn infant. *New England Journal of Medicine, 283,* 344–349.

Kephart, W. M. (1950). Status after death. *American Sociological Review, 15,* 635–643.

King, A. (1990). A Samoan perspective: Funeral practices, death and dying. In J. K. Parry (Ed.), *Social work practice with the terminally ill: A transcultural perspective* (pp. 175–189). Springfield, IL: Charles C Thomas.

Kirp, D. L. (1989). *Learning by heart: AIDS and schoolchildren in America's communities.* New Brunswick, NJ: Rutgers University Press.

Kitagawa, E. M., & Hauser, P. M. (1973). *Differential mortality in the United States: A study in socioeconomic epidemiology.* Cambridge, MA: Harvard University Press.

Kitano, H.H.L. (1976). *Japanese-Americans: The evaluation of a subculture* (2nd ed.). Englewood Cliffs, NJ: Prentice-Hall.

Klagsbrun, F. (1976). *Too young to die: Youth and suicide.* New York: Houghton Mifflin.

Klass, D. (1982). Elisabeth Kübler-Ross and the tradition of the private sphere: An analysis of symbols. *Omega, 12,* 241–261.

Klass, D. (1985a). Bereaved parents and the Compassionate Friends: Affiliation and healing. *Omega, 15,* 353–373.

Klass, D. (1985b). Self-help groups: Grieving parents and community resources. In C. A. Corr & D. M. Corr (Eds.), *Hospice approaches to pediatric care* (pp. 241–260). New York: Springer.

Klass, D. (1988). *Parental grief: Solace and resolution.* New York: Springer.

Klass, D., & Hutch, R. A. (1985). Elisabeth Kübler-Ross as a religious leader. *Omega, 16,* 89–109.

Klass, D., & Shinners, B. (1983). Professional roles in a self-help group for the bereaved. *Omega, 13,* 361–375.

Klaus, M. H., & Kennell, J. H. (1976). *Maternal-infant bonding.* St. Louis: C. V. Mosby.

Kliever, L. D. (Ed.). (1989). *Dax's case: Essays in medical ethics and human meaning.* Dallas: Southern Methodist University.

Kluge, E-H. W. (1975). *The practice of death.* New Haven, CT: Yale University Press.

Knapp, R. J. (1986). *Beyond endurance: When a child dies.* New York: Schocken.

Knope, L. (Ed.). (1989). *Facilitator's training manual.* Portland, OR: The Dougy Center.

Kohlberg, L., & Gilligan, C. (1971). The adolescent as a philosopher: The discovery of the self in a postconventional world. *Daedalus, 100,* 1051–1086.

Kohn, J. B., & Kohn, W. K. (1978). *The widower.* Boston: Beacon Press.

Koocher, G. (1973). Childhood, death, and cognitive development. *Developmental Psychology, 9,* 369–375.

Koocher, G. P., & O'Malley, J. E. (1981). *The Damocles syndrome: Psychosocial consequences of surviving childhood cancer.* New York: McGraw-Hill.

Koocher, G. P., O'Malley, J. E., Foster, D., & Gogan, J. L. (1976). Death anxiety in normal children and adolescents. *Psychiatria clinica, 9,* 220–229.

Koop, C. E. (1988). *Understanding AIDS.* HHS Publication No. (CDC) HHS-88-8404, U.S. Department of Health and Human Services. Washington, DC: U.S. Government Printing Office.

Koop, C. E., & Samuels, M. E. (1988). The Surgeon General's report on AIDS. In I. B. Corless & M. Pittman-Lindeman (Eds.), *AIDS: Principles, practices, and politics* (pp. 5–18). New York: Hemisphere.

Krasinski, K., Borkowsky, W., & Holzman, R. S. (1989). Prognosis of human immunodeficiency virus infection in children and adolescents. *Pediatric Infectious Diseases, 8,* 216–220.

Krementz, J. (1981). *How it feels when a parent dies.* New York: Knopf.

Krementz, J. (1989). *How it feels to fight for your life.* Boston: Little, Brown.

Kübler-Ross, E. (1969). *On death and dying.* New York: Macmillan.

Kübler-Ross, E. (1983). *On children and death.* New York: Macmillan.

Kübler-Ross, E. (1987). *AIDS: The ultimate challenge.* New York: Macmillan.

Kulka, E. (1986). *Escape from Auschwitz.* South Hadley, MA: Bergin & Garvey.

Kurtz, L. P. (1934). *The dance of death and the macabre spirit in European literature.* New York: Institute of French Studies.

Kurtz, D. C., & Boardman, J. (1971). *Greek burial customs.* Ithaca, NY: Cornell University Press.

Kushner, H. S. (1981). *When bad things happen to good people.* New York: Avon.

Lack, S. A. (1977). I want to die while I'm still alive. *Death Education, 1,* 165–176.

Lack, S. A. (1979). Hospice: A concept of care in the final stage of life. *Connecticut Medicine, 43,* 367–372.

Lack, S. A., & Buckingham, R. W. (1978). *First American hospice: Three years of home care.* New Haven: Hospice, Inc.

Ladd, J. (1979). *Ethical issues relating to life and death.* New York: Oxford University Press.

LaGrand, L. E. (1980). Reducing burnout in the hospice and the death education movement. *Death Education, 4,* 61–76.

LaGrand, L. (1981). Loss reactions of college students: A descriptive analysis. *Death Studies, 5,* 235–247.

LaGrand, L. (1986). *Coping with separation and loss as a young adult: Theoretical and practical realities.* Springfield, IL: Charles C Thomas.

Lamb, J. M. (Ed.). (1988). *Bittersweet . . . hellogoodbye.* Belleville, IL: SHARE National Office.

Lamers, E. P. (1986). Books for adolescents. In C. A. Corr & J. N. McNeil (Eds.), *Adolescence and death* (pp. 233–242). New York: Springer.

Lamont, C. (1954). *A humanist funeral service.* New York: Horizon Press.

Lang, A. (1975). *Blue fairy book.* Ed. B. Alderson. Illustrated by J. Lawrence. Harmondsworth, Middlesex: Penguin Books, Ltd. (Original work published 1889.)

Lang, L. T. (1990). Aspects of the Cambodian death and dying process. In J. K. Parry (Ed.), *Social work practice with the terminally ill: A transcultural perspective* (pp. 205–211). Springfield, IL: Charles C Thomas.

Langone, J. (1972). *Death is a noun: A view of the end of life.* Boston: Little, Brown.

Langone, J. (1974). *Vital signs: The way we die in America.* Boston: Little, Brown.

Larson, L. E. (1972). The influence of parents and peers during adolescence. *Journal of Marriage and the Family, 34,* 67–74.

Lattanzi, M. (1982). Hospice bereavement services: Creating networks of support. *Family and Community Health, 5,* 54–63.

Lattanzi, M. E. (1983). Professional stress: Adaptation, coping, and meaning. In J. C. Hanson & T. T. Frantz (Eds.), *Death and grief in the family* (pp. 95–106). Rockville, MD: Aspen Systems Corp.

Lattanzi, M. E. (1985). An approach to caring: Caregiving concerns. In C. A. Corr & D. M. Corr (Eds.), *Hospice approaches to pediatric care* (pp. 261–277). New York: Springer.

Lattanzi, M., & Cofelt, D. (1979). *Bereavement care manual.* Boulder, CO: Boulder County Hospice.

Lattanzi, M., & Hale, M. E. (1984). Giving grief words: Writing during bereavement. *Omega, 15,* 45–52.

Lazar, A., & Torney-Purta, J. (1991). The development of the subconcepts of death in young children: A short-term longitudinal study. *Child Development, 62,* 1321–1333.

Lazarus, R. S., & Folkman, S. (1984). *Stress, appraisal, and coping.* New York: Springer.

Leach, C. (1981). *Letter to a younger son.* New York: Harcourt Brace Jovanovich.

Lear, M. W. (1980). *Heartsounds.* New York: Simon & Schuster.

Lee, A. S. (1977). Maternal mortality in the United States. *Phylon, 38,* 259–266.

Lee, E. (1986). Chinese families. In M. McGoldrick, P. Hines, E. Lee, & N. Garcia-Preto, Mourning rituals: How cultures shape the experience of loss. *The Family Therapy Networker, 10*(6), 35–36.

Lee, P.W.H., Lieh-Mak, F., Hung, B.K.M., & Luk, S. L. (1984). Death anxiety in leukemic Chinese children. *International Journal of Psychiatry in Medicine, 13,* 281–290.

Leenaars, A. A., & Wenckstern, S. (Eds.). (1991). *Suicide prevention in the schools.* Washington, DC: Hemisphere.

Leininger, M. (1978). *Transcultural nursing: Concepts, theories, and practices.* New York: Wiley.

Leininger, M. (1988). Leininger's theory of cultural care diversity and universality. *Nursing Science Quarterly, 1,* 152–160.

Leininger, M. (1991). Transcultural nursing: The study and practice field. *Imprint, 38,* 55–69.

Lerner, G. (1978). *A death of one's own.* New York: Simon & Schuster.

Lerner, M. (1970). When, why, and where people die. In O. Brim, H. Freeman, S. Levine, & N. Scotch (Eds.), *The dying patient* (pp. 5–29). New York: Russell Sage Foundation.

Lerner, M. (1990). *Wrestling with the angel: A memoir of my triumph over illness.* New York: Norton.

LeShan, E. (1976). *Learning to say good-by: When a parent dies.* New York: Macmillan.

LeShan, L. (1964). The world of the patient in severe pain of long duration. *Journal of Chronic Diseases, 17,* 119–126.

Lester, B. (1989). *Women and AIDS: A practical guide for those who help others.* New York: Continuum.

Lester, D. (1983). *Why people kill themselves* (2nd ed.). Springfield, IL: Charles C Thomas.

Lester, D. (1990). *Understanding and preventing suicide: New perspectives.* Springfield, IL: Charles C Thomas.

Lester, D., & Beck, A. T. (1981). What the suicide's choice of method signifies. *Omega, 11,* 271–277.

Lesy, M. (1973). *Wisconsin death trip.* New York: Pantheon.

Levi, P. (1986). *Survival in Auschwitz; and, The reawakening: Two memoirs.* Trans. S. Woolf. New York: Simon & Schuster.

Levinson, D. J. (1978). *The seasons of a man's life.* New York: Knopf.

Leviton, D. (1978). The intimacy/sexual needs of the terminally ill and widowed. *Death Education, 2,* 261–280.

Leviton, D. (Ed.). (1991a). *Horrendous death, health, and well-being.* Washington, DC: Hemisphere.

Leviton, D. (Ed.). (1991b). *Horrendous death and health: Toward action.* Washington, DC: Hemisphere.

Levy, J. A., Hoffman, A. D., Kramer, S. M., Landis, J. A., Shimabukuro, J. M., & Oshiro, L. S. (1984). Isolation of lymphocytopathic retroviruses from San Francisco patients with AIDS. *Science, 225,* 840–842.

Levy, J. E., & Kunitz, S. J. (1987). A suicide prevention program for Hopi youth. *Social Science and Medicine, 25,* 931–940.

Lewis, C. S. (1976). *A grief observed.* New York: Bantam Books.

Lewis, O. (1970). *A death in the Sanchez family.* New York: Random House.

Ley, D.C.H., & Corless, I. B. (1988). Spirituality and hospice care. *Death Studies, 12,* 101–110.

Lieberman, M. A., & Borman, L. (1979). *Self-help groups for coping with crisis.* San Francisco: Jossey-Bass.

Liegner, L. M. (1975). St. Christopher's Hospice, 1974: Care of the dying patient. *Journal of the American Medical Association, 234,* 1047–1048.

Lifton, R. J. (1964). On death and death symbolism: The Hiroshima disaster. *Psychiatry, 27,* 191–210.

Lifton, R. J. (1967). *Death in life: Survivors of Hiroshima.* New York: Random House.

Lifton, R. J. (1979). *The broken connection.* New York: Simon & Schuster.

Lifton, R. J. (1986). *The Nazi doctors: Medical killing and the psychology of genocide.* New York: Basic Books.

Lindemann, E. (1944). Symptomatology and management of acute grief. *American Journal of Psychiatry, 101,* 141–148.

Lindemann, E., & Greer, I. M. (1972). A study of grief: Emotional responses to suicide. In A. C. Cain (Ed.), *Survivors of suicide* (pp. 63–69). Springfield, IL: Charles C Thomas. (Reprinted from *Pastoral Psychology,* 1953, *4,* 9–13)

Lindstrom, B. (1983). Operating a hospice bereavement program. In C. A. Corr & D. M. Corr (Eds.), *Hospice care: Principles and practice* (pp. 266–277). New York: Springer.

Linn, E. (1986). *I know just how you feel . . . Avoiding the clichés of grief.* Incline Village, NV: The Publisher's Mark.

Lipman, A. G. (1980). Drug therapy in cancer pain. *Cancer Nursing, 3,* 39–46.

Litman, R. E. (1967). Sigmund Freud on suicide. In E. S. Shneidman (Ed.), *Essays in self-destruction* (pp. 324–344). New York: Science House.

Lonetto, R. (1980). *Children's conceptions of death.* New York: Springer.

Lonetto, R., & Templer, D. I. (1986). *Death anxiety.* Washington, DC: Hemisphere.

Lopata, H. Z. (1973). *Widowhood in an American city.* Cambridge, MA: Schenkman.

Lorimer, D. (1989). The near-death experience: Cross-cultural and multi-disciplinary dimensions. In A. Berger, P. Badham, A. H. Kutscher, J. Berger, M. Perry, & J. Beloff (Eds.), *Perspectives on death and dying: Cross-cultural and multi-disciplinary views* (pp. 256–267). Philadelphia: The Charles Press.

Lowenthal, M., & Weiss, L. (1976). Intimacy and crisis in adulthood. *Counseling Psychologist, 6*(1), 10–15.

Lum, D. (1974). *Responding to suicidal crisis: For church and community.* Grand Rapids, MI: Eerdmans.

Lund, D. A. (1989). *Older bereaved spouses: Research with practical applications.* Washington, DC: Hemisphere.

Lund, D. A., Dimond, M., & Juretich, M. (1985). Bereavement support groups for the elderly: Characteristics of potential participants. *Death Studies, 9,* 309–321.

Lustig, A. (1977). *Darkness casts no shadow.* New York: Inscape.

Luterman, D. M. (1991). *Counseling the communicatively disordered and their families* (2nd ed.). Austin, TX: Pro-Ed.

Lynn, J. (Ed.). (1986). *By no extraordinary means: The choice to forgo life-sustaining food and water.* Bloomington, IN: Indiana University Press.

Lynn, K. S. (1987). *Hemingway.* New York: Simon & Schuster.

Lynn, R. J. (1992). *Introduction to estate planning in a nutshell* (4th ed.). St. Paul, MN: West.

Lyons, J. S., Larson, D. B., Anderson, R. L., & Bilheimer, L. (1989). Psychosocial services for AIDS patients in the general hospital. *International Journal of Psychiatry in Medicine, 19,* 385–392.

Mace, N. L., & Rabins, P. V. (1991). *The 36-hour day: A family guide to caring for persons with Alzheimer's disease, related dementing illnesses, and memory loss in later life* (rev. ed.). Baltimore: Johns Hopkins University Press.

Mack, A. (Ed.). (1974). *Death in American experience.* New York: Schocken.

Mack, J. E., & Hickler, H. (1981). *Vivienne: The life and suicide of an adolescent girl.* Boston: Little, Brown.

MacMillan, I. (1991). *Orbit of darkness.* San Diego: Harcourt Brace Jovanovich.

Magee, D. (1983). *What murder leaves behind: The victim's family.* New York: Dodd, Mead.

Mahoney, M. C. (1991). Fatal motor vehicle traffic accidents among Native Americans. *American Journal of Preventive Medicine, 7,* 112–116.

Maizler, J. S., Solomon, J. R., & Almquist, E. (1983). Psychogenic mortality syndrome: Choosing to die by the institutionalized elderly. *Death Education, 6*, 353–364.

Malinowski, B. (1954). *Magic, science, and religion and other essays.* New York: Doubleday.

Mandelbaum, D. (1959). Social uses of funeral rites. In H. Feifel (Ed.), *The meaning of death* (pp. 189–217). New York: McGraw-Hill.

Mandell, H., & Spiro, H. (Eds.). (1987). *When doctors get sick.* New York: Plenum.

Manio, E. B., & Hall, R. R. (1987). Asian family traditions and their influence in transcultural health care delivery. *Children's Health Care, 15*, 172–177.

Mann, J. M., Tarantola, D.J.M., & Netter, T. W. (Eds.). (1992). *AIDS in the world: A global report.* Cambridge, MA: Harvard University Press.

Mann, T. C., & Greene, J. (1962). *Over their dead bodies: Yankee epitaphs and history.* Brattleboro, VT: Stephen Greene Press.

Mann, T. C., & Greene, J. (1968). *Sudden and awful: American epitaphs and the finger of God.* Brattleboro, VT: Stephen Greene Press.

Manning, D. (1979). *Don't take my grief away from me: How to walk through grief and learn to live again.* Hereford, TX: In-Sight Books.

Manning, J. A. (1991). *Estate planning* (4th ed.). New York: Practising Law Institute.

Marcel, G. (1962). *The philosophy of existentialism* (2nd ed.). Trans. M. Harari. New York: Citadel Press.

Marcia, J. (1980). Identity in adolescence. In J. Adelson (Ed.), *Handbook of adolescent psychology* (pp. 159–187). New York: Wiley.

Margolis, O., & Schwarz, O. (Eds.). (1975). *Grief and the meaning of the funeral.* New York: MSS Information.

Maris, R. W. (1969). *Social forces in urban suicide.* Homewood, IL: Dorsey Press.

Maris, R. W. (1981). *Pathways to suicide: A survey of self-destructive behaviors.* Baltimore: Johns Hopkins University Press.

Maris, R. W. (1985). The adolescent suicide problem. *Suicide and Life-Threatening Behavior, 15*(2), 91–109.

Maris, R. W. (Ed.). (1988). *Understanding and preventing suicide.* New York: Guilford Press.

Maris, R. W., Berman, A. L., Maltsberger, J. T., & Yufit, R. I. (Eds.). (1992). *Assessment and prediction of suicide.* New York: Guilford Press.

Markel, W. M., & Sinon, V. B. (1978). The hospice concept. *CA—A Cancer Journal for Clinicians, 28*, 225–237.

Markides, K. (1981). Death-related attitudes and behavior among Mexican Americans: A review. *Suicide and Life-Threatening Behavior, 11*, 75–85.

Marks, A. S., & Calder, B. J. (1982). *Attitudes toward death and funerals.* Evansville, IL: Northwestern University, Center for Marketing Sciences.

Marks, R., & Sachar, E. (1973). Undertreatment of medical inpatients with narcotic analgesics. *Annals of Internal Medicine, 78*, 173–181.

Marquis, A. (1974). *A guide to America's Indians.* Norman, OK: University of Oklahoma Press.

Marshall, J. R. (1975). The geriatric patient's fears about death. *Postgraduate Medicine, 57*(4), 144–149.

Martin, B. B. (Ed.). (1989). *Pediatric hospice care: What helps.* Los Angeles: Children's Hospital of Los Angeles.

Martinson, I. M. (Ed.). (1976). *Home care for the dying child.* New York: Appleton-Century-Crofts.

Martinson, I. M., Davies, E. B., & McClowry, S. G. (1987). The long-term effects of sibling death on self-concept. *Journal of Pediatric Nursing, 2,* 227–235.

Martinson, I. M., Martin, B., Lauer, M., Birenbaum, L. K., & Eng, B. (1991). *Children's hospice/home care: An implementation manual for nurses.* Alexandria, VA: Children's Hospice International.

Maslow, A. (1968). *Toward a psychology of being* (2nd ed.). Princeton, NJ: Van Nostrand.

Maslow, A. (1971). *The farther reaches of human nature.* New York: Viking Penguin.

Matchett, W. F. (1972). Repeated hallucinatory experiences as a part of the mourning process among Hopi Indian women. *Psychiatry, 35,* 185–194.

Matse, J. (1975). Reactions to death in residential homes for the aged. *Omega, 6,* 21–32.

Mauk, G. W., & Weber, C. (1991). Peer survivors of adolescent suicide: Perspectives on grieving and postvention. *Journal of Adolescent Research, 6,* 113–131.

Maurer, A. (1964). Adolescent attitudes toward death. *Journal of Genetic Psychology, 105,* 75–90.

Maurer, A. (1966). Maturation of the conception of death. *Journal of Medical Psychology, 39,* 35–41.

Mayer, R. A. (1990). *Embalming: History, theory, and practice.* Norwalk, CT: Appleton & Lange.

Mbiti, J. S. (1970). *African religion and philosophy.* Garden City, NY: Doubleday Anchor.

McCaffery, M., & Beebe, A. (1989). *Pain: Clinical manual for nursing practice.* St. Louis: C. V. Mosby.

McClowry, S. G., Davies, E. B., May, K. A., Kulenkamp, E. J., & Martinson, I. M. (1987). The empty space phenomenon: The process of grief in the bereaved family. *Death Studies, 11,* 361–374.

McCord, C., & Freeman, H. P. (1990). Excess mortality in Harlem. *New England Journal of Medicine, 322,* 173–177.

McCormick, R. (1974). To save or let die. *Journal of the American Medical Association, 224,* 172–176.

McCray, E. (1986). Occupational risk of the acquired immunodeficiency syndrome among health care workers. *New England Journal of Medicine, 314,* 1127–1132.

McEntire, R. (1991). For my broken heart. *For my broken heart.* Universal City, CA: MCA Records International.

McGoldrick, M. (1988). Women and the family life cycle. In B. Carter & M. McGoldrick (Eds.), *The changing family life cycle: A framework for family therapy* (2nd ed., pp. 29–68). New York: Gardner.

McGoldrick, M., & Gerson, R. (1985). *Genograms in family assessment.* New York: Norton.

McGoldrick, M., & Gerson, R. (1988). Genograms and the family life cycle. In B. Carter & M. McGoldrick (Eds.), *The changing family life cycle: A framework for family therapy* (2nd ed., pp. 164–189). New York: Gardner.

McGoldrick, M., Pearce, J. K., & Giordano, J. (Eds.). (1982). *Ethnicity and family therapy.* New York: Guilford.

McGoldrick, M., & Walsh, F. (1991). A time to mourn: Death and the family life cycle. In F. Walsh & M. McGoldrick (Eds.), *Living beyond loss: Death in the family* (pp. 30–49). New York: Norton.

McGuffey, W. H. (1866). *McGuffey's new fourth eclectic reader: Instructive lessons for the young* (enlarged ed.). Cincinnati: Wilson, Hinkle & Co.

McIntosh, J. L. (1983). Suicide among Native Americans: Further tribal data and considerations. *Omega, 14,* 215–229.

McIntosh, J. L. (1985a). Suicide among the elderly: Levels and trends. *American Journal of Orthopsychiatry, 56,* 288–293.

McIntosh, J. L. (1985b). *Research on suicide: A bibliography.* Westport, CT: Greenwood Press.

McIntosh, J. L. (1989a). Suicide: Asian-American. In R. Kastenbaum & B. Kastenbaum (Eds.), *Encyclopedia of death* (pp. 233–234). Phoenix, AZ: Oryx Press.

McIntosh, J. L. (1989b). Trends in racial difference in U.S. suicide statistics. *Death Studies, 13,* 275–286.

McIntosh, J. L., & Santos, J. F. (1981a). Suicide among minority elderly: A preliminary investigation. *Suicide and Life-Threatening Behavior, 11,* 151–166.

McIntosh, J. L., & Santos, J. F. (1981b). Suicide among Native Americans: A compilation of findings. *Omega, 11,* 303–316.

McIntosh, J. L., & Santos, J. F. (1982). Changing patterns in methods of suicide by race and sex. *Suicide and Life-Threatening Behavior, 12,* 221–233.

McNeil, J. N. (1986). Talking about death: Adolescents, parents, and peers. In C. A. Corr & J. N. McNeil (Eds.), *Adolescence and death* (pp. 185–201). New York: Springer.

McNeil, J. N., Silliman, B., & Swihart, J. J. (1991). Helping adolescents cope with the death of a peer: A high school case study. *Journal of Adolescent Research, 6,* 132–145.

McNeill, W. H. (1976). *Plagues and peoples.* Garden City, NY: Doubleday.

McNurlen, M. (1991). Guidelines for group work. In C. A. Corr, H. Fuller, C. A. Barnickol, & D. M. Corr (Eds.), *Sudden Infant Death Syndrome: Who can help and how* (pp. 180–202). New York: Springer.

Mead, M. (1973). Ritual and social crisis. In J. D. Shaughnessy (Ed.), *The roots of ritual* (pp. 87–101). Grand Rapids, MI: Eerdmans.

Medical ethics, narcotics, and addiction [Editorial]. (1963). *Journal of the American Medical Association, 185,* 962–963.

Melzack, R. (1990, February). The tragedy of needless pain. *Scientific American*, pp. 27–33.

Melzack, R., Mount, B. M., & Gordon, J. M. (1979). The Brompton mixture versus morphine solution given orally: Effects on pain. *Canadian Medical Association Journal, 120,* 435–438.

Melzack, R., Ofiesh, J. G., & Mount, B. M. (1976). The Brompton mixture: Effects on pain in cancer patients. *Canadian Medical Association Journal, 115,* 125–129.

Melzack, R., & Wall, P. D. (1989). *The challenge of pain* (rev. ed.). New York: Penguin. (Originally *The puzzle of pain,* 1973)

Melzack, R., & Wall, P. D. (Eds.). (1991). *Textbook of pain* (3rd ed.). Edinburgh: Churchill Livingstone.

Mendelson, M. A. (1974). *Tender loving greed.* New York: Knopf.

Menninger, K. (1938). *Man against himself.* New York: Harcourt, Brace & World.

Metzger, A. M. (1979). A Q-methodological study of the Kübler-Ross stage theory. *Omega, 10,* 291–302.

Meyer-Baer, K. (1970). *Music of the spheres and the dance of death: Studies in musical iconology.* Princeton, NJ: Princeton University Press.

Michalek, A. M., & Mahoney, M. C. (1990). Cancer in native populations—Lessons to be learned. *Journal of Cancer Education, 5,* 243–249.

Mike and the Mechanics. (1988). The living years. *Living years.* New York and Los Angeles: Atlantic Records.

Miles, M. S. (n.d.). *The grief of parents when a child dies.* Oak Brook, IL: The Compassionate Friends.

Miles, M. S. (1984). Helping adults mourn the death of a child. In H. Wass & C. A. Corr (Eds.), *Childhood and death* (pp. 219–241). Washington, DC: Hemisphere.

Miles, M. S., & Demi, A. S. (1984). Toward the development of a theory of bereavement guilt: Sources of guilt in bereaved parents. *Omega, 14,* 299–314.

Miles, M. S., & Demi, A. S. (1986). Guilt in bereaved parents. In T. A. Rando (Ed.), *Parental loss of a child* (pp. 97–118). Champaign, IL: Research Press.

Miller, M. (1979). *Suicide after sixty: The final alternative.* New York: Springer.

Miller, P. H. (1983). *Theories of developmental psychology.* New York: W. H. Freeman.

Mills, L. O. (Ed.). (1969). *Perspectives on death.* Nashville: Abingdon.

Milofsky, C. (1980). *Structure and process in self-help organizations.* New Haven, CT: Yale University, Institution for Social and Policy Studies.

Mindel, C. H., Habenstein, R. W., & Wright, R. (1988). *Ethnic families in America: Patterns and variations* (3rd ed.). New York: Elsevier.

Minkoff, H. L. (1989). AIDS in pregnancy. *Current Problems in Obstetrics, Gynecology and Fertility, 12,* 205–228.

Minnich, H. C. (1936a). *Old favorites from the McGuffey readers.* New York: American Book Company.

Minnich, H. C. (1936b). *William Holmes McGuffey and his readers.* New York: American Book Company.

Mitchell, L. (1977). *The meaning of ritual.* New York: Paulist Press.

Mitford, J. (1963). *The American way of death.* New York: Simon & Schuster.

Moffat, M. J. (1982). *In the midst of winter: Selections from the literature of mourning.* New York: Vintage.

Molinari, G. F. (1978). Death, definition and determination of: I. Criteria for death. In W. T. Reich (Ed.), *Encyclopedia of bioethics* (pp. 292–296). New York: Free Press.

Momeyer, R. W. (1988). *Confronting death.* Bloomington and Indianapolis: Indiana University Press.

Monat, A., & Lazarus, R. S. (Eds.). (1991). *Stress and coping: An anthology* (3rd ed.). New York: Columbia University Press.

Monette, P. (1988). *Borrowed time: An AIDS memoir.* San Diego: Harcourt Brace Jovanovich.

Monette, P. (1992). *Becoming a man: Half a life story.* San Diego: Harcourt Brace Jovanovich.

Moody, H. R. (1984). Can suicide on grounds of old age be ethically justified? In M. Tallmer, E. R. Prichard, A. H. Kutscher, R. DeBellis, M. S. Hale, & I. K. Goldberg (Eds.), *The life-threatened elderly* (pp. 64–92). New York: Columbia University Press.

Moody, R. A. (1975). *Life after life.* Covington, GA: Mockingbird Books. (Reprinted New York: Bantam, 1976)

Moore, J. (1980). The death culture of Mexico and Mexican Americans. In R. A. Kalish (Ed.), *Death and dying: Views from many cultures* (pp. 72–91). Farmingdale, NY: Baywood.

Moos, R. H., & Schaefer, J. A. (1986). Life transitions and crises: A conceptual overview. In R. H. Moos & J. A. Schaefer (Eds.), *Coping with life crises: An integrated approach* (pp. 3–28). New York: Plenum.

Morgan, E. (1990). *Dealing creatively with death: A manual of death education and simple burial* (12th ed.). Ed. J. Morgan. Bayside, NY: Barclay House.

Moroney, R. M., & Kurtz, N. R. (1975). The evolution of long-term care institutions. In S. Sherwood (Ed.), *Long-term care: A handbook for researchers, planners, and providers* (pp. 81–121). New York: Spectrum.

Morris, R. A. (1991). Po Starykovsky (The old people's way): End of life attitudes and customs in two traditional Russian communities. In D. R. Counts & D. A. Counts (Eds.), *Coping with the final tragedy: Cultural variation in dying and grieving* (pp. 91–112). Amityville, NY: Baywood.

Moss, F., & Halamanderis, V. (1977). *Too old, too sick, too bad: Nursing homes in America.* Germantown, MD: Aspen Systems Corp.

Moss, M. S., Lesher, E. L., & Moss, S. Z. (1986). Impact of the death of an adult child on elderly parents: Some observations. *Omega, 17,* 209–218.

Moss, M. S., & Moss, S. Z. (1983). The impact of parental death on middle-aged children. *Omega, 14,* 65–75.

Moss, M. S., & Moss, S. Z. (1984). Some aspects of the elderly widow(er)'s persistent tie with the deceased spouse. *Omega, 15,* 195–206.

Mount, B. M., Jones, A., & Patterson, A. (1974). Death and dying: Attitudes in a teaching hospital. *Urology, 4,* 741–747.

Muwahidi, A. A. (1989). Islamic perspectives on death and dying. In A. Berger, P. Badham, A. H. Kutscher, J. Berger, M. Perry, & J. Beloff (Eds.), *Perspectives on death and dying: Cross-cultural and multi-disciplinary views* (pp. 38–54). Philadelphia: Charles Press.

Myers, E. (1986). *When parents die: A guide for adults.* New York: Viking Penguin.

Nabe, C. M. (1981). Presenting biological data in a course on death and dying. *Death Education, 5,* 51–58.

Nabe, C. M. (1982). "Seeing as": Death as door or wall. In R. A. Pacholski & C. A. Corr (Eds.), *Priorities in death education and counseling* (pp. 161–169). Arlington, VA: Forum for Death Education and Counseling.

Nagy, M. A. (1948). The child's theories concerning death. *Journal of Genetic Psychology, 73,* 3–27. (Reprinted with some editorial changes as "The child's view of death" in H. Feifel [Ed.], *The meaning of death* [pp. 79–98]. New York: McGraw-Hill, 1959.)

National Center for Health Statistics. (1991). *Vital Statistics of the United States, 1988.* Hyattsville, MD: United States Department of Health and Human Services, Public Health Service, Centers for Disease Control.

National Center for Health Statistics. (1993). Advance report of final mortality statistics, 1990. *Monthly Vital Statistics Report, 41*(7) (Supp.). Hyattsville, MD: United States Department of Health and Human Services, Public Health Service, Centers for Disease Control and Prevention.

National Hospice Organization. (1987). *Standards of a hospice program of care.* Arlington, VA: Author.

National Research Council. (1990). *AIDS: The second decade.* Washington, DC: National Academy Press.

National Safety Council. (1991). *Accident facts, 1991 edition.* Chicago, IL: Author.

Neaman, J. S., & Silver, C. G. (1983). *Kind words: A thesaurus of euphemisms.* New York: Facts on File Publications.

Neimeyer, R. A. (1988). Death anxiety. In H. Wass, F. M. Berardo, & R. A. Neimeyer (Eds.), *Dying: Facing the facts* (2nd ed., 97–137). Washington, DC: Hemisphere.

Nelson, T. C. (1983). *It's your choice.* Glenview, IL: AARP, Scott, Foresman.

Neugarten, B. L. (1974). Age groups in American society and the rise of the young-old. *Annals of the American Academy of Political and Social Science, 415,* 187–198.

Neugarten, B. L., & Datan, N. (1973). Sociological perspectives on the life cycle. In P. B. Baltes & K. W. Schaie (Eds.), *Life-span developmental psychology: Personality and socialization* (pp. 53–69). New York: Academic Press.

Neuringer, C. (1962). Methodological problems in suicide research. *Journal of Consulting Psychology, 26,* 273–278.

New England Primer (1962). New York: Columbia University Press. (Original work published 1727)

Nichols, S. E. (1985). Psychosocial reactions of persons with the Acquired Immunodeficiency Syndrome. *Annals of Internal Medicine, 103,* 765–767.

Nieburg, H. A., & Fischer, A. (1982). *Pet loss.* New York: Harper & Row.

Noppe, L. D., & Noppe, I. C. (1991). Dialectical themes in adolescent conceptions of death. *Journal of Adolescent Research, 6,* 28–42.

Noss, D., & Noss, J. (1990). *A history of the world's religions* (8th ed.). New York: Macmillan.

Nouwen, H. (1974). *Aging: The fulfillment of life.* New York: Doubleday.

Novack, D. H., Plumer, R., Smith, R. L., Ochitill, H., Morrow, G. R., & Bennett, J. M. (1979). Changes in physicians' attitudes toward telling the cancer patient. *Journal of the American Medical Association, 241,* 897–900.

Noyes, R., & Clancy, J. (1977). The dying role: Its relevance to improved patient care. *Psychiatry, 40,* 41–47.

O'Carroll, P. W. (1989). A consideration of the validity and reliability of suicide mortality data. *Suicide and Life-Threatening Behavior, 19,* 1–16.

O'Connor, M. C. (1942). *The art of dying well: The development of the ars moriendi.* New York: Columbia University Press.

Offer, D., Ostrov, E., & Howard, K. I. (1981). *The adolescent: A psychological self-portrait.* New York: Basic Books.

O'Gorman, B., & O'Brien, T. (1990). Motor neurone disease. In C. Saunders (Eds.), *Hospice and palliative care: An interdisciplinary approach* (pp. 41–45). London: Edward Arnold.

Oken, D. (1961). What to tell cancer patients: A study of medical attitudes. *Journal of the American Medical Association, 175,* 1120–1128.

Olson, L. M., Becker, T. M., Wiggins, C. L., Key, C. R., & Samet, J. N. (1990). Injury mortality in American Indian, Hispanic, and non-Hispanic White children in New Mexico, 1958–1982. *Social Science and Medicine, 30,* 479–486.

Oltjenbruns, K. A. (1991). Positive outcomes of adolescents' experience with grief. *Journal of Adolescent Research, 6,* 43–53.

Opoku, K. A. (1978). *West African traditional religion.* Singapore: Far Eastern Publishers.

Opoku, K. A. (1987). Death and immortality in the African religious heritage. In P. Badham & L. Badham (Eds.), *Death and immortality in the religions of the world* (pp. 9–21). New York: Paragon House.

Orbach, I. (1988). *Children who don't want to live: Understanding and treating the suicidal child.* San Francisco: Jossey-Bass.

Osbourne, O. (1981). Suicide solution. *Blizzard of Oz.* Los Angeles: CBS Records.

Osgood, N. J. (1985). *Suicide in the elderly: A practitioner's guide to diagnosis and mental health intervention.* Rockville, MD: Aspen Systems Corp.

Osis, K., & Haraldsson, E. (1977). *At the hour of death.* New York: Avon.

Osmont, K., & McFarlane, M. (1986). *Parting is not goodbye.* Portland, OR: Nobility Press.

Osterweis, M., Solomon, F., & Green, M. (Eds.) (1984). *Bereavement: Reactions, consequences, and care.* Washington, DC: National Academy Press.

Palgi, P., & Abramovitch, H. (1984). Death: A cross-cultural perspective. *Annual Review of Anthropology, 13,* 385–417.

Papadatou, D. (1989). Caring for dying adolescents. *Nursing Times, 85,* 28–31.

Papadatou, D., & Papadatos, C. (Eds.). (1991). *Children and death.* Washington, DC: Hemisphere.

Parkes, C. M. (1970). "Seeking" and "finding" a lost object: Evidence from recent studies of reaction to bereavement. *Social Science and Medicine, 4,* 187–201.

Parkes, C. M. (1971). The first year of bereavement: A longitudinal study of the reaction of London widows to the death of their husbands. *Psychiatry, 33,* 444–467.

Parkes, C. M. (1975). Determinants of outcome following bereavement. *Omega, 6,* 303–323.

Parkes, C. M. (1979). Evaluation of a bereavement service. In A. DeVries & A. Carmi (Eds.), *The dying human* (pp. 389–402). Ramat Gan, Israel: Turtledove.

Parkes, C. M. (1980). Bereavement counselling: Does it work? *British Medical Journal, 281,* 3–6.

Parkes, C. M. (1981). Evaluation of a bereavement service. *Journal of Preventive Psychiatry, 1,* 179–188.

Parkes, C. M. (1987a). *Bereavement: Studies of grief in adult life* (2nd ed.). Madison, CT: International Universities Press.

Parkes, C. M. (1987b). Models of bereavement care. *Death Studies, 11,* 257–261.

Parkes, C. M., & Weiss, R. (1983). *Recovery from bereavement.* New York: Basic Books.

Parry, J. K. (Ed.). (1990). *Social work practice with the terminally ill: A transcultural perspective.* Springfield, IL: Charles C Thomas.

Parsons, T. (1951). *The social system.* New York: Free Press.

Partridge, E. (1966). *A dictionary of slang and unconventional English.* New York: Macmillan.

Pattison, E. M. (1977). *The experience of dying.* Englewood Cliffs, NJ: Prentice-Hall.

Pawelczynska, A. (1979). *Values and violence in Auschwitz: A sociological analysis.* Trans. C. S. Leach. Berkeley & Los Angeles: University of California Press.

Peabody, B. (1986). *The screaming room: A mother's journal of her son's struggle with AIDS.* San Diego: Oak Tree Publications.

Peck, M. L., Farberow, N. L., & Litman, R. E. (Eds.). (1985). *Youth suicide.* New York: Springer.

Pellegrino, E. (1988). Altruism, self-interest and medical ethics. *Journal of the American Medical Association, 258,* 1939–1940.

Pendleton, E. (Comp.). (1980). *Too old to cry, too young to die.* Nashville, TN: Thomas Nelson.

Peppers, L. G. (1987). Grief and elective abortion: Breaking the emotional bond. *Omega, 18,* 1–12.

Peppers, L. G., & Knapp, R. J. (1980). *Motherhood and mourning: Perinatal death.* New York: Praeger.

Pfeffer, C. R. (1986). *The suicidal child.* New York: Guilford Press.

Pfeffer, C. R. (Ed.). (1989). *Suicide among youth: Perspectives on risk and prevention.* Washington, DC: American Psychiatric Press.

Piaget, J., & Inhelder, B. (1958). *The growth of logical thinking from childhood to adolescence.* Trans. A. Parsons & S. Milgram. New York: Basic Books.

Piaget, J. (1960). *The child's conception of the world.* Trans. J. Tomlinson & A. Tomlinson. Totowa, NJ: Littlefield, Adams.

Piaget, J. (1973). *The child and reality—Problems of genetic psychology.* Trans. A. Rosin. New York: Grossman.

Piel, J. (Ed.) (1989). *The science of AIDS.* New York: W. H. Freeman.

Pike, M. M., & Wheeler, S. R. (1992). *Bereavement support group guide: Guidebook for individuals and/or professionals who wish to start a bereavement, mutual, self-help group.* Covington, IN: Grief, Ltd.

Pindyck, J. (1988). Transfusion-associated HIV infection: Epidemiology, prevention and public policy. *AIDS, 2,* 239–248.

Pine, V. R. (1975). *Caretaker of the dead: The American funeral director.* New York: Irvington.

Pine, V. R. (1977). A socio-historical portrait of death education. *Death Education, 1,* 57–84.

Pine, V. R. (1986). The age of maturity for death education: A socio-historical portrait of the era 1976–1985. *Death Studies, 10,* 209–231.

Pine, V. R., Kutscher, A. H., Peretz, D., Slater, R. C., DeBellis, R., Volk, A. I., & Cherico, D. J. (Eds.). (1976). *Acute grief and the funeral.* Springfield, IL: Charles C Thomas.

Pine, V. R., Margolis, O. S., Doka, K., Kutscher, A. H., Schaefer, D. J., Siegel, M-E., & Cherico, D. J. (Eds.). (1990). *Unrecognized and unsanctioned grief: The nature and counseling of unacknowledged loss.* Springfield, IL: Charles C Thomas.

Pinsky, L., & Douglas, P. H. (1992). *The essential HIV treatment fact book.* New York: Pocket Books.

"Pitch of Grief" [Videotape]. (1985). Newton, MA: Newton Cable Television Foundation and Eric Stange.

Plath, S. (1964). *Ariel.* New York: Harper & Row.

Plath, S. (1971). *The bell jar.* New York: Harper & Row.

Plato. (1948). *Euthyphro, Apology, Crito.* Trans. F. J. Church. New York: Macmillan.

Plato. (1961). *The collected dialogues of Plato including the letters.* Eds. E. Hamilton & H. Cairns. New York: Bollingen Foundation.

Platt, M. (1975). Commentary: On asking to die. *Hastings Center Report, 5*(6), 9–12.

"Please Let Me Die." [Videotape]. (1974). Galveston, TX: University of Texas Medical Branch.

Plumb, M. M., & Holland, J. (1974). Cancer in adolescents: The symptom is the thing. In B. Schoenberg, A. C. Carr, A. H. Kutscher, D. Peretz, & I. K.

Goldberg (Eds.), *Anticipatory grief* (pp. 193–209). New York: Columbia University Press.

Pojman, L. P. (1992). *Life and death: Grappling with the moral dilemmas of our time.* Boston: Jones & Bartlett.

Poland, S. (1989). *Suicide intervention in the schools.* New York: Guilford Press.

Polednak, A. P. (1990). Cancer mortality in a higher-income Black population in New York State: Comparison with rates in the United States as a whole. *Cancer, 66,* 1654–1660.

Porter, J., & Jick, H. (1980). Addiction rare in patients treated with narcotics. *New England Journal of Medicine, 302,* 123.

Pound, L. (1936). American euphemisms for dying, death, and burial: An anthology. *American Speech, 11,* 195–202.

Powell-Griner, E. (1988). Differences in infant mortality among Texas Anglos, Hispanics, and Blacks. *Social Science Quarterly, 69,* 452–467.

Prashad, J. (1989). The Hindu concept of death. In A. Berger, P. Badham, A. H. Kutscher, J. Berger, M. Perry, & J. Beloff (Eds.), *Perspectives on death and dying: Cross-cultural and multi-disciplinary views* (pp. 84–88). Philadelphia: Charles Press.

President's Commission for the Study of Ethical Problems in Medicine and Biomedical and Behavioral Research. (1981). *Defining death: A report on the medical, legal and ethical issues in the determination of death.* Washington, DC: U.S. Government Printing Office.

President's Commission for the Study of Ethical Problems in Medicine and Biomedical and Behavioral Research. (1982). *Making health care decisions: A report on the ethical and legal implications of informed consent in the patient-practitioner relationship.* Vol. 1, *Report;* Vol. 3, *Studies on the foundation of informed consent.* Washington, DC: U.S. Government Printing Office.

President's Commission for the Study of Ethical Problems in Medicine and Biomedical and Behavioral Research. (1983a). *Deciding to forego life-sustaining treatment: A report on the ethical, medical, and legal issues in treatment decisions.* Washington, DC: U.S. Government Printing Office.

President's Commission for the Study of Ethical Problems in Medicine and Biomedical and Behavioral Research. (1983b). *Summing up: Final report on studies of the ethical and legal problems in medicine and biomedical and behavioral research.* Washington, DC: U.S. Government Printing Office.

Preston, R. J., & Preston, S. C. (1991). Death and grieving among northern forest hunters: An East Cree example. In D. R. Counts & D. A. Counts (Eds.), *Coping with the final tragedy: Cultural variation in dying and grieving* (pp. 135–155). Amityville, NY: Baywood.

Preston, S. H. (1976). *Mortality patterns in national populations: With special reference to recorded causes of death.* New York: Academic Press.

Preston, S. H., & Haines, M. R. (1991). *Fatal years: Child mortality in late nineteenth-century America.* Princeton, NJ: Princeton University Press.

Prestopino, D. J. (1989). *Introduction to estate planning* (2nd ed.). Homewood, IL: Irwin.

Puckle, B. S. (1926). *Funeral customs: Their origin and development*. London: Laurie.

Purtillo, R. B. (1976). Similarities in patient response to chronic and terminal illness. *Physical Therapy, 56*, 279–284.

Qtoby, M. J. (1990). Perinatally acquired human immunodeficiency virus infection. *Pediatric Infectious Diseases, 9*, 609–619.

Quackenbush, J. (1985). The death of a pet: How it can affect pet owners. *Veterinary Clinics of North America: Small Animal Practice, 15*, 305–402.

Queensryche. (1988). Operation mindcrime. *Operation mindcrime*. Hollywood, CA: Capitol Records.

Quinlan, J., Quinlan, J., & Battelle, P. (1977). *Karen Ann: The Quinlans tell their story*. Garden City, NY: Doubleday.

Quinn, T. C., Mann, J. M., Curran, J. W., & Piot, P. (1986). AIDS in Africa: An epidemiologic paradigm. *Science, 234*, 955–963.

Rachels, J. (1975). Active and passive euthanasia. *New England Journal of Medicine, 292*, 78–80.

Radhakrishnan, S. (1948). *The Bhagavadgita: With an introductory essay, Sanskrit text, English translation and notes*. New York: Harper & Brothers.

Radhakrishnan, S., & Moore, C. (1957). *A sourcebook in Indian philosophy*. Princeton, NJ: Princeton University Press.

Radin, P. (1973). *The road of life and death: A ritual drama of the American Indians*. Princeton, NJ: Princeton University Press.

Raether, H. C. (Ed.). (1989). *The funeral director's practice management handbook*. Englewood Cliffs, NJ: Prentice-Hall.

Rahner, K. (1973). *On the theology of death*. Trans. C. H. Henkey. New York: Seabury Press.

Rakoff, V. M. (1974). Psychiatric aspects of death in America. In A. Mack (Ed.), *Death in American experience* (pp. 149–161). New York: Schocken Books.

Ramsey, P. (1970). *The patient as person: Explorations in medical ethics*. New Haven, CT: Yale University Press.

Rando, T. A. (1984). *Grief, dying, and death: Clinical interventions for caregivers*. Champaign, IL: Research Press.

Rando, T. A. (1985). Creating therapeutic rituals in the psychotherapy of the bereaved. *Psychotherapy, 22*(2), 236–240.

Rando, T. A. (Ed.). (1986a). *Parental loss of a child*. Champaign, IL: Research Press.

Rando, T. A. (1986b). Death of the adult child. In T. A. Rando (Ed.), *Parental loss of a child* (pp. 221–238). Champaign, IL: Research Press.

Rando, T. A. (Ed.). (1986c). *Loss and anticipatory grief*. Lexington, MA: Lexington Books.

Rando, T. A. (1988a). Anticipatory grief: The term is a misnomer but the phenomenon exists. *Journal of Palliative Care, 4*(1/2), 70–73.

Rando, T. A. (1988b). *Grieving: How to go on living when someone you love dies*. Lexington, MA: Lexington Books.

Rando, T. A. (1993). *Treatment of complicated mourning*. Champaign, IL: Research Press.

The Random House Dictionary of the English Language (2nd ed.). (1987). New York: Random House.

Raphael, B. (1983). *The anatomy of bereavement.* New York: Basic Books.

Rawson, H. (1981). *A dictionary of euphemisms and other doubletalk.* New York: Crown.

Reddin, S. K. (1987). The photography of stillborn children and neonatal deaths. *The Journal of Audiovisual Media in Medicine, 10*(2), 49–51.

Redmond, L. M. (1989). *Surviving: When someone you love was murdered.* Clearwater, FL: Psychological Consultation and Education Services.

Rees, W. D. (1972). The distress of dying. *British Medical Journal, 2*, 105–107.

Rees, W. D., & Lutkins, S. (1967). The mortality of bereavement. *British Medical Journal, 4*, 13–16.

Reich, W. (Ed.). (1978). *Encyclopedia of bioethics* (4 vols.). New York: Free Press.

Reitlinger, G. (1968). *The final solution: The attempt to exterminate the Jews of Europe 1939–1945* (2nd rev. ed.). London: Vallentine, Mitchell.

Resnik, H.L.P. (Ed.). (1968). *Suicidal behaviors: Diagnosis and management.* Boston: Little, Brown.

Resnik, H.L.P. (1972). Psychological resynthesis: A clinical approach to the survivors of a death by suicide. In A. C. Cain (Ed.), *Survivors of suicide* (pp. 167–177). Springfield, IL: Charles C Thomas.

Retherford, R. D. (1975). *The changing sex differential in mortality.* Westport, CT: Greenwood Press.

Reynolds, F. E., & Waugh, E. H. (Eds.). (1977). *Religious encounters with death: Insights from the history and anthropology of religion.* State College, PA: Pennsylvania State University Press.

Reynolds, S. E. (1992). *Endings to beginnings: A grief support group for children and adolescents.* Minneapolis: HRG Press.

Rhoden, N. (1989). Litigating life and death. *Harvard Law Review, 102*, 375–446.

Richardson, D. (1988). *Women and AIDS.* New York: Methuen.

Rieder, I., & Ruppelt, P. (Eds.). (1988). *AIDS: The women.* San Francisco: Cleis Press.

Riley, M. W., Ory, M., & Zablotsky, D. (Eds.). (1989). *AIDS in an aging society.* New York: Springer.

Ring, K. (1980). *Life at death: A scientific investigation of the near-death experience.* New York: Coward, McCann & Geoghegan.

Ring, K. (1984). *Heading toward omega: In search of the meaning of the near-death experience.* New York: Morrow.

Ring, K. (1989). Near-death experiences. In R. Kastenbaum & B. Kastenbaum (Eds.), *Encyclopedia of death* (pp. 193–196). Phoenix, AZ: Oryx Press.

Robertson, J. A. (1991). Second thoughts on living wills. *Hastings Center Report, 21*(6), 6–9.

Rochlin, G. (1967). How younger children view death and themselves. In E. A. Grollman (Ed.), *Explaining death to children* (pp. 51–85). Boston: Beacon Press.

Rodin, J., & Langer, E. J. (1977). Long-term effects of a control-relevant intervention with the institutionalized aged. *Journal of Personality and Social Psychology, 35,* 879–902.

Rogers, M. F. (1985). AIDS in children: A review of the clinical, epidemiologic and public health aspects. *Pediatric Infectious Diseases, 4,* 230–236.

Rollin, B. (1985). *Last wish.* New York: Simon & Schuster.

Roman, J. (1980). *Exit house: Choosing suicide as an alternative.* New York: Seaview Books.

Romond, J. L. (1989). *Children facing grief: Letters from bereaved brothers and sisters.* St. Meinrad, IN: Abbey Press.

Ropp, L., Visintainer, P., Uman, J., & Treloar, D. (1992). Death in the city: An American tragedy. *Journal of the American Medical Association, 267,* 2905–2910.

Rosen, E. J. (1990). *Families facing death: Family dynamics of terminal illness.* Lexington, MA: Lexington Books.

Rosen, H. (1986). *Unspoken grief: Coping with childhood sibling loss.* Lexington, MA: Lexington Books.

Rosenbaum, E. E. (1988). *A taste of my own medicine: When the doctor is the patient.* New York: Random House.

Rosenberg, C. E. (1987). *The care of strangers: The rise of America's hospital system.* New York: Basic Books.

Rosenblatt, P. C. (1983). *Bitter, bitter tears: Nineteenth-century diarists and twentieth-century grief theories.* Minneapolis: University of Minnesota Press.

Rosenblatt, P. C., Walsh, P. R., & Jackson, D. A. (1976). *Grief and mourning in cross-cultural perspectives.* Washington, DC: Human Relations Area Files.

Rosenthal, N. R. (1986). Death education: Developing a course of study for adolescents. In C. A. Corr & J. N. McNeil (Eds.), *Adolescence and death* (pp. 202–214). New York: Springer.

Rosenthal, T. (1973). *How could I not be among you?* New York: George Braziller.

Rosenwaike, I., & Bradshaw, B. S. (1988). The status of death statistics for the Hispanic population of the Southwest. *Social Science Quarterly, 69,* 722–736.

Rosenwaike, I., & Bradshaw, B. S. (1989). Mortality of the Spanish surname population of the Southwest: 1980. *Social Science Quarterly, 70,* 631–641.

Ross, C. P. (1980). Mobilizing schools for suicide prevention. *Suicide and Life-Threatening Behavior, 10,* 239–243.

Ross, C. P. (1985). Teaching children the facts of life and death: Suicide prevention in the schools. In M. L. Peck, N. L. Farberow, & R. E. Litman (Eds.), *Youth suicide* (pp. 147–169). New York: Springer.

Ross, E. S. (1967). Children's books relating to death: A discussion. In E. A. Grollman (Ed.), *Explaining death to children* (pp. 249–271). Boston: Beacon Press.

Ross, J. W. (1988). An ethics of compassion, a language of division. In I. B. Corless & M. Pittman-Lindeman (Eds.), *AIDS: Principles, practices, and politics* (pp. 81–95). New York: Hemisphere.

Roth, J. S. (1989). *All about AIDS*. New York: Harwood Academic Publishers.

Rozovsky, F. A. (1990) *Consent to treatment: A practical guide* (2nd ed.). Boston: Little, Brown. (Also see 1991 Supplement)

Rubin, B., Carlton, R., & Rubin, A. (1979). *L.A. in installments: Forest Lawn*. Santa Monica, CA: Hennessey & Ingalls.

Ruby, J. (1984). Post-mortem portraiture in America. *History of Photography, 8*, 201–222.

Ruby, J. (1987). Portraying the dead. *Omega, 19*, 1–20.

Ruby, J. (1991). Photographs, memory, and grief. *Illness, Crises and Loss, 1*, 1–5.

Ruby, J. (in press). *Secure the shadow ere the substance fade: Death and photography in America*.

Rudolph, M. (1978). *Should the children know? Encounters with death in the lives of children*. New York: Schocken.

Ryan, C., & Ryan, K. M. (1979). *A private battle*. New York: Simon & Schuster.

Rynearson, E. K. (1978). Humans and pets and attachment. *British Journal of Psychiatry, 133*, 550–555.

Sabatino, C. P. (1990). *Health care powers of attorney: An introduction and sample form*. Washington, DC: American Bar Association.

Sabom, M. B. (1982). *Recollections of death: A medical investigation*. New York: Harper & Row.

Sahler, O.J.Z. (Ed.). (1978). *The child and death*. St. Louis: C. V. Mosby.

Salcido, R. M. (1990). Mexican-Americans: Illness, death and bereavement. In J. K. Parry (Ed.), *Social work practice with the terminally ill: A transcultural perspective* (pp. 99–112). Springfield, IL: Charles C Thomas.

Sande, M. A. (1986). The case against casual contagion. *New England Journal of Medicine, 314*, 380–382.

Sanders, C. M. (1979). A comparison of adult bereavement in the death of a spouse, child and parent. *Omega, 10*, 303–322.

Sanders, C. M. (1980). Comparison of younger and older spouses in bereavement outcome. *Omega, 11*, 217–232.

Sanders, C. M. (1989). *Grief: The mourning after*. New York: Wiley.

Sanders, C. M. (1992). *Surviving grief . . . and learning to live again*. New York: Wiley.

Saul, S. R., & Saul, S. (1973). Old people talk about death. *Omega, 4*, 27–35.

Saunders, C. M. (1967). *The management of terminal illness*. London: Hospital Medicine Publications.

Saunders, C. M. (1976). The challenge of terminal care. In T. Symington & R. L. Carter (Eds.), *Scientific foundations of oncology* (pp. 673–679). London: William Heinemann.

Saunders, C. M. (Ed.). (1984). *The management of terminal malignant disease* (2nd ed.). London: Edward Arnold.

Saunders, C. M. (Ed.). (1990). *Hospice and palliative care: An interdisciplinary approach*. London: Edward Arnold.

Schaefer, D., & Lyons, C. (1986). *How do we tell the children? A parent's guide to helping children understand and cope when someone dies*. New York: Newmarket.

Schatz, W. H. (1986). Grief of fathers. In T. A. Rando (Ed.), *Parental loss of a child* (pp. 293–302). Champaign, IL: Research Press.

Scheible, S. S. (1988). Death and the law. In H. Wass, F. M. Berardo, & R. A. Neimeyer (Eds.), *Dying: Facing the facts* (2nd ed., 301–319). Washington, DC: Hemisphere.

Scheper-Hughes, N. (1992). *Death without weeping: The violence of everyday life in Brazil.* Berkeley: University of California Press.

Schiamberg, L. B. (1985). *Human development* (2nd ed.). New York: Macmillan.

Schiff, H. S. (1977). *The bereaved parent.* New York: Crown.

Schiff, H. S. (1986). *Living through mourning: Finding comfort and hope when a loved one has died.* New York: Viking Penguin.

Schilder, P., & Wechsler, D. (1934). The attitudes of children toward death. *Journal of Genetic Psychology, 45,* 406–451.

Schindler, R. (1990). Terminal illness and bereavement: A Jewish-Israeli view. In J. K. Parry (Ed.), *Social work practice with the terminally ill: A transcultural perspective* (pp. 83–98). Springfield, IL: Charles C Thomas.

Schneider, J. M. (1980). Clinically significant differences between grief, pathological grief, and depression. *Patient Counseling and Health Education, 2,* 161–169.

Schodt, C. M. (1982). Grief in adolescent mothers after an infant death. *Image, 14,* 20–25.

Schoenberg, B., Carr, A., Kutscher, A., Peretz, D., & Goldberg, I. (Eds.). (1974). *Anticipatory grief.* New York: Columbia University Press.

Schulz, R. (1976). Effect of control and predictability on the physical and psychological well-being of the institutionalized aged. *Journal of Personality and Social Psychology, 33,* 563–573.

Schulz, R., & Aderman, D. (1974). Clinical research and the stages of dying. *Omega, 5,* 137–144.

Schwiebert, P., & Kirk, P. (1986). *Still to be born: A guide for bereaved parents who are making decisions about the future.* Portland, OR: Perinatal Loss.

Scott, G. B., Hutto, C., & Makuch, R. W. (1989). Survival in children with perinatally acquired human immunodeficiency virus type 1 infection. *New England Journal of Medicine, 321,* 1791–1796.

Seiden, R. H. (1977). Suicide prevention: A public health/public policy approach. *Omega, 8,* 267–276.

Seligman, M.E.P. (1975). *Helplessness: On depression, development, and death.* San Francisco: W. H. Freeman.

Selkin, J. (1983). The legacy of Emile Durkheim. *Suicide and Life-Threatening Behavior, 13,* 3–14.

Selye, H. (1978). *The stress of life* (rev. ed.). New York: McGraw-Hill.

Shenson, D. (1988, February 28). When fear conquers: A doctor learns about AIDS from leprosy. *New York Times Magazine,* pp. 35–36, 48.

Shephard, D.A.E. (1977). Principles and practice of palliative care. *Canadian Medical Association Journal, 116,* 522–526.

Shield, R. R. (1988). *Uneasy endings: Daily life in an American nursing home.* Ithaca, NY: Cornell University Press.

Shilts, R. (1987). *And the band played on: Politics, people, and the AIDS epidemic.* New York: St. Martin's Press.

Shirley, V., & Mercier, J. (1983). Bereavement of older persons: Death of a pet. *The Gerontologist, 23,* 276.

Shneidman, E. S. (1971). Prevention, intervention, and postvention of suicide. *Annals of Internal Medicine, 75,* 453–458.

Shneidman, E. S. (1973). *Deaths of man.* New York: Quadrangle.

Shneidman, E. S. (1978). Some aspects of psychotherapy with dying persons. In C. A. Garfield (Ed.), *Psychosocial care of the dying patient* (pp. 201–218). New York: McGraw-Hill.

Shneidman, E. S. (1980). *Voices of death.* New York: Harper & Row.

Shneidman, E. S. (1983). Reflections on contemporary death. In C. A. Corr, J. M. Stillion, & M. C. Ribar (eds.), *Creativity in death education and counseling* (pp. 27–34). Lakewood, OH: Forum for Death Education and Counseling.

Shneidman, E. S. (1985). *Definition of suicide.* New York: Wiley.

Shneidman, E. S., & Farberow, N. L. (1961). "Some facts about suicide" (PHS Publication No. 852). Washington, DC: U.S. Government Printing Office.

Showalter, J. E. (1983). Foreword. In J. H. Arnold & P. B. Gemma, *A child dies: A portrait of family grief* (pp. ix–x). Rockville, MD: Aspen Systems Corp.

Shrock, N. M. (1835). On the signs that distinguish real from apparent death. *Transylvanian Journal of Medicine, 13,* 210–220.

Shryock, H. S., Siegel, J. S., & Associates. (1980). *The methods and materials of demography* (2 vols.; 4th printing, revised). Washington, DC: U.S. Government Printing Office, U.S. Bureau of the Census.

Shulman, W. L. (Ed.). (1993). *Directory: Association of holocaust organizations.* Bayside, NY: Holocaust Resource Center and Archives, Queensborough Community College.

Siegel, K., & Weinstein, L. (1983). Anticipatory grief reconsidered. *Journal of Psychosocial Oncology, 1,* 61–73.

Siegel, R. (1982). A family-centered program of neonatal intensive care. *Health and Social Work, 7,* 50–58.

Siegel, R., Rudd, S. H., Cleveland, C., Powers, L. K., & Harmon, R. J. (1985). A hospice approach to neonatal care. In C. A. Corr & D. M. Corr (Eds.), *Hospice approaches to pediatric care* (pp. 127–152). New York: Springer.

Siggins, L. (1966). Mourning: A critical survey of the literature. *International Journal of Psychoanalysis, 47,* 14–25.

Silver, R. L., & Wortman, C. B. (1980). Coping with undesirable life events. In J. Garber & M.E.P. Seligman (Eds.), *Human helplessness: Theory and applications* (pp. 279–340). New York: Academic Press.

Silverman, P. R. (1969). The widow-to-widow program: An experiment in preventive intervention. *Mental Hygiene, 53,* 333–337.

Silverman, P. R. (1974). Anticipatory grief from the perspective of widowhood. In B. Schoenberg, A. Carr, A. Kutscher, D. Peretz, & I. Goldberg

(Eds.), *Anticipatory grief* (pp. 320–330). New York: Columbia University Press.

Silverman, P. R. (1978). *Mutual help groups: A guide for mental health workers.* Rockville, MD: National Institute of Mental Health.

Silverman, P. R. (1980). *Mutual help groups: Organization and development.* Newbury Park, CA: Sage.

Silverman, P. R. (1986). *Widow to widow.* New York: Springer.

Silverman, P. R., & Worden, J. W. (1992). Children and parental death. *American Journal of Orthopsychiatry, 62,* 93–104.

Silverman, P. R., Nickman, S., & Worden, J. W. (1992). Detachment revisited: The child's reconstruction of a dead parent. *American Journal of Orthopsychiatry, 62,* 494–503.

Simeone, W. E. (1991). The Northern Athabaskan potlatch: The objectification of grief. In D. R. Counts & D. A. Counts (Eds.), *Coping with the final tragedy: Cultural variation in dying and grieving* (pp. 157–167). Amityville, NY: Baywood.

Simon, N. (1979). *We remember Philip.* Chicago: Whitman.

Simon, P., & Garfunkel, A. (1970). Bridge over troubled water. *Bridge over troubled water.* New York and Los Angeles: Columbia Records.

Simonds, W., & Rothman, B. K. (Eds.). (1992). *Centuries of solace: Expressions of maternal grief in popular literature.* Philadelphia: Temple University Press.

Simos, B. (1979). *A time to grieve.* New York: Family Service Association of America.

Simpson, J. A., & Weiner, E.S.C. (1989). *The Oxford English dictionary* (2nd ed.; 20 vols.). Oxford: Clarendon Press.

Simpson, M. A. (1976). Brought in dead. *Omega, 7,* 243–248.

Simpson, M. A. (1979). Social and psychological aspects of dying. In H. Wass (Ed.), *Dying: Facing the facts* (pp. 108–124). Washington, DC: Hemisphere.

Sloane, D. C. (1991). *The last great necessity: Cemeteries in American history.* Baltimore: Johns Hopkins University Press.

Smart, N. (1976). *The religious experience of mankind* (2nd ed.). New York: Scribners'.

Smeltzer, S. C., & Whipple, B. (1991a). Women with HIV infection: The unrecognized population. *Health Values, 15,* 41–48.

Smeltzer, S. C., & Whipple, B. (1991b). Women and HIV infection. *Image: Journal of Nursing Scholarship, 23,* 249–256.

Smilansky, S. (1987). *On death: Helping children understand and cope.* New York: Peter Lang.

Smith, A. A. (1974). *Rachel.* Wilton, CT: Morehouse-Barlow.

Smith, I. (1991). Preschool children "play" out their grief. *Death Studies, 15,* 169–176.

Society for the Right to Die. (1991). *Refusal of treatment legislation: A state by state compilation of enacted and model statutes.* New York: Author.

Solomon, K. (1982). Social antecedents of learned helplessness in the health care setting. *The Gerontologist, 22,* 282–287.

Sontag, S. (1978). *Illness as metaphor*. New York: Farrar, Straus & Giroux.

Sontag, S. (1989). *AIDS and its metaphors*. New York: Farrar, Straus & Giroux.

Soto, A. R., & Villa, J. (1990). Una platica: Mexican-American approaches to death and dying. In J. K. Parry (Ed.), *Social work practice with the terminally ill: A transcultural perspective* (pp. 113–127). Springfield, IL: Charles C Thomas.

Souter, S. J., & Moore, T. E. (1989). A bereavement support program for survivors of cancer deaths: A description and evaluation. *Omega, 20,* 31–43.

Spiegelman, V., & Kastenbaum, R. (1990). Pet Rest Cemetery: Is eternity running out of time? *Omega, 21,* 1–13.

Spinetta, J. J. (1978). Communication patterns in families dealing with life-threatening illness. In O. J. Sahler (Ed.), *The child and death* (pp. 43–46). St. Louis: C. V. Mosby.

Spinetta, J. J., & Deasy-Spinetta, P. (1981). *Living with childhood cancer*. St. Louis: C. V. Mosby.

Spinetta, J. J., & Maloney, L. J. (1975). Death anxiety in the out-patient leukemic child. *Pediatrics, 56,* 1034–1037.

Spinetta, J. J., Rigler, D., & Karon, M. (1973). Anxiety in the dying child. *Pediatrics, 52,* 841–849.

Stannard, D. E. (Ed.). (1975). *Death in America*. Philadelphia: University of Pennsylvania Press.

Stannard, D. E. (1977). *The Puritan way of death: A study in religion, culture, and social change*. New York: Oxford University Press.

Stark, E. (1991). Preventing primary homicide: A reconceptualization. In D. Leviton (Ed.), *Horrendous death, health, and well-being* (pp. 109–136). Washington, DC: Hemisphere.

Starr, P. (1982). *The social transformation of American medicine*. New York: Basic Books.

Start, C. (1968). *When you're a widow*. St. Louis, MO: Concordia.

Staudacher, C. (1991). *Men and grief*. Oakland, CA: New Harbinger Publications.

Stedeford, A. (1978). Understanding confusional states. *British Journal of Hospital Medicine, 20,* 694–704.

Stedeford, A. (1979). Psychotherapy of the dying patient. *British Journal of Psychiatry, 135,* 7–14.

Stedeford, A. (1984). *Facing death: Patients, families and professionals*. London: William Heinemann.

Stehr-Green, J. K., Holman, R. C., Jason, J. M., & Evatt, B. L. (1988). Hemophilia-associated AIDS in the United States, 1981 to September 1987. *American Journal of Public Health, 78,* 439–441.

Stengel, E. (1964). *Suicide and attempted suicide*. Baltimore: Penguin.

Sternberg, F., & Sternberg, B. (1980). *If I die and when I do: Exploring death with young people*. Englewood Cliffs, NJ: Prentice-Hall.

Stevens, C. (1970). But I might die tonight. *Tea for the tillerman*. Los Angeles: A & M Records.

Stevens, R. (1989). *In sickness and in wealth: American hospitals in the twentieth century.* New York: Basic Books.

Stevens-Long, J. (1988). *Adult life* (3rd ed.). Palo Alto, CA: Mayfield.

Stevenson, A. (1989). *Bitter fame: A life of Sylvia Plath.* Boston: Houghton Mifflin.

Stillion, J. M. (1985). *Death and the sexes: An examination of differential longevity, attitudes, behaviors, and coping skills.* Washington, DC: Hemisphere.

Stillion, J. M. (1986). Examining the shadow: Gifted children respond to the nuclear threat. *Death Studies, 10,* 27–41.

Stillion, J., McDowell, E., & May, J. (Eds.). (1989). *Suicide across the life span: Premature exits.* Washington, DC: Hemisphere.

Stinson, R., & Stinson, P. (1983). *The long dying of Baby Andrew.* Boston: Little, Brown.

Stoddard, S. (1992). *The hospice movement: A better way of caring for the dying* (rev. ed.). New York: Vintage.

Stone, H. (1972). *Suicide and grief.* Philadelphia: Fortress Press.

Stroebe, W., & Stroebe, M. S. (1987). *Bereavement and health: The psychological and physical consequences of partner loss.* Cambridge: Cambridge University Press.

Sudnow, D. (1967). *Passing on: The social organization of dying.* Englewood Cliffs, NJ: Prentice-Hall.

Sugar, M. (1968). Normal adolescent mourning. *American Journal of Psychotherapy, 22,* 258–269.

Suicide is painless. (1980). *M*A*S*H.* New York & Los Angeles: Columbia Records.

Swenson, W. M. (1961). Attitudes toward death in an aged population. *Journal of Gerontology, 16,* 49–52.

Tabachnick, N. (Ed.). (1973). *Accident or suicide?* Springfield, IL: Charles C Thomas.

Tatelbaum, J. (1980). *The courage to grieve.* New York: Lippincott & Crowell.

Templer, D. (1971). Death anxiety as related to depression and health of retired persons. *Journal of Gerontology, 26,* 521–523.

Terkleson, K. (1980). Toward a theory of the family life cycle. In B. Carter & M. McGoldrick (Eds.), *The family life cycle: A framework for family therapy* (pp. 21–52). New York: Gardner.

Thomas, W. C. (1969). *Nursing homes and public policy: Drift and decision in New York State.* Ithaca, NY: Cornell University Press.

Thompson, B. (1990). Amyotrophic lateral sclerosis: Integrating care for patients and their families. *The American Journal of Hospice and Palliative Care, 7*(3), 27–32.

Thompson, J. W., & Walker, R. D. (1990). Adolescent suicide among American Indians and Alaska natives. *Psychiatric Annals, 20,* 128–133.

Thrush, J. C., & Paulus, G. S. (1970). The concept of death in popular music: A social psychological perspective. *Popular Music and Society, 6,* 219–228.

Thurman, H. (1953). *Meditations of the heart.* New York: Harper & Row.

Tishler, C. L., McHenry, P. C., & Morgan, K. C. (1981). Adolescent suicide attempts: Some significant factors. *Suicide and Life-Threatening Behavior, 11,* 86–92.

Tolstoy, L. (1960). *The death of Ivan Ilych and other stories.* Trans. A. Maude. New York: New American Library. (Original work published 1884)

Toynbee, A. (1968a). The relation between life and death, living and dying. In A. Toynbee, A. K. Mant, N. Smart, J. Hinton, S. Yudkin, E. Rhode, R. Heywood, & H. H. Price, *Man's concern with death* (pp. 259–271). New York: McGraw-Hill.

Toynbee, A. (1968b). Traditional attitudes towards death. In A. Toynbee, A. K. Mant, N. Smart, J. Hinton, S. Yudkin, E. Rhode, R. Heywood, & H. H. Price, *Man's concern with death* (pp. 59–94). New York: McGraw-Hill.

Toynbee, A., Koestler, A., & others. (1976). *Life after death.* New York: McGraw-Hill.

Toynbee, A., Mant, A. K., Smart, N., Hinton, J., Yudkin, S., Rhode, E., Heywood, R., & Price, H. H. (1968). *Man's concern with death.* New York: McGraw-Hill.

Turner, C. F., Miller, H. G., & Moses, L. E. (1989). *AIDS: Sexual behavior and intravenous drug use.* Washington, DC: National Academy Press.

Turner, R. E., & Edgley, C. (1976). Death as theatre: A dramaturgical analysis of the American funeral. *Sociology and Social Research, 60,* 377–392.

Twain, M. (1962). *Letters from the earth.* Ed. B. Devoto. New York: Harper & Row.

Twycross, R. G. (1976). Long-term use of diamorphine in advanced cancer. In J. J. Bonica & D. Albe-Fessard (Eds.), *Advances in pain research and therapy, Vol. 1* (pp. 653–661). New York: Raven Press.

Twycross, R. G. (1977). Choice of strong analgesic in terminal cancer: Diamorphine or morphine? *Pain, 3,* 93–104.

Twycross, R. G. (1979a). The Brompton Cocktail. In J. J. Bonica & V. Ventafridda (Eds.), *International symposium on pain of advanced cancer: Advances in pain research and therapy, Vol. 2* (pp. 291–300). New York: Raven Press.

Twycross, R. G. (1979b). Overview of analgesia. In J. J. Bonica & V. Ventafridda (Eds.), *International symposium on pain of advanced cancer: Advances in pain research and therapy, Vol. 2* (pp. 617–633). New York: Raven Press.

Twycross, R. G. (1982). Principles and practice of pain relief in terminal cancer. *Cancer Forum, 6,* 23–33.

Twycross, R. G., & Lack, S. A. (1983). *Symptom control in far advanced cancer: Pain relief.* London: Pitman.

Uhlenberg, P. (1980). Death and the family. *Journal of Family History, 5,* 313–320.

United Nations. (1992). *Demographic yearbook, 1990* (42nd ed.). New York: Author.

United States Bureau of the Census. (1975). *Historical statistics of the United States, colonial times to 1970, bicentennial edition* (2 parts). Washington, DC: U.S. Government Printing Office.

United States Bureau of the Census. (1991). *Statistical abstract of the United States: 1991* (11th ed.). Washington, DC: U.S. Government Printing Office.

United States Congress. (1986). *Indian health care.* Washington, DC: U.S. Government Printing Office.

Until We Say Goodbye [Film]. 1980. Washington, DC: WJLA-TV.

Vachon, M.L.S. (1979). Staff stress in care of the terminally ill. *QRB/Quality Review Bulletin, 6,* 13–17.

Vachon, M.L.S. (1987). *Occupational stress in the care of the critically ill, the dying, and the bereaved.* Washington, DC: Hemisphere.

Valente, S. M., & Saunders, J. M. (1987). High school suicide prevention programs. *Pediatric Nursing, 13*(2), 108–112, 137.

Valente, S. M., & Sellers, J. R. (1986). Helping adolescent survivors of suicide. In C. A. Corr & J. N. McNeil (Eds.), *Adolescence and death* (pp. 167–182). New York: Springer.

Van der Maas, P. J., Van Delden, J.J.M., Pijnenborg, L., & Looman, C.W.N. (1991). Euthanasia and other medical decisions concerning the end of life. *Lancet, 338,* 669–674.

Van Gennep, A. (1961). *The rites of passage.* Trans. M. B. Vizedom & G. L. Caffee. Chicago: University of Chicago Press.

Van Tassel, D. (Ed.). (1979). *Aging, death, and the completion of being.* Philadelphia: University of Pennsylvania Press.

Van Winkle, N. W., & May, P. A. (1986). Native American suicide in New Mexico, 1957–1979: A comparative study. *Human Organization, 45,* 296–309.

Veatch, R. M. (1972). Brain death: Welcome definition or dangerous judgment? *Hastings Center Report, 2*(5), 10–13.

Veatch, R. M. (1975). The whole-brain-oriented concept of death: An outmoded philosophical formulation. *Journal of Thanatology, 3*(1), 13–30.

Veatch, R. M. (1976). *Death, dying, and the biological revolution: Our last quest for responsibility.* New Haven, CT: Yale University Press.

Veatch, R. M. (1978). Death and dying: Euthanasia and sustaining life: Professional and public policies. In W. Reich (Ed.), *Encyclopedia of bioethics* (pp. 278–286). New York: Free Press.

Veninga, R. (1985). *A gift of hope: How we survive our tragedies.* New York: Ballantine Books.

Vernick, J., & Karon, M. (1965). Who's afraid of death on a leukemia ward? *American Journal of Diseases of Children, 109,* 393–397.

Verwoerdt, A. (1976). *Clinical geropsychiatry.* Baltimore: Williams & Wilkins.

Verwoerdt, A., Pfeiffer, E., & Wang, H. S. (1969). Sexual behavior in senescence. *Geriatrics, 24,* 137–154.

Vicchio, S. J. (1979). Against raising hope of raising the dead: Contra Moody and Kübler-Ross. *Essence, 3*(2), 51–67.

Vicchio, S. J. (1981). Near-death experiences: A critical review of the literature and some questions for further study. *Essence, 5*(1), 77–89.

Viorst, J. (1986). *Necessary losses: The loves, illusions, dependencies and impossible expectations that all of us have to give up in order to grow.* New York: Simon & Schuster.

Vladeck, B. C. (1980). *Unloving care: The nursing home tragedy*. New York: Basic Books.

Volkan, V. (1970). Typical findings in pathological grief. *Psychiatric Quarterly, 44*, 231–250.

Volkan, V. (1985). Complicated mourning. *Annual of Psychoanalysis, 12*, 323–348.

Waechter, E. H. (1971). Children's awareness of fatal illness. *American Journal of Nursing, 71*, 1168–1172.

Waechter, E. H. (1984). Dying children: Patterns of coping. In H. Wass & C. A. Corr (Eds.), *Childhood and death* (pp. 51–68). Washington, DC: Hemisphere.

Wald, F. S., & Bailey, S. S. (1990, November). Nurturing the spiritual component in care for the terminally ill. *Caring Magazine, 9*(11) pp. 64–68.

Wallace, S. E. (1973). *After suicide*. New York: Wiley-Interscience.

Walsh, F., & McGoldrick, M. (1988). Loss and the family life cycle. In C. J. Falicov (Ed.), *Family transitions: Continuity and change over the life cycle* (pp. 311–336). New York: Guilford Press.

Walsh, F., & McGoldrick, M. (1991a). Loss and the family: A systemic perspective. In F. Walsh & M. McGoldrick (Eds.), *Living beyond loss: Death in the family* (pp. 1–29). New York: Norton.

Walsh, F., & McGoldrick, M. (Eds.). (1991b). *Living beyond loss: Death in the family*. New York: Norton.

Walton, D. N. (1979). *On defining death: An analytic study of the concept of death in philosophy and medical ethics*. Montreal: McGill-Queen's University Press.

Walton, D. N. (1982). Neocortical versus whole-brain conceptions of personal death. *Omega, 12*, 339–344.

Wass, H. (1984). Concepts of death: A developmental perspective. In H. Wass & C. A. Corr (Eds.), *Childhood and death* (pp. 3–24). Washington, DC: Hemisphere.

Wass, H., Berardo, F. M., & Neimeyer, R. A. (1988). *Dying: Facing the facts* (2nd ed.). Washington, DC: Hemisphere.

Wass, H., & Cason, L. (1984). Fears and anxieties about death. In H. Wass & C. A. Corr (Eds.), *Childhood and death* (pp. 25–45). Washington, DC: Hemisphere.

Wass, H., & Corr, C. A. (Eds.). (1984a). *Childhood and death*. Washington, DC: Hemisphere.

Wass, H., & Corr, C. A. (Eds.). (1984b). *Helping children cope with death: Guidelines and resources* (2nd ed.). Washington, DC: Hemisphere.

Wass, H., Corr, C. A., Pacholski, R. A., & Forfar, C. S. (1985). *Death education II: An annotated resource guide*. Washington, DC: Hemisphere.

Wass, H., Corr, C. A., Pacholski, R. A., & Sanders, C. M. (1980). *Death education: An annotated resource guide*. Washington, DC: Hemisphere.

Wass, H., Miller, M. D., & Stevenson, R. G. (1989a). Factors affecting adolescents' behavior and attitudes toward destructive rock lyrics. *Death Studies, 13*, 287–303

Wass, H., Raup, J. L., Cerullo, K., Martel, L. G., Mingione, L. A., & Sperring, A. M. (1989b). Adolescents' interest in and views of destructive themes in rock music. *Omega, 19*, 177–186.

Wasserman, H., & Danforth, H. E. (1988). *The human bond: Support groups and mutual aid.* New York: Springer.

Waugh, E. (1948). *The loved one.* Boston: Little, Brown.

Webb, J. P., & Willard, W. (1975). Six American Indian patterns of suicide. In N. L. Farberow (Ed.), *Suicide in different cultures* (pp. 17–33). Baltimore, MD: University Park Press.

Webster, B. D. (1989). *All of a piece: A life with multiple sclerosis.* Baltimore, MD: Johns Hopkins University Press.

Wecht, C. H. (1974). The coroner and death. In E. A. Grollman (Ed.), *Concerning death: A practical guide for the living* (pp. 177–185). Boston: Beacon Press.

Weinberg, J. (1969). Sexual expression in late life. *American Journal of Psychiatry, 126,* 713–716.

Weir, R. F. (Ed.). (1980). *Death in literature.* New York: Columbia University Press.

Weisman, A. D. (1972). *On dying and denying: A psychiatric study of terminality.* New York: Behavioral Publications.

Weisman, A. D. (1977). The psychiatrist and the inexorable. In H. Feifel (Ed.), *New meanings of death* (pp. 107–122). New York: McGraw-Hill.

Weisman, A. D. (1984). *The coping capacity: On the nature of being mortal.* New York: Human Sciences Press.

Weisman, M-L. (1982). *Intensive care: A family love story.* New York: Random House.

Weizman, S. G., & Kamm, P. (1985). *About mourning: Support and guidance for the bereaved.* New York: Human Sciences Press.

Wentworth, H., & Flexner, S. B. (Eds.). (1967). *Dictionary of American slang (with supplement).* New York: Crowell.

Wertenbaker, L. T. (1957). *Death of a man.* New York: Random House.

Weseen, M. H. (1934). *A dictionary of American slang.* New York: Crowell.

Westberg, G. (1971). *Good grief.* Philadelphia: Fortress Press.

Westerhoff, J. H. (1978). *McGuffey and his readers: Piety, morality, and education in nineteenth-century America.* Nashville: Abingdon.

Westphal, M. (1984). *God, guilt, and death.* Bloomington, IN: Indiana University Press.

White, R., & Cunningham, A. M. (1991). *Ryan White: My own story.* New York: Dial Press.

White, R. B., & Engelhardt, H. T. (1975). A demand to die. *Hastings Center Report, 5*(3), 9–10, 47.

White, R. H. (1974). Strategies of adaptation: An attempt at systematic description. In G. V. Coelho, D. A. Hamburg, & J. E. Adams, (Eds.), *Coping and adaptation* (pp. 47–68). New York: Basic Books.

Whitfield, J. M., Siegel, R. E., Glicken, A. D., Harmon, R. J., Powers, L. K., & Goldson, E. J. (1982). The application of hospice concepts to neonatal care. *American Journal of Diseases of Children, 136,* 421–424.

Whitmore, G. (1988). *Someone was here: Profiles in the AIDS epidemic.* New York: New American Library.

Whitney, S. (1991). *Waving goodbye: An activities manual for children in grief.* Portland, OR: The Dougy Center.

Wiesel, E. (1960). *Night.* Trans. S. Rodway. New York: Avon.

Wilcoxon, S. A. (1986). Grandparents and grandchildren: An often neglected relationship between significant others. *Journal of Counseling and Development, 65,* 289–290.

Wilkes, E., et al. (1980). *Report of the working group on terminal care of the standing sub-committee on cancer.* Her Majesty's Stationary Office.

Wilkes, E., Crowther, A.G.O., & Greaves, C.W.K.H. (1978). A different kind of day hospital—For patients with preterminal cancer and chronic disease. *British Medical Journal, 2,* 1053–1056.

Willans, J. H. (1980). Nutrition: Appetite in the terminally ill patient. *Nursing Times, 76,* 875–876.

Williams, G. (1958). "Mercy-killing" legislation—A rejoinder. *Minnesota Law Review, 43,* 1–12.

Williams, P. G. (1989). *Life from death: The organ and tissue donation and transplantation source book, with forms.* Oak Park, IL: P. Gaines Co.

Williams, P. G. (1991). *The living will and the durable power of attorney for health care book, with forms* (rev. ed.). Oak Park, IL: P. Gaines Co.

Wilson, M. (1981). Suicidal behavior: Toward an explanation of differences in female and male rates. *Suicide and Life-Threatening Behavior, 11,* 131–140.

Wishner, A. R., Schwarz, D. F., Grisso, J. A., Holmes, J. H., & Sutton, R. L. (1991). Interpersonal violence-related injuries in an African-American community in Philadelphia. *Public Health Briefs, 81,* 1474–1476.

Wolfelt, A. (1983). *Helping children cope with grief.* Muncie, IN: Accelerated Development.

Wolfenstein, M. (1966). How is mourning possible? *Psychoanalytic Study of the Child, 21,* 93–123.

Wolfenstein, M., & Kliman, G. (Eds.). (1965). *Children and the death of a president.* Garden City, NY: Doubleday.

Wolff, J. R., Nielson, P. E., & Schiller, P. (1970). The emotional reaction to a stillbirth. *American Journal of Obstetrics and Gynecology, 108,* 73–77.

Woman in machine, subject of suit, dies. (1975, November 10). *New York Times,* p. 36.

Woodson, R. (1976). The concept of hospice care in terminal disease. In J. M. Vaeth (Ed.), *Breast cancer* (pp. 161–179). Basel: Karger.

Woodward, K. (1986). Reminiscence and the life review: Prospects and retrospects. In T. R. Cole & S. A. Gadow (Eds.), *What does it mean to grow old? Reflections from the humanities* (pp. 135–161). Durham, NC: Duke University Press.

Worden, J. W. (1982). *Grief counseling and grief therapy: A handbook for the mental health practitioner.* New York: Springer.

Worden, J. W. (1991a). *Grief counseling and grief therapy: A handbook for the mental health practitioner* (2nd ed.). New York: Springer.

Worden, J. W. (1991b, April 27). Bereaved children. Keynote presentation at the Thirteenth Annual Conference of the Association for Death Education and Counseling, Duluth, MN.

Wortman, C. B., & Silver, R. C. (1989). The myth of coping with loss. *Journal of Clinical Consulting Psychology, 57,* 349–357.

Wrobleski, A. (1984). The suicide survivors grief group. *Omega, 15,* 173–183.

Yalom, I. (1985). *The theory and practice of group psychotherapy* (3rd ed.). New York: Basic Books.

Yalom, I. D., & Vinogradov, S. (1988). Bereavement groups: Techniques and themes. *International Journal of Group Psychotherapy, 38,* 419–446.

York, J. L., & Calsyn, R. J. (1977). Family involvement in nursing homes. *The Gerontologist, 17,* 500–505.

Yu, E. (1982). The low mortality rates of Chinese infants: Some plausible explanatory factors. *Social Science and Medicine, 16,* 253–265.

Yu, E.S.H. (1986). Health of the Chinese elderly in America. *Research on Aging, 8,* 84–109.

Zalaznik, P. H. (1992). *Dimensions of loss and death education* (3rd ed.). Minneapolis: Edu-Pac.

Zambelli, G. C., & DeRosa, A. P. (1992). Bereavement support groups for school-age children: Theory, intervention, and case example. *American Journal of Orthopsychiatry 62,* 484–493.

Zanger, J. (1980). Mount Auburn Cemetery: The silent suburb. *Landscape, 24*(2), 23–28.

Zerwekh, J. V. (1983). The dehydration question. *Nursing 83, 13,* 47–51.

Zielinski, J. (1975). *The Amish: A pioneer heritage.* Des Moines, IA: Wallace-Homestead Book Co.

Zinner, E. S. (Ed.). (1985). *Coping with death on campus.* San Francisco: Jossey-Bass.

Zipes, J. (1983). *The trials and tribulations of Little Red Riding Hood: Versions of the tale in sociocultural context.* South Hadley, MA: Bergin & Garvey.

Zisook, S., & DeVaul, R. A. (1983). Grief, unresolved grief, and depression. *Psychosomatics, 24,* 247–256.

Zisook, S., & DeVaul, R. A. (1984). Measuring acute grief. *Psychiatric Medicine, 2,* 169–176.

Zisook, S., & DeVaul, R. A. (1985). Unresolved grief. *American Journal of Psychoanalysis, 45,* 370–379.

Zittoun, R. (1990). Patient information and participation. In J. C. Holland & R. Zittoun (Eds.), *Psychosocial aspects of oncology* (pp. 27–44). Berlin: Springer Verlag.

Zolotow, C. (1974). *My grandson Lew.* New York: Harper & Row.

Zorza, V., & Zorza, R. (1980). *A way to die.* New York: Knopf.

Name Index

Subject Index

Credits

This page constitutes an extension of the copyright page.

Text Credits

We have made every attempt to trace the ownership of all copyrighted material and to secure permission from copyright holders. In the event of any question arising as to the use of any material, we will be pleased to make the necessary corrections in a future printing.

Photo Credits